T5-BQA-242

Cooperation and Conflict in Southern Africa:

Papers on a Regional Subsystem

Edited by

Timothy M. Shaw

Kenneth A. Heard

Published by University Press of America for the Centre for African Studies and the Centre for Foreign Policy Studies, Dalhousie University, Halifax, Nova Scotia, Canada, in association with Dalhousie University Press.

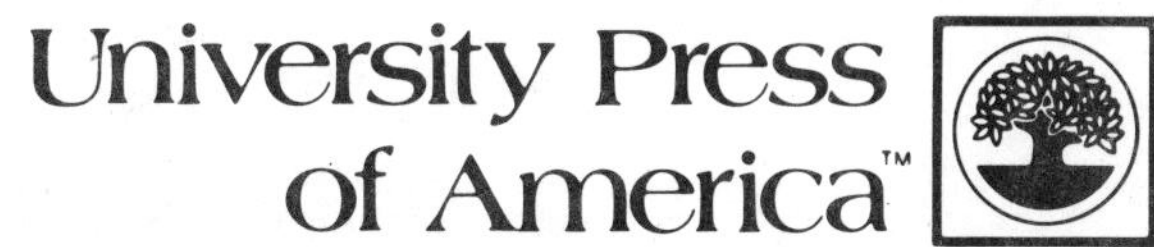

University Press of America™
division of
R.F. Publishing, Inc.
4710 Auth Place, S.E., Washington, D.C. 20023

Printed in the United States of America
0-8191-0005-6

Library of Congress Catalog Card Number: 76-27625

TABLE OF CONTENTS

PREFACE

In mid-August 1973 a modest workshop on Southern Africa was held on the campus of Dalhousie University. It was designed to provide a relaxed and intimate environment in which specialists in the area could collectively re-examine approaches to the analysis of Southern African society in a relatively intensive and protracted interaction. The essays included here are largely revised versions of the papers originally presented at the workshop, since rewritten in response to suggestions and criticisms made by participants at the meeting. The collection also includes two papers prepared for, but regrettably not presented at, the workshop (Chapters Ten and Eleven), two reprints of particularly salient and suggestive articles which originally appeared elsewhere (Chapters One and Two), and four essays prepared after the workshop by participants (Chapters Nine, Thirteen, Fourteen and Fifteen).

The intellectual stimulus for the workshop was our dissatisfaction with previous attempts to explain the slow and devious rate of change in Southern Africa. We were also critical of the absence of rigorous interdisciplinary analysis of the region and the artificial state-centric focus of most research. We structured the workshop to direct discussion away from this inheritance of orthodox approaches and instead suggested that we should examine patterns of interaction in the region in several issue areas; our set of three issue areas was clearly related to substantive and analytic "disciplinary" interests - i) culture, race and history; ii) economic and infrastructural linkages; and iii) political and military systems. We also wanted to "test" in an informal manner the utility of the subsystemic approach to explanation. The seminar was structured so that we considered both regional and extra-regional patterns of behaviour. We informally analysed the behaviour of actors in the region both within the subsystem and in the larger global system; we were examining, therefore, the degree of autonomy of the subsystem in each of its issue areas. We were able to consider a wider range of actors than is possible in a more orthodox conceptual framework - liberation movements, multinational corporations and other transnational organisations as well as regimes, leaders and parties.

The workshop was proposed and designed, therefore, to re-examine the subordinate state system of Southern Africa which had been initially and suggestively anal[illegible]

[illegible] In doing so, however, it went [illegible]

largely vindicated and new insights into the subsystem were generated.

All participants shared an awareness that our analytic approach to the explanation of the slowness of change in the region was related to our individual definitions of the desirability of change. We did not, nor cannot or should not, disregard the normative and policy implications of research. However, we regard our primary task as that of the collection and analysis of data to explain, and hopefully to predict, behaviour. Our training and temperaments fit us best for this role. However, we also recognize that we cannot be neutral or uncommitted, and hope that our findings are both relevant and suggestive. We have no control over the use to which our findings are put. We appreciate that past and present strategies of social engineering in Southern Africa, as well as preferred alternatives, are in part based on "academic" data. They have already made simplistic solutions inappropriate and increased the social complexity of the region. We all have different definitions of the desirability, rate and goal of change in the region; we have alternative conceptions of desirable futures for Southern Africa and may dispute whether liberation movements, Bantustan leaders and western pressure groups are compatible and are likely to open up a reformist option to the present patterns of confrontation and enforced cooperation.

The workshop took place before the April 1974 coup in Portugal which has led to independence in Mozambique and Angola and to diplomatic activity over Zimbabwe (Rhodesia) and Namibia (South West Africa). Some of our essays incorporate these changes while others were revised earlier. However, we believe that the collection points to important continuities and discontinuities in regional relations. The constraints on the new black regimes in Southern Africa, and the reassessment of the remaining minority governments both support our general approach; change in any part of the subsystem leads to change in the region as a whole. The dominance of South Africa and the dependence of many states in the region on it will not change rapidly no matter what the colour or ideology of leadership.

We would like to acknowledge the support of a variety of individuals and institutions without whose stimulation and assistance the workshop would not have been held. Firstly, we appreciate the continued collaboration of colleagues at Dalhousie University in both the Centre for Foreign Policy Studies and the Centre for African Studies. Secondly, the workshop could not have been held without the financial support of the Canada Council, the Faculty of Graduate Studies at Dalhousie University, and the Centre for Foreign Policy Studies. And thirdly, we are indebted to the participants at the workshop for contributing to a lively but always friendly seminar from a variety of disciplinary and national perspectives and for agreeing to the inclusion of their work in this collection; we also appreciate their tolerance over the much-delayed appearance of this volume.

The usual warning should perhaps be given, namely that the views expressed in each chapter are those of the author only and are not necessarily shared by the other contributors or by the editors. Finally, but by no means least, it is a pleasure for us both to acknowledge the love and tolerance of our wives and families in the neglect of domestic duties, and to express our gratitude to George Braden, Malcolm Grieve and Mary Nzomo-Mugomba for editorial assistance, and to Doris Boyle, Ann MacCallum, Lorna Cross, Marlene Brooks, Wilhelmena Ross and July Campbell for invaluable secretarial services.

Timothy M. Shaw and Kenneth A. Heard

Halifax, July 1976.

Map of Southern Africa

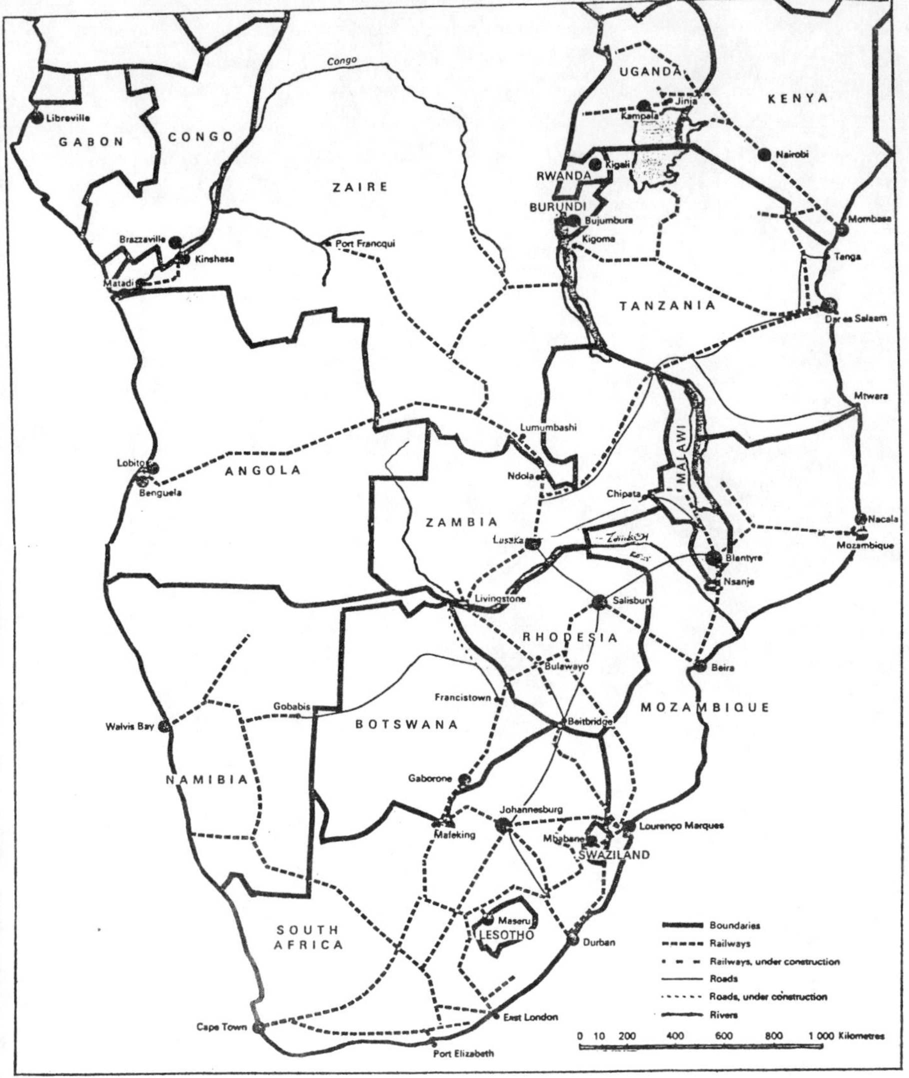

INTRODUCTION TO SOUTHERN AFRICA AS A REGIONAL SUBSYSTEM

Timothy M. Shaw

This set of papers is an attempt to explain the halting and uneven pace of change in Southern Africa. We have adopted an interdisciplinary and subsystemic approach both to understand Southern African society and to discover if this level of analysis yields new insights. Our conceptual framework does not exclude relations between the states of Southern Africa and the larger global system but suggests that the region as a whole, rather than merely discrete units within it, are affected by extra-regional, intrusive relations. We distinguish, therefore, between three types of interaction -- intra-regional relations, ties between the region and the international system, and linkages between the global system and individual actors in Southern Africa. We also informally hypothesise that the importance of these relations varies between issue areas.

The first part of this collection consists of five essays which suggest alternative, and largely complementary, approaches to the study of Southern Africa. A new generation of students of the region have heeded Larry Bowman's advice in his land-mark essay on "The subordinate state system of Southern Africa" to abandon historical-constitutional, racial and state-centric approaches. This collection is intended as one contribution to these revisionist designs as well as a pause for reflection on the ground covered and the new peaks to be scaled. Although many of the references in it are now dated, and some of his predictions have not been fulfilled, Bowman's suggestive article is reprinted here as our first chapter because its mode of analysis remains appropriate and because many other contributions are developments of its original insights.

Bowman was interested in the prospects for stability and unity in Southern Africa as well in the advocacy of a new level of analysis. His definition of the region excluded Zambia, which has successfully implemented a strategy of disengagement from the subsystem. Otherwise, the region exhibits a remarkable continuity from its origins in the Central African Federation, the High Commission Territories, the Portuguese Empire and the old Union of South Africa plus its mandated territory, South West Africa. However, stability is threatened by new discontinuities, notably the threat to the incumbent white regimes from the liberation movements and the growth of black power in South Africa with its institutional form in the leadership of South Africa's Bantustans. New strategies of disengagement and confrontation, unlike those of Zambia, may emerge from the growing complexity of actors and interactions in Southern Africa. Subsequent political change in Portugal has had a profound effect on the balance of power between black and white regimes in the region. The vulnerability of Rhodesia with a FRELIMO government in Mozambique has led to diplomatic detente between Prime Minister Vorster and President Kaunda. If progress towards majority rule is maintained in Rhodesia then Zambia may yet become reintegrated into Southern Africa. Its crucial copper industry depends on technology and equipment from South Africa and, TAZARA notwithstanding, renewed communication across the Zambesi will help Zambia to contain the impact of inflation. However, Zambia and South Africa may be interested in the same markets for their manufactured goods such as Botswana, Malawi and Mozambique.

The dominance of South Africa in the region was noted by Bowman and is analysed further in our first section. In the economic and infrastructural issue area, BLS and South Africa are "a mini-Southern African system" (21), or the core of the subsystem. The findings of both Boyd and Shaw are supportive of this distinction, although their conceptual approaches differ from Bowman's. Boyd's innovative use of events data, Bowman's interest in labour migration, and Shaw's use of institutional and transactions analysis yield a fundamentally compatible finding -- that the communication between, and dependence on, South Africa and BLS are essentially one-way and unequal. In the study of regional subsystems, insufficient attention has been given to structures of regional dependence. While it is recognised that the ruling elites and other groups in BLS share with the South African elite an interest in the perpetuation of the present system, the relationship between them is clearly asymmetrical. As Bowman and others have noted, the strategic choices of the four black states of the region are constrained: "they are all exceedingly poor countries, land-locked and underdeveloped" (28). The new states of Mozambique and Angola have ports but the former is much poorer than the latter. Botswana, after the discovery of highly significant mineral reserves, has perhaps the least limited geo-political alternatives. The two papers on Botswana in Part Three, by Christopher Hill and by Donald Rothchild and Robert Curry, both analyse Botswana's ideological and economic development. In particular, Hill points to the similarities and contrasts between Botswana and the Bantustans; Rothchild and Curry examine the dilemmas of Botswana's mushrooming mineral complexes and the possibilities of greater independence. Johns also examines the constraints on Botswana in his contribution on opposition to white power.

In his original essay, Bowman suggested that the strategy of coexistence followed by the new black regimes in the region, plus the distinctions and tensions between the white rulers, tend to erode the racial dialect of the area. The more recent detente between the super-powers combined with a growing western ambivalence about the automaticity of support for South Africa further detract from the prospects of race war in the region. Bowman argues that the peripheral strategic status of the subsystem, combined with significant western investments in Southern Africa, enhance South Africa's middle power role in the region: "The lack of great power interest in a Southern African military adventure is a central pillar of support for the system" (35). Bowman concludes that the stability of the region is a function of the maintenance of white power in South Africa. The perpetuation of the white oligarchy is a function of its economic and military power. The essays by Kenneth Grundy and Tim Shaw in Section Three update and develop this thesis.

In his suggestive paper which analyses structural change in the "mini-Southern African system", John Barratt is essentially concerned with regional economic relations. He focuses on the prospects of converting dependence into interdependence, of South Africa responding positively to the demands of BLS. He suggests that the interests of stability demand that relationships centred on South Africa become both two-way and multilateral; he proposes a regional development agency to distribute South African assistance to both BLS and the homelands. He recognises that the African environment discourages the black states from maximising cooperation with South Africa and that more than rhetorical change in the structure of racial supremacy is necessary to eliminate their misgivings: the "conflict between regional loyalties and African unity is aggravated by the issue of South Africa's internal policies, which issue has effectively isolated the Republic from Africa as a whole" (59). The conflict between the OAU and the white regimes, which may force the black states of the region to choose between continued economic interdependence in the region and PanAfrican respectability, is noted in Zdenek Cervenka's paper on incompatible organisations in Part Four. However, diplomatic initiatives in the region in November and December 1974 may soften the confrontation and lead to new forms of coexistence between black and white polities.

Political change in South Africa's 'coprosperity sphere' contributed to the demise of its outward-looking policy, which was always ambivalent about whether its goal was economic cooperation or military coexistence through association with white and/or black states. However, the Vorster/Kaunda 'understanding' over Rhodesia and South West Africa may revive South Africa's regional diplomacy based on coexistence and exchange. Although Barratt may over-estimate China's intrusive role in the region, he correctly points to an emerging western response to domestic pressures to disengage. Many western states have expanded their strategies of multiple advocacy to include the region, by increasing aid and relations with BLS. In the future these ties with black regimes may be expanded to include recognition of, and the provision of assistance to, the Bantustans. A paradoxical situation would then arise: South Africa has become a regional imperial power as Britain has withdrawn from Southern Africa; but because of internal political constraints the Republic cannot fully implement even the Tomlinson Commission's recommendations for the development of the Bantustans; instead, the west may assist their development and by doing so improve their bargaining positions with the Republic.

Barratt's interest in patterns of regional behaviour is shared by Tim Shaw in his attempt to distinguish between relations of dependence, interdependence and independence in different subsystemic issue areas. His paper is essentially pre-theoretic and proposes a conceptual framework for the analysis of regional politics and a typology of regional actors. Shaw suggests that interdependencies and dependencies affect the independence of national actors (82). Patterns of regional conflict and cooperation are important foci of linkage politics in all states in the subsystem. National elites in the region are interested in the perpetuation of the subsystem but the intensity of domestic opposition affects their willingness to take political risks in advancing this stability. The neutrality of BLS in the regional military confrontation is challenged not only by guerrilla strikes and the intervention of white soldiers but also by the determination of their oppositions to adopt more PanAfrican postures. In the military issue area there were two sets of confrontational transnational coalitions - the "unholy alliance" of the white regimes and the dominant "Khartoum alliance" of the liberation movement. These unequal alliances, which are investigated in more depth in Chapter Eight by Sheridan Johns in Part Two, are in turn partially dependent on extra-regional support and supplies. The white armies are dependent on western equipment and technology; the guerrillas were dependent on either Soviet and/or Chinese material but are now successfully diversifying their sources to include groups and states in the west.

These extra-regional association are also related to the tolerance extended by the crucial group of host states in 'frontier' Africa -- Tanzania, Zambia and Zaire. Shaw presents data on the revised Southern African Customs Union and on the importance of regional trade to regional actors. He notes that over a variety of indicators the black states of the subsystem are more vulnerable and dependent than the white regimes on the perpetuation of regional structures --

trade, labour, and customs revenue. Tim Thahane examines these relations more comprehensively in Chapter Ten in Part Three. Shaw also points to the interests of regional and global multinational corporations in the advocacy of regional integration. Finally, he presents data on the diplomatic advantage possessed by the black states in being able, unlike the while regimes, to secure international recognition and hence into international circles for the presentation of their pleas for special consideration in their regional predicament. He concludes, like Bowman that constitutional schemes to avoid majority rule will not contribute to regional stability unless accompanied by redistributive justice. However, the liberation movements recognise that, at least in the short term, Bantustanisation detracts from their appeal to African nationalism and liberation.

The innovative methodology of Barron Boyd yields compatible results to the more orthodox and selective data used by Shaw. The latter provides some indicators of the constraints under which national decision-makers operate; Boyd presents events data to test the hypothesis that Southern Africa, as defined by Bowman, exists. He is concerned with the boundaries, structure and environment of the subsystem. Through the use of graphic techniques he discovers two distinct patterns of interaction in Southern Africa; only South Africa participates in both the "mini-Southern African system" with BLS, while it also interacts with the white regimes plus Malawi. These two sets of actors exhibit different patterns of behaviour. As also suggested by Bowman, Barratt and Shaw, the ties between BLS and South Africa are essentially dyadic rather than multilateral, dependent and not particularly cooperative or cohesive. Conversely, the relations between South Africa, Rhodesia, Angola, Mozambique and Malawi (the 'unholy alliance' plus the most cooperative black state) are multilateral, cooperative and cohesive; this is supportive of Shaw's suggestion that interdependence exists in the military issue area. Boyd also points out that "the dominating structural characteristic of relations between states in Southern Africa is the importance of South Africa" (113). He is modest in his claims for his methodology but justifiably asserts that a beginning has been made to verify empirically the attributes of subsystemic relationships. Clearly, events data could also be used to discover the frequency and characteristics of extra-regional relations and to determine whether regional cooperation has an impact on the general foreign policies of each regional unit. Problems of events data research in addition to the accuracy of sources include the coding of guerrilla conflict, an artificial nation-state focus, and the assumption that all reported interactions in any issue area are of equal importance. Relations in Southern Africa are characteristically confidential or unreported; 'soft' analysis is required to supplement more rigorous procedures; economic relations are of particular importance and are not 'captured' by this technique. Boyd's findings may also be indicative of the important variable of the race of the ruling elite: one set of actors is largely the white regimes, the other is largely black. Interaction among the white governments is more interdependent; that between black and white regimes is characterised by dependence. Both of the papers by Shaw and Boyd raise issues of the interpretation and validity of data. They also are relevant to the larger debate over approaches to the analysis of international politics: is the international system characterised by cooperation or conflict; are theories of neo-functionalism or war most salient?

In his innovative attempt to abstract trends in the development of the subsystem, Christian Potholm uses Kaiser's typology and distinguishes between six regional issue areas. He suggests that the willingness of the white regimes to offer rewards for cooperation rather than punishments for intransigence are generative of stability; threats, which may be responses to the imperatives of white politics, lead to regional disintegration and disturb patterns of communication. He points to a contemporary divergence of practice between the white regimes: "Both the Portuguese and the South African governments are currently far more inclined than Rhodesia to promote economic (and hence systemic) integration and to avoid, insofar as possible, punishment" (124). Potholm notes that one gap in research on the region is on the transnational ties between national elites and the impact of different ideologies and perceptions; will South Africa export its racial prejudices to Rhodesia and Portugal or will the nonracial examples of BLS be influential? Potholm suggests that incompatible and inflexible core values discourage integration. He concludes that the present pattern of behaviour in Southern Africa is most like Kaiser's intergovernmental regional subsystem type, rather than his transnational societal or comprehensive regional systems. His findings constitute a critique of neo-functional hypotheses; increased regional economic and infrastructural cooperation has not lead to socio-political integration. Perhaps major regional development projects serve merely to limit disintegration.

The papers in Part Two are concerned with the historical, racial and political continuities and discontinuities in the region, in examining the origins and development of the subsystem. Arthur Keppel-Jones uses evidence submitted to the Lagden Commission as an indicator of changing attitudes to race and culture at the turn of the century. His essay also raises the more general issue of the salience of class or colour as the basis of socio-political organisation in South Africa. He suggests that the relatively permissive and enlightened white attitudes expressed in evidence were related to calculations of the unlikelihood of real black equality for decades. 'Westernisation' was encouraged to force Africans into the market system; in a true *laissez-faire*, but nevertheless hypocritical, spirit the emergent black middle class was offered the rewards of upward social mobility but no special facilities were provided to advance this transition. Equality was acceptable as a white philosophy so long as it was believed that Africans could not achieve an elevated status. Few whites accepted that South Africa was to become one community; rather they welcomed social Darwinism and customary discrimination as evidence of natural social forces which did not challenge their intellectual acceptance of human equality. The Afrikaners refused to accept such English-speaking distinctions and in their characteristic quest for honesty and order have changed South Africa's legal system to reflect white practice rather than liberal ideas of permissive equality.

We need more research on black perspectives and opinions to understand contemporary black strategies towards the Republic. Black academics in Africa and the United States have a particular interest in the rediscovery of black history in Southern Africa. Such research will contribute to an understanding of the historical dimensions of Southern Africa and allow us to compare, for instance, Moshoeshoe's diplomacy with that of Buthelezi. We also need to recognise the imperative of power in understanding the evolution of core values, especially about race, over time. The contribution of Keppel-Jones may be usefully compared with that of Charles Harvey (Chapter Sixteen in Part Four) as disbelief continues to be one rationalisation for being permissive about black advancement.

The suggestive contribution by Lawrence Schlemmer considers a variety of theoretical approaches to race and conflict in Southern Africa. His explication of pluralism retrieves some of its utility after the onslaught of more critical and radical analysts of the class school of historical interpretation. He asserts that race and economic interests are reinforcing and superimposed. He is concerned to integrate these comments into the fabric of pluralism: "the presence of cultural differences, and the operation of cultural influences, have imparted a particular quality and flavour to inter-racial and inter-class relations in South Africa" (163). In his review of the historical origins of discrimination he suggests that religious rationalisations of colour prejudice followed rather than preceded racial attitudes; race conflict was caused by both Dutch and British settlers and was pre-industrial. Fear of black uprisings in the nineteenth century, the hate of blacks by the dispossessed and impoverished poor whites, and the racism of the South African mineral revolution all contributed to the development of discrimination and apartheid. In particular, urban Afrikaners felt threatened by black labour.

Following this historical and theoretical introduction, Schlemmer presents data on opinion research in Durban. Most respondents support notions of race supremacy; a minority of Afrikaner 'enlightened separatists' and English-speaking progressives, for reasons of ethnic autonomy and equality, favour race separation. The survey provides evidence supportive of pluralist theory; white opinion distinguishes clearly between the black and white community. Schlemmer also presents a suggestive typology of white voters based on a factor analysis of his survey; these composite groups have been labelled verkramptes, pragmatics, pluralists and liberal paternalists. Only the latter two groups are permissive towards the development of the Bantustans even if this demands sacrifices from the white community. The regime is responsive to verligte demands over the development of the homelands and there is evidence that the black middle class is abandoning majority rule in favour of homeland referents, at least in the short-term. This may increase conflict between the Bantustan leadership and the central government. Schlemmer concludes his provocative paper by returning to pluralism and South African history in which ethnicity, material interests and status-concern have become articulated into a coordinated and "self-reinforcing process, which in turn has produced a 'culture of racism'" (180). His data provide an interesting and topical background to South Africa's recent diplomatic initiatives following political change in Mozambique and Angola.

White politics and prosperity conflict with notions of substantive separate development; hence the South African regime's preoccupation with constitutional and administrative change rather than with redistributive justice. In future the demands of the white electorate for status and of the black leadership coalition for land and improved migrant labour facilities will conflict. Economic growth has led to greater tolerance over changes in the colour bar but not over the distribution of land. The contributions by Sheridan Johns and Christopher Hill both indicate the constraints on opposition and on development in the subsystem.

In his regional review of opposition in Southern Africa, Sheridan Johns proposes six categories of groups. These include the ruling parties in BLS, and now Mozambique and Angola, who within the limitations of regional integration provide respectability and access for other oppositional movements. Legal non-governing parties in BLS are actors in linkage politics of the region but all, like the Progressive Party in the Republic, have limited impact and resources. Legal extra-parliamentary political associations have a chequered history in the minority-ruled states, but the African National Council in Rhodesia, the Bantustan leadership and the Black People's Convention in South Africa, and the National Convention in Namibia, keep African demands and hopes alive. The most effective and threatening opposition to white power are the liberation movements, illegal political associations, which are typically direct descendants of previously legal extra-parliamentary political associations; these have also formed informal, transnational counter-alliances to the white coalition. These explicitly political organisations receive support from racially-based non-political associations such as the "black consciousness movement" and emergent labour organisations in South Africa. Finally, a less effective group is the multi-racial non-political associations such as student and church organisations in South Africa. Johns suggests that few transnational links have been forged between opposition groups, although the leadership of Botswana and Lesotho is moving towards recognition of the liberation movement and the Bantustan leaders hope for linkages with BLS. There are also few linkages across categories of oppositions. The modes of behaviour vary between groups, from the symbolic and verbal to the violent, but Johns concludes that the tenuousness of established linkages "make the likelihood of a strong and cohesive region-wide opposition movement remote" (224). However, some groups are more effective than others and have isolated vulnerable targets -- e.g., FRELIMO in Tete Province, before the coup, and the Bantustan leadership. So. although formal links may be minimal, there are multiple relationships of influence and collective pressure. Whether all opposition pressures are mutually supportive or contradictory is debatable. Both regional and global influence vectors have to be considered in the evaluation of likely developments in Southern Africa.

The final contribution in Section Two is an exhaustive analysis of the disengagement by Zambia from its inherited dependence on Southern Africa by Douglas Anglin. The quality of leadership and the high price of copper have propelled Zambia towards terminating its established ties with the Federation and South Africa and into developing new relations and infrastructure with states of the East African Community, especially with Tanzania. However, integration with East Africa has not been formalised outside bilateral institutions with Tanzania and participation in the East African National Shipping Line. Zambia is determined never to repeat its inherited dependence for trade, capital and labour on the white South, especially on Rhodesia. It has developed diversified relations with Zaire, Malawi and Botswana and will likely increase its cooperation with Mozambique and Angola once black governments are established. Zambia was an example and diplomatic centre for the region before its recent locus as centre of negotiations over Mozambique, Angola and Rhodesia. The comprehensive transactions analysis presented by Anglin is important not only for its theoretical insights, but also because it describes an alternative strategy to the tolerance of dependence on Southern Africa. Zambia continues to be dependent on copper, but copper has enabled it to disengage in important ways from Southern Africa.

The five essays in Part Three focus on the political economy of Southern Africa. Regional cooperation does not necessarily lead to advantages for all participants; in this section we begin to analyse who gets what from the partial integration of the region. Timothy Thahane presents an overview of the financial, communications and labour transactions in the subsystem. He presents data on the development of South Africa's financial and economic dominance over time and on both the dependence and challenges of the black states. He analyses the costs and benefits of participation in regional trade, finance and migration and examines the impact of poverty and land-lockedness on BLS. Communications and exchange focus on South Africa, but the infrastructure of the region offers the prospect of more multilateral relations. Thahane underlines the impact of race on the level of regional integration and points to the potential for regional development once political change makes it more desirable.

Chapters Eleven and Twelve both deal with the most interesting and dynamic ex-High Commission Territory, Botswana. Donald Rothchild and Robert Curry analyse the new choices and constraints on Botswana now that its beef potential has been supplemented by significant mineral reserves. The sensitive and courageous style of government under President Khama has served to maximise Botswana's options and maintain development while avoiding new forms of dependence on the white states. The poverty of Botswana has been reduced by a renegotiated Customs Union agreement and exports of diamonds, copper, manganese and nickel. Botswana has increased its ties with black Africa, especially with Zambia and will soon possess both road, rail, air and telecommunications links northwards. Botswana has 'struck it rich' in two ways -- it has discovered vast mineral reserves to augment its ranching and water resources, and the white power structure of the region is no longer so cohesive or threatening. Botswana is now less vulnerable, both economically and strategically. However, Rothchild and Curry are cautious about new forms of dependence and the impact of mining complexes on Botswana's fragile pastoral society; they are hopeful that Botswana will avoid growth without development.

Christopher Hill is also concerned with the possible 'underdevelopment' of Botswana as the benefits from its mineral resources leave the country, but he is confident about the diplomatic and administrative skills of the President and government. Both Zambia and Botswana have been able to disengage from regional dependence because of their political and mineral resources, as indicated in the chapters by Anglin and Hill. Hill, like Johns, also adopts a comparative approach to the development of black governments and parties; he focuses on Botswana and the Transkei. He suggests that the ethic of the ruling Botswana elite is essentially liberal; capitalism is accepted in a controlled environment. It welcomes growth in the mining industry and hopes to prevent the rise of new urban classes and distorted development; mining revenue will finance rural projects. Hill argues that Botswana can exploit a variety of necessary transnational ties with the white regimes while at the same time reducing dependence on them by accepting extra-regional investment. Like Shaw, he attaches importance to Botswana's diplomatic astuteness and diversification, and he draws a clear distinction between a dependent and a "stooge" state. He concludes with a comparison between Botswana and the Bantustans. Botswana is constitutionally and politically more free than the Transkei because of its international status and nonracial society plus its mineral and agricultural resources. However, the gap between the two systems could be narrowed if Bantustan independence is secured on terms acceptable to the black leadership. Conversely, South Africa may have an interest in retarding growth in BLS to speed the advance of the Bantustans to a comparable status. It may be able to reduce its responsibilities for rural unemployment and poverty in the Bantustans by providing formal independence and allowing western aid to flow to them as well as to BLS. Although the South African regime is not monolithic and is responsive to white interest group pressures, it would clearly be able to exploit the multiplicity of black units in a future Southern Africa. Whether it will be able successfully to divide-and-rule the region in a quasi-feudal style is partially dependent on the degree of cohesiveness that may develop within the emerging black caucus of Bantustan and BLS leaders.

Kenneth Grundy in Chapter Thirteen exposes the contradiction between South Africa's regional hegemony and its rhetoric of anti-neo-colonialism. His analysis of South Africa's foreign policy looks at the dilemmas of playing a "middle power" role. The Republic is dependent on the western economies while the region is dependent on it. Settlers in Southern Africa have always had an ambivalent relationship with their metropoles. The Boer War, UDI and the ineffective settler protest against black government in Mozambique and Angola all support Grundy's contention that simplistic imperialism is only a partial explanation. The tradition of anti-colonialism in South Africa, associated with Afrikaner political dominance, has led to a rejection of claims of South African imperialism in the subsystem. The political and strategic isolation of the Republic reinforce this rhetoric and world view; South African paranoia may not be completely unjustified. South Africa has assumed many roles vacated by Britain in the region, but her offers of dialogue and detente are combined with a massive arms build-up and internal oppression. Political change in Portugal has largely resolved the issue of how best to defend the laager -- through alliances or tactical retreat. However, as long as South Africa can maintain its economic links with the capitalist world economy it will be able to afford a combination of economic seduction and military deterrence in Southern Africa and overlook its history of anti-colonialism.

In Chapter Fourteen, Tim Shaw also analyses the dependence of South Africa and the bases of its regional dominance. Grundy focuses on the ideological aspects of this sub-imperial role; Shaw analyses the political economy of South Africa's hegemony. He examines the development of Afrikaner state capitalism in the Republic and the impact of new railways and energy sources on the region. His investigation of the limitations on South Africa, and its inability or unwillingness to prevent the emergence of black governments in the subsystem, indicates that it is moving towards a neo-colonial strategy. Although, as Grundy suggests, such a policy is a contradiction given its historical opposition to imperialism, nevertheless, if its middle power role is to be perpetuated it may have to accept the influence of foreign entrepreneurs and financiers. If South Africa can no longer protect white affluence by military or political means, it has the potential to maintain it by economic measures. South Africa needs the collaboration of the ruling elites in Southern Africa if its relationship with the western economy is to be secured. Interdependence is a relationship of mutual dependence.

In the final section, Part Four, we present four essays which further analyse the place of South Africa and Southern Africa in world politics. Zbigniew Konczacki in Chapter Fifteen analyses the weakness of Portugal and contradictions in its colonial policy. He suggests that the dependent status of Portugal in Europe prevented it from either increasing its exploitation or strengthening its control in Angola and Mozambique. It had insufficient economic resources to advance a neo-colonial solution and so attempted to defeat nationalism by military means. It mortgaged its metropolitan and colonial economies to pay for the anti-guerrilla wars; the cost of the wars prevented growth in Portugal and encouraged the dissatisfaction which led to the April 1974 coup. Portuguese colonialism was both unprofitable for the state and unattractive for the people. The transnational interests of the African nationalists and Portuguese people led to support for the military regime and to rapid decolonisation. Konczacki analyses the limited colonisation of Angola and Mozambique and the costs both to the colonies, to the metropole and ultimately to the anachronistic imperial elite.

Our primary subsystem level of analysis does not exclude extra-regional linkages but draws attention to intrusive pressures which act on the subsystem as a whole and those which influence individual actors within the region. Charles Harvey's study of British investment in South Africa presents data on the impact of British capital and management in South African society. He is sceptical of the political power allegedly wielded by corporations and in his review of possible strategies for foreign investors rejects withdrawal, except as a tactic. He indicates that pressure on foreign investors from active domestic constituencies is moderately effective whereas the denial of new investment is unlikely to have significant effects because of the amount of capital already committed; he advocates pressure for incremental change in a situation characterized by immobility rather than revolutionary potential. His paper is a valuable contribution to the debate on forces of change and the role of external capital. Harvey concludes that the quality and attitude of management is the crucial variable in the rate of black advance; overseas pressure encourages foreign investors to make good their claim to be agents of black improvement rather than mere supporters of the status quo. Of course, British investment in South Africa is of less economic importance than its trade with the Republic. Any strategy of change needs to be multilateral, to prevent other companies from taking advantage of withdrawal, and to deploy policies with respect to the region rather than employing less effective tactics against only national targets.

Although South Africa is the fortress of the region, its nuclear programme has evolved under significant economic and political constraints. In his paper, Jack Spence is concerned with South Africa's ability to enrich uranium and the likelihood of its substantiating its claim to regional hegemonic status by producing a nuclear weapon. It has not become a party to the nuclear non-proliferation treaty and has advanced the likely date by which it could achieve a nuclear capability to less than a decade. Spence traces the development of the Republic's nuclear programme since 1949. It exports uranium and may become self-reliant in energy resources with its own enrichment technology. Although it has no military alliances with major states it has entertained nuclear collaboration with the west. It refused to sign the

Non-Proliferation Treaty on four grounds: i) it is discriminatory against small states; ii) it is discriminatory against technologically underdeveloped states; iii) inspection would infringe South Africa's sovereignty; and iv) it does not have confidence in UN security guarantees. Spence argues that a nuclear capability is inappropriate given the nature of the threat to South Africa, as outlined in Johns' paper; it would not enhance, and may detract from, its potential to launch a pre-emptive attack against African cities and staging areas. No major power would be interested in a nuclear confrontation or alliance with South Africa and a nuclear South Africa would complicate the justificatory arguments of its major trade partners. Both Britain and South Africa are interested in keeping their relations at a level of relatively undisturbed normality, although nuclear status would enhance South Africa's ability to participate as a regional power within the framework of the Nixon Doctrine. However, it would also undermine the co-existence goals of the outward-looking policy. Spence concludes that South Africa is unlikely to become the seventh nuclear power because of political constraints; if gross proliferation occurred, the costs to its orthodox diplomatic stance would be reduced. However, South Africa's enforced isolation could lead it to act irrationally and to both acquire and employ nuclear weapons.

The essay by Zdenek Cervenka on the OAU analyses the organisational aspects of the confrontation between independent and white Africa. The African states have reluctantly advocated armed resistance as a strategy of change in the region, according to the Lusaka Manifesto. The OAU policy is based on the collective experience of its membership of colonialism and racial discrimination. Its military approach has been based on support for the liberation movements rather than the commitment of national armies to the confrontation. The marginal role of the OAU in Southern Africa is due to factionalism within the Liberation Committee and its lack of appropriate military resources. Although western interests discourage African states from military involvement in the region, they have belatedly afforded some recognition and assistance to the dominant liberation movements. Cervenka argues that given the disproportionate repression of guerrillas in South Africa and Rhodesia, non-violent techniques of resistance have been most effective to date. However, he predicts future racial conflict and bloodshed. The OAU's strategy has led to new policies in BLS and it hopes to liberate the region during its second decade. The OAU's goal of PanAfrican autonomy is presently dependent on extra-continental support for the liberation movement and African armies. It is particularly dependent on the continuation of its compatibility with the UN system. There are dangers in its organisational rigidity and the advocacy of platitudes of violence. There are many voices in Southern Africa pleading for better incomes and housing as well as for independent Bantustans or majority rule. Reform may lead to, rather than away from, revolution if the dissatisfied proletariat in South Africa becomes pre-revolutionary rather than merely dissatisfied.

This volume is concerned with the level and direction of cooperation and conflict in Southern Africa. These relationships coexist in several issue areas and are likely to continue despite political or economic change. Indeed, the interdependence of the region, and South Africa's dominance in it, may be increased as black governments are formed and detente progresses. We hope that this collection helps in the understanding and prediction of directions of change and continuity in Southern Africa.

1. Interaction and Integration in Southern Africa

Chapter One

THE SUBORDINATE STATE SYSTEM OF SOUTHERN AFRICA*

Larry W. Bowman

This paper hypothesizes the existence of a subordinate system in Southern Africa.[1] Evidence will be produced to show that this system can be described as an entity, that it operates quite independently of the dominant world power blocs, and most importantly, that it can best be analyzed and understood in terms of its own interrelations. Having postulated this system, I will then analyze the forces and pressures, both on and within the system, in an effort to assess the system's prospects for stability.

The idea of joining the notion of an integrated system with that of a discussion about the possibility of future stability in the area seems particularly useful. For far too long, events in Southern Africa have been viewed in a discrete manner, with little consideration given to the interaction of the countries concerned. However, recent political events, combined with a re-evaluation of historical factors, provide a persuasive basis for a new analysis of political relations in this very complex and interesting area of the world.

I. Introduction

The study of Southern African politics has always been fragmented because of the differing histories of the various countries and the wide variety of constitutional and legal forms under which they have been governed. To recount briefly: South Africa has been fully independent since 1910. South-West Africa was first a German colony and was then mandated to South Africa after the First World War. Though its legal status is now confused (since the United Nations General Assembly voted to terminate South Africa's mandate in October 1966), South Africa remains in effective control. The three former High Commission territories (Bechuanaland/Botswana, Basutoland/Lesotho, and Swaziland) were British protectorates or colonies from the end of the nineteenth century. The long-held tacit assumption that they would be turned over to South Africa faded in the 1950's, and both Lesotho and Botswana were brought to full independence in October 1966;

Swaziland will follow the same road this year. The gigantic territories of Mozambique and Angola are administered as integral parts of Portugal. Northern Rhodesia/Zambia and Nyasaland/Malawi were British colonies from the end of the nineteenth century and Southern Rhodesia was a self-governing colony after 1923. Linked together in the now defunct Federation of Rhodesia and Nyasaland from 1953-63, Malawi and Zambia both became independent in 1964; and Southern Rhodesia unilaterally declared itself independent in November 1965.

Scholars and political commentators have tended to shape their analyses around the prevailing constitutional forms. The area once called Central Africa (Zambia, Malawi, and Rhodesia) has often been handled as a unit, but seldom have its links to either the Portuguese territories or to South Africa been well described.[2] Many good studies of South African politics have been written, but little analysis exists of South Africa's economic and political penetration of the neighbouring countries.[3] The High Commission territories and South-West Africa have normally been studied in isolation, and the Portuguese territories have the even more dubious distin tion of virtually never having been studied by non-Portuguese scholars.[4] Recently two books with Southern Africa in their titles have been published, but in both cases the identification is basically geographic, rather than in terms of an integrated political analysis of the whole area.[5]

The few studies that have attempted to transcend the confines of the historical-constitutionalist approach and link the area in a meaningful fashion have not gone very far.[6] Concern has generally centered on a consideration of the white-dominated Southern African states and in particular upon the chances for political change or revolution within these states. The linkages considered have amounted to little more than the domino theory applied to Southern Africa. Thus Colin and Margaret Legum, perhaps the most influential British commentators on Africa could write in 1963:

> How long will it take to reach this point (of a liberation struggle beginning within South Africa)? Here one can only guess: perhaps two or three years before the collapse of Angola; another year for Mozambique and Southern Rhodesia - if they have survived that long. Thus one would fix the crisis point at between 1966-68. But, by then, the pattern of violence inside South Africa will have passed the point at which one can hope for any reasonable settlement between the races.[7]

Both historical-constitutional approaches and the approaches focusing essentially on racial questions have failed to delineate many of the social, political, and economic links that bind the area. This has led to an underestimation of some factors which make for stability and unity in Southern Africa. The determination of the whites to stay, fight, and rule has been underestimated, and the anticipated timetable for African nationalist victories has been very unrealistic. A set of expectations concerning change in the area was established that was completely out of touch with the realities of the situation. The result was poor political analysis during some crucial years in Southern Africa. Scholars, politicians, governments, and citizens have all contributed to the litter of discarded assumptions and expectations about the area.

I would support this statement with two of many examples of the political results of misperception. Rhodesia offers an unparalleled and continuing case of British inability or unwillingness to come to terms with the realities of Southern African politics. "Partnership" - the secret password to the Federation of Rhodesia and Nyasaland - served as a ten-year blinder to the constantly deteriorating racial situation in Rhodesia. Since Federation, Rhodesia's unilateral declaration of independence (UDI) has come, but Britain continues to search for "moderate" members of the Rhodesian Front to which to entrust an independent, legal Rhodesian government. Despite repeated British promises of imminent success, sanctions have not yet proved effective. It may well be at the present time that Britain sees the status quo as the best of a bad set of alternatives. Nevertheless, it is difficult to blame the Rhodesian Europeans alone for their actions - they have merely persisted in a policy condoned by Britain since 1923.

Similar illustrations can be produced relating to the South-West Africa case at the International Court of Justice. This case, argued at the World Court from 1960-66, was essentially intended to determine whether or not _apartheid_ in South-West Africa negated South Africa's obligations under the League of Nations mandate to "promote to the utmost the moral and material well-being and social progress" of the inhabitants of South-West Africa.[8] Numerous articles and books appeared, each dealing knowledgeably with various aspects of the case, but all assumed that the judgement would go against South Africa. The possibilities that South Africa would win the case or that the Court would refuse to pass judgement (which is what happened) were never really considered.[9] Neville Rubin has pointed out that on the day the South-West Africa judgement was announced, the U.S. State Department was unable to comment because the only prepared statement assumed that the judgement would go against South Africa.[10] The title of Ernest A. Gross's article in the prestigious _Foreign Affairs_, "The South-West Africa Case: What Happened?", captured the mood of bewilderment.[11]

It is now time to stop and reassess the political alignments in Southern Africa. White resistance to change has proven formidable, and neither in Rhodesia nor in the Portuguese territories is there any imminent sign of collapse. Malawi,

Botswana, Lesotho, and Swaziland are adjusting to the political realities of their geographic and economic positions and are not proving to be the political wedge of liberation that some had expected. The unwillingness of the big powers to intervene themselves, and their restraining influence in the United Nations on questions of intervention, necessarily limit the possibilities for change in Southern Africa. Furthermore, militant Pan-Africanism seems clearly on the decline. Thus political order in Southern Africa must be re-examined, for there is every reason to believe that for the foreseeable future the existing constellation of power must be dealt with. This point is made not in despair, but simply because Southern Africa is not intelligible unless it is seen as it is, rather than as one might hope it to be.

II. The Southern African State System

In considering Southern Asia, Brecher suggested that for a subordinate system to exist, the following six conditions would have to be present:

1. There should be a delimited scope with primary stress on a geographic region;
2. There should be at least three actors;
3. Taken together the actors should be objectively recognized by other actors as constituting a distinctive community, region, or segment of the global system;
4. The members should identify themselves as such;
5. The units of power should be relatively inferior to units in the dominant system (taken to mean the major world blocs); and
6. Changes in the dominant system should have a greater effect on the subordinate system than the reverse.[12]

He suggested that these characteristics would define the system in space and time and that two other sets of features, relating to "structure" and "texture," should be added to complete the description of a subordinate system. "Structure" would denote the basic patterns of relations among and between the units of the system, and "texture" would delineate the broad characteristics of the environment in which these relations function.[13] I have drawn heavily on Brecher's ideas in shaping my evidence for a Southern African state system.

I would suggest that the following states comprise the subordinate system in Southern Africa: South Africa, South-West Africa, Rhodesia, Angola, Mozambique, Lesotho, Botswana, Swaziland, and Malawi. Together these nine countries cover an area of over two million square miles (nearly twice the size of the Indian sub-continent, or two-thirds the size of the continental United States). They have a population of nearly forty million. Whereas prior to Rhodesia's UDI Zambia was fully a member of the Southern African system, this is no longer the case. Zambia's unique position will later be described in depth. The Congo (Kinshasa) might be considered a peripheral member of the system, but is is reasonably self-sufficient in enough ways (power, transportation, labor, finance) so that it cannot really be included in the Southern African system. The following table summarizes the demographic data:

Table 1

The States of Southern Africa

	Area (in sq. miles)	Pop. Est. 1/1/64	Pop. (per sq. mile)	Ratio of whites to non-whites
South Africa	472,926	17,330,000	36.0	1 to 4
South-West Africa	317,887	565,000	1.8	1 to 7
Angola	481,351	5,050,000	10.0	1 to 22
Mozambique	297,486	6,900,000	23.0	1 to 69
Lesotho	11,716	725,000	62.0	1 to 428
Botswana	275,000	365,000	1.3	1 to 143
Swaziland	6,705	290,000	43.0	1 to 28
Rhodesia	150,333	4,080,000	27.0	1 to 18
Malawi	45,747	3,200,000	70.0	1 to 400
Total	2,059,511	38,505,000	18.7	
By comparison:				
India	1,227,275	467,700,000	381.0	
United States	3,675,633	190,700,000	52.0	
Africa (total)	11,685,000	278,000,000	24.0	

Source: E. B. Espenshade, Jr. (ed.) Goode's World Atlas (12th ed., Chicago: Rand McNally and Co., 1965).

South Africa's economic dominance. The overwhelming structural characteristic of Southern Africa, and the one that more than anything else makes the system unified, is the domination of the area by South Africa's economic wealth and economic demands. South Africa holds an economic stranglehold over the neighboring states of Swaziland, Lesotho, and Botswana and exercises a significant influence within Malawi, Rhodesia, and Mozambique. South-West Africa is almost totally economically integrated with South Africa. Angola alone is completely viable without heavy interaction with the Republic.

South Africa's hold on the three ex-high Commission territories derives from their disadvantageous geographical locations, from their need to export labor to South Africa, and from their lack of resources.[14] Only Swaziland is in any way free from these controls, but other controls take their place. Extensive land alienation has occurred in Swaziland, and all mines and major industrial works are in the hands of South African capital. The Swazi traditionalists, who are in complete control of the Swazi political system, are determined to preserve the present close relations with the Repuplic.[15]

Lesotho is totally dependent on exporting her labor to South Africa. At any one time nearly 50% of all Lesotho's males are away at work in South Africa; their remittances home form an essential part of Lesotho's gross domestic product. Botswana must also export labor to South Africa although only about 20% of her males are normally away. As with Lesotho, Botswana cannot afford to risk the repatriation of her labor as a retaliatory move in a political quarrel. The societal crisis this would provoke internally in both countries would be vastly greater than any political harm these countries could do to South Africa.[16]

In addition, these three countries share with South Africa both a common currency (even after independence) and a 1909 customs and excise agreement (due to be re-negotiated with each independent country). Under this agreement South Africa distributes 1.3% of her customs and excise revenue among the three countries. This amount provides 53% of Lesotho's ordinary revenue, 10% of Botswana's, and 7% of Swaziland's.[17] A common currency of course prevents the three countries from having monetary policies of their own.

Whatever political changes occur in Southern Africa, Lesotho, Botswana, and Swaziland must look forward to a lengthy, if not perpetual, dependence on the goodwill and favour of South Africa, whoever the South African rulers are. These four countries form in essence a mini-Southern African system under any foreseeable circumstances.

South-West Africa should also be included within this smaller system for she has been fully incorporated into South Africa's economic and political structure. South-West Africa sends representatives to the South African Parliament, and South Africa has publicly stated that it will defend South-West Africa against any external aggression. One can only assume that South Africa is serious in this regard. Recently, Prime Minister Vorster has made a lengthy tour of South-West Africa and has offered Ovamboland, in Northern South-West Africa, Bantustan status, similar to that of the Transkei. It may well be that this is the first step in South Africa's implementation of the Odendaal Report which advocated Bantustans for South-West Africa.[18] Despite the United Nation's efforts to strip South Africa of her mandate and establish a United Nations administration for South-West Africa, all the evidence points to a hardening of South Africa's attitude regarding South-West Africa and the continued political integration of the two countries.[19]

South Africa and Mozambique have economic links that go back to the nineteenth century. The most important tie between these two countries is codified in the Portuguese-South African convention of 1909 (as amended). This convention allows the Witswatersrand Native Labor Association (WNLA) to recruit, for work in the mines, up to 100,000 Africans annually in Mozambique south of 22° latitude. In return for this labor, the South African government guarantees that 47.5% of the import-export traffic of the Rand area will pass through the port of Lourenço Marques. It is certain that far more than 100,000 Mozambique laborers are annually in South Africa, and Marvin Harris has estimated that up to 400,000 or two-thirds of the adult males of Southern Mozambique are employed in foreign territories.[20]

As Portugal has slowly moved to open up Mozambique for investment, new opportunities have been given South Africa to extend her influence within the country. A natural gas pipeline is now being laid between Moambo, sixty miles from Lourenço Marques, and the Rand. The cost of $140,000,000 is largely being met by South Africa.[21] It has also recently been reported that Portugal and South Africa have agreed to go ahead with the Cabora-Bassa hydro-electric scheme on the Zambezi above Tete. The estimated cost of $364,000,000 will partly be met by South Africa.[22]

Although presently South Africa has far fewer connections with Angola than with Mozambique, potentially Angola can be very important to South Africa. Oil has been discovered in Angola, and in the event of an oil boycott against South Africa, the Portuguese territory could be a crucial source of supply. The oil could be transported from Angola to South Africa within twelve-mile territorial limits without necessitating any travel in international waters where ships could be legally intercepted.

Malawi is primarily linked with South Africa through her need to export labor to the mines. Approximately 80,000 Malawians are recruited each year by WNLA and taken to the Rand. Indeed it is labor, above everything else, that ties the poor countries of Southern Africa to the dynamic, growing economic machine of South Africa. In 1963 the Froneman Committee reported to the South African government on foreign Africans within the country. This committee estimated (conservatively, it thought) that there were 836,000 foreign-born Africans in South Africa in 1960. The origins of these Africans were as follows:

Table 2

Foreign Africans in South Africa - 1960

Birthplace	Persons	% of total African pop. of South Africa
South-West Africa	6,000	.06
Lesotho	280,000	2.60
Swaziland	66,000	.61
Botswana	85,000	.79
Rhodesia	75,000	.69
Malawi	73,000	.68
Mozambique	220,000	2.04
Other	31,200	.31
Total	836,000	7.78

Source: Ken Owen Foreign Africans: Summary of the Report of the Froneman Committee (Johannesburg: South Africa Institute of Race Relations, 1963) 3.

The small percentage figures belie the crucial role of this foreign labor in the economic system of South Africa. These Africans, when distributed, comprise over 25% of the agricultural working force, and in the mines they make up a far higher percentage.

Based on the recommendations of the Froneman Committee, it has been the stated policy of the South African government to replace foreign labor with indigenous workers whenever possible. This policy has been a cause of great concern in all the labor-exporting countries, but to date it has not been seriously implemented. Nevertheless, the repatriation of foreign labor, or even the cutting back on foreign recruitment, remains one of the most powerful controls that the South African government holds over its smaller and less wealthy neighbours.

Table 3

Origin of Labor in Gold and Coal Mines - 1960

	Affiliated Gold Mines	Affiliated Coal Mines
South Africa	37.8%	37.7%
High Commission Terr.	19.5%	16.6%
East Coast-Mozambique	22.4%	45.3%
Other Africa	20.3%	.4%
Total	100.0%	100.0%

Source: Ken Owen, op.cit., 10.

Prior to her unilateral declaration of independence (UDI) on November 11, 1965, Rhodesia traded heavily with South Africa, but in no sense could it have been called economically dependent upon her southern neighbour. This is no longer the case. Rhodesia is now absolutely beholden to South Africa for her ability to survive the economic sanctions applied by most of the world's countries.[23] South Africa has done two crucial things which have allowed Rhodesia to stay on her feet economically: she has provided oil and petroleum products, and she has permitted the unlimited exchange, at par value, of the Rhodesian pound for the South African rand (one Rhodesian pound = two South African rand).

It is difficult to know which of these services has been more important. It seems clear that Rhodesia's contingency planning for UDI, such as it was, had not seriously considered the possibility of oil sanctions. Thus, once they were implemented in December 1965, and Beira, Mozambique, was closed as an import route, Rhodesia had to reorient her supply route to South African supplies by road and Mozambique supplies by rail from Lourenço Marques.[24] Rationing was imposed in Rhodesia, but it was never a hardship and it is now thought highly likely that Rhodesia is stockpiling oil.[25]

The credit arrangements made possible by South Africa's acceptance of the Rhodesian pound have allowed Rhodesia to maintain relatively normal trading relations with much of the world. Dummy corporations have been established in South Africa as middlemen for imports and exports to Rhodesia. By accepting payment in pounds for oil and other purchases, South Africa has freed Rhodesia's limited foreign exchange for essential purchases that South Africa cannot supply. This is in part good business (in being a middleman at premium prices), but it has also been estimated that Rhodesia's trading deficit to South Africa in 1966 was approximately $70,000,000.[26] Whether South Africa will be willing to carry and increase this type of deficit indefinitely is a matter of conjecture.[27] What is clear, however, is that South Africa is in a position to exercise a virtual life or death control over Rhodesia's economy.

In addition to the broad variety of economic links that tie nearly all Southern African countries to South Africa, two other internal ties within the system should be noted. As in their relations to South Africa, both Mozambique and Malawi also export significant amounts of labor to Rhodesia. J. Clyde Mitchell has estimated that in 1956, 48% of the Africans in wage-earning employment in Rhodesia were non-indigenous.[28] In the farming and forestry industries, 60% of Rhodesia's labor comes from outside the country, and in mining the percentage is even higher. The 1962 Rhodesian African census put the number of Malawians in Rhodesia at 200,000 and Mozambiquans at 117,620. Zambia exports about 50,000 laborers to Rhodesia. Rhodesia has threatened to repatriate this foreign labor if their home countries press sanctions against Rhodesia, but this threat has not as yet been implemented.

<u>Zambia's disengagement from Southern Africa</u>. An unforeseen, and to date the most important, effect of Rhodesia's UDI was the impetus given to Zambia to cut her links with the South and move into the East African trading and supply orbit as quickly as possible. This is necessarily a long-term proposition, but there is little doubt that Zambia is committed to this course and will not be likely to alter this decision, regardless of any change in governments in Rhodesia.

At the time of UDI, Zambia was absolutely dependent on Rhodesia. Her trading deficit to Rhodesia in 1965 was $110,000,000. All Zambia's copper was exported through Rhodesia; Wankie Colliery in Rhodesia supplied 100,000 tons of coal monthly to keep the Copperbelt mines and other industries running; Kariba Dam, controlled by Salisbury, supplied 75% of the Copperbelt's power; 40% of Zambia's imports and all of her oil came from Rhodesia.[29]

Since UDI Zambia has made phenomenal progress in extricating herself from Rhodesia's control.[30] Since mid-December 1965, all of Zambia's petroleum products have been supplied from sources other than Rhodesia. Zambia has had to live under much stricter rationing than Rhodesia, but her oil supply is now firmly tied to Tanzania. An Italian consortium is presently constructing a pipeline from Dar es Salaam to the Copperbelt. It is hoped that this will be completed by September 1968 and replace the inconvenient road and air imports that now take place.

Zambia's dependence on Rhodesian coal has been partially eliminated by the opening of two coal fields within Zambia. It has been estimated that Zambia halved its normal coal imports from Rhodesia in 1966, and it is projected that by the end of 1968, Zambia will fully supply her own coal requirements.[31] As far as power is concerned, Zambia has continued to draw from Kariba as was done before UDI. However, Zambia intends to dam the Kafue river near Lusaka and thus partially construct a power alternative to Rhodesia. Nothing has as yet been firmly settled but it appears Yugoslavia will get the contract and that Zambia hopes to complete the project by 1971.

These projects aside, the most remarkable achievement of Zambia's policy has been her ability to shift export and import markets away from Rhodesia. In 1965, Zambia imported about $128,000,000 worth of goods from Rhodesia; in 1966 Zambia's imports from Rhodesia were off 35% and in 1967 they were off 55%. This downward trend should continue. Before UDI, 98% of Zambia's imports came through Rhodesia; this has now dropped to 75%.

As far as exports are concerned, copper is the lifeblood of Zambia. Copper accounts for 95% of Zambia's exports; the revenues received comprise 50% of the total domestic product and 70% of the government's revenue. During 1966, Zambia slowly developed alternative export routes to the usual rail route through Rhodesia. By the end of the year, over 50% of Zambia's 60,000 tons per month exports were going out via Lobito in Angola, via Beira through Malawi, and via road or air to Tanzania. By mid-1967 not even a third of the copper exports passed through Rhodesia. As the Great North Road is improved and Dar es Salaam's harbor is expanded, the rest of the copper as well may find an alternative to the Rhodesian route.

Taken together, Zambia's actions are dramatically reshaping long-standing political and economic patterns in Southern Africa. With all of these projects unfolding (and Zambia is one of the few African countries with the resources to make them a reality), we can say with some confidence that in the not distant future Zambia will be freed from dependence on many of her former southern trade and supply routes. But it will take time. Zambia's trade with Rhodesia has altered substantially but South Africa has largely filled the void (Zambia's imports from South Africa rose from $58 million in 1965 to $120 million in 1967).

The key to the timetable of Zambia's disengagement lies in the transport problem. An all-weather road north to Tanzania is a minimum requirement; the proposed TanZam railroad would be better. China appears ready to finance and build this rail link, but there are still too many uncertainties about the project to make any firm predictions. Nevertheless, Zambia's commitment to turn north seems firm.

Despite her lingering and important ties to the south, Zambia's relations with Rhodesia and South Africa are distinctly cool. Zambia has applied for membership in the newly formed East African Community and this has important implications for Zambia's long-range plans. Rhodesia's cutting of supplies to land-locked Zambia following UDI taught Zambia to make trade relationships with solid friends and this is what she is doing to the north. Zambia's actions are drawing a line at the Zambezi and further throwing Rhodesia into the arms of South Africa.

The expansion of political interaction. The economic structure of the area plus the emergence in recent years of independent African-governed states has given rise to broadly expanded political intercourse in Southern Africa. These political interchanges, going far beyond mere perfunctory meetings, are of critical importance in describing the evolution of the Southern African state system. Because of South Africa's long-standing position as the *pariah* of the world community, both her friends and enemies have generally been reluctant to be publicly associated with her. It is a political change worthy of some comment that neighboring countries (both black and white) are now prepared to interact more openly with the South African government.

Malawi and Lesotho are the two independent African-governed countries that, to date, have sent official diplomatic missions to South Africa. It is likely, however, that Botswana and Swaziland will also do so. Chief Jonathan, Prime Minister of Lesotho, was the first African leader to meet formally with Dr. Verwoerd. He paid a state visit to Pretoria on September 2, 1966, four days before Verwoerd was assassinated. Chief Jonathan has since returned to South Africa to pay an official call on Mr. Vorster, South Africa's new Prime Minister. On both occasions Lesotho's black leader was received with full diplomatic honors, and *apartheid* was relaxed to accommodate him. Malawi subsequently entered diplomatic negotiations with South Africa and in March 1967 three Malawi ministers paid a state visit to Cape Town.

These visits have been major diplomatic breakthroughs for South Africa, which has always sought to expand its diplomatic activity with the rest of Africa. The political effect of these exchanges has been to crack the solid phalanx of African countries lined up against the white-ruled Southern African states at the United Nations.[32] Malawi has gone the farthest in this respect. With Britain and France, Malawi abstained on the United Nations General Assembly motion to strip South Africa of her South-West Africa mandate. (The vote was 114 for, two - Portugal and South Africa - opposed, with three abstentions.) Lesotho and Botswana were conveniently not present for the vote. President Banda of Malawi has been sharply critical of other African states for their attitude toward his regime's relations with South Africa. He has claimed that Malawi would never join "the Hypocrisy Club" like other African countries who "are criticizing me for trading openly with South Africa (while) they themselves are trading with South Africa secretly. While they are decrying South Africa, they are doing so on stomachs full of South African meat." Trading with South Africa did not mean Malawi supported apartheid "but one has to be realistic, for South Africa is here to stay and is the most powerful country in Africa industrially, economically, financially, and the most militarily powerful."[33]

Malawi, Lesotho, and Botswana have broken sharply with the African states on other issues as well. They have refused full compliance with the United Nation's vote of mandatory sanctions against Rhodesia and are publicly opposed to the use of force to bring down the Smith government. Malawi has also shattered precedent by being the first African-governed state to send an official mission to Lisbon, and Portugal's Foreign Minister Noqueira has visited Malawi.[34] A wide variety of other contacts (both official and unofficial) are maintained within the region. South African businessmen regularly visit the adjoining African states, and South Africa's Foreign Minister Muller attended independence celebrations in both Botswana and Lesotho. He has since made a return visit to Lesotho. Chief Jonathan and Prime Minister Khama of Botswana both visited Malawi in 1967, and Malawi ministers have visited Lesotho and Botswana in addition to making contacts with the white governments.

It is difficult to see how Malawi, Lesotho, and Botswana could order their relations in Southern Africa in any other way. They are all exceedingly poor countries, land-locked and underdeveloped. Unlike Zambia, they do not have the financial resources to pull themselves out of the Southern vise. Their only major export (aside from Malawi's tea) is their labor, and the internal stability of each society demands that this labor be exported. Each country is free to maintain its own internal non-racial policy, but none is in a position to push change upon its surrounding neighbor. As Seretse Khama put it in a recent article, his country must follow "a policy of prudence."[35]

South Africa and Portugal have both been delighted to find black friends on an otherwise hostile continent. South Africa's Muller termed the Malawian visit to South Africa "of historic importance, and one that should serve, we hope, as an example to others that peaceful coexistence is possible in Southern Africa ..."[36] South Africa has signed trade agreements with both Malawi and Lesotho, and a South African firm has undertaken to plan and design Malawi's new capital in Lilongwe. Portugal and Malawi have signed a major transportation agreement and a short railroad connection is now being built to link the Malawi railroad to the Mozambique port of Nacala (in addition to the present links to Beira). It is much too early to determine the lasting impact of South Africa's open relations with black states but there is an obvious optimism emanating from Pretoria.[37]

Interaction between the white-ruled states is also increasing. This too is a new development, at least in its public aspects, for the whites have traditionally been adverse to acknowledging their common interests. It is, of course, obvious that Portugal, Rhodesia, and South Africa are drawn together by their common defense of racial privilege. But it is by no means so apparent to what, if any, extent they would be prepared to defend one another militarily.

Until recently it could be said with some degree of certainty that Angola and Mozambique were the most underdeveloped areas in Africa. The colonial wars, although a serious drain on Portugal's national budget, have ironically given a much needed injection of manpower, skill, interest, and money to the long-neglected territories. The European population of both countries has risen sharply, and antiquated financial policies which have long impeded the exploration for and development of resources are gradually giving way. As has been noted, this has resulted in new opportunities for South African investment.

On the political side, South Africa has tended to be skeptical about Portugal's willingness to defend her African territories. A recent trip to Lisbon, however, by South Africa's Defense Minister, Piet Botha, sheds new light on South Africa's rising confidence in Portugal's determination. For the first time the two countries publicly alluded to joint defense cooperation, and Botha noted that "our task has been greatly facilitated by the strength and resolution of our Portuguese neighbors in Angola and Mozambique."[38] Portugal's ability to withstand African nationalist pressure has, if anything, increased over the years. The appointment, late in 1966, of Lt. Col. C. A. Rebocho Vaz as the Governor-General of Angola was expected to bring an even tougher line to Angola.[39]

Rhodesia's UDI has presented Southern Africa collectively with its most vexing problem. UDI was undertaken as a pre-emptive political step because the Rhodesian Front government had convinced itself that independence of any kind was the only alternative to an African nationalist government in Rhodesia. The illegality of the move established a new and uncertain political situation in the area and has since led to major political and economic restructuring - the importance of which should not be underrated.

As noted, Malawi, Lesotho, and Botswana have refused to comply fully with the Security Council's call for mandatory sanctions against Rhodesia. Although none of these countries likes the present Rhodesian government, trade and transport links have not been broken except when suitable and viable alternatives exist. Unlike Zambia, these countries have not quickly and visibly broken ties with Rhodesia whenever possible.

The Portuguese and South Africans have been put in an awkward position by UDI. Their own ideological position has been newly exposed by the Rhodesian move, and the illegal status of the Smith regime established the possibility of international intervention in Southern Africa. Both countries have been cautious in their relations with Smith's government; Rhodesia has not been diplomatically recognized, but sanctions have not been imposed. Both countries defend their domestic policy, and the foreign policy which flows from it, on a strict interpretation of Article 2 (7) of the United Nations Charter which states, "Nothing contained in the present Charter shall authorize the United Nations to intervene in matters which are essentially within the domestic jurisdiction of any state ..."[40] As they consider the Rhodesia question a domestic dispute between Britain and Rhodesia, they do not support UN involvement. Neither country supports trade boycotts, so they have maintained normal commercial dealings with Rhodesia. Portugal has been rather more harassed in this regard than South Africa, for Britain has chosen to apply pressure against the much weaker Portuguese. Portugal has not had the political or military power to prevent Britain from blocking oil shipments to Beira for trans-shipment to Rhodesia, but Britain has not disturbed the main Mozambique port of Lourenço Marques, from which most of Rhodesia's oil now derives.[41]

South Africa's relations with the Smith government are the most important to note. From the beginning South Africa feared UDI because of the possibility that sanctions against Rhodesia might expand to include herself as well. Whereas Rhodesia was prepared to gamble that South Africa would come to her assistance, South Africa was reticent about aiding Rhodesia until it became obvious that Britain was neither prepared to use force against Rhodesia nor willing to contemplate an economic confrontation with South Africa over the Rhodesian question.[42] This being the case, South Africa was more than prepared to assist Rhodesia, for, all things being equal, Smith was preferable to any African leader. Furthermore, helping Smith was good domestic politics[43] and offered the possibility of discrediting sanctions as a weapon for coercing political change in Southern Africa. If no n^w international political debts were to accrue from helping Smith, the cost to South Africa in comparison to the advantages gained was not great.

It is nevertheless possible that South Africa's support for Smith is not without bounds. The fervent ideologues of _apartheid_ are contemptuous of Rhodesia's verbal adherence to multi-racialism, and the politicians continue to see UDI as an unnecessary and dangerous step. As Rhodesia's economy becomes ever more dependent upon South African support, its need to remain white may diminish. Although the loss of Rhodesia to an African government would be a psychological blow to South African whites (and perhaps politically impossible to accept unless imposed by the great powers), it is highly questionable whether it would affect South Africa's security at all. It should also be pointed out that when the need arises (as in the development of good relations with the new African states) South Africa has been able to bend apartheid with striking pragmatism.

A black Rhodesia might even offer political advantages. Many white Rhodesians would leave Rhodesia for South Africa and thus bolster that country's racial equation. South Africa would no longer bear the opprobrium of supporting an illegal regime. But the most important point is that once the economies of the two countries are inter-locked, it is largely irrelevant whether Rhodesia is ruled by whites or blacks. As Allistair Sparks, foreign editor of the Rand Daily Mail (Johannesburg) has pointed out, "In many ways, a ring of black states economically beholden to South Africa can provide a far better protective cushion against the North than the odd arc of white colonies which, being colonies, tend to invite attention and trouble ..."[44] This sort of reasoning may have been behind the blunt editorial in Die Burger (Cape Town) on December 22, 1966, which suggested that Rhodesians should ask themselves whether UDI has not become an empty shell - something which could have had its uses, but which in the time ahead can become more and more of a hindrance .... Independence has not been gradually accepted internationally and the chances that it will be recognized by even a single state in the world in the present and expected circumstances are negligible. Normal economic relations with her become less defensible if she maintains that she is a sovereign state.[45]

As long as sanctions continue against Rhodesia, the political fact to note is that it is Pretoria, rather than London or Salisbury, that ultimately controls the destiny of the Rhodesian state. In the absence of direct military force, it is South Africa alone which has the power to coerce political change in Rhodesia. It is interesting to speculate, if nothing else, that if Rhodesia continues to grow in dependence upon South Africa, it may one day be Pretoria, far more than London, which will put a black government into Rhodesia.

The character of the system. From the foregoing discussion it is apparent that the dominating characteristic of the relation between states in Southern Africa is the dependence of most of the states within the system on South Africa. Angola alone is included solely out of political affinity and Zambia, the only state in the area with any potential to be a countervailing political or economic force, has instead chosen to begin to disengage from Southern Africa.

It would be wrong, in my opinion, to emphasize the racial characteristics of Southern Africa to the exclusion of a thorough analysis of the other unifying factors which are indigenous to the area. Racism gives a distinctive tone to the area, but by looking closely at the economic and social structure one quickly discovers that government changes from colonial status to independent African rule have not seriously altered the pattern of relations among states. In fact, it is certain that the new African rulers are interacting more, and taking a far more practical and intelligent look at their position, than Britain ever did on their behalf. Rather than further polarizing the area, the emergence of African governments in Malawi, Botswana, Lesotho and Swaziland has served an integrating function in Southern Africa and led to meaningful discussions across racial lines at the governmental level.

It could be expected that this same pattern would occur if African governments emerged in Rhodesia or the Portuguese territories. Mozambique under African leaders would in all probability want to continue to export labor to South Africa and Rhodesia. Further, the economic viability of Mozambique is closely linked to its trade and transport ties to the interior, and an African government would be unlikely to jeopardize these links. Rhodesia's future rulers whether white or black, will have to deal with the vast reorientation and partial destruction of the Rhodesian economy brought by UDI. Rhodesia's land-locked status necessarily limits the extent to which she could be antagonistic toward Mozambique or South Africa. All the states in the region will have to come to terms with the reality that, without the full support of the great power, they have no future prospects of changing the political structure of South Africa. The system is drawn together by powerful economic demands that are met in spite of fundamental political differences. Barring the economic destruction of South Africa, this pattern of economic and political relations can be expected to continue indefinitely.

All of the countries in Southern Africa seek to extend their influence beyond the boundaries of Southern Africa. Malawi, Botswana, and Lesotho are members of the United Nations, of the Organization of African Unity, and of the Economic Commission for Africa. In these organizations they have sought to explain their difficult position and asked for understanding when their geographic and economic position forces them to deviate from the solid anti-colonial line.

In addition to its massive economic ties to all the major Western countries, South Africa, particularly in recent years, has assiduously attempted to develop ties with other African states. Although the results of these diplomatic and trade initiatives are shrouded in secrecy by both the South Africans and the African states, there is evidence that South Africa is having some success in breaking out of her isolated position. Dr. Muller, South Africa's Foreign Minister, attended the Independence Day celebrations in both Lesotho and Botswana, where he met African leaders from all over the continent. He subsequently reported that in 1966, fifty African Ministers passed through Jan Smuts Airport in Johannesburg and that South Africa sent eight official or semi-official delegations to African states in 1966.[46] In Parliament on January 31, 1967, Dr. Muller said that "Those countries willing to cooperate with South Africa are increasing. Contact on different levels has increased day by day." This statement is at least partially substantiated by reference to South Africa's trade figures with the rest of Africa. Although for political reasons South Africa does not break down her African trade on a country-by-country basis, there have been sharp increases in recent years.

Table 4

South African Trade with Africa (in rand)
(1 rand = $1.40 US)

	Imports from	Exports to
1964	90,139,717	113,883,538
1965	108,825,982	147,137,428
1966	129,000,000	192,000,000*

Source: Republic of South Africa *Monthly Abstract of Trade Statistics* (Pretoria: Government Printing Office, 1964-65). *The Daily Telegraph* (London) February 28, 1967.

* The much expanded trade figures in 1966 reflect for the most part South Africa's growing trade with Rhodesia and Zambia.

With the preceding evidence of economic and political relations in mind, how do Brecher's six conditions for the existence of a subordinate system hold up? There can be no question that conditions one and two prevail. The area is delineated and fully integrated, and there are more than three actors. Points three and four deal with the question of identity. Internally there is no question of the fact that the actors see themselves as members of a Southern African system and realize that their own relations to others within the system are critical to their success or failure. Externally South Africa is trying to improve her image as an African country, and the African-governed countries are everywhere undertaking the difficult task of explaining to the world the real dynamics of the Southern African system. Point six, that "changes in the dominant system have a greater effect on the subordinate system than the reverse," also applies. It is obvious that any major world power shift against the West would have an unsettling effect upon the system, whereas internal political changes within any member state (outside of South Africa) would have relatively little impact upon the dominant system.

Point five, that "the units of power are relatively inferior to units in the dominant system" is the most interesting to handle. Though it is clear that the dominant system has far greater power than the subordinate system, it is also true that the dominant system, short of military action, has little influence over the political pattern in Southern Africa. The deviant racial stance of South Africa, Portugal, and Rhodesia is a source of embarrassment to the West and, within the confines of the anti-communist bloc, puts the West in the somewhat uncomfortable position of supporting racism. Nevertheless, there is little disposition in the West to challenge the *status quo* in Southern Africa. Can we draw any conclusions from this relating to dominant system/subordinate system relations?

Cuba offers one example of how the West punishes those who deviate within the system. Sanctions were applied (unsuccessfully) and total exclusion ultimately followed. But it is clear from the pattern of events that the West is only prepared to punish deviance to the left (Dominican Republic, Cuba, Vietnam) whereas Argentina and Greece are only the latest examples of continued Western support for fascistic-type governments. Southern Africa draws great strength from these historic parallels. In 1966, the year following UDI and the imposition of economic sanctions against Rhodesia, France, West Germany, and the United States all increased their trade with Rhodesia. Early figures from the first quarter of 1967 (after the imposition of mandatory sanctions by the Security Council) indicate that these same countries (with Japan added) have *increased* their trade with Rhodesia above 1966 levels.[47]

Aside from the West's preoccupation with left-wing disturbances (a major qualification, to be sure) the general pattern seems to be for increasing latitude within extant subordinate systems. France is clearly making her own way in Western Europe and Rumania is doing much the same in Eastern Europe. The Middle East is the most relevant recent example of a subordinate system completely out of control.

The Southern African system, however, draws strength from the West's rigidity toward change. The dominant and subordinate systems are drawn together on basic Cold War issues, but the West's power to reshape the deviant racial ideology (outside of sanctions, blockade, and in all likelihood war) is very small. In addition, a shift in power between the dominant systems is not likely to change Southern Africa unless the above military operation is carried out. Ideological adherence to the Western position on communism combined with a strong and integrated economic structure gives a hard core of unity to the Southern African subordinate system. What are this system's chances for stability?

III. The Prospects for Stability

In his conclusion Brecher alludes to several questions around which one could frame an analysis of the stability of a subordinate state system. Three of these seem particularly useful: (1) Does the system have the power to impede intervention and ensure its own independence? (2) Is internal stability of member states necessary for systemic maintenance? (3) Does systemic maintenance create a condition for greater world stability?

Many factors lead to the conclusion that Southern Africa, as a system, is strong enough to impede intervention. Much of its strength is of a negative variety. The unpredictability of the direction of coerced change mediates against intervention, and in a troubled world no great power is eager to start a war in Southern Africa. The lack of great power interest in a Southern African military adventure is a central pillar of support for the system. The reasons for this resistance to fundamental change are obvious and well-documented. Britain and America both have sizeable financial investments in the area, particularly in South Africa.[48] South Africa is part of the Western world's defense chain. This fact is sometimes scoffed at, but it is not to be discounted when the Suez Canal is closed and Britain is withdrawing from East of Suez. South Africa is a crucial market for Britain and the supplier of most of the non-communist world's gold. For all these reasons the West would be loath to mount a military operation without a clear idea of the outcome that would follow from the inevitable chaos. The South African defense establishment is large, well-equipped, mobile and dedicated; it is certain that any invasion would meet strong resistance. With much smaller military forces, the Portuguese in both Angola and Mozambique have demonstrated their ability to repel external forces, and Rhodesia is now doing the same.

It has long been believed that if an invasion were to be mounted against Southern

Africa, the United Nations should play a leading role. A cost analysis of a projected invasion has even been made.[49] But it is not a likely proposition. The great powers would have to concur, and it is inconceivable that Britain or America would support an invasion of South Africa. In addition, France and the Soviet Union very definitely seek to limit the United Nation's role in matters involving peacekeeping and military operations. Even on the question of South-West Africa, where the United Nations is on stronger legal grounds, the desultory debates of the special South-West African session (April-May 1967) demonstrate the unreality of the whole question of intervention. The shadow of the Congo operation hangs heavily over all suggestions that the United Nations be used in a military role. Barring the unlikely possibility of external aggression by a Southern African white state, United Nations military action can probably be ruled out.

Sanctions too have been thoroughly discussed as a possible method of coercing internal change.[50] The conclusion reached in the Leiss volume was that

> Based on purely economic calculations and assuming determination on part of the South African government to resist the measures taken, it becomes reasonably clear that no single economic measure would be likely to have a sufficiently powerful impact to force acquiescence. Indeed, South Africa could probably hold out against a complete boycott and embargo reasonably well for several years, possibly longer.[51]

Mandatory sanctions against Rhodesia were voted in December 1966. Their lack of effect to date against a much smaller country can give little encouragement to those seeking political change in South Africa via the sanctions route. In the absence of effective sanctions we are thrown back to the question of enforcement, where we again encounter the slim likelihood that the great powers would concur. Perhaps the death knell of sanctions was sounded in March 1967, when Dr. Robert Gardiner, a Ghanaian and the Executive Secretary of the United Nations Economic Commission for Africa, visited Southern Africa. He encouraged increased contact between South Africa and the rest of Africa and stated, "Greater economic cooperation in Southern Africa is to our mutual advantage."[52] Following his return to ECA Headquarters in Addis Ababa, Gardiner even suggested that the ECA would reconsider admitting South Africa back into the ECA from which she had been suspended in 1963. These are remarkable and surprising statements in light of what the United Nations has traditionally said about South Africa.

For the foreseeable future at least, Southern Africa's ability to impede intervention seems clear. Eleven military coups in Africa since June 1965 have curbed the militant foreign policies of individual African states and of the Organization of African Unity. The anti-colonial consensus at the United Nations remains fairly intact, but its ability to escalate activity beyond the verbal stage is highly questionable. An economically and militarily strong South Africa, surrounded by client states, befriended by the great powers, and geographically isolated from any significant political enemy would be a difficult foe in time of war, let alone when no encounter is projected.

Is internal stability of member states necessary for systemic maintenance? Here we must, as we have in other places, make a sharp distinction between South Africa and the other states of the system. Malawi, Lesotho, Swaziland, and Botswana can be endemically unstable without greatly affecting the overall stability of Southern Africa. Angola, Mozambique, Rhodesia, and even South Africa have all sustained periods of internal unrest without endangering the nature of the system as it now exists. Containable instability does not affect the system but what would be the effect of revolutionaly change?

Here we can only speculate. One could presume, though not with complete certainty, that if one Portuguese territory was lost, the others would quickly follow. Angola under an African government could cause serious trouble for South-West Africa, because South Africa's controls over Angola are very limited and the defense of South-West Africa would be a distant and difficult problem. Mozambique under an African government would ease the geographical dependence of Malawi and Swaziland on the white countries, but Mozambique's important labor and transport ties to Rhodesia and South Africa would probably prevent overt hostility toward white governments in Rhodesia and South Africa. If Rhodesia became black before Mozambique, its militance would necessarily be tempered by its transport needs. If Mozambique and Rhodesia were both African-governed, they could over time reduce their own and their neighbor's vulnerability vis-à-vis South Africa. In the last analysis, however, it is my conclusion that internal stability, up to and including internal revolution, could be sustained within the system for all countries other than South Africa. As far as South Africa is concerned, the result of change to a ruling group other than the United Party would be incalculable, and the effect on the system would depend entirely on how it was achieved. The system is essentially stable as long as South Africa remains stable; if South Africa undergoes radical change, it is certain that the South African system will change as well, though the direction of the change is unpredictable.

Does systemic maintenance create a condition for greater world stability? The answer to this question must provisionally be yes. For all reasons adduced in this paper, we can only conclude that the system is stable. Though we can deplore its racial characteristics and be disheartened by the stability of such a system, this does not detract from its stable nature. The foes of South Africa, Portugal, and Rhodesia hope to justify intervention on the assertion that "a threat to the peace"[53] exists and that under Articles 41 and 42, the United Nations should undertake military action. Under present circumstances, a Security Council approval of intervention does not appear likely.[54]

It is the tragedy of Southern Africa that, at least to date, the growing, almost thriving, inter-country relationships across racial lines have not led to an easing of intra-country racial tensions. As such, the operation of the Southern African subordinate system gives a gloss of respectability to the area which is unwarranted in terms of most of its human relationships. For the moment, however, it would probably be most realistic to take notice of Prime Minister Vorster's assertion that it is for the "independent states in Southern Africa (to) prove to the world that racial groups with different policies can live together alongside one another in the same geographic area."[55] There may be more of this going on than one ever would have imagined.

NOTES

* An earlier draft of this paper was presented at the African Studies Association meeting in New York City, November 3, 1967. I am indebted to Professors Kenneth N. Waltz and Sheridan W. Johns III, both of the Department of Politics, Brandeis University, for their extensive and helpful comments on various drafts of this paper.

"The Subordinate State System of Southern Africa" by Larry W. Bowman is reprinted from International Studies Quarterly 12(3), September 1968, 231-261 by permission of the publisher, Sage Publications Inc., and the author.

1. There is virtually no literature on the subject of subordinate international systems. I am aware of only two pioneering articles: Leonard Binder "The Middle-East as a Subordinate International System" World Politics 10, April 1958, 408-429 and Michael Brecher "International Relations and Asian Studies: The Subordinate State System of Southern Asia" World Politics 15, January 1963, 213-235. Most texts on international politics deal with major world areas either in terms of their relationship to the dominant power blocs (their relative independence being described in terms of tight or loose bi-polarity) or as part of the Third World or neutralist bloc. Southern Africa fits awkwardly into either category, for it is certainly not neutralist and the persistent racial stance of its major members sets it apart from the dominant system to which it belongs.

2. For a brief survey of most of the existing literature see Robert I. Rotberg "Colonialism and After: The Political Literature of Central Africa - A Bibliographic Essay" Africa Forum 2, Winter 1967, 66-73.

3. For bibliographic information on South Africa see Leonard M. Thompson The Republic of South Africa (Boston: Little, Brown, 1966) and Gwendolen M. Carter The Politics of Inequality: South Africa Since 1948 (London: Thames and Hudson, 1958).

4. For the High Commission territories see Leslie Rubin "South Africa and her Immediate Neighbours - A Bibliographic Essay" African Forum 2, Fall 1966, 78-84; Jack Halpern South Africa's Hostages (Baltimore: Penguin, 1963) and R. P. Stevens Lesotho, Botswana and Swaziland (New York: Praeger, 1967). Two English-language sources for Portuguese Africa are James Duffy Portuguese Africa (Cambridge: Harvard University Press, 1959) and R. H. Chilcote Portuguese Africa (Englewood Cliffs: Prentice-Hall, 1967). Both of these books are up-dated by the excellent November 1967 issue of Africa Report, which deals entirely with contemporary trends in Portuguese Africa.

5. See J. A. Davis and James K. Baker (eds.) Southern Africa in Transition (New York: Praeger, 1966) for a very uneven set of articles on the area; and W. A. Nielsen African Battleline: American Policy Choices in Southern Africa (New York: Harper and Row, 1965). A new book, William A. Hance (ed.) Southern Africa and the United States (New York: Columbia University Press, 1968) came to the author's attention only after this article had gone to press.

6. An exception to this critique is Hilda Kuper "The Colonial Situation in Southern Africa" Journal of Modern African Studies 2, 1964, 149-164.

7. Colin and Margaret Legum South Africa: Crisis for the West (London: Pall Mall, 1964) 5.

8. Neville Rubin "South-West Africa from Courtroom to Political Arena" Africa Report 11, December 1966, 12.

9. See, for instance, C. W. De Kiewiet "South Africa's Gamble with History" The Virginia Quarterly Review 41, Winter 1965, 1-17 and W. A. Nielsen Africa Battleline 110-126. "It is, of course, possible that the Court may rule in favour of South Africa, but this is generally considered unlikely." (116).

10. Neville Rubin "South-West Africa from Courtroom to Political Arena" 12.

11. Ernest A. Gross "The South-West Africa Case: What Happened?" Foreign Affairs 45, October 1966, 36-48. See also Rosalyn Higgins "The International Court and South-West Africa: The Implications of the Judgement" International Affairs 42, October 1966, 573-599.

12. Michael Brecher "International Relations and Asian Studies: The Subordinate State System of Southern Asia" 200. Brecher identified five existing subordinate systems: Middle Eastern, American, Southern Asian, West European and West African. The list seems questionable in that it is difficult to say why Eastern Europe is excluded if an American system is included. The line between the dominant system and subordinate systems (turning on the degree of the dominant systems penetration of the other system) is most difficult to draw. Furthermore, West Africa has little real unity, certainly less than Southern Africa, and at this point in time could be hardly called a system.

13. Ibid. 218. Structural features incorporate the configuration of power, organizational integration (political, judicial and economic, but not social), the character and frequency of interaction between actors, and the extra-state relationship with the dominant system. Textual features include the intensity of communication and transport, common and conflicting ideologies and values, the diversity of political systems, and the internal instability within member states. These features are elaborated upon in pages 221-233.

14. The most comprehensive single work on the three territories is J. Halpern's South Africa's Hostages. Also see Leonard M. Thompson "South Africa's Relations with Lesotho, Botswana, and Swaziland" Africa Forum 2, Fall 1966, 65-77.

15. See R. P. Stevens "Swaziland Political Development" Journal of Modern African Studies 1, 1963, 327-350 and Christian P. Potholm "Swaziland: Changing Political Configurations" Journal of Modern African Studies 4, 1966, 313-322.

16. In addition to Halpern's coverage, recent events in Botswana and Lesotho have been discussed in R. P. Stevens "The New Republic of Botswana" Africa Report 11, October 1966, 15-18 and R. Weisfelder "Power Struggle in Lesotho" Africa Report 12, January 1967, 5-13. Michael Ward's recent "Economic Independence for Lesotho?" Journal of Modern African Studies 5, 1967, 355-368, further demonstrates the inherent limitations of Lesotho's economic position.

17. Leonard M. Thompson "South Africa's Relations with Lesotho, Botswana, and Swaziland" 73.

18. See Anthony A. D'Amato "Bantustan Proposals for South-West Africa" Journal of Modern African Studies 4, 1966, 177-192.

19. See Financial Times (London) October 27, 1966; The Observer (London) October 30, 1966 and The Johannesburg Star, September 2, 1967.

20. Marvin Harris Portugal's African "Wards" (New York: American Committee on Africa, 1958) 29. Also see Marvin Harris "Labour Emigration Among the Mocambique Thonga: Cultural and Political Factors" Africa 20, January 1959, 50-66; Douglas L. Wheeler "The Portuguese and Mozambique: The Past Against the Future" in Davis and Baker (eds.) Southern Africa in Transition, and On the Situation of the Workers in Portuguese Colonies, an International Confederation of Free Trade Unions Memorandum to the XVIII Session of the General Assembly of the United Nations, 1963.

21. South African Financial Gazette (Johannesburg) September 2, 1966.

22. The Financial Times (London) March 22, 1967.

23. See Larry W. Bowman "Rhodesia Since UDI" Africa Report 12, February 1967 for a detailed discussion of Rhodesia's efforts to withstand sanctions. For a much more theoretical approach to the question of sanctions, see Johan Galtung "On the Effects of International Economic Sanctions with Examples from the Case of Rhodesia" World Politics 19, April 1967, 378-416. See Sunday Times (London) August 27 and September 3, 1967 for a detailed report on how sanctions are circumvented.

24. See Portugal Some Portuguese Documents on the Questions of Rhodesia (Lisbon: Ministry of Foreign Affairs, 1967) and The News (Lisbon) February 25, 1967 for angry Portuguese documentation on the detrimental effects sanctions against Rhodesia have had on trade and transport through Mozambique. Under Chapter 50 of the United Nations Charter, the Portuguese have asked the United Nations for $28 million in damages.

25. Rhodesia's annual consumption of 400,000 tons is less than the annual increase in South Africa's rate of consumption. The Financial Times (London) January 27, 1967.

26. Ibid.

27. See, for instance, The Observer (London) April 9, 1967, which speculated that Vorster had told Smith at their meeting at the end of March that South Africa's subsidization of Rhodesia could not be permanent and that Rhodesia should re-enter negotiations with Britain, with the intention of reaching a settlement.

28. J. Clyde Mitchell An Outline of the Sociological Background to African Labour (Salisbury: Ensign, 1961) 77.

29. See Richard Hall "Zambia and Rhodesia: Links and Fetters" Africa Report 11, January 1966, 8-12, for an appreciation of Zambia's difficult position following UDI.

30. See F. Taylor Ostrander "Zambia in the Aftermath of Rhodesia UDI: Logistical and Economic Problems" Africa Forum 2, Winter 1967, 50-65 for the most complete survey of Zambia's post-UDI efforts.

31. Ibid. and the Times of Zambia (Lusaka) November 17, 1966.

32. The general unity of African states has been documented in Edward T. Rowe "The Emerging Anti-Colonial Consensus in the United Nations" The Journal of Conflict Resolution 8, 1964, 209-230 and A. Lijphart "The Analysis of Bloc Voting in the General Assembly" American Political Science Review 57, 1963, 902-917.

33. See Africa Report 12, April 1967, 26 and Africa Report 12, May 1967, 26.

34. See Portugal Noticias de Portugal (Lisbon: Boletime Semanal de Secretariado Nacional da Informacao, 1967) Nos. 1037-38 for information on the warm Portuguese reception given to Malawi ministers.

35. Seretse Khama "A Policy of Prudence" Africa Report 11, October 1966, 19-20.

36. Africa Report 12, May 1967, 26.

37. See Allistair Sparks "South Africa: A View from Within" Africa Report 12, March 1967, 40-45, for an assessment of the new trends in Southern African politics.

38. New York Times, April 9, 1967. The possibility of a white military alliance has always been the charge of critics of South Africa, Portugal and Rhodesia. See especially Rosalynde Ainslie The Unholy Alliance (London: The Anti-Apartheid Movement, 1962). Tangible evidence to support this claim has emerged with South Africa's continuing presence in anti-guerrilla operations in Rhodesia. See The Observer (London) and the Sunday Times (London) of August 27, 1967. Edwin S. Munger has brought to my attention the further interesting point that in 1966-67, Portugal was the foremost supplier of immigrants to South Africa.

39. See Vaz's fighting speech "Cerrar Fileiras e Machar" (Close Ranks and March) in Boletim Geral de Ultramar (Lisbon) 42, Nos. 497/498, November-December 1966.

40. Charter of the United Nations and Statute of the International Court of Justice (New York: United Nations, 1965) 9.

41. South Africa's foreign policy has been put forward in Eric H. Louw The Case for South Africa (New York: Macfadden Books, 1963) and examined critically by J. E. Spence Republic Under Pressure: A Study of South African Foreign Policy (London: Oxford University Press, for Royal Institute of International Affairs, 1965). Portuguese foreign policy is summarized in two documents by the Portuguese government Portuguese Foreign Policy (Lisbon: Ministry of Foreign Affairs, 1965) and Some Portuguese Documents on the Question of Rhodesia (Lisbon: Ministry of Foreign Affairs, 1966).

42. It is worth noting which country had a sensible perspective on the forthcoming sanctions battle. Prime Minister Wilson in Lagos in January 1966 said that the victory over Rhodesia would be won in a matter of weeks, not months. Dr. Verwoerd in his only major address on the Rhodesian crisis said on January 26, 1966 "I do not expect a speedy climax." Republic of South Africa Hansard 16, Col. 47.

43. South Africa had an election of March 30, 1966. The opposition United Party desperately tried to outflank Verwoerd to the right by accusing him of not openly recognizing Rhodesia or helping her enough.

44. Allistair Sparks "South Africa: A View from Within" 40.

45. Die Burger (Cape Town) December 22, 1966. Die Berger is generally accepted as the spokesman for the "liberal" Cape Province viewpoint of the Nationalist Party.

46. The Times (London) January 25, 1967.

47. See the Financial Times (London) July 1, 1967 and the Times of Zambia (Lusaka) July 21, 1967. Though subsequent American trade figures show a decline, it is impossible to know how much has simply been absorbed through

dummy corporations into the trade figures of other countries. There is certainly no sign that Rhodesia is hurting.

48. See Dennis Austin *Britain and South Africa* (London: Oxford University Press, 1966) and Dennis Austin "A Special Report on American Involvement in the South African Economy" *Africa Today* 13, January 1966.

49. See Amelia C. Leiss (ed.) *Apartheid and United Nations Collective Measures* (New York: The Carnegie Endowment for International Peace, 1965) 165-170.

50. *Ibid*. 95-130 and Ronald Segal *Sanctions Against South Africa* (Baltimore: Penguin, 1964).

51. Amelia C. Leiss (ed.) *Apartheid and United Nations Collective Measures*, 130.

52. *Johannesburg Star*, March 18, 1967 and April 1, 1967.

53. *Charter of the United Nations* 24.

54. This present hands-off policy is not without its own dangers. The greatest long-term threat which Southern Africa poses to world stability is, in my opinion, the very real possibility that left-leaning guerrilla movements will one day be near success, only to have the West intervene on the side of the whites.

55. Republic of South Africa *Hansard* 17, Col. 2606, September 21, 1966.

Chapter Two

SOUTHERN AFRICA:

INTRA-REGIONAL AND INTERNATIONAL RELATIONS*

John Barratt

Introduction

A study of the foreign policies and international relations of the various states of the African sub-continent is not a simple matter, because there are no clear-cut and consistent policies that can be summarised and analysed. The foreign policies of individual countries amount in each case to numerous decisions on specific issues. For a thorough study one must understand who makes the decisions, how they are arrived at, i.e. by what process, and what are the influences brought to bear on the decision-makers - external and internal - and their relative strength. All this is complicated by the fact that the environment in which these decisions are taken - i.e. all the internal and external influences and pressures - is not static. There is constant change, and what may be especially relevant one day is not so the next. This is true of all states, but perhaps even more so of African states, where change can be rapid and where, therefore, one notable characteristic of politics is its unpredictability.

To attempt a thorough study of all these factors in this paper is not possible. But it is intended to try to indentify some of the major determinants in the foreign policies of the independent Black states of the African sub-continent, which have a bearing on relations between the countries of this region. This means inevitably mainly their relations with South Africa as the strong power centre of the region.

The theme of the conference - Intra-Regional Dependence and the Quest for Self-determination - implies a possible conflict between the forces pulling the countries together and those tending to pull them apart, i.e. the centripetal and the centrifugal forces. The foreign policies of the states concerned, as well as the various external pressures on the region as a whole, will therefore be looked at in this paper with that possible conflict in mind.

It is assumed that South Africa, and the South African government in particular, desires closer regional co-operation for a variety of possible reasons. It is not necessary to dwell on this; there are many policy statements and decisions which clearly indicate closer regional co-operation as a goal. What is more important for our subject is to determine to what extent South African actions contribute towards the achievement of this goal, and what seems to stand in the way of closer co-operation in the light of the policies and attitudes of Black states. It must be expected that, as with the other states concerned, and with all states in fact, South Africa's own interests will be paramount in determining policies. But, if closer regional co-operation is considered to be one of South Africa's major interests, then some adaptation of other interests lower on the scale of priorities may be involved. The same holds true for the other states concerned. However, the necessary accommodation of the interests of all these countries, in order to achieve this intra-regional co-operation, will depend on the relative importance attached to it as a goal in each case. There may be goals which have a much higher priority for certain countries at the present time, and to judge this it is necessary to try to look at the situation from the point of view of all concerned and not simply from the standpoint of what we in the Republic may wish to achieve and what we may think is the best for the other countries of the sub-continent. This does not mean that South Africa must adopt all its policies to suit others, but, if it is hoped to find common interests and to build on them, then in the first place we must honestly try to understand what the interests of the other countries are.

As it is expected that this paper should deal with political factors, it is necessary to say something about the relationship of politics and economics. The pattern of relationships between the countries of the sub-continent, and between each of them and other countries in Africa and overseas, is largely based on, and continually concerned with, economic matters. These economic factors have been shown in other papers and elsewhere to have created a considerable number of links between the Southern African states and territories. They are extremely important factors for the development of each of the countries and of the sub-continent as a whole, as well as for the relationship between these countries. Therefore, although this paper is focussed on political factors, the economic factors can never be lost sight of. Moreover, they influence politics to a large degree; in fact it is not really possible to separate the two completely. But it is necessary to try to identify the political factors - external and internal - influencing the direction the countries are taking. It is also necessary to recognise that while economics influence politics, and vice versa, it is ultimately the political decisions which determine a country's direction. In some cases economic considerations may be the over-riding factor.

This seems to be true often in the case of Malawi, for instance, as expressed in Dr. Banda's remark, "No country can reasonably be expected to cut its own throat,"[1] - in spite of the strong commitment during his career to African solidarity and to African independence. But there are many cases in Africa where economic interests have apparently taken second place. President Idi Amin's current behaviour in Uganda is one rather extreme example which comes easily to mind, but there are less dramatic indications of the paramountcy of political considerations, even in the affairs of Southern Africa.

There are, of course, also cultural factors which influence decisions on foreign policy and, as with the economic factors, it is not possible neatly to separate the cultural factors from the political. "A particular foreign policy position may reflect personal convictions or cultural ties of the members of the leadership group, which have little or no obvious connection with the problem under discussion".[2] Another problem is that the distinction between foreign and domestic policies is often difficult to establish. "Activities and decisions, which on the surface fall within the realm of foreign policy, may well be designed as much or more for internal consumption as for their effect on relations with other states".[3] This is a problem in examining the foreign policy of any state and must always be borne in mind. Examples of the clear influence of domestic considerations will appear in the course of the paper, but sometimes these are not easily discernable to the outside observer.

Finally, it should be explained that this is not intended to be a theoretical study, as it concerns practical matters of vital importance to all those living in this sub-continent. Although certain concepts will have to be dealt with in fairly general terms, the discussion of this subject should be made as relevant as possible to current developments, even at the danger of seeing some aspects out of proportion in the long term view. In other words, the subject of our discussion is academic in the sense that it should be as objective and well informed as possible, but it is not a subject on which one can adopt in any way an "ivory tower" mentality, as it is one of immediate and urgent relevancy for all.

Some Factors Affecting Foreign Policies

Geography

In determining their policies towards each other and towards states outside this region, the governments of the countries of Southern Africa have to take into account certain basic considerations, which limit or extend their freedom of action. One of these which they cannot escape, is the fact of the geographical situation of each country in the region and in relation to the rest of the world. The size of a country is not by itself a determining factor; but smallness combined with a geographical situation such as that of Lesotho - with no outlet to the sea and surrounded on all sides by one relatively very powerful neighbour - imposes severe limitations on the exercise of fully independent policies. Swaziland is in a similar position, although it has some advantage in sharing borders with two countries, which gives it somewhat more flexibility.

Botswana is by no means small in size, having an area nearly nineteen times greater than that of Lesotho and over thirty-three times that of Swaziland, but it has a small population and suffers from the same disability of being landlocked and surrounded on three sides by South African, or South African-administered, territory and on the fourth by Rhodesia - with a tiny, disputed outlet to Zambia.

Uner the circumstances, these three Black states are locked into South Africa, and it is impossible for them to make decisions about their international relations without bearing in mind the proximity of South Africa, and to a lesser extent that of Rhodesia and the Portuguese territories. This does not mean that they have no way of asserting their independence, but it does mean that their foreign policies are inseparably linked, for better or for worse, in peace or in conflict, with those of the powerful neighbour which surrounds them geographically.

This limiting factor does not apply to the other countries of the sub-continent to anything like the same extent. Rhodesia, Zambia and Malawi are also landlocked, it is true, and this does provide problems, but on a geographical basis (leaving current political questions aside for the present) their choices are wider.

Economics - Dependence or Interdependence

Another basic factor which policy makers in the countries of the sub-continent must bear in mind in most foreign policy decisions, is their degree of economic independence now, as well as their potential for economic development leading to a greater independence in the future. This is a wide subject, already dealt with in other papers at this Conference, and it is only intended to pursue certain aspects here, which have a bearing on the political decisions taken in regard to intra-regional and wider international relations.

Economic dependence of a weak country on a much stronger neighbour obviously imposes a limitation on the freedom of action of the former. This is a condition which applies in Southern Africa in regard to several countries in relation to South Africa. They are naturally sensitive about this, especially the three neighbour states, and they are trying to diversify their economic links to the extent that they are able to do so. Botswana hopes to become more independent as a result of the development of its mineral resources. Swaziland is already in a more favourable position, with considerable natural resources and with 85% of its exports going to countries outside the Southern African Customs Union area. It also has an active policy of developing new industries, and of further expanding its trade relations with countries overseas and with other African countries outside the southern African region.[4] Lesotho's opportunities are much more limited, but even there attempts are being made to diversify economic relations. In reviewing recently the work of the Lesotho National Development Corporation, Chief Jonathan spoke of his country's development taking place in association with a variety of older countries, and he mentioned prospecting agreements with American and Canadian companies. He noted that the Corporation was "in stiff competition for investments with territories and other countries of Southern Africa", and he made no mention at all of South Africa's role in Lesotho's development.[5] But in spite of all these efforts, there is - and will remain - a considerable degree of dependence on the one economically strong country in the region, which in effect limits the political freedom of these smaller countries in intra-regional relations and in the international sphere, too.

This condition of dependence is often loosely described as <u>inter</u>dependence which is the ideal for all those who wish to see closer co-operation, as it does not involve the same type of limitation, but rather implies more equality between the parties - a two-way rather than a one-way dependence. It also, implies a dependence more or less freely accepted for the mutual benefit of both or all parties concerned. A distinction should be drawn between these two concepts, and the temptation should be avoided of confusing dependence with interdependence. While economic dependence may be unavoidable in some cases, it is a condition which any self-respecting nation will want to change if at all possible, and it will be tempted to try to compensate by aggressively asserting its political independence. This may already be happening in the case even of Lesotho, the most economically dependent of these states. In any case, it must at least never be assumed that economic dependence of one state on another ensures political friendship between the two.

On the other hand, interdependence, while it still involves limitations for the interdependent partners, is a positive concept which can bind the states concerned together in a more healthy relationship. There are obvious difficulties in converting dependence into interdependence. Even without the political difficulties which will be dealt with later, there is the relatively overwhelming economic strength of South Africa. There are, however, examples of attempts to create greater interdependence, which have been supported and even initiated by South Africa. Cabora Bassa and the Kunene River scheme are such examples, but, as these both at present mainly involve Portugal and South Africa, they do not directly approach the real problem. A better example would be the exploitation of Lesotho's water resources in the proposed Malibamatso scheme. This would involve South Africa becoming dependent to some extent on Lesotho's resources, while Lesotho would become dependent on the revenue earned from South Africa. There may have been some reluctance in South Africa to become dependent in this way for such a vital resource as water, but it is in fact a mutual dependence, and in any case some risks have to be taken for a greater long-term benefit. There are also advocates of a scheme which would involve bringing water from the Okavaŋgo Delta in Botswana, but in this case it is probably reluctance on the side of Botswana to become so closely interdependent with South Africa, which is preventing serious consideration of such a scheme.[6]

A relevant example of interdependence is perhaps the Customs Union Agreement and especially South Africa's willingness, after lengthy negotiations, to revise the Agreement so that the terms became much more favourable to the three smaller partners than previously. Labour relations, too, which have been dealt with in a separate paper, involve elements of interdependence. The co-operation involved in the work of the South African Regional Committee for the Conservation and Utilization of Soil (SARCCUS), on the basis that the problems dealt with are not contained by national boundaries, is a recognition of interdependence.[7] It is hoped that in the future the proposed organisation to co-ordinate tourism, namely the Southern African Regional Tourist Conference (SARTOC), will come into being and further foster interdependence.

Because of its powerful position, the onus rests primarily on South Africa to go out of its way to create conditions for interdependence, even if this means sacrificing some of its own independent advantages. If it is desired, for reasons of South Africa's own national interest, that there should be co-operative relations between the states of the sub-continent, then all past experience in relations between states dictates that the degree of simple dependence on South Africa should be lessened as far as possible. In Botswana's National Development Plan, 1970-75, as published in September 1970, this paragraph appears (after enumeration of the advantages and disadvantages to Botswana of the Customs Union and joint monetary system):

> Thus Botswana's economic dependence on South Africa is great. It is considered to be in the interest of both countries to transform this dependence into a relationship of interdependence. Despite the differences in political and social systems, and the disparity of wealth and resources

> between the two countries, and given the close economic links, Botswana and South Africa have achieved, and wish to maintain a stable relationship based on inter-dependence, co-existence and mutual non-interference.[8]

This is surely a definition of policy that should be accepted by all, and although directly concerned with economic matters, it has important implications for healthy political relations between the countries of the sub-continent. It is in line with the South African Government's aims, as expressed on numerous occasions. For example, in April 1970, Dr. Hilgard Muller said in an important speech at the University of South Africa:

> As is generally known, the Government's standpoint is that international friendship and co-operation must at all times be based on mutual respect, the recognition of the sovereign independence of states and non-intervention in the domestic affairs of others. Differences in political concepts and approaches in respect of internal affairs should not be obstacles to fruitful co-operation between governments in matters of common interest. It goes without saying that no country should strive to dominate another in the political, economic or any other terrain. Where one country helps another the main aim of such help must be to enable the recipient to help itself. South Africa is strongly opposed to any form of neo-Colonialism or economic Imperialism.[9]

To find more effective ways of applying this policy of interdependence in practice is a matter for the economists to pursue further. But political decisions are also required in South Africa, as well as in the other countries concerned, to make the policy of greater interdependence effective in the economic sphere generally, and in particular in important areas such as the Customs Union, where regular consultation is now required by the Agreement, and in the monetary union, where no formal machinery for consultation exists, but seems to be wanted by the smaller partners.[10] There is also the question as to what extent industrial development in the neighbouring states is being encouraged or frustrated by South Africa.[11] These are all matters which are hopefully receiving attention, in order gradually to make economic interdependence a practical reality, and they are all matters which profoundly affect inter-regional relations on a political level.

Development Assistance

Apart from the full recognition of the formal independence of our neighbour states there is no doubt that South Africa desires to co-operate in aiding their development. Already much is being done[12] and the philosophy behind the assistance is not designed to create more dependence.[13] This type of co-operation has helped to link the countries of Southern Africa closer together, and some governments clearly see advantages for their countries in technical assistance and financial aid from South Africa. Malawi is probably the prime example. But for them to accept South African assistance requires a positive decision by each of these governments, as distinct from the unavoidable necessity of continuing economic links of various kinds (because of dependence on South Africa), and there is obvious sensitivity and hesitancy on this point. Take the example of Botswana again. President Seretse Khama has said (March 28, 1970): "We do not intend to seek aid from South African official sources. It would not be in the interest of either country to increase Botswana's dependence on South Africa. We are determined that no word or deed on Botswana's part will give comfort to the advocates of race supremacy."[14] On another more recent occasion (Sept. 1971) Sir Seretse is reported to have said that in skills, knowledge of African conditions and proximity to Black Africa, South Africa has much to offer. But Botswana was morally and politically unable to accept official South African aid.[15] However, Malawi, in particular, Lesotho and Swaziland are recipients of some official South African assistance, financial and technical. In the case of Swaziland, the Prime Minister, Prince Makhosini Dlamini, referred during a visit to Cape Town in March 1971, for talks with Prime Minister Vorster, to various examples of assistance which, he said, showed "the considerable contribution which your country (South Africa) is making towards my country's development . . .".[16]

This question of development is the crucial one with which all governments in the sub-continent are concerned, including South Africa where the progress of the Homelands is a sine qua non for the evolution of the Government's internal policies, as well as for an improvement in its international relations. For the Black states their policies for accelerated development are intimately linked with their foreign policies. They are all actively seeking development assistance from governments outside Africa, as well as from international organisations. In fact they are considerably more active in seeking such outside assistance than assistance from South Africa, probably because they accept that South Africa's ability to assist them is limited, in view of the development needs within the Republic, but also for political motives - including the desire to diversify their sources of aid and not be limited to dependence on South Africa (in the same way as they are trying to diversify their trade). While it is not intended to compare the value of aid from different sources - even if this were possible - it may be useful to give an indication, by means of some examples, of the extent of development assistance which is being received from outside sources by all the independent Black states of the sub-continent.

(a) International Organisations

The United Nations Development Programme (UNDP)[17] coordinates the work of the UN and the Specialised Agencies in developing countries throughout the world. It has a regional office in Lusaka, responsible for Botswana, Lesotho, Swaziland, Malawi and Zambia, and there are also separate offices in all these countries. The UNDP representatives in the five countries meet two or three times each year to discuss, in particular, projects covering more than one country of the region. The Specialised Agencies, notably the Food and Agricultural Organisation (FAO), also have their own representatives in some of the countries. The UNDP regional office cooperates closely with the headquarters of the Economic Commission for Africa (ECA) in Addis Ababa.

The extent of the UNDP assistance to the five independent Black states of Southern Africa is illustrated by the following Indicative Planning Figures for the current five-year period, beginning January 1972: (These are estimates of the resources allocated to these countries, for the purpose of advanced planning.)

Botswana - $5.8 million; Lesotho - $8.3 million;
Swaziland - $5.7 million; Malawi - $7.5 million,
Zambia - $15 million.

(As Botswana, Lesotho and Malawi have been included in a UN list of "least developed" countries, they are able to receive further UN funds over and above these amounts.)

The approximate numbers of expert personnel in these five countries, financed by UNDP and provided by the various international organisations in the UN family, are currently as follows:

Botswana - 41; Lesotho - 50; Swaziland - 45;
Malawi - 35; Zambia - 150.

(As compared with the total of 321 UNDP personnel currently operating in Southern Africa, there were altogether 28 seconded South African officials working in Lesotho, Swaziland and Malawi in February, 1972.)[18]

As an illustration of the type of international assistance to these countries, further details are now given of the projects in one country, namely Botswana, where the UNDP provided technical assistance during 1971 worth over R700,000. This assistance was channelled through the FAO (for a project "Surveys and Training for the Development of Water Resources and Agricultural Production"), the ILO (for a Co-operative Development Centre and a National Vocational Training Scheme) and UNESCO (for the Teacher Training College in Francistown), as well as WHO, WMO, ITU and the World Bank. About 40 technical assistance experts were provided during 1971 by these agencies, and in addition the UN Office for Technical Cooperation (UNOTC) provided an expert and two consultants plus 5 fellowships from its own funds (outside UNDP). Other UN assistance came from the UN Children's Fund and the UN Fund for Population Activities. These UN technical assistance activities are continuing this year, and from next year (1973) a new, more effectively co-ordinated Country Programme will be introduced, planned for a 5-year period.[19]

The most important international financial aid in the sub-continent is the loan of R23 million arranged in 1971 by the World Bank for the Shashe Project in Botswana. Another example is the R2,9 million loan from the International Development Association for the tarring of the 89-mile Leabua Jonathan Highway in Lesotho.[20]

By far the largest amount of international assistance is received by Zambia. In 1970 the UN and its Specialised Agencies spent nearly K3 million on technical assistance activities, to which was added over K4 million in Zambian Government counterpart funds. The organisations operating in Zambia through the UNDP include: FAO, the World Food Programme, UNICEF, WHO, UNESCO, ILO, ITU, UPU, ICAO, WMO, IAEA, and UNIDO (UN Industrial Development Organisation). Most of these bodies have experts stationed in Zambia, totalling 123 in April 1971, and approximately 150 a year later. In 1969-70 World Bank loans to Zambia totalled K7,6 million, for the purpose of education and of commercial farming.[21]

(b) Bilateral Assistance

As all the independent Black states in the sub-continent are ex-British colonies or protectorates, it is not surprising that the United Kingdom has been the major donor in all these countries. British financial aid has been in the form of direct budgetary grants and development loans. The budgetary grants have been of considerable importance, because most of these countries were not able to balance their budgets from their own revenue when they became independent. But they have all now substantially reduced or even eliminated their deficits, and the increased revenue resulting from the revised Customs Union Agreement of December 1969, has been a major cause of this improvement for Botswana, Lesotho and Swaziland. Lesotho, for instance, has reduced its dependence on external budgetary aid from over 50% five years ago to 10% now.[22]

Examples of annual British development assistance to all these countries are loans of R2 million to Lesotho for the 1969/70 year[23] and nearly R4 million to Botswana for the 1972/73 year.[24] The Commonwealth Development Corporation is doing important work in all the independent Black states of the sub-continent.[25]

For its 1972/73 Development Fund Botswana is also receiving grants and loans totalling R16,4 million from Denmark, Sweden, the Netherlands, Canada and the United States; by far the largest amount (over R10 million) is from Canada, followed by the United States with nearly R3,8 million and Sweden with over R2 million.[26]

In addition, an agreement was recently signed with the United States for a loan of R9 475 000 for the construction of the BotZam road, to which further reference is made later in this paper.[27]

Several of the above countries, notably the United States, are active in providing financial and technical assistance in Lesotho and Swaziland, too, as well as in Malawi and Zambia.

These examples - not an exhaustive account - indicate the importance to the other independent states in Southern Africa of their relations with a number of countries overseas, as well as with the United Nations and the Specialised Agencies. The degree of the influence on intra-regional relations of this outside assistance, including the growing number of experts and advisers from international bodies, as well as from individual foreign countries, who are working in all these states, can only be guessed at. But it must be considerable and it is an influence with which South Africa has no connection at all, and with which it cannot compete at its present level of development assistance. However, looking to the future, it can be suggested that although South Africa is not in a position to compete in quantity with all the aid - technical and financial - from extra-regional sources, it could perhaps contribute more effectively in quality, if there were more overall planning and co-ordination of development assistance. Clearly it is the Government's policy to assist other African states, and the foreign policy implications of such assistance are recognised, as evidenced by the fact that the Economic Co-operation Promotion Loan Fund is administered by the Department of Foreign Affairs. (This Fund was established in 1968, with an initial capital of R5 million, and it has had further amounts allocated to it since then.[28]) But there does seem to be a need for co-ordinated planning and for the establishment of guidelines for the most effective use of the resources, financial and technical, which South Africa is able to contribute in this field. Has the time perhaps not arrived for an international or regional development agency in South Africa, such as exists in several western countries? The role of such an agency would be to plan and channel South African development assistance to developing states and territories in the sub-continent, including the emerging Homelands at present within South Africa's borders (as soon as they reached a certain stage of self-government). This agency could be linked to or eventually replaced by, a multi-national organisation, so that the development assistance could become largely multi-lateral, at least in its planning and allocation (assuming that South Africa would remain the largest contributor). In his proposal for the establishment of an Economic Commission for Southern Africa[29], Professor J.L. Sadie suggests that its main functions should include the provision of development aid, as well as the creation of an Institute of Development Studies. (The first function he mentions is that of promoting intra-regional and external trade.) He points out that the advantage of a multi-lateral operation of this kind, rather than the continuation of bilateral arrangements between South Africa and other countries, is that the latter "lacks generalised mutuality, and economically, administratively and diplomatically is less efficient".[30]

The aspect of "mutuality" is important for the success of such a multi-national organisation from the political point of view, and is linked with the need for greater interdependence, as discussed above. This should be the goal in all thinking about the effective co-ordination of development assistance in the future. In the meantime, however, while the creation of a multi-national organisation (which would include the independent Black states of the sub-continent) remains inpracticable mainly because of differing political approaches, the establishment of a South African agency for international development assistance might be a constructive beginning.[31]

The African Environment - Nationalism and Unity

We have dealt at some length with the implications for intra-regional relations of the economic dependence on South Africa and the need for more interdependence as well as the striving of the Black states to diversify their economic links, both in trade and in satisfying their needs for development assistance. These are basic questions underlying the decisions which they must take on their external relations, both within the region and outside, and running through them all one sees the urge to consolidate their formal independence and to determine more effectively their own destiny. While the economic dependence and the elements of interdependence certainly create strong intra-regional links and constitute centripetal forces within the sub-continent,[32] this urge to exercise self-determination more effectively has centrifugal effects. These centrifugal forces are strengthened by certain aspects of the particular environment in which these states are evolving - an environment which links them with Black Africa as a whole, as well as with the White-ruled countries of the sub-continent.

One of these aspects is African nationalism, and linked with this is the aspiration for greater African unity. These are in a sense ideological aspects, the effects of which on intra-regional relations are difficult to measure, but which nevertheless do have a political influence on relations, as evidenced by many statements of Black leaders. Moreover, these influences - of African nationalism and African unity - are not generally shared by the Whites of Africa, who tend to have a more pragmatic approach and regard economic realities as the ones which should be paramount when policy decisions are made.

This complex subject deserves fuller treatment than can be given it here, but some light may be thrown on it by considering what Doudou Thiam, who was Foreign Minister of Senegal, has referred to as the two forms which nationalism takes in Africa, namely micro-nationalism and macro-nationalism.[33] The first is concerned with the nation in terms of its territory, with boundaries settled during the colonial period, and with the maintenance of sovereign independence. The second is the movement towards a greater African unity - in its more radical form known as Pan-Africanism. While there has been some conflict between these two forms of nationalism during the past decade, they do not seem to be contradictory in the African context. They are both a reflection of an African nationalism which seeks to defend and consolidate its independence, while at the same time recognising that this concept is wider than the individual state. This wider African nationalism resulted partly from the common independence struggle, and it has therefore lost some of its momentum during the past decade. But it remains a reality, and it is reflected in the constant concern expressed for those African peoples who are considered not yet to be free.[34] It is seen too, as a means of safeguarding independence. When the new African states continue to denounce colonialism (or neo-colonialism) and racism, they may be considered by outsiders to be governed by an obsession or to be reacting to an imaginary threat. But their attitude that independence is not final, and must be continually safeguarded and extended, is a reality and is an important ideological base for the foreign policies of many states. Even those states which are not extreme in this respect are nevertheless affected by this ideology and are therefore suspicious of, or at least sensitive about, anything which they may regard as being an infringement of their independence, and/or a denial of self-determination and independence for other Black Africans.

In its extreme form this is best reflected in Nkrumah's philosophy, which has had a considerable influence on the political development of Africa, even though Nkrumah himself was personally discredited after his fall from power in Ghana. His admonition, "Seek ye first the political kingdom and all things shall be added to you", has had wide currency in Africa and is felt by many to have been borne out in practice, because in some cases the achievement of self-determination and independence has in fact provided the motivation and means for more all-round development. In any case, whatever the results, this nationalism as defined by Nkrumah and others, does not put economic considerations first, it seeks effective independence and equality, with economic development as a means to that end. As Rupert Emerson commented in an article written in 1960: "The prime rival to nationalism as a driving force is presumed to be the desire for an improved standard of living. From time to time, it is asserted that the ordinary poverty-stricken Asian and African is really interested only in seeing an end put to his poverty. This is a highly dubious proposition. The evidence indicates that he regards at least temporary economic privation as an appropriate price to pay for national salvation. It has also been contended that his real demand is for a transition to modernity, as manifested in economic and social development. In some part the pressure for economic development derives from the same root as the desire for an improved standard of living. However, it also has nationalist implications in its drive for equality."[35]

Economic development has come to absorb much more of the attention of most African leaders than it did in the first years of independence, and it is clearly of the highest priority for the leaders of all the Black states of the sub-continent. But even today this question is inseparably linked with the urges of nationalism for self-determination and full independence.[36]

Nkrumah was also an apostle of African unity, and the social "revolution" which he advocated was seen as an instrument of genuine African unity. "Every African regime should be concerned with its success in every other state and is consequently justified in taking steps to protect it where it has occurred or to foster it where it has not yet been fully realised."[37] Nkrumah's position, as thus defined, is an extreme one, and has certainly not been accepted generally in Africa in that form, because of the implication of interference in the internal affairs of those Black states not considered to be carrying out the "revolution". But it is nevertheless an extension of the widespread conviction that the social, economic and political problems of African states are common African problems that must be solved together.

The desire which Black Africans have for unity is possibly confused, often emotional and seemingly divorced from reality. But it is nevertheless real. It may still remain simply a vague aspiration, but, as Doudou Thiam states, whenever African unity is mentioned "it strikes a powerful chord in the minds of the people".[38]

In practical terms and in relation to our subject this all means that on the one hand the Black states of Southern Africa will jealously guard their independence, and on the other hand they will always be conscious of their links with the rest of Black Africa. For instance, one of the strongest arguments used in the OAU against dialogue with South Africa has been that African unity on the issue should not be broken. This has been an effective argument, and several governments claiming to be in favour of dialogue in principle, have nevertheless argued that they will not undertake this on their own. Even Chief Jonathan has been speaking more in this vein recently and has reportedly tried to prevent other individual states, such as the Ivory Coast, from starting bilateral dialogue.[39] That he nevertheless still favours dialogue is shown by the efforts which he has made in the past to encourage a unified approach and to oppose confrontation and violence. But this means that such dialogue will have to be on the basis of the Lusaka Manifesto which all Black African states, with the possible exception of Malawi, now seem to have accepted as a starting point for any substantive discussions. The Botswana Government has always based its position on the necessity of African unity in general and on the Lusaka Manifesto in particular, and now this appears to be true of Swaziland and Lesotho, too. (Further reference to the dialogue issue, and, in particular, to the Lusaka Manifesto is made later in this paper.)

The possibility of closer political relations must therefore be seen in the context of this African environment, which exerts such a strong pull on the Black African states, and on their leaders especially. There are many in South Africa who have recognised the strength of African nationalism, and this is reflected to some extent in the separate development policy. But this seems to be a recognition only of the micro-nationalism[40] to which Doudou Thiam refers, and not the equally strong macro-nationalism.

External Pressures - Africa

The discussion above of the African environment in which the independent Black states make their foreign policy decisions, has already indicated some of the general pressures on them, tending to militate against closer regional links which might be considered to be contrary to general African unity. This would apply also to other regional groupings, as for instance in West Africa, which might be considered to be pulling away from a wider unity, as expressed through the OAU. But in the sub-continent this potential conflict between regional loyalties and African unity is aggravated by the issue of South Africa's internal policies, which issue has effectively isolated the Republic from Africa as a whole.

It is not necessary now to go into the history of this conflict in any detail, as it has developed since the fifties and in particular since the crucial year of 1960.[41] During this period South Africa, for its part, has moved from a defensive position in the early sixties to a more dynamic policy of attempting to build links in various ways with other African states. This policy has been assisted by the presence in Southern Africa of several Black states with which the Republic has so far been able to maintain at least satisfactory working relationships, based mainly, of course, on the fact of their economic dependence. In the case of Malawi, the relations could even be said to be cordial. Madagascar did, until a few months ago, provide a special example of progress in this outward movement into Africa, as it was a country not dependent on South Africa, which nevertheless saw advantages in closer economic relations and inevitably - because they cannot be completely separated - closer political relations, too. Madagascar was also providing a potential bridge for contacts further afield in Africa. But for the time being at any rate, progress in that direction has been halted by the new government which has found it necessary to bow to strong internal pressures linked with the general African pressure on countries communicating with South Africa.

Most of the African states for their part have during the past decade or more developed their policy of hostility into one of confrontation as expressed mainly through the OAU. Since the formation in 1963 of this Organisation, of which all African states except South Africa are members, its major objectives have been to remove Portugal from Africa, to bring about majority rule in Rhodesia and to effect a revolutionary change in South Africa (although there have been many differences and no clear exposition of what is envisaged in place of the present system).

The official instrument established to carry out these objectives is the Liberation Commmittee, which has existed since the beginning of the OAU, with its headquarters in Dar-es-Salaam. Its functions include the co-ordination of operations against the White South, the distribution to national liberation movements of funds received from African states, as well as from other outside sources, the overseeing of guerilla training and the care of refugees. This

Committee has, however, not received support from all OAU members. A few states have contributed funds regularly, more have supported it with words, but not with money, and a few have disagreed with its activities in principle. In addition, there have from the beginning been differences within the Committee, and in the OAU itself, over which nationalist or guerrilla movements to support, and about the administration of the Committee's affairs.[42] As a result the Liberation Committee has not been an effective instrument, but it remains more than simply a symbol of the OAU majority policy of confrontation, including the use of force, against the White South, and in recent times the more radical states have been making a concerted effort to obtain meaningful support for the Committee.

The last OAU summit meeting (June 1972) paid special attention to this matter, as did the recent summit meeting (early September 1972) of the East and Central African States in Dar-es-Salaam. At the former meeting it was decided to increase by 50% the Liberation Committee's annual budget, and several Heads of State were reported ready to make special individual contributions. This included King Hassan of Morocco who pledged $1 million and who also maintained that African States bordering on countries under colonial rule should allow liberation movements to install military bases on their territories. (No decision was, of course, taken on this suggestion.) Membership of the Committee was increased from 11 to 17. This more aggressive tone was evident amidst much talk of 1972 as being a "year of reconciliation" among African states. Malawi was the only country not represented at the meeting.[43]

At the Dar-es-Salaam meeting there was agreement among the 15 states represented that their arrears of dues to the Liberation Committee would be paid, that members of liberation movements would be given free passage through their countries; and that other aid should be given to "frontline" countries bordering on White-ruled areas, so that the latter in turn could assist the liberation movements.[44]

The Southern African independent Black states, with the exception of Zambia, have not given support to the liberation movements or other subversive activities they have made it clear that their territories cannot be used for these purposes, and they have claimed that in any case they do not approve of the use of force to solve problems of the sub-continent. The public explanations of their policies have varied, however. President Banda of Malawi has been most openly critical, and has poured scorn on the efforts of certain African leaders, which, he has often said, amount to empty threats which will not influence South Africa. Sir Seretse Khama of Botswana has often spoken against violence as a means of bringing about change, but he has commented that he was not condemning those who had to resort to violence when all other paths were closed.[45] At an African-American conference held in Lagos in March 1971, he is reported to have said: "We can no more condemn those who resort to violence to gain freedom (in Southern Africa) than we could condemn the violence of European resistance movements against German occupation or the violence of the Hungarians against the Russians in 1956.[46]

The Swazi Prime Minister, Prince Makhosini, seems to have consistently adopted a low profile on this question and, while certainly not supporting the use of violence, has shown more reluctance to comment on the liberation movements than the other leaders. He has, however, spoken strongly at meetings of the OAU in favour of the need for OAU members to do "all in their power" to ensure freedom and self-determination for peoples in every part of Africa[47], without being specific on the means to be employed.

Chief Jonathan's attitude at the present time is not clear. While he has spoken strongly in the past against terrorism and subversion, there has been a change in the tenor of his more recent statements. He is reported to have said that the "freedom fighters", who should no longer be called "guerillas" or "terrorists", feel frustrated by the absence of constitutional machinery and therefore take refuge in violence.[48] His Foreign Minister went further in a statement at the Non-Aligned Conference in Georgetown, Guyana, in August 1972, referring specifically to the Portuguese territories: "The African majorities in these countries are involved in a military struggle against the imposed Portuguese administration. My government will continue to lend its whole-hearted support to these freedom movements."[49]

The conclusion which must be reached from the public statements of these leaders is that, with the exception of President Banda, they are at least reluctant to criticise the militant position of the OAU in general and the "liberation movements" in particular, although they do not give any indication of changing their basic policy of not allowing their own countries to become involved in subversive activities against their neighbours, including South Africa. This policy would seem to be based on a realistic assessment of their geographic and economic dependence on South Africa. (The apparent shift in the attitude of the Lesotho Government is still not clear.)

A notable development in the campaign against the "White South", on what may be termed the diplomatic front, was the adoption of the Lusaka Manifesto. This Manifesto was first adopted at a meeting between the East and Central African States in Lusaka in April 1969. It was reported to have been drafted mainly by Presidents Nyerere and Kaunda. It was then approved by the OAU as a whole, and finally endorsed by the UN General Assembly towards the end of 1969. There is no doubt that the Lusaka Manifesto has become an important basic document in the policies of African states, explicitly endorsed and frequently referred to by most of them - again Malawi is probably the only exception - including South Africa's three immediate neighbours. Botswana has always approved of it, but the approval of Lesotho and Swaziland only became clear more recently.

While the Manifesto is perhaps open to different interpretations, depending on which sections of it are emphasised, it is claimed by African states to represent their common attitude towards the White-ruled countries and to indicate the minimum change required in those countries before their governments can be accepted in Africa. The Manifesto says that the African states would prefer to achieve "the objectives of liberation" without physical violence. "We would prefer to negotiate rather than destroy, to talk rather than kill. We do not advocate violence...." However, the Manifesto goes on to say that "while possible progress is complicated by actions of those at present in power in the states of Southern Africa, we have no choice but to give the peoples of these territories all the support of which we are capable in their struggle against the oppressors." It is true that it recognizes "that all the peoples who have made their homes in the countries of Southern Africa are African, regardless of the colour of their skins". It also recognizes that "for the sake of order in human affairs, there may be transitional arrangements while a transformation from group inequality to individual equality is being effected", and it acknowledges that within the states which issued the Manifesto, "the struggle towards human brotherhood and unchallenged human dignity is only beginning". But the Manifesto does not contain the slightest indication that the Black African states recognise a possibility that these principles may be given effect to under present policies in the White-ruled states. For instance, there is no hint that the policy of separate development in South Africa, even if carried out at a faster rate and more equitably, may provide a solution. On the contrary, the Manifesto maintains that the South African government's policy, supported to a greater or lesser extent by all the White citizens, "is based on a rejection of man's humanity" and "on the denial of human equality". The Manifesto goes on to say:

> South Africa should be excluded from the United Nations Agencies, and even from the United Nations itself. It should be ostracised by the world community. It should be isolated from world trade patterns and left to be self-sufficient if it can. The South African government cannot be allowed both to reject the very concept of mankind's unity, and to benefit by the strength given

> through friendly international relations. And certainly Africa cannot acquiesce in the maintenance of the present policies against people of African descent.[50]

The actual effectiveness of the OAU's actions against the White South has been in inverse proportion to the torrent of words, condemnations, resolutions, etc., which have come from OAU meetings (as well as from UN meetings where OAU proposals have received strong support in the General Assembly). Nevertheless, the Organisation has created serious problems for healthy intra-regional relations in Southern Africa. Its political and material support has helped to maintain guerilla wars against Portugal in Mocambique and Angola, which show no signs of ending, even if they are not at present seriously threatening Portugal's position in Africa; it has mobilised opinion against the Rhodesian Government to such an extent that a settlement of the Rhodesian constitutional question is not possible without a complete reversal of policy in that country; and it has kept South Africa largely isolated politically and economically from the rest of Africa.[51] Its militant position has meant, too, that the Black states of Southern Africa are continually being forced to choose between their allegiance to the OAU and to the concept of African unity, on the one hand, and the development of their relations with the White-ruled States of their region on the other. Every time the need for a decision arises, involving closer contacts with South Africa, for instance, these governments have to take into account the possible reaction in the rest of Africa, as well as the reaction of their own people who are also influenced by the political currents in Black Africa.

An important change in the seemingly solid anti-South African stand of the rest of Black Africa has, however, appeared in recent years with the evolution of a new line of thinking among some African states. This has come to be known as the movement for "dialogue", and it broke into the open with the announcement by President Felix Houphouët Boigny of the Ivory Coast in November 1970, that he was planning to urge other African leaders to have direct talks with the South African Government, because he considered that force would not solve the problems of apartheid. His country, he said, supported negotiation and dialogue. "We hope to succeed by dialogue. For seven years we have had nothing but grand and violent speeches, with tragic and sometimes ridiculous results. We cannot make threats without the means to apply them."[52] Strong support came from several other French-speaking African states, including Madagascar, and from Malawi and Lesotho. (President Banda and Chief Jonathan, however, justifiably claimed that they had been saying much the same thing for several years.) President Houphouët Boigny's initiative was cautiously welcomed by the South African Government.

A separate initiative was taken by Prime Minister Busia of Ghana, who at about the same time suggested that African states should negotiate with the South African Government while encouraging "constitutional and moral change" from within.[53] He also maintained that the policies of violence and isolation were not the only ones on which African states should rely.[54]

This dialogue movement appeared to be gathering strength particularly among the French-speaking states, and it was introduced by the Ivory Coast at the OAU Summit Meeting in June 1971. Although President Houphouët Boigny himself was not present, he explained the motives of his dialogue proposals in a message to the Conference. The main theme was the need for a "true neutrality" in Africa which "will put each of us in a position to break the alliance we have with the blocs and which will from this point be likely to take our Africa away from the consequences of this divided world and away from war". To obtain this objective there must be peace and, "peace is set up and maintained by dialogue".[55]

Although the dialogue proposals were rejected by the OAU, 11 of the 41 states either supported them or abstained from voting against them (and 2 states were absent). The countries which did not oppose dialogue included Lesotho, Swaziland, Malawi and Madagascar. That more than one quarter of the Black states were willing to take this moderate position in the face of all the pressures which had been built up within the OAU, was seen as an indication that a new wind of change was blowing in Africa, which might reduce the pressures on the sub-continent and also South Africa's own outward movement to progress further into Africa. This, it was felt by many in South Africa, would be to the benefit of Africa as a whole and would reduce the dangers of outside intervention, in line with President Houphouët Boigny's philosophy. However, during the past year there has been little positive development and, if anything, the dialogue movement has lost strength. Two important countries, mainly Ghana and Madagascar, have withdrawn their support for any form of dialogue as a result of sudden changes of government caused by internal dissatisfaction and frustrations. Though President Houphouët Boigny has not changed his policy, other French-speaking African states appear to have lost their enthusiasm. President Senghor of Senegal stated in July 1972, that it was clear that there was now a less lenient attitude towards South Africa among African states. He said he was himself in favour of a united, well-balanced, and even "moderate" attitude to South Africa, and he proposed a three-point plan, which he felt OAU members would accept. (He explained that he would have submitted it to the last OAU summit meeting in June 1972, if President Houphouët Boigny had been present). The three points are (a) that all OAU members must jointly confirm that the Lusaka Manifesto (meaning, in his view, Black/White dialogue within South Africa before external dialogue) is the basis of OAU policy towards South Africa; (b) that OAU members must all agree that the only proper dialogue would be one which included the "lawful representatives of the Black majority"; and (c) all OAU members must agree that to bring about this type of dialogue "each African state must be free to work out its own tactics". On this third point President Senghor explained that, if the whole plan were supported, individual African leaders, such as himself, could then make unilateral proposals to South Africa (and also to Portugal and Rhodesia). But all this would have to take place within the framework of the OAU.[56]

In Southern Africa Botswana has not changed its policy, namely that dialogue is not possible except on the basis of the Lusaka Manifesto, and both Lesotho and Swaziland have now moved closer to that position. Malawi has not changed, and only recently President Banda told the annual congress of his party that good neighbourly relations would be maintained with South Africa, Rhodesia and Portugal because "screaming against the Whites of Southern Africa would not effect any change".[57] Malawi, however, seems to have become reconciled to "going it alone" in its relations with the White-ruled countries.

As a result of this decline of support for dialogue over the past year, the matter has not again been seriously discussed in the OAU or even in OCAM, the grouping of French-speaking African states. This may be a temporary lull, or even setback, in a movement which may later gather strength again, on the basis perhaps of President Senghor's proposals. But it does mean that for the present there is no further reduction in the pressures from Africa, which are making it difficult to build meaningful links between the Black and White-ruled states of the sub-continent.

External Pressures From Outside Africa

The pressures from outside the continent, namely from the United Nations, the Communist powers, the United States and some other Western countries, cannot all be dealt with in any detail here. They are in any case closely related to the conflict in Africa itself. In other words, it is safe to conclude that, if there were to be an improvement in relations between the White-ruled countries and the rest of Africa the pressures from outside the continent would immediately decrease. For instance, the multifarious statements and resolutions emanating from United Nations bodies, including the threats of sanctions (with the actual imposition of sanctions by the Security Council in the case of Rhodesia), are largely sponsored by the Black states and supported by other groups of states for that reason.

It is intended therefore simply to deal here with the intervention of China in Africa, as this is an issue of some immediate concern in Southern Africa, and the influence of the United States.

Not the least of the pressures which are affecting the pattern of relationships in Southern Africa, is the increasing involvement of China in Africa, particularly in the affairs of Tanzania and Zambia, and the support being given by China to action against the White-ruled states. In China's search for status and power in the world, its attention is directed at influencing the peoples of the Third World which in Mao's philosophy constitutes the countryside encircling and eventually overcoming the "cities" of the industrialised first and second worlds. The two worlds of the American led West and the Soviet bloc fall into the same category in Chinese eyes, and it is the Third World led by China, which will eventually - in the long-term historical process - overcome them. But first China must extend its influence in this Third World, of which Africa is such a significant part.

China's prime interest, therefore, is not in taking over Southern Africa, but rather in becoming the dominant influence over the peoples of Black Africa, which in the long run would mean the whole of Africa. But one of the means of increasing this influence, which comes most easily to hand at relatively little cost, is to lend support - moral and material - to the campaign against the White South. In this way the Chinese combine with Black states against what is considered to be the common enemy, while at the same time they are infiltrating the Black states themselves. (This was a tactic employed in China itself in the struggle against the Nationalists, with Japan in the role of common enemy.) Chinese forces are unlikely to become involved in this particular struggle; Africans are to undertake the struggle themselves, but with strong Chinese backing. Then, in terms of the Chinese scenario China will take the credit and Africa will be indebted to and more dependent on China.

It does not particularly matter to the Chinese how long this struggle is drawn out. In fact, it is probably a case of the longer the better, because then there is more time for Chinese influence to increase and become entrenched. And the more fuss made about their presence in Africa by White governments in Africa and elsewhere, the more progaganda value can be squeezed out of the exercise. In all this it must not be forgotten that the Chinese are able to take a very long-term view, and they are no doubt convinced that in this long-term the world is moving steadily in their direction.

In terms of Chinese communist strategy employed elsewhere, it has been suggested by experts on this strategy that the process could be speeded up in Africa, if the White governments could be provoked into retaliating, thus weakening the Black governments and making it easier for Chinese trained persons to take over in the Black states, under the pretext that they will be more effective.

This all means for the countries of Southern Africa that, as long as there are strong differences between the so-called White South and most Black states, these differences will be exploited by China in the form of aid for liberation movements and in other ways calculated to encourage confrontation rather than accommodation. Such aid projects as the Tanzam railroad, the naval base and factories in Tanzania, radio transmitters and an important road in Zambia, and so one, as well as the training of the army and guerillas in Tanzania, are all designed to this end.

Having given this brief assessment of China's aims in Africa, and Southern Africa in particular[58], one must also briefly consider the position of the African states themselves vis-a-vis China, especially the countries of Southern Africa. It must be said immediately in this connection that the Black African states are not passive subjects for Chinese exploitation, as the history of Chinese/African relations during the past decade or more has shown. Both the Soviet Union and China - as well as the United States and other lesser powers for that matter - have not found that their attempts to win influence in Africa plain sailing. They have all had their ups and downs, as a result of the strength of African nationalism and the resentment of foreign domination, and also as a result of the unpredictability of African politics.

Therefore it must not be assumed that Tanzania will forever remain subject to Chinese influence, or that this influence will continue to increase in Zambia. Furthermore, there are at present a number of important African countries strongly opposed to the extension of Chinese influence, notably Zaire which stands in the way of the probable Chinese policy of establishing a zone of influence right across Africa from Tanzania to the Peoples Republic of the Congo - which would effectively cut off Southern Africa. In our immediate neighbourhood the Black states all still recognise the Republic of China (Taiwan) and have no dealings with mainland China. There are no indications of changes of policy in this regard, even though Botswana voted in the UN last year for the seating of the Communist Chinese representatives at the expense of the Republic of China. The one important shift in policy has occurred in Madagascar, where the new Foreign Minister recently indicated that relations might be established with Communist countries and clearly hinted, after a visit to Tanzania, that this might include China.[59] If this happens, it will be a considerable advance for China and will pose an increased threat to Southern Africa, not only in the abvious strategic sense, but also because it might encourage future changes of policy elsewhere in the southern part of Africa.

In sum, the indications are that, while China does not dominate the scene as far as the external pressures on Southern Africa are concerned, Chinese influence on the borders of Southern Africa is increasing and is likely to continue for the foreseeable future. Under normal conditions this type of external pressure, originating moreover from outside the African continent, could be expected to increase the cohesiveness of countries within the region, and it is only to be expected that those in South Africa, seeing this threat and wishing to promote closer ties, will argue that the other states should turn to South Africa for protection. Thus, for instance, Mr. Theo Gerdener, when still Minister of the Interior, said earlier this year that the five Black states and the future independent Homelands could play a decisive role in the defence and security of the sub-continent. It was, therefore, in the best interests of South Africa as well as the other states that there should be co-operation, when threatened by a common enemy, and he referred in this connection to the terrorists movements operating from Tanzania and to Communist China.[60] Mr. R.F. Botha, MP, has referred to the "message" which he feels must be conveyed to Africa and the world, namely that South Africa seeks to promote the peaceful co-existence of different nations in this region of Africa, and thereby to halt the danger of Communist penetration.[61] The Prime Minister has himself spoken in a similar vein on several occasions.

Unfortunately, however, it has to be admitted that, because of political differences within the region, the potentially positive results of this alien pressure are not being achieved, except between the White-ruled states themselves, plus to some extent Malawi which is in an especially exposed position. Because the Chinese-supported action is directed ostensibly against the policies of the White governments, and because it is being carried out by certain Black African governments, the tendency of Black governments in Southern Africa is to maintain neutrality as far as possible, lest they be considered in the rest of Africa to be succumbing too much to South African influence. In other words, their opposition to the internal policies of South Africa, Rhodesia and Portugal, is still such that it prevents the development of a sense of common purpose - even against a potentially serious external threat. While they act correctly, in the sense for instance, that there is no question of their territories being used for subversion against

South Africa, and while they are opposed to Communism within their own countries, their reaction to the outside threat tends to be that there should be change within the White-ruled states, thus removing the object of the threat. So, to some extent the Chinese-supported policy of confrontation is serving to keep alive, and perhaps even deepen political differences within the region, rather than lessen them.

The question of United States relations with the countries of Southern Africa, and with South Africa in particular, is a wide and complex one, and it is intended to mention only certain aspects here, which have a direct bearing on the theme of this paper.

It is difficult to define United States/South Africa relations, they certainly cannot be described as "normal" bilateral relations on the political level. Although South Africa is not high on the list of priorities in American foreign policy, it does receive special attention, because of concern about the racial issue. According to Mr. David Newsom (Assistant Secretary of State in the U.S. State Department), the American official attitude towards this issue has been constant, and he has said that there is "no question of us condoning or acquiescing in these policies. We stand on the side of fundamental human rights in Southern Africa as we do at home and elsewhere."[62] In fact, however, the expressions of concern about South African domestic policies have increased over the years in number and strength, in proportion to the rise of Black nationalism and independence on the African continent and to the development of Black influence in the domestic politics of the United States itself. This is borne out by Mr. Newsom's statement that American policy "springs from our own ethnic composition in the U.S., and from our very keen and appropriate interests in the many independent countries of Black Africa."[63]

Apart from condemnations of South African domestic policies in the UN and elsewhere, American policy includes the maintenance of an arms embargo, in terms of the UN Security Council's recommendation of 1963, and a refusal since 1967 to allow American warships to visit South African ports. These moves were indicative of a tendency in American policy towards isolation of South Africa internationally. Although these specific moves have not been reversed, there has been a shift in policy in recent years, during the Nixon Administration. The policy is now described as one of "communication" rather than isolation, and it is clear that this is conceived of not simply as between governments, but between peoples, at various levels.[64] The implication in this policy of communication is that American influences can assist in a process of change in South African society. In fact the policy has been referred to as "communication for change".[65]

The area where it has been clearly claimed that American official policy could help toward bringing about change, is in U.S. relations with South Africa's three neighbours - Botswana, Lesotho and Swaziland. During recent years the United States has considerably developed its relations with these countries, both on the level of its diplomatic representation and in the financial assistance given to them. In September 1971, the first American Ambassador to the three countries referred, in presenting his credentials to the President of Botswana, to the "unique role" of the new states of Southern Africa, and in particular to Botswana's non-racial democracy which, he said, constituted "a model that might well be studied by other African states". In his reply the President, Sir Seretse Khama, welcomed American assistance "because it serves to demonstrate that the U.S.A. shares our desire that the values of non-racialism and democracy ... should eventually triumph throughout Southern Africa."[66]

United States policy is consciously directed towards strengthening the independence of Botswana, Lesotho and Swaziland vis-a-vis South Africa, as well as their associations with other African states, and this policy fits in with the urges of the countries themselves, as indicated above. This policy includes financial aid which has increased considerably in recent years, totalling approximately $10 million in 1971.[67]

The bulk of this American aid is going to Botswana. It has included a substantial loan for the development of the Selebi-Pikwe copper/nickel project and an even larger amount for the construction of the so-called BotZam road from Nata to Kazungula.[68] This project is intended to provide Botswana with an all-weather road link with Zambia, using the ferry crossing of the Zambesi at Kazungula. While the potential economic value of the road is not clear, there is no doubt that the Botswana Government attaches great importance to it, for reasons which are probably mainly political. It is in fact a symbol of Botswana's intention to lessen its dependence on the south and to develop as far as possible its links with Zambia and other African countries to the north.[69] To assist Botswana in this direction is clearly an element in American policy.[70]

In so far as the United States is supporting the efforts of Botswana, Lesotho and Swaziland to lessen their dependence on South Africa, its policy can be considered as an influence which is weakening the intra-regional ties in Southern Africa, at least in the short term. Coupled with this are its cool political relations with South Africa and its oft-expressed moral disapproval of South African domestic policies. But in the long-term it may be that the encouragement of greater independence on the part of South Africa's neighbours, will help to make possible a healthier interdependent relationship, if and when the racial issue looses its diversive strength.

Furthermore, United States policy does not support violence as a means of bringing about change, and it is not opposed to "dialogue" as such - although American spokesmen have insisted that this is a matter to be resolved between African states themselves,[71] implying that the United States will not use its influence either for or against such dialogue proposals as those of President Houphouët Boigny or President Senghor, in view presumably of the strong differences between African states on this issue.

Internal Pressures

As indicated in the Introduction above, the influence of domestic considerations on the foreign policies of the states of the sub-continent must be mentioned as one of the political factors affecting intra-regional relations, even though it is often difficult to distinguish between domestic and foreign policies. References has already been made to the link between the development needs of African states and foreign policies. Likewise the striving to assert independence, which is no noticeable in these states, is intimately connected with internal nation-building.

Sometimes a foreign policy position may be taken directly for domestic purposes. For instance, in Lesotho Chief Jonathan is making a major effort to effect "reconciliation" between various conflicting groups or forces. In this process he is trying to bring members of the former opposition Congress Party closer to his own government, with the aim of developing some form of national movement and returning the country to a more democratic form of government. One of the differences between the parties has been their respective attitudes to South Africa, with the Congress Party more radical in its African nationalist position. It is not surprising, therefore, that a change in attitude towards South Africa should now be observable as part of this reconciliation process - especially as the process has also included the shedding by Chief Jonathan of what can be termed his "right wing".[72]

More obvious even, was the result on Madagascar's foreign policy - in particular its attitude towards South Africa - of the change in government there in May 1972.

In South Africa itself the effect of domestic pressures on foreign policy is a factor constantly to be borne in mind. It has been especially relevant to the question of relations with Black African states, and, although the outward policy has not been an issue between the main political parties, the Government has clearly been sensitive to possible reaction from the White electorate. In this regard the increasing assertion of their independence by our Black neighbouring states and their more critical statements about South African policies may well have an effect on the White electorate which will make it harder for the Government to develop constructively its relations with other African states. The importance of these relationships, not only for their own sake, but also because of their effect on South Africa's wider international relations, will therefore mean that strong and imaginative leadership will be needed to educate the electorate and to counter the possible reaction.

Concluding Comments

The main focus of this paper on political factors affecting the intra-regional and international relations of the states of the African sub-continent has been on the independent Black states. The consideration of the political factors has been directed mainly at the relations of these states with South Africa. But references to Rhodesia and to the Portuguese states of Mozambique and Angola have inevitably occurred throughout this discussion, and there is no need to stress the fact that Rhodesia and Portugal are linked to South Africa in the attitudes of Black African states when the latter refer to the "White South" or the "White-ruled states".

The same factors *mutatis mutandis* apply to relations with Rhodesia and Portugal as to relations with South Africa. However, it must be noted that the disputes or conflict situation in which they are involved are themselves factors influencing the other states of the sub-continent, which aggravate the general centrifugal forces dealt with above, and further complicate South Africa's own difficult international relations. These disputes also create centres of instability of potential instability within the region and provide opportunities for outside intervention. Moreover there is the constant threat for South Africa of being drawn unavoidably into deeper involvement in these specific issues, even in the military sense.

If the settlement terms between the British and Rhodesian Governments had been found by the Pearce Commission to be acceptable to the people of Rhodesia as a whole, and a settlement of the dispute had followed, the pressure would have been reduced, allowing for a possible gradual relaxation of attitudes on the part of the Black states. But this would not have happened immediately, because officially even Botswana, Lesotho and Swaziland condemned the proposed settlement and welcomed the Pearce Commission's Report. It is one of the strange contradictions of Southern Africa that Botswana, which must have daily dealings with Rhodesian authorities - for instance in regard to the railways - is the country with the strongest political stand on this issue in the sub-continent. President Banda of Malawi, on the other hand, is prepared to admit that he has communication with Mr. Smith's government, although there has been no suggestion that Malawi recognises Rhodesia as an independent state.

It is no doubt the hope of Portugal that the economic and social development of Angola and Mozambique, together with greater autonomy for these territories, will gradually convince the African states, inside and outside the sub-continent, that Portugal's place in Africa should be accepted. The issue with the Black Africans in this regard is "colonialism", not "racism" as in South Africa's case. The two are closely linked, of course, in Black African attitudes, but Portugal makes every effort to avoid being identified with South Africa in respect of internal "racial" policies.

Zambia has a crucial strategic position in regard to Rhodesia, Angola and Mozambique (as well as South West Africa). Although Zambia is geographically part of Southern Africa and is still linked economically to other countries of the sub-continent - including primarily South Africa and Rhodesia - it has turned radically away politically. However, Zambia's future development, both economically and politically, is highly uncertain, and it is by no means clear what role it will be playing within a few years time. In any case its role is and will be extremely important, and it will have direct bearing on the political and economic development of the sub-continent as a whole.

South West Africa remains a vital issue for South Africa. Although special attention has not been given to this issue in this paper, its bearing on South Africa's general international relations must be recognised. No countries - and this includes the other independent Black states of Southern Africa - acknowledge South Africa's right de jure to administer the Territory. There are at present important negotiations with the UN Secretary-General in progress, holding out the possibility of some form of accommodation between UN and South African positions, if sufficient time is allowed for the negotiation process. In any case, the fact that there are negotiations, has meant a reduction of pressure on this score for the time being.

However, the issue of South West Africa remains part of the central issue on which attention is constantly focussed, namely the separate development policies ofthe South African Government, which are known in the outside world simply as "apartheid". That this is the central issue is obvious, but it serves no purpose simply to say, therefore, that the answer to the problems of Southern Africa is for South Africa to remove that issue. The big question would still remain, namely, <u>how</u> this is to be done, given the realities of the situation. A discussion of this question is beyond the limits drawn for this paper, although it is necessary to recognise clearly that this is the basic political factor in South Africa's relations with its Black neighbours in the sub-continent, and that it has strong centrifugal effects. While this remains true, there will never be a deep commitment to regionally oriented development - economic or political - in the sub-continent of Africa.

NOTES

* Reprinted by permission of the author. This paper was presented at a Conference on Southern Africa organised by the Africa Institute of South Africa in September 1972 and was published in its Bulletin 10(10), November/December 1972; it was also published as a monograph of the same title by the South African Institute of International Affairs in January 1973.

1. Quoted by Andrew M. Kamarch "Economic Determinants" in Vernon McKay (ed.) African Diplomacy (London: Pall Mall Press, 1966) 55.

2. L. Gray Cowan "Political Determinants" in Vernon McKay (ed.) African Diplomacy, 120.

3. Ibid.

4. See, for instance, the interview with the Minister of Commerce, Industry and Mines, the Hon. Sishayi S. Nxumalo, entitled "Swaziland and Inter-African Trade" Swaziland Today 1, February 1972, and also the paper by Mr. Nxumalo entitled International Trade and Investment: The Case of Swaziland, presented at the Conference on "Accelerated Development in Southern Africa", Johannesburg, March 1972.

5. Statement published in Lesotho National Development Corp., Maseru, August 11, 1972.

6. See, for instance, paper (mimeographed) by Professor D.C. Midgley presented at a Symposium on Natural Resources in Southern Africa, organised by the South African Institute of International Affairs in December, 1971. Comments on this paper by a participant from Botswana indicated that, in addition to political factors, there was concern in Botswana about the ecological effects of drawing water from the Okavango Delta.

7. The South African Minister of Agriculture, Mr. Hendrick Schoeman, when he opened the 13th meeting of SARCCUS on September 18, 1972, pointed out that all Southern African countries were striving towards economic viability and independence. But to achieve this, he said, they would have to acknowledge their mutual interdependence. He praised the "dialogue" conducted by SARCCUS and wondered whether this could not be emulated in other fields of science and technology which were raising standards of all the peoples of Southern Africa. Noting that SARCCUS is a non-political organisation which aims at ensuring the best use of natural resources through international co-operation, Mr. Schoeman said it had functioned for 22 years and it would be accepted that its work was appreciated by member governments. Otherwise they would cease supporting it. (From a report in Rand Daily Mail (Johannesburg) September 19, 1972, 4.) For an account of the origins, history and work of SARCCUS, see the background paper by Dr. D.M. Joubert (Secretary-General of SARCCUS), prepared for the Symposium Natural Resources in Southern Africa, organised by the South African Institute of International Affairs in December, 1971.

8. Botswana National Development Plan, 1970-75 (Gaborone: Government Printer, September 1970).

9. Africa Institute of South Africa Bulletin 10(6), July 1970, 256. Among other relevant policy statements see the Prime Minister's speech of July 1969 entitled "South Africa's Outward Policy" in Die Suid Afrikaanese Akademie vir Wetenskap en kuns South Africa in the World (Cape Town: Tefelberg Uitgewers, 1970) 101.

10. Botswana officials, for instance, expressed concern over the fact that South Africa suspended foreign currency dealings in December 1971, without informing Botswana (or presumably the other two monetary union partners) and the same occurred when the subsequent rand devaluation was announced. See report in The Star (Johannesburg) March 8, 1971, 28. Similar concern has been expressed by Lesotho officials. See report in The Star, July 20, 1972, 27.

11. There have been reports about difficulties created by South Africa in regard to the proposed establishment of certain factories in both Swaziland and Lesotho. See, for instance, the Financial Mail (Johannesburg) February 4, 1972, 283, South African Financial Gazette, April 21, 1972, 7, The Star, July 20, 1972, 27 and September 11, 1972, 23. See also in this connection P.M. Landell-Mills "The 1969 Southern African Customs Union Agreement" The Journal of Modern African Studies 9(2), 1971, 269.

12. See for instance G.M.E. Leistner Co-operation for Development in Southern Africa, paper (No. DEV/72/C2/2) presented to Conference on "Accelerated Development in Southern Africa", Johannesburg, March 1972.

13. Ibid., 2.

14. Kutlwano, May 1970, p. 20, quoted in paper by Dr. P. Smit in Samewerking in Suidelike Afrika (Potchefstroom: Sentrum vir Internasionale Politiek, 1971)

15. The Star, September 7, 1971, 25.

16. Rand Daily Mail, March 27, 1971.

17. The following summary of UNDP activities in the Southern African region is based on information provided by the UNDP Regional Representative in Lusaka, which is set out more fully in the Appendix to a paper (No. DEV/72/03/3) by David Hirschman, entitled The Policies, Interests and Attitudes of Donor and Recipient Countries; and the Role of Multilateral Aid presented to the Conference on "Accelerated Development in Southern Africa", Johannesburg, March 1972.

18. G.M.E. Leistner Co-operation for Development in Southern Africa, 17.

19. The above details from Botswana Daily News, Weekly Edition (19), April 5, 1972.

20. Barclays Bank D.C.O. Lesotho: An Economic Survey (London: Barclays Bank, February 1970) 26.

21. Zambia Activities of the UN and its Family Agencies in Zambia (Lusaka: Government Printer, April 1971).

22. Koenä News (Maseru) 6(162), August 25, 1972.

23. Barclays Bank D.C.O. Lesotho: An Economic Survey, 26.

24. Botswana Estimates of Revenue and Expenditure for the Development Fund (Gaborone: Government Printer, 1972).

25. See, for instance, Commonwealth Development Corporation Annual Report (London: Her Majesty's Stationery Office, December 31, 1971). The work of the Corporation in Africa is organised in four regions: Southern Africa, covering Botswana, Lesotho, Swaziland and Rhodesia (although it is apparently not operating in the latter country at present); Central Africa, covering Zambia and Malawi; East Africa and West Africa.

26. Zambia Estimates of Revenue and Expenditure for the Development Fund, 1972-73.

27. Botswana Daily News (140), September 6, 1972.

28. See G. M. E. Leistner Co-operation for Development in Southern Africa, 18.

29. J. L. Sadie "An Economic Commission for Southern Africa" South Africa International 1(4), April 1971, 167-75.

30. Ibid., 169.

31. An interesting recent development has been the establishment of a new development bank for Southern Africa--Economic Development for Equatorial and Southern Africa (EDESA)--with the object of assisting developing states, including the Homelands. It is registered in Luxembourg with capital of $25 million (± R20 million). See report in The Star, September 19, 1972, 28.

32. As Chief Jonathan said in 1967 in respect of Lesotho, ". . . you cannot build Utopia overnight, and you cannot ignore the facts of geography and economics." Quoted in M. C. Eksteen Lesotho in Uitwaartse (Johannesburg: Perskor-Uitgewery, 1972) 127.

33. Doudou Thiam The Foreign Policy of African States (London: J. M. Dent & Sons Ltd., 1965) 5 et seq.

34. Ibid., 15.

35. Rupert Emerson "Nationalism and Political Development" in John H. Hallowell (ed.) Development: For What? (Durham: Duke University Press, 1964) 4.

36. Even Nigeria, which has fuller economic and political independence than most African states, is an illustration of this point. The late Olasupo Ojedokun, who was Director of the Nigerian Institute of International Affairs, wrote earlier this year: "Increasingly, economics have come to dominate modern international relations. Not that there was a time when nations ignored economic considerations in their daily contacts; however the extensive percolation of economic issues into all aspects of international affairs is of a recent origin. Nigeria'a external relations have shown traces of this trend. Indeed, the most marked feature of her foreign and domestic policies in the last quarter has been the prominence of economic issues. The drive for a truly non-aligned position in world affairs, and the pursuit of the objectives of the Organisation of African Unity are only matched by a derermination to secure economic independence at home.

There is now a feeling of self-assurance and self-reliance--a widespread realisation, that, in the words of General Gowon, "our only way to development lies through self-reliance and a determination of the part of all of us to make it on our own." Nigerian Institute of International Affairs Nigeria: Bulletin on Foreign Affairs 1(4), May 1972, editorial.

37. L. Gray Cowan "Political Determinants" in Vernon McKay (ed.) African Diplomacy, 125.

38. Doudou Thiam The Foreign Policy of African States, 117.

39. See, for instance, a report in The Star, March 6, 1972, 1. Previously, Chief Jonathan had spoken about the need for African states to find a basis for unity on the dialogue issue before approaching White governments. See, The Star, December 3, 1971, 7; Rand Daily Mail, December, 17, 1971,2; The Star, December 17, 1971, 11. Even earlier, in September 1970, Chief Jonathan was reported to have told an OAU conference in Addis Ababa that Lesotho was the only country qualified to speak with authority on the problems of Southern Africa and he requested that Lesotho be consulted on any decision taken by the OAU or individual member states on proposed solutions to these problems. See report in Rand Daily Mail, September 9, 1970.

40. Thiam's "micro-nationalism", however, refers to the states inherited from the colonial powers, within their presently recognised boundaries. So it would not, strictly speaking, allow for partition and independence of various nations within these present international boundaries, as envisaged in South African policy for South West Africa and the Republic itself.

41. For background and further details see, among others, J. E. Spence Republic Under Pressure (London: Oxford University Press, 1965); Gail-Maryse Cockram Vorster's Foreign Policy (Pretoria and Capetown: Academica, 1970); Amry Vandenbosch South Africa and the World (Lexington: University of Kentucky Press, 1970); Gerrit Olivier "South African Foreign Policy" in Denis Worrall (ed.) South Africa: Government and Politics (Pretoria, Van Schaik, 1971) 285-331; and John Barratt "South Africa's Outward Policy: From Isolation to Dialogue" in Nic Rhoodie (ed.) South African Dialogue (Johannesburg: McGraw-Hill, 1972) 543-561.

42. Zdenek Cervenka The Organization of African Unity and Its Charter (London: C. Hurst & Co., 1968) 26 et seq., and L. Gray Cowan "Political Determinants" in Vernon McKay (ed.) African Diplomacy, 138.

43. See discussion entitled "OAU Ministerial and Summit Conferences" Africa Research Bulletin 9 (6), July 15, 1972, 2497, 2498 and 2499; The Times (London) July 16, 17 and 20, 1972.

44. The Star, Septmeber 11, 1972, 23. Malawi was not represented at the meeting, although President Banda has acknowledged the special efforts of President Nyerere to persuade Malawi to attend, which President Banda regarded as a sign of improving relations with Tanzania.

45. The Star, December 15, 1970.

46. The Star, March 9, 1971

47. Die Transvaler (Johannesburg), September 3, 1970.

48. Die Vaderland (Johannesburg), September 12, 1972.

49. Translated from Afrikaans report in Die Vaderland, August 11, 1972, 5.

50. Extracts from the text of the Lusaka Manifesto as reproduced in South Africa Institute of International Affairs Questions Affecting South Africa at the 24th Regular Session of the United Nations General Assmebly (1969) (Johannesburg: South Africa Institute of International Affairs, 1970) Annexure I.

51. While South African trade with Africa as a whole has steadily increased, this has been the result of the development of trade in the sub-continent only. Trade with the rest of Africa has in fact declined. See, for example, "Afrika-handel is 'n Tasie" in Rapport (Johannesburg) September 3, 1972.

52. Malawi News, November 17, 1970.

53. The Times (London) November 11, 1970.

54. From a statement made in December 1970, quoted in The Star, March 23, 1971.

55. From the text of a message as reproduced in Africa Institute of South Africa Bulletin 9(6), July 1971, 250-251.

56. From a report in Die Burger (Cape Town) July 4, 1972. This policy statement was given in an interview to "Le Monde" of Paris, after President Senghor's meetings with President Pompidou of France and also with British Prime Minister Heath. President Senghor's stature in Africa and his closer relations in recent times with President Houphouet-Boigny made this a significant statement.

57. Die Vaderland, September 11, 1972.

58. For a fuller analysis, which has been drawn on for the above summary, see the lecture in "Chinese Foreign Policy" given by W. A. C. Adie to the South Africa Insitute of International Affairs, Witwatersrand and Pretoria Branches, July 1972. The text is to be issued by the South Africa Insitute of International Affairs, Johannesburg.

59. See article entitled "Political Relations Between African States, Madagascar-South Africa" Africa Research Bulletin 9(6), July 15, 1972, 2501A; Die Transvaler, September 2, 1972, 3 and The Star, Septmeber 5, 1972.

60. Die Transvaler, June 1, 1972.

61. Die Transvaler, May 5, 1972.

62. From statement made during press conference in Johannesburg, November 10, 1970, as reproduced in South Africa Institute of International Affairs Newsletter (8), December 1970, 12.

63. Ibid., 15

64. See, for instance, remarks of Assistnat Secretary of State David Newsom to the African Affairs Sub-committee of the U.S. House of Representatives in December 1970, as quoted in South Africa Institute of International Affairs Newsletter (1), February 1971, 20 et seq.

65. U.S. Secretary of State William Rogers has, for instance,referred to the "continued contacts with South Africans of all races in the belief that this is the most effective way of assisting in this process" of change. U. S. Department of State U.S. Foreign Policy 1971: A Report of the Secretary of State Department of State Publication No. 8634, March 1972.

66. Botswana Daily News, September 15, 1971. U.S. President Nixon has also said: "We have sought to provide assistance and encouragement to Botswana, Lesotho and Swaziland in their efforts to prove the viability of multiracial societies in the heart of Africa." The Times (London) September 11, 1972, Special Supplement, 1.

67. The Times (London) September 11, 1972, Special Supplement, 1.

68. The agreement for the latter loan of R9,475 million was signed only in September 1972. It is therefore not included in the total figure for 1971 given above.

69. The Botswana Vice-President, Mr. Masire, has recently described the road as a "major landmark" in the development of Botswana. "Hitherto we have had to rely on the minority regimes of Rhodesia and South Africa for all our means of communications and trading links with the rest of the world. Now we shall have a direct all-weather road to Zambia, a country with which we have close friendship." Botswana Daily News (140), September 6, 1972, 2.

70. When the loan agreement was signed, U.S. Ambassador Charles Nelson assured Botswana of American co-operation in achieving the goal of closer links with countries north of the Zambezi. "This closer association with a majority-ruled state in Southern Africa is an objective which I feel merits the support of all African nations." Ibid., 1.

71. See, for instance, Mr. David Newsom's Johannesburg press conference as referred to above (note 62).

72. The Times (London), September 11, 1972, Special Supplement, 4.

Chapter Three

SOUTHERN AFRICA: DEPENDENCE, INTERDEPENDENCE AND INDEPENDENCE IN A REGIONAL SUBSYSTEM*

Timothy M. Shaw

In the preceding chapter on the regional and global interactions of Southern African states, John Barratt made a plea for a clear distinction between the concepts of dependence and interdependence.[1] This brief essay is presented as a small contribution to the understanding of the politics of Southern Africa. It suggests that one fruitful approach to the analysis of this, and other, international subsystems is the adoption of an issue-area framework. Regional subsystems have been conceived as patterns of interaction between a set of states over all social values. The case of Southern Africa, characterised by a high degree of both conflict and cooperation, leads us to question this approach. Instead, we suggest that patterns of interaction in the region differ between issue areas in terms of both their mode and actors. There are significant discontinuities of scope between different issue areas. We propose distinguishing between military, economic and political issues areas and the type of interaction in each; Table 1 presents our analytic framework:

Table 1

Issue Areas and Mode of Interaction in the Regional Subsystem of Southern Africa

Issue Area	Mode of Interaction
Military	Interdependence
Economic	Dependence
Political	Independence

Interdependence has been defined by Oran Young as

> the extent to which events occurring in any given part or within any given component unit of a world system affect (either physically or perceptually) events taking place in each of the other parts or component units of the system.[2]

We suggest in Section 1 below that the military subsystem of Southern Africa is characterised by interdependence; in the confrontation between two transnational alliances, the white entente and the liberation movement, the strategies of both sets of actors are affected by actions of the other.

In contrast to this confrontational military interdependence, the regional economic issue area is characterised by relations of dependence. Most states in the region are dependent on the regional economic power, South Africa, and indirectly on the dominant economies of the western capitalist system, in this instance, Britain, Japan and the United States. dos Santos has defined dependence as

> a conditioning situation in which the economies of one group of countries are conditioned by the development and expansion of others.[3]

Interdependence is a relationship of mutual interaction; dependence is characterised by the subordination of some economies to the growth of others. It is an unequal relationship. Interdependencies and dependencies determine the degree of independence of national actors.

Independence is a condition of formal sovereignty and national equality; but the territorial and political integrity of all states is an ideal notion. In practice, because of the activities of international and transnational organisations and because of intervention or penetration, some states are more dependent than others. In Southern Africa, the small landlocked, "least-developed" states are vulnerable and possess only a tenuous independence. However, the white regimes are increasingly interdependent in the military issue area and are in varying degrees penetrated by guerrilla activities. Regime control in Rhodesia, Angola and Mozambique is threatened both by the development of liberated areas and by the related interdependence of the white regimes. In the economic issue area, South Africa's designs for a "Southern African Commonwealth" and a wider "Co-prosperity sphere" have forced it to be more tolerant of the demands of its weaker economic partners; the verkramptes resent the impact of interdependence on white prosperity and authority. However, the peripheries in Southern Africa are not impotent and possess certain countervailing resources which constrain the regional imperialism of the Republic.[4] Both black and white states provide labour, mineral and water resources and markets for South Africa. These reduce its own dependence on the western capitalist system and serve to support its claim to benevolent regional policies, even if these are associated with heightened internal oppression. The national elites in the region have a collective interest in transforming inherited structures of dependence into relationships of interdependence which pose less threat to their independences. The present black leadership in the region is as concerned with exploiting, as with destroying, inherited structures.

Table 2

The Military and Other Resources of the White, Frontier African and Neutral States in Southern Africa

Alliance and State	GNP ($m)	Population (in millions)	Military Expenditure ($m)	As % GNP	Men in Security Forces (and reserves in thousands)	Number of Military Planes
White entente						
South Africa (including South West Africa)	18,400	21	448	3	109(80)	515
Portugal (Angola and Mozambique	850	(A) 5 (M) 7	150	20	140	900
Rhodesia	1,440	6	25	2	13(45)	74
Totals for white entente	20,690	39	623	25	387	1,489
Frontier Africa						
Tanzania	1,300	14	27	2	11	30
Zambia	1,500	4	25(est.)	2	6	30
Zaire	1,900	23	84	5	50	100
Liberation movements	-	-	6	-	30	-
Totals for frontier Africa	4,700	41	142	9	97	160
Neutral States						
Malawi	200	5	2	1	1	-
Botswana	70	0.7	-	-	-	-
Lesotho	90	1	-	-	-	-
Swaziland	140	0.5	-	-	-	-
Totals for neutral states	500	7.2	2	1	1	-

Source: Timothy M. Shaw "South Africa's Military Capability and the Future of Race Relations" in Ali A. Mazrui and Hasu H. Patel (eds.) Africa in World Politics: the next thirty years (New York: Third Press, 1973) 58-59.

Table 3

Principal Liberation Movements in Southern Africa, With Their Transnational Associations

Country	Movement and Acronym	
	a) Major Faction	b) Minor Faction
South Africa (Azania)	African National Congress (ANC)*	Pan-African Congress (PAC)*
South West Africa (Namibia)	South West African People's Organisation (SWAPO)*	South West African National Union (SWANU)
Rhodesia (Zimbabwe)	Zimbabwe African People's Union (ZAPU)*	Zimbabwe African National Union (ZANU)*
Angola[1]	Movimento Popular Para a Liberatacio de Angola (MPLA)*	Frente Nacional Liberatacao de Angola (FNLA)*
Mozambique	Frente de Libertacao de Mocambique (FRELIMO)*	Comite Revolutionario de Mocambique (COREMO)

* Groups recognised and supported by the OAU Liberation Committee.

1 Uniao National Pro Independencia Total de Angola (UNITA) also operates in Angola.

Source: Shaw, "South Africa's Military Capability and the Future of Race Relations," 57; and Kenneth W. Grundy *Guerrilla Struggle in Africa: An Analysis and Preview* (New York: Grossman, for World Law Fund, 1971) 191-195.

1. Military Interdependence: The White Entente

Conflict in Southern Africa occurs between races, classes and states. The primary confrontation is between black and white, which is institutionalised in the clash between transnational associations of freedom fighters and the white military entente. Table 2 presents data on the unequal resources of 'frontier' Africa and the liberation movements compared with the capabilities of the white regimes; BLS and Malawi have declared their neutrality in this confrontation. The strategy of guerrilla conflict erodes the military superiority of the white entente and South Africa has had to commit increasing troops and equipment outside the *laager*. In response to the emerging but heterogeneous alliance between the white regimes, the liberation movement has developed a set of trans-national factions, the basic division being between the Khartoum and Congo Alliances, as outlined in Table 3. There are also tactical relationships between ZANU and ZAPU

Table 4

Liberation Movement, Sanctuary, Training Ground, Headquarters, Source of Assistance, and Year Military Campaign Begun

Party	Sanctuary	Training	Headquarters	Support	Military Campaign Begun
a) Major Faction, the "Khartoum Alliance"					
ANC	Zambia	Tanzania	Tanzania	USSR	1961
SWAPO	Zambia	Tanzania	Tanzania	USSR	1966
ZAPU	Zambia	Tanzania	Zambia	USSR	1967
MPLA	Zambia	Internal	Zambia	USSR	1961
FRELIMO	Tanzania	Tanzania	Tanzania	USSR and China	1964
PAIGC	Guinea	Guinea and Internal	Guinea and Internal	USSR	1963
b) Minor Faction, the "Congo Alliance"					
PAC	Zambia	Tanzania	Tanzania	China	?
ZANU	Zambia	Tanzania	Zambia	China	1966
GRAE	Zaire	Zaire	Zaire	Zaire	1961
COREMO	Zambia	Internal	Zambia	China	1965
Unaffiliated groups:					
UNITA	Zambia	Internal	Internal	China	1966
SWANU	Tanzania	Tanzania	?	China	?

Source: Shaw "South Africa's Military Capability and the Future of Race Relations," 57; Grundy Guerrilla Struggle in Africa 191-195; and Bruce D. Larkin China and Africa 1949-1970: The Foreign Policy of the People's Republic of China (Berkeley: University of California Press, 1971) 188.

in the Zimbabwe People's Liberation Army, ANC and ZAPU, MPLA and FNLA, and MPLA, FRELIMO and PAIGC in CONCP. The opposing military factions, which may now be fragmenting, reflect diverse extra-regional sources of support. The white entente depends on military equipment and expertise from NATO, primarily through Portugal, but also through the close Franco-South African working relationship. The liberation movement is dependent primarily on support and equipment from Russia and Eastern Europe, and China and its allies as indicated in Table 4. However, the revival of African interest and unity may improve contributions to the Liberation Committee and make extra-African support less crucial, thus removing the threat to Africa's unity of extra-African states working through their African dependencies to influence factional conflict within the movements.[5]

2. Economic Dependence: The Coprosperity Sphere

Integration in Southern Africa is highest in the economic issue area. Economic cooperation incorporates all states in the region but is formalised only between South Africa and BLS. One indication of South Africa readiness to fill the vacuum left by Britain's departure as colonial power in the subsystem is the renegotiation of the Southern African Customs Union Agreement in 1969. The improved terms for BLS reduce the need for grants-in-aid from Britain and enhance their development resources; conversely, their dependence on South Africa is increased and the underdevelopment of their economies perpetuated by the absence of potent redistributive mechanisms. The original 1910 Agreement was the first attempt at regional integration in Africa although it failed to produce the anticipated federation or incorporation.

The absence of development or fiscal discretion for BLS, because of South Africa's dominance in the Customs Union and the Rand Monetary Area, was underlined by South Africa's surprise unilateral introduction of a new sales tax. In the revised Agreement,

> The most significant victory for BLS was the implicit acceptance by South Africa of the principle of compensation for polarization of development, price-raising effects and the loss of fiscal discretion.[6]

The new Agreement includes a self-adjusting formula for the distribution of revenue, consultation within the Customs Union Commission, the freedom for BLS to impose extra duties and to develop their own transport fleets, and freedom of transit within the customs area despite South Africa's refusal to sign the UN Convention on Landlocked States. Substantive trade agreements with non-member states must be approved by the contracting parties; South Africa has trade agreements with Rhodesia and Malawi and all the partners hope for some form of association with the EEC. Under the new formula for the distribution of customs, excise and sales revenues, BLS are to receive a greater proportion of growing revenue of the Customs Union as indicated in Table 5.

Landell-Mills concludes that although the Agreement will not tackle regional imbalances rapidly it does contain advantages for the small partner states:

> The free access to the South African market, guaranteed to BLS under the new Agreement, is of key significance for their long-term development.[7]

Table 5

The Distribution Formulae and Revenues Under the Southern African Customs Union

State	1 Percentage Shares: 1910 Formula	2 1969 Agreement	3 Customs & Excise Revenue Budgeted (1910 Formula)	4 Actual (1969 Agreement)	5 Actual 1971
South Africa	98.68903	97.42	na	na	na
Botswana	0.27622	0.74	R 1, 870,000	5,030,000	8,290,000
Lesotho	0.88575	0.89	R 1, 850,000	4,900,000	5,930,000
Swaziland	0.14900	0.95	R 2, 710,000	7,080,000	8,490,000

Source: P. M. Landell-Mills "The 1969 Southern African Customs Union Agreement" Journal of Modern African Studies 9(2), August 1971, 264 and 276 and IMF Surveys of African Economics 5 (Washington: IMF, 1973) 16.

Selwyn is critical of the impact of the customs union and Rand currency area on BLS because of the dominance of South African resources and interests. These institutions perpetuate dependence rather than advance development. The peripheral states have not been allowed to industrialise through sales in the regional market. BLS "are probably net exporters of capital to the Republic" also, they "normally have a substantial deficit on their transactions with South Africa, and a surplus on their transactions with the outside world, and are thus net-foreign currency earners for the Rand Area."[8] South Africa has tried to expand its co-prosperity sphere by the provision of aid from its Economic Cooperation Promotion Loan Fund; an Economic Commission for Southern Africa has been proposed to confront the OAU-ECA continental structures.

Trade within the region is less than 5% of the region's total international trade. Although South Africa and Rhodesia are the largest traders in the region (see Table 6) they, along with Angola and Mozambique, are the least dependent on regional trade (see Table 7). Moreover, those states which are most dependent on trade within the region and especially on trade with South Africa are also those which supply labour for agriculture and mining in South Africa. Table 8 indicates that Lesotho and Mozambique receive most income from labour migration, along with substantial revenues for Botswana, Malawi and Swaziland. Trade, customs revenues and labour migration are the primary interests of BLS in the perpetuation of their dependence in the region.

All the states in Southern Africa, except for South Africa and Rhodesia, are

Table 6

Intra-regional Trade in South Africa (in US $000's) 1964 Exports

Imports	Angola	Botswana	Lesotho	Malawi	Mozambique	South Africa	Rhodesia	Swaziland	Zambia	Total Import in Region
Angola		-	-	-	1,700	1,000	100	-	200	3,000
Botswana	-		-	-	-	300	500	-	300	1,100
Lesotho	-	-		-	-	4,000	-	-	-	4,000
Malawi	-	-	-		200	1,300	2,600	-	700	4,800
Mozambique	2,000	-	-	400		5,700	2,200	100	100	10,500
South Africa	1,700	3,700	12,200	900	14,600		48,000	12,600	12,900	119,600
Rhodesia	400	3,200	-	11,600	1,900	17,600		100	65,200	100,000
Swaziland	-	-	-	-	100	6,600	100		100	6,900
Zambia		100	-	800	100	16,000	8,700	-		25,700
Total Exports in Region	4,100	7,000	12,200	13,700	18,600	52,500	62,200	12,800	79,500	

Total regional trade - 275,600

Total international trade of region - 5,685,000

Table 7

Dependence on Regional Trade in Southern Africa

	Imports %	Exports %
Angola	04	02
Botswana	94	50
Lesotho	90	95
Malawi	60	25
Mozambique	19	16
Rhodesia	35	29
South Africa	01	29
Swaziland	84	37

Source: Timothy M. Shaw and Terry L. Evans "Towards a Comparative Analysis of Regional Integration in Southern and Eastern Africa" African Studies Association meeting, Philadelphia, November 1972, 5.

Table 8

Labour Migration to South Africa: Employment and Income for Country of Origin, 1964

	1	2	3			6
	Sector of Employment		Total Employed*	Sector of Earnings (R,000)		Total Amount to Country of Origin*
	Agriculture	Mining				
Botswana	20	23	52	360	1,495	2,279
Lesotho	63	74	164	1,134	4,885	7,319
Swaziland	7	7	18	126	472	766
Rhodesia	8	14	27	144	929	1,073
Malawi	15	26	49	270	1,725	1,995
Mozambique	25	106	135	450	6,943	7,393

* Includes employment/earnings in other sectors.

Source: G. M. E. Leistner "Foreign Bantu Workers in South Africa: Their Present Position in the Economy" South African Journal of Economics 35(1), 1967, 49 and 52.

Table 9

Export Commodity Concentration in Southern Africa, East Africa, Canada, the United States and Japan

	1	2	3	4
State	Top Three Commodities	Top Commodities as % of Total Exports		Food and "Raw Material" Exports (SITC Codes 0-4) as % of Total Exports
		Top 1	Top 3	
South Africa	Diamonds, copper, maize	10	25	55
Rhodesia	Tobacco, asbestos, copper	33	43	66
Angola	Coffee, diamonds, iron ore	45	71	99*
Mozambique	Cashews, cotton, sugar	15	39	99*
Botswana	Cattle, hides, manganese	66	75	99*
Lesotho	Cattle, wool, mohair	31	71	99*
Swaziland	Sugar, iron ore, wood	24	61	99*
Malawi	Tobacco, tea, ground-nuts	31	74	99*
Zambia	Copper, zinc, cobalt	95	97	99*
Uganda	Coffee, cotton, copper	46	73	84
Kenya	Coffee, tea, petroleum	14	38	69
Tanzania	Cotton, coffee, sisal	17	42	81
Canada	Wood, wheat, iron ore	10	18	41
United States	Wheat, oilseeds, maize	3	8	28
Japan	Fish, rubber, petroleum	1	1	4

* The figure of 99% is approximate and indicative only. Data are for 1968.

Sources: United Nations *Yearbook of International Trade Statistics*, 1968; *United Nations Yearbook of National Accounts Statistics*, 1971; Colin Legum (ed.) *Africa Contemporary Record, Annual Survey and Documents, Volume 5: 1972-73*; Jan Jorgensen and Timothy M. Shaw "International Dependence and Foreign Policy Choices: The Political Economy of Uganda" *Canadian Association of African Studies*, Ottawa, February 1973, 8.

Table 10

Trading Partner Concentration for Southern Africa, Canada, the United States and Japan

State	1 Trade / GDP (%)	2 Trading Partner Concentration (% of total trade) Top 1	3 Top 3	4 Column 2 as % of main trading partner's total trade	5* Column 2 / Column 4
South Africa	41	9	17	4	2
Rhodesia	23	na	na	na	na
Angola	54	35	61	11	3
Mozambique	41	34	53	7	5
Botswana	65	na	na	na	na
Lesotho	40	na	na	na	na
Swaziland	53	na	na	na	na
Malawi	41	38	60	0.1	380
Zambia	88	27	53	0.8	34
Uganda	42	22	53	0.1	220
Kenya	49	24	41	0.5	48
Tanzania	60	23	39	0.1	230
Canada	38	70	82	25	3
United States	8	25	42	70	0.4
Japan	18	30	39	10	3

* Column 5 presents the ratio of Column 2 and Column 4, a measure of the imbalance in the relative importance of trade to both states; the larger the ratio, the more unequal the states.

Data are for 1968.

Source: United Nations *Yearbook of International Trade Statistics 1968*; Jan Jorgensen and Timothy M. Shaw "International Dependence and Foreign Policy Choices: The Political Economy of Uganda" *Canadian Association of African Studies* Ottawa, February 1973, 5.

Table 11

International Trade and Debts of Southern Africa, 1970
(in R Millions)

State	1 Exports	2 Imports	3 Trade Balance	4 External Debt (1971)
South Africa	1,524.3	2,068.3	-543.5	104
Rhodesia	97.4	103.5	-6.1	na
Angola	360	310	+50	na
Mozambique	190	274	-84	na
Botswana	20.7	48.4	-27.7	12
Lesotho	3.7	22.9	-19.2	6
Swaziland	50.2	42.7	+7.5	30
Malawi	40.0	65.5	-25.5	na
Zambia	715	341	+374	na

Source: IMF Surveys of African Economies 5

dependent on the export of food and raw materials. Moreover, as indicated in Table 9, they are all highly vulnerable to market conditions for their top three commodity exports, which are in general agricultural products rather than minerals. Their vulnerability as independent states is heightened by their associated dependence on external trade, as indicated in Table 10. Although data are incomplete, BLS all trade mainly with Britain and South Africa and so would also have a high score of the importance of trade to pairs of trading partners, as contained in Column 5. It is instructive to note the much greater vulnerability of BLS, Malawi and Zambia to fluctuations of trade with Britain than of South Africa and Angola-Mozambique with Britain and Portugal respectively. Trade between BLS and Malawi with Britain and South Africa is more important to the former than to the latter; they are subordinate to Britain and South Africa; In contrast, South Africa's trade is more diversified than that of Canada or Japan; Angola's is as diversified as that of Canada and Japan.

Most states in Southern Africa have considerable and continual imbalances in thei external trade and are vulnerable, therefore, to changes in the international economy. Table 11 is indicative of the dependence of most of the region's economies on external economic support; it also suggests that Angola, Swaziland and Zambia possess the strongest economies, which is a factor in their regional

Table 12

Balance of Trade, Payments and External Exchange in Southern Africa, 1970 (in R Millions)

State	1 Trade Balance	2 Invisible Balance	3 External Exchange Balance (Column 1 minus Column 2)
South Africa	-1,159	-521	-843[1]
Rhodesia	+20	-35	-15
Angola	+50	-90	-40
Mozambique	-84	-39	-113
Botswana	-24	-8	-32
Lesotho	-19	0	-14[2]
Swaziland	+8	-8	0
Malawi	-20	-20	-40
Zambia	+527	-189	+338

1 Includes income from gold sales of R837 m.

2 Includes remittances from migrant workers of R5 m.

Source: Africa South of the Sahara, 1973

policies and behaviour. Angola's importance has been heightened by the global energy crisis and the discovery of new oil reserves off Cabinda; Botswana will shortly have a significant trade balance as its large copper and diamond reserves are exploited. All states of Southern Africa have significant imbalances on their invisible accounts; they pay more for transport, financial services, profit, etc., than they receive. Moreover, their dependence on the international economy is such that their invisible imbalances transform all their external exchange totals into deficits, except for Swaziland and Zambia. Table 12 gives an indication of the dependence of the states of Southern Africa on extra-regional capital, skills and services.

One cause of the continuing imbalance of payments of the states of Southern Africa and, hence their dependence on the sterling and escudos payment areas, is the low level of domestic investment in the region, as indicated in Table 13.

One other structure of dependence in the subsystem is the role of global and regional multinational corporations.[9] American and European companies play an

Table 13

Gross Domestic Investment as a Percentage of Gross Domestic Product in Southern Africa, 1968

State	1 Gross Domestic Product	2 Gross Domestic Investment	3* Column 2 / Column 1
	(in R Millions)		
South Africa	10,152	2,316	22
Rhodesia	780	170	21
Angola	750	na	na
Mozambique	1,000	na	na
Botswana	46	11	16
Lesotho	46	5	11
Swaziland	56	11	19
Malawi	223	37	17
Zambia	989	265	26

* Column 3 presents the ratio of Column 2 to Column 1, a measure of the investment generated domestically; the larger the ratio, the more self-reliant the economy.

Source: IMF Surveys of African Economies, 5; IMF International Financial Statistics 26(8), August 1973; Africa South of the Sahara, 1973.

increasingly important role in the economic growth of Angola, Mozambique and South Africa; South African corporations, notably Oppenheimer's Anglo-American and Rupert's Rembrandt Corporations, are in the vanguard of their government's outward looking policy. Rupert claims to have originated the multi-national corporate concept and is the Industrial Adviser to the Lesotho Government: Anglo-American is developing the mineral reserves of Botswana and is the major shareholder in the ZAMCO consortium which is building the Cabora Bassa Dam in Tete Province, Mozambique. Regional infrastructural plans also include the Kunene dam between Angola and Ovamboland in Namibia, the Ox-Bow scheme between Lesotho and South Africa, and designs for road, rail and power transmission development. Multinational corporations, along with the white armies, migrant labourers and national elites, are the major functional equivalents or identifiable interests which advocate regional cooperation.

3. Political Independence: Conflict and Cooperation Among Unequal States

Military confrontation and economic integration in Southern Africa have not produced significant changes in organisational or political linkages. The status of plans for the 'dialogue club' and proposals for the federation of the emergent Bantustans plus the present set of small black states is that of highly problematic schemes. Although the black states in the coprosperity sphere have been offered non-aggression pacts and aid in exchange for diplomatic links, all except Malawi have declined South Africa's overtures. All the black states are members of the OAU despite Tanzania's proposal that new membership criteria should include non-cooperation with the white regimes. Table 14 indicated that tremendous growth of diplomatic representation by the black states of the subsystem, mainly in Africa and the rich states.

Table 14

Diplomatic Missions Operated by Southern African States

Location	Africa		Other Third World		Rest of World		Totals	
	1965	1971	1965	1971	1965	1971	1965	1971
Angola	0	1	0	0	0	2	0	3
Botswana	0	6	0	0	0	6	0	12
Lesotho	0	6	0	0	0	7	0	13
Malawi	0	3	0	0	3	13	3	16
Mozambique	0	1	0	0	0	2	0	3
Rhodesia	3	0	0	0	0	0	0	0
South Africa	1	1	1	2	16	18	18	21
Swaziland	0	3	0	0	0	3	0	6
Totals	4	21	1	2	19	51	24	74

Source: Shaw and Evans "Towards a Comparative Analysis of Regional Integration" 7.

In contrast, despite tremendous diplomatic efforts, South Africa's international recognition has increased only marginally. Rhodesia belongs to no international organisations, and South Africa and Portugal are treated like lepers in those organisations in which they retain membership. The black states attach importance to access to international organisation; this is a potential counter-balance to their economic dependence on the region and may modify their neutrality. Participation in the global system serves to substantiate their independence and attracts aid and investment to check the dominance of South African capital. Zambia's disengagement from the regional subsystem serves as an example of how to gradually escape the web of interdependence and substitute communications and societal links with East Africa, especially with Tanzania and Kenya.

Elites in the region share a common interest in the maintenance of order and authority. The white regimes are attempting to perpetuate this regional coexistence by changing the basis of nationalism away from race and towards ethnicity. Schemes for Bantustanisation and provincialisation in South Africa and Rhodesia, and the development of 'home rule' in Angola and Mozambique are alternative methods of belatedly forcing the growth of a visible but compliant black 'middle class'. The devolution of power (and poverty) to the leaders of the black mini-states in the region may transform the structures of conflict and cooperation in the subsystem; national identity based on ethnic groups may replace a socio-racial identity in the unitary systems of South Africa and Rhodesia. However, the perpetuation of ethnic stratification is an unstable basis for both regional coexistence and white prosperity. Only a regional order characterised by redistributive justice is likely to divert popular support away from the black majoritarian order advocated by the liberation movement.[10]

NOTES

* An earlier version of this paper was presented at the annual Social Science Conference of the East African Universities, Dar es Salaam, December 1973. Support from Dalhousie University is gratefully acknowledged.

1. See John Barratt "South Africa: Intra-regional and International Relations" South African Institute of International Affairs Johannesburg, January 1973, especially 1-9; reprinted in this collection as Chapter Two.

2. Oran R. Young "Interdependencies in world politics" International Journal 24(4), Autumn 1969, 726; cf. the definition of interdependence in Barratt's article and in Marshall R. Singer Weak States in a World of Powers: the dynamics of international relationships (New York: Free Press, 1972) as a relationship in which "the advantages of reciprocal dependence" are recognised (44). His fourth category of "counter-dependence" (42-43) is applicable in Southern Africa because of the dominance of South Africa.

3. T. dos Santos "The Crisis of Development Theory and the Problem of Dependence in Latin America" in Henry Bernstein (ed.) Underdevelopment and Development: The Third World Today (Harmondsworth: Penguin, 1973) 76.

4. See also my note on "The International Subsystem of Southern Africa" in Zdenek Cervenka (ed.) Land-locked Countries of Africa (Uppsala: Scandinavian Institute of African Studies, 1973) 161-164.

5. See Yashpal Tandon "Nasser and the African Liberation Movements" Third International Congress of Africanists, Addis Ababa, December 1973.

6. Biff Turner "A Fresh Start for the Southern African Customs Union" African Affairs 70(280), July 1971, 273.

7. Landell-Mills "The 1969 Southern African Customs Union Agreement" 279; see also E. J. van der Merwe "The Customs Union Agreement Between Botswana, Lesotho, Swaziland and the Republic of South Africa" South African Journal of African Affairs 2, 1972, 65-75; and A. M. R. Ramolefe and A. J. G. M. Sanders "The Structural Pattern of African Regionalism" The Comparative and International Law Journal of South Africa 6(1), March 1973, 82-105.

8. Percy Selwyn "Core and Periphery: A Study of Industrial Development in the Small Countries of Southern Africa" IDS Discussion Paper Number 36, November 1973, 78 and 177.

9. See N. M. Shamuyarira "Inter-penetration of the Southern African State System" Ninth Congress of the International Political Science Association Montreal, August 1973.

10. For a suggestive and comprehensive review of the varieties of foreign policies and political interests in the subsystem see Kenneth W. Grundy Confrontation and Accommodation in Southern Africa: The Limits of Independence (Berkeley: University of California Press, for the Center of International Race Relations, University of Denver, 1973).

Chapter Four

SOUTHERN AFRICAN INTERACTIONS: THE FOREIGN POLICY PERSPECTIVE*

J. Barron Boyd, Jr.

> The regional subsystems ... are now coming more and more into their own as a complement to the global nature of the overall international system.[1]

Recently the investigation of the subsystem has assumed an increasingly prominent place in the study of international relations. The reasons for the emergence of the subsystem as a unit of analysis are relatively straightforward; while great strides have been made in the work of general systems theorists it remains true that the theoretical and analytic difficulties posed by dealing with the total system of states are immense and seem to defy facile solution.[2] Reacting against the dilemmas posed by looking at the total system, a number of analysts have sought to reduce the "complexity, generality and abstraction"[3] found when attempting to view international relations from a general systems perspective by focusing their attention on partially self-contained geographically localized groups of states such as those found in the Middle East, South East Asia, Africa, and elsewhere.[4]

The postulated benefits that should accrue from this shift of perspective are two-fold. From a theoretical standpoint, it is hoped that the problems of understanding and comprehending international actors and their activities in regional subsystems are less formidable than those encountered in studies of the total system. Arguments for the subsystemic view tend to hypothesize that the complexity of research design and validation are ameliorated by the relatively small sample size found in such groupings. The limited number of cases and the limited number of transactions that must be evaluated aid in the isolation of independent variables, the identification of patterns and regularities in state interaction; and will thus facilitate "the formation of tentative hypotheses about unit behavior in comparable milieu."[5] The ultimate theoretical aim is to move beyond the study of a particular case of particular subsystem to higher levels of generalization about state behavior in the international environment.

From another standpoint there would seem to be certain implications for understanding the behavior of a state which is the member of a subsystem. In seeking to understand, explain, or predict the activity of a state, it is most unwise to consider the state apart from the environment in which it functions. If it can be established that a state is the member of a subsystem, subject to the pressures, attractions, and demands emanating from the other members of its subsystem, then a portion of that environment can be isolated. Further, if the nature of the interaction within that subsystem, the kinds of demands made by other subsystem members on the subject state, the types of ties with its other subsystem partners, etc., can be defined, a better estimate of how that state will behave can be made.

It has been asserted that the states of Southern Africa form one such subsystem; that they are not a loose congregation of states who share little except the accident of geographic proximity. On the basis of economic ties, migration patterns, and salient political occurrences some authors have concluded that the states of Southern Africa (Rhodesia, Angola, Mozambique, South Africa, Malawi, Swaziland, Lesotho, and Botswana) form a subsystem whose unity and stability has been underestimated by other observers of the area.[6] It is the purpose of this exercise to investigate the nature of the foreign policy interactions which characterize that subsystem. Such an endeavor will augment the considerable transactional and attribute data which has been collected and analyzed with reference to the states of Southern Africa. Transaction data links states on the bases of physical exchanges, economic and trade ties, migration flows, political meetings, and the like. Attribute data, on the other hand, compares and contrasts units along a range of variables: population, per capita income, GNP, industrial levels, homegeneity of cultural and historical traits, etc.[7] While these are all essential aspects of subsystemic interaction, the use of such data alone gives a somewhat distorted view of the subsystem by stressing only one aspect of the total spectrum of international intercourse; that of situational givens and non-verbal transactions.

It would seem important to support such data with an assessment of the foreign policy interactions which characterize the subsystem of Southern Africa, for foreign policy forms a primary means of contact between states which may be quite independent of both attributes and transactions. It is through this medium that states inform others of their desires, signal their intentions, and attempt to attain their goals in the international environment. Foreign policy is also the means through which states attempt to "control" the actions of others; it is the channel used for the explicit purpose of getting others to do what they would not otherwise do.[8] Therefore to ignore foreign policy, or to give it only marginal consideration in a study of the subsystem would be to overlook a significant aspect of subsystemic interaction.

A subsystem is a multi-dimensional and multi-faceted entity; there are cultural, historical, transactional, political, and many other aspects of systemic form and function.[9] If a full understanding of the dynamics of that regional entity is to be approached, considerable energy must be expended to explore as many of these facets as possible.

This effort will proceed in three steps: first, the conceptual groundwork will be laid for the subsequent inquiry; we will determine which aspects of the subsystem should be developed if that unit is to have more than marginal analytic utility; second, a framework for analysis will be developed which should allow for the illumination of these aspects; and finally, the hypothesized subsystem of Southern Africa will be evaluated using that framework.

If the subsystem is to be an analytically fruitful unit of analysis there are at least two aspects of this unit which must be developed: the "state" or structure of relationships between subsystem members must be identified; and the content of intra-systemic interaction must be evaluated. Knowledge of these two factors is essential if the environment in which the system members operate is to be fully illuminated.

Identifying the structure of relationships among the members of a particular subsystem is of primary importance. Any valid research scheme must attempt to isolate the variables that could affect a state's behavior.[10] With the subsystem as a focus for analysis, it is possible to identify many of the factors which condition a state's behavior by virtue of its membership in a subsystem and which would likely have been missed had a general systems or a nation-state perspective been adopted. For example, there would be different pressures on an environed state which functioned in an hierarchical subsystem as opposed to one with actors equal. In a similar fashion, knowledge of a system's structure could tell whether it is dense or diffuse, whether all states interact with one another, or whether certain states are focal points for interaction. Each of these situations will exert different forces on the system members and hence will have different behavioral manifestations. Elaboration and illumination of the structural qualities of the subsystem is essential if the environment in which actors function is to be fully explored.

Similarly, if the nature of the environment is to be determined the content of intra-systemic interaction must be developed. Structure is essentially a non-qualitative aspect of the subsystem and needs to be augmented with more qualitative information than an assessment of the content of actor interaction could provide. If the _nature_ of the pressures, demands, and forces which are brought to bear on the environed states are to be established, the content of intra-systemic interaction must be developed.

At this point it becomes necessary to begin the development of a framework which will allow the analyst to combine the specific foreign policy focus of the work with the more general conceptual need to study the explicit structure of interactions within a system and to assess the frequency and content of intra-systemic activity.

The Framework

A basic postulate of this framework is that the identification of communicative interaction within a hypothesized subsystem will enable the student to develop the structural qualities of that subsystem and to ascertain the content of interaction between the members of that group. In spite of the diversity in approach and conclusions, one element seems common to the conceptualizations of most systems theorists: the importance of information flows.[15] Interaction among the units of a system occurs as a result of a communication process in which information is passed between and among the elements of that system. In light of this, the viewpoint of cybernetics and communication theory, as best expressed in the works of Karl Deutsch and Norbert Weiner,[12] provide a particularly fruitful set of insights. These approaches suggest that all systems are alike in certain fundamental characteristics and that every system is held together by communication.[13] To quote Norbert E. Weiner:

> The existence of social science is based on the ability to treat a social group as an organization and not as an agglomeration. Communications is the cement that makes organizations. Communications alone enables a group to think together, to see together and to act together.[14]

Communications are crucial to the preservation and the sustained dynamics of an international system. As the core element of any system, analysis of intra-systemic communication flows can form the basis for an evaluation of the subsystem. The intensity, the content, and the pattern of communications will all tell us about the nature of interaction between members of an hypothesized subsystem. In addition, many analytic techniques developed by other disciplines to deal with information flows can be adapted for use in a study of political communication within a regional group.

As information is communicated between member states, a channel or network is formed to carry that information. If these channels are isolated, the particular structure of communicative interaction within a system can be defined. Network analysis, a tool developed by sociologists, makes it possible to chart the patterns of contact between members of a particular social group.[15] By conceiving of the members of a subsystem as a "social group," an adaptation of network analysis can be the means of specifically defining the structure of interaction within a subsystem. Representing states as nodes, or points, in a network, and the complex communicative relationships between those states as lines, it is possible to graphically map the actual or potential patterns of interaction between members of any sample group.

This analytic method is essentially am amplification of mathematical graph theory, and with this basis a whole series of operations can be carried out which further develop the structural aspects of subsystemic interaction. The theorems of this branch of mathematics will serve to call attention to important structural attributes of interstate communication. Graphically representing interaction serves clearly to define patterns within the communication network, to isolate peculiar configurations of interaction, and empirically to establish the structure of intra-systemic contact.

However, before we can employ network analysis to map the structure of interaction within the subsystem of Southern Africa, some easily identifiable measure of interstate communication must be found. At this juncture the foreign policy focus of the present inquiry becomes eminently compatible with its conceptual basis, for foreign policy is one of the primary modes of communication between states. As Charles McClelland has observed:

> The communications perspective in the international system is not limited to the meanings and content of written and spoken words or to the encoding and decoding of explicit messages. . . Thus the deploying of troops, the conferring of government officials, the traveling of diplomats and heads of state, and other physical manifestations are regarded as indirect means of conveying information between governments . . . A proposal, a protest, an accusation, a threat, or an act of force can be envisioned as a coded message.[16]

All of these are foreign policy activities, but before they can be used in our study some means of operationally defining foreign policy of this sort must be found. In recent years this question has been addressed by an increasing number of scholars who have come to form the events data "movement."[17] In search of means to define the foreign policy behavior of nations, devotees of this data mode have come to conceptualize foreign policy as a series of events which are

> The <u>acts</u> initiated by national governments on behalf of their societies, and pursued beyond their national boundaries, to affect changes in the behavior of other nation-states and international actors in the international system.[18]

The data itself is generated from publicly available sources - newspapers, periodicals, indexes, and other collections dealing with international affairs.

Elaborate procedures have been developed to identify, abstract, and code the actions and activities of nations along a range of variables. Events data thus provide the analyst with an easily identifiable measure of a nation's foreign policy behavior, but it must be pointed out that this sort of data represents a particular aspect of international relations.

Because events are extracted from public sources, they are deemed to be the type of activities which attract the attention of those public sources. They are the non-routine, newsworthy, out of the ordinary, foreign policy happenings which do not correspond to the routinized, ongoing transactions or the long-term relationships which form the bulk of international relations. Events data represent the international political activities of states, the efforts at control, the efforts to persuade other states, or the efforts to effect a change in the behavior of other actors in the international system. Hence the use of event data limits the range of this particular inquiry to a study of the international political activities of states which must be supplemented with detailed investigations of transactions and ongoing relationships if the full range of international relations for a specific set of actors is to be assessed.

Recall that in addition to determining the structure of relationships within the subsystem of Southern Africa, this work seeks to define the content of those same relationships. Foreign policy, and event data, can also be used in this aspect of the study, but some means must be devised which will allow the analyst to treat an event as something whose meaning is explicitly established. This involves transforming an event into a quantity so that events can be aggregated and not treated as discrete acts.

There have been several efforts aimed at developing scales which transform events into numerical quantities along a conflict-cooperation continuum.[19] One of the most interesting methods has been devised by Herbert Calhoun in which he uses the semantic differential to develop a scale for the previously defined types of foreign policy events.[20] Without going into detail, the semantic differential seeks to quantitatively define - to measure the meaning of - words and concepts.[21] This approach seems to avoid many of the problems encountered by others who have sought to develop similar scales,[22] and hence was chosen as the medium to employ in developing the content of interaction among our sample group of Southern African states.

Taken together, this series of operations forms the analytic framework for a study of interaction between and among a small group of states. Before moving on to an actual application of this technique, let us briefly review the major components of the paradigm. Subsystems are seen *as* being "held together" by communication.

Foreign policy, specifically foreign policy events, will allow the evaluation of communications within the sample group of states. The structure of interaction within the subsystem can be evaluated using an adaptation of sociological network analysis. And the content of foreign policy communication can be determined by assigning scale values to each event and then aggregating them.

A Methodological Application

The next step in this exercise will be an application of the framework to the foreign policy activities of the states in the Southern African area in an attempt to formalize the nature of regional foreign policy interaction. We took as our sample group the states cited by Larry W. Bowman as belonging to the subsystem of Southern Africa.[23] Consequently, foreign policy events between the states of South Africa, Rhodesia, Malawi, Angola, Mozambique, Swaziland, Lesotho, and Botswana were coded from the Africa Research Bulletin and the African Recorder for the year 1971.[24] A list of all possible dyadic relationships was constructed, and each event was assigned to the particular dyad (pair of states) involved in the event transaction. This operation specifies the communication that flowed between the regional actors during the cited time period. On the basis of this, a graphic representation of the interactive network of the Southern African states was drawn.

An analysis of this graph, based on the principles of mathematical graph theory, yields information about the essential configuration of relationships in the region.

In the terms of graph theory the resultant network forms a dual component graph.[25] This means that the graph indicates the existence of two subgraphs within the total graphic representation. The points P_1 (South Africa), P_2 (Lesotho) P_3 (Swaziland), and P_4 (Botswana), form one component of the graph (C_1). While the points P_1 (South Africa), P_5 (Mozambique), P_6 (Angola), P_7 (Rhodesia), and P_8 (Malawi) form the other (C_2).

Further, the subgraph C_1 is a rooted graph - one in which one of the points is singled out; in this case P_1 (South Africa). On the other hand, C_2 is a complete graph; one in which all points are connected. It is obvious that point P_1 (South Africa) is central to the structure of the entire graph. If point P_1 were removed, the resultant graph would be separated into two disjointed parts. Such a point is known as the articulation point of the graph.

We have thus clearly and concisely defined the major structural characteristics of the Southern African area, and with the graph as a point of departure our

Interactive Network of Southern African States

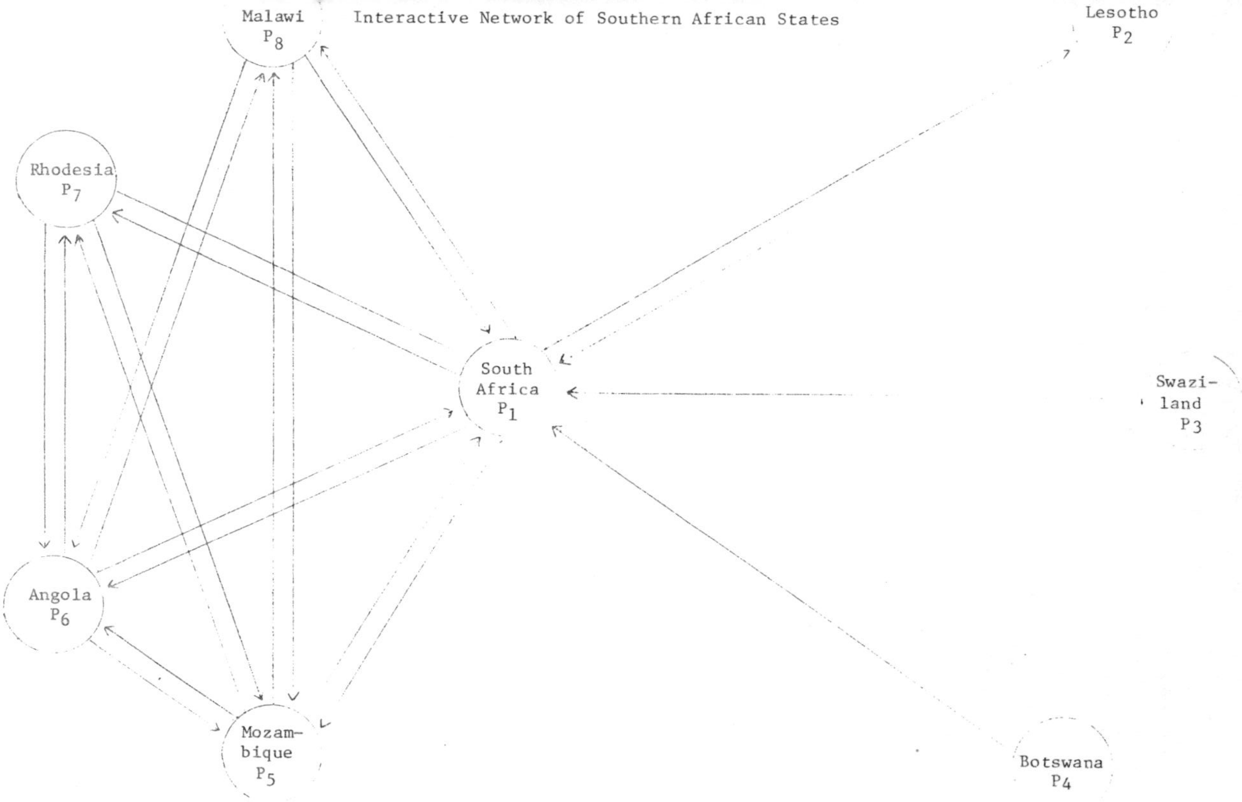

Malawi P_8

Lesotho P_2

Rhodesia P_7

South Africa P_1

Swazi-land P_3

Angola P_6

Mozam-bique P_5

Botswana P_4

Figure 2

Components of Interactive Network

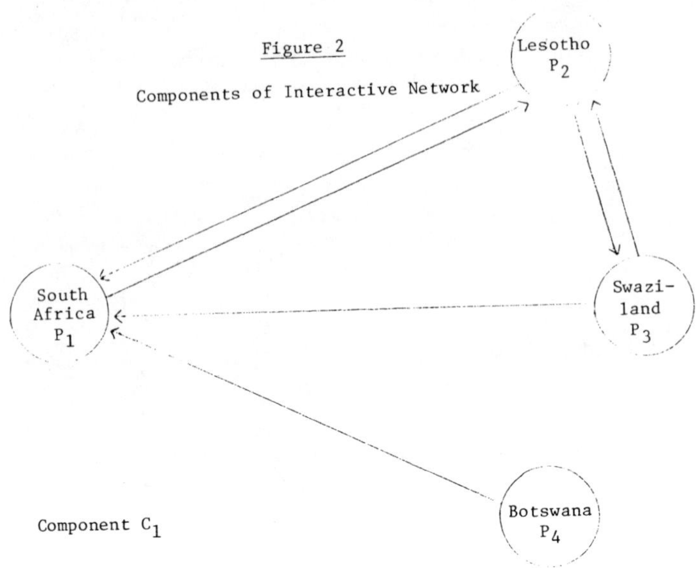

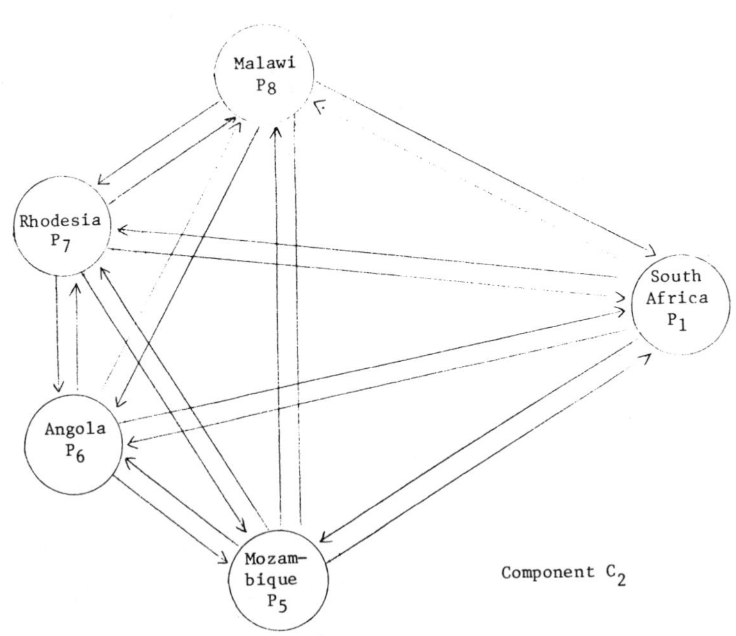

approach allows the augmentation of this purely structural pattern with more qualitative information. The density of any network can be defined as the ration of actual links to all possible links. The overall density of the graph of Southern Africa is 0.45 (26:56). Taking each of the isolated components separately , it is found that the density of C_1 is 0.50 (6:12), while C_2 is 1.00 (20:20). Density is a rather gross measure of intra-systemic communication. A simple frequency count of events passing between members of the respective components will yield additional information about the intensity of interaction. Of the 93 events coded, 23 took place within C_1, while the remaining 70 involved members of C_2. Comparing the percentages of total interactive frequency for the components (75% for C_2 to 25% for C_1) indicated not only that C_2 exhibits optimum density of communication but also that the points in C_2 engaged in significantly more intense interaction with one another.

Table 1

Ranking of Interaction Among Southern African States

Rank	Concept	Value	$(\text{Value})^2$
1	Cooperate	4.674	21.79
2	Bargain	3.531	12.49
3	Reward	3.387	11.41
4	Negotiate	3.058	9.30
5	Consult	2.942	8.59
6	Agree	2.780	7.73
7	Propose	2.568	6.59
8	Grant	2.518	6.34
9	Approve	2.514	6.30
10	Participate	2.459	6.05
11	Request	1.241	1.54
12	Promise	1.018	1.04
13	Yield	0.720	0.52
14	Comment	0.108	0.01
15	Origin	0.000	0.00
16	Reduce	-1.070	-1.15
17	Warn	-1.668	-2.78
18	Demonstrate	-1.807	-3.26
19	Deny	-1.966	-3.48
20	Protest	-1.982	-3.92
21	Accuse	-2.653	-7.05
22	Reject	-2.884	-8.32
23	Expel	-3.062	-9.34
24	Demand	-3.181	-10.05
25	Threat	-3.342	-11.30
26	Conflict	-3.441	-11.75
27	Seize	-3.503	-12.50
28	Force	-4.044	-16.78

The status of P_1 (South Africa) as an articulation point makes it the single most important member of the graph from a structural standpoint. But if the full importance of P_1 to the subsystem is to be ascertained, a more detailed study of its role is necessary. The numbers in the upper right hand corner of each cell in Figure 3 give the event frequency for each dyad. Looking at the total column and row frequency counts for P_1 we find that P_1 initiated 23 of the 93 events (25%) and was the object of 39 events (43%). The correlation between influence and communications flows in small groups has been well established by psychologists; the greater a group member's influence over the other group members, the higher the proportion of communications he tends to receive from them rather than send to them.[26] The rather large difference between the event-outputs and the event-inputs for P_1 indicates that its influence in the subsystem is great. In addition to being the most influential actor in the system, P_1 is the most predominant actor, being involved in 62% of all event/transactions during the time period under study. Because it is the key point that holds the graphic structure together, the most influential actor, and the most predominant actor in Southern Africa, the importance and centrality of P_1 to the subsystem cannot be denied.

By assigning Calhoun's scale values to each recorded event we can operate at the interval level, as shown in Table 1. Consequently a number of operations are possible which will serve to develop the more qualitative aspects of the <u>content</u> of relations within the structural confines defined above. As a first step a weighted average was computed for each pair of states with the following formula:

$$WA = \frac{f.w - u.w}{f + u}$$

where WA = weighted average
f = favorable events
u = unfavorable events
w = weight for each event

To see if the structural differentiation cited before had any ramifications for the behavior of the members of each respective component, the weighted averages were represented in matrix form and the two components were isolated. The average content of interaction was found to differ significantly for each group. The average for C_1 is +2.07 (the + sign indicates cooperative behavior) while that for C_2 is a more cooperative +5.80.

To develop this apparent disparity in behavior more fully, another series of operations was carried out. Using a small model, Burgess has developed a series o indices that are based on the disposition of members of an alliance toward one another.[27] For Burgess the basis for calculating alliance disposition is events data. Since the framework used herein also makes use of Burgess, it is based on

Figure 3

Weighted Averages of Interaction

	Botswana P_4	Lesotho P_2	Swaziland P_3	South Africa P_1	Angola P_6	Mozambique P_5	Rhodesia P_7	Malawi P_8
Botswana P_4			4 7.23	3 -2.88				
Lesotho P_2				8 0.65				
Swaziland P_3	3 6.77			4 .667				
South Africa P_1			1 0.01		4 3.72	5 4.36	4 6.87	9 2.98
Angola P_6				1 8.59		1 8.59	1 8.59	3 7.82
Mozambique P_5				4 .29	1 8.59		2 7.45	3 6.07
Rhodesia P_7				1 8.59	1 8.59	3 12.23		1 8.59
Malawi P_8				18 6.44	2 3.15	5 3.60	1 0.01	

the proportion of positive and negative events for a particular transactional exchange divided by 100. Our framework makes use of weighted events data; it is thus proper that Calhoun's "Tension Index" be used in the calculation of mutual disposition within a subsystem:[28]

$$T = \frac{P - n}{P + n + \frac{ne}{2}}$$

where T = tension (or disposition)
P = total scaled positive events
n = total scaled negative events
ne = total scaled neutral events

Figure 4

Disposition Matrix for Southern African States

	Botswana P_4	Lesotho P_2	Swaziland P_3	South Africa P_1	Angola P_6	Mozambique P_5	Rhodesia P_7	Malawi P_8	
Botswana P_4			1.00	.666					1.666
Lesotho P_2				.623					.623
Swaziland P_3	1.00			-.093					.007
South Africa P_1					1.00	1.00	1.00	.969	3.969
Angola P_6				1.00		1.00	1.00	1.00	4.00
Mozambique P_5				.586	1.00		1.00	1.00	3.586
Rhodesia P_7				1.00	1.00	1.00		1.00	4.00
Malawi P_8				1.00	1.00	1.00	1.00		4.00

This formula yields a normalized disposition scale value which ranges between +1. and -1.0. The magnitude of the values for T shows the degree to which a pair of states are favorably or unfavorably disposed toward one another.

By computing the tension-disposition index for each state in the subsystem of Southern Africa, it is possible to construct a disposition matrix for that group of national actors; this is shown in Figure 4. With this matrix forming the bas one can amplify the content of intra-systemic interaction by applying a series o operations that expand on dyadic disposition. These operations are outlined bel

1. Cohesiveness Index for the Subsystem

This index establishes the level of cohesiveness or solidarity within the subsystem. It is derived by computing the mean of all dispositional indices. The disposition scores for all dyads are summed and divided by N(N-1). Subsystemic cohesiveness index ranges from -1.- (disintegration) to +1.0 (consolidation).

2. Esteem for Subsystem Index (E)

The row marginals of the dispositional matrix allow the calculation of an index that describes the behavior of a subsystem member with regard to the other subsystem members. The mean of the dispositional scores:

$$\frac{\text{(sum of disposition indices from A)}}{\text{N-1}}$$

provides a measure of the value placed upon the entire subsystem or the overall esteem in which the fellow subsystem members are held. It also ranges from -1.0, indicating that a member is generally unfavorably disposed toward other system members; to +1.0, indicating that a member is generally favorably disposed toward other system members.

Table 2

Disposition Index for Southern African States

Cohesiveness for total region = .407

	Esteem	Acceptance
South Africa	.567	.680
Angola	.571	.571
Rhodesia	.571	.710
Malawi	.571	.567
Mozambique	.512	.571
Botswana	.380	.142
Lesotho	.089	.000
Swaziland	.001	.142

3. Acceptance Index (A)

The column marginals of the disposition index matrix quantitatively illustrate subsystem and subsystem-member behavior. The mean of each column values indicates the degree to which each subsystem member is accepted or rejected by its fellow subsystem members. This index also ranges from -1.0 to +1.0.

The results of these operations are presented in Table 2.

Our structural analysis has indicated that the two components of the total graph of Southern African interaction must be considered separately. The above operation is thus repeated considering the two components as separate entities. The results of that analysis are presented in Table 3.

Table 3

Disposition Index by Component Groups

Cohesiveness for C_2 = +.975

	Esteem	Acceptance
South Africa	.990	.896
Angola	1.000	1.000
Mozambique	.896	1.000
Rhodesia	1.000	1.000
Malawi	1.000	.990

Cohesiveness for C_1 = +.266

	Esteem	Acceptance
South Africa	.0	.399
Botswana	.555	.337
Swaziland	.302	.302
Lesotho	.208	.0

Conclusions

Having completed the analysis of interactive structure and content between the states of Southern Africa, a number of substantive conclusions can be drawn from the data.

A glance at the graphic representation of interaction (Figure 1) makes it apparent that a marked structural cleavage exists within the region. The states of South Africa, Botswana, Lesotho, and Swaziland are clustered together in one group; while South Africa, Malawi, Rhodesia, Angola and Mozambique form the other.

Besides being structurally distinct entities, these two groups of states exhibit significantly different traits of interactive contact among themselves. South Africa, Lesotho, Botswana and Swaziland do not show a great deal of intra-componen interaction with a density of only 0.50. Similarly, event interaction frequency is low accounting for only 25% of the total interaction within the sample group of states. The quality of relations shows a low level of average cooperation, +2.07 on a conflict-cooperation continuum ranging from -16.78 (force) to +21.79 (cooperate). Intra-group cohesion hovers around the level of indifference toward the other members at +2.66 on a -1.0 to +1.0 scale, and finally, the individual states exhibit low levels of esteem for other group members as well as being only marginally accepted by their fellows.

Relations between South Africa, Rhodesia, Malawi, Angola, and Mozambique are quite different: structurally, quantitatively, and qualitatively. The members of this group interact quite heavily with one another. This grouping exhibits the optimum density of communications of 1.00. In addition, these states account for 75% of all interaction within the sample group. Qualitatively, relations are more cooperative than are those in the other segment with these states averaging cooperation at the +5.80 level. The component is quite cohesive, C = +9.75, and these states generally hold other states in the common group in high esteem and are highly accepted by others in the same cluster.

Indeed, there would appear to be a foreign policy political subsystem within the total Southern African subsystem. Karl Deutsch has postulated that a "group" can be defined in terms of the greater relative intensity and frequency of communication within the community compared with that outside the group.[29] In other words, group members, and hence subsystem members, communicate more with other group members than with those outside of that group. An alternate conceptualization of the subsystem is found in Oran R. Young's "Discontinuities Model."[30] Young hypothesizes that a subsystemic configuration can be identified on the basis of state behavior; that states within a subsystem behave differently toward one another than toward states outside that system.

On both counts the states of South Africa, Mozambique, Angola, Rhodesia, and Malawi form a distinct entity from the foreign policy perspective. They exhibit significantly more frequent and intense communication with each other than do the other states in the region, and the content of the intra-group interaction is quite different from that between structural groupings.

The dominating characteristic of political relations between states in Southern Africa is the importance of South Africa. The "articulation point" of South Africa in the graphic representation makes it the state that can be said to hold the region together from a structural standpoint. Once the qualitative aspects of South Africa's role were developed it was found to be the most influential actor in the region as well as the predominant state in terms of event-messages sent and received.

The data also indicate that Botswana, Swaziland, and Lesotho are prepared to interact with South Africa. They have all shown a relatively high frequency of interaction with South Africa with fully 65% of all interactions within this group being directed toward South Africa. Significantly, while the frequency of interaction is rather high, the content of that interaction has not been characterized by high levels of cooperation. In fact, one state, Botswana, has shown a somewhat conflictual stance (-2.88) in its relationship with South Africa. This observation is of some interest since the overwhelming dependence, in economic and transactional terms, of these states on South Africa would seem to imply that they should be acting in an acquiescent manner toward the Republic in order to placate her.

Another interesting observation concerns the nature of relationships between the two groups in the region. While there has been a good deal of interaction betweer the BLS states and South Africa, there has been no "spin-off effect" with regard to the forging of foreign policy links with the other states in the region; e.g., although Lesotho interacts with South Africa, it does not interact with Rhodesia, Mozambique, and the others in their group.

A number of interesting lines of investigation are suggested by these observations Why has Malawi, alone of all the black states in the region, chosen to answer the call of dialogue and to enter into an intense, cooperative relationship with South Africa? Economic dependence on South Africa offers a partial explanation, but why has she chosen to maintain favorable foreign policy relations not only with South Africa, as the other black states have done, but also to enter into a close relationship with the other members of the white-dominated group? It would also be of value to explain why Malawi has seen fit to break off foreign policy contact with the other black states in the area.

Another set of questions concerns the behavior of Lesotho, Swaziland, and Botswana. Although clearly dependent on South Africa, their foreign policy does not appear to reflect total acquiescence and a perceived need to placate South Africa with cooperative interaction. Why? Although they interact with South Africa, why have they not followed the lead of Malawi and begun to interact with the other states of Southern Africa? And, although they share a common set of attributes, and a similar dependence on South Africa, why do they not interact more heavily among themselves?

The framework developed herein obviously cannot answer these and many other essential questions about the Southern African region. However, it has enabled us to determine the structure and content of the foreign policy interactions which cha acterize Southern Africa. When coupled with examinations of the financial, trade, attribute, and military inter-relationships of the subsystem, we have a beginning in the effort to unfold the broad spectrum of international relations which characterize the Southern African geographic region.

NOTES

* The author would like to express his thanks to Robert M. Rood and to the members of the Workshop on Southern Africa, especially Douglas Anglin and Immanuel Wallerstein, for their very helpful comments on an earlier draft of this paper. Data sources for this paper were Africa Research Bulletin, 1971 and African Recorder, 1971.

1. Oran R. Young "Political Discontinuities in the International System" in James N. Rosenau (ed.) International Politics and Foreign Policy (New York: Free Press, 1969) 342.

2. Jerone Stephens "An Appraisal of Some Approaches in the Study of International Systems" International Studies Quarterly 16(3), September 1972, 321-349.

3. Michael Brecher "The Subordinate State System of South Asia" in James N. Rosenau (ed.) International Politics and Foreign Policy (New York: Free Press, 1969) 153-166.

4. Pioneers of this approach include Leonard Binder (1958), Michael Brecher (1968), George Modelski (1961), I. William Zartman (1967) and Larry Bowman (1968); most of these seminal articles are reprinted in Richard A. Falk and Saul H. Mendlovitz (eds.) Regional Politics and World Order (San Francisco: Freeman, 1973).

5. Michael Brecher "The Subordinate State System of South Asia" in Rosenau (ed.) International Politics and Foreign Policy 156.

6. See Larry W. Bowman "The Subordinate State System of Southern Africa" International Studies Quarterly 12(3), September 1968; reprinted as Chapter One in this collection.

7. Charles F. Hermann "What is a Foreign Policy Event?" in Wolfram F. Hanreider (ed.) Comparative Foreign Policy: Theoretical Essays (New York: David McKay, 1971) 299-300.

8. James N. Rosenau The Scientific Study of Foreign Policy (New York: Free Press, 1971) 197-283.

9. William R. Thompson "The Regional Subsystem: A Conceptual Explication and a Propositional Inventory" International Studies Quarterly 17(2), March 1973, 89-117.

10. Fred M. Kerlinger Foundations of Behavioral Research (New York: Holt, Rinehart and Winston, 1964) 228.

11. James E. Dougherty and Robert L. Pfaltzgraff, Jr. Contending Theories of International Relations (Philadelphia: Lippincott, 1971) 103.

12. See Karl W. Deutsch Nationalism and Social Communication (Cambridge: MIT Press, 1966), Nerves of Government (New York: Free Press, 1966) and Norbert Weiner The Human Use of Human Beings (Boston: Houghton and Mifflin, 1950).

13. Karl W. Deutsch Nationalism and Social Communication 77.

14. Communication from Weiner cited in Karl W. Deutsch Nerves of Government 77.

15. J. Clyde Mitchell (ed.) Social Networks in Urban Situations (Manchester: Manchester University Press, 1969).

16. Charles A. McClelland Theory and the International System (New York: Macmillan, 1966) 134.

17. Edward Azar, Richard A. Brody and Charles A. McClelland "International Events Interaction Analysis: Some Research Considerations" in Vincent Davis (ed.) Professional Papers in International Studies 2(1) (Beverly Hills: Sage, 1972) 14-15.

18. Charles W. Kegley "Toward the Construction of an Empirically Grounded Typology of Foreign Policy Behavior (unpublished Ph.D. Dissertation, Syracuse University, 1971) 119.

19. See Edward Azar "Analysis of International Events" Peace Research Reviews 4(1), November 1970, L. E. Moses, R. A. Brody, O. R. Holsti, J. B. Kadane and J. S. Milstein "Scaling Data on Inter-Nation Action" Science 155(26), May 1967 and W. Torgenson The Theory and Method of Scaling (New York: John Wiley, 1967).

20. Herbert L. Calhoun "Exploratory Applications to Scaled Event Data" International Studies Association Convention, Dallas, March 14-18, 1972.

21. Charles E. Osgood, G. J. Suci and Perch H. Tannenbaum The Measurement of Meaning (Urbana, Ill.: University of Illinois Press, 1967).

22. Alan H. Peterson "Measuring Conflict Cooperation in International Relations: A Methodological Inquiry" John Hopkins School of Advanced International Studies, Fall 1971.

23. Larry W. Bowman "The Subordinate State System of Southern Africa" 237.

24. The codebooks and manuals of Patrick J. McGowan's Africa Foreign Behavior Study were used in the coding process.

25. Frank Harary and Robert Z. Norman Graph Theory as a Mathematical Model in Social Science (Ann Arbor: University of Michigan Press, 1953).

26. Stephen J. Brams "The Structure of Influence Relationships in the International System" in James N. Rosenau (ed.) International Politics and Foreign Policy 584.

27. Philip M. Burgess, Raymond W. Lawton and T. P. Kridler "Indicators of International Behavior: An Overview and Re-Examination of Micro-Macro Designs" International Studies Association Convention, Dallas, March 14-18, 1972.

28. Herbert L. Calhoun "Exploratory Applications to Scaled Event Data" 24.

29. Karl W. Deutsch Nationalism and Social Communication.

30. Oran R. Young "Political Discontinuities in the International System" in Rosenau (ed.) International Politics and Foreign Policy 336-345.

Chapter Five

THE LIMITS OF SYSTEMIC GROWTH: SOUTHERN AFRICA TODAY*

Christian P. Potholm

Since World War II, much of the literature dealing with Southern Africa has been concerned with discrete entities such as South Africa or Southern Rhodesia, or with bilateral relations between various dependencies and their colonial authority such as the High Commission Territories and Great Britain.[1] More recently, scholars have turned to an analysis of the interrelationships among the various entities in Southern Africa, even carrying the process back through time.[2] In fact, this very collection and its emphasis on the comprehensive nature of the existing subsystem of Southern Africa is indicative of the extent to which these new approaches have affected the way in which we look at the region.

I am concerned here not with establishing the existence of the subsystem, but rather to indicate the kind of system which seems to be evolving in the area. In the process, I shall be examining some relevant models of international subsystems and the not inconsiderable literature dealing with regional integration in general. Hopefully this exercise will provide a basis for understanding the long-term implications for South Africa and the subsystem. With regard to the Republic, most authors who have recently dealt with the area have - quite rightly I think - stressed the centrality of South Africa to the subsystem and the considerable economic, political, military and diplomatic influence which it exerts in varying degrees upon the other units in the subsystem. In an attempt to redress this analytical imbalance, I am also concerned here with considering the existing and possible influences which are exerted by the other units and the feedback effect of South African policies (both private and governmental) which in turn may impinge upon the Republic.[3]

Karl Kaiser in his "The Interaction of Regional Subsystems,"[4] outlines three ideal types of regional subsystems which are of value in setting the stage for our discussion. The first is the transnational societal system in which "... relations between national systems are handled and decided upon by nongovernmental elites and pursued directly by social, economic and political groups in the participating societies."[5] In this model, investment, trade and migration patterns are established by nongovernmental groups, as transnational assemblages act more or less independently in by-passing traditional decision-making institutions within the individual units. The second model is that of the intergovernmental regional subsystem in which "... the relations between national systems are handled and decided upon by elites located in governmental institutions."[6] In this type of system, most decisions of import are formulated by representatives of the various governments; there is tight governmental control over nongovernmental groups and their interactions with counterparts elsewhere. Kaiser's third model, the comprehensive regional system, is characterized by a combination of governmental and nongovernmental decision making as the system goes through a "federalizing process."[7]

While Kaiser's data are drawn primarily from the experiences of the European Economic Community and in their simplicity, the models represent a beginning, not a concluding, theoretical setup, his constructs are not without relevance for our analysis of Southern Africa since they offer both indications of the type of system currently operative in the region, as well as important benchmarks on the way to further integration (or disintegration) of the subsystem. With regard to the current status of the Southern African system, there are strong elements of both the intergovernmental and comprehensive regional models although the former are clearly the predominant. Yet the situation is in flux. Some units, such as Zambia are attempting to withdraw from the system, to reverse the direction of their major transaction flows and to establish new patterns of interaction with other African subsystems.[8] At the same time, there are strong extrasystemic pressures, primarily military, which are pushing at least the white minority governments in the region toward closer cooperation. Internal changes within South Africa, primarily the implementation of the bantustan policy, also offer the intriguing possibility of closer interaction with Lesotho, Botswana and Swaziland. In addition, there is increased economic integration of the region, both in terms of governmental policy and private investment decisions.

In order to provide a comprehensive analysis of these forces and influence vectors and in an attempt to gauge their relative importance in determining the future type of subsystem which will obtain in the region, we have separated them into six categories: (1) military/paramilitary, (2) intergovernmental/diplomatic, (3) philosophical/ideological, (4) economic/investment, (5) infrastructural/communications, and (6) demographic. In actuality of course those are not discrete categories. Rather, they are overlapping, mutually interacting and more often than not, complementary. But capturing the essence of the present state of the Southern African subsystem and the parameters of its future development is facilitated by their use rather than by the traditional method of summarizing bilateral trends and relations among the nine units which currently make up the system. In addition, because of the cumulative nature of the categories, even such a limited conceptual framework should enable us to identify more readily those developments which are most likely to influence the future course of events in the Republic of South Africa, which remains the heart of the subsystem.

Military/Paramilitary

The strength of South Africa's military establishment is well known.[9] In terms of its cohesion, mobility, equiment and training, it is the premier force in Africa south of the Sahara. Its very existence bolsters the status quo, not only within the Republic but also within the larger subsystem. Yet there are situations in Angola, Mozambique and Rhodesia which are capable of generating pressures that could have the most serious ramifications for the military capabilities of the Republic. The present situation of simmering guerilla wars in all three offer the distinct possibility of greater South African involvement in the future. Since a number of developments could occur quite apart from South African designs, it is important to sketch briefly the present situation in each of the three areas.

In Angola, despite 12 years of struggle, the forces of the African nationalists appear to be stalemated.[10] This is due in large part to the heavy Portuguese military commitment to the area and to the successful adoption of a counter-insurgency strategy which has kept the various guerrilla groups penned up in the north end east of the country, away from the more populous coastal zone. But the present stalemate also owes a good deal to the nationalists' persistent pattern of fratricide, division and disloyalty. Indeed, the Popular Movement for the Liberation of Angola (MPLA) led by Agostinho Neto, the Angolan National Liberation Front (FLNA) led by Holden Roberto and the National Union for the Total Independence of Angola (UNITA) led by Joseph Savimbi have spent almost as much time plotting and fighting against one another as they have against the Portuguese.

This situation may be changing. On December 13, 1972, an agreement was reached in Kinshasa, Zaire, which set up a joint Supreme Council for the Liberation of Angola with MPLA and FLNA each sending 14 members to the 28-man council. In addition, there are to be a United Military Command (led by MPLA) and an Angolan Political Council (led by FLNA). This merger could be interpreted as a sign that FLNA is hard pressed indeed. Increasingly isolated in the Carmona region, cut off from its bases in Zaire and lacking the international support afforded MPLA by the Organization of African Unity and the Soviet Union, FLNA may have moved toward merger to avoid oblivion. Also, Zaire may have played a considerable role in the merger as one important military ramification will be a shifting of activities away from the borders of Zaire to the Moxico province which abuts Zambia. Thus these events might well indicate that the Portuguese position is stronger, not weaker, than in previous years.

At the same time, these first hesitant steps toward merger could herald a rejuvenation of the nationalist struggle. If in fact the nationalist movement is on the upsurge and able to sustain a high level of fighting in southeastern Angola, pressures on South Africa to intervene militarily could mount. Currently, there is some infiltration by the forces of the South West African People's Organization (SWAPO) from Zambia through Angola into Ovamboland and the Caprivi strip. To date, South African security forces have kept the situation well in hand. But unlike the situation in Mozambique where the Portuguese are the strongest in the areas immediately adjacent to the South African frontier, there is already something of a power vacuum in southeastern Angola. Vast stretches of wilderness in this area are beyond effective Portuguese control. Were the military situation in the region to deteriorate further, and South African commitment to the area (as in the Kunene hydroelectric project)[11] rise, the resulting mix could have a serious disequilibrating effect on the entire subsystem.

While these possibilities lie in the future, the contemporary military situations in Mozambique and Rhodesia indicate that time may well be speeded up by events, and South Africa may be faced with a choice of substantially increasing its military commitment or see the military balance decline still further.[12] For several years, it appeared that the major African liberation movement in Mozambique, the Mozambiquean Liberation Front (FRELIMO) was on the defensive. Following the assassination of its leader, Dr. Eduardo Mondlane in 1969, there were severe internal difficulties within the group and major defections to the Portuguese. Taking advantage of the situation, the Portuguese launched a series of major counteroffensives which disrupted FRELIMO's control over much of Cabo Delgado province and pushed many of the insurgents back across the border into Tanzania. Yet FRELIMO proved to be resilient, opening a new front in the province of Tete, site of the Cabora Bassa dam and by early 1973, the nationalists had opened up two new fronts in the areas of Manica and Sofal, circumventing the he Portuguese defensive positions to the north and outflanking the Rhodesian-outh African forces in the Zambezi valley.

he altered situation in Rhodesia is potentially the most explosive for the sub-ystem. Here the South Africans are most directly involved and far more committed to the existence of a white-controlled Rhodesia than previously. At the time of the Rhodesian Unilateral Declaration of Independence in 1965, one could well argue that a black Rhodesia ruled by a Dr. Banda type leader might be preferable in the long term to South African interests than an outlaw regime which was the focus of international attention and sanctions. Time has changed this assumption. The Rhodesian government has survived and with the rejection of the Pearce Commission recommendations, settlement with Great Britain seems distant indeed. Moreover, by sending police and paramilitary units to Rhodesia, the South African government has a visible and important symbolic commitment to the Smith regime.

Thus recent military events in Rhodesia while inconclusive, do suggest the possibility of major changes in the military posture of the subsystem. The Zimbabwe African Peoples Union (ZAPU, Zimbabwe African National Union (ZANU) and the Front for the Liberation of Zimbabwe (FROLIZI) have all been more active recently and, under OAU auspices, ZANU and ZAPU signed an agreement in March, 1973 calling for a joint military command and a unified political council. More significant perhaps was the outbreak of new fighting in the Matusadonha mountain region near the Chiweshe tribal homeland. Although opinions differ as to just which groups should get credit for the action[13] the movement of guerrillas through liberated portions of Mozambique into northeast Rhodesia offers a challenge to the current military strategy of the Rhodesians and the South Africans. Some observers believe that if these new efforts can be sustained, they would raise serious questions about the ability of the Rhodesians to contain the uprising with existing force levels.[14] While the Rhodesians could call up additional reserves, they would be hard pressed to match much in the way of escalation without substantial South African assistance, in both men and material.

The military situation in northeast Rhodesia and north central Mozambique could thus throw South Africa on the horns of a most unpleasant dilemma. Previous South African strategy has assumed that with modest South African input - some police and paramilitary units, a sharing of intelligence data and modest logistical support, the guerrilla movements could be confined to remote areas and kept under control by the Portuguese and Rhodesians. If these assumptions are no longer valid, South Africa could be faced with a choice of drastically increasing its commitment.[15] Interestingly enough, it would seem that South Africa has little or no control over whether or not such a crisis will take place. Faced with a substantial escalation of its commitment or the loss of Rhodesia and perhaps the partitioning of Mozambique,[16] the decision makers in the Republic might well rethink Prime Minister Vorster's assertion that if one's neighbor's house is on fire, one helps him out. One may think twice about helping, for example, if one is likely to do mortal damage to oneself.[17]

But what of the rest of the subsystem? If there are substantial potential dangers to the Republic and to the entire subsystem in the existing "frontier" situations in Angola, Mozambique and Rhodesia, there are countervailing, stabilizing aspects to the military situation elsewhere. Vis à vis its neighbors in Swaziland, Lesotho and Botswana, South Africa enjoys overwhelming military superiority and, given the traditional character of the first two regimes, a good deal of support for the status quo in Southern Africa. All three former High Commission Territories lacked armies until recently, when the Swazi king, Sobhuza II created one out of his tribal impis. Not by chance, these levies are to be armed with South African weapons. At the present time, none of the three territories poses a military threat to the Republic. All are free from guerrilla activities and all have sharply curtailed the activities of refugees from South Africa. In addition, South Africa has already demonstrated a considerable paramilitary capability of penetrating Lesotho and Swaziland to acquire both information and prisoners.[18] It seems highly unlikely that either of these two states would challenge the status quo.

In terms of the military/paramilitary category then, the subsystem is moving toward closer defensive cooperation (especially among Portugal, Rhodesia and South Africa) and increasing reliance on South Africa (rather than Great Britain) to maintain the status quo (especially in Lesotho and Swaziland). Botswana's posture, while somewhat ambivalent, seems to indicate that the present government prefers the status quo to initiating intrasystemic violence. While most of this increased interaction is of Kaiser's intergovernmental type and seems to be leading toward increased integration, there are indications that this drawing together is not without problems, inertia and hesitation.[19] Ironically enough, the very extra-systemic pressures that currently provide the major impetus for military cooperation, and at least one level of intergovernment integration, seem potentially capable of generating the most centrifugal of pressures, pressures which provide the greatest threat to the existing status quo and the continuing integration of all nine units.

Intergovernmental/Diplomatic

While full coverage of South Africa's outward strategy lies beyond the scope of this paper, there can be little question that during 1971 and 1972 South Africa took diplomatic initiatives that threw black Africa onto the defensive.[20] Although the Organization of African Unity subsequently rejected the concept of "dialogue" with South Africa and two major proponents of it, Dr. Kofi Busia of Ghana and President Philibert Tsiranana of the Malagasy Republic were overthrown, South African initiatives clearly had an effect within the Southern African subsystem.

This is especially true in the case of Malawi. Following Prime Minister Vorster's visit in 1970, Dr. Kamuzu Banda journeyed to the Republic in 1971, the first head of state to make such a trip since 1947. These initial contacts were followed up by subsequent visits (including that of President J. J. Fouche in 1972), financial and trade agreements and the establishment of formal diplomatic relations. For the very modest price of technical assistance and financial support for the building of the new Malawian capital at Lilongwe, South Africa gained considerable diplomatic insulation both within the Organization of African Unity and the United Nations and certain military prerogatives, including landing rights at Lilongwe. While Dr. Banda has subsequently hedged his bets through increased diplomatic contact with Zambia (and according to one report, some liberation movements[21]), and the <u>détente</u> may not survive his government, it seems clear that for the foreseeable future, South Africa has, through diplomatic initiatives, increased the stability of the area, thereby underscoring the observation of George C. Homans that rewards tend to produce stability and continued interaction.[22]

In terms of international relations theory, it is instructive that contrary to the *a priori* assumptions of many political scientists and historians, the exchange of punishments tends toward instability and the eventual reduction in integration.[23]

In the Southern African context, this latter hypothesis has most recently been borne out by the contemporary relations between Rhodesia and Zambia, Ever since the breakup of the Central African Federation, but more intensively since UDI, both Zambia and Rhodesia have attempted to use punishments against one another in an attempt to alter governmental policy. The destabilizing effect of punishments and the threat of punishments (in systemic terms at least) seems quite clear. Most recently, the closing of the Zambian border by Rhodesia, especially the entry and exit posts at Chirundu, Kariba and Victoria Falls, led to a subsequent reorientation of Zambian copper cargoes through Angola to the port of Lobito. Both the Portuguese and the South African governments are currently far more inclined than Rhodesia to promote economic (and hence systemic) integration and to avoid, insofar as possible, punishment.[24]

While South African trade statistics with the various countries of Black Africa are buried under generic headings, one can ascertain certain broad trends and these support the proposition that South Africa is not only seeking to expand its trade with the African states beyond the subsystem particularly in the area of exports,[25] but it has markedly increased its trade with the African states within the system. In the case of Malawi, for example, 1972 imports rose by 50% over those of 1970 and exports doubled.[26]

The increasing implementation of the bantustan program within South Africa has als produced some important and interesting diplomatic aspects to the situation in Southern Africa. The espousal of the bantustan program and the independence of t three High Commission Territories reversed a decades-old pattern of South African interest in incorporating them into the Union. In addition, the bantustan's very evolution has given the South African government considerable bargaining power with Lesotho, Swaziland and Botswana. For example, there are currently some 450,000 Swazis living in the Republic, most of them in the Transvaal. Although there has been little public sentiment in Swaziland for a "gathering in" of these Swazis, it seems clear that South Africa and the present regime in Swaziland see some mutual benefit in discussing the possibility of transferring at least some of the South African Swazis to the jurisdiction of Swaziland. Late in 1972, the Deputy Minister of Bantu Development, J. J. Raubenheimer indicated that there might be future homelands for the Swazis which could then affiliate with Swaziland.[27] This announcement followed an October 1972 meeting near Plaston between the Commissioner General for the Swazis, Mr. P. H. Forlage and the Swazi council of the Nsikzai regional authority.

As I have indicated elsewhere,[28] the relationship between Swaziland and South Africa is a complicated one, containing strong undercurrents of complementarity. Although the Swazi government is opposed to apartheid, there are areas of substantial agreement which it shares with the Republic, most notably in the areas of economic integration, the avoidance of guerrilla warfare in Southern Africa and keeping South African refugees in Swaziland out of politics. At the same time, one has to be careful not to misperceive the kind and amount of direction which Pretoria is able to give the Swazi government. As David Baldwin has so lucidly pointed out, influence and intervention are complex concepts which are often imprecisely handled by scholars and one should carefully distinguish between the fact that nation A wants nation B to take action x from the fact that B actually does x. There may be little causal connection between A's wants and B's action since "getting" B "... to do what it would have done anyway can hardly be considered intervention."[29]

At the same time, South Africa cannot have been displeased with recent events in Swaziland and there is some evidence that South Africa either initiated diplomatic inquiries or proved most receptive to Swazi interests in acquiring South African arms for its new army.[30] The South African government also looked with favor on the subsequent banning of political parties in Swaziland, including the Ngwane National Liberatory Congress (NNLC) of Dr. Ambrose Zwane, and the suspension of the 1968 constitution. Sobhuza's action strengthened the hand of the conservative elements within the Imbokodvo National Movement and the pro-Sough African elements within the government. Indicating that the present constitution was divisive because it "... permitted the importation into our country of highly undesirable political practices alien to, and incompatible with the way of life in our society and designed to disrupt and destroy our own peaceful and constructive and essentially democratic methods of political activities,"[31] Sobhuza suggested that a new constitution would be drawn up which would more fully reflect the realities of Swazi national life. It should be noted that as far back as the government of Prime Minister Hendrick Verwoerd, South Africa indicated that the multiracial constitutions based on one man one vote ran counter to South African interests and it will be most interesting to watch further constitutional activities in Swaziland and their possible relationship to the acquisition of additional Swazis and land from the Republic.

If the contemporary military situation is providing an impetus for more substantial governmental interaction among Portugal, Rhodesia and South Africa, and if such units as Malawi and Swaziland are increasing the intensity as well as the frequency of their contacts with the Republic, and that in general, these phenomena indicate greater integration of the subsystem, current diplomatic relations between Lesotho and the Republic are more ambiguous. The present government of Chief Leabua Jonathan and his ruling Basutoland National Party, which seized power in 1970 following their loss in the national elections to the Basutoland Congress Party, have spent several years in attempting to work out a government of national reconciliation. The Interim Assembly which was opened in April 1973 by King Moshoeshoe II indicated the means by which Chief Jonathan has attempted to reassert the legitimacy of his government. Of the ninety three members, 19 were from former opposition parties including four from the Marematlou Freedom Party, two from the United Democratic Party and others from the Basutoland Congress Party.

Although the political situation in Lesotho has always been far more complicated than in Botswana or Swaziland,[32] and prediction as to the course of Lesotho-South Africa relations is hazardous at best, it does seem that in order to broaden the support for his government, Chief Jonathan was forced to move away from his earlier pro-South African stance. In recent months, Lesotho has disavowed the dialogue concept and its delegation to the United Nations has been noticeably cooler toward the Republic, particularly after the kidnapping of Fanele Mbale in 1973. While Lesotho's economic dependence and military vulnerability continue to be overriding influences propelling Lesotho into continuing docility, recent diplomatic/ intergovernmental relations have been strained compared with previous years.

On balance, the current thrust of diplomatic and intergovernmental activities within Southern Africa seems to indicate that the subsystem as a whole is moving in rather pronounced ways toward greater interregional cooperation and intergovernmental activities of the type outlined by Kaiser in his second model. While there may indeed be individuals and groups of a nongovernmental nature who are positive influences on the pattern, their impact seems markedly reduced in comparison with governmental principals.

Philosophical/Ideological

If extra-systemic pressures from without and intergovernmental cooperation from within are both moving the region toward a more extensive pattern of interaction, there are nevertheless some distinctly countervailing philosophical and ideological currents which militate against the region as a whole moving toward the true comprehensive system outlined by Kaiser. These have to do with the fundamental assessments about the nature of human collectivities which the various entities have made and with the nature of the power diffusion within them. Four states (Lesotho, Botswana, Swaziland and Malawi) have governments which stress nonracial societies and economic and political systems based, at least in theory, on non-racial criteria for advancement. Three entities (South Africa, Namibia and Rhodesia) have pronounced philosophies of racial separation and racial exclusivity while two (Angola and Mozambique) stress a type of multiracial society where the cultural values of the one racial group, the Europeans, are held to be superior, but, where assuming one adopts these values, one can be accepted as a social and political equal.

While many of the diplomatic and military aspects of the Southern African situation have been extensively probed, comparatively little has been done dealing with these various philosophical and ideological strands on a cross-country basis, and we have little practical data such as attitudinal surveys with which to fill in the blank spaces on the current cognative map of Southern Africa. Therefore, the observations which follow are both preliminary and tentative.

Although some African nationalists would argue that in the case of the Portuguese theory of assimilation, even Africans who have adopted European values are not accepted as equals and that true political power is denied them, it seems clear that many Portuguese do not perceive the situation in this fashion.[33] As far as the Portuguese in Africa are concerned, the theory - and to a certain extent even the practice - of race relations has stressed a fundamental societal assumption that the less racial consciousness the better. This contrasts most sharply with the South African (and increasingly Rhodesian) assumption that racial-ethnic consciousness is a desirable good in and of itself.[34] Thus in the Southern African context, Portuguese officials worry about those Africans from Angola and Mozambique who go to work on South African mines and farms returning with a heightened sense of racial consciousness. For their part, many South Africans have substantial reservations about racial theory and actual societal interaction which in Angola and Mozambique have an economic or class aspect to them which overshadows any racial ingredient.

This divergence in societal core values helps to explain, I believe, the unwillingness of the Portuguese to enter into an open and formal military alliance with the South Africans and the Rhodesians. Because there is a common strand of repression among the white-dominated regimes in Southern Africa there has been a tendency on the part of some observers to misread some of the existing data. Despite the military cooperation among the three regimes and the pooling of intelligence data, what some have called "a growing and ominous collaboration,"[35] there is little reason to doubt the sincerity of the Portuguese Foreign Minister, Dr. Rui Patricio when he declared in March, 1973 that he hoped such an alliance would never become necessary.[36] While the South Africans have certain military reservations about a formal alliance, it is psychological and philosophical aspects to such an alliance which seem most troubling to the Portuguese. And, since the Rhodesians are moving toward the South African core values rather than toward a nonracial society, the Portuguese are also reluctant to support the Smith government without reservation.

There are of course crosscurrents. The long drawn out guerrilla wars in Angola and Mozambique have tended to raise racial consciousness quite apart from Portuguese designs. In addition, the 100,000 Portuguese troops in these areas, few of which are there by choice, develop perceptions of their own since the enemy they face is invariably nonwhite. As some areas such as Lourenço Marques have had distinctly increased contacts with South Africans in large numbers, there are sharpened racial attitudes from a decade ago and it is quite possible that Portuguese racial theory aside, any substantial accommodation with the guerrillas would lead to a Universal Declaration of Independence (UDI) by white settlers in southern Mozambique. Now it may well be that should Angola and Mozambique come under African rule, the European residents in these two countries would be treated as well as were their counterparts in Kenya or Senegal following independence, but there is little evidence that the settlers believe they would be.[37]

The Portuguese government also has some substantial ideological views concerning the diffusion of power within the collectivities which run counter to those of the Rhodesians and the South Africans. The recent devolution of some power from the <u>métropole</u> to the local governments in Angola and Mozambique does not have as its ultimate objective the political and territorial fragmentation of those areas as do the South African bantustan proposals. Under the new decrees from Lisbon promulgated in December of 1972, there are to be local legislative assemblies in Angola and Mozambique with the power to set their own budgets, pass local laws and enact taxation measures. In addition, these areas are designated "states" within the new Portuguese "framework" and have expanded representation in the Portuguese National Assembly. This accent on the unity of the colonial areas, of course, runs diametrically counter to current South African thinking which endorses Africans out of the South African national politi arena and into their own political homelands.[38] The lack of day-to-day racial segregation, the underlying nature of a multiracial collectivity and the devolution of metropolitan power to a multinational unit, all distinguish the Portuguese approach from that of the South Africans and, in this writer's opinion at least, offer very substantial impediments to the evolution of a true comprehensive regional subsystem.

There area also the very definite commitments to nonracial society already made by Lesotho, Malawi, Swaziland and Botswana. Because of the small number of Europeans resident in the first two, we shall concentrate on the latter for the purpose of indicating the extent to which at least some philosophical core values seem currently non-negotiable.

Of these two, Swaziland seems to have the greatest impact on South African consciousness in terms of the image of a nonracial society. The country is readily accessible from the Republic, there is a burgeoning tourist trade which, taken together with Swazi receptivity to visitors, makes for a greater impact than the more remote and less accessible Lesotho or Botswana. As stated earlier, the present Swazi government is conservative and not inclined to challenge the status quo overtly. At the same time, the nonracial character of its society seems far less negotiable than other aspects of its political and military posture. In recent years there have been many aspects of the Swazi situation which have displeased officials in the Republic. The South African government at various times since 1968 exerted pressures on the Swazis to reduce the blatantly non-racial interaction which seems so troubling to the Republic. At times they have been successful, but more often than not, the Swazis have avoided jeopardizing their philosophical core values. While Sobhuza II remains strong enough to reshape the political system to his liking, and the South Africans could offer territory and large numbers of expatriate Swazis as bargaining chips in exchange for the political exclusion of Europeans from the Swazi political scene, it seems unlikely that the Swazis would willingly accept any substantial alteration of their present pattern of race relations and the philosophical assumptions on which this is based.

Botswana too stands for a genuinely nonracial society and political system. Its philosophical basis is too well-known to require elaboration here[39] except to reiterate the extent to which Sir Seretse Khama both in word and in deed has placed himself in strong opposition to the core values of all three white-dominated regimes in Southern Africa. As will be seen in the following section on economics and investment, Botswana's room for maneuver vis à vis these regimes is somewhat limited. The Botswana self-image remains one of a poor, weak African nation linked in important symbolic ways to black Africa to the north.

The "coordination of national policies"[40] which is such an important and integral part of Kaiser's comprehensive regional subsystem model is simply not present in the Southern African situation at this time. Some writers[41] have indeed suggested that a true federation for Southern Africa is the best solution for a variety of its economic, political and extra-systemic problems. Yet it would seem that the basic core values which form the basis for at least three different types of societies within that subsystem strongly militate against its passing from an intergovernmental type to a comprehensive type. I would like to submit that the varying philosophies and ideologies present in Southern Africa are far less malleable than has been previously suggested. The core values of principal decision makers, be they white South Africans or Rhodesians, black Swazis or Batswana or the various racial types within the Portuguese colonial system represent one of the more fundamental "givens" in the present situation. The pattern of racial dominance found in South Africa and the colonial patterns in Angola and Mozambique are centuries old.[42] And for at least a hundred years, Africans have sought to alter or escape the implications of these patterns. African fear of domination remains strong, especially in Lesotho, Swaziland and Botswana. It is only in the last decade, for example, that these three areas have managed finally to achieve independence and avoid incorporation into the Republic. It would take extremely powerful and at this moment unforeseen forces to get them to consider any arrangement which would jeopardize the type of society they have attained, just as it would take truly momentous changes in the white electorate of South Africa to move toward African majority rule or a non-racial society. Now it may well be that a type of comprehensive regional subsystem could be evolved which would satisfy all parties concerned but I for one am at a loss to conjecture on what philosophical underpinnings it would be based.[43]

Economic/Investment

If the strands of military integration and diplomatic cooperation are in some fundamental sense bounded by the *a priori* philosophical assumptions of the variou[s] entities in Southern Africa, they are indeed reinforced and accelerated by curren[t] economic trends within the region. There is little question but that Southern Africa is drawing closer together economically and that this increased integratio[n] is taking place as a result of both governmental and nongovernmental impetus.[44]

The availability of capital and skilled manpower, technical assistance and [eco]nomic planning guidance give South Africa an attractive aid package to offer the surrounding, poorer nations and the Republic has not been averse to using that package for diplomatic advantage. For example, during 1970 at the height of the dialogue strategy, South Africa and the government of Philibert Tsiranana concluded an agreement which called for economic cooperation between the two countries and for the development of a tourist industry on Madagascar. With the coming to power of General Gabriel Ramanantsea many of the projects, including the development of Nossi-Be Island were terminated and in June of 1972 the South African government announced the suspension of the agreement. This set of developments clearly underscores the fragility of South Africa's outward movement once one gets beyond the confines of the subsystem.

Within the subsystem, however, there continues to be further economic integration. This is particularly true in the case of the three former High Commission Territories. Despite their attempts to diversify the sources of both their aid and their export markets, Swaziland, Botswana and Lesotho find themselves more intrinsically bound up with the Republic than ever before. The new customs agreement which came into effect on March 1, 1970 sharply revised upward the annual portion of the customs revenues due each territory. The previous agreement was based on the ratio of total customs duties collected by each territory to the total customs revenue for the entire area during 1906-1908. This meant that Swaziland had been receiving .53% annually, Botswana .31% and Lesotho .47%.

Because of the common currency and the post-1960 upsurge in exports from Swaziland and Botswana, the leaders of the three territories argued that since they were now more substantial earners of foreign exchange and trying to develop their own infant industries, a new arrangement had to be worked out. The 1969 agreement kept the common currency, common customs pool and duty-free interchange of domestic products, allowed for some modest protection for the territories' infant industries and a revised method for the calculation of the division of customs, excise and duty revenues. In place of the old percentage figures, each territory was to get a share based on a complex formula involving a number of variables. As a result of the new arrangement, Swaziland's yearly revenues jumped by over 100% and those of Lesotho 500%. But ironically enough, these new revenues only increase the territories' dependence on the Republic since previous British grants-in-aid necessary to balance their budgets are now no longer necessary and the British have been able to scale down the level of their aid.

While the levels of dependence vary from territory to territory, they are generally considerable. Lesotho takes nearly 80% of its imports from South Africa and sends over 60% of its exports to the Republic. In addition, the South African government will provide the major financing for Lesotho's Maliba-

Matso water development project. In the case of Swaziland, South Africa continues to provide 80% of the country's imports although Japan, Great Britain and the United States take a major portion of its exports. In the case of Botswana, it is interesting to note that despite the government's more independent diplomatic stance, its level of economic dependence remains considerable. In fact, knowledgeable observers have concluded that the recent economic boom in the country has increased, not decreased, its reliance on South Africa.[45]

The exploitation and development of the mineral resources in Botswana seem to offer the hope that Botswana, now one of the poorest countries in the world, can improve its economic situation. Nickel and copper deposits at Selibe Pikwe, coal at Morupule and diamonds at Orapa are extensive and accessible as major amounts of venture capital have flowed in from the United Nations, United States, Great Britain, Canada, Germany and South Africa. It is anticipated that the total investment package will exceed $150 million.[46] The Anglo American Corporation emerges as the major private investment source.

The importance of Anglo American to the development of Botswana's mineral riches underscores the perspicacious insights of Samuel P. Huntington in his examination of transnational organizations.[47] Anglo American, like its American and European counterparts, is able to move personnel and resources from one portion of its holdings to another, across national frontiers, seeking access rather than territorial holdings thus providing impetus for the development of the type outlined in Kaiser's transnational society subsystem. Huntington suggests an index of development by which generally speaking, the more developed the country economically, the higher its price of access. In this regard, it is instructive that the government of Botswana's share of the proposed project is distinctly a minority one, 20%. Huntington also suggests that while these corporations both seek and initially reinforce the status quo, in the long run, by creating new demands, new styles of life, and new ideas, their activities are destabilizing. Because of the dychronic and dysrhythmic impact of investment, the transnational corporations are sowing the seeds of future social and political upheaval at the very time they are creating new linkages among the units in which the transnational organization operate.

Without subscribing entirely to the Huntington hypothesis, we can project the possible future impact on South African foreign policy as economic development proceeds throughout the subsystem. In the case of Botswana, while the near term brings greater dependence, it is by no means clear that the long term continues this pattern and there are situations, particularly in the Portuguese-controlled territories, where increasing economic integration leads to diplomatic and political interdependence which, from the South African point of view may be dysfunctional indeed.[48] For example, the $350 million project at Cabora Bassa in Mozambique and the $200 million hydroelectric facility at Kunene, together with the South African-sponsored pipeline to transport natural gas from Mozambique all involve substantial investment by South African firms and all anticipate South Africa taking major portions of the energy generated from all three projects. Thus South Africa becomes more involved in the fate of the Portuguese-held areas and as a result of these projects, military and political events far from the Republic have potentially more resounding implications than they would have a decade ago. While it is speculation at this point as to the extent to which these projects will become hostages to, or important influence vectors upon, South Africa's foreign policy, the increasing economic integration of the region is not without considerable importance for the future diplomatic posture of the Republic and may have as yet unseen consequences for its domestic scene.

There is also another dimension to all of this. Many exponents of development overlook what Gunnar Myrdal has called "backwash" effect from development.[49] This backwash is produced by the spread effect of a wealthy core area like South Africa which may eventually lead to a highlighting of regional disparities rather than producing a decrease in them. In terms of Kunene and Mozambique, for example, the skilled labor and capital which flow toward these projects at their inception may well flow back toward the Republic when the projects are completed and local labor which has become more highly skilled in the course of the projects' development then seeks employment at the same level, a level which is now obtainable, not in the local region, but in the Republic.

Thus one could argue that what is taking place in Southern Africa is sector economic integration (i.e. between target points in Angola and target points in Namibia, or between southern Mozambique and the Rand) not total economic integration and this coupled with the permeation of race as a crucial variable in the more highly developed region may politicize many functional issues. For the short term then, economic integration is proceeding apace and should continue to do so. What is less clear is what impact this particular type of economic integration will have on the political and social aspects of regional integration over the long term.

Infrastructural/Communications

In terms of the communications and transportation infrastructure of Southern Africa, South Africa continues to stand at its heart and centre. In particular, the degree of reliance of the former High Commission Territories is considerable. In the case of Lesotho, its only railroad which runs to the capital at Maseru is South African. Air service from Lesotho currently runs through the Republic and flights in and from Lesotho must use South African facilities in order to overfly that country. Telex and telephone lines run through South Africa as well. For Lesotho, there are no viable alternatives at this time.

For its part, Swaziland is also hightly dependent on South Africa. Its major transportation links, road net, bus lines and cable car system all terminate in South Africa and together they carry nearly 80% of Swaziland's imports (and in the case of the cable car, represent the primary export vehicle for asbestos). The Swaziland railroad built in 1964 connects the central portion of the country with Lourenço Marques and thus gives the country some alternatives to total dependence upon South Africa although to date the rail line is primarily important for Swaziland's exports. During 1973, the South African Railway Board indicated that to link the Swaziland railroad with the South African rail net was not feasible at this time.[50] South Africa continues to stand astride most of Swaziland's links with the outside world. All international telephone traffic is routed through Johannesburg, while mail and telex go through Pretoria. Although weekly flights to Lourenço Marques began in 1973, most of Swaziland's air traffic continues to be routed through Durban and Johannesburg.

There are currently no infrastructural changes planned which will redirect the existing patterns for Lesotho and Swaziland and these are likely to persist into the future, giving South Africa important leverage over both territories and thereby effecting systemic stability. In the case of Botswana, however, while it is currently highly dependent on the Republic for its lines of communication, there are indications that this may be changing.

Except for a narrow strip of land several hundred yards wide where Botswana abuts Zambia, the country is surrounded by South Africa (including Namibia) and Rhodesia. Most of its population lives within 50 miles of the Republic and the country's only rail line runs from Rhodesia and through South Africa, as do most of its telecommunication links with the rest of the world. Botswana is attempting to reduce this level of dependence. Of major symbolic importance for the country and subsystem is the proposed tarred highway which will link Gaberone and the southern portion of Botswana with Livingstone in Zambia via the Kanzangula ferry (there is also the possibility the ferry will be replaced by a bridge). Ever since its inception, the project has been strenuously opposed by South Africa. Nevertheless, with American, British, World Bank and Swedish assistance, the tarring and extension of the road continues and the completion date is set for mid-1975.

The completion of the road and the options it will provide for the Botswana could alter the infrastructural patterns of that portion of the subsystem and, in time, reorient some of Botswana's trade toward Zambia and the emerging eastern African subsystem. As indicated above, the Rhodesian railroad runs through the country and together with Rhodesian rail lines which connect with their Mozambiquean counterparts, represent that country's access to the sea. Were Botswana able to reduce its dependence on the railroad, especially that portion which runs through South Africa, it could then take advantage of Rhodesian dependence by threatening to nationalize that portion of the Rhodesian rail line which goes through Botswana or actually doing so.[51]

It is worth noting that the links the subsystem has with Zambia whether forged by Botswana or broken by Rhodesia represent important barometers for extra-systemic pressure. In addition to the possible military implications of Botswana's new road to Zambia, there are significant infrastructural aspects which should be borne in mind. As Zambia has broken away from Southern Africa, reducing its links and its dependence by reorienting its transaction flows toward East Africa via its existing road net and the forthcoming TanZam railroad, it is able to exert some steady though relatively minor gravitational pull on the remaining black states in the subsystem. In addition to these aspects affecting Botswana, the Zambian situation is of importance for Swaziland and Malawi; Swaziland has already signed a series of trade agreements calling for meat and vegetable exports to Zambia by plane.

While one can speculate about the future course of infrastructural and communications patterns within the subsystem, it seems clear that for the present, their possible changes are hardly momentous. South Africa and Mozambique, as systemic units, will continue to dominate the transportation and communication patterns for the foreseeable future and with regard to the subsystem as a whole, provide the major influences on it.[52] This is in no way to denigrate the symbolic and psychological importance of such initiatives as those of Botswana but physically, and in terms of the holistic subsystem, they are of marginal importance.

Demographic

There are two major demographic aspects which are of importance in assaying the future of the subsystem. The first of these is the international transfer of labor, primarily through the device of contract labor agreements but also in terms of informal, often individual, migration to seek employment. The second is the movement of refugees across international borders within the Southern African subsystem.

The first category, that of labor migration, is important both for the Republic of South Africa and the surrounding territories. It is estimated that there may be up to one million nonindigenous Africans present in South Africa at the present time.[53] The numbers of Africans who come to South Africa just on a contract basis indicates their considerable importance for the economy of their home countries. In 1972 there were over 130,000 from Lesotho, 120,000 from Mozambique, 130,000 from Malawi, 32,000 from Botswana, 10,000 from Swaziland and 6,200 from Rhodesia.[54] A good deal has been written about the importance of these workers in terms of income remitted, reduction in high unemployment rates in the home country and the learned skills with which they return. Although this line of argument has been vigorously challenged,[55] there remains considerable validity in the notion that the labor-exporting countries are highly dependent upon South Africa at the present time.[56] For our purposes, we are interested in the impact, present and future, which these workers have on South Africa. Larry Bowman has speculated that "... the repatriation of foreign labor, or even the cutting back on foreign recruitment, remains one of the most powerful controls that the South African government holds over its smaller and less wealthy neighbors."[57] But what conclusions can be drawn by looking at this aspect from the other direction? For one thing, the migrant workers are of considerable value to the Republic, not just as bargaining chips in the international politics of the region. Because these workers come from other countries and return there following the expiration of their contracts, they are far less likely to become mobilized and politicized than their South African counterparts and highly vulnerable to forced repatriation. While these target workers are less productive and less efficient than permanent workers, they are politically more reliable and far less likely to challenge the status quo. Now it may well be that if and when the bantustans attain their independence, there will be considerable political appeal in using their labor "units" as contract workers but for the present, the migrant workers seem preferable, particularly in the coal and gold-mining industries.

Not that the migrant worker system is not without problems. As in the case of Zambia, which prohibited the Witwatersrand Native Labor Association (WNLA) from recruiting following independence, or more recently when over 13,000 contract workers went out on strike in Namibia during January, 1973 it is possible that these policies can have important feedback consequences for South Africa. If Malawi, Lesotho, Swaziland and Botswana were to act in concert, for example, they could exert considerable leverage back upon South Africa. While under the headin of intergovernmental/diplomatic, it is worth noting that the present demographic configurations represent an important variable in the interaction of the subsystem.

The situation with regard to refugees is less clear. Following the outbreak of violence in South Africa during 1960, numerous refugees fled to the High Commission Territories. Due to the permeable nature of the frontiers, the lack of receptivity on the part of the eventual ruling parties (especially in Lesotho and Swaziland) and the generally isolated position of these refugees, many of them left the subsystem for Zambia and Tanzania. As a result of the more recent fighting in Mozambique and Angola, other refugees fled to both countries, although some from Angola settled in Botswana. While those that eventually settled in Zambia and Tanzania represent something of an ongoing pressure group in those countries' support for the eventual liberation of Southern Africa, by and large, the refugees as a group exercise little or no influence on the subsystem *per se*. Should their numbers increase substantially over the next decade or two, their role could approximate that played by the much larger numbers of Palestinian refugees in their host countries of Egypt, Jordan and Lebanon. That is, depending upon time and place and the strength of the host government, they could influence the amount of pressure and force committed to the alteration of the subsystem. For the foreseeable future, however such a magnified role seems unlikely indeed.

On balance then, while aspects of the present demographic situation seem to be pushing the subsystem toward greater integration, at least economically and in the international transfer of persons, there is little to suggest that the present pattern of intergovernmental interaction, rather than comprehensive, nongovernmental interaction, will change. Moreover, given the nature of the yearly migration patterns, these demographic concerns seem stabilizing rather than destabilizing in character.

Conclusion

Where then are we? Totalling up the various factors moving the subsystem toward greater integration, subtracting those countervailing influences which seem to be acting in a centrifugal fashion, and bearing in mind the types of systemic outcomes, we come to the following conclusion. Although there are some factors which seem to suggest the possibility of a comprehensive system and although there are some nongovernmental actors (such as the transnational companies and their directors) who are pressing for greater integration, on balance one is struck by both the persistent strands of the intergovernmental model and the definite parameters to sustained further integration.

The greater economic integration of the region which seems heralded by the hundreds of millions of dollars to be invested in Angola, Mozambique and Botswana could change this but, as indicated in the philosophical/ideological section, there are some definite and I would argue compelling reasons why the economic factors cannot be assumed to be all powerful. In fact, in terms of the subsystem as a whole, it may well be that except for economic cooperation, the limits of systemic integration are already being approached. If South Africa and Namibia proper are to be genuinely fragmented with individual non-European units attaining _de facto_ as well as _de jure_ independence, there could be some new variables whose impact would be most difficult to structure at this point. These could unleash a powerful ground swell for some type of federation, although this might be confined to non-European units. In all of this, one should keep in mind the assessment of Ernst Haas and Philippe Schmitter:

> Linkages between economic objectives and politics, on the one hand, and political consequences of a disintegrative or integrative nature, on the other, are of a "functional" character; they rest very often on indirection, on unplanned and accidental convergence in outlook and aspiration amoung the actors, on dialectical relations between antagonistic purposes.[58]

Technical, infrastructural and economic integration may well lead to more thinking about political integration and even federation. And just as strong actors in Southern Africa could view "federation" as a method of maintaining the _status quo_ of their elites, so weak actors might perceive that they could better their present situation - demographically, territorially, or economically by some new arrangement. But for the present, there is little evidence to refute the hypothesis that a stable subsystem is not necessarily an increasingly politically integrated subsystem. Moreover, if the individual actor governments in Southern Africa seek to go beyond the present limits of integration, the odds are they will do so rather in the fashion of porcupines making love: very slowly, very carefully and without passion.

Notes

* The author is indebted to the research assistance and thoughtful comments of Ms. Jane Titcomb.

1. For an overview of the literature see Richard Dale, "South Africa and the International Community", World Politics 18(2), January 1966, 297-313, and C.P. Potholm "After Many a Summer: The Possibilities of Political Change in South Africa", World Politics 24(4), July 1972, 613-638.

2. In this regard, Larry Bowman's "The Subordinate State System of Southern Africa", International Studies Quarterly 12(3), 231-261, and reprinted in this volume, turns out to be seminal indeed. See also, C. P. Potholm and Richard Dale (eds) Southern Africa in Perspective: Essays in Regional Politics (New York: The Free Press, 1972).

3. This latter theme is explored more fully in my study "Process and Feedback: The Effects on South Africa of Changes in Contiguous States and Territories" presented at the Conference on Change in Contemporary Southern Africa, Yale University, April 1974.

4. Karl Kaiser, "The Interaction of Regional Subsystems", World Politics 22(10), October 1968, 84-107.

5. Karl Kaiser, "The Interaction of Regional Subsystems", 90.

6. Ibid., 92.

7. Kaiser is thus suggesting a combination of Donald J. Puchala's "international community formation or the linking of peoples", and "international amalgamation or the linking of governments", Donald J. Puchala, "Integration and Disintegration in Franco-German Relations, 1954-1965", International Organization 24, 1970, 184.

8. For a superb analysis of this phenomenon, see Douglas Anglin, "Zambia's Disengagement from Southern Africa: A Transaction analysis", paper prepared for delivery at the Canadian Association of African Studies annual meeting, Ottawa (February 1973), revised version in this volume. See also John Leech, "Zambia Seeks a Route to Fuller Independence", Issue 2(4), Winter 1972, 6-11.

9. J.E. Spence and Elizabeth Thomas, South Africa's Defense: The Problem of Internal Control, Security Studies Paper #8 (Los Angeles: University of California at Los Angeles, 1968), J. E. Spence, "Southern Africa: The Military and Political Framework" in J. E. Spence The Strategic Significance of Southern Africa (London: Royal United Service Institution, 1971) 22-32, and Charles Peterson, "The Military Balance in Southern Africa" in Potholm and Dale (eds) Southern Africa in Perspective, 298-317.

10. As a detailed description of the military situation in Angola falls beyond the purview of the paper, the interested reader should consult the following works: Ronald Chilcote, Portuguese Africa (Englewood Cliffs: Prentice Hall, 1965), John Marcum, The Angolan Revolution (Cambridge: MIT Press, 1969), Douglas Wheeler and Rene Pelissier, Angola (New York: Praeger Publishers, 1971), David Abshire and Michael Samuels (eds) Portuguese Africa (New York: Praeger Publishers, 1969), MPLA Revolution in Angola (London: Merlin Press, 1972), Richard Gibson African Liberation Movements (London: Oxford University Press, 1972), 197-242, Kenneth Grundy Guerrilla Struggle in Africa (New York:

Grossman Publishers, 1971), 91-107, and Don Barnett and Roy Harvey (eds) The Revolution in Angola: MPLA, Life Histories and Documents (New York: Bobbs Merrill, 1972).

11. There have been allegations that South Africa already has an air base in the area: Le Monde (Paris), January 22, 1971. As will be seen in the section dealing with economic/investment factors, the Kunene project could loom large in South African thinking. Unlike the Cabora Bassa project in Mozambique, Kunene would involve a series of smaller, less easily defended sites.

12. For relevant background material see the Chilcote, Wheeler and Abshire books listed above as well as Gibson African Liberation Movements, 265-290, Grundy Guerrilla Struggle in Africa, 91-107, Eduardo Mondlane The Struggle for Mozambique (Baltimore: Penguin Books, 1969), Barbara Cornwall The Bush Rebels (New York: Holt, Rinehart and Winston, 1972) and FRELIMO Mozambique Revolution (Dar es Salaam: FRELIMO, yearly).

13. The San Francisco Chronicle reported on May 15, 1973, that most of the recent fighting was done by FROLIZI and ZANU while Peter Niesewand gave primary credit to ZANU and ZAPU: Peter Niesewand,"What Smith Really Faces", Africa Report 18(2) March-April 1972, 16-20. Winter Lemba gave credit to ZANU: Winter Lemba, "Liberation Rivalry Buried", Africa Report 18(3), May-June 1973, 15.

14. Rhodesian security forces are already stretched thin, with a single white battalion of light infrantry and an additional white-officered battalion of Rhodesian African Rifles along with some black African units already deployed.

15. Portugal has over 140,000 troops in Africa, at least 60,000 of which are in Mozambique, while South Africa has but 10,000 men in a standing army and 80,000 in reserve: The Institute of Strategic Studies The Military Balance: 1972-1973 (London: The International Institute of Strategic Studies, 1972), 23 and 29.

16. It could be argued that South Africa could and would tolerate a partitioned Mazambique with a northern black-run portion and a southern, white-run zone. There are, of course, a great variety of possibilities most of which go beyond the scope of this paper, although the growing importance of the Cabora Bassa dame could substantially narrow the acceptable possibilities.

17. This is not to say that there are not very considerable handicaps which would-be revolutionaries in Southern Africa must overcome: John Marcum, "The Exile Condition and Revolutionary Effectiveness", in Potholm and Dale (eds) Southern Africa in Perspective, 262-275, C. P. Potholm, "The International Transfer of Insurgency Techniques; SubSaharan Pathologies", Plural Societies Autumn 1972, 3-21, and Sheridan Johns, "The Obstacles to Revolutionary Guerrilla Struggle: A Southern African Case", Journal of Modern African Studies 11(2), June 1973, 267-303. In addition, there is a most poignant portrait of the exile dilemma in Ezekiel Mphahlele The Wanderers (New York: MacMillan Company, 1971).

18. For a celebrated instance of South African penetration into Lesotho see Jeffrey Butler "South Africa and the High Commission Territories: The Ganyile Case, 1961", in Gwendolen M. Carter (ed) Politics in Africa: Seven Cases (New York: Harcourt, Brace and World, 1966) 245-283. 1973 saw a similar case when the South African police crossed into Lesotho and departed with one Fanele Mbale. In the recent history of Swaziland, there have been a variety of similar incidents when refugees from the Republic have either been abducted or have disappeared under mysterious circumstances: see C. P. Potholm Swaziland: The Dynamics of Political Modernization (Berkeley: University of California Press, 1972), 144-145.

19. Many of the pitfalls to closer military cooperation are not exclusively endemic to the area but lie in the very character of the process. Michael Brenner "Strategic Interdependence and the Politics of Inertia: Paradoxes of European Defense Cooperation", World Politics 23(4), July 1971, 635-644.

20. Amry Vandenbosch South African and World: The Foreign Policy of Apartheid (Lexington: University Press of Kentucky, 1970), Larry Bowman South Africa's Outward Strategy: A Foreign Policy Dilemma for the United States. Papers in International Stuties, Africa Series #13 (Athens: Ohio University Center for International Studies, 1971) and Aristide Zolberg, "Military Decade in Africa", World Politics 25(2) January 1973, 309-331. Interestingly enough, Zolberg indicates that the benign neglect of the great powers promoted interest in a "dialogue" with South Africa.

21. Africa Confidential 13(19), September 22, 1972, 1-2.

22. Quoted in David Baldwin "The Power of Positive Sanctions", World Politics 24(1) October 1972, 35.

23. Baldwin is most persuasive that punishments tend toward instability and rewards toward stability.

24. And, when they have attempted punishments and the threat of punishments against Zambia and Tanzania, they too have been unsuccessful in promoting systemic stability.

25. State of South Africa Economic, Financial and Statistical Yearbook for the Republic of South Africa (Johannesburg: De Gama Publishers, 1973), 198-199.

26. Standard Bank Review, May 1973, 39. It should be pointed out, however, that Malawian trade with the United Kingdom and Japan also showed major advances during this period.

27. Times of Swaziland 70(47), November 24, 1972, 1.

28. C. P. Potholm "Swaziland", in Potholm and Dale (eds) Southern Africa in Perspective, 141-153.

29. David Baldwin "Foreign Aid, Intervention and Influence", World Politics 21(3), April 1969, 429.

30. Johannesburg Star, 24 March 1973. There is additional evidence that the King had been planning his moves for quite some time. Late in January he told a gathering of the Emabutfo that one of the duties of the young men was to deal with any trouble which might threaten the peace of the nation. He also indicated that the men would be called upon the near future: Times of Swaziland 71(5), February 2, 1973, 1.

31. King Sobhuza II Proclamation to All My Subjects - Citizens of Swaziland (Lobamba: mimeographed, 1973), 1.

32. J. E. Spence Lesotho: The Politics of Dependence (London: Oxford University Press, 1968), B. M. Khaketla Lesotho 1970: An African Coup Under the Microscope (Berkeley: University of California Press, 1972), Richard F. Weisfelder "Lesotho" in Potholm and Dale (eds) Southern Africa in Perspective, 125-140, "Power Struggle in Lesotho" African Report 12(1), January 1967, 5-13, and The Basotho Monarchy: A Spent Force of A Dynamic Political Factor? Papers in International Studies, Africa Series, #16 (Athens: Ohio University Center for International Studies, 1972).

33. See, for example, the highly intriguing portrait of Portuguese-African society at war found in A. J. Venter Portugal's War in Guine-Bissau (Pasadena: Munger Africana Library Notes, 1973).

34. Although it should be pointed out that Heribert Adam has argued that racial consciousness among non-whites may ultimately prove counterproductive to the Republic's plan for the full implementation of apartheid and the maintenance of white supremacy. Heribert Adam Modernizing Racial Domination (Berkeley: University of California Press, 1971).

35. Mohamed El-Khawas, "Mozambique and the United Nations", Issue 2(4), Winter 1972, 30-35.

36. Rand Daily Mail, 6 March 1973.

37. Rita Cruise O'Brien has written a provocative book about the continued high status of Europeans in African-ruled Senegal justaposed with the settlers' views concerning the precariousness of their long-term position: Rita Cruise O'Brien White Society in Black States: The French of Senegal (Evanston: Northwestern University Press, 1972).

38. Depending upon how far Lisbon is prepared to go with the autonomy of these "states", their evolution could offer some intriguing possibilities. For example, what if one or more of the bantustans wanted to be affiliated with the state of Mozambique? Both Kaiser Matanzima and Gatsa Buthelezi have already indicated an interest in linking up various bantustans into a federation with later links to one or more of the former High Commission Territories.

39. Sir Seretse Khama Botswana: A Developing Democracy in Southern Africa (Uppsala: Scandinavian Institute of African Studies, 1970), Richard Dale Botswana and its Southern Neighbor: The Patterns of Linkage and the Options in Statecraft. Papers in International Studies, Africa Series, #6 (Athens: Ohio University Center for International Studies, 1970) and The Racial Component of Botswana's Foreign Policy, Studies in Race and Nations 2(4), 1970-71, 1-29, and Edwin S. Munger Bechuanaland: Pan-African Outpost or Bantu Homeland (London: Oxford University Press, 1965), 86.

40. Kaiser "The Interaction of Regional Subsystem", 93.

41. Leo Marquard A Federation of Southern Africa (London: Oxford University Press, 1971).

42. Parenthetically, one important aspect of the psychological situation in South Africa and the problems of raising forces to alter the status quo by military means has to do with the number of military defeats suffered by the Africans over the centuries. An interesting question thus arises. Would the defeatism which currently saps the strength of the nationalist forces be overcome by African victories in Guine-Bissau or northern Mozambique?

43. We have not discussed the economic underpinnings of the present subsystem but the transformation from a capitalist to a socialist economy might produce some important structural changes and closer integration although as the experience of eastern Europe indicates, it is by no means clear that this would lead ipso facto to a comprehensive-type system.

44. Peter Robson "Economic Integration in Southern Africa", Journal of Modern African Studies 5(4), 1967, 469-490, P. Smit and E. J. van der Merwe "Economic Cooperation in Southern Africa", Journal of Geography and Eschel M. Rhoodie

"Southern Africa: Towards a New Commonwealth" in Potholm and Dale (eds) Southern Africa in Perspective, 276-297.

45. Sheridan Johns "Botswana's Strategy for Development: An Assessment of Dependence in the Southern African Context", Journal of Commonwealth Political Studies 11(3), November 1973, 214-230.

46. Standard Bank Review, December 1971, 29.

47. Samuel P. Huntington "Transnational Organizations in World Politics", World Politics 25(3), April 1973, 333-368.

48. Although Edward Morse has indicated in his "Crisis Diplomacy, Interdependence and the Politics of International Economic Relations", World Politics 24, Supplement, 1970, just how rudimental is our understanding of the interaction between the economic and political aspects of statecraft.

49. Gunnar Myrdal Economic Theory and Under-Developed Regions (New York: Harper and Row, 1957), 23-39.

50. Times of Swaziland 71(3), January 19, 1973, 1.

51. This helps to explain Rhodesian interest in linking up directly with South Africa via the Beit bridge route. Although expensive, this extension would reduce Rhodesian dependence on Botswana and a potentially hostile government. Ironically enough during 1971-1972, the Batswana found themselves lobbying privately to get the United States to sell new rolling stock to Rhodesia in spite of existing sanctions since Botswana was so dependent on the Rhodesian railroad for its export trade with South Africa.

52. For its part, South Africa is somewhat dependent upon Malawi, at least for refueling and landing rights which, together with South African privileges at Sal Island in the Cape Verde Islands enable South Africa to fly to Europe despite the opposition of other African states.

53. The African Institure of Pretoria puts the figure at more than 800,000 while those strictly on a contract basis for 1972 numbered 441,148: South African Digest 22 June 1973, 3.

54. Ibid.

55. Robert Molteno African Labor and South Africa (London: Africa Bureau, 1971).

56. In the case of Lesotho, for example, current figures indicate that there are five or six times as may jobs available in the Republic as in Lesotho itself. Lesotho is obviously the extreme case, but Botswana and Mozambique are also considerably dependent.

57. Bowman, "Subordinate State System of Southern Africa", 242.

58. Ernst Haas and Philippe Schmitter "Economic and Differential Patterns of Political Integration: Projections About Unity in Latin America", International Organization 18, Autumn 1964, 707.

2. Continuities and Discontinuities in the Region

Chapter Six

CULTURE, RACE AND HISTORY: A QUESTION WITHOUT AN ANSWER

Arthur Keppel-Jones

In his standard work on *Race Attitudes in South Africa* Professor I. D. MacCrone has ascribed the origin and development of the attitudes of white to black to the need of a community to preserve its identity. The white colonists, being a societ distinct from the indigenous society around them, had to emphasize the differences between the two in order to save their own group from being swallowed up. The dif ference that was emphasized was, in the beginning, religion. In the end it was ra

Race is the difference that is emphasized now. As the word is generally used in a broad and loose sense, it has obscured instead of illumining the nature of the antipathy which the members of one group may feel for those of another. If the word race is used in a strict sense it releases another element in the antipathy - culture - for separate consideration.

Racial characteristics are genetic and ineradicable, like the leopard's spots and the Ethiopian's skin. Culture is of the mind and in some circumstances can be controlled. Group hostility can be based on either, but the reactions in the two cases are different. Where the differences are cultural, the more powerful group usually tries to assimilate the other - in language, customs, values, even in religion. Where the differences are racial the dominant group tries at all costs to prevent assimilation.

The problems arising in the first case are, in principle, soluble. Our civilizat has found ways of dealing with cultural differences. They may be eliminated, as the American melting-pot; or they may be preserved within a single state by such devices as federalism, official bilingualism, religious toleration or constitutio guarantees. No such device makes it possible to preserve racial differences with a single state. If two races are to be kept genetically separate, they must be mutually independent, and separated by a Chinese Wall or an Iron Curtain. The or alternative is the oppression of one by the other, which is not a solution.

The differences between white and black in South Africa are of course both racial and cultural; but which of these is primary? Did white antipathy begin as a dislike of, and defence against, values, habits, and a way of life, and then tur by association into a dislike of shapes and pigments? The question does not ref basically to historical time. We know that in Van Riebeeck's colony the only recognized difference was that of religion. The change from a cultural to a racial emphasis could occur in the experience of every generation and of every individual. It could be a change in the opposite direction; or the two aspects could be unrelated.

The practical importance of the question is obvious. If the root of the antipathy is some biological gut reaction, it is incurable, and the problem is insoluble. If the root is cultural, then as the groups are drawn closer together in cultural standards their obsession with race may fade away.

Every generation has experienced the double relationship of race and culture; but every generation has done so in a different set of contexts from its predecessors. A series of studies in which the group attitudes of a generation are related to their contexts would throw some light on this important question. The present paper attempts to do this for one short period before and after the beginning of this century.

We happen to possess for that period a source of information on this question which heavily outweighs all other such sources for many decades, namely the three volumes of evidence given to the Lagden Commission, or Intercolonial Native Affairs Commission of 1903-5. The witnesses included officials, missionaries and other clergy, tribal chiefs and headmen, white farmers, progressive African farmers, politicians, journalists, lawyers, merchants, teachers, indeed an excellent cross-section of the public, though not numerically in proportion to the groups represented. Their views on many aspects of race relations were solicited, often one may say dragged out of them, by the Commissioners.

This valuable collection, eked out by newspaper reports and editorials and some other sources, is examined here to find an answer to our basic question. Can we discover from the statements of the witnesses, or from the overtones, or by readin between the lines, how far the supposedly racist antipathies of the whites were really that, and how far they were rooted in cultural differences?

Black and white were two distinct social groups; there had been absolutely no fusion of the two. That being so, the members of each were naturally conscious of a conflict of interests between their group and the other. The whites were afraid to give the blacks the vote because "they are so numerous they may out-vote us". Another witness would concede political rights "in the very far distance ... after an enormous preponderance of the European population over the Native".[1]

The great majority of witnesses advocated an emphasis on practical or industrial training in African education. Some argued that Africans were better suited to practical than to academic education, but the usual reason given was that the training should be geared to the job market. Industrial training for Africans, however, would enable them to compete with European artisans. That was why the Acting Chief Justice of Natal objected to it in a colony with responsible government: "the voice of the [white] artisan has to be heard".[2] A missionary thought that industrial education for Africans was desirable only "if this is to be a black man's country". If it was to be a white man's country, he would hesitate to give such education, "otherwise you will displace the white man and make it impossible for the white mechanic to live".[3] Most witnesses had no fear of this. Among the reasons for their complacency were: that it would be impossible to train enough Africans to have this effect; that the demand for their labour would increase at least as fast as the supply; and "if we are wise, we shall create amongst them the demand for the productive capacity of a very much larger area of white industry than they themselves are ever likely to take by supplanting white workers". A Kingwilliamstown merchant did not object to the supplanting of white artisans by black - he wanted cheaper labour.[4]

The danger which worried most of the farmers - and some of the Commissioners - in this regard was not the ousting of white mechanics, but the further diminution of the supply of farm labourers. Though some advanced the old weatherbeaten argument that the educated African was spoilt and useless, too proud to work, fit only to strut about in idleness, the vast majority of witnesses of all types agreed that this generalization applied only to the semi-educated. Even farmers admitted that workers properly grounded, even in no more than the three R's, were better motivated and generally more useful, though not usually suited to mere rough labour. Education, industrial or other, must not be given so lavishly as to dry up the supply of that.

In all of these cases the arguments relate to the economic interests of a class, and the fact that the class was also a race is coincidental. The upper classes of Europe had for centuries shown a similar concern to be assured of the services of the lower orders, which were of the same race as themselves. Another and more generalized example of the bearing of economic interest on South African policy was the attitude of the witnesses to African education of all kinds. Most advocated it, and one of the reasons adduced was that education would foster new wants among them, and so promote trade and industry.

The fostering of new wants would have an even more fundamental effect: it would promote cultural assimilation. There were both black and white witnesses who explained in detail, and with strong approval, how Africans were adopting European standards in housing, furniture, clothing and food - including an egg for breakfast and a cup of tea at eleven o'clock. It was John X. Merriman (perhaps a little biased) who spoke with pride of an African who bought a farm for £3500, and of another who both bought land and invested in a coal mine - all the result of the Cape's enlightened policy.[5]

Such opinions and such development were less common outside the Cape Colony; but denunciations of Africans were almost always expressed in cultural terms. "They are savages; they are uneducated", said J. W. Shepstone, a man of somewhat blemished reputation in the history of race relations in Natal.[6] R. J. Dick of Kingwilliamstown objected to the intonjani and abakweta dances and to the large beer-drinking assemblies. He was disappointed that missionary influence had not been more effective. He would have expected "larger results, and that you would not have had still those barbarous masses of heathen Natives practising their customs to the full".[7] A Natal solicitor drew the conclusion: "When a Native can come up to what we are in education and civilisation, I do not mind the colour, but until he does that, I object to his being placed on a level with us".[8]

If these opinions were sincere, the corollary would be a demand to educate Africans as far and as fast as possible. Few witnesses were quite as daring as that, but the great majority favoured both the basic primary schooling already offered by the missions and practical training in trades, all subsidized by the state. Advanced education should be available to those Africans who wanted it, but at their own expense. "I am firmly of the opinion," said a Kingwilliamstown merchant, "that a great deal more can be done for them in the way of educating and civilising them. It is absolutely necessary, unless they are to remain uncivilised you cannot have them civilised without education."[9] Sir Liege Hulett, the sugar magnate, spoke appreciatively of schools and missionaries, adding "that the natural result of that is the elevation of character, or the increase of opportunity; and it must raise and elevate the people as a whole, and naturally their aspiration towards assimilating themselves more to European surroundings is an inevitable result of that policy."[10] Even a bloated landowner like Donald Strachan of Griqualand East was enthusiastic about the effects of education and Christianity.[11]

The two went together, because virtually all African schools were mission schools. The Methodist D. B. Davies of the Glen Grey district was not unrepresentative, only more specific, when he gave a catalogue of the results of their combined influence. It included the diminution or disappearance of "smelling out" and other superstitions, of tribal animosities, of the depredations of one man on the stock of another. There was "peace between man and man." Other changes were the increasing observance of the sabbath; a growing sense of decency represented by divisions in the huts for the separation of the sexes and of parents and children; improvement in homes and in habits and cleanliness; an improvement in the status of women; a desire for education for the children; a growing spirit of generosity; kindness to animals.[12]

In the opinion of many, these views were too optimistic. A few offered hostile criticism: Kaffirs were impossible to teach, or often reverted to savagery when they had left school. Most of the criticism was made more in sorrow than in anger. One missionary thought that the work of the schools was like "writing on the sand," chiefly because it was conducted in English.[13] Harriette Colenso said that "we have done as much harm as good."[14] Tengo Jabavu was disappointed. "The great mass of the Natives," he thought, "have not made such progress as one would like to see them do - they are making very slow progress indeed."[15] The comment that "as it took the white man hundreds of years to attain the present point of civilisation, so the natives must be prepared to take it step by step, and that it is impossible to bring out a perfect type at once" was made, not by a white farmer, but by a black journalist from the Gold Coast.[16]

In all the discussion of education, barbarism, Western values and civilised standards, the centre of interest was invariably "the dignity of labour." The schools, it was said, must teach, above all, the dignity of labour. Does the educated African despise work? The trouble with the Kaffir is that after a short spell of work he goes back to the kraal and lives in idleness on the product of his wives' industry. On this theme the changes were rung at length.

One might guess that these were the views of farmers who believed that the primary purpose of government was to provide them with cheap, plentiful and reliable labour. Many such farmers did express their views - and those were their views. But concern with the dignity of labour affected a much wider constituency. It perfectly illustrates a conflict between two cultures with different values, and need not have involved the element of race at all. People belonging to an industrial society with a Puritan background found idleness infuriating, and the feeling was shared by Africans who had been converted to those values. It is hardly an exaggeration to say that every one of the witnesses before the Commission was obssessed by this question. The farmers who objected to idleness because they happened to be short of labour were merely exploiting the universal belief in the "work ethic".

The Rev. P. K. Kawa, an African priest, thought that while the Christians were improving the heathens were not. What, he was asked, would you do to improve the heathen? "Teach him to work ...he spends most of his time in doing nothing."[17] The Gold Coast journalist gave exactly the same answer.[18] The Rev. Charles Pamla, a Methodist missionary of Fingo origin, thought that "the best thing to make a Native work is to give him a good education, to enlighten him."[19] Where education was favoured because it would increase the African's wants, it was always borne in mind that an increase in wants would force him to work in order to satisfy them. To some extent this argument was a rationalization of the real motive, which was expressed by an Anglican missionary, W. A. Goodwin: "I think, myself, that a man is to a certain extent educated when he has learned to love work for work's sake, and not only because he must do it. I do not think a Native, until he becomes Christianised, and has come into contact with hard-working white men, realises at all that work is of any pleasure for its own sake."[20] He might have noted that much progress had been made in that direction. An old headman from Middledrift assured the Commission that whereas the women formerly did the work, "the custom has been changed, and now the men must also work; even the 'red' Kaffirs despise a man who does not work."[21]

It was easy to preach the congenial doctrine of the dignity of labour; only a few witnesses noticed that the whites were losing this virtue almost as fast as the blacks were acquiring it. It was not so easy to devise an electoral system that honestly took account of the rise of the Africans (however slowly) in the scale of civilization.

The question of the franchise, destined to a greater notoriety during the century then opening, was not in itself a racial question. The history of Great Britain in the century just closed had shown that. One of our witnesses, who agreed that the black vote could be a danger, pointed to the Labour Party as an analogous danger. But the question could not be dodged. It was generally agreed that the whites, as the bearers of a superior civilization, had a duty to share it with the blacks, and to raise them to the level that the whites had already reached.[22] When a black man reached it, he would be entitled to exactly the same rights as the white. Even, a Natal merchant and politician was asked, the vote? Certainly, he replied, "if he had attained that position." Even voting alongside a white man on the same roll? "If he had attained that position, I should not have the slightest objection." This seems a very liberal position for a Natal politician, but it is explained by his postscript: "the time will come when they can claim that right; certainly not now."[23] This was the usual alibi. "It is such a long way off," said another advocate of the principle.[24] A mine manager thought that "it must come after my time; I do not think it will come in my time."[25] Even a Free State farmer like G. H. Turvey, who thought that giving the vote to an

African was like letting a child play with fire, was not speaking in absolute terms: "I do not think that the time has come. I do not say that it will not come."[26]

White South Africans were accustomed to thinking in ways, and subscribing to values, which they or their ancestors had brought from Europe; in the case of most of these witnesses, from Britain. British society was highly stratified. The privileges of the upper classes were jealously defended. The lower orders were expected to touch their caps and keep to their proper stations. But there was also social mobility. The son of a coal-factor could become the Earl of Eldon and Lord Chancellor of England. The most crusted Tory never suggested that the vote should be denied to anyone who acquired the qualifications. This background helps to explain why witness after witness before the Commission insisted on one hand that the supply of cheap and reliable labour must be maintained, respect and obedience inculcated, seditious thoughts stamped out, and no half-educated "blanket Kaffirs" allowed to vote; and on the other that every African should be allowed, encouraged and helped to rise as high in the cultural and economic scale as his talents would permit.

Yet all the witnesses knew that the cases were not analogous. This put them in a difficulty; if British precedents did not apply, they were at a loss to know where to turn. The confusion and floundering of those who ventured into the field of social and political philosophy throw a vivid light on the evolution of white South African thinking.

Sir Henry Elliott was living in retirement in Natal, but had been Chief Magistrate of the Transkei. The Commissioners were not altogether pleased with his evidence, because when asked whether he saw a danger "in the extension of the franchise to the probably increasing number of educated Natives," he replied "I do not; but I see great danger in withholding it." For a long time they pressed, almost bullied him, in the hope of getting him to admit the danger. After discussing other subjects they came back to this one. Did he not think it dangerous that the black voters held the balance of power between the parties in a number of Cape constituencies? No, he said, "I think it matters little so long as they can vote with Europeans."

What could you do with such an obstinate fellow? The inquisitors pressed him again. He had to agree that the Cape system was not calculated to secure European predominance, and that this might be threatened in about fifty years' time. Did he not think that for the sake of future generations this catastrophe should be prevented? "With that," said Sir Henry, "I entirely concur. I have never approved of the levelling policy ...I do not think that the Native voter should be brought into conflict with the white voter. To that I am strongly opposed; and I have seen some degrading spectacles on the part of men who stand high in the country. The depths of which they would descend to secure two or three black votes is [sic] disgraceful."[27]

Or listen to Henrique Shepstone. When asked whether an African with industrial training would not take the bread out of white artisans' mouths, he replied, "Why should he not have it? He is a fellow subject, and why should he not be in the same position as an ordinary white man? Why should you keep him under?" A few minutes later the same witness, when asked about the franchise, said flatly "I would not give the franchise to them." Not on any conditions.[28]

The Mayor of Kokstad thought that "if we are to grant the franchise to Natives ...they should be placed on exactly the same level as Europeans in respect of other conditions of life," and added that "they must inevitably fit themselves for it, and they are fitting themselves for the exercise of the franchise continuously." Pressed further, he said that African representation should be either by government nominees or by members elected on a separate roll.[29]

The Commissioners would not leave it at that. As the Mayor persisted in his advocacy of equal opportunities, equal rights balanced by equal responsibilities, he was asked what the position of the white man would eventually be, given the numerical superiority of the blacks. "The white man," he replied, "will still be the superior." How so? His answer is worth quoting in full: "By virtue of his mental superiority and higher intellect, and the fact that he is the white man in the country. The Native is only a hewer of wood and drawer of water. He is a subordinate people, and why he should be placed in this position of equality I cannot quite understand. You will say at once that I advocate equality. I say that I do not; but I do say that if they want equality they must have it. If the Native is capable of attaining to this position of equality then he must also undertake the responsibilities as well as the advantages."[30] The horns of the dilemma were sharp.

Why were they all caught on them? The reason, from which they carefully steered clear in their answers, was that they were trying to justify in class and cultural terms an exclusiveness which, in the recesses of their minds, they knew and intended to be racial. No other explanation fits the case. If the British precedent applied there would be no problem: the new voter would be absorbed into the class of the old voters and would become indistinguishable from them. The barriers separated classes, but could be crossed by individuals. It was because they did not intend this to happen that these witnesses saw the black voters as a separate community, threatening to out-vote the white.

One of the reasons why many saw no danger to white artisans in the competition of black was their belief that the African was congenitally incapable of rising to the intellectual level of the European, so that the latter had nothing to fear.[31] A reason for opposing that kind of training was that white artisans would not work alongside black. Mr. Justice Boshoff, of the Natal Native High Court, was a firm advocate of rights, including the franchise, for all who could qualify. An African with an LL.B. should, he thought, be allowed to practise at the bar. Asked whether that would not imply social equality, Boshoff replied, "I am afraid we would have to guard against that ...The Native does not seem to recognise the fact that the Great Designer intended them to be an absolutely distinct section of the community for all of their existence."[32]

An obstacle to federation with the Cape Colony, even if that Colony's franchise were not extended to the others, was that in the federal Parliament you might "have a coloured man sitting alongside of you." One witness was shocked that white and black convicts were imprisoned together, and even marched through the streets in gangs together. Worst of all, white criminals were sometimes under the charge of black policemen, thus lessening the respect which the black ought to have for the white. A shocking thing could be seen in Pietermaritzburg: "The White boys play with the Natives in the streets; you can see them playing every day in the streets here, football, cricket and marbles." Scott, the solicitor, could see no objection to the advancement of a talented African to any position he was able to reach, but he drew certain lines: "I would not dine with him, I would not drink with him, and I would not associate with him, but I would have no objection to walking on the pavement with him."[33]

It was the insistence on the social colour bar that made all the other problems seem insoluble; but how is this insistence to be interpreted?

The overtones of the witnesses' replies show convincingly that they did not regard inter-racial social intercourse as a danger that had to be fought with all their might. Rather it was a fantasy that to many or most was not even conceivable. The turn of the century, however, was a time of transition, and not only in terms of the calendar. Many of the witnesses who described the advance of Africans in civilization dated this advance to "the last twenty years" or thereabouts. Thus it was about the turn of the century that the cultural advance began to have social implications on a noticeable scale. Evidently the inconceivable could happen. People to whom this possibility had never occurred were forced to think about it. We heard some of them thinking on their feet before the Commissioners.

Some thinking had been provoked by a bizarre incident in 1897, when the British Empire, at its apogee, celebrate the Queen's Diamond Jubilee. On June 21 of that year about seven thousand schoolchildren assembled on the grounds of Government House, Cape Town. Milner made a speech. Mrs. Hanbury Williams, wife of the Military Secretary, acted as hostess for the bachelor Governor. Two little girls stepped up to present bouquets to her, one on behalf of the white and the other on behalf of the Coloured children. Mrs. Williams graciously received the bouquets and kissed each of the little girls.

According to various sources, including Milner himself, the kissing of the Coloured girl by Mrs. Williams released a flood of denunciations from outraged white citizens. The columnist of the Cape Argus described their reaction, which he treated with contempt, as one of "pious horror". For his comments he was then attacked in what he called "the language of the gutter."[34]

In 1901 John Tengo Jabavu, the editor of Imvo Yabantsundu, applied to Dale College, Kingwilliamstown, to admit his son (the future Professor). The Board of Management rejected the application on the ground that a precedent would be set. The guarded language of the Board was elaborated by the newspapers, most of which expressed with restraint the opinions that their readers would have voiced in grosser language. If Africans were admitted to Dale College, the white parents would by degrees withdraw their sons, so that "the status of the school would rapidly degenerate from that of a first-class school to that of a mission school." The words of W. B. Shaw, who said in a sermon that "the recent conduct of the trustees of Dale College ...is directly opposed to the Gospel of Paul and the professed doctrine of the Catholicity of the Christian religion" fell on very stony ground.[35]

Both these incidents were breaks with tradition which suddenly revealed that social segregation was not an immutable system. The immediate defensive reaction of the more responsible whites was to clutch at the nearest straw, which was the interest of the Coloured races themselves. "A moment's thought," said the Cape Argus about the Dale College affair, "will show that for the sake of the coloured races themselves, a mixture would be undesirable in the highest degree, if not actually repugnant." Another paper thought Jabavu ill-advised to make the application; still another could not "understand why Mr. Jabavu should wish to send his son to a European school."[36]

The Argus columnist who defended Mrs. Williams for kissing the Coloured girl thought that the compliment would be appreciated by that community, but - he could "only hope that they will have the sense and good taste not to pressure upon it." Similarly a witness told the Lagden Commission that though the blacks had the right, and in some places the power, to elect one of their own number to Parliament, they were unlikely to do so. "as their common sense and their political instinct would dictate otherwise." In their clutching the whites were helped by the Coloured people themselves. One of their leaders, in a speech in 1909, assured them that "the coloured people had times without number stated in the most explicit and emphatic manner that they had no desire for social equality; indeed, would infinitely prefer that there should be none."[37]

This straw would not keep anyone afloat for long. Though the Uitenhage Times left the future open in the customary way ("our social system does not at present admit of innovations like that which Mr. Jabavu's request involved"), the loop-hole seemed to be closed again by the East London Daily Dispatch, which found it "hard to think that the time will ever be ripe."[38] Was the obstacle something immutable like the leopard's spots, or mutable like attitudes to labour, clothing or eleven o'clock tea? Would ever the twain meet?

What we are trying to discover is the real reason for the objections to social intercourse between black and white. Why would white parents withdraw their boys from Dale College if black boys were admitted? An answer of sorts can be deduced from remarks made to the Lagden Commission by F.R. Moor, the future Premier of Natal who was to be one of the most unbending white supremacists at the National Convention. His ingenious and plausible solution to the dilemma on which they were all impaled was that "civilization" was not a quality to be found in an individual. Because it was essentially characteristic of social relationships, it was a condition that could be found only in "the whole of a people." Therefore an individual could not be raised from his subordinate status "until the whole of his fellows are equally civilised." The process would take time, because "the present effects of religion and education are not very deep; the whole thing is mere veneer."[39] This was a neat way of shifting the burden on to "the broad shoulders of a later generation," but the important point in the present context is that even Moor put the emphasis on culture and allowed for the theoretical possibility of racial equality in the remote future. His theory also fits the facts of social segregation as they were at the time he was speaking.

The little boy whom Dale College rejected grew up to be a professor and to have a daughter who married an Englishman of eminent family, which would almost certainly not have happened if her father had been educated in Kingwilliamstown instead of at Colwyn Bay. Yet this was the very kind of disaster which above all the College authorities and the white parents were anxious to prevent.

English-speaking colonists were reluctant to put this fear into words; Afrikaners were less inhibited. In Natal both Schwikkard the farmer and Rudolph the magistrate thought that sexual relations between black and white, whether marital or otherwise, should be prohibited.[40] In the Cape Colony, with its infinite variety of colours, such prohibition was out of the question, but missionaries and others deplored the extra-marital relations though not inter-racial marriage.

Generalizations were made to the Commission about "white men consorting with Kaffir women," but for specific information about this we have to look elsewhere. At first sight this form of immorality would seem to prove that whites could have felt no antipathy to the black race as such. In the long run it probably does prove just that, but in its immediate context it does not. On the mining and other frontiers, where there were few white women, the black concubine or harem was a regular appurtenance of the white frontiersman. Melina Rorke asserts this of Kimberley, and there is overwhelming evidence of it in Matabeleland. White opinion tolerated it, but was almost pathologically hostile to the opposite offence, where the man was black and the woman was white. There were many reasons for this: the superior role of the male in the relationship; the Victorian idealization of the woman; the fact that the woman was tied to the offspring, who would be incorporated in her own social group. (In Natal an illegitimate child belonged by law as well as custom to the mother's racial group).[41] Thus it was one thing to tolerate the wild oats of a young man, who could go his way and put the incident behind him; another to accept a coloured child into a white community.

It was essentially for this reason that, according to Melina Rorke "when a white man so far forgot himself as to marry a Kaffir girl the public rose in its wrath and blotted him out of the social picture."[42] The public would have found it hard to give a coherent explanation of why it did this, and we are left with an unanswered question. Was it a concern with genetics or with culture? Did it reflect Moor's idea that all must be civilized first?

At least we can say that in Matabeleland absolutely, and in Kimberley with very rare exceptions, white men and black women were then separated by a cultural gulf which would have made marriage between them an almost empty relationship, and which must have reduced extra-marital relations to a very low moral level. In Matabeleland the girls, who were generally shameless in flaunting their attractions before white male visitors, tried to make themselves irresistible by wearing little bags of scent round their necks. Having no access to the perfumes of Araby they used a local product, which travellers described as smelling like a mixture of human excrement and rotten flesh.[43] The device was not only counter-productive, but left the intended objects of seduction in what may be called a state of culture-shock. Social separation at this stage can be explained without recourse to racial theories.

In 1909, when all South Africa was excited by the Draft Act produced by the National Convention and published on February 9, many citizens were forced to think more clearly about their social philosophy. In later years the centre of interest in the South Africa Act would be the Cape franchise and its entrenchment. Though this came in for a good deal of discussion in 1909, it was not the chief focus of debate or of anger in Cape Town. That focus was the clause which limited membership of the Union Parliament to persons of European descent. Although no Coloured or black person was ever elected to the old Cape Parliament there was no law to prevent it. This clause in the Act was the first legal imposition of a racial distinction affecting Coloured people or, except for the special case of the liquor laws, Africans in the Cape. The reaction to it was vehement.

The protests of the Coloured people were supported by white crowds at meetings and by many leading whites in and out of Parliament, from Schreiner and Sauer downwards. Was this hypocrisy? Had they not managed to achieve a racially exclusive system in the past without putting it into words? It did not appear as hypocrisy to the people affected. Dr. Abdurrahman, speaking for the Coloured people, said that he had read many constitutions, but "had never read one so unjust and so wicked as this" - the main ground of his attack being the clause about European descent. His attitude to the practical, but not legal, exclusion of the past was quite different. The Coloured people, he said, "were living at present under conditions which gave freedom and privilege to all men, despite colour, race and creed. They were now asked to wipe all that out and accept the new."[44]

Among Abdurrahman's white supporters on the City Hall platform when that speech was made was Dr. Jane Waterston, who five and a half years earlier had given evidence to the Lagden Commission. At that time she had said that "you cannot allow the white to be overbalanced by the coloured ...I do see the danger. I hav seen it for some time. Everybody in South Africa must see the danger."[45] In 190 she stood up to be counted among the defenders of the Cape franchise and of a non racial Parliament. She had been forced to think; so had many others.

A week earlier, at the graduation ceremony of the University, the High Commissioner Lord Selborne had received an honorary degree and made a speech, which the Cape Argus called "a fearless statement of views not entirely palatable to the white man." His main theme was that the African was advancing in civilization whether his white neighbours liked it or not, and whether they helped him or not. If the whites did not positively assist and guide this process, they "would forfeit the right to be surprised at the appearance of a foolish and seditious native press, or at the spirit of what is called 'Ethiopianism'." He had, however, no fear for the future of the whites, who had advantages that they would never lose, "except by being mollycoddled out of existence by artificial protection against the competition of the black man," or by "surrendering to the black man the larger portion of the field of honourable labour."

Having been living in the Transvaal, Selborne attacked such evils as the pass laws and what he called "pin-pricks," known to a later generation as petty apartheid. Perhaps it is encouraging to note that criticisms which would seem commonplace to-day, and would hardly be questioned in the English press or universities of South Africa, were then received as a bombshell. The Cape Argus rushed to the defence of the Whites and their system. It defended the pass laws on the ground that "cattle thieving has been bred into the Kaffir," and the by-laws excluding Africans from sidewalks in some towns by citing the case of two white girls in Kingswilliamstown who were rudely pushed off the pavement by some Africans. This was because in tribal custom women had to give way to men. And so forth. The arguments were all derived from cultural traits and differences.[46]

Those were the arguments, but where were the explicit doctrines? There were very few whites in that decade who could conceive of any kind of fusion of the races, within a measurable period of time, into a single society. Very few? Of the witnesses at the Lagden Commission possibly only one, Harriette Colenso. Her statement would have sounded strange to the Commissioners:

> I think that the Natives and we are parts of one community out here. I think we mislead ourselves when we talk about the Native question. It is an odd way of putting it when you come to think of it, because they were here first. It is rather a question of how Europeans are best to live in this country, and we have not only to fit them to our ways, but to accommodate ourselves to a certain extent to their ways and to their country.[47]

This was a rare opinion indeed.

If there were few who thought in terms of "one community," there were not many more who frankly professed racial theories. Most of those were in the ex-republics, and more might have been heard of this point of view if more Boer witnesses had appeared before the Commission. As it was, they were ably represented by R. K. Loveday, who in the days of the South African Republic had been the only English-speaking member of the Volksraad. If you give a black man the vote, Loveday thought, "you will force him upon the white races socially, and the question is, can you accept that - will you accept that? I say, you cannot do it. As I have pointed out, we should take every precaution to prevent the fusion of the two races ...You cannot get away from it, that the negro races occupy the lowest position in the evolutionary scale. If we are going to believe scientists, anthropologists, they tell us that they are a lower order of beings than ourselves, and, if they are a lower order of beings, is it not very foolish of us to try and force them to an absolutely impossible position? Are you not flying in the face of Divine Providence in attempting to do such a thing?"[48] That was a formidable combination to oppose - God, Darwin and the anthropologists.

Return, however, to loyal little Natal, where there was still some hesitation about frankly abandoning the respectable ground of culture for the possibly un-English and certainly un-Christian doctrines of new fangled science. The last word may be given to H. D. Winter, farmer and ex-Minister of Agriculture, who in the course of interrogation arrived at a conclusion which was probably representative, in its clarity, of white South Africa in general.

> Do you think that they are an inferior race, given the same environment and the same opportunities as we have? - I think that they are an inferior race. We look upon them as an inferior race. They cannot do what the civilised people do, therefore they are bound to be an inferior race.
>
> The ancient Egyptians could do many things that out ancestors could not do. Are we an inferior race because of that? - We have lived since then; that was many centuries ago.
>
> Yes, that is so. When you speak of an inferior race, do you mean of inferior capacity, or do you mean inferior for the moment for the want of training? - Yes, inferior for the want of training, in knowledge of things and in civilisation generally.
>
> When you speak of these people as an inferior race, you do not mean that they are inferior in potential power, but simply inferior in efficiency for the moment? - They are inferior to the whites.
>
> But in what sense; in which of those two senses do you use the word inferior? - In the sense that I have just explained.
>
> There are only two senses, it appears to me, to choose between: the one is the sense of inferiority in capacity, and the other is inferiority in efficiency at the moment. In which of those respects do you apply the term inferiority to these people? - I will give you an answer in this way: their position generally.
>
> Anyway, your whole policy in regard to them would be based upon the view that they are an inferior race, and incapable of reaching to our standard? - They are incapable of reaching civilisation for many years to come, and, therefore, they must be an inferior race.
>
> When you say for many years to come, do you think that ultimately they may come to it? - They will, but not in my time, I am certain of that.[49]

NOTES

1. Q.24798, 25648. All footnotes in this form will refer to the numbered questions (and answers) in the Volumes of Evidence attached to the Lagden Report.
2. Q.23705
3. Q.9661. Cf. Q.19032.
4. Q.8391, 21136.
5. Q.5088-90, 5305, 5626, 9414-6, 9546-7, 16913-7.
6. Q.18733.
7. Q.5680, 5849.
8. Q.21837.
9. Q.8341, 8343.
10. Q.20314.
11. Q.15288.
12. Q.12660.
13. Q.9595.
14. Q.23890.
15. Q.9990.
16. Q.4017.
17. Q.8522-6.
18. Q.3938.
19. Q.16343.
20. Q.27966, 28001-4.
21. Q.9844.
22. A view expressed even by a Natal farmer with the opinions of his class. See Q.22916-7.
23. Q.23269-73, 23278.
24. Q.23179.
25. Q.23664, and cf. 21243.
26. Q.38799.

27. Q.20504, 20648, 20687-91.

28. Q.19123, 19151-2.

29. Q.16242, 16246.

30. Q.16255-9.

31. Q.1917, 2480-4, 2488-90, 11029-31, 16507-15, 21140, 21321-3.

32. Q.23063, 23093-9, 24584.

33. Q.21879, 22441-5, 24813, 27765, 27864.

34. Cape Argus June 21, 26 and July 17, 1897 (the last two in the column called "Saturday Sallies"); Cecil Headlam (ed) The Milner Papers 1897-1905 (London: Cassell and Co., 1931, 1933) Vol. 1, 50, 180.

35. D.D.T. Jabavu John Tengo Jabavu (no publisher: no date) 71, 73, 75.

36. Ibid., 72, 74-5.

37. Q.8794. Cape Argus June 26, 1897 and February 1, 1909.

38. D.D.T Jabavu op.cit., 72, 74.

39. Q.20811, 20919.

40. Q.22086, 22192-5.

41. Q.27825-34, 27842-3.

42. Melina Rorke The Story of Melina Rorke: Her Amazing Experiences (London: George Harrap, 1939) 47-48.

43. H. Vaughan-Williams A Visit to Lobengula in 1889 (Pietermaritzburg: Shuter and Shooter, 1947) 100.

44. Cape Argus, March 6, 1909.

45. Q.2974, 2977.

46. Cape Argus, February 27 (late edition and March 2, 1909.

47. Q.24015.

48. Q.40606.

49. Q.25215-22.

Chapter Seven

RACIAL ATTITUDES IN SOUTHERN AFRICA: THE CONTRIBUTIONS OF CULTURE, ECONOMIC INTERESTS AND HISTORY

Lawrence Schlemmer

In this paper I will attempt what may be the impossible task of disentangling the elements of culture, politics and economic interest which have been so closely inter-woven in the formation of race attitudes in Southern Africa, past and present. This task is made difficult by a variety of things, not the least of which is that culture or ethnicity has all too often paraded itself on the front stage of history in Southern Africa drawing attention away from more salient and greedy machinations taking place on the backstage. But culture as justification for domination, through its influence on ideology, has also at times been somewhat of a self-fulfilling prophecy, and consequently neat distinctions between culture and class, or between culture and power are impossible to make. My own attempts to isolate specific factors, for this reason are largely heuristic in purpose. My last complaint is that the subject matter is material enough for a substantial book; hence my approach will be conceptual and selective in the extreme.

I. My selectivity, broadly, is linked to the basic thrust of a particular theoretical framework - the theory of Pluralism as it applies to post-colonial societies. Even critics of theory of the plural society acknowledge that it does offer a useful comprehensive framework for the analysis of deeply divided societies[1] and I consider that I can do no better than to make my analysis sensitive to the issues raised by this conceptual approach. My use of the concept Pluralism here refers to the more recent use of the concept, i.e. that relating to deeply divided composite societies marked by social separation and inequality, and does not refer to the pattern of cross-cutting checks and balances found in stable democracies.

Theories of the plural society owe their origin mainly to Furnivall, who wrote about the colonial societies in South-East Asia,[2] and M. G. Smith, who elaborated the theory after extensive study in the Caribbean.[3] I do not consider it necessary to outline these theories; it will be more economical if I sketch some of the major issues arising out of this broad approach which seem most applicable to the topic under consideration.

There seem to me to be two important points of debate around the theory of the plural society which must be considered. The first relates to the question of whether or not cultural pluralism, in itself, is sufficient as an explanation of the social cleavages and the associated conflicts which plural societies tend to evince. The second point of debate is concerned with the relative importance of competing economic interests in causing or exacerbating conflict between ethnic segments in the populations of composite societies. Furnivall himself was quite clear on this point, claiming for the societies he studied, that cleavages along racial or cultural lines are accompanied by economic tensions and patterns of economic exploitation basic to the colonial process, and that such tensions are not counteracted or constrained by social norms and the integrating factors which exist in metropolitan capitalist society - *inter alia* common citizenship and an awareness of shared loyalties, values and institutions.[4] John Rex, although he does not recognise how much emphasis Furnivall placed on the economic factor, criticises theories of *Pluralism* for ignoring the nature of the economy and the manifestations of class-conflict in many of the plural societies studies.[5] A few additional comments around these two issues are necessary.

Smith's development and exposition of the theory of *Pluralism* certainly does not rest on simple cultural determinism. Ethnic heterogeneity, he maintains, does not necessarily lead to plural structures; if there is agreement on basic institutional forms, as among whites in the United States of America, for example, ethnic diversity gives rise to a range of secondary differences but not to *Pluralism*. According to Smith, *Pluralism* can be *cultural*, i.e. relating to things like family type, religion, language, etc., or *social*, resulting in differences in corporate group identity.[6] If the basic institutional system is plural in nature, there is likely to be both social and cultural *Pluralism*. The most marked form of *Pluralism*, however, occurs when there is significant exclusion of one or more segments of the population from political participation. Smith appears to claim that where this differential incorporation of segments into society exists (he calls it *structural pluralism*) there *must* of necessity also exist social and cultural cleavages. This is an interesting but very debatable point which requires very careful examination. Smith, therefore, seems to be presupposing a very particular type of divisive principle operating in plural societies which has a consistent manifestation at both higher and lower levels of structure, as it were.

Since Smith does not take full account of economic interests (indeed, he criticises Furnivall for over-emphasising them) one is left with a very large and important question. Do ethnic divisions involving differences in basic institutions contain the potential for such basic and inevitable incompatibility between groups as to provide a sufficient explanation for the serious conflict encountered, say, in South African society? Does ethnicity, in itself, have the salience to cleave society so deeply? My own interpretation of Smith leads me to conclude that his answer to this question, sufficiently qualified, would be yes. If, on the other hand, this is not the general thrust of his analyses, then his exposition of the theory is basically no more than a system of classification; an analytical paradigm. Malcolm Cross opts for the latter alternative when he argues that the theory of Smith does not tell us ..."how ethnic identity came to occupy the importance which it may ...have".[7] Smith either assumes that this importance is implicit in the nature of ethnic identity itself, or else has failed to provide a theory with explanatory value. Kuper's interpretation of Smith suggests the former, when he says of the theory that "cultural diversity or pluralism automatically imposes the structural necessity for domination by one of the cultural sections".[8] In another paper, Kuper seems to align himself with Smith when he says that "cultural pluralism has intrinsic significance in the sense that objective consequences flow from the fact of cultural difference, regardless of the meanings attached by the actors".[9] However, Kuper also seems to qualify the significance of race and ethnicity when he says the "It is the interaction within (the) context of the plural society which affects the significance attached to race and ethnicity, the ideological emphases on these identities, and their structural implications."[10] Hence one is left with some uncertainty as to Kuper's position in this argument. Rex, by firmly introducing the additional and interrelated concepts of labour exploitation and economic interest avoids the assumption of ethnic or cultural determinism and lays down a basis for elaborating the theory in such a way as to provide explanatory power vis-à-vis the South African situation.[11]

While I completely accept these qualifications of Smith's position, the question posed earlier which arises out of Smith's own analysis nevertheless demands some closer attention. I am not suggesting that ethnic identity and cultural differences automatically predispose men to erect social barriers between groups or to dominate and exclude others in political affairs. However, it is probable that the presence of cultural differences, and the operation of cultural influences, have imparted particular characteristics of inter-racial and inter-class relations in South Africa. It is this particular influence which might give theories of Pluralism a particular significance worth exploring in the context of Southern African society.

II. The Formation of Race Attitudes: A Brief Historical Consideration

Today the race attitudes of whites in South Africa are often seen as a phenomenon of rather outlandish proportions, which they undoubtedly are. When I consider the circumstances of our history, on the other hand, I am often surprised that inter-racial hostility in South Africa is not even more intense than it is.

Initial contacts between white Dutch East India Company officials and Khoi tribesmen held a mixed promise for the future.[12] Prior stereotypes of African aboriginals as cannibals and barbarians had existed in Europe. The story of the curse of Ham, the association of blackness with evil, and misconceptions regarding the sexual inclinations of Negroes were familiar features of medieval and post-medieval Europe.[13] The Dutch East India Company, however, was insistent that the rights, dignity and territorial integrity of the indigenous peoples had to be respected as far as possible. Van Riebeeck pursued this policy with barely concealed irritation but great patience. However, the wide difference in appearance, in culture and personal habits (made wider still by mutual ignorance resulting from partial, segmental contact), distinctions between heathen and protestant Christian which were especially deeply felt by the Europeans because their own ethnic and national identity was very closely bound up with protestant concepts of salvation,[14] and a polarity of material interests arising out of the issues of rights over land and the terms of the cattle trade, made anything other than a plural situation with intense latent conflict impossible. If at this early point there could have been some incorporation of Khoi peoples and their interests into the affairs of the refreshment station, and some social integration other than exploitative sexual and trading relationships, the subsequent history of South Africa might have been different.

With the advent of the free burghers, certain aspects of the situation changed. It seems likely that the early white population at the Cape was composed of people relatively lacking in the idealism, rationality and refinement of the Dutch parent culture - they were probably marginal individuals who had not been able to prosper in the full, competitive society in Holland.[15] But they had also probably been influenced by the opportunity in bourgeois Dutch society and appear to have had high material aspirations, if one is to judge by the amount of cattle trading, hunting, and private inn-keeping which existed, often against the wishes of the Company. Despite what might have been relatively high material aspirations, the free burghers displayed no rare passion for work, and a constant need for servants (knechten), slaves and cheap Khoi labour seemed to exist. It would seem that fairly soon, the genesis of the South African white's dependence on cheap, subservient labour had occurred.[16]

A sexual factor probably played a part in the evolution of race attitudes as well. It has been suggested that the easy sexual exploitation of black women by white men was regarded as a threat by European women when they began arriving in substantial numbers. White women were far from subservient and docile in the settler society, and were in an excellent position to encourage racial 'distance' in an effort to protect their own interests.[17]

Later, the lure of cattle trading and breeding, barter, and hunting caused a land hunger to develop among a section of the burghers with a consequent rapid expansion of the settlement. The loan-farm tenure system spread throughout the territory, displacing more and more indigenous peoples.[18] In the course of occupying and exploiting the land, the expanding settler frontier was the scene of bitter and long drawn out hostility between first Khoi peoples and the whites and later between San (Bushmen) peoples and the settlers. The small-group social organisation of the San peoples inevitably meant that their resistance to the settlers took the form of cattle theft and surprise attacks. This was not perceived by the settlers as activity which, although antagonistic, might have the legitimacy of warfare in defence of territory. It was seen as criminal and barbarous activity carried out with the stealth and cunning of marauding predators. The Bushmen were perceived as sub-humans to be eradicated like vermin.[19]

Maccrone's account contains some evidence that while the Khoi peoples were visibly organised in strong tribal units they were treated with a measure of very reluctant and artificial respect, but this respect soon disappeared when these communities became disorganised and atomised, and smaller groups and individuals without tribal backing interacted with the Dutch settlers. At this stage the real contempt for the character of the Hottentots emerged.[20]

What evolved very rapidly was a very strong prejudice among the Dutch settlers with regard to the Khoisan peoples of the Cape, which combined elements of strong and open animosity, dehumanisation, contempt, feelings of ethnic superiority, and, particularly regarding the Bushmen, fear. Initially, this was not colour prejudice as such. It is well known that during the 17th and even the early 18th century, certain free burghers and other people of colour were accorded social acceptance if they were Christians and, presumably, if they shared the life-style of the whites.[21] However, by a process of association which was inevitable given the constant reinforcement of impressions, pigmentation itself came to be associated with the characteristics perceived in the indigenous ethnic groups. Maccrone expresses it as follows: "Christianity and skin colour, membership of a particular group, and social superiority, became so closely associated with one another that any one by itself could serve as a criterion of group membership."[22]

Associated with, or perhaps accompanying this process, were changes in the perceptions of slavery. The impression one gains is that in the early period of slavery, it was seen as a status from which a deserving individual could escape by diligent behaviour, loyalty and baptism. However, as time went by the vested interests in the property which slaves represented, as well as impressions formed by certain inevitable characteristics which slave classes possessed, like dependency or recalcitrance, led to the view that slavery was appropriate to the inherent nature of the slave class. Because all slaves were black, and because it was easy for settlers to imagine that the only worth of the indigenous peoples was the providing of very cheap and useful manual labour, "the view began to be held and asserted that slavery was the proper condition of the black race".[23] The labour market for indigenous labour, once the traditional structure of indigenous society had been destroyed, was such as to make of the employment of black labour an institution closely akin to slavery.[24] Hence a continuity came to exist betwen perceptions of slave status and perceptions of non-white status. This, coupled with the attitudes of labour which the economic circumstances encouraged (already discussed above) led to a particular perception of the appropriate occupational role and social position of black people. This was to combine with hostility and contempt to form a complex of stereotypes which, in the time to come, would establish firmly in the consciousness of whites the stigma of moral, social, cultural, personal an economic inferiority in blacks.

In interpretations of South Africa's early colonial history, much has been made of the factor of the 18th Century Cape burghers' conservative Calvinist religion.[25] Maccrone refers to the very much quoted Anna Steenkamp, the Voortrekker leader Piet Retief's sister, in support of his contention that a narrow Calvinist concept of Christian identity and destiny underlay the racial exclusiveness which evolved among the frontier farmers of Dutch origina during the 18th Century.[26] Van Jaarsveld also quotes evidence to show that the view that coloured people bore the curse of Ham and that it was God's will that they should be subservient was an important factor in shaping the race attitudes of the nascient Afrikaner group at that stage.[27]

There might be two elements of misplaced emphasis in this interpretation. Firstly it cannot be claimed that a firmly established and uniform response to people of colour had developed among all Cape burghers by the beginning of the 19th Century. (I will return to this point presently). More importantly, though, it would seem that religious rationalisations of colour prejudice <u>followed</u> the formation of of racial attitudes rather than shaping it. Certainly the official attitude of the Dutch Reformed Church in the Cape in the 18th Century and even in the 19th Century, on the whole, seemed to support the principles of equality in the eyes of

God, mixed worship, and the dignity of all men.[28] Maccrone's own evidence suggests that while the principle of the changed status of blacks after baptism was upheld in official church policies, community pressures were increasingly such as to prevent slaves from becoming baptised, hence blocking access to improved social status for slaves.[29] This viewpoint is strongly argued by Haasbroek, who rejects the notion that the Calvinist religion was the powerful factor <u>shaping</u> race attitudes which it is claimed to be.[30]

It would seem possible, then, that aspects of culture and material interest were more important than religious views as factors giving initial content to race attitudes, and it is probable that popular interpretations of Old Testament doctrines were invoked to rationalise and justify these attitudes. It should be conceded, however, that a simple dichotomous status distinction between Christian and heathen provided one basis for the ascribing of lower status to indigenous communities from the very beginning of early Cape history. Since this type of distinction does not necessarily block the acquisition of Christian status and therefore of civilised status by individual non-whites, however, it is not in itself sufficient as a basis for the formation of hostile relations and caste-like distinctions based on pigmentation; one has to look at other factors as well. These factors, one may suggest, were labour, land, and a more or less inevitable tendency to have contempt for peoples who presented relatively few outward signs of religion (no churches), few signs of rights over or possession of land (no established farm-houses, towns or land improvements), possessed hardly any technology and 'civilisation' (no fine clothing, literature, objects d'art, etc.). Perceptions of this basic cultural rift were not made any the less salient by the fact that very many of the settlers themselves were illiterate and lived in wagons or wattle and daub houses. They saw themselves as identified with a "superior" culture.

Such perceptions of a very fundamental incompatibility were immeasurably reinforced by later contacts with Bantu-speaking tribesmen on the Eastern frontier, since conflicts over land, cattle, or, at best, an uneasy trading relationship characterised this contact from the outset. The so-called Kaffir Wars, of course, set the seal on the patterns of racial enmity which had developed in the earlier period.

I have expanded a little on the history of white-black contact in South Africa simply to show how certain material interests and cultural differences made race conflict more or less inevitable, and established a basic pattern of response towards blacks among rank and file Afrikaners.

Despite the liberal thrust in policies emanating from London after the British occupation of the Cape and the influence of the British humanitarian and philanthropic movement, the rank and file English-speaking settlers in the Cape and Natal revealed basically the same sort of reaction to indigenous peoples as was the case among Afrikaners. Thompson remarks that "The British settlers were not slow in acquiring a pride in colour comparable with that of the Afrikaners."[31] Robert Godlonton, of the Graham's Town Journal, one of the prominent leaders of the English settler community in the Eastern Cape, led perhaps the majority of the rank and file English settlers in a campaign against black franchise in the early 1850's. Godlonton, with strong public support had been very critical of British missionaries and their stand on behalf of Coloured people and Africans. The Piet Retief manifesto of 1837 setting out the grievance of those Afrikaners who joined the Great Trek, read like a repetition of the complaints of English-speaking settlers which appeared in the columns of the Graham's Town Journal. It is interesting that for a time the majority of the Coloureds in the Eastern Cape supported Andries Stockenström against the candidates of the English settlers.[32]

Some of the basic issues raised in the foregoing account are further elucidated by aspects of the history of 19th Century Natal. There the attitudes of the colonists, supported by editorials in the Natal Mercury, seem to have been compounded of fear of the overwhelming numbers of Africans, a fundamental disapproval of African customs and laws (which were regarded as barbarous and immoral), a cynical desire to exploit the labour of Africans, and a resistance to the setting aside of land for tribesmen in terms of the resettlement policies of Shepstone. There was a strong body of opinion in favour of westernising the Zulu tribesmen; as Welsh puts it, "...the colonists' rhetoric about civilising and improving Africans did not really mean assimilation in the sense of eliminating cultural differences between white and black; rather they wished to entrench a new difference: that between a class of masters and a class of servile labourers." Welsh goes on to say that "Racialist views were widespread among the colonists and most would have agreed with an editorial comment in the Natal Mercury in 1858: "We believe in the divinely purposed supremacy of the white over the black race" ..."[33] Some of the evidence put forward by Welsh attests to the quite breathtaking cynicism of white colonist spokesmen in defending the view that the only proper role for blacks in the colony was to perform menial labour for whites. Welsh quotes De Kiewiet in pointing out to what extent morally-based revulsion of African customs accorded well with the need to rationalise the desire for a cheap and obedient labour force.[34] The arguments put forward by colonists' representatives in favour of imposing curbs on the voting rights of Africans in order to effectively disenfranchise them, revealed rather ruthless sentiments of white racial superiority and exclusiveness coupled with cynical materialism.[35]

Hence we see that both Dutch and British settler communities, at the level of rank and file community perceptions, responded to indigenous peoples with a measure of "culture shock". The value of black labour in both settings and the devaluation of indigenous culture produced an ambivalence which, after various types of conflicts had displaced Khoisan and African people from their land and forced them to seek work in settler communities, could not but result in highly unequal and authoritarian master-servant relations between white and black.

Space does not permit an assessment of developments in racial attitudes in the Voortrekker Republics nor in the early period of Union. Suffice to say that one author has made out a fairly strong case for saying that it was partly as a result of both English and Dutch Eastern Cape settler influences that the Reverend van der Hoff was encouraged to agitate for formal racial segregation in Dutch Reformed Church in the Transvaal.[36] Although it was only in 1883 that the Dutch Reformed Church in the Transvaal finally and formally resolved to permit no integration of races in the church, the Transvaal Constitution of 1858 contained the famous clause permitting no equality between Coloured and white people in church or State. Their independence of Britain enabled the Boer Republic to codify what the majority of settlers in Natal and in the Cape (outside of the urban area of Cape Town perhaps) would have supported. Cape Afrikaners in particular were successful in influencing the colonial government to tighten the voting qualification for non-whites in 1887 and 1892. Cape 'liberalism' and the enlightened policies of the Afrikaner Bond in that province were powerfully inspired by outstanding Cape politicians (Merriman, Solomon, Hofmeyr, Sauer, etc.), whose political and intellectual abilities enabled them to shore up the colour-blind legal system at the Cape despite resistance from rank and file supporters. Cape liberalism and the tradition of the Afrikaner Bond appear to have been relatively superficial and, to a considerable extent, paternalistic and conservative.[37] The Afrikaner Bond, for example, did not have the vitality or the grass roots strength to maintain its tradition successfully after amalgamation with the northern parties, 'Het Volk' and 'Oranje Unie', after Union. As Lord elborne and Churchill pointed out, just before Union, in terms of popular white entiments, "the politics of the Transvaal are the politics of South Africa".[38] t the National Convention in 1908, Moor, the Natal Prime Minister, dogmatically choed the mythical beliefs of most whites in all territories that "the black man as incapable of civilisation".

onflicts between Boers (who made notoriously inefficient use of their extensive land holdings) and African tribes over land in the Transvaal, and parts of Natal before Union reinforced sentiments which had come to exist in the old colony. Here an element of naked fear was important. The Boers in parts of the Transvaal feared the military threat of the Pedi tribesmen in Sekhukuneland. The same could be said of the colonists in Natal.[39] Fear tends to brutalise attitudes - note the ruthlessness with which the Natal settlers responded to the Bombatha rebellion by the Zulus in 1906. Also, the transformation of defeated tribesmen into a landless class of tenant farmers and labourers reinforced the same sort of stereotypes which had come to be held in regard to Coloured farm-labour in the old colony. The fact that in many instances the African tenant farmers were better agriculturalists than the white owners and were responsible for a major part of the land production may have created a sense of threat and hostility among the Boer farmers. Certainly, persisting conflicts existed over the extent of livestock ownership to which the African squatters were entitled and other similar issues. Hence, the defeat and subsequent transformation of African tribesmen into a rural 'underclass' did not necessarily alleviate economic tension between white and black.[40]

The new role of Africans on the farms was also one of the factors preventing even the poorest white farmers from acquiring habits of labour which might have alleviated another problem which was to have an enormous impact on race attitudes - urban white poverty.

Already at the turn of the century, an impoverished class of landless _byowner_ and nomad whites had become conspicuous.[41] The poverty which degraded so many Afrikaners had been caused, _inter alia_, by pressure on land, uneconomical subdivision of farms, the advent of the railways which made the occupation of "transport-riding" redundant, and the cattle disease "rinderpest" which killed off two-thirds of Boer cattle in 1896. From my own experience I know that many of them had an "oral tradition" of bitterness against the British for preventing their fathers and forefathers from alienating the land of Africans in the Western Transvaal and elsewhere. A bitter, discontented, resentful and degraded stratum of people, their collective attitudes became a repository of the crudest forms of racial envy and antagonism. As people firmly identified with Boer farming traditions, they abhorred the objective similarity of their circumstances to those of the hated Africans.

The most dramatic new injection of racialism into the popular culture of whites, however, occurred on the mines and in the urban industrial setting. The discovery of diamonds and the commencement of the industrial revolution in South Africa brought the first white blue-collar workers - South Africa's first industrial working class - who tended to be British miners and artisans, notably from Cornwall. These men, who were steeped in a tradition of trade unionism, were thoroughly orientated towards protectionism and to an all-embracing defence of their own occupational interests. One striking early manifestation of the effects of these orientations on race relations was attempts by white diggers to exclude Coloured diggers from the Kimberley diamond claims.[42] One must assume that in situations of that sort, any differentiating-factor becomes important if it can be seized upon to eliminate material competition or protect material interests.

Among the majority of these new settlers, the typically working class spirit and socialist inclinations proved to have rigid ethnic boundaries which excluded blacks. An important factor was the fact that Africans were prepared to accept lower pay and poorer conditions. The whites could legitimately claim a superiority of skills, experience and technological expertise over African unskilled labour. Hence they had some basis for a claim of "cultural" superiority, and they utilised this fully in their negotiations with employers who, like their counterparts today, would have liked to reduce production costs by employing greater proportions of black skilled labour. This notion of 'cultural' superiority or of so-called 'civilised labour' became the conerstone of the policy of the South African Labour Party, which at one stage controlled the Transvaal Provincial Council. The same rationalisations for demanding protection against black competition were, however, taken over by the far less-skilled (mainly Afrikaans) white workers who were streaming into the early mines and industries from impoverished and highly attenuated "cultural" circumstances on the platteland. This type of justification for the protection of white labour was facilitated by the pact between the Labour Party and the Nationalist Party (the party of poor Afrikaners) in the period following 1924. The notorious speeches of people like Walter Madeley and Colonel Cresswell which, in blatant terms, protested the racial superiority of the white and the need for complete social, economic and political segregation of the Africans, seeped into the economic vocabulary of white workers and provided a decisive influence in the maturation of the political ideal of the separation of races.[43]

Hence it was the "craft union" tradition of British workers coupled with the urbanisation and industrialisation of impoverished unskilled Afrikaners who had only their white skins to protect them, and the turbulent labour conflicts of the twenties that provided a very definite mould for popular white race attitudes after Union.

One other powerful movement - the most spectacular of all - converged on the labour movement in the twenties with momentous implications for subsequent events.

Starting from intellectual, literary, rural pioneer and quasi-theological beginnings in the 18th Century, the spirit of Afrikaner identity and patriotism was fanned by the winds of British imperialism and the Federation Movement in the 19th Century. The British annexation of the Transvaal, the Jameson Raid, and finally the Anglo-Boer War injured the group-feeling of Afrikaners and a full-blown nationalism within a heterogeneous region developed, which fed back into the Cape Colony, eliminating most vestiges of Cape liberalism from rank and file white political sentiment.

Inevitably, a strong central ideology becomes a peg on which a community can hang a variety of issues crucial to its own interests. Thus the colour issue and the issue of Afrikaner poverty in the cities became integrated into a fairly consistent pattern of ideological thinking during the twenties. General Hertzog provided this thinking with political thrust, and in the thirties, the secret Afrikaner organisation, the Broederbond, through a network of influence at high level, commenced to steer the political destiny of Afrikaners. The segregationist policies of the Labour Party, inasmuch as they had influenced popular Afrikaans thinking, accorded well with the principles of separation and cultural autonomy which were evolving within the powerful Afrikaans intellectual and religious establishment. So did the thinking of Shepstone in regard to the question of dispensation for Africans - Shepstone's policies had been imposed on the Transvaal after the first British Occupation.[44] A central political theme of this movement has emerged in the form of the conviction that the Afrikaner, as well as other ethnic groups in South Africa, each have a distinct and separate heritage and destiny. The belief which emerged among architects of Afrikaner Nationalist political thinking was that problems of race relations and the economic circumstances of people in South Africa should be approached within a context of ethnic separation and cultural perservation.[45] That this type of thinking, even if nobl inspired, is convenient as a justification for a variety of other political and economic motives goes without saying. What was significant, however, was the process of a coherent articulation of cultural beliefs and ethnic stereotypes and myths into an all-embracing ideological prescription for a highly complex and heterogeneous social, economic and political order.

More broadly, the status threats and economic competition which the Afrikaners experienced in the cities, both from immigrant whites and unskilled blacks (but mainly from the latter since the Afrikaner could not really even begin to compete with the former) sharpened their ethnocentricism and deepened their hostility and prejudice towards blacks.[46]

The brief and highly selective historical account suggests the following broad conclusions. Initial perceptions of group distinctiveness when whites encountered blacks in South Africa rested largely on the protestant-heathen dichotomy and on dissimilarities of appearance and culture. The religious distinction in particular but also the absence of technology in the culture of the indigenous peoples led to the ascription by whites of a lower status to the blacks. This was probably reinforced by the association of pigmentation with slave status once black slaves were imported by the settlers. Later, the conquest of blacks and the destruction of their social and political organisation allowed the lower status ascribed to them to be enforced. Cultural differences (whether or not the whites lived up to the prescriptions of their culture notwithstanding) were an obvious basis for the justification of domination of blacks by whites.

Once a lower status has been ascribed to a group and it has been successfully enforced, the lack of power, esteem and resources tend to become self-reinforcing. The morale of the underclass declines and, as we have seen, even the sexual exploitation of black women encourages the vilification of the black group.

Inter-group distinctions and social cleavages such as these meant that the white elite came to see its material interests in ethnic terms. At different stages of history the material interests of whites in land, cattle, cheap labour, wage levels and occupations imbued racial differentiation with a powerful economic basis, and this in turn was a potent reinforcement of the prior differences in culture and ethnicity. Economic interests and ethnic differences became superimposed by virtue of the congruity of ethnic, social and class status. The Christian tradition shared by most whites, with its discouragement of material selfishness and greed, probably encouraged the white elites to defend their identities and interest in terms of culture and nationalism rather than in terms of what had become the more salient issues of material privilege and the power to ensure it.

III. Race Attitudes Among Whites Today

Today, one would expect to find the historical components of culture, nationalism and material privilege intertwined in the anatomy of race attitudes among whites. Moodie has described in great historical and conceptual depth the nature of Afrikaner Nationalist ideology, which he describes as a "civil religion". This ideology was forged in opposition not only to English influences, but also in opposition to the earlier evangelical Calvinism of the Dutch Reformed Churches and the more liberal and rational nationalism propounded by Hertzog and his followers.[47] The influence of this ideology is undoubtedly one of the factors which make Afrikaans-speaking whites more candid and consistent in the expression of separationist ideals. However, of equal valence in historical terms, is the rather more general and certainly more negative element of the simple cultural stereotyping of black peoples as backward and incompatible with white 'civilisation'. Then again, the era of white labour 'protest' in the thirties is an immediate memory for many whites, and this aspect of the past as well as the long history of white interests in cheap black labour and in land should be as strongly evident in the composition of white racialism as the other factors mentioned.

Very few studies have been conducted with a view to disentangling the components of racialism among whites. We have attempted one such study recently in Durban, where by means of selective sampling, a fairly balanced random sample of English and Afrikaans-speaking white male voters was drawn.[48] For the purposes of this paper an additional analysis - a 'Factor Analysis' - of the responses of the 155 English and 105 Afrikaans-speaking subjects has been undertaken. Subjects had been presented with 90 carefully worded statements, covering virtually the entire spectrum of major political, social and race relations issues in South Africa. The statements were required to be accepted or rejected by subjects after they had been put at their ease and carefully motivated to respond authentically in personal interview situations. I will attempt, briefly, to summarise some of the major conclusions as well as the implications emerging from this study. Within the scope of this paper it is impossible to give examples of the quantitative findings. The results suggest that a majority of both English and Afrikaans-speaking whites support the broad notion of race separation, although for different reasons. For the majority, it is a means of maintaining white political integrity and power in the major part of the country. For a minority of Afrikaners (in Durban ± 20% of this group but elsewhere probably somewhat more) it seems to be associated with a genuine desire to grant autonomy and opportunitie for development to black ethnic groups, independent of whites. This group of 'separationist' progressives is the equivalent among Afrikaners of the roughly 30% of enlightened, tolerant, and integration-orientated voters that one finds among English-speakers. The lack of colour prejudice and the degree of willingne to make material sacrifices on behalf of blacks among this group of Afrikaners almost matches that among English-speaking progressives. Yet there appears to be a very clearly-formulated conception of the importance of ethnic autonomy and a notion of the basic significance of separate destinies for the different ethnic groups in South Africa (often defined by this group as "nations"). This probably is evidence of the effect on popular attitudes of the "civil religion" of Afrikaners which Moodie refers to.[49] However, this spirit of enlightened separatism appears mainly among better-educated Afrikaners (as do progressive sympathies among English-speakers). This same spirit becomes "corrupted" with a number of other political motivations among less well-educated Afrikaners, as I will outline presently.

The results support the findings of most other investigations of race attitudes in South Africa in showing the English-speaking white group generally to be less inclined to prejudice and hostility towards blacks than the Afrikaans-speaking group. Our results also show, not unexpectedly, however, that a majority in both groups have a consistent tendency to distantiate themselves from black South Africans. Indeed the differences between the language groups are in many ways superficial. Apart from the liberally-oriented and "progressive" groups that I have described, the differences between English and Afrikaans-speaking whites generally tend to become insignificant when the issue being responded to involves any sacrifice of material welfare or political influence. Both groups are distinctly white supremacist in orientation; the rank and file English-speaker not quite as aggressively so as the Afrikaans-speaker.

A strong feeling for Afrikaans group identity appears to be a phenomenon found mainly among an Afrikaner elite and upper-middle class. The vast majority of middle and lower-middle class respondents reject the need for divisions between English and Afrikaans-speaking whites. We would guess that the reason why most Afrikaners consistently support the Nationalist Party has more to do with ingrained voting habits, with the party's "image" of determination and strength and with its policy generally in regard to the handling of the colour issue rather than with the maintenance of Afrikaans group identity. The "high-priests" of Afrikanerdom who publicly defend the principles of the "civil religion" in terms of white language-group differences do not appear to have a large popular following <u>on this issue</u>.

Our results suggest that the popular "political ideologies" of whites in both groups, <u>apart from issues relating to race</u>, are broadly democratic in flavour, emphasising freedom of speech, the rule of law, and rights of protection for interest groups. Totalitarian thinking or authoritarian political ideology generally has not penetrated the rank and file of white voters to any significant degree, despite all outward appearances of the South African political system. A clear (almost "schizoid") distinction is made between 'white politics' and "colour politics", and in the sphere of the former our respondents could hardly be distinguished, I am sure, from, say, a typical North American sample. However, the perceptions among whites of deep divisions between a "white community" on the one hand, and "black communities" on the other are very pervasive, even among some of those whites whose ideal inclinations are for racial integration. This essentially "plural" perception of politics and society is very basic to an understanding of the situation in Southern Africa.

The "factor analysis" of our findings[50] can only be presented in very broad terms in this paper. The aim of the factor analysis was to establish whether or not different specific components of race attitudes could be identified. Among both English and Afrikaans-speaking voters the single most powerful factor appears to be a compound of social distance from blacks, hostility towards blacks, occupational exclusiveness, and a white power-supremacy component. Among Afrikaners the element of social distance or separation from blacks is stronger than among the English. This appears to be the most general factor and seems to indicate that a spirit of *white exclusiveness and dominance* has emerged from history as a powerful dynamic, incorporating and obscuring any more specific cultural, economic and political motivations.

Distinct from this dominance factor, but less powerful in the group as a whole, is a factor of *racism* or racial stereotyping. This involves a vilification of the inherent character of black people. It is also present among the English and Afrikaners, but appears somewhat more clearly in the results for the English-speaking group.

Thirdly, there is a factor, also present among both white language groups, which has strong elements of white dominance combined with a pragmatic and compromising stance on issues of race separation. We can call this a *pragmatic white leadership* factor. It is rather stronger in the English group than in the Afrikaans group.

Fourthly, among both groups once again, there is a factor which can only be described as *liberalism cum paternalism*, involving no insistence on rigid race separation. This is considerably stronger among English-speakers than among Afrikaans-speakers.

Fifthly, a factor appears, overwhelmingly among Afrikaans-speakers, which we can term a *pluralism* factor. This involves separation of white and black with no insistence on continued white domination or privilege.

This factor analysis, combined with other results in our survey, as well as a broad assessment of opinion poll results[51] has allowed us to construct a broad typology of white voters as well as assessments of relative numerical strength along the following lines: (the estimates of numerical strength are very tentati since we are extrapolating from the results of a sample in one city, albeit ver carefully).

"Verkramptes"*: (materially self-interested; unenlightened, prejudiced, white dominance-orientated voters). Approximately one-half of the Afrikaans group and one-fifth of the English-speaking group.

Pragmatics: (materially self-interested; not insistent on rigid race discrimination, favouring separation but only where practical; tolerant of black occupational advance; white leadership-orientated). Approximately one-quarter of the Afrikaans group and just under one-half of the English group.

Pluralists: (insistent on group separation; not insistent on white domination or material exploitation of blacks). Roughly one-fifth of the Afrikaans group.

Liberal paternalists and liberals: (not insistent on separation; progressive, demanding of justice in South Africa). Approximately one-third of the English-speaking group and roughly one-twentieth of the Afrikaans group.

It must be emphasised that, despite differences in the relative size of racial-political types in the two white language groups, the basic variations in racial attitudes appear to be shared by the two groups. The differences which do exist can be seen as resulting from specific aspects of South African history which I have discussed and from the still wide differences in average socio-economic and educational level which exist between English and Afrikaans.

The typology and the factor analysis described above do not give much prominence to the factor of material interests. However, a perusal of the detailed responses to items indicates quite clearly that an insistence on white privileges is a very strong component of those factors and orientations which involve racialism, white domination, segregation, and even the pragmatic stance. One might also add that a powerful element of white status exclusiveness exists which, although it does not appear in these results, is strongly evident in the orientations of representatives of lower-skilled white workers.[52]

In another analysis[53] I have taken results from the study quoted above and from other surveys conducted recently to show that the grand designs of Separate Development, involving the need for considerable sacrifices from whites for the development and consolidation of "Homelands", accord only with the orientations of our pluralist group and with the progressive attitudes to black development of the liberal/paternal voter group. The rank and file English and Afrikaans-speaking voters are tolerant of and support the policy only as a means of maintaining segregation and avoiding the political dangers of continuing territorial and economic interdependence of the races.

---

*An Afrikaans term meaning narrow, rigid, unenlightened.

IV. Implications Within the Geo-Political Region of Southern Africa

My own observations, which unfortunately cannot be substantiated by any systematic evidence other than widening occupational opportunity for blacks and a definite shift in government thinking on the issue of occupational mobility for Africans,[54] is that the pragmatism outlined above is definitely on the ascendancy at the moment. This is possible, of course, within a period of economic growth which, despite recent setbacks, can generally guarantee white prosperity. The main consequence of this for black people will be significantly enhanced occupational opportunity and improved occupational skills, but within a context of sustained relative inequality. However, the bargaining power of blacks on the labour market must increase as a result of this. The strikes among 60,000 African workers in Durban in February 1973 is evidence of a growing capacity among blacks to act without community-wide leadership and without the disastrous consequences of victimisation which have characterised earlier strikes. If pragmatism among whites does gain strength, the possibilities of an era of negotiation between white and black in the market place could eventuate.

Pragmatism will not spell the downfall of the present regime in the near future. The only real dangers of a split in the ranks of government supporters appears to come from a type of "pluralist" orientated "verligte" (enlightened person) among professional and academic Afrikaners. The main opposition party is showing a more serious form of ideological disunity than any difference in the ranks of the governing party. The government can to some degree avoid open opposition from the "pluralist" intellectuals if it places additional emphasis on "Homeland" development. Furthermore, outside pressures on South Africa may have the effect of encouraging greater emphasis on Homeland development as well, as has been the case ever since Dr. Verwoerd, a former Prime Minister, admitted in Parliament in 1961 that the policy was partly a response to criticism from a hostile world. In any event, the degree of autonomy already granted to the African "homelands" and the privileges and perks for many middle-class Africans associated with homeland development has meant that the policy has a momentum and impetus which cannot any longer be halted.

Observations in Durban, as well as the results of systematic research[55] suggest very strongly that more and more urban Africans, while remaining committed to the principle of racial justice in the whole of South Africa, are taking the "homeland" administrations and their leaders as a political reference. It seems to be inevitable that the political aspirations of Africans are going to be articulated by and directed through the emergent "homeland" leadership. There are also signs in Durban, for example, that black worker organisation will associate itself in various ways with "homeland" leadership. The present trend towards increasing co-operation between leaders of different "Homelands" is another development with significance.

The grass-roots supporters of the government are not likely to allow substantial sacrifices of land or resources to be made to the homeland territories. The potential conflict between homeland leadership and the central government cannot, therefore, be alleviated by significant concessions. The conflict between homeland leaders and the government is likely to increase. One of the more important points at issue is likely to become the rights of migrant workers from the homeland territories. This is merely one of the issues on which homeland leaders can make common cause with South Africa's "hostages", the former High Commission Territories of Botswana, Lesotho and Swaziland. If and when the issues of land and labour are taken up in concert by homeland leaders Lesotho, and perhaps to a lesser extent, Swaziland and Botswana as well, might start articulating their own demands. Historically these territories have been involved in the conflicts in Southern Africa, and any escalation of black political activity in the region should tempt them to participate. Naturally, the South African government has the means of imposing coercive restraints. However, in the current climate of world opinion and in view of the increasing prominence of some homeland leaders, these avenues of action cannot be contemplated too lightly. Historical issues in the region seem likely to raise their gory heads again.

V. Brief Conclusions Relevant to the Theory of Pluralism

The evidence from South African history points to the importance of distinctions between groups existing at the time of the very earliest contact between the different population segments of the plural society. This accords with a point which John Rex makes in developing his theoretical views on race relations.[56] These distinctions involve differential evaluation of the cultures of the groups making contact. It is not the characteristics of the culture as such, but how they are viewed by the groups involved which is critical. The group which has the most power, whether in the form of war technology or appropriate internal organisation, will be able to impose, in Rex' terms, an ascriptive role, or a lower status, on other groups. Very early on in the history of colonial settlement in South Africa, an inferior status-role in community interaction was allocated to (indeed, enforced upon) the Khoisan peoples and the black slaves, setting a pattern of white dominance which has been reinforced by historical events right up to the present.

However, the South African situation provides evidence that this type of cultural distinction, and the differences in basic institutions which may accompany it, may not be sufficient to maintain the rigid segmentation in the absence of other factors. The discussion of the early history suggests that acculturation was fairly widespread, and that social acceptance of freed slaves and people of mixed blood was not unusual at a certain stage. It seems that the society might have undergone a process of <u>depluralisation</u> if frontier conflict and the economic value of subservient Coloured labour had not reinforced distinctions based on pigmentation and ethnic identity. The early history of Natal shows how positive attempts on the part of colonists to encourage deculturation and acculturation to western values among Zulus were in no way associated with any later social acceptance of 'westernised' Zulus on a basis of equality. If South Africa is an important example of the Plural Society, it suggests that culture or ethnicity alone is not sufficient in itself as an analytical basis for a deeply divided society with a hierarchical ordering of the component communities.[57]

The results of the empirical study of white voter attitudes, and in particular the <u>general</u> factor isolated by means of the factor analysis, mirror the consequence of South Africa's historical development in which ethnicity, nationalism, material interests, and status-concern have become articulated into a complex and internally self-reinforcing process, which in turn has produced a general "culture of racism" in which the original parameters of the constituent factors have become obscured. A clearly identifiable "ethos" of cultural pluralism exists in the attitudes of only a minority of white Afrikaners, albeit a significant minority.

Political developments in recent years and likely future trends, however, appear likely to reinforce the ethnic basis of conflict in the unified economy of Southern Africa. While it is incorrect to see the genesis of conflict in Southern Africa only in terms of cultural or ethnic Pluralism, such divisions have remained so salient to structure and processes within the society that the theories of the Plural Society have a critical relevance to the situation. Despite this assertion, however, this analysis suggests that it is incorrect to assume that cultural and ethnic differences in themselves and by themselves can offer a basis for complete explanation of South Africa's divided society.

NOTES

1. Malcolm Cross "On Conflict, Race Relations, and the Theory of the Plural Society", *Race* 12(4), 1971, 492.

2. J. S. Furnivall *Colonial Policy and Practice* (London: Cambridge University Press, 1948).

3. M. G. Smith's main theoretical contributions in Leo Kuper and M. G. Smith (eds.) Pluralism in Africa (Berkeley: University of California Press, 1969), 27-65, 91-151 and 415-458.

4. Furnivall, *op.cit*., 311.

5. John Rex "The Plural Society: The South African Case", *Race* 12(4), 1971, 402-413.

6. M. G. Smith "Some Developments in the Analytic Framework of Pluralism" in Kuper and Smith (eds.), *op.cit*., 415-458.

7. Cross, *op.cit*., 485.

8. Leo Kuper "Plural Societies: Perspective and Problems" in Kuper and Smith (eds.), *op.cit*., 14.

9. Leo Kuper "Political Change in White Settler Societies: The Possibility of Peaceful Democratisation" in Kuper and Smith (eds.), *op.cit*., 174.

10. Leo Kuper "Ethnic and Racial Pluralism" in Kuper and Smith (eds.) *op.cit*., 460.

11. Rex, *op.cit*.

12. The major part of ensuing discussion draws heavily on the material in I. D. Maccrone *Race Attitudes in South Africa* (Johannesburg: Witwaterstrand University Press, 1957).

13. Winthrop Jordan *White over Black: American Attitudes Toward the Negro 1550-1812* (Baltimore: Penguin, 1968) Chapter 1.

14. Maccrone, *op.cit*., 41.

15. Leonard Thompson "The South African Dilemma" in Louis Hartz (ed.) *The Founding of New Societies* (New York: Harcourt Brace, 1964) 182 and F. A. van Jaarsveld *The Afrikaner's Interpretation of South African History* (Cape Town: Simondium, 1964) 5.

16. Maccrone, *op.cit*., 33, 74, 123.

17. Based on thoughts expressed in E. Wester "The Origin of South African Racism, 1652-1850" (unpublished paper, Department of Sociology, University of Natal, 1973) following an analysis by Stanislav Andreski "Reflections on the South African Social Order from a Comparative Viewpoint" in Heribert Adam (ed.) *South Africa: Sociological Perspectives* (London: Oxford University Press, 1971).

18. Maccrone, _op.cit._, 93.

19. _Ibid._, 123.

20. _Ibid._, 44, 47-49.

21. _Ibid._, 70-73, and van Jaarsveld, _op.cit._, 5.

22. Maccrone, _op.cit._, 130.

23. G. M. Theal _History of South Africa South of the Zambesi, 2_ (London: Allen and Unwin, 1922) 465.

24. Maccrone, _op.cit._, 113.

25. _Ibid._, 126, _passim_ and van Jaarsveld, _op.cit._

26. Maccrone, _op.cit._, 127, 129.

27. van Jaarsveld, _op.cit._, 6.

28. See the decisions of the Cape Synod in 1820 and 1857 and the official resistance to segregation. T. N. Hanekom (ed.) _Ons Nederduitse Gereformeerde Kerk_, 319.

29. Maccrone, _op.cit._, 135.

30. D. J. P. Haasbroek "The Interpretation of Race Attitudes by African Historians" _Humanitas_ 2(1), 1972, 47-52 and Haasbroek "The Origins of Apartheid in South Africa" _Historia_ 16(1), 1971, 9-29.

31. Thompson, _op.cit._, 206.

32. Robert Godlonton _Irruption of the Kaffir Hordes_, discussed in Haasbroek "Origins of Apartheid", _op.cit._

33. David Welsh _The Roots of Segregation_ (Cape Town: Oxford University Press, 1971) 41.

34. _Ibid._,

35. _Ibid._, Chapter 4.

36. Haasbroek, _op.cit._

37. P. Lewsen "The Cape Liberal Tradition: Myth or Reality?" ISMA paper No. 26, 1969, Institute for the Study of Man in Africa, Johannesburg: and T. R. H. Davenport _The Afrikaner Bond, 1880-1911_ (London: Oxford University Press, 1966).

38. N. Mansergh _South Africa, 1906-1961: The Price of Magnanimity_ (London: Allen and Unwin, 1962) 72, (quoting Churchill).

39. D. Denoon _Southern Africa Since 1809_ (London: Longman, 1972) 69, 71, 79, 94

40. C. W. de Kiewiet _A History of South Africa: Social and Economic_ (London: Oxford University Press, 1957) Chapter 8, and Denoon, _op.cit._, Chapter 13.

41. de Kiewiet, _op.cit._, 181.

42. Denoon, _op.cit_., 67.

43. Haasbroek, _op.cit_.

44. _Ibid_.

45. N. J. Rhoodie _Apartheid and Racial Partnership in Southern Africa_ (Pretoria: Academica, 1969) Chapter II (i).

46. G. V. Doxey _The Industrial Colour Bar in South Africa_ (Cape Town: Oxford University Press, 1961) Chapter 6.

47. T. Dunbar Moodie _Power, Apartheid and the Afrikaner Civil Religion_ (Berkeley: University of California Press, 1974) Chapter 2.

48. L. Schlemmer _Privilege, Prejudice and Parties_ (Johannesburg: South African Institute of Race Relations, 1973). The co-author, Dr. Rick Turner, is banned and his name is not associated with the publication, with his agreement). A comparison of our sampling results and responses with the results of opinion polls showed that the responses tend to be representative of the country as a whole. The sample was a two-stage randam sample of white dwelling units in Durban. Interviews were conducted by trained interviewers who motivated respondents to complete the 90 statement attitude inventory.

49. Moodie, _op.cit_.

50. Standard Varimax programme. The Factor Analysis of 90 attidudinal and 7 demographic variables yielded 26 factors with 70% explanation of total variance. The 5 factors discussed in the test were those with the highest explanation of variance; the percentage for the 5 being ± 30%.

51. Mainly those conducted by Mark en Meningsopnames, published in _Rapport_, 1970, 1971, 1972.

52. L. Schlemmer _Employment Opportunity and Race in South Africa_ (University of Denver: Centre for International Relations, Studies in Race and Nations Series, 1973).

53. L. Schlemmer "White Interests and the Bantustans" _Third World_ 2(6), June 1973.

54. L. Schlemmer _Employment Opportunity and Race in South Africa_.

55. L. Schlemmer "City or Tribal Homeland" _Social Forces_, 51, December 1972.

56. John Rex _Race Relations in Sociological Theory_ (London: Weidenfeld and Nicholson, 1970) 132.

57. Here I am substantially in agreement with Rex "The Plural Society: The South African Case" _op.cit_.

Chapter Eight

OPPOSITION IN SOUTHERN AFRICA: SEGMENTS, LINKAGES, AND COHESION

Sheridan Johns

White power in Southern Africa is no longer so securely entrenched as it was at the start of 1974. The immediate catalyst for its present erosion came not from within the region, but from within the ranks of the Portuguese armed forces. Yet without the sustained guerrilla challenge to continued white Portuguese domination in Mozambique and Angola it is not likely that the Armed Forces Movement within Portugal would have moved so quickly to oust the Caetano regime. In Rhodesia, the success of the African nationalist movement in neighboring Mozambique and determined pressure from both guerrilla forces directed by exiled nationalist leaders and the barely-tolerated legal African opposition organizations within the country have unquestionably contributed to the testy willingness of the Rhodesian government to sit at a conference table with all African opposition groups. Further south, the "black consciousness movement", black workers' groups and the actions of Chief Gatsha Buthelezi, as well as other Bantustan leaders, indicate a new black assertiveness in the South African heartland of white power. With the withdrawal of the Portuguese from the region, and the apparent readiness of the white Rhodesian and South African governments to explore possibilities for accommodation with black Africa, opposition groups within the region assume even greater importance. It is to an examination of the nature and structure of opposition within particular territories of the region, as well as the linkages between groups within the region as a whole, that the following analysis is directed.

Several problems immediately present themselves in any effort to analyze opposition within Southern Africa. Initially, there is the question of definition -- what is meant by opposition? To examine opposition to the *status quo* in the broadest sense is perhaps an impossible task -- certainly one beyond the scope of the present analysis. Instead the focus will be upon organized groups which have indicated their disagreement with the principle of white-minority rule as it is (or was) practised in South Africa, South African-controlled South West Africa, Rhodesia, and the Portuguese ex-colonies of Angola and Mozambique. In selecting such an approach it is recognized that concentration upon organizations may lead to an overemphasis upon their importance in a situation where developments beyond the organizational realm may have great significance for the overall evolution of the opposition movement. For example, an articulate "black power" group, such as the "black consciousness movement" in South Africa, even if suppressed by white authority, might have a great impact upon popular moods which would be difficult to detect and measure as well as being slow to translate itself into organizational structures or cohesive support for such structures. Similarly, widely-reported successful challenges by guerrilla movements in one territory have undoubtedly had considerable impact elsewhere in the region (for whites as well as blacks), with the most spectacular example being the reaction by black South Africans to the announcement that FRELIMO would come to power in an independent Mozambique. Accordingly, efforts will be made to assess the likelihood and significance of such developments although the center of analysis will be organized opposition as defined.

Even by restricting attention primarily to organizations, it is impossible to escape further problems. It has always been difficult to obtain accurate information upon the activities of opposition groupings, particularly in white-ruled territories where, of necessity, certain black political organizations must operate illegally or semi-legally, and other groups do not receive regular attention from the press or political analysts. Perforce reliance must be placed upon journalistic reports, controlled government press releases, and partisan political tracts. Yet within the limitations imposed by the nature of the data available, it is possible to obtain sufficient information to indicate the configuration of opposition organizations becomes controversial in relation to those groups which seem to have accepted elements of the established system and operate within it, yet simultaneously express their disagreement with specific policies or even broader principles underlying the existing order. Whether or not such groups should be considered part of the organized opposition will be determined by an examination of the specifics of the group and its situation.

Rather than focusing discussion upon opposition groups on a territory-by-territory basis, it seems more useful for analytical purposes to suggest broader categories which would apply to groupings in several, if not all, of the territories within the region (i.e. Angola, Botswana, Lesotho, Mozambique, Rhodesia, South Africa, South West Africa and Swaziland). One component of the opposition is governments and ruling parties, a category until 1975 comprising the governments and the dominant parties of the three black-ruled states of the region, Botswana, Lesotho, and Swaziland. With the changes in the status of Mozambique and Angola governments of quite different origin are being added to this grouping. A second category of the opposition is _legal non-governing parties_ which includes both the opposition parties in Botswana and Lesotho as well as opposition parties in South Africa and Rhodesia committed to movement away from white-minority rule. A third component of the opposition is _legal extra-parliamentary_ political associations, a classification which encompasses specifically political organizations operating outside of the national parliamentary arena, either because they are excluded by law from national parliamentary competition or because they do not accept white-defined political structures; within this category fall such diverse groups as the African National Council of Rhodesia and the Black People's Convention of South Africa as well as the Transkei National Independence Party and other Bantustan leadership groupings which by South African law are restricted to participation in the government-recognized institutions of separate development. A quite different fourth category of opposition is _illegal political associations_, comprised of specifically political organizations which have been or remain banned from operation in their own territories; among the organizations in this category would be the African National Congress (ANC) of South Africa, Pan-Africanist Congress (PAC) of South Africa, Unity Movement of South Africa, the South African Communist Party, Zimbabwe African National Union (ZANU), Zimbabwe African People's Union (ZAPU), Front For the Liberation of Zimbabwe (FROLIZI), _Frente de Libertacao de Mocambique_ (FRELIMO), _Comite Revolucionairio de Mocambique_ (COREMO), _Movimento Popular de Libertacao de Angola_ (MPLA), _Frente Nacional de Libertacao de Angola_ (FNLA), and _Uniao Nacional para a Independencia Total de Angola_ (UNITA). The fifth component of the opposition is _uniracial non-political associations_, a category including groups whose membership is defined in some fashion in racial terms and whose goals are not primarily or exclusively political; examples of organizations falling within this category would be the Black Sash, the South African Student Organization (SASO), and black trade unions. The sixth and final component of the opposition is _multiracial non-political associations_, a category comprised of groups whose membership is either explicitly multi-racial or non-restrictive in terms of race and whose goals are also not primarily or exclusively political; the most prominent groupings under this heading would be various religious and student organizations.

Governments and Ruling Parties

To what extent the governments and ruling parties of the initial three black-ruled states of Southern Africa can be considered part of the opposition to the maintenance of white-minority rule in the region is a matter of subjective judgement in the case of each government and its ruling party. Each of the parties (Bosotho National Party - Lesotho, Botswana Democratic Party - Botswana, Imbokodvo National Movement - Swaziland) and the governments which they formed and have controlled since before the independence of their countries have exhibited a pattern of both collaboration and dissociation with the white-minority regimes of southern Africa. It is possible, however, to discern in the actions of the parties and the governments differences in nuance, if not in substance, which allow judgements to be made about their potential as foci of opposition to the existing system.

The Botswana Democratic Party and the government of Botswana, which the former has led since 1965 as a result of successive victories in three general elections, seem to have established the most consistently outspoken stance of opposition to white-minority rule.[1] Although the Botswana Democratic Party was received favorably by the Nationalist Party government of South Africa after its initial electoral campaign against rival parties which at the time had strong pan-Africanist links, the actions of the party since its assumption of power have been in the direction of disengagement from the white minority regimes of the region.

In symbolic terms, the Botswana Democratic Party and the government of Botswana have quietly but unequivocally distanced themselves from their neighbours and associated themselves with independent black Africa to the north of the Zambesi. At its first postindependence annual conference, the Botswana Democratic Party pointedly invited leaders of the then multi-racial opposition Progressive Party of South Africa as featured foreign guests. Three years later in 1970, a high-level representative of TANU of Tanzania addressed the conference and in 1973 the featured foreign speaker was the vice-president of Zambia. Government leaders have repeatedly reaffirmed their commitment to non-racial democracy and their condemnation of <u>apartheid</u> and the Unilateral Declaration of Independence (UDI) in Rhodesia. President Seretse Khama has never travelled to South Africa to meet the head of the Nationalist Party government, and his government has declined to exchange diplomats upon a regular basis until South Africa can guarantee that Botswana diplomats will in all respects, at all times, and in all places be treated the same as diplomats from any other country. Botswana has been unwilling to accept bilateral financial and technical aid directly from the South African government.

Although Botswana has always articulated its preference for a non-violent transition to majority rule in Southern Africa, it has refused to endorse South African initiatives for dialgoue without pre-conditions. Instead, after a brief period during which Botswana offered its territory as a meeting place for white and black Africa, Botswana gave unqualified endorsement to the proposal that white-minority governments should be required to accept the principle of majority rule as a precondition for dialogue. More recently, President Seretse Khama expressed "Full support for the struggle the oppressed peoples are waging in all the unliberated areas of Africa".[2] On two other diplomatic fronts Botswana has also asserted its sovereignty to the evident displeasure of its white-ruled neighbours: links with Zambia have been progressively expanded and non-resident diplomatic relations have been established with the Soviet Union (and several other European communist states); in early 1974 Botswana recognized the People's Republic of China.

In certain vital political matters, however, Botswana has been careful not to stretch its links with South Africa and Rhodesia to the breaking point. It has maintained correct relations with South Africa through direct personal contact and by telephone upon an *ad hoc* basis. While Botswana has refused to deal with the government of post-UDI Rhodesia, forbidden the transport of petroleum goods and military items across its territory to Rhodesia, and limited its purchases from Rhodesia, it has continued to break sanctions when it has deemed it absolutely essential for its own interests. It has maintained the policy of the British colonial administration in granting asylum to political refugees while simultaneously denying to them opportunity to organize for political action against any other state.

In the economic realm the Botswana government has embarked upon a far-reaching development plan designed to transform the economy from a stagnant pastoral appendage of South Africa to a mineral and beef exporting state linked to the major economic powers of Western Europe and North America. With the prospects of significantly increased internally-generated revenue at hand the Botswana government has been able to assert more forcefully its desires for revision of the quadripartite customs agreement with South Africa, Lesotho, and Swaziland (successfully renegotiated to the advantage of Botswana, Lesotho, and Swaziland in 1969), and for changes in transportation arrangements through South Africa. With the failure to negotiate an acceptable revision of the nature of the Rand monetary zone, the Botswana government announced in 1974 its decision to establish its own currency. Yet Botswana simultaneously recognizes that it will remain dependent upon South Africa (and to a far lesser extent Rhodesia and Mozambique) for its access to the sea and for a substantial portion of its manufactured imports. Indeed, its accelerated economic development, financed in the vital mineral sector primarily by South African private capital, im many ways ties Botswana even closer within the Southern African system -- although it does also open new possibilities for diversification of Botswana's dependence beyond the region.

While Botswana has sought to reorient itself away from the white-minority regimes of Southern Africa to the extent deemed compatible with its economic and geographical inextricability, the ruling party and government of Lesotho initially sought affinity with South Africa to a degree judged by many to be unnecessary even given the apparently intractable economic and geographical disabilities from which Lesotho suffers.[3] In the territory's first general election in 1965, the Basotho National Party under Chief Leabua Jonathan willingly accepted material support from the Nationalist government of South Africa. Although Chief Jonathan criticized _apartheid_ he advocated the strongest possible economic ties with South Africa. Once in office at the head of a government based upon a narrow parliamentary majority but a minority electoral vote, Chief Jonathan proceeded to act in a fashion seemingly designed to secure South African aid in return for support from his government.

Although the Lesotho government participated in the Organization of African Unity (OAU) and sought to expand diplomatic contacts in independent black Africa, the leadership of the Basotho National Party made little effort to establish links with other African parties, most of which, in any case, looked askance upon the line which the Basotho National Party continued to espouse. Concerning the sensitive question of political refugees from South Africa, the government maintained an official posture similar to that of Botswana, but certain refugees, many of whom had been sympathetic to the opposition parties in Lesotho, were harassed by the government and even a few, with apparent particularly close association with Chief Jonathan's domestic political enemies, were deported to South Africa. At one time, Chief Jonathan threatened to deport all political refugees whether or not they could obtain safe conduct from South Africa. Although Lesotho has yet to exchange diplomats with its neighbour, Chief Jonathan travelled to South Africa twice for official meetings with the republic's Prime Minister. Lesotho accepted direct financial assistance from the South African government as well as the secondment of South African civil servants to key posts within the Lesotho government, but it was unsuccessful in negotiating sufficient aid to proceed with the vital Malibamatso hydroelectric project which would supply power and water to the energy-hungry Witwatersrand. In a number of instances, Chief Jonathan endorsed proposals of the South African government for closer economic cooperation within Southern Africa. The apogee of Lesotho's identification with South Africa's diplomacy came in the wake of Chief Jonathan's preemptive coup d'etat of January, 1970, in which he blocked the opposition Basutoland Congress Party from taking the reins of government which it had apparently won in the country's second general election. In the year and a half following the coup the Lesotho government prominently pressed efforts to further dialogue between South Africa and independent black Africa, associating itself with initiatives of the Ivory Coast and Malawi.

Yet since late 1971 Chief Jonathan and the Lesotho government have veered away from their earlier apparent closeness to South African regime. The signal of the shift in Lesotho's position came in a particularly sharp attack upon _apartheid_ delivered by Chief Jonathan at Lesotho's fifth independence anniversary celebrations. At about the same time, Lesotho apparently successfully persuaded the Ivory Coast and its Francophone supporters to drop their courtship of South Africa; subsequently government spokesmen have openly criticized a range of South African policies including attempts to block industrial developments in Lesotho which would compete against established South African entrepreneurs. South African civil servants upon secondment have been removed in a number of instances. Government spokesmen have also publicly affirmed their moral support of African liberation movements.[4]

The changed stance of the Lesotho government does not mark a complete _volte face_. Chief Jonathan and his government have never wavered in their declared opposition to _apartheid_. Even in the years of Lesotho's apparent closeness to South Africa, Chief Jonathan resisted attempts of the republican government to have him visit the nearby Transkei and thus associate himself with the policy of separate development. Lesotho has also been forthright in its condemnation of Rhodesian UDI. Nevertheless, the more recent escalation of verbal confrontation with South Africa does represent a shift from the past. It has been suggested that it is a tactic to rally support within Lesotho for Chief Jonathan's policies of enforced national reconciliation and to press South Africa to come to terms upon the key Malibamatso hydroelectrical scheme.[5] Whether or not Chief Jonathan is now operating from a position of increased strength within Lesotho as a consequence of the authoritarian structure which he has consolidated since his 1970 coup, the new posture is likely to continue. In symbolic terms Lesotho's opposition to white minority rule has now become more salient.

Such a pose does not mean, however, that Lesotho will move beyond verbal challenges to South Africa; it remains in economic thralldom to its neighbour and, if anything, further development will add to the links between the two economies.

Swaziland initially steered a course between the positions of Botswana and Lesotho.[6] In the early 1960s King Sobhuza and the traditional Swazi elite associated with him accepted advice and support from resident white settlers and South Africans associated with the Nationalist Party; when they formed the Imbokodvo National Movement to block pan-Africanist opposition parties support was accepted from white South African sources. Yet, even prior to independence, once King Sobhuza and the Imbododovo National Movement had secured their base of power against challengers within Swazi society, they moved away from close association with their erstwhile white allies within Swaziland. In external affairs the Swazi government has neither sought close identification with South Africa nor has it attempted to question sharply the broader status quo within Southern Africa. Rather, it has concentrated its efforts internally to strengthen its rule and to continue diversified economic development within a pattern of more complex dependence upon South Africa and Mozambique.

In many ways, Swaziland's stance seems closer to that of Lesotho, prior to late 1971. Like Lesotho, Swaziland has accepted South African financial and technical assistance and its prime minister has travelled to South Africa to meet with his republican counterpart. Swaziland has continued to give asylum to political refugees, but it has been generally unwilling to allow them to remain in the country, particularly since many of them have given support to the opposition to the Swazi government. Thus, Swaziland has deported many refugees, for the most part getting them safe conduct northward to Zambia or Tanzania. Like Lesotho, Swaziland has also sought to extend diplomatic contact in independent Africa, especially to east and central Africa which offer potentially profitable markets for Swazi minerals and agricultural products. Swaziland, like Lesotho, has also made no move to establish links with communist countries. In intra-African and international councils Swazi diplomats, like those of Lesotho, have strongly condemned the white Rhodesian regime, while voicing more muted opposition to apartheid. (Understandably, the Swazi government refused to condemn Portugal upon which it was dependent for its rail access to the sea through neighboring Mozambique.)

Yet Swaziland's diplomatic posture differed in emphasis from the pre-1971 stance of Lesotho. The distinctiveness of its position became evident during South Africa's campaign to open a dialogue with black Africa. Unlike Botswana, Swaziland did not fully associate itself with the majority of the OAU in opposition to dialogue on South Africa's terms. At the same time Swaziland, unlike Lesotho, did not actively identify itself with the efforts of the Ivory Coast to accept South Africa's proferred hand of friendship. Instead, in the key OAU vote Swaziland abstained and subsequently maintained a low profile on the matter.

The potential role of the government and the ruling party of Swaziland in any opposition to the existing system of white-minority rule in Southern Africa was revealingly suggested by events surrounding the abrogation of the Swaziland constitution and the assumption of full power by King Sobhuza II in April, 1973. In response to what was apparently perceived as a threat to the maintenance of royal power King Sobhuza II acting on his own established a small Swazi army with weapons bought from South Africa. Shortly thereafter, he repealed the independence constitution under which the opposition party had gained three out of twenty-four elected seats in parliament in the second general election held in May, 1972 and government efforts to prevent the seating of an opposition member had been blocked by the courts. Taking all powers of government into his own hands King Sobhuza II banned political parties and promised a new constitution in accord with traditional Swazi practices.

The actions of King Sobhuza II once again spotlighted his paramount concern to secure the power of the traditionally-based Swazi political structure over modernizing Swazi society. To further this end, he apparently had no qualms to use arms from South Africa's insurance for his move in the same fashion that earlier in the 1960s he had sought and accepted South African aid to block the pan-Africanist challengers to his position. The government of Swaziland remains preoccupied with the internal political dynamics of its own country, and not with the possibilities for transformation throughout Southern Africa. Undoubtedly it will continue to voice its opposition to white-minority rule in South Africa and Rhodesia, but it is improbable that it will give high priority to articulating even a symbolic campaign of verbal challenge to its neighbors.

The government and ruling parties of the three long-established black-ruled states in Southern Africa unquestionably pose no military challenge to the might of their white-ruled neighbors, nor are they likely to be focal points for significant political pressures of other types against the regimes of South Africa and Rhodesia. With the exception of Swaziland, none of the states maintains an army -- and Swaziland's recent tiny force was created with help from South Africa. There are no indications that any of the regimes will change their existing policies to allow refugee opposition groups to organize openly within their borders for political action against their neighbors. Although their economic fortunes are rising, the three states remain economically beholden to their neighbors, perhaps even more so as development schemes fuelled by outside capital begin to gather momentum. Yet within the differing constraints faced by each state the three regimes have maneuvered to assert patterns of sovereignty contrasting with those of their white-ruled neighbors. Particularly in the case of Botswana symbolic assertions of independence have provoked unhappiness from the dominant white power. To the degree that the governments have been regarded as successful by opponents of white-minority rule they have served as demonstrations of the viability of a black-dominated multiracial alternative within Southern Africa. To this extent the government and ruling parties of Botswana, Lesotho, and Swaziland continue to have a potential as a possible psychological rallying point for opposition to the status quo -- either in a multiracial context or from a black-oriented perspective. Yet even if such a potential could be realized it would be, at best, only a preliminary way station -- albeit possibly a necessary one -- on the path to a broader direct organizational challenge to the remaining centre of white power.

With the change in status of the previously illegal political associations of the former Portuguese colonies of Angola and Mozambique (see below) there are appearing within the region governments and ruling parties with histories sharply at variance with those of their counterparts in Botswana, Lesotho, and Swaziland. Achieving power through armed struggle and the willingness of the new Portuguese government to grant independence to them, the governments of Mozambique and Angola represent movements which successfully challenged the prior status quo in the vast northeastern and northwestern areas of the Southern African region. In their struggles they were dedicated to a radical transformation of their own societies and allied with illegal political associations from the remaining white-ruled territories enunciating similar goals. Once in power, it is unlikely that they will abandon these goals. Yet in the case of Mozambique much of its economy, symbolized by the now operative Cabora Bassa hydroelectric project, is presently closely linked with South Africa and Rhodesia; it is possible that the Mozambique government, like that of newly-independent Zambia a decade earlier, will not move precipitously to direct confrontation --

thus its challenge to its white-ruled neighbors is likely to be carefully structured to avoid provoking unduly harsh retaliation while slowly, but steadily, seeking disengagement and the achievement of its long-term goal of the end of white-minority rule in the region. In the case of Angola, more distant from the heartland of white power and contiguous only to Namibia, it can be surmised that a more militant stance might be maintained but its impact may be limited to the extent that the three liberation movements within the territory become preoccupied with either their pre-independence antagonisms or a concerted effort at national reconciliation. Although this focus upon domestic affairs would be rooted in a completely different situation from that of Swaziland or Lesotho, its consequences, in the short run, with respect to a further direct challenge to continuing white might within the region might be similar.

Legal Non-Governing Parties

Legal non-governing parties within the states of Southern Africa are in an even weaker position than the governing parties to challenge the existing *status quo* in the region. Yet many of the parties have been on record for more than a decade in favour of forthright moves to dismantle the structure of white hegemony. Their lack of success in achieving any influence is a testament to their generally peripheral nature within the existing system. If anything, most legal non-governing parties have lost any minimal potential to influence events which they might once have possessed.

In the black-ruled states of Botswana, Lesotho, and Swaziland the parties which came to be the opposition parties after the first general elections held in the mid-1960s were the earliest political parties, or splinters thereof, in each of the territories (Botswana - Bechuanaland People's Party headed by Philip Mantante, Botswana Independence Party headed by Motsamai Mpho; Lesotho - Basutoland Congress Party headed by Ntsu Mokhehle, Marematlou Freedom Party headed by Dr. Seth Makotoko; Swaziland - Ngwane National Liberatory Congress headed by Dr. Ambrose Zwane).[7] The leaders were relatively well-educated men involved in the small modern sectors of territorial life; they directed the appeals of their parties particularly to the minority of the population resident in towns and engaged in salaried work or industrial labor. Many of the leaders had been previously directly involved in African nationalist politics in South Africa or they had links with either the ANC or the PAC which had broken from it in 1959. From the inception of political activity in their territories the parties put forth programs which demanded rapid moves to full independence and radical changes in the existing colonial structure of society. The parties identified fully with the efforts of other African nationalist organizations, particularly in South Africa and Rhodesia, to end white-minority rule. Much of their platforms were couched in the rhetoric of anti-imperialism and pan-Africanism, and all of the parties maintained links with pan-Africanist groupings in independent black Africa and with international anti-imperialist organizations in which communist and third world militants were dominant.

Their political strategies were to a large extent modelled upon those pursued by the mass-based nationalist parties which had gained independence from colonial rule in west and east Africa. Yet the inappropriateness of such strategies for Botswana and Swaziland, if not Lesotho, was made apparent when the parties were defeated by the present ruling parties. The latter cast their appeal to the more traditionally-based groups in each country, eschewed radical rhetoric for more moderate language and explicitly expressed their willingness to work with neighboring white-minority governments, of which they did not approve, to the extent necessary for the development of their countries. Once defeated, the earliest nationalist parties were cast in an opposition role and cut off from the resources of government which their victorious opponents used in various fashions to enhance their power. To the degree that the ruling parties were able to take credit for the achievement of independence and for what economic development followed in its wake the opposition parties were additionally weakened. Furthermore, their pan-Africanist credentials were undercut to the extent that the new governments were able to establish their *bona fides* among independent black states and within the OAU.

Only in Lesotho, where the major opposition groups, the Basutoland Congress Party, and its smaller ally, the Marematlou Freedom Party, had actually won a majority of the votes cast in the 1965 general election did prospects for the opposition remain promising. Yet the very possibility of achieving electoral success in the general election to be held by 1970 encouraged the Basutoland Congress Party to moderate its stance. Acceptance by the Basutoland Congress Party of the post-independence constitutional rules of the game also led the party to mute its previous policy of outspoken antagonism to South Africa. In Swaziland and Botswana the opposition parties also seemed to recognize uneasily that they would have to accept the necessity of working within the regional *status quo*.

Presently the opposition political parties of the three countries are even more insignificant elements of any opposition within the region to white-minority rule. In Swaziland political parties have been banned, and the government has proclaimed that the country's new constitution will be based upon traditional Swazi political practices. In Lesotho, Chief Jonathan declared a five-year "holiday" on partisan political activity. Although the leaders of the opposition parties were released from detention and some accepted Chief Jonathan's invitation to participate in a process of national reconciliation the present Lesotho government has made it clear that the country will not return to a Westminister model in any future constitution. Only in Botswana are there still fully legal non-governing parties. Each of the three parties, including the Botswana National Front, an uneasy amalgam of traditionalists and modernists formed in 1965 in addition to the two pre-existent opposition parties, has at least one seat in parliament. Yet the apparent continuing strength of the ruling Botswana Democratic Party as manifest in its strong electoral victory in 1974 and the inability of the fragmented opposition to cooperate effectively make it unlikely that any of the present legal non-governing parties will influence policy, let alone accede to power.

The prospect of legal non-governing parties in the white-ruled states emerging as a component of significant opposition to the regional status quo is probably limited, yet cannot be fully ruled out. In the former Portuguese territories there were no such organizations. In Rhodesia the white opposition parties that have existed, including the present Rhodesian Party, not only have drawn little support among the whites, but, more significantly in this context, they have been concerned primarily with achieving settlement with Britain. Only the small Centre Party, now multiracial, has shifted to question some of the premises of white dominance; it is conceivable, although unlikely in the light of Zambian experience, that it could play a role in any transition to African majority rule. The African parliamentary parties which have been permitted to exist have to varying degrees offered verbal challenges to the government, but they, too, draw little support from their own small black constituency and thus have no possibility of making their challenges more credible. In South Africa, the situation is perhaps slightly different. No black parties, of course, have been permitted to operate in the national parliamentary arena. The white-led parties which have advocated a reversal of present government policy -- the multiracial Liberal Party which disbanded in 1968 in response to government legislation barring multiracial political parties, and the now all white Progressive Party -- have never received more than a small minority of white votes. (In the 1974 general election however, the Progessive Party sharply increased its vote, six new MP's being elected to join its longtime lone parliamentary representative, Helen Suzman). Although the Progessive Party continues its outspoken condemnation of many apartheid policies it remains powerless to bring about change within South Africa or the region which it dominates. By its continued existence it testifies that a minority of whites seem willing to entertain the possibility of a radical shift from the *status quo*, yet its very whiteness precludes it from ever becoming even a symbolic focal point for a majority-based movement to challenge white hegemony. It is possible, nevertheless, that it could play an intermediary role in the seemingly unlikely event that South Africa were to veer from its present political system.

Legal Extra-Parliamentary Political Associations

In the Southern African region there is a long and uneven history of activity by black extra-parliamentary political associations seeking expanded participation in government. In South Africa, the earliest center of such activity, the long-established African National Congress was the most prominent of the organizations pressuring white authority. Since 1960, however, the South African government has ruthlessly suppressed national black political organizations. In Rhodesia extra-parliamentary political associations emerged later than in South Africa, but they also achieved prominence in the postwar until they were choked off in the early 1960s. In the former Portuguese territories, however, organizations of this type were never allowed to develop.

Despite the suppression of most national extra-parliamentary political associations in the white-ruled states of the region there still remains a potential for such organizations in the short run to become a salient component of opposition to the *status quo* in South Africa and Rhodesia.

In Rhodesia the pre-December, 1974 experience of the African National Council indicated the range within which legal extra-parliamentary political associations could serve as centers of opposition to the regime. As long as the Rhodesian government left open the possibility of settlement with Britain and Britain demanded that any settlement have the approval of the African population there was a narrow field of maneuver outside of parliament, but within the law, for black political bodies. It is within this political space that the African National Congress was born and operated in the wake of the tentative agreement negotiated by Rhodesia and Britain in late 1971. Brought into existence specifically to oppose the agreement, the African National Council successfully mobilized African opposition before the Pearce Commission with the result that the latter body declared that the terms of the agreement had been rejected by the African population. Yet the very success of the African National Council brought it close to the limits of its power to influence events within Rhodesia. The white authorities stepped up their harrassment of the organization in 1973-74. Nevertheless, the African National Council sustained a sense of solidarity among

Africans; to this extent it had symbolic utility in the further development of organized opposition in Rhodesia. Its role was further legitimated by the Lusak unity agreement of December, 1974, under which the illegal bodies of ZANU, ZAPU, and FROLIZI placed themselves within the African National Council. It is evider that the reorganized African National Council, as long as it remains tolerated by the Rhodesian regime, has the potential to serve as a vehicle for the further mobilization of the African population in support of demands for the achievement of majority rule.

In South Africa it is the "latent dynamics of the contradictions of apartheid"[8] which provide an unevenly wider arena within which legal extra-parliamentary political associations can operate. Under the canons of apartheid Africans have been closed out of even indirect token participation in national political institutions and restricted to the subordinate institutions of separate development centered in the Bantustans. In order to maintain a modicum of credibility with Africans within the country as well as with key foreign supporters, the government has an incentive to appear to demonstrate that it is genuinely devolving some power to Africans who have accepted separate development. Bantustan leaders thus have a platform for political maneuver which is denied other Africans in South Africa. By demanding that the Nationali Party government implement fully its promises they have the potential to expose the inconsistencies of apartheid or to push the government into minor concessior which it otherwise might not make. Simultaneously with the relative immunity offered by their official positions within government-sanctioned institutions Bantustan leaders have the possibility to question Nationalist Party policies in a fashion that might not be tolerated from Africans outside Bantustan institutions.

It has taken some time for Bantustan leaders to begin to stretch the tether by which they are tied to the South African government. During the 1960s when the Transkei was the lone Bantustan with internal self-government there was litt effort made to challenge the fundamentals of Nationalist Party policy. Althougl the government of Kaiser Mantanzima did reverse Nationalist educational policy by substituting English for Xhosa as the medium of instruction, for the most part spokesmen of the Transkei government restricted their questioning to the pace and details of the implementation of separate development. Thus, their most noticed demands were those for an extension of the borders of the Transkei to include white-owned lands claimed as a part of the Xhosa patrimony.

With the quickening of the pace of Bantustanization in the late 1960s -- (very probably as part of a coordinated government policy to prettify South Africa's image as a prospective partner in dialogue with black Africa) -- new platforms were created and additional opportunities were opened for articulation of African demands. The spotlight quickly shifted from Chief Kaiser Matanzima of the Transkei to Chief Gatsha Buthelezi of the newly-constituted KwaZulu Territorial Authority. Chief Buthelezi explicitly accepted his position as a Bantustan leader only when he felt all other possibilities for the advancement of his people's interests had been closed. He has not only sharply questioned the manner in which the South African government was attempting to impose its definition of separate development upon the Zulus in the matters of internal autonomy and the granting of land, but he has also moved to question some of the central tenets of government policy.[9]

Chief Buthelezi has argued forcefully that the inadequacy of funding from the South African government demands that Bantustan leaders have direct access to private South African capital as well as foreign capital and governmental assistance without going through white administrators. Refusing to accept the lines of racial separation drawn by the government, he has proposed that whites should be granted full citizenship to KwaZulu and that representatives of all South African racial groups should meet in a national convention to decide the future of the country. Perhaps more significantly in terms of African solidarity within South Africa he has rejected the ethnic compartmentalization upon which the Bantustans are based in calling for consultation among all Bantustan leaders to devise a coordinated strategy vis-a-vis the government to further accelerate the process of devolution of power to Africans. He has moved completely outside of the Bantustan framework to endorse the cultural dimensions of the "black consciousness movement" (see below); simultaneously, he has encouraged KwaZulu involvement in efforts to represent African workers and to strengthen their organizational capabilities.

Chief Buthelezi's forthrightness seems to have spurred Chief Matanzima to sharpen his demands upon Pretoria for more land, greater autonomy, and increased funds. But Chief Matanzima has also shifted to argue that resident whites could be citizens of the Transkei and that cooperation among Africans should be furthered to advance towards an eventual federation of black-ruled political units in southern Africa, including the presently independent states of Botswana, Lesotho, and Swaziland. Other Bantustan leaders have not sought so directly to question central elements of the Bantustan policy, but they have been increasingly forceful in their articulation of African demands concerning the need for more African land, the necessity for increased funds, and their unwillingness to accept decisions unilaterally imposed by white administrators.

There is no indication that the South African government is willing to concede any substance of its powers in realms which it considers essential. Thus, it is standing firm on its insistence that the land area of the Bantustans will not be enlarged beyond the relatively small increment authorized under legislation passed in 1936 (which would raise African-controlled land to only 13.7% of the total area of South Africa). Likewise, it has brusquely rejected suggestions for a national convention of all races to consider the future of the country, and it has also indicated its disagreement with the idea of citizenship for whites in the Bantustans. It has, however, apparently shifted its position to consider the possibility of direct foreign economic involvement with the Bantustan governments -- perhaps figuring that any outside funds attracted would both help its exchequer and its image while not diluting dangerously its control. It has also indicated its willingness to negotiate a speedup in the rate of the devolution of power to the point where political independence will be granted before the achievement of economic viability. Yet government spokesmen clearly indicate that they recognize that any such arrangements would leave any newly-independent former Bantustan overwhelmingly dependent upon South Africa despite the fact of its political sovereignty.

The South African government now finds itself faced with far more complications in conducting its policy of separate development, but it still commands the means and shows the determination to contain the new currents which have appeared. There is little prospect that the Bantustans will in the foreseeable future provide any bases for more than verbal confrontations with (and occasional embarrassment of) the South African government, yet the recent assertiveness of Bantustan leaders is not without significance in the long range evolution of opposition to the existing order within Southern Africa. In a situation where almost all other avenues for aboveground African political maneuver within the heartland of white power remain closed, the leaders of the Bantustans can serve not only as foci for the heightening of existing ethnic feeling, but also as centers around which new patterns of trans-ethnic African solidarity might coalesce. To the extent that they rise above the government-defined ethnic divisions upon which their offices formally rest and seek to exploit, within the constraints of their position, contradictions of apartheid, the leaders of the Bantustans can further African unity consciously (and even possibly unconsciously). Should their efforts to push the government to fulfil its promises for separate development meet increasing resistance from white authority, their activities may also have the unintended by-product of making non-legal alternatives more attractive for a new generation of Africans despite the evident obstacles to such a course of action.

The opportunities for black extra-parliamentary political associations outside of the Bantustan structures are paradoxically both greater and lesser than those within the structures. Unencumbered by any allegiance to the framework of separate development, such bodies have more latitude to question directly the basic principles of apartheid. On the other hand, should such associations move to mount what the government would perceive as even a potential threat to its control, it would not hesitate to suppress the association or its leadership. The symbolic potential and the organizational weakness of such groups are illuminated in the activities of the Black People's Convention within South Africa and the National Convention of South West Africa.

The Black People's Convention represents the first national black specifically political organization formed since the banning of the ANC and the PAC.[10] Including in its membership not only Africans, but also Indians and Coloureds; the inaugural conference of the Black People's Convention met in July, 1972, to unite South African blacks into a single political organization to realize "liberation and emancipation from both psychological and physical oppression." In line with the tenets of the broader "black consciousness movement" (see below) of which it can be considered a part, the Black People's Convention has rejected participation in the Bantustans and stated its intention of developing programs to stimulate black pride and to further cooperative self-reliance among blacks. To date the organization seems to have caught the imagination of elements of the black urbanized elite, but it apparently has not openly undertaken any exclusively political activity which could challenge the government outside of the symbolic realm. Yet the arrest of its secretary-general in late 1974 indicates its exposed position. Should the articulation of its position even at the symbolic level seem further to threaten the government, there seems little doubt that the government would move to decapitate the entire leadership through banning orders, house arrest, or imprisonment (as it has done with the leadership of the South African Student Organization), or, if it considers it necessary, to ban the organization completely (as it did with the ANC and the PAC).

Although South West Africa in so many respects has been integrated into the system prevailing within South Africa, the Nationalist Party government still apparently retains some inhibitions against complete integration out of deference to particular United Nations interest in the former mandated territory. Thus, neither the South West African People's Organization (SWAPO) nor the quiescent South West African National Union (SWANU), whose external representatives advocate and organize for armed struggle within the territory, have been banned in South West Africa. Local representatives of both organizations, along with representatives of ethnically-based groups which, however, reject separate development (e.g. Chief Clements Kapuuo of the Herero Council, leaders of the Rehobeth Volksparty) joined together in February, 1972, to form the National Convention. When Dr. Alfred Escher, the special representative of the United Nations Secretary-General, visited the territory in October, 1972, the Convention led a delegation to protest against South African policies in the territory. Yet were the Convention (or any other legal extra-parliamentary political organization) to organize what the government considered to be a potentially effective political force, it is doubtful that the government would hesitate to act against the key leaders of the organization -- although it might not ban the body outright. Recent government moves against SWAPO youth meetings and the arrest of selected SWAPO leaders point up the narrow parameters within which aboveground politics can take place. Nevertheless, the distinctive "international" status of South West Africa probably gives legal black political bodies slightly more latitude for manoeuver than the analgous bodies would have in South Africa. Accordingly they have significance out of proportion to their limited resources and their organizational weaknesses in the context of South Africa's ongoing "dialogue" with the United Nations and the outside world. Yet the constraints which such bodies face in organizing a direct frontal challenge to South African authority without outside support remain formidable, if not insuperable.

Illegal Political Associations

It is barely more than a decade that illegal political organizations have been important in the opposition to white-minority rule in Southern Africa. Their appearance followed directly from the continuing determination of the Portuguese, Rhodesian, and South African authorities to suppress all aboveground organizations and activities which might conceivably pose a challenge to the security of the established order. In the case of the ex-Portuguese colonies extra-parliamentary political associations were only occasionally tolerated, and they never established themselves firmly on a territorial basis. Thus, nationalist leaders in the late 1950s and early 1960s turned to underground organizations, dedicated to the mobilization of the population on a territory-wide basis. In contrast, in Rhodesia, South Africa, and South West Africa territorial-wide extra-parliamentary organizations were allowed to operate although under accelerating government harrassment with the exception of the Communist Party of South Africa which was banned in 1950. The leaders of these organizations clung to their legal existence. Only when they were banned by the white authorities in the early 1960s did they attempt to transform themselves into underground nationalist movements to carry on their opposition to minority rule.

In consequence of the absence of any legal avenues outside of government-sponsor organizations for expression of opposition in Angola and Mozambique illegal political associations took center stage. From their inception underground (MPLA - 1956) or in exile (FNLA - 1958; UNITA - 1966; FRELIMO - 1962; COREMO - 1964) these underground organizations committed themselves to the organization of armed struggle and the mobilization of the population in support of their activities to oust the Portuguese regime. Although unburdened by a "reformist" past, both Angolan and Mozambican organizations suffered from internal frictions, fragmentation, and other problems of what John Marcum has identified as the "exile condition".[11] Yet all of the groups, with the exception of COREMO, were able to surmount their problems to organize increasingly effective challenges to the Portuguese regime.

The Portuguese responded to the armed challenge of the African nationalist parties by intensification of their counter-insurgency programs. Quickened economic and social development, in tandem with harsher and more extensive methods of control, were employed to blunt the appeal of the nationalist parties in rural areas. The Portuguese were largely successful in retaining their preeminence in the major cities and in the most significant agricultural areas. Yet despite deep divisions between the nationalist bodies in Angola, and sometimes even within the movements, all of them stayed in the field. In Mozambique FRELIMO continued steadily to consolidate its position and in 1973-74 it dramatically expanded its activities southward and stepped up its military pressure on the Portuguese. The April 25 coup by the Armed Forces Movement in Portugal was, in large part, a testament to the success of FRELIMO and the Angolan guerrilla movements and they were quickly recognized by the new Portuguese government in its moves to decolonization. The rapid dismantling of the Portuguese colonial political order marks a dramatic transformation of the pre-coup regional system. In the process the previously illegal political associations have now been transformed into governments and ruling parties (although in Angola some of the nationalist groups or segments thereof may find themselves in opposition to a postindependence regime dominated by their longtime rivals).

In Rhodesia and South West Africa the experiences of illegal political organizations have been quite different from those of the former Portuguese colonies. Unlike in Angola and Mozambique illegal political associations in Rhodesia and South West Africa are direct descendants of extra-parliamentary political associations which were either banned by the government (ZAPU and ZANU in Rhodesia; FROLIZI was created by dissidents from the two organizations in exile) or so constricted by the shrinking parameters of legally allowable activity that elements of the leadership decided to go underground or into exile to more directly challenge the regime (SWAPO and SWANU in South West Africa). In both countries the now illegal political associations transferred their headquarters into exile from whence they reorganized for armed struggle. Like their counterparts in Angola and Mozambique the Zimbabwean and Namibian groups have experienced the syndrome of problems which mark the "exile condition". Their operations have been further complicated by the shift from non-violence to violence, the transition from legal to illegal activity, and the distinctive "international" statuses of both territories. In moving to organize for armed struggle the leaderships of the groups had to overcome the habits of the past as well as reservations among some of their supporters about the legitimacy and the efficacy of the new tactics. Their past legal existence initially left them much more exposed not only to police surveillance but to the full weight of the coercive machinery of the Rhodesian and South African regimes than might have been the case had they been illegal organizations from their birth. In South West Africa the remaining aboveground branches of SWAPO and SWANU have been severely constrained in their activities; whatever relationship they have with the internal underground organization and the exiled center must be greatly complicated. Hopes that the United Nations or Great Britain (in the case of Rhodesia) might act as an outside force to induce change without the territory very probably inhibited initial efforts to organize armed struggle; in any case efforts to influence the United Nations and British public opinion have demanded attention from the leaderships of the organizations which might otherwise have been directed towards internal activities.

Despite the difficulties under which they operated ZANU, ZAPU, and SWAPO all managed to initiate guerrilla actions within their countries in the mid-1960s. The catalysts of the undertakings were party militants infiltrated from exile, although in the case of the SWAPO actions in northern South West Africa it seems that considerable preparations were made within the territory utilizing locally-recruited manpower. After a brief period the counter-insurgency forces of the white regimes were able to defeat the guerrilla bands whose activities were limited mostly to relatively sparsely populated areas bordering upon, or close to, friendly foreign sanctuaries in Zambia or parts of Angola then dominated by friendly guerrilla forces. In 1967, however, Rhodesia was forced to call upon supplementary forces from South Africa to repel the thrusts of guerrilla bands comprised of members of both ZAPU and the ANC of South Africa; since that date South Africa has maintained an undisclosed number of police and soldiers in Rhodesia which it claims it will withdraw when fighting stops.

Before the early 1970s, the guerrilla actions of the nationalist groups in South West Africa and Rhodesia did not appear to have the potential to expand into a sustained challenge to white authority in the fashion that such challenges

were being maintained in Mozambique and Angola. There was little evidence that the guerrillas had strong support or firm organization in the areas in which they undertook operations; their activities seemed limited to sporadic hit-and-run attacks. Yet the mere fact that these actions occurred did force the white regime to extend and intensify their counter-insurgency preparations at the same time that they also perhaps served a symbolic purpose for segments of the African population.

Recent developments in the two territories suggest that they do possess the potential for a more effective challenge. In South West Africa, SWAPO has sustained guerrilla activity within the Caprivi Strip to the extent that South African forces have been substantially reinforced. At the same time within Ovamboland in northern South West Africa opposition to South African-backed leaders of the Ovambo Bantustan has been growing in tandem with group defiance of the strengthened police forces stationed in the area under terms of a state of emergency declared by the South African government.[12] These incidents do suggest the development of a situation in which it might be possible to mobilize elements of the population into underground nationalist structures which at some future date could confront white authority and its black allies, particularly if the South African government does not move to meet Namibian demands. During 1969-71 both ZAPU and ZANU exile groups were plagued by publicly visible internal dissensions which in the case of ZAPU led to a split in the organization followed by the creation of FROLIZI which also initially attracted to its ranks some supporters of ZANU. Nevertheless, from mid-1972 guerrilla activity intensified, particularly in the northeastern region adjoining Mozambique. For the first time it seems that the guerrillas in the region, affiliated with ZANU, received active support from the local population, suggesting that the armed encounters were preceded by more careful attention to underground mobilization and organization. Elsewhere in the country other guerrilla attacks continued, although not with the same intensity. The impact of the heightenend guerrilla activity in Rhodesia can be seen in the willingness of the Rhodesian regime to enter into negotiations with Zimbabwean nationalists, including the ZAPU and ZANU leaderships, in return for a ceasefire in the armed struggle. It remains to be seen whether, and at what speed, the Rhodesian regime will accede to the unchanged Zimbabwean demand for an end to white-minority rule. Should a mutually-acceptable compromise for evolution to majority rule be agreed upon by the Rhodesian regime and the enlarged ANC, the legal extra-parliamentary political association which now includes the illegal political associations of ZANU, ZAPU, and FROLIZI, it is probable that illegal political associations will no longer be so central to further change in the status quo in Rhodesia. Yet should negotiations fail it seems certain that once again they will reassert themselves, although perhaps not in the same organizational form, in armed struggle against white domination. In South West Africa, the immediate future is even more hazy, but it would seem safe to suggest that illegal political associations, committed to military confrontation, will attempt to expand their challenge unless the South African government, like the Rhodesian authorities, shows a willingness to enter into direct negotiations with Namibian nationalists.

In South Africa the most prominent illegal political associations (ANC, PAC, Unity Movement, and the South African Communist Party), like those in South West Africa and Rhodesia, are direct descendants of previously legal extra-parliamentary political associations whose leaders and membership had long histories of aboveground political activity prior to the banning of their organizations. Like their Namibian and Zimbabwean counterparts they, too, have suffered from the disabilities of their past orientation in attempting to mobilize and organize for armed struggle, largely under the direction of their exiled leaders. The leaderships of these organizations also initially clung to the hope that either changes in the international environment would lead the Nationalist Party government to modify its policies or limited acts of organized violence within the country would induce a shift in government policy out of fear of internal and external loss of confidence. Yet unlike their counterparts in South West Africa and Rhodesia, the South African illegal organizations have not yet been able to mount any challenge which seems to threaten white hegemony even at the periphery of territory controlled by their opponents.

It is beyond the purview of this analysis to examine in detail the reasons for the failure to date of South African illegal political organizations,[13] but in order to estimate the place of these groups within the ongoing opposition to white-minority rule it is relevant to delineate some of the features of their activities and their consequences for the future potential of the organizations. Whereas in the Portuguese colonies, and to a lesser extent in Rhodesia and South West Africa, the level of visible confrontation on the part of illegal political associations has risen, in South Africa a contrary pattern has prevailed. Frontal challenges to the regime peaked in the early and mid-1960s and since that time have declined. In the forefront of these activities were the sabotage campaigns organized jointly by the ANC and the Communist Party under the aegis of _Umkhonto we Sizwe_ and the more uncoordinated outbreaks of violence against white authority carried out by _Poqo_, an offshoot of the PAC. Both efforts suffered from internal frictions and organizational weaknesses, but ultimately both were unsuccessful in the face of ruthless government determination to crush any opposition. Subsequently South African security forces broke the underground organization of the Communist Party.

Forced increasingly to shift to distant exile headquarters in countries not even contiguous to South Africa the illegal political associations have continued attempts to devise means to organize some form of armed challenge to the South African regime. Their problems have had three major foci -- the organization and maintenance of effective headquarters and trained personnel in exile, the infiltration of personnel and resources from exile into South Africa, and the reconstruction within South Africa of an effective organizational base to support any confrontation with government forces. All of the organizations in exile, with the apparent exception of the Communist Party, have suffered from the hazards of the "exile ondition", with the PAC exhibiting the greatest tendency to internecine struggles and fragmentation. Both the PAC and ANC have turned to allies among the exiled nationalist movements of other territories in the region in efforts to return their men to South Africa, yet both groups were unsuccessful. A PAC group being shepherded through Mozambique by COREMO members were intercepted by Portuguese troops in 1967; the more extensive joint guerrilla campaign by ANC and ZAPU in Rhodesia in 1967-69 was blocked by joint Rhodesian-South African forces and foundered further with the disintegration of ZAPU in 1969-71. Periodical political trials within South Africa testify to continuing efforts by all of the illegal political associations to reorganize within the country, but to date there is no indication that any of the groups have been particularly successful. From time to time the ANC and the Communist Party surreptitiously distribute anti-government propaganda, but this does not pose more than nuisance value to the regime -- although it may serve some limited symbolic value in keeping the organizations before sections of the African public. It is possible that deep underground, the very difficult task of building an organizational structure secure from government penetration is proceeding, but in view of the determination and resources in the hands of the government, it would seem that such an effort could succeed only over a long period of time. Unlike the Zimbabwean and Namibian organizations the South African groups have not had the benefit of friendly African regimes along at least a part of their borders. With the recent independence of Mozambique, the boundary situation has changed, yet it is unclear presently to what extent the new Mozambican regime will allow South Africa exile groups to operate in view of its considerable dependence in the short run upon the South African economy and the stated intention of the South African government to retaliate against guerrilla incursions over its borders. Although in the long run the situation may change, it would seem that the existing South African illegal political associations do not have the capability in the immediate future to organize any widespread direct confrontation of white authority in South Africa.

It might well be that when a challenge of this sort comes in South Africa, it will originate with an illegal political association not descended from the legal political associations of the past. It also seems possible that such an organization might have little or no links with presently exiled nationalists--very possibly such a group would be one which is not yet in existence. The experience of the peasant revolt in the Transkei in the early 1960s suggests a pattern which, in a new form, might be the catalyst for a presently unforeseen confrontation with the regime.[14] Although the locally-based rural movement which then arose to challenge the imposition of Bantustan rule was contained and suppressed, during its existence, it did pose a direct challenge to South African authority. It is difficult to estimate the likelihood of an analogous movement emerging now or in the near future in the changed context of intensified Bantustanization, but the possibility should not be completely ruled out, particularly if the apparent devolution of power aggravated existing cleavages among Africans in the Bantustans. Another possibility might be urban-based illegal groups, linked perhaps with black workers' organizations which are likely to assert themselves in the future (see below). It is impossible to estimate the evolution of such movements should they ever emerge, but it does seem sure that they would be met with repression at every stage by the white regime.

Uniracial Non-Political Associations

Almost by definition the ultimate challenges to the established political order in Southern Africa will come from explicitly political organizations. Yet a vital component in the strength of any such bodies is likely to be support derived from groups which are not primarily political. Such groups will either provide an undergirding solidarity upon which the political associations can build or specific organizational blocs which will be linked to the structure of the political associations.

In the polarized racial context of the white minority-ruled states of southern Africa there are almost no exclusively white non-political associations which are pushing for radical change towards majority rule -- although the Black Sash, an organization of white women in South Africa, has long stood on a platform of non-violent opposition to *apartheid*. Yet there are black non-political associations which probably have considerable potential for mobilizing opposition in the short run. Their actions might possibly further modification of government policy, although they are also likely to result in harsh government repression if perceived as threatening. It is unlikely that they will bring about a direct broad confrontation of white political authority, but they may change the pattern of the dynamics of opposition politics in a fashion which might subsequently permit wider challenges to the *status quo*.

It seems highly improbable that associations of this sort anchored in officially-sponsored uniracial institutions (e.g. teachers organizations, civil servant bodies) will be important in the development of opposition; on the contrary, such groupings can be expected to be primarily concerned with their own narrow group interests and as such defenders of the framework of separate development in which they have found a niche of subordinate security. Instead, significant questioning of existing institutions will originate with vanguard organizations dedicated to the mobilization of broader patterns of black solidarity or with larger social forces groping for means to secure improvement in their living conditions. It is also possible that more narrowly-based associations, rooted within a single ethnic group or its cultural tradition, can be utilized for explicitly oppositional ends.

The hardening of white determination in the 1960s and early 1970s brought further limitations upon tolerated multiracial organization in both South Africa and Rhodesia. Simultaneously, black public opinion shifted in favor of racially-exclusive organizations. Some reluctantly accepted the government-approved framework of separate development as the only remaining alternative for action, no matter how limited. For others participation in government-backed institutions, despite the paucity of alternatives, remained an anathema tantamount to the acceptance of white supremacy. It is within this latter approach that the "black consciousness movement"emerged in South Africa at the end of the 1960s.[15]

The organizational core of the new mood has been the South African Student Organization (SASO), formed in 1969 by black students (Africans, Indians, Coloureds) outside of the multi-racial, but white-led, National Union of South African Students (NUSAS). Leaders of SASO have forcefully stated the need for the assertion of black pride and group solidarity; simultaneously they have been outspoken in their opposition to white domination. Support for their viewpoint has come from churchmen engaged in the formulation of black theology and from other public figures some of whom are associated with the explicitly political Black People's Convention. The "black consciousness movement" has been able to articulate both the aspirations and frustrations of blacks within a rhetoric of racial separateness without accepting the terms upon which the Nationalist Party government has defined *apartheid*. But there is little evidence to suggest that this distinctive South African version of "black power" has yet taken firm organizational root outside of the small black student and professional elite where it originated.

Despite the limited base of its support the "black consciousness movement" has already received backhanded recognition from white authority for its potential as a rallying point for opposition. In early 1973, the South African government banned and restricted the top leadership of SASO, and subsequently in 1974 it moved against other prominent figures associated with organizations linked to the "black consciousness movement". The government may still regard it useful to tolerate limited activity within SASO and other segments of the loose "black consciousness movement" in order to provide a safety valve for frustration and a vehicle through which potentially significant opposition leaders may expose themselves to easier surveillance. Yet the mere existence of a barely tolerated platform from which verbal opposition can be forcefully articulated outside the officially-accepted ethnically-based framework provides an important pole of attraction for blacks seeking broader black unity within South Africa and the region, even if only at the symbolic level. If the "black consciousness movement" continues in existence it could also develop even a rudimentary organizational skeleton and a network of contacts which might be of utility for some future broader specifically political organization. The organizational impotence of the movement at its present stage, however, has been demonstrated by its inability to challenge the government's decapitation of the leadership of SASO and other "black consciousness" groups. The government has clearly put the "black consciousness movement" on notice that it, and not the "black consciousness movement", will set the limits within which the latter can operate as a legal non-political association. The fate of the Nucleo dos Estuadantes Africanos Secundarios de Mocambique (NESAM) at the hands of the Portuguese authorities when they realized its role in providing support for FRELIMO argues that the South Africans will be no less ruthless if they deem it necessary.[16]

A potentially broader-based challenge to white authority in Southern Africa, very probably less amenable to control by the government without considerable social dislocation, could emerge from within the ranks of the black labor force upon which the economies of the region depend. The major strikes of black workers in South West Africa (December, 1971) and in Durban, South Africa (February, 1973) indicated that new patterns of class action could elicit broad support.[17] Subsequently widespread, but smaller-scale, labor disruptions point to fertile soil for the growth of black labor organizations. Such groups could evolve into bodies which would significantly expand the nature and scope of black-white confrontation.

In contrast to the "black consciousness movement" which originated among the most privileged segments of the subordinate groups of South African society, the strike actions of the Ovambo work force in South West Africa and the largely Zulu laborers in Durban appear to have had their impetus within the rank-and-file of the workers. Despite the harsh restrictions upon labor organization and the absolute ban upon strikes by African labor, workers found the ad hoc organizational means to take effective collective action against deeply-resented poor working conditions and scandalously low wages. There is little or no evidence to suggest that the first major strikes were organized by representatives of illegal political organizations; rather they seem to have been spontaneous outbursts led by men thrown up by the workers as a group. The strike actions caught white employers and state authority by surprise and effectively halted economic activity. Ultimately the strikers agreed to new terms for a return to work far below their original demands, but the mere fact that they were granted concessions in response to their actions marked a departure from the pattern that has generally prevailed in both South Africa and South West Africa.

In the wake of the major strikes existing black trade union groups, the most prominent of which is the Black Allied Workers' Union formed in August, 1973, extended their organizational efforts. For the first time in history, many white trade unions, willing to recognize that black workers should be allowed greater latitude for organization and expression of their grievances. The government has responded by proposing an upgrading of works committees already permitted and a recognition of a right to strike under certain limited conditions. It is too early to tell what will be the consequences of these developments. Yet it does semm that perhaps certain barriers blocking organization and collective bargaining by black workers may have been broken. Although it is clear that the government will still exert its power to control any reforms or activities deemed threatening (e.g. the banning in 1974 of Drake Koka, leader of the Black Allied Workers' Union), it may be possible that some shifts in the existing system of black-white labor relations will be tolerated.

Yet the recent strike actions have a significance beyond their immediate impact upon any reforms in industrial relations; they demonstrate that the latent power of segments of the black working force can be mobilized at least upon an ad hoc basis. This need not necessarily lead to a politically militant black trade union movement -- in Rhodesia black labor organizations narrowly concerned with working conditions have been tolerated for decades. Nevertheless, in the context of the South African economy which has grown ever more dependent upon black labor, the potential for black trade unionism remains substantial. Models for future organizers to build upon were delineated as long ago as the 1920s with the Industrial and Commercial Workers Union (ICU) of Clements Kadalie.

In the contemporary situation trade unions upon the hitherto tolerated Rhodesian model may make significant gains. Yet it is also possible that their appeal might be even further enhanced were it pitched within a broader and more explicitly political strategy.

While the potential base of support for both the "black consciousness movement" and black labor organizations lies in social groupings which cut across existing ethnic divisions other uniracial non-political associations which draw their support more narrowly, often from within one particular ethnic group, also have the potentiality of becoming components of an opposition movement. In South West Africa the Herero Council has long been in the forefront of organizations protesting South African rule, cooperating on an *ad hoc* basis with other legal extra-parliamentary organizations, most recently in the National Council. The original core of SWAPO was the Ovambo People's Organization. In Angola Bakongo-based organizations in the northern part of the territory and among Bakongo imigrants in Zaire have provided the foundation for FNLA. Other ethnically-based examples could be cited from within the Southern African region.

Reliance upon ethnically-based groups for a broader territorially-based opposition political movement is, of course, fraught with difficulties of the sort which other African nationalist movements have encountered further north on the continent. In the case of FNLA the predominantly Bakongo composition of the organization has probably been one of the greatest barriers to the extension of its influence throughout Angola. Ethnically-based cleavages within the exiled ZAPU leadership in Zambia apparently were at the root of the disputes within the organization of 1969-1971. Yet FRELIMO, in particular, was not apparently significantly hampered in the extension of its base by ethnic particularism. It would seem, that as elsewhere on the continent, ethnically-based groups can contribute to, as well as hinder, the process of the creation of broader patterns of national integration within an opposition movement challenging white rule.

The organizational potential of illegal political associations (as well as other types of organizations) can also be strengthened by groups or cultural phenomena which, while based within a particular ethnic group or its cultural traditions, do not speak in explicitly ethnic terms. In northern Mozambique FRELIMO was able to gain support among the Makonde through a grass-roots cooperative movement in the region which had unsuccessfully led demonstrations against the Portuguese. In northeast Rhodesia, spirit mediums have been utilized by the guerrilla movement to mobilize support among the local Shona-speaking population.[18] In this instance, the illegal political organizations would seem to have placed reliance upon African institutions which earlier played a central role in resistance to the imposition of white rule. It is possible only to suggest that such types of racially-based non-political associations may continue to provide building blocks for the construction of broader specifically political organizations; the precise nature of the role that they might play and the actual potential which they have for the creation of a more effective organizational challenge to the regional status quo remains to be seen.

Multiracial Non-Political Associations

While black non-political associations to varying degrees seem to have the potential for the generation of support for broader opposition movements, it would seem that the role of multiracial non-political associations, most of which are white-led, is more limited. Nevertheless, the continued existence of multiracial groups questioning the existing order provides a focal point for those whites who wish to express or act upon their moral objections to present arrangements and for those whites who, perhaps from a different perspective, foresee the inevitability of change and thus the necessity of action to ease the future transition away from white-minority rule. Simultaneously, such multiracial bodies also are important for blacks concerned for various reasons that organization for change should not be defined in exclusively racial terms.

The most consistently active multiracial non-political associations concerned with opposition to the present system have been those representing elements of the university student population and segments of Christian groups in Southern Africa. The center of activity of groups of this type has been South Africa, and to a lesser extent, Rhodesia, while in the Portuguese territories there were only rare challenges from associations of this sort.

The focal point for opposition activity among students in South Africa has for many years been NUSAS.[19] Drawing its active supporters primarily from the English-medium universities NUSAS has sought in defiance of apartheid to include within its membership representatives of students of all racial groups within the country. It has not only opposed the Nationalist Party government on matters concerning education, but it has also issued forceful verbal condemnations of other government policies. Upon a number of occasions it has led peaceful demonstrations to protest government action. Although its efforts to include blacks within its membership have been rebuffed by SASO, the organization has maintained contact with the new black body and has continued its defiance of government. The banning of its leadership in early

1973 testified at least to its nuisance capability in the eyes of the government, as well as its unacceptability as a symbol of white non-violent defiance upon an explicitly multiracial platform.

Since the advent of apartheid in South Africa certain Christian bodies, particularly those centered among the English-speaking population, have been forceful in their verbal condemnation of government policy upon religious grounds.[20] Individual churchmen have taken their opposition further from time to time against particular government actions (e.g. Father Trevor Huddleston, Bishop Colin Winter) or in other fashion giving support to opposition activities (e.g. Dean G.A. ffrench-Beytagh). An organizational foundation for opposition was provided in 1963 by the banding together of individual concerned Christians into the Christian Institute of South Africa which has not only questioned the canons of apartheid and exposed the inhumanity of its implementation, but more recently has encouraged active investigation of the means by which a change in the status quo might be realized. Its efforts have received increasing support from the South African Council of Churches which joined the Institute in Apartheid Society (Spro-Cas). The non-denominational University Christian Movement played a vanguard role in furthering ecumenical activities, particularly among black Christians. Certain denominations have taken increasingly forthright stands in opposition to government policy and have also stepped up their programs to combat racism in their own ranks. The result has been an increasingly direct confrontation between the church leadership and the government over the policies and activities of certain individuals and specific Christian groups.

Religious leaders have been banned or restricted (e.g. Father Cosmos Desmond, Rev. Basil Moore, Rev. Manas Buthelezi) and the residence permits of foreign churchmen have not been renewed (e.g. Bishop Colin Winter). In the wake of the decision of the World Council of Churches to grant funds to various Southern African nationalist movements dedicated to violent overthrow of white minority-rule, the government threatened action against churches which did not denounce the decision and withdraw from the World Council; subsequently, however, it pulled back from direct confrontation, allowing contact between the World Council and South African bodies to continue. The Christian Institute and the University Christian Movement (along with NUSAS and the South African Institute of Race Relations) were investigated by a special parliamentary commission (Schlebusch Commission). More recent government restrictions upon individuals associated with the Christian Institute underline its determination that even religious leaders dedicated to non-violence and speaking in the name of Christian ethics will be strictly limited in their verbal confrontations and organizational challenges of apartheid.

The individual white Christians and multi-racial Christian groups which have challenged the government do not seem in any instance to have directly threatened government control. Yet because they speak and act from a Christian perspective against a self-professed Christian regime, they have a potential moral authority among the white population which other critiques of government action might not carry. In addition, when black churchmen publicly question the policies of the regime in Christian terms, as have Bishop Leonard Auala and Pastor Paulus Bowaseb of South West Africa since 1971, their arguments might be heard more readily than criticism from an explicitly black political perspective.[21] On the symbolic plane, the actions of certain denominations in moving towards racial integration of their leaderships and assertion of a more activist program to combat racism challenge the basic fundamentals of racial separation advocated by the regime. In a country where a substantial proportion of the African population considers itself Christian and many of them, in turn, are affiliated with denominations which recognize no formal racial distinctions, the shift of churches towards a more explicit questioning of government might have greater significance than elsewhere on the continent. There seems no likelihood, however, that multiracial religious bodies will ever provide either the organizational means or the financial support for a direct frontal political challenge to the regime. Yet by their generally more outspoken opposition to the government they do undoubtedly sustain some in a situation where few legal channels for action are open. They perhaps also provide important psychological support for individual acts of confrontation against an apparently overpowering opponent.

In Rhodesia many church leaders have also been forthright in their opposition to many steps taken by the government towards an even more fully segregated society. In the absence of other significant outspoken multiracial or white-led opposition groups, their voices and actions have stood out, but they have had little success in deflecting the government from its policies. In the changed situation of negotiations between the enlarged African National Council, headed by the Methodist Bishop, Rev. Abel Muzorewa, and the Rhodesian government over acceptable terms for a new Rhodesian constitution, multiracial Christian groups might become a useful bridge between racial communities and thus contribute to the modification of the status quo. But if negotiations fail and guerrilla actions resume, it would seem that multiracial Christian groups will have little role to play in confrontation with the government.

In the former Portuguese territories church organizations, per se, generally remained neutral or actively supported government policy. The Portuguese

Catholic hierarchy was a strong defender of the colonial system in which the church was given a central role by the Portuguese authorities, although individual Catholics, such as the former Bishop of Beira, Monsigneur Sabastiao Soares de Resenda, offered criticism of aspects of the regime's policy. The decision of the White Fathers in 1971 to withdraw from further mission activity within Mozambique in protest against government policy represented the viewpoint of a predominantly non-Portuguese segment of the church. Foreign Catholics were similarly in the forefront of those accusing the regime of massacres of Africans in the Tete region. Their actions were of symbolic interest, but they did not signal any general reversal of policy by the Portuguese hierarchy of the Catholic Church in Mozambique. Protestant churches, representing a small minority of the population and long under suspicion by the government, particularly in Angola, as an alleged source of subversive ideas, were generally careful to restrict their activities to strictly religious spheres. The churches in Angola and Mozambique made no direct contribution to the success of organized opposition to Portuguese colonialism.

Linkages and Regional Cohesion

From the foregoing survey of organized groups opposed to minority-rule in the Southern African region it is evident that opposition varies widely in internal cohesion and intensity within the region and that the nature of its potential for the strengthening of a broad opposition movement to the remaining centers of white power is sharply differentiated. Further examination will show that linkages between territories and between groups in different classifications are often non-existent, or if existent, intermittent and weakly structured. Although in certain areas there are signs of intensifying opposition and new broader patterns of cohesion, the prospects of movement towards an overarching self-conscious and cohesive opposition within the region seem remote. Further analysis will also indicate that not the least of the obstacles to any development of a broader and more powerful coordinated regional opposition movement is the nature of linkages between certain opposition groups and the forces of white dominance within the region. For the foreseeable future, the forces of white dominance will probably continue to exert great influence upon the configuration of any opposition to them in the region.

It is striking, but not surprising, that there are so few interterritorial links between opposition groups. The present pattern is largely that which has prevailed for more than a decade.

Only in the case of illegal political organizations have there been significant or potentially significant linkages between bodies in Angola,

Mozambique, Rhodesia, South Africa, and South West Africa. Even in this instance the strongest linkages have been between the exiled leaderships of the organizations; they seemed primarily directed towards better coordination of activities _outside_ the region, rather than for the coordination of activities _within_ the region. Both MPLA and FRELIMO joined with the _Partido Africano da Independencia da Guine a Cabo Verde_ (PAIGC) and the small _Comite de Libertacao de Sao Tome e Principe_ (CLSTP) in the _Conferencia das Organizacoes Nacionalistas das Colonies Portuguesas_ (CONCP), a grouping designed to achieve interterritorial cooperation in advancing the common anti-Portuguese cause. More embracing was the informal alliance of ANC, ZAPU, FRELIMO, MPLA, SWAPO, and PAIGC, which was most in evidence in 1969 at an international conference on Southern Africa convened in Khartoum by Soviet-oriented anti-imperialist bodies. Yet such alliances were probably designed primarily to attract outside support; they did not immediately translate themselves into strengthened solidarity of the organizations for any kind of direct joint struggle against white power in Southern Africa.

Where patterns of organizational cooperation between illegal bodies developed _within_ the region they seem to have been on an _ad hoc_ basis between two organizations, and until recently, enjoyed limited success. The fate of the joint ANC-ZAPU campaigns in Rhodesia illustrated some of the pitfalls which could arise. Similarly, it seems that the possibilities for cooperation between SWAPO and logical allies within Angola were hindered by rivalry between MPLA and UNITA, both of which operated in areas of Angola astride the approaches to South West Africa from Zambia. Only the more recently forged link between FRELIMO and ZANU showed direct results in northeastern Rhodesia in 1973-74 and ironically FRELIMO seemed previously to have been associated with ZAPU in more loose cooperation outside the region whereas ZANU had been grouped with COREMO. Yet the _ad hoc_ cooperation between FRELIMO and ZANU could set a pattern for new effective linkages between other movements in the region, although the changing status of Angolan, Mocambican, and possibly Zimbabwean movements, makes prospects uncertain.

Interterritorial linkages otherwise are rather limited, particularly in the case of the former Portuguese territories, Rhodesia, and South West Africa. There are some regular ties between members of particular Christian denominations which are organized upon a regional basis primarily to include all English-speaking territories, but these linkages are not exclusively concerned with matters of opposition to white-minority rule although such questions do sometimes arise. Most other types of groups which have taken opposition stances pay little attention to establishing ties across the borders of the territory in which they operate. Even in South West Africa, which is under South African rule, opposition groups within the territory have relatively few linkages with South African bodies -- and almost none with those of other territories.

Only in the case of South Africa and its three black-ruled neighbors of Botswana, Lesotho, and Swaziland does there appear to be slightly less territorial segmentation, reflecting both the colonial political patterns of the past as well as the new circumstances of the present. During the late 1950s and early 1960s there was considerable interaction between members of black extra-parliamentary associations in South Africa (in particular, the ANC and the PAC, which, in 1960, became illegal associations) and political parties in the three territories. Yet when the parties to which the ANC and the PAC looked became the opposition non-governing parties, and more particularly after independence was achieved under ruling parties which, in most instances, were not friendly to the ANC and the PAC, links between the latter two parties, by then illegal, and the non-governing parties of Botswana, Lesotho, and Swaziland atrophied. Because of the position of the three governments and ruling parties on refugee political activity no visible links have developed between them and illegal political associations -- although in the case of Botswana the Rhodesian authorities have asserted (and Botswana authorities have denied) that Botswana has provided sanctuary for members of Rhodesian illegal associations. Nevertheless, general statements of support for African liberation movements made by spokesmen for the Botswana and Lesotho governments since the early 1970's suggest a new willingness on the part of the latter to make explicit their affinity with the goals of the illegal associations while carefully refraining from establishing more specific and open organizational linkages which would threaten reprisal from their white-ruled nieghbors.

Within the context of the Southern African region taken as a whole and in isolation from factors external to the region the governments and ruling parties of Botswana, Lesotho, and Swaziland have assumed a salience which they did not have before their independence. The simple facts that they are black-controlled governments and their political sovereignty is internationally recognized made them objects of interest for opponents of the system of white-minority rule. It is quite clear that they provide models for Bantustan leaders such as Chief Kaiser Matanzima who talks of an eventual federation of African states to include the three now independent states. For their part, the governments and ruling parties of Botswana, Lesotho, and Swaziland have been careful to avoid any official recognition of the Bantustan leaders; they recognize that this would be construed as an endorsement of the system of separate development. Yet it can be presumed that they have respect for the assertiveness of Chief Gatsha Buthelezi although this is unlikely to be stated explicitly.[22] The linkages between the parties of Botswana, Lesotho, and Swaziland are presumptive and symbolic in an uneven relationship in which the independent governments would never specifically recognize the linkages or give them organizational form whereas the Bantustan leaders would very probably wish to have their affinity underpinned with explicit recognition and organizational ties.

There are, however, linkages between opposition groups in the four territories which are quite open. Many multiracial non-political associations centered in South Africa, particularly religious denominations, have long-established branches in one or more of the territories. Thus, there are regular interchanges between members of such groups which would be relevant to the development of opposition across territorial lines to the extent that the groups involve themselves in defiance to the status quo. By pointed hospitality to members of the progressive Party, the government and ruling party of Botswana have shown their respect for the white-led non-racial opposition in South Africa. Outside a multiracial context informal linkages have always existed across the borders between certain uniracial non-political associations (e.g. black separatist churches); their broad potential for the development of interterritorial opposition to white-minority rule is impossible to estimate. More specifically suggestive of possibilities, at least on the symbolic level, is the Southern African Students Movement linking the four territories for which Abraham Tiro of SASO (of South Africa) was working at the time of his murder in Botswana early in 1974.

While linkages between opposition organizations in South Africa and its small neighboring black-ruled states may be more established than interterritorial ties elsewhere in the region they are, nevertheless, not particularly strong. It does seem, however, that in recent years for the first time the initiative for the establishment of links is coming more from South Africa than from the three territories. Botswana, Lesotho, and Swaziland have served as poles of attraction out of proportion to their relative size and strength in the region simply by virtue of their existence as black-ruled states in the closest proximity to the citadel of white might.

Not only are linkages across territorial lines within the region limited, but linkages between various categories of opposition groups within particular territories (and within the region as a whole) are also limited. To a certain extent the lack of linkages (and the difficulty of obtaining information about linkages that do exist) flows out of the very nature of the type of organizations and their consciousness of proximate white power. Thus, for instance, government and ruling parties in dependent black-ruled states would not establish visible links with political associations illegal in the eyes of their powerful white-ruled neighbors. Similarly, neither legal political associations, whether non-governing parties or extra-parliamentary groups, nor non-political associations, whether uniracial or multiracial would openly establish ties with illegal parties. For quite different reasons uniracial associations are unlikely to establish close ties with multi-racial organizations. Yet there are linkages between different types of opposition groupings and even where linkages do not exist there is evidence of important affinities which suggest presumptive linkages or potential support for linkages in the future.

Some of the strongest established links between categories of organizations are those which probably have the least potential for extension to other categories. Many of the whites active in multiracial non-political associations in South Africa have been for a long time active supporters of white-led non-governing parties in South Africa. Upon a number of occasions parties have joined with non-political associations to sponsor various activities critical of _apartheid_, ranging from study groups to demonstrations. Yet in a situation of racial polarization where black organizations are excluding white participation or at a minimum accepting whites and their organizations as junior partners or auxiliaries, the well-established linkages between white-led non-governing parties and generally white-led multiracial non-political associations would seem to have a limited potential in any broader black-based and black-oriented opposition movement which might conceivably develop.

Within the legal political arena the other focal points for linkages are the extra-parliamentary political associations. Linkages centering around the extra-parliamentary political associations are much more in a state of flux, and many of them are of a symbolic type based upon some sort of affinity rather than regular organizational links. Inasmuch as extra-parliamentary politicial associations eschew the use of violence they cut themselves off from links with illegal political associations. Nevertheless, in situations where the utility of direct violent confrontation seems marginal or hazardous at present, or where unexpected prospects for change materialize, specific extra-parliamentary political associations can become vehicles for illegal political associations of their supporters. Thus, in Rhodesia it seems that Africans with broad allegiances to both ZANU and ZAPU became involved in the African National Council after its formation in 1971; with the Lusaka Unity greement of December, 1974, both ZANU and ZAPU (along with FROLIZI) agreed to place themselves under the African National Council. In South Africa, the ANC indicates that some use might be made of Bantustan institutions to advance the longer range goal of the total destruction of apartheid.[23] In a reverse direction, as was noted previously, government and ruling parties of Botswana, Lesotho, and Swaziland, have become poles of attraction for African groups operating within the framework of separate development.

There is otherwise a variegated pattern of linkages, few regular or organizational, between specific Bantustan leaders with specific uniracial non-political associations and also with specific multiracial non-political associations. For example, Chief Gatsha Buthelezi endorses the cultural dimensions of the platform enunciated by leaders of the "black consciousness movement" and asserts a role for KwaZulu in black-white labor relations at the same time that he maintains at least personal ties with such multiracial organizations as the South African Institute of Race Relations. Other Bantustan leaders may not have yet been so active in striving to create a network of interpersonal and inter-organizational contacts, but there are signs that they are moving to emulate the examples of Chief Gatsha Buthelezi. In addition, it seems that there is interest in establishing linkages between Bantustan leaders and between certain African, Coloured, and Indian groups in order to present a more united front to white authority. The pattern of the linkages centered around black extra-parliamentary political associations, in particular the Bantustans, is clearly shifting; new linkages are in the process of being created and the few previous linkages are being stretched.

In many respects the illegal organizations are without visible linkages to the other types of opposition groups. Yet in areas where illegal organizations have undertaken mobilization for armed struggle they have utilized various uniracial non-political associations as organizational building blocks to extend themselves into new areas (e.g. FRELIMO's use of the cooperative movement in northern Mozambique, ZANU's ties with particular spirit mediums in northeastern Rhodesia). In South Africa, where the task of mobilization is much more difficult, the ANC has not only suggested that limited use might be made of Bantustan institutions, but it has specifically made the organization of the black working force one of its prime goals and it has also indicated that it regards the leadership of the "black consciousness movement" of particular importance.[24] What linkages, if any, have been established between the ANC and black non-political associations within South Africa is impossible to determine, but it would seem most likely that the ANC will attempt to create such ties. Other illegal organizations in South Africa and the remaining white minority-ruled territories would probably also try to link themselves with black non-political associations which they estimate could be fruitfully harnessed in their confrontation with white might.

The tenuous nature of existing linkages between different types of opposition organizations and between organizations in different territories is further weakened by the ties between many existing opposition groups and the forces of white authority within the region. Only the illegal political associations completely reject the established order and organize exclusively to confront and destroy it. To various degrees all of the other organizations which oppose the principle of white minority-rule accept elements of the established system. The governments and ruling parties of Botswana, Lesotho, and Swaziland are painfully aware of the geographical and economic realities which force them to maintain a pattern of dependent co-existence with South Africa and Rhodesia. In Lesotho and Swaziland the governments have also opted upon occasion to seek support from South Africa to secure their own positions against internal challenges. In Botswana the government has carefully avoided seeking political support for its position from neighbors, but it is impossible for it as well to dispense with all of its economic linkages to its neighbors. All non-governing parties also are embedded in the existing political arrangements within which they seek or have sought to oust the existing governments through recognized constitutional procedures. (Segments of the opposition parties in Lesotho and Swaziland might possible organize in defiance of the new political orders decreed respectively by Chief Jonathan and King Sobhuza II; such seems to have been the case in Lesotho in 1973-74. In this fashion, they place themselves within the ranks of the illegal political organizations.) Likewise other aboveground associations, whether specificially political or non-political, have accepted the need to work at least partially within the existing political order in order to change it. The acceptance may vary from those which participate within the institutions of separate development in lieu of any suitable alternative to those which on tactical grounds accept only the constraints against the use of violence to bring about change. But by their involvement, even if limited, in the established order the various opposition associations are subject to the control and manipulation of white authority which can vary from suppression, if the group or its leaders are estimated to be a potential threat, to more sophisticated limitations imposed through the screen of separate development. It is the white authorities which largely determine the limits within which legal and non-violent opposition activity can occur, although it would seem that for those in South Africa working within the institutions of separate development the range of accepted activity is broader than for those rejecting the Bantustan framework.

It is outside the scope of this discussion to analyze the nature of, and the linkages between, the military and political means which the remaining white minority-rule regimes have at their disposal to maintain their hegemony. The coup by the Armed Forces Movement in Lisbon and the subsequent rapid dismantling of the Portuguese colonial empire have dramatically shifted the balance of power within the region. Yet the initiative from within the ranks of the dominant whites for change in the regional status quo came from outside the region in the Portuguese metropole. With the withdrawal of the Portuguese "external" factor, attention more than ever before focuses upon white power within the region, and upon South Africa in particular. Its actions since the change of government in Portugal, especially those reported in connection with the unexpected shift of the Rhodesian government to accept negotiations with the African opposition, suggest that Pretoria is willing to encourage further modification of the regional status quo, possibly even to the extent of tolerating black participation in a Rhodesian government, provided that it believes that the white position within South Africa remains secured. If, as seems likely despite protestations to the contrary, the South African government has applied pressure to Rhodesia, its overwhelming power within the white laager is made even more evident. It would seem that in the short run its vast military power and great economic strength pose insurmountable obstacles to any successful direct confrontation of the white bastion.

Opposition nevertheless will continue and intensify. In the short run, however, organized opposition in the Southern African region will remain fragmented. Activity will cluster around three nodal points. As they have done for decades in South Africa and Rhodesia (and to a much lesser extent in South West Africa) white-led non-governing parties and multiracial non-political associations will continue to question the status quo. Yet they have neither the means nor the will to organize more than a verbal confrontation with white authority. In the peripheries of the remaining white-ruled territories of the region -- (South West Africa, and Rhodesia if a negotiated settlement is not reached or collapses) - guerrillas of illegal political associations will soon be able to mobilize organizationally to mount a direct armed challenge. Instead the initiative there will be taken by barely tolerated uniracial non-political bodies (black trade unions, "black consciousness movement") and by extra-parliamentary political associations (African National Council in Rhodesia and Bantustan governments in South Africa). The latter have a modicum of immunity by virtue of their recognition by white authority, but for all groups the arena for political maneuver remains limited -- although it could expand in Rhodesia if and when agreement is made upon steps toward majority rule. Nevertheless, within the narrow parameters of white-tolerated activity these groups still have the potential to create new bonds of solidarity and organizational nuclei for future broadened opposition activities. In an analagous fashion at the symbolic level Botswana, Lesotho, and Swaziland have also probably contributed to this end; henceforth, however, Angola and especially Mozambique are more likely to be poles of attraction for groups within South Africa, Rhodesia, and South West Africa.

A complex and uncoordinated pattern of symbolic challenge, verbal confrontation, organizational experimentation, and armed struggle is in prospect for the opposition in the remaining redoubts of white-majority rule. The possibilities for the emergence of a cohesive region-wide opposition movement still seem remote. Yet consolidation of the recent unity of the Zimbabwean nationalists in the context of steps towards majority rule in Rhodesia, new challenges by Namibian opposition groups in orchestration with heightened diplomatic pressure spearheaded by the United Nations, or the coalescence of more permanent politically-oriented black trade unions in South Africa might set in motion additional currents which could quicken the erosion of white power. The apparent preeminence of white South African might is not necessarily a permanent feature of Southern African politics.

NOTES

1. For discussion of Botswana's efforts to disengage from its neighbors see the following studies by Richard Dale: "Botswana and Its Southern Neighbor: The Patterns of Linkage and the Options in Statecraft", Ohio University Center for International Studies, Papers in International Studies, Africa Series 6, 1970 "The Racial Component of Botswana's Foreign Policy", Center on International Race Relations, University of Denver, Studies in Race and Nations, 2, 1970-71; "Botswana" in Potholm and Dale (eds.) Southern Africa in Perspective: Essays in Regional Politics (New York: Free Press, 1972), 110-124. A slightly more recent analysis can be found in Sheridan Johns, "Botswana's Strategy for Development: An Assessment of Dependence in the Southern African Context", The Journal of Commonwealth Political Studies, 11 (3), November 1973, 214-230.

2. Botswana Daily News, September 5, 1973; September 10, 1973.

3. Lesotho's closely intertwined internal and external policies are analyzed in John D. Holm, "Political Stability in Lesotho", Africa Today 19, Fall 1972, 3-16; Richard Weisfelder, "Lesotho and South Africa: Diverse Linkages", Africa Today 18, Spring 1971, 48-55; Richard Weisfelder, "Lesotho" in Potholm and Dale (eds.), Southern Africa in Perspective 125-140.

4. For an early summary of the deterioration in relations between Lesotho and South Africa see X-Ray 3, December 1972, 2-3.

5. Holm, "Political Stability in Lesotho" 12-13.

6. Discussion of Swaziland's foreign policy is to be found in Christian P. Potholm, Swaziland: The Dynamics of Political Modernization (Berkeley: University of California Press, 1972) 139-156.

7. The development of political parties in the three countries is dealt with in detail in Jack Halpern South Africa's Hostages: Basutoland, Bechuanaland, and Swaziland (Harmondsworth: Penguin, 1965), and Richard P. Stevens Lesotho, Botswana, and Swaziland: The Former High Commission Territories in Southern Africa (London: Pall Mall, 1967). Discussions of party activity in the context of a broader analysis of political modernization in Swaziland is available in Potholm Swaziland 47-130.

8. Heribert Adam, "The Rise of Black Consciousness in South Africa" (Paper presented at the Third Annual Conference of the Canadian Association of African Studies, Ottawa, 16-18 February 1973) 2.

9. To follow the development of Chief Buthelezi's thinking it is necessary to pay close attention to a number of South African and overseas publications in which his statements have been reported on an irregular basis. Such publications would indicate The Star (Johannesburg), The Post (Johannesburg), Sunday Tribune (Durban), X-Ray (London), Southern Africa (New York). A presentation of a range of his earlier views drawn from diverse sources is to be found in "The Buthelezi Factor: Hope for the Bantustans?" Africa Today 18, July 1971, 53-59.

10. For an authoritative account of the genesis of the organization and its first year of activities see Black Review 1972 (Durban, 1973) 8-15. A short sympathetic evaluation of the organization is available in Alfred Kgokong "The Black People's Convention" Africa Today 19, Summer 1972, 31-38.

11. John Marcum "The Exile Condition and Revolutionary Effectiveness: Southern African Liberation Movements" in Potholm and Dale (eds.) Southern Africa in Perspective 262-275.

12. African Research Bulletin - Political Social and Cultural Series 10(6), 15 June 1973, 2869A.

13. Ananalysis of the difficulties encountered by the underground ANC leadership and its allies is presented in Edward Feit Urban Revolt in South Africa, 1960-1964: A Case Study (Evanston: Northwestern University Press, 1971). A briefer discussion covering a longer time period is available in Sheridan Johns, "Obstacles to Guerrilla Warfare - a South African Case Study", Journal of Modern African Studies 11(2), June 1973, 267-303.

14. The most extensive account of the disturbances in the Transkei has been by Govan Mbeki, an ANC official now serving a life sentence in a South African prison. See South Africa: The Peasants' Revolt (London: Penguin 1964).

15. The growth of the movement through 1972 is outlined in Black Review 1972, 40-54. For further surveys see Alfred Kgokong "The Black People's Convention" and Heribert Adam "The Rise of Black Consciousness in South Africa".

16. An evaluation of the role of NESAM in extending the underground network of FRELIMO within Mozambique is found in Eduardo Mondlane The Struggle for Mozambique (London: Penguin, 1969) 113-114.

17. For a succinct summary of the South West African strike see "Namibia: The Ovambo Challenge to South Africa" Africa Bureau Fact Sheet, 18, February 1972; a brief analysis of the Durban strike is to be found in Benjamin Pogrund "The Durban Strikes" Africa Report 18, March - April, 1973, 25-26.

18. Peter Niesewand, "What Smith Really Faces" Africa Report 18, March-April 1973, 18.

19. The highlights of its history and its immediate prospects were surveyed in a recent issue of South African Outlook (Mowbray) 104 (1232), January 1974.

20. Perhaps the most useful regular source of information upon the outlook and activities of various South African church groups is to be found in the annual Survey of Race Relations in South Africa compiled by Muriel Horrell for the South African Institute of Race Relations; see especially the section, "The Churches".

21. For Bishop Awala's statement see South African Outlook 102 (1210), February 1972.

22. In this context see the general remarks of President Seretse Khama of Botswana concerning the significance of the Bantustans Africa Today 18, July 1971, 33.

23. Oliver Tambo, acting president of the ANC, has observed, "The Bantustans are dangerous to the extent that they break up a nation born in 1912, and those who work the system in conscious support of the South African Government are collaborators in oppression. We must exclude from this attack those who have no choice but to work within the Bantustan framework and those who use the Bantustan platform to attack apartheid and supplement our demands." Quote in "Bantustans: The Current Position", *Africa Bureau Fact Sheet* 21, July 1972.

24. See, for example, *Sechaba* 6, February 1972, 4-5; *ibid*, 6, May 1972, 18-20.

Chapter Nine

ZAMBIAN DISENGAGEMENT FROM SOUTHERN AFRICA AND INTEGRATION WITH EAST AFRICA, 1964-1972: A TRANSACTION ANALYSIS

Douglas G. Anglin

Few countries have undergone as deliberate and dramatic a reorientation in their external relations as has Zambia in the brief period since Independence in 1964. During this decade, the search for an alternative to the inherited dependence on Southern Africa has constituted the central thrust of foreign policy. Almost everything else - relations with the rest of the continent and with countries overseas - has reflected the pervasive impact of this central national preoccupation. This paper attempts (1) to assess the scope of Zambia's disengagement from the Southern African system and of its integration with East Africa, (2) to compare the extent of change in different functional issue areas, and (3) to distinguish between behavioural patterns at the governmental and societal levels.

Historically, Zambia formed an integral part of the Southern African regional system, principally because of the contributions of its copper to the region's wealth and its landlocked condition. South Africa constituted the core of this constellation, economically, socially and to some extent politically, although Zambia's closest direct ties were with Rhodesia. Typically, Zambia interacted with South Africa only indirectly through Salisbury - known disdainfully as Bamba Zonke or "Grab-All". To adopt a commercial analogy, Zambia was merely a local office of a Rhodesian branch plant of a South African parent company. Zambia also had long-standing contacts with Angola and especially Mozambique, particularly in the field of transportation. This vast area embracing South Africa (and Namibia), Rhodesia and the Portuguese colonies, all subject to minority rule, collectively comprise the Southern African sub-system for the purpose of this study.

The hardening of racial attitudes in the South, coupled with the spread of African majority rule throughout Black Africa in the 1960's, rendered the perpetuation in Zambia of any hegemonial relationship increasingly intolerable. A deeply felt sense of economic grievance combined with a re-awakened ethnic pride reinforced the growing nationalist pressures for self-determination. Freedom from Britain and disengagement from Southern Africa, and especially Rhodesia, were seen as opposite sides of the same political coin. The initial phase of disengagement was political: the dissolution at the end of 1963 of the Federation of Rhodesia and

Nyasaland (ironically originally conceived by the British as a check on the ini tious spread of apartheid ideas northward). This paved the way for Independenc the following year and a shift in the focus of attention to the promotion of ecc omic independence from the South. "We are embarking on very bold schemes," President Kaunda announced on the morrow of Independence, "which I hope very soor will lessen our dependence on Southern Rhodesia, South Africa, Angola and Mozambique."[1] Yet his new Government managed to make comparatively little progress towards realizing that goal during its first crowded year in office. Rhodesia's unilateral declaration of independence in November 1965 transformed the situation dramatically. UDI supplied not only a powerful new political incentive to disengagement but also the economic compulsion. When Lusaka supported UN sanctions, Salisbury retaliated swiftly by cutting off completely the flow of oil to Zambia.

The corollary of the policy of disengagement was the political and economic reorientation of the country towards East Africa and especially Tanzania. In 1961, the United National Independence Party joined the Pan African Freedom Movement of East. Central and Southern Africa (PAFMECSA) and, the following year, Kenneth Kaunda became its chairman. Also, as early as 1962, UNIP called for a rail link with Tanzania.[2] "This railway is a political necessity," Kaunda declared. "Even after Rhodesia wins majority rule, there will be Mozambique and South Africa between ourselves and the sea."[3] Once Independence had been achieved, Lusaka joined eagerly in the efforts of the UN Economic Commission for Africa to promote economic integration within Eastern Africa. In April 1965, it sponsored an Interterritorial Conference on Trade Expansion between Zambia and East Africa and, in October 1965, hosted an ECA subregional Conference on Harmonization of Industry.[4] Yet, as with disengagement, there were few concrete achievements to record prior to UDI.

However, during the course of the next five years, the Zambian economy underwent an unprecedented structural transformation as the Government struggled to extricate itself from dependence on the South.[5] Trade with Rhodesia in particular declined dramatically, as did reliance on the Rhodesia Railways for copper exports. At the same time, important new links were forged with Tanzania. Initially these were of an emergency character but, with time, permanent new infrastructures have emerged: an oil pipeline, a modern highway and the prospect of early completion of the railway. Moreover, in December 1967, Zambia formally applied for membership of the East African Community.[6]

The achievements of this period were all the more remarkable as they coincided with the implementation of an impressive development programme. In 1969 alone, the gross domestic product at factor cost recorded a phenomenal 23.2% increase.[7]

Yet, within a year, the economic outlook deteriorated drastically. A collapse of the copper market sent world prices plunging from over $1,800 per tonne in April 1970 to under $1,000 per tonne nine months later.[8] Then, in September 1970, a massive cave-in occurred at Mufilira, one of the world's largest copper mines. The impact of these twin calamities on export earnings and even more on government revenues was devasting. Copper, which in 1969 provided over half the country's net domestic product, contributed less than one quarter in 1971.[9] At the same time, a critical maize shortage following the disastrous drought of 1970 compelled the country to turn temporarily to foreign markets, including Rhodesia, for massive supplies of its staple diet. With exports declining and imports mounting, foreign exchange reserves dwindled to one-quarter of their value less than two years earlier. In the circumstances, the Government had no alternative but to curtail imports severely. At the same time, to ease dangerous inflationary pressures, it announced in February 1972 that henceforth importers would be encouraged to buy from the cheapest source, which in many cases meant South Africa.[10] For all these reasons as well as the intense frustration stemming from the continued failure of the world community to deal effectively with the Rhodesian rebellion, the momentum of disengagement gradually slackened. Enthusiasm for integration with East Africa also appeared on the wane.

Negotiations with the East African Community opened in November 1968, but soon bogged down as Zambians came to appreciate the full implications of common market membership for an interior state with a high-cost economy. Active efforts to achieve even a limited form of associate membership ended early in 1971 following the Uganda coup, though this development was more a convenient pretext for suspending negotiations than an adequate explanation of Zambia's declining interest in Community participation. On the other hand, the strains which the emergence of Amin created within East Africa, as well as the growing realization in Lusaka that its primary concern was with improved communications rather than economic advantages, served to draw Tanzania and Zambia even closer together.[11]

In January 1973, relations with Southern Africa were again transformed with Rhodesia once more providing the catalyst compelling Zambia to turn its back on the South. Ian Smith's ill-considered action in suddenly closing the frontier along the Zambezi effectively cut off the flow of imports to Zambia from and through the whole of the southern part of the continent. At the same time, it provoked President Kaunda to respond with a ban on the export of copper through Rhodesia, and to refuse to resume trade across the border when Smith realized the magnitude of his miscalculation and sought rather clumsily to back down. From Rhodesia's point of view the attempt at economic blackmail proved thoroughly counterproductive. Not only did the rebel regime lose in copper traffic a major source of foreign exchange, but it compelled Zambia to accept risks which until then it had not felt economically and politically able to do prior to the completion of the Tanzam railway in 1975. In the circumstances, the Zambian reaction to this formidable challenge was courageous - but inevitable. No country could safely allow its lifeline to the sea to remain at the mercy of a malevolent neighbor if there were any conceivable alternatives. As a result, the goal of disengagement, at least with respect to Rhodesia, has virtually been achieved.

The Lusaka-Dar es Salaam entente also reached new peaks of cordiality and mutual support, and to some extent this harmony has split over to relations with Kenya and even Uganda. Nevertheless, the outlook for further substantial integration with East Africa is now less certain. The idea of formal association with the East African Community has for the present been abandoned. Moreover, the periodic inability of Dar es Salaam port to cope adequately with Zambia's present transit trade, let alone the additional traffic the Tanzam railway (TAZARA) will generate, is a constant worry. In addition, the prospect of far-reaching political changes in Southern Africa may revive interest in options which are currently politically unacceptable. There will, however, be no return to the pre-independence situation. In particular, Zambia has no intention of becoming ensnared in the Southern African economic community that Pretoria is promoting so optimistically. The impact of structural changes of the past decade on the pattern of Zambia's interactions with its neighbours is permanent.

Disengagement and Integration

Disengagement denotes a systematic reduction by one actor in a system of the scope and intensity of its positive interactions with the other actors in that system. Integration, on the other hand, can be defined as the calculated increase in the scope and intensity of an actor's positive interactions with other actors or with a system of actors.[12] Thus, the two terms are essentially opposites. This is not to suggest that the simultaneous pursuit by Zambia of disengagement from Southern Africa and integration with East Africa has been merely a matter of seeking to replace one hegemonial relationship with another; there is no intention of leaping from the frying pan into the fire. Fortunately, there is little danger of replicating the past as the two situations are vastly different.

To begin with, the element of dependence and disparity is not so great. Every landlocked country is to some extent at the mercy of transit states, but the degree of Zambian dependence on East Africa is bound to be far less and its scope more limited than it was in relation to Southern Africa. The latter exercised a predominant influence in the spheres of investment and labour as well as trade and communications. Similarly, the asymmetrical character of the relationship is much less marked. By most measures, Southern Africa commands five to fifth times the resources and the corresponding benefits available to Zambia, whereas the ratios of disparity with East Africa range only from one to eight (Table 1). The relative imbalance is particularly striking when Zambia is compared with South Africa and Tanzania respectively. Clearly East Africa lacks the capability, even if it had the inclination, to exploit Zambia to the extent that Southern Africa has in the past. There are now too many options available to Zambia for it to allow history to repeat itself.

Table 1

Indicators of Asymmetry: Zambia in Relation to Southern Africa and East Africa, 1972

	Ratio of Zambia and:			
	Southern Africa	East Africa	South Africa	Tanzania
Area	1: 5.9	1:2.3	1: 1.6	1:1.2
Population	1:10.0	1:8.2	1: 5.2	1:3.2
Gross Domestic Product	1:14.8	1:2.9	1:12.6	1:0.9
Trade	1: 7.0	1:1.4	1: 5.2	1:0.5
Post-Secondary Students	1:50	1:5.3	1:47	1:1.2
Armed Forces	1.54	1:6.9	1:25	1:2.5

Sources: UN Statistical Yearbook 1973; The Military Balance, 1972-73 (London: Institute for Strategic Studies, 1973).

Secondly, there is no ideological barrier to cooperation with East Africa. On the contrary, particularly in the case of Tanzania and Zambia, the personal philosophies and political programmes of the leaders have been strikingly similar.[13] With respect to Southern Africa, on the other hand, racialism, colonialism and tyranny have rendered impossible any relationship based on equality and mutual respect.

A third distinction stems from the voluntary character of the partnership being forged with East Africa. Admittedly, following UDI, Zambia had only two alternative outlets to the sea through independent Africa: through Tanzania or through Zaire, and conditions in the latter were still too chaotic to offer a reliable lifeline. Nevertheless, Zambia eagerly seized on the necessity of appealing to Tanzania for assistance to foster a relationship it favoured on other grounds.

Clearly, the inducements to participation in the East African community were predominantly non-coercive.[14] By way of contrast, Zambia's earlier "engagement" to the South was a colonial imposition. The Federation of Rhodesia and Nyasaland, in particular, arose out of a betrothal arranged between the parents and the groom over the fierce protests of the bartered bride.

This is not to suggest that the political and emotional incentives to integration have been anything like as powerful or sustained as the determination to disengage. Subordination to the South has been a searing experience that has left an indelible imprint on the Zambian consciousness, whereas the full implications of closer association with East Africa are still difficult to visualize. Moreover, nationalism reinforces the drive for disengagement, but inhibits enthusiasm for integration. This is the dilemma of the Pan-Africanist that President Nyerere has so clearly recognized. "As each of us develops his own state," he observed, "we raise more and more barriers between ourselves ... It is not impossible to achieve African unity through nationalism ... [but] it is difficult."[15] Finally, the historical context in which the urge for integration with East Africa has emerged has insured that Zambians view it at least as much as a means to the end of disengagement as an end in itself. On the other hand, disengagement is also in an important sense an instrumental value in that it constitutes a precondition for effective confrontation with the minority regimes south of the Zambezi. The Zambian Government and President Kaunda in particular are firmly committed to political transformation in Southern Africa. Yet, to the extent that Zambia remains dependent on the White South, its support for the liberation struggle there is necessarily constrained.

The indicators employed to operationalize the concepts of disengagement and integration are, in the absence of alternatives, principally transaction flows. The theoretical and practical problems inherent in this form of analysis are formidable. Apart from the complexities of the phenomena being measured, the empirical data available on developing African countries is frequently deficient, quantitatively and qualitatively. Moreover, there is growing scepticism among scholars concerning the precise significance of transaction data.[16] To compensate for these liabilities, or at least to minimize them, a multi-indicator, multi-measurement, multi-dimensional approach has been adopted. In the case of indicators, an effort has been made to tap as wide a range as possible in the hope that these might reveal some convergence, or at least that composite indices will prove less subject to error than single indicator indices. Inevitably, the principal focus is on trade, communications and migration but, where feasible, other measures including political transactions are utilized. As the approach is from the perspective of a single state, not a region, the comparative element in the data is provided longitudinally (since Independence in 1964) rather than cross-sectionally.

As a further check on the validity of indicators, a variety of scoring technique is employed as appropriate and their congruence noted. Each of these has its theoretical and practical advantages and disadvantages.[17] Raw scores are easies to calculate, and often the only available data. On the other hand, they are susceptible to a variety of extraneous influences. A decline in Zambian copper shipments through Rhodesia, for example, might merely reflect a shortfall in production, not a deliberate diversion of exports to alternative routes. Relati scoring procedures overcome some of these difficulties by instituting various co trols. Control for size is achieved by calculating transactions with the target states as a proportion of total transactions or of some alternative base.

Nye has argued persuasively in favour of disaggregating integration into its economic, social and political components, and others have emphasized the need t distinguish between societal and governmental actors.[18] These functional categories and levels of analysis are also relevant as dimensions of disengagement. Accordingly, they have been combined in the simple matrix in Table 2. The essen of this study is to obtain appropriate indices for each of the cells.

Table 2

Dimensions of Disengagement/Integration

Functional Dimensions / Actor Level	Disengagement from Southern Africa/ Integration with East Africa		
	Political System	Society	Economy
Governmental			
Societal: Zambian			
Societal: European			

It is important to appreciate that in the Zambian environment, "society" (conceived as the "attentive public) effectively excludes the bulk of the subsistenc sector, comprising two-thirds of the population. The peasant masses are, for al practical purposes, outside the decision-making process on national issues and sufficiently independent of the money economy not to be greatly affected by, for example, increases in the cost of living resulting from disengagement. Moreover even the modern sector is far from homogeneous. In particular, recognition must be accorded to the realities of race even with a government dedicated to the ide of non-racialism. Accordingly, allowance is made for the differential behavior patterns of Zambians and Europeans.

Intergovernmental Transactions

Common Services

The breakup of the Federation of Rhodesia and Nyasaland at the end of 1963 was preceded by prolonged negotiations on the nature and scope of the intergovernmental arrangements to replace it. In the past, Federal apologists had "tended to argue that where a low level of regional identity exists, the creation of strong central institutions is necessary to provide the framework for its growth."[19] When this failed to materialize, they retreated to a neo-functional position. The British in particular pressed for "effective new forms of collaboration between the territories" so that "the benefits of association might be preserved."[20] This aroused Zambian suspicions that, in Nye's words, "the neo-functionalists were federalists in functionalist clothing, pursuing federal ends through what appeared to be functionalist means." Or, more colourfully, neo-functionalism was "a strategy for attacking the castle of national sovereignty by stealth, with interest groups as mercenaries and technocrats as agents within the walls to open the gates quietly."[21]

Ideally, Zambia would have preferred no formal ties with Rhodesia because of their potential spillover effects. Consequently, a Common Service Organization on the East African model (as proposed by the British) was out of the question. Even the revival of the purely advisory and consultative Central African Council which had served as a forum for functional cooperation from 1945 to 1953 was more than Zambian leaders were prepared to accept. At the same time, they were sufficiently realistic to acknowledge the need for some joint decision-making machinery to maintain certain essential shared services, at least during a transitional period. The Siamese twins could not be surgically separated immediately. "You cannot build a wall across Kariba like the Berlin wall," Kaunda admitted. "We must have some tie-up with Southern Rhodesia, whether we like it or not."[22]

The British (and Rhodesian) negotiators considered that the "essential core" of any future association lay in "the shared economic arrangements, such as the common market in goods and labour, and the joint banking, credit, exchange and currency facilities." Yet, the most Lusaka would concede in the financial sphere was "the possible need for interim joint arrangements in such matters as currency."[23] Accordingly, provision was made for the central Bank of Rhodesia and Nyasaland to function for two years beyond the end of the Federation.[24] In only four fields - three commercial and one technical - was Zambia prepared to contemplate continuing collaboration with Rhodesia, and then only on the basis of strict quality of ownership and control, and on the understanding that the commercial enterprises would be run as purely business operations. As a result, joint statutory corporations were established for Rhodesia Railways,[25] the Central African Power Corporation (Kariba),[26] Central African Airways (with Zambia Airways as a jointly and wholly owned subsidiary),[27] and the Agricultural Research Council of Central Africa.[28] The latter two were tripartite bodies with Malawian participation. A number of factors contributed to Zambia's willingness to compromise, among them respect for the expressed concern of the World Bank for protection of its rail and power investments,[29] the realization that the headquarters and most of the shared assets and staff were physically located in Rhodesia, and the opportunity which membership offered of influencing political developments in Rhodesia by promoting non-racialism in the common services.[30] The decisive consideration, however, was political: anxiety not to prejudice or delay a break-up of the Federation in any way. Acceptance of certain common services was a price Zambia was prepared to pay to secure British and Rhodesian agreement on defederation.

Table 3

Dissolution of Post-Federal Common Services

Common Service	Zambian Decision to Withdraw	De Facto Dissolution	De Jure Dissolution
Bank of Rhodesia and Nyasaland	June 28, 1963	June 1, 1965	June 30, 1965
Agricultural Research Council	March 30, 1967	Sept. 30, 1967	Sept. 30, 1967
Rhodesia Railways	Nov. 8, 1965	June 30, 1967	-
Central African Airways	Aug. 30, 1966	Dec. 31, 1967	-
Central African Power Corporation	-	-	-

Although dissolution of the common services was always regarded as a possibility, it was nevertheless confidently assumed even in Lusaka that the post-Federal agreements would provide a mutually satisfactory basis for cooperation for the foreseeable future, especially in the case of the airways and Kariba which were financially independent. This did not prove to be the case (Table 3). In mid-1965, the Bank of Rhodesia and Nyasaland was formally wound up, six months ahead of schedule. More significant, as early as April 1965, the Rhodesian government proposed the break-up of the unified railway system, to which Zambia agreed in principle three days before UDI.[31] But it was the Rhodesian rebellion, more thar anything else, which destroyed the basis for continued cooperation across the Zambezi. Even the comparatively innocuous Agricultural Research Council succumbed to the inexorable pressures in Zambia to disengage. The only common service to survive in recognizable form has been the Central African Power Corporation, and with the commissioning of the Kariba North power station expected by early 1977, the fate of this last institutional legacy of Federation remains in some doubt. In the meanwhile, Zambia remains heavily dependent for power on the jointly owned Kariba South generating station in Rhodesia.

The major common services dissolved were the railways and the airways. Both ceased joint operations in 1967, though in neither case has final agreement been reached on the division of assets and liabilities among the national successor organizations. Eventual dissolution of Central African Airways was perhaps predictable, in view of the prestige attached to national airlines. Nevertheless, the economic significance of Rhodesia Railways was much greater, and controversy concerning its operation correspondingly more intense. This accords with Nye's Law of Inverse Salience: "the more important the task by nature or impact, the weaker the authority of the organization will be."[32]

One measure of the extent of Zambian disengagement from inter-governmental cooperation with Rhodesia is the decline in the number of meetings of joint decision-making organs. The agreements establishing the common services typically provided for a policy-making Higher Authority (except in the case of the Agricultural Research Council) at ministerial level and a board of management composed essestially of civil servants.

The only joint body with an element of supernational political authority was the Higher Authority for Civil Air Transport which exercised "the powers of the Government of any Territory" in the matter of international air traffic rights, though only on the basis of unanimity.[33] The other higher authorities were at Zambian insistence deliberately endowed with minimal powers to ensure that ministers would have to confer only infrequently. Even so, business was normally transacted by circulating resolutions for signature - a form of conference by correspondence. As a result, the only ministerial meeting held prior to the Rhodesian rebellion was a brief meeting of the Higher Authority for Railways on November 8, 1965 on the eve of UDI, and it adjourned without issuing any policy directive.[34] Thereafter, Zambian ministers refused to sit down with "rebel ministers."[35] On one occasion shortly after UDI, the Railways Authority reverted to the practice of circular resolutions. However, on February 25, 1966, Zambia advised the Railways Board that this procedure was no longer acceptable.[36] This action finally ended any prospect of the Higher Authority for Railways ever functioning. In any case, with the *de facto* division of the railways (and the airways) the following year, the need for ministerial bodies in these fields lapsed. Accordingly, they were replaced by Dissolution Committees.[37]

Zambia had repeatedly urged the British Government "to appoint lawful members to the Higher Authority [for Railways] to act on behalf of Rhodesia" as had been done with the Reserve Bank of Rhodesia, but, according to President Kaunda, "our requests were answered by a mixture of lies and evasion."[38] In the case of the Higher Authority for Power, London eventually relented following the return of the Conservative Government to office and, in October 1970, named two British members in place of the Rhodesian ministers. The Higher Authority was then able to reconstitute the Central African Power Corporation with a quorum of legal members. This was a necessary preliminary to the decision authorizing construction of a power station on Kariba North Bank.[39]

Although the Zambian Government attempted to extend its ban on direct dealings with "ministers" of the illegal Salisbury regime to include relations between officials, this did not always prove practicable. Contact continued at three levels: at policy conferences concerned with the future of the common services, at regular meetings of boards of management, and in periodic consultations at the operational level.

In July 1966, Lusaka approached London (rather than Salisbury) concerning the dissolution of the unitary railway system but, as in the case of membership of the Higher Authority for the Railways, the response was "a mixture of deceit and weakness, coupled with platitudes allied to evasion." Eventually, in November, President Kaunda presented the British with an ultimatum: either they agreed within seven days to negotiate the break-up or "we may be obliged to negotiate directly with the rebel regime in Rhodesia, unpalatable as that would be."[40] Needless to say, London merely protested its helplessness. Accordingly, talks between Zambian and Rhodesian officials commenced the following month. The agreement that finally emerged took the form of virtually identical letters, dated May 22, 1967, from the delegation heads to their respective governments.[41] Subsequently, similar discussions took place on the dissolution of Central African Airways.

Following UDI, the boards of the various common service organizations also continued to meet (Table 4). Only with the break-up of three of them in 1967 did the frequency of meetings decline significantly. Nevertheless, Zambian qualms about acquiescing in anything that might imply recognition of the rebels necessitated resort to a variety of procedural devices. In the case of the Railways Board, the legal requirement of Higher Authority approval for deficit budgeting and capital expenditures was simply ignored. In letters to the two governments

Table 4

Meetings of Boards of Common Services, 1964-72

Year	Bank of Rhodesia and Nyasaland Board	Agricultural Research Council	Central African Airways Board	Rhodesia Railways Board of Management	Central African Power Corporation: Corporation	Central African Power Corporation: Committee	Total	Index 1964 = 100
1964	10	3	13	16	11	-	53	100
1965	5	2	11	17	14	-	49	92
1966	-	3	9	14	1	9	36	68
1967	-	1	12	8	0	12	33	62
1968	-	-	9	3	0	8	20	38
1969	-	-	9	3	0	11	23	43
1970	-	-	9	4	1	12	26	49
1971	-	-	6	4	0	10	20	38
1972	-	-	4	3	0	11	18	34
Total	15	9	82	72	27	73	278	

on May 11, 1966, the Board argued boldly that, despite the Higher Authority's persistent failure to function, the Board was still bound to carry out its statutory obligations - "making decisions where compelled to do so without Higher Authority approval."[42] The Central African Power Corporation, on the other hand, adopted the subterfuge of a "Committee" composed of members of the Corporation to circumvent the awkward legal vacuum created by the expiration on December 20, 1965, of the appointments of its Rhodesian members. On two occasions, however, Zambian members did participate in formal Corporation meetings.[43] Moreover, when in November 1969 the Rhodesian membership of the Railways Board changed, Lusaka quietly overlooked the illegality of the new appointments.[44] The pursuit of political purity was not pressed to the point of seriously interfering with vital national interests, especially as no other government was prepared to take a stand on principle.

Another indicator of the extent of Zambia's institutional disengagement from Rhodesia is the size of the common service bureaucracies, as measured by their

Table 5

Zambia-Rhodesia Common Services Bureaucracies

Year	Senior Administrative Staff		Administrative Expenditure*		Mean Index 1964 = 100
	No.	Index	US$	Index	
1964	529	100	8,310,000	100	100
1965	581	110	10,449,000	126	118
1966	563	106	10,629,000	128	117
1967	594	112	10,955,000	132	122
1968	31	6	872,000	10	8
1969	30	6	641,000	8	7
1970	29	6	698,000	8	7
1971	31	6	748,000	9	7
1972	32	6	891,000	11	8

* Year ended June 30th. The 1972 increase reflects the devaluation of the dollar.

Sources: Annual Reports of common services.

administrative budgets and staffs (Table 5). After an initial build-up during the early years of the organizations, a sharp decline in their human and financial resources set in, particularly following the break-up of the railways and airways in 1967. The shrinkage is even more marked when compared to the spectacular growth of the size of and expenditure on the Zambian bureaucracy, and when allowance is made for inflation.

At the time of Independence, there were no institutional links at governmental level between Zambia and East Africa. Various schemes had been proposed in the past, but consideration of these ended with the commitment of Northern Rhodesia to the Federation of Rhodesia and Nyasaland. UDI and the search for alternative routes, however, led to the emergence of a number of common services with East Africa and especially Tanzania. These have been of two types: public corporations and private limited liability companies (Table 6). In addition, several intergovernmental committees exist at ministerial or official level to deal with common problems such as security and shipping.

The scale of operation of the three Zambia-Tanzania common services are expanding steadily in terms of numbers of employees and the value of their fixed assets, and should eventually approach, in size, the three joint Zambia-Rhodesia organiza

Table 6

Zambia-Tanzania Common Services Organizations

Common Service	Date Established	Headquarters	Zambian Participation US$	Zambian Participation %	Other Partners	Corporate Structure
Zambia Tanzania Road Services Ltd.	12 May 1966	Lusaka	$ 980,000(1966) $1,470,000(1968)	35%	Tanzania 2 Italian firms	Private Company
Eastern Africa National Shipping Line Ltd.	28 June 1966	Dar es Salaam	$ 280,000	17%	Kenya Tanzania Uganda Southern Line	Private Company
Tazama Pipelines Ltd.	8 Dec. 1966	Ndola/ Dar es Salaam	$ 467,000	67%	Tanzania	Private Company
Tanzania Zambia Railway Authority (TAZARA)	3 Oct. 1968 (reconstituted 17 Dec. 1972)	Dar es Salaam		50%	Tanzania	Public corporation

tions at their peak (Table 7). As was the case with Rhodesia, the railway will be by far the largest of the enterprises shared with Tanzania.[45] Completion of the railway to Dar es Salaam will also mean the running down or winding up of Tanzania Zambia Road Services as a jointly owned company, thus leaving only two common services: Tazara and Tazama.

Zambia has also sought to strengthen its bonds with the East African Community as a whole. However, the relatively low level of integration achieved so far contrasts sharply with the rhetoric of Government spokesmen. Although until recently Lusaka still professed to favour eventual full membership of the Community, no real progress was made towards even the more modest objective of joining some of the East African common services. In November 1968, Zambian negotiators indicated an interest in the Harbours Corporation, the Posts and Telecommunications Corporation, the Research and Social Council and possibly East African Airways - but not East African Railways.[46] Zambian interest in the East African Harbours Corporation is obvious. This has been demonstrated as early as 1967 when the Government

Table 7

Scale of Operations of Zambian Common Services with Rhodesia/Tanzania

Year	Employees				Fixed Assets				Mean Index	
	Zambia-Rhodesia		Zambia-Tanzania		Zambia-Rhodesia		Zambia-Tanzania		Zambia-Rhodesia	Zambia-Tanzania*
	No.	Index	No.	Index	US$m	Index	US$m	Index*		
1964	30,424	100	-	-	$439	100	-	-	100	-
1965	30,900	102	-	-	438	100	-	-	101	-
1966	31,104	102	950	3	456	104	$ 7	2	103	2
1967	31,662	104	2,200	7	456	104	28	6	104	7
1968	654	2	2,300	8	205	47	60	14	24	11
1969	649	2	2,600	9	202	46	60	14	24	11
1970	666	2	9,700	32	199	46	70	16	24	24
1971	686	2	37,000	122	204	47	100	23	24	72
1972	708	2	34,000	112	228**	52	200	46	27	79
-			-	-	-	-	-	-	-	-
1976	0	0	10,000	33	0	0	480	109	0	71

* Based on Zambian-Rhodesian figures for 1964 = 100.

** 1972 increase reflects devaluation of dollar.

Sources: Annual Reports of Zambia-Rhodesia common services; Annual Reports of Indeco. Figures for Zambia-Tanzania common services must be regarded as only approximate in view of the wildly differing estimates available, particularly concerning TAZARA employees.

provided a grant of $1,400,000 and a loan of $4,800,000 towards the cost of development of the port facilities of Dar es Salaam and Mtwara.[47]

Political Transactions

Interstate agreements, diplomatic exchanges and heads of state contact provide further measures of Zambian interaction at the governmental level with Southern Africa and East Africa. During the final months of the Federation and with the full concurrence of Zambian leaders, Northern Rhodesia concluded a number of agreements with its southern neighbours, notably those with Rhodesia establishing common services. However, the great majority of the international obligations Zambia inherited at Independence were incurred by the Federal or British governments. Lusaka undertook to honour all of these (without being quite certain what they were) pending a review to assess their implications. As a result, over half the agreements with Southern Africa have since been abrogated - and only two new ones negotiated, in June 1969 and June 1971. Both of these involved undertakings by Portugal to cease "retaliatory" action against Zambia in return for assurances concerning guerrillas allegedly harboured on Zambian territory. The majority of the pre-independence agreements retained related to boundaries.

Table 8

Zambian Agreements with Southern Africa and East Africa: 1964-72

Year	Southern Africa		East Africa*		Rhodesia		Tanzania*	
	No.	Index	No.	Index	No.	Index	No.	Index
1964	23	100	2	9	13	100	2	15
1965	20	87	5	22	12	92	5	38
1966	16	70	10	44	9	69	10	77
1967	13	57	13	57	6	46	13	100
1968	13	57	18	78	6	46	18	138
1969	13	57	18	78	6	46	18	138
1970	13	57	19	83	6	46	19	146
1971	13	57	20	87	5	38	20	154
1972	13	57	20	87	5	38	20	154

* Index calculated on the basis of the number of agreements with Southern Africa/Rhodesia in 1964 = 100

Of the twelve agreements that have been terminated, two dealt with trade relations with South Africa and Portugal. (Zambia has no trade agreement with Rhodesia as, under the Federation, the two countries formed a customs union and later, when Salisbury offered an agreement, Lusaka spurned it.) Four agreements were in the communications field: these concerned the railways and airways (and are in practice, if not legally, inoperative), and membership of the (Southern) African Posta Union and the (Southern) African Telecommunications Union.[48] Zambia also withdrew from the Agricultural Research Council of Central Africa and later the International Red Locust Control Service based in Mbala, following the creation of a new body which excluded the southern African minority regimes from membership. Finally Zambia terminated the various arrangements with Rhodesia, South Africa and Portugal governing visas, extradition and fugitive offenders.[49]

The pattern of treaty relations with East Africa has been very different (Table 8) At the time of Independence, few agreements existed, but since then their number has steadily increased. A majority, reflecting Zambia's search for alternative routes, have concerned communications. Most have also taken the form of bilateral arrangements with Tanzania, though several, mainly dealing with security matters, have been concluded with the East African states collectively. Curiously, there appear to have been no purely bilateral agreements so far with either Kenya or Uganda.

Except for treaty relations, there has been less scope for inter-governmental disengagement from South Africa and Portugal than in the case of Rhodesia as ther was never the same degree of political integration. Until 1963, the jurisdiction of the South African Accredited Diplomatic Representative in Salisbury embraced Zambia, but this lapsed with the dissolution of the Federation. Shortly afterwards, in January 1964, Dr. Kaunda offered to exchange ambassadors with Pretoria provided the Zambian envoy was assured equality of treatment with other diplomats in South Africa.[50] This condition was evidently unacceptable as the initiative was ignored.

The only official representation Zambia had in South Africa was the Government Labour Office opened in Johannesburg before the Second World War to deal with contract labour on the mines. In late 1965, following the South African decisio to require all foreign Africans to carry passports, the office was strengthened with the appointment of a Senior Passport Officer with consular responsibilities limited to the issuing of travel documents to expatriate Zambians.[51] The Zambia Labour Department Representative (also a European) resident in Salisbury since 1938 assumed similar functions after UDI. Both offices were closed in 1968.

With the end of the Federation, the Portuguese consul in Ndola was withdrawn.

However, Lisbon repeatedly pressed Lusaka to exchange ambassadors, or at least accept consular representation, which Zambia equally firmly refused. The only continuing forum for consultation with the Portuguese at the intergovernmental level, therefore, was the monthly meeting of the Beira Port Traffic Advisory Committee where deliberations among the port users (including Rhodesian and railway representatives) are normally confined to technical issues. The so-called Mixed Luso-Zambian Commission which the Portuguese claimed existed consisted of a series of four ad hoc meetings in 1968 and 1969 to investigate violations of Zambia's borders.[52]

The absence of direct diplomatic relations has not entirely precluded high-level Zambian contacts with Pretoria, Lisbon and even Salisbury. Yet, relations have at best been sporadic and hardly qualify as the "beneficial communication" spanning "a period of several years" that Alker and Puchala consider the test of significant transaction flows.[53] On the contrary, these encounters have been more comparable to the peaking of diplomatic exchanges during a disintegrating relationship on the eve of conflict. Between April and August 1968, President Kaunda and Prime Minister Vorster engaged in a fairly extensive exchange of correspondence exploring Southern African issues. Moreover, on five occasions between June 1968 and March 1971, the Zambian President received South African emissaries, who appeared primarily interested in securing his consent to a meeting with Vorster. The missions were uniformly unsuccessful.[54] Similar intermittent contact was maintained with the Portuguese government. Dr. Kaunda corresponded on at least two occasions with successive prime ministers and, in March 1971, his Special Assistant on Foreign Affairs visited Lisbon. These exchanges undoubtedly paved the way for the constructive role Zambia was able to play in facilitating Portuguese decolonialization following the 1974 military coup.

Diplomatic linkages between Zambia and East Africa have evolved only gradually (Table 9). Missions were first exchanged with Tanzania and then with Kenya, though in each case Zambia acted several years before the recipient state reciprocated. No resident High Commissioners have yet been exchanged with Uganda and even Zambia's non-resident representation established in 1966 lapsed following the Amin coup of 1971.[55] One reason for the comparatively slow pace of development of official relations is paradoxically the very closeness of political relations. These have been regarded as too important and too intimate to be entrusted to diplomats. The East African Community members do not exchange diplomats among themselves. Of greater significance, therefore, as indicators of political integration may be the summit meetings of heads of state (Table 10). Two trends are apparent here: President Kaunda has had closer direct contact with President Nyerere than with either of the other East African leaders, and

Table 9

Government Representatives: Zambia and Southern Africa/East Africa, 1964-1972

Year	Zambia - Rhodesia		Zambia - Southern Africa		Zambia - Tanzania		Zambia - East Africa	
	No.	Indices*	No.	Indices*	No.	Indices*	No.	Indices*
1964	1	7	2	5	0	0	0	5
1965	1	7	3	7	2	14	2	5
1966	1	7	3	7	3	21	5	12
1967	1	7	3	7	4	29	6	14
1968	1	7	2	5	9	64	13	31
1969	0	0	0	0	9	64	13	31
1970	0	0	0	0	14	100	24	57
1971	0	0	0	0	14	100	26	62
1972	0	0	0	0	13	93	25	60

* Assumes full complement of a mission is 7; hence with an exchange of missions, 14 = 100 or 42 = 100 for a region. In the case of Zambian non-resident representation in Kenya (1966-68 and Uganda (1966-71), only the High Commissioner is recorded.

Sources: Diplomatic Lists and Government Directories.

Table 10

Meetings Between Zambian and East African Heads of State: 1964-1972

Year	Kaunda - Nyerere	Kaunda - Kenyatta	Kaunda - Obote	Zambia - East Africa Summits	Total*
1964	3	3	3	2	9
1965	8	3	3	2	14
1966	10	1	3	1	14
1967	8	5	8	4	21
1968	3	4	2	0	9
1969	6	2	4	2	12
1970	6	0	3	1	9
1971	8	1	1	0	10
1972	4	0	0	0	4

* Summit meetings excluded to avoid duplication.

the frequency of personal encounters has tapered off since the peak year of 1967. The explanation of this decline is to be found in the passing of the immediate crisis engendered by the Rhodesian rebellion, growing preoccupation with domestic affairs, particularly since 1971, improved telecommunications and greater reliance on diplomatic channels.

Economic Transactions

The long and sorry history of Zambia's absorption into the Southern African economic empire in general and the Rhodesian economy in particular underlines the significance of economic indicators as a measure of disengagement from the South. Two of these have special relevance: trade (imports and exports) and energy (electricity, coal and oil).

Statistics on financial transactions might also prove revealing if more data were available. A qualitative assessment, however, suggests that considerable progress has already been made in reducing Zambia's financial ties with Southern Africa. On May 26, 1965, national foreign exchange controls were instituted in place of the federal regulatory machinery which had continued to function for nearly a year and a half following the dissolution of the Federation. Also, overseas companies were urged to establish "truly Zambian offshoots" in place of mere order offices of their Southern African subsidiaries. The Government was especially anxious that foreign businesses in Zambia should dissociate themselves administratively from Rhodesia.[56] As a result, most multinational corporations transferred supervisory responsibility for their Zambian branches to Nairobi or London. Finally, a series of economic reforms were instituted between April 1968 and November 1970. These led to agreements on 51% government participation in a large number of companies ranging from the giant mining corporations to comparatively small-scale concerns. Admittedly, this action was not directed specifically at foreign control emanating from any particular quarter. Nevertheless, the predominance of Southern African investments in Zambia ensured that the greatest impact would fall on them. Zambianization of the economy has been primarily at the expense of Rhodesian and South African financial interests.

Trade

Table 11 demonstrates both the nature and the extent of previous Zambian trade dependence on the South, particularly with respect to imports, and also the degree of disengagement so far achieved. Although at Independence Southern Africa provided a market for only 12% of Zambian exports (mainly copper), nearly sixty percent of imports originated there, with Rhodesia directly or indirectly providing

Table 11

Zambian Trade with Southern Africa: 1964-1972
(by value)

Year	Imports			Exports			Trade		
	% Total Imports	Indices: 1964 = 100		% Total Exports	Indices: 1964 = 100		% Total Trade	Indices: 1964 = 100	
		Value	%		Value	%		Value	%
1964	58.2	100	100	12.0	100	100	26.2	100	100
1965	51.6	121	89	9.4	89	79	24.1	111	92
1966	40.7	112	70	6.8	83	57	17.8	103	68
1967	31.3	106	54	5.9	69	49	15.6	94	60
1968	27.4	98	47	2.4	32	20	11.5	77	44
1969	26.5	91	46	1.1	22	9	8.2	69	31
1970	20.3	76	35	1.4	25	12	7.3	60	28
1971	18.6	83	32	2.3	28	19	9.5	66	36
1972	16.9	78	29	2.3	31	19	8.3	62	32

Sources: <u>Annual Statement of External Trade</u>; <u>Monthly Digest of Statistics</u>.

Table 12

Zambian Trade with Rhodesia and South Africa: 1964-1972

Year	Zambian Trade with Rhodesia			Zambian Trade with South Africa		
	% Total Imports	% Total Exports	% Total Trade	% Total Imports	% Total Exports	% Total Trade
1964	36.1	4.1	13.9	21.9	7.8	12.1
1965	30.9	2.9	12.6	20.5	6.5	11.4
1966	15.9	1.0	5.8	24.7	5.7	11.8
1967	6.3	0.4	2.7	24.7	5.4	12.8
1968	2.4	0.2	1.0	24.5	2.1	10.3
1969	2.0	0.1	0.6	23.5	1.0	7.3
1970	1.4	0.1	0.5	18.2	1.2	6.5
1971	2.2	0.1	1.0	15.7	2.1	8.1
1972	1.3	0.3	1.0	14.9	1.9	7.5

Sources: <u>Annual Statement of External Trade</u>; <u>Monthly Digest of Statistics</u>

over three-fifths of this amount. (Imports of Rhodesian electrical energy have been excluded from all trade calculations as the Kariba generators, while physically located on the south bank of the Zambezi, are jointly owned with Zambia.)

During the first eight years of Independence and especially since 1966, trade with the South decreased by nearly one-third in money terms and by two-thirds in relation to total Zambian trade. If national income is used as a control, the dimensions of the decline are even more dramatically revealed. Aggregate indicators for Southern Africa as a whole, however, obscure some significant variations in the separate patterns of trade with Rhodesia and with South Africa. The former (Table 12) has on every scale lost out heavily. Both imports and exports have dwindled to the point that they are now almost insignificant.[57] During 1971-72, a slight recovery occurred when, faced with a disastrous drought, Zambia was compelled to purchase substantial quantities of Rhodesian maize but this represented no more than a temporary setback. In any case, with the closing of the border in January 1973 - initially by Rhodesia and then permanently by Zambia - direct trade (except for Zairois transit traffic) effectively ceased.

The trade pattern with South Africa (Table 12) is more complex, particularly with respect to imports. During the Federal period, South Africa lost out relative to Rhodesia which was able to exploit the tariff advantages of a customs union to expand its markets in Zambia greatly. Consequently, the proportion of imports from Rhodesia increased two-and-a-half times, while the proportion from South Africa fell by a quarter. The South African share continued to decline during the first year after Independence, though not as rapidly as Rhodesia'a. However, following UDI, South African sales to Zambia recovered as Zambia shifted part of its purchases away from Rhodesia to South Africa. In practice, this often meant merely dealing with the Johannesburg head office instead of the Salisbury branch. In cash terms, sales more than doubled between 1964 and 1967. Nevertheless, the extent of this reallocation of purchases within Southern Africa should not be exaggerated. The percentage of South African imports increased only modestly and, since 1967, has declined. As indicated in Table 13, South Africa reaped only a fifth of the windfall from UDI.

Moreover, by 1969, the value of imports from South Africa had begun to decline absolutely as well as relatively, and continued to do so until 1972. The relaxation of restrictions on trade with South Africa instituted in 1971 and formally acknowledged in February 1972 following the collapse of world copper prices, revived hopes in South Africa of a restoration of its profitable market in Zambia. This failed to materialize. Moreover, prospects were seriously impaired when Rhodesia closed its northern border. Despite the resort to circuitous routes

Table 13

Diversion of Zambian Imports from Rhodesia: 1965-1967

Years	Decrease in Rhodesia's % share of Zambian imports	Diversion of Zambian purchases to:	
		South Africa	Elsewhere
1965 to 1966	15.3	4.2	11.1
1966 to 1967	9.3	0.0	9.3
Total	24.6	4.2	20.4

Source: Table 12.

through Angola and Malawi, the re-opening of Dar es Salaam to South African goods designated as essential, and the improvisation of an airlift, the additional transport costs incurred more than cancel out South Africa's previous natural advantage due to proximity. As a result in 1973, imports from South Africa fell by more than 30%. Once Zambia's immediate supply crisis is surmounted, the outlook for those who envisage Zambia as the gateway to the economic penetration of Black Africa will be even bleaker.

The Portuguese colonies have never been a significant factor in Zambian trade. Total trade still amounts to less than $3 million per year. Nevertheless, a gradual expansion has occurred over the years, particularly on the import side and with Mozambique, and trade is now over four times what it was in 1964.

Much oratory and considerable energy has been expended in promoting trade between Zambia and East Africa. The inspiration behind this drive has come from a combination of ideology and economic necessity: it is welcomed as both a practical expression of pan-Africanism and a partial solution to the search for alternative markets and sources of supply.

The obstacles to closer economic collaboration with East Africa - in ascending order of potency - have been fiscal, physical, informational and structural. As early as February 1964, Zambia lowered its tariffs on certain Kenyan and Zanzibar commodities.[58] On the other hand, East Africa lost the competitive advantage it enjoyed under Commonwealth preferences when, in pursuance of a policy of non-alignment, Zambia introduced a single column customs tariff at the beginning of 1966.[59] Nevertheless, the Zambian tariff level is, for historical reasons, approximately half that prevailing in East Africa.[60] Another positive manifestation of Lusaka's intentions was the decision in September 1967 to admit goods of

East African origin under Open General Licenses. Unfortunately, for administrative reasons this concession had to be revoked fourteen months later.[61]

Meanwhile, some of the communication problems inhibiting expansion of inter-regional trade were being overcome. Although Central African Road Services had pioneered a scheduled freight service to Nairobi since 1957, as late as 1963 traffic on the Great North Road to Dar es Salaam averaged only eight lorries per week.[62] Yet, within a few months of UDI, a fleet of over a thousand giant vehicles was plying this route regularly. Under this punishment, the road soon disintegrated into the Hell Run but, as a result of a major reconstruction operation, a modern hardtopped highway capable of withstanding the massive tonnages using it now links Zambia with Dar es Salaam.

Table 14

Trade Disengagement and Integration: 1964-1972
(by value)

Year	*Indices of Zambian Trade (Imports and Exports) with:							
	Rhodesia		Tanzania		Southern Africa		East Africa	
	Value	% Total	Value	% Total	Value	% Total	Value	% Total
1964	100	100	1.0	1.0	100	100	1.2	1.2
1965	109	91	1.7	1.4	111	92	1.6	1.3
1966	62	41	1.8	1.2	103	68	2.6	1.7
1967	30	19	2.7	1.7	94	60	4.1	2.6
1968	13	7	2.8	1.6	77	44	5.1	2.9
1969	9	4	7.0	3.2	69	31	9.5	4.3
1970	8	4	6.3	2.9	60	28	10.3	4.8
1971	13	7	9.6	5.3	66	36	13.1	7.3
1972	10	5	6.8	3.5	62	32	9.1	4.7

* Indices for Rhodesia and Tanzania based on Rhodesia 1964 = 100; indices for Southern Africa and East Africa based on Southern Africa 1964 = 100. Imported "Rhodesian" electricity and East African oil are excluded.

Sources: Annual Statement of External Trade; Monthly Digest of Statistics.

Inaccessibility also bred ignorance of the potential for mutual exploitation of markets in Zambia and East Africa. The initiative in exploring these opportunities came from Lusaka. In 1964, the Government mounted an exhibition at the

Nairobi Agricultural Show.[63] The following year, it convened a conference in Lusaka on interregional trade and despatched a trade mission to East Africa capitals. Trade commissioners were also appointed to Dar es Salaam in 1967 and to Nairobi in 1970. In return, beginning in 1965 a succession of Kenyan and Tanzanian trade missions descended on Zambia. (Uganda continues to evince little real interest in commercial relations with Zambia or, for that matter, with Tanzania.) Although no formal trade agreements emerged from these visits, imports from East Africa doubled in 1966 and again in 1967. As a result, a substantial trade deficit developed with Kenya and Tanzania. One reason for this was that, after UDI, Zambia's most pressing need was for alternative sources of supply, not new markets. It is not surprising, therefore, that the Zambian Industrial and Commercial Association (ZINCOM) delegation that toured East Africa in 1968 was more concerned with imports than exports. In any case, the Government was eager to encourage businessmen in Zambia to break their traditional ties with Southern Africa. Gradually under pressure, the structural orientation of the Zambian economy began to veer eastward.

Table 15

Diversion of Zambian Trade from Southern Africa to East Africa
(by value)

	Imports Diverted*			Exports Diverted*			Trade Diverted*		
Years	From Southern Africa	To East Africa	% Diverted to East Africa	From Southern Africa	To East Africa	% Diverted to East Africa	From Southern Africa	To East Africa	% Diverted to East Africa
1964-69	-31.8	+2.8	+8.7%	-10.9	+0.08	+0.7%	-18.0	+0.97	+5.4%
1969-72	- 9.6	-0.9	-8.8%	+ 1.2	+0.05	-	+ 0.2	-0.05	-
1964-72	-41.3	+1.9	+4.7%	- 9.7	+0.13	+1.3%	-17.8	+0.92	+5.2%

* As % of total imports/exports/trade, excluding "Rhodesian" electricity and East African oil.

Sources: Tables 11 and 14.

Nevertheless, the extent of economic integration achieved with East Africa must be kept in perspective. While the percentage increase in trade is impressive, and in 1969 and 1970 the value of trade with Tanzania approached that with Rhodesia, the level of trade with East Africa as a whole was in 1972 still only a fraction of the <u>residue</u> of Zambian trade with Southern Africa (Table 14). Expressed differently, by 1969 the East African Community had managed to fill less than 9% of the market vacuum created by Zambia's policy of squeezing out imports from the South, and since then the East African share has actually declined. Success in diverting Zambian exports eastward has been even more modest (Table 15). It seems unlikely that East Africa can ever hope to provide an adequate alternative to Southern Africa as a trading partner. Certainly to date, Europe not Africa has been the principal beneficiary of economic disengagement.

Energy

At Independence, Zambia was dependent on Rhodesia for all its major sources of industrial energy. The Kariba hydro-electric generating station, though jointly owned, was situated on the South Bank; the high-grade coal and coke essential to the refining of copper and lead came from Wankie; and oil for the railways, road transport and the mines flowed through the Beira-Umtali pipeline to the Feruka refinery.[64]

The rebellion in Rhodesia directly threatened each of these pillars of the Zambian economy. With the reported mining of the approaches to Kariba (and the refusal of the British to respond effectively), the Salisbury regime acquired the capability of closing down the Copperbelt with impunity at any time it wished merely by pulling a switch - though for its own reasons it chose not to do so. In the case of coal, Ian Smith on December 17, 1965 suddenly boosted the royalty a hundredfold from 14 cents to $14.00 a ton and introduced a new export tax on coke of over $22 a ton. Although he was forced to climb down two weeks later when President Kaunda called his bluff, the oil embargo instituted at the same time, allegedly in retaliation against British sanctions, continued.

The resulting oil drought was the most critical energy problem to confront the Zambian Government. On January 13, 1966, petrol stocks in the country amounted to less than three days' consumption.[65] Nevertheless, the oil crisis proved the easiest and quickest to solve (Table 16). As an immediate palliative, an Anglo-American-Canadian airlift was mounted to ferry in oil from Kinshasa, Nairobi and Dar es Salaam.[66] By the time it wound up in October 1966, considerable progress had been made in introducing alternative surface routes. Moreover, strict rationing (over a period of 33 months) ensured that available supplies were allocated to the most essential services. Finally, in September 1968, the oil pipeline, constructed from Dar es Salaam to Ndola in record time, was opened. Thus, within three years of UDI, Zambia had succeeded in completely overcoming the effects of the Rhodesian ban on transit traffic in oil.

The search for satisfactory alternative supplies of coal proved more difficult.

Table 16

Stages in Zambian Disengagement from Rhodesian Sources of Energy

Date	Oil	Coal	Electricity
December 1965	Rhodesian oil embargo Anglo-American-Canadian airlift (ended October 1966)		
June 1966		Nkandabwe mine in production	
September 1968	Tazama pipeline from Dar es Salaam opened		
November 1970		Maamba coal washing plant opened	
October 1971		Imports of Wankie coal ended	Kafue power available
February 1977			Kariba North Bank in operation

It was also a matter of increasing urgency as successive railway crises interfere with normal Wankie traffic. So serious did the shortage become that in October 1966 the mines were forced to cut back production by one quarter for a period of seven months. To meet the immediate situation, small amounts of coal were imported at great expense through Lobito from South Africa and West Germany, but the final answer lay in discovering a dependable domestic source. Exploration began even before UDI and in anticipation of it, but it was mid-1966 before the first mine was in production. Even so, output was disappointing, costs were high and the quality was low. Gradually, however, the numerous difficulties were overcome until, in October 1971, Zambia felt able to dispense entirely with imports of Wankie coal. On the other hand, dependence on Wankie coke continued, with nearly 100,000 tons of coke valued at $2.5 million imported in 1971.[67] No way has yet been found to dispense with it; nor has a domestic source been discovere The financial and logistic problems of securing supplies from elsewhere constituted one of the most serious consequences for Zambia of the closure of the

Table 17

Zambian Dependence on Rhodesia for Energy, 1964-1972
(by quantity)

	Oil		Coal		Electricity	
Year	Total Imports (million gallons)	% Via Rhodesia	Total Supply (thousand tonnes)	% Wankie Coal	Total Supply (m kwh)	% Kariba Power
1964	40.2	100.0	977.8	99.6	2726.8	67.8
1965	52.8	99.8	1160.4	99.7	2919.4	69.6
1966	48.8	1.2	1024.4	85.7	2984.9	69.9
1967	82.9	0.0	1382.4	70.8	3230.3	81.3
1968	92.6	0.0	1266.7	52.7	3409.2	79.5
1969	107.0	0.0	1078.4	61.9	3635.2	79.0
1970	109.3	0.0	956.8	33.6	3999.7	72.6
1971	63.4	0.0	860.6	5.6	4371.3	68.0
1972	65 est.	0.0	936.5	0.0	4715.4	31.2

Sources: Annual Statement of External Trade; Monthly Digest of Statistics.

Rhodesian border in January 1973.

While oil imports through Rhodesia were cut off almost overnight as a result of UDI, and Wankie coal imports declined to zero over a period of six years, imports of electrical power - the major energy resource at the time of Independence - increased sharply until 1972 (Table 17). Only with the expansion of the capacity of the Victoria Falls power station in 1969 and especially the completion of Kafue State One in 1971 has the trend been reversed. If, as expected, Kariba North comes into operation in early 1977, Zambia will at last achieve self-sufficiency in electrical energy and cease to be a hostage of Kariba South Bank.

East Africa has not offered an alternative source of supply for either electrical power or coal. Extensive deposits of coal exist in the Ruhuhu Valley within 100 miles of the Great North Road, but these remain unexploited. Tanzania did, however, replace Rhodesia quickly and, by 1968, completely as a supply route for Zambia's rapidly growing imports of oil.

An analysis of the sources of Zambia's aggregate energy supply (Table 18) highlights the drastic changes that have occurred since Independence. The extent of

Table 18

Zambian Energy Sources, 1964-1976
(by value)

Year	Total Energy Supply 1964 = 100	Energy Source (%)			
		Domestic	Southern Africa	East Africa	Other External
1964	100	19.5	74.6	0.0	5.9
1965	106	17.1	78.4	0.1	4.4
1966	108	23.1	56.4	9.6	10.9
1967	148	21.3	51.0	26.9	0.8
1968	155	23.5	49.2	26.2	1.1
1969	159	20.7	47.8	30.1	1.4
1970	158	22.7	45.4	30.0	1.9
1971	163	24.9	40.1	32.4	2.6
1972	175	36.9	27.7	35.0	0.4
...	...	...	...	...	...
1976 (est)	323	62.4	0.0	37.5	0.1

Sources: Annual Statement of External Trade; Monthly Digest of Statistics; Second National Development Plan.

reliance on Southern Africa has declined from 75% in 1964 to 25% in 1972. With the closure of the Rhodesian border in early 1973, Kariba power remained the only significant energy import for which Zambia still looked southward. Even this residual element of dependence is diminishing and, by 1977, will finally cease. Thus, with respect to primary energy requirements, complete disengagement from Southern Africa is within sight of achievement. At the same time, dependence on East Africa is only half as great as it was with respect to Southern Africa at Independence.

Two developments have made this radical restructuring of the national energy picture possible: import substitution (in the case of coal and electricity) and alternative routes (for oil). Whereas in 1964 domestic resources accounted for less than 20% of Zambian consumption, in 1972 37% was provided internally, and by 1976 the proportion is expected to exceed 60%. Moreover, with the switch from thermal generation to hydro power, electricity production is becoming much more economical. Even more striking is the crucial new importance of East Africa in Zambia's national energy policy. In terms of its total requirements, dependence here has increased dramatically from zero at Independence to 35%, a level at which it seems likely to stabilize.

Communications

All countries aspire to assured, efficient and economical means of international communication but, for Zambia, this is a condition of national survival. It is not simply the fact of being landlocked geographically and hemmed in on three sides by hostile neighbours. Equally important is the heavy export orientation of the country's economy. Zambia's economic and political viability as a state rests on its ability to deliver its copper to the markets of the world.

Table 19

Zambian Transit Traffic Through Southern Africa: 1964-1972
(by value)

Year	Imports			Exports			Trade		
	% of Total Imports	Indices: 1964 = 100		% of Total Imports	Indices: 1964 = 100		% of Total Imports	Indices: 1964 = 100	
		Value	%		Value	%		Value	%
1964	40.6	100	100	87.2	100	100	73.0	100	100
1965	47.4	159	117	89.0	115	102	74.6	123	102
1966	56.7	222	140	81.7	138	94	73.6	153	101
1967	42.1	204	104	63.3	101	73	57.9	120	80
1968	43.1	223	106	62.2	115	71	55.3	134	76
1969	38.7	190	95	65.6	171	75	58.1	175	80
1970	39.1	211	97	62.4	153	71	55.2	162	75
1971	45.1	290	111	63.2	105	73	55.2	136	76
1972	55.0	362	135	70.7	131	81	64.1	170	88

Sources: Annual Statement of External Trade; Central Statistical Office, Route Analysis; figures for 1972 are provisional.

Transit Traffic

Zambia's traditional outlet to the sea has been the southern route through Rhodesia to Mozambique and South African ports. From the first, political and commercial interests have conspired to ensure that Zambia and especially the Copperbelt were tied in tightly to the Southern African transport network. Any outside challenge, even from the Lisbon-based Benguela Railway, was fiercely resisted by a combination of subtle pressures and ingenious economic inducements in the form of railway freight rate and ocean shipping tariff penalties and concessions.[68]

Table 19 analyzes the process of Zambian disengagement from dependence on transit routes through Southern Africa (including Angola). Whereas, with respect to trade with Southern Africa, imports have always exceeded exports, in terms of transit traffic the opposite is the case. In 1964, 41% of Zambia's imports and 87% of its exports transited Southern Africa. Moreover, the volume of the transit trade in monetary terms increased steadily until 1969, reflecting the rapid expansion of the Zambian economy. On the other hand, the proportion of total trade passing through Southern Africa is now below the level at the time of Independence, and exports are substantially lower. In practice, it has been easier to divert exports, mainly copper, to alternative routes than imports, principally because port facilities at Dar es Salaam and Lobito are less versatile in handling goods than at Beira. This explains why, during the domestic maize shortage of 1971-72, dependence on the southern route for imports increased dramatically.

Aggregate data on regional transit obscures the fact that ideologically there was less objection to the use of the Zaire-Angola and Malawi-Mozambique routes than to the traditional outlet through Rhodesia. On the Zambian scale of political acceptability, the Rhodesian route ranked lowest and the Tanzanian route highest. Portuguese east and west coast ports fell somewhere in between. They were welcome as short-term expedients pending completion of the TAZARA railway and the development of adequate port capacity in Dar es Salaam.

When data on transit traffic through Rhodesia is extracted from that of the Southern African region as a whole (Table 20), its crucial importance to Zambia is readily apparent. In 1964, 61% of imports and 95% of exports used the southern route. Yet, by 1972, these proportions had been reduced to approximately 50%. Moreover, the increase in the value of imports in transit was much smaller than for Southern Africa as a whole and, in the case of exports, the value has actually declined. Disengagement from Rhodesia, as a first step towards disengagement from the whole of the White South, was fast becoming a reality even before the final cutoff in January 1973.

The corresponding increase in dependence on East African ports is dramatic. Whereas, prior to UDI, transit traffic through Tanzania was virtually non-existent in 1972 a quarter of imports and exports travelled this route, despite all the difficulties encountered. The East African transit trade accounted for fully one-third of Southern Africa's 1964 share and, in the case of imports, over one-

Table 20

Zambian Transit Traffic Through Rhodesia and Tanzania: 1964-1972
(by value)

Year	% of total imports through:		% of total exports through:		% of total trade through:	
	Rhodesia	Tanzania	Rhodesia	Tanzania	Rhodesia	Tanzania
1964	61	0	95	0	85	0
1965	65	0	96	0	85	0
1966	60	1	69	10	66	7
1967	51	14	52	29	52	23
1968	55	17	41	35	46	28
1969	51	18	51	32	51	28
1970	42	23	43	36	43	32
1971	42	20	47	33	44	27
1972	51	24	51	26	51	25

Sources: As in Table 19.

Table 21

Zambian Transit Traffic Through East Africa: 1964-1972
(by value)

Year	Imports			Exports			Trade		
	% of Total Imports	Indices: Southern Africa: 1964 = 100		% of Total Exports	Indices: Southern Africa: 1964 = 100		% of Total Trade	Indices: Southern Africa: 1964 = 100	
		Value	%		Value	%		Value	%
1964	0.0	0	0	0.0	0	0	0.0	0	0
1965	0.0	0	0	0.0	0	0	0.0	0	0
1966	1.2	5	3	10.0	17	11	7.2	15	10
1967	12.7	62	31	28.9	46	33	22.7	48	31
1968	15.6	80	38	34.5	63	39	27.6	66	38
1969	15.8	78	39	31.6	82	36	27.2	81	37
1970	20.4	110	50	35.4	85	40	30.8	90	42
1971	18.2	117	45	32.6	53	37	26.2	65	36
1972	22.7	150	56	25.8	47	30	24.5	65	34

Sources: As in Table 19.

half (Tables 20 and 21).

The radical reorientation of export routes for Zambian copper provides, in perhaps the most sensitive sphere of all, a further measure of the extent of disengagement from the South (Table 22). Up until UDI, all copper was exported through Rhodesia. By 1968, Rhodesia's share amount to only one-third of the total. Another third reached world markets through Angola, and the balance - the "largest third" - used the Great North Road to Dar es Salaam. When Lusaka attempted to increase Lobito's quota at the expense of Rhodesia even further, Salisbury reacted on November 1, 1968 with a prohibitive 50% surcharge applicable whenever its allocations of copper fell below 25,000 tons per month. As Zambia was not yet in a position to dispense with the southern route entirely, it was compelled to comply with Rhodesia's demands. As a result, Rhodesia recaptured nearly one half of the lucrative Zambian copper traffic.

Table 22

Zambian Copper Exports by Routes: 1964-1972
(by weight)

Year	Total Copper Exports metric tonnes	Through Rhodesia		Through Southern Africa		Through Tanzania/ East Africa	
		% of Total	Indices of Weight 1964 = 100	% of Total	Indices of Weight 1964 = 100	% of Total	Indices of Weight SR1964 = 100
1964	681,000	100.0	100	100.0	100	0.0	0
1965	683,000	100.0	100	100.0	100	0.0	0
1966	599,000	68.6	58	89.2	75	10.8	9
1967	601,000	43.5	39	68.7	62	31.3	28
1968	643,000	33.0	31	62.1	59	37.9	36
1969	730,000	49.4	51	66.2	69	33.8	35
1970	684,000	41.7	42	61.6	62	38.4	38
1971	635,000	47.2	44	68.5	64	31.5	29
1972	711,000	49.4	51	71.9	75	28.1	29

The extent of integration into the Southern African transportation system can be seen in even clearer perspective by relating Zambia's transit traffic through the South to its direct trade with the region. As shown in Table 23, in 1964 99% of Zambian imports and exports came from, went to or passed through Southern Africa.

Since then, these percentages had been reduced by more than one quarter. Expressed differently, the proportion of Zambian trade that was wholly outside white minority control has, since Independence, risen spectacularly from under 1% to nearly 30%. Most of this massive shift is accounted for by the decline in trade with the South and the diversion of overseas exports through Dar es Salaam. On the other hand, the diminished dependence on Southern Africa is only relative to total trade. In monetary terms, trade with and through the South in 1972 was still above the 1964 level. Moreover, even the proportion of imports transiting Southern Africa increased after 1969, though it did not return to the peak percentage of 1966.

Table 23

Zambian Trade by Routes: 1964-1972

Year	% of Total Imports (by value):			
	From Southern Africa	Transiting Southern Africa	From and Through Southern Africa	From and Through East Africa
1964	58.2	40.6	98.8	0.5
1970	20.3	39.1	59.4	23.9
1972	16.9	55.0	71.9	25.1

Year	% of Total Exports (by value):			
	To Southern Africa	Transiting Southern Africa	To and Through Southern Africa	To and Through East Africa
1964	12.0	87.2	99.2	0.2
1970	1.4	62.4	63.8	37.5
1972	2.3	70.7	73.0	26.1

Border Traffic

The altered character of Zambia's external communication links is further illuminated by isolating indicators of Zambia's total trade with and through Rhodesia and Tanzania (Table 24). In 1964, virtually all Zambia's external trade crossed the Zambezi border with Rhodesia, whereas eight years later only half of it used this route and, since January 1973, effectively none. Trade across the Tanzanian border, on the other hand, developed from almost nothing to nearly 40% of the total.

Table 24

Zambian Trade With and Through Rhodesia and Tanzania: 1964-1972
(by weight)

Year	Rhodesia			Tanzania		
	% of Total Trade	Indices: 1964 = 100		% of Total Trade	Indices: SR1964 = 100	
		Weight	%		Weight	%
1964	99.8	100	100	0.0	0	0
1965	99.1	106	99	0.0	0	0
1966	85.1	89	85	6.8	7	7
1967	68.8	83	69	15.0	18	15
1968	68.9	77	69	21.5	24	22
1969	61.9	68	62	27.2	30	27
1970	58.9	62	59	29.3	31	29
1971	50.5	53	51	32.3	34	32
1972	47.8	47	48	37.0	37	37

Sources: Annual Statement of External Trade: Central Statistical Office, Route Analysis; Report of the Security Council Mission (S/10896/Add.1); A Challenge to the Nation.

The final abandonment of the southern route in January 1973 has merely accelerated and completed the process of disengagement from Rhodesia. Admittedly, Zambia was once again compelled to pay a much higher economic cost to preserve its political freedom of action than if the path had been more orderly. Nevertheless, the country was in a far stronger position to meet this challenge than during the precarious months following UDI. Whereas the attempt to dispense completely with the use of Rhodesia Railways failed in 1966,[69] it succeeded in 1973. On the other hand, part of the price of independence from Rhodesia was greater dependence on Angola; in 1973 nearly two-thirds of all imports came through Lobito.[70] This, however, is a case of one step backwards in preparation for two steps forward. The completion of the TAZARA railway, possibly as early as the end of 1975, should finally enable Zambia to cut its communication ties with the whole of Southern Africa - though whether the Government will decide actually to do this, in view of political changes in Angola and Mozambique, is by no means certain. Moreover, it is understandably reluctant to replicate the pre-UDI situation of having all its transportation eggs in one (chronically congested basket when it is at last presented with a choice of competitive routes.[71]

Table 25

Scheduled Air Connections Between Zambia and Southern Africa/
East Africa, 1963-1972
Weekly Flights

Year (January)	Rhodesia		Tanzania		Southern Africa		East Africa	
	No.	Indices*	No.	Indices*	No.	Indices*	No.	Indices*
1963	33	67	4	8	37	71	10	19
1964	49	100	2	4	52	100	8	15
1965	41	84	2	4	43	83	11	21
1966	53	108	2	4	54	104	10	19
1967	40	82	4	8	42	81	12	23
1968	26	53	10	20	30	58	20	38
1969	27	55	10	20	29	56	21	40
1970	14	29	20	20	22	42	42	33
1971	21	43	10	20	24	46	15	29
1972	25	51	9	18	31	60	25	48

* For Rhodesia and Tanzania, Rhodesia 1964 = 100; for Southern Africa and East Africa, Southern Africa 1964 - 100.

Source: ABC World Airways Guide

Air Communications

Air travel has long superseded rail and even road transportation as the major means of communication between Zambia and neighbouring states, especially for the expatriate and business communities. Moreover, politics appears to have had a less lasting effect on the flow of traffic than might have been expected. Certainly, there has been no complete severance of all air connections, as once seemed likely. In 1964, Zambia Airways flights to South Africa were withdrawn and, following the break-up of Central African Airways at the end of 1967, all direct flights between Zambia and Rhodesia ceased (along with passenger train service). However, more circuitous and expensive alternative routes through Malawi and Botswana and by bus between Livingstone and Victoria Falls were quickly devised, and eventually serviced by larger and faster aircraft. Moreover, a growing number of private companies acquired their own planes or patronized air charter firms. The Government even offered UTA and Alitalia fifth freedom privileges in 1967 to operate between Lusaka and Johannesburg, partly to cater for children attending South African schools. Nevertheless, the frequency of flights across the Zambezi has been reduced bv nearly 60%, and in the case of Rhodesia even more (Table 25).

The significance of the volume of air traffic between Zambia and East Africa is more difficult to gauge as many passengers are merely in transit. There has, however, been a fairly steady increase in the frequency of flights except for a period during 1966 and 1967 when, in accordance with an OAU resolution, Zambia Airways planes were banned from East Africa (and Zaire) as they were registered in Rhodesia.[72] As a result, flights to East Africa are now almost as numerous as to Southern Africa and passenger capacity is probably greater (Table 25).

In other aspects of air communications, disengagement from Rhodesia has been virtually complete. This is particularly true of air traffic control which previously had been centred in Salisbury. Zambians, not unnaturally, found it intolerable that the RAF Javelin squadron, invited in after UDI to defend the country against a possible Rhodesian air strike should be subject to rebel operational control. Even prior to this, the Government had pressed for its own Flight Information Centre in Lusaka and, despite fierce resistance within ICAO, this was achieved at the beginning of 1967.[73]

Table 26

Foreign Radio Audience in Zambia, 1971

Radio Station	% of Zambian Population Listening to Foreign Broadcasts	
	Including "music only" listeners	Excluding "misic only" listeners
Tanzania	9.4%	5.6%
Southern Africa		
South Africa	8.8%	5.9%
Rhodesia	3.8%	2.8%
Mozambique	2.8%	1.4%
	15.4%	10.1%
Other	28.7%	
Total*	24.8%	

* Excludes duplication; no data available on Radio Angola audience.

Source: Graham Mytton Report on the National Mass Media Audience Survey, 1970-1971 (Lusaka: Institute of African Studies, University of Zambia, 1972) pp. 77-81.

Table 27

Import of Books, Periodicals and Newspapers, 1964-1970
(by value)

Southern Africa					
Year	% from Rhodesia	% from South Africa	Imports from Southern Africa		
			%	Indices: 1964 = 100	
				Value	%
1964	9.1	10.1	19.2	100	100
1965	9.3	7.7	17.0	151	89
1966	1.0	8.3	9.3	135	49
1967	2.1	11.0	13.1	141	69
[illegible]	[illegible]	1.2	1.4	12	8
[illegible]	[illegible]	3.9	4.0	29	21
[illegible]	[illegible]	5.8	6.0	52	31
1971	0.0	3.7	3.7	51	19

East Africa					
Year	% from Tanzania	% from Kenya	Imports from East Africa		
			%	Indices: 1964 = 100	
				Value	%
1964	1.0	25.4	26.4	100	100
1965	0.1	16.7	16.8	108	64
1966	0.2	12.2	12.4	130	47
1967	1.3	11.4	12.8	100	48
1968	4.3	10.3	14.6	91	55
1969	2.2	18.8	21.0	112	79
1970	1.9	26.5	28.5	179	108
1971	0.1	26.7	28.9	267	102

Source: Annual Statement of External Trade. Item code was revised slightly in 1970.

nformation

nformation flows represent another element in communications. Unfortunately ittle data are available on broadcasts across Zambia's borders, and none over ime. What evidence does exist suggests that a quarter of the adult population r half of all radio listeners tune in to foreign stations. Radio Tanzania Dar es

Salaam's overall popularity rating is slightly higher than Radio South Africa but, when those whose interest is confined to music are excluded, the rankings are reversed (Table 26). Moreover, in areas of the country where ZBS reception has been poor, reliance on Southern African sources for news and opinion has been heavy. With the introduction of the powerful new Chinese transmitters in April 1973, Zambia is in a much stronger position to compete effectively with foreign broadcasts both inside the country and in neighbouring states.

If the flow of books, periodicals and newspapers is easier to measure, their significance is more difficult to interpret. Nevertheless, it seems reasonable to assume that the level of literature imports is primarily an indicator of the extent of European societal interaction, at least with respect to Southern Africa. The data suggest (Table 27) a somewhat erratic pattern, principally because during 1968 and 1969 the introduction of import route controls temporarily disrupted normal commercial channels. When allowance is made for this, however, a distinct trend is apparent, revealing a marked reduction in the value and especially the proportion of printed matter emanating from the South. This decline is particularly striking in the case of Rhodesia, which has almost ceased to serve as a source.

In the case of East Africa, no simple conclusions emerge from the confusing data available. In the base year 1964, the value (though not the weight) of imports actually exceeded that of imports of Southern African origin. Moreover, the ethnic origins of consumers of East African literature in Zambia are by no means clear. What can be said is that East Africa and especially Kenya continues to corner a substantial share of the Zambian market and that, since Independence, the increase in the value (and weight) of imports has been significant - even if less dramatic than the drying up in the flow of print across the Zambezi.

People

The flow of persons across boundaries is evidence of societal interaction, though not necessarily cooperation. Yet, it represents more than this. Data on population movements record not only the cumulative effects of the decisions of individuals, but also the influence of government policy expressed in terms of visa requirements, restrictions on recruitment, currency regulations and tourism promotion. It is not always easy, therefore, to decide precisely what it is tha migration measures. In the case of Zambia, the analysis is further complicated by the need to disaggregate flows in terms of race and nationality.

Table 28

African Population of Zambia Born in Southern Africa and East Africa

Country of Birth	1963 Census		1969 Census		Indices: 1963 = 100	
	Persons	% of Foreign born Africans	Persons	% of Foreign born Africans	Number	%
Southern Africa	130,000	57.2%	99,675	39.9%	76	70
Rhodesia	52,230	22.9%	57,781	23.1%	110	101
South Africa/ Namibia	600	0.3%	5,002	2.0%	834	762
Angola/Mozambique	77,660	34.0%	36,892	14.8%	48	43
East Africa			22,833	9.1%		
Tanzania	12,990	5.7%	22,423	9.0%	173	158
Kenya			292	0.1%		
Uganda			118	0.05%		
Total Alien Africans	228,130	100.0%	249,637	100.0%	109	100

Sources: Census returns. Some Zambian citizens "by birth" were born outside Zambia and some alien African residents of Zambia were born in Zambia. The number of alien African residents in 1969 who were citizens of southern African territories was 49,180 - only half the number of foreign born.

African Migration

Alien Southern Africans[74] constitute a tiny and declining proportion (2.5%) of the Zambian population. Nevertheless, except for the Angolans, they have, at least in the past, played a more important part in the economy of the country than their numbers might suggest. A comparison between the 1963 and 1969 censuses (Table 28) indicates that the size of the foreign-born Southern African community declined by one-quarter during the intervening years. This is more than accounted for by the reduction in the migrant peasant population from neighbouring Portuguese territories. At the same time, a modest increase in the number of Rhodesians was recorded along with the emergence, for the first time, of a sizeable black South African community, many of whom are more or less refugees who fled northwards in the exodus of the mid-1960's. This should not be interpreted as evidence of any significant strengthening of societal links with the South. On the contrary, quite apart from the smallness of the numbers involved, the growing public demand for Zambianization of the jobs of non-citizens indicate that alien Africans are under increasing pressure. This is as true of Tanzanians, the only significant East African community in Zambia, and even the tiny but highly visible group of Kenyan traders as it is of Southern Africans.

Table 29

Estimates of Zambian Africans Resident in Southern Africa, 1962-1972

Year (December)	Rhodesia		South Africa		Southern Africa	
	Persons	Index: 1964 = 100	Persons	Index: 1964 = 100	Persons	Index: 1964 = 100
1960*			11,600	75		
1962	69,740	113				
1964	61,500	100	15,500	100	77,000	100
1965	59,600	97				
1966	52,300	85				
1967	48,100	78				
1968	45,100	73				
1969*	44,510	72				
1969	42,500	69				
1970	40,000	65	5,000	39	46,000	60
1971	37,500	61				
1972	35,700	58				

* Census returns: South Africa, September 1960 and Rhodesia, April-May 1962 and March 1969; December estimates for other years calculated on basis of migration statistics.

Sources: Rhodesian census returns and Migration Report for Rhodesia; G. M. E. Leistner "Foreign Bantu Workers in South Africa" South African Journal of Economics 25 (March 1967) 47, 49 and Southern African Data (Pretoria: Africa Institute, 1970), Labour" 10.

More significant as a measure of Zambia societal sentiment towards Southern Africa is the decline in the number of Zambians living south of the Zambezi. During colonial days, Zambians regularly migrated south in search of employment. No reliable figures exist as to the magnitude of this movement, but the evidence suggests that at the time of Independence at least 75,000 Zambians resided in Southern Africa, 80% of them in Rhodesia (Table 29). Since then, these communities have dwindled to little more than half their former size, and even less

Table 30

Zambian Contract Labour in Southern Africa, 1963-1969

	South Africa (WENELA)			Rhodesia	Total	
Year	Engaged	Repatriated	Net	Farm Contracts	Recruits	Index: 1964 = 100
1963	5395	6657	-1262	1392	6787	118
1964	5380	5329	+51	387	5767	100
1965	5982	5492	+490	0	5982	104
1966	4446	5744	-1298	0	4446	77
1967	0	4730	-4730	0	0	0
1968	0	139	-139	0	0	0
1969	0	0	0	0	0	0

Sources: Department of Labour Annual Report; WENELA.

in the case of South Africa.[75]

Many of those lured south had been recruited on contract specifically to work in the South African gold mines or on Rhodesian farms. With the coming of Independence, the Zambian Government intervened to end what it considered an unacceptable form of indentured labour. Arrangements had already been made to terminate the Rhodesian labour draft in 1964, and, in September 1966, the recruitment agreement with the Witwatersrand Native Labour Association (WENELA), which had operated in the Western Province since 1938, was abruptly abrogated (Table 30). However, the inability of the authorities to provide adequate alternative employment opportunities immediately produced a minor political backlash that contributed to the Government's electoral setback in that province in 1968.[76]

This might seem to suggest that the attempt to sever societal ties with the South was not universally welcomed. Certainly, a fair proportion of those who ventured south on their own, particularly those who settled in Rhodesia, appear to have established roots there, and are unlikely to return until they retire. Nevertheless, the incentive in the migratory labour system has always been more economic than social. In any case, the link was primarily of regional significance within Zambia. It is now of little importance and is becoming steadily less so.

A similar decline has occurred in the number of Zambians employed in Tanzania.[77] This has been particularly marked since 1964 following the abolition of contract recruitment of foreign labour and the widening of the disparity in living stan-

Table 31

African Business Visitors to Zambia, 1966 and 1968

Nationality	1966	1968	Index 1966 = 100
Southern African			
South African	1010	642	63
Rhodesian	890	580	65
Angolan/Mozambique	820	79	10
Total	2720	1301	48
East African			
Tanzanian	920	15916*	
Kenyan		2510	
Ugandan		106	
Total		18532	
Africa	7350	23816	324

* Appears to reflect lorry traffic on Great North Road.

Sources: Migration Statistics, 1966 and 1968. Figures for 1966 are based on August-December data.

dards in the two countries. The recruitment of Zambians to work in Tanzania on the TAZARA railway represents a temporary reversal of the trend, but even here the numbers involved are far smaller than originally anticipated.

Another dimension of interaction comprises private Zambian economic ties with neighbouring states. In the past, little interest has been evinced in this, partly no doubt because of its supposed limited scope, but also because of the colonial legacy of generally underrating all African economic activity. As a result, the data that exists is quantitatively sparse and qualitatively uneven (Table 31). What statistics are available suggest, first, that contacts with East Africa have been somewhat closer than with Southern Africa and, secondly, that the latter have diminished substantially, at least over the brief period 1966 to 1968. At the same time, a tiny but significant group of Zambian business executives associated with companies with South African connections now exists, and this emerging elite finds it expendient to maintain personal contact with their head offices in Johannesburg.

European Migration

The most dramatic change in the expatriate community in Zambia since Independence has been the reduction in both the numbers and the proportion of white Southern Africans (Tables 32 and 33). Although the total European population declined 42% between 1961 and 1969 - from roughly 2% of the country's population to 1% - the numbers of those born in South Africa or Rhodesia fell 76%. This amounts to a major structural transformation in the composition of the European sectcr. On

Table 32

European Population of Zambia by Place of Birth

Country of Birth	1961 Census		1969 Census		Indices: 1961 = 100	
	Persons	% Eur.pop.	Persons	% Eur.pop.	Persons	% Eur.Pop.
South Africa	25,211	33.8	5,779	13.3	23	39
Rhodesia	5,856	7.8	1,352	3.1	23	40
Southern Africa	31,530	42.3	7,474	17.2	24	41
Zambia	16,127	21.6	7,274	16.8	45	77
East Africa	311	0.4	417	1.0	134	230
All Europeans	74,549	100.0	43,390	100.0	58	100

Sources: Census reports for 1961, 1969.

the one hand, Rhodesian railway workers and South African miners and commercial farmers trekked south and, on the other hand, a smaller but significant number of Europeans were recruited overseas on contract to assist with the expansion of the public service, the secondary schools and industry. The number of East African Europeans in Zambia has remained infinitesimal.

Table 34 provides additional evidence of the altered pattern of European migration. The heavy net outflow of Europeans mainly to the South began in 1963 and in fact peaked before Independence. Nevertheless, during the next couple of years, substantial numbers of immigrants continued to come from South Africa and especially Rhodesia. As with several other indicators, the fall off from Rhodesia came sooner and was sharper than for Southern Africa as a whole. One factor in this was government policy on the recruitment of skilled labour from the South. Al-

Table 33

Country of Citizenship	1961 Census		1969 Census		Indices: 1961 = 100	
	Persons	% Eur.pop.	Persons	% Eur.pop.	Persons	% Eur.pop.
South Africa	19,417	26.0	4,006	9.2	21	35
Rhodesia			434	1.0		
Southern Africa			4,785	11.0		
Zambia			4,343	10.0		
East Africa			90	0.2		
All Europeans	74,549	100.0	43,390	100.0	58	100

Sources: Census reports for 1961, 1969.

Table 34

Estimates of European Immigration into Zambia from Southern Africa: 1964-1970 (by citizenship)

Year	South Africans		Rhodesians		Southern Africans	
	Immigrants	Index: 1964 = 100	Immigrants	Index: 1964 = 100	Immigrants	Index: 1964 = 100
1964*	1060	100	670	100	1730	100
1965	460	43	200	30	660	38
1966	980	92	233	35	1213	70
1967	-	-	-	-	-	-
1968	127	12	46	7	173	10
1969	33	3	7	1	41	2
1970	61	6	9	1	70	4

* By country of birth.

Sources: Migration Statistics.

though the Minister of Home Affairs insisted in 1967 that there was no discrimination against Rhodesians and South Africans in the issuance of visas and employment permits and certainly there appear to have been no formal instructions issued to companies, "employers were advised to recruit elsewhere if possible".[78] As a result, as early as 1965, the two mining companies ceased entirely to seek employees in Rhodesia and turned to South Africa only for highly specialized personnel.

As a consequence of these changes, the European community's close societal ties with the South have in some respects been progressively attenuated.[79] A larger proportion of the expatriate population now seems to feel a substantial, though in most cases only a short term, commitment to the country. Moreover, ten per cent of Europeans have acquired Zambian citizenship. Nevertheless, 11% (in 1969) remained citizens of Southern African countries, 17% were born there and an even larger proportion maintain family educational or family ties with the South. Many plan to retire there. The vitality of the residual links, especially with South Africa, is reflected in the continuing, if diminishing, flow of visitors southward.

Table 35

Zambia Visitors to South Africa by Motivation, 1964-1972

Year	Business			Holiday			Education			Total		
	No.	Indices: 1964=100		No.	Indices: 1964=100		No.	Indices: 1964=100		No.	Indices: 1964=100	
		No.	%*		No.	%*		No.	%*		No.	%*
1964	1,297	100	100	26,825	100	100	2,366	100	100	30,488	100	100
1965	1,361	105	109	26,033	97	101	2,310	140	146	30,704	101	105
1966	1,847	142	156	28,021	104	115	4,219	179	196	34,087	112	123
1967	2,206	170	210	25,607	95	118	4,743	200	248	32,556	107	132
1968	2,229	172	244	23,855	89	126	3,386	143	203	29,470	97	137
1969	2,086	161	267	19,663	73	122	2,648	112	185	24,397	80	133
1970	2,445	188	348	16,905	63	116	2,543	108	198	21,893	72	133
1971	1,350	104	208	14,926	56	111	1,636	69	138	17,912	59	117
1972	1,049	81	172	13,002	48	103	1,709	72	153	15,760	52	109

* Index based on Zambian visitors to South Africa as a % of the European population of Zambia in 1964=100.

Source: South African Tourist Corporation, Annual Report.

If we can assume that the vast majority of recorded visitors to Southern Africa are Europeans, then there has undoubtedly been an absolute decline in their number. Whereas in 1964 there were over 100,000 visits by Zambian residents to Rhodesia - three times as many as to South Africa - two years later there were only half that number and, since then, visits have decreased even further. Nevertheless, the level of personnel contact remains high, as is quickly apparent whenever a threat arises to the seasonal mass movement of expatriate school-children across the Zambezi. In the case of South Africa, a similar trend has

Table 36

Visitors to Zambia, 1964-1972
(by country of last permanent residence)

Year	Total No. of Visitors	Southern African Visitors		Southern Africans		East African Visitors	East Africans	
		Rhodesians	South Africans	No.	Index: 1964=100	Tanzanians	No.	Index: 1964=100
1964	92,099	35,093	14,622	51,800	100	1,902	3,400*	7
1965	118,366	29,017	17,000*	46,000*	88			
1966	108,469	15,000*	19,000*	34,000*	66	2,300*	4,200*	8
1967	67,535							
1968	96,696	11,512	5,237	17,128	33	25,332**	30,723**	59
1969	37,723	7,163	2,879	10,212	20	6,418	9,122	18
1970	46,814	8,988	3,388	12,486	24	5,908	8,941	17
1971	62,441	13,425	4,466	18,144	35	6,735	9,687	19
1972	61,638	10,429	4,240	14,862	29	4,368	6,188	12

* Estimates based on incomplete data.

** Appears to reflect heavy lorry traffic on Great North Road.

Sources: Migration Statistics.

occurred, with the fall off in the volume of holiday traffic particularly striking (Table 35). Yet, if account is taken of the dwindling size of the European population of Zambia, it is evident that the level of interaction on a per capita basis has actually increased especially in the case of businessmen. Certainly, the southward flow of visitors is still many times greater than that heading eastward. Although visits to East Africa have more than doubled since Independence, their number has yet to total four thousand a year.

A final measure of migration trends is the flow of Southern African visitors to Zambia. Statistics here are unusually sketchy and unreliable. Nevertheless, it is clear that a dramatic drop in numbers has occurred (Table 36). This appears to have been especially pronounced among Europeans. Once again, Rhodesia has led the way in terms of time and percentage reduction. Statistics on business visits by Southern African Europeans suggest a remarkable 79% decline between 1966 and 1968, and a 85% decline in the case of Rhodesians.[80] However, this data is based on nationality, not residence, and fails to reflect the fact that many Rhodesian and South African businessmen are British, or dual citizens who, with the connivance of their governments, travel on British passports.

One group of visitors has presented Zambia with an acute dilemma. The Government has been anxious to exploit the country's unrivalled tourist potential much more fully than in the past in order to boost foreign exchange earnings, generate employment, and diversify the economy. Yet, it is confronted with the unwelcome fact that, for geographical reasons, the most obvious target group is the white community in Southern Africa. As late as 1966, as many as eighty per cent of tourists visiting Victoria Falls came from the South,[81] and the prospects of increasing the flow were good. Nevertheless, Lusaka resisted the temptation and even took positive steps to discourage holiday visitors from the South. When, in November 1966, a system of tourist visas available at the port of entry was introduced, this facility was specifically denied to South Africans, Rhodesians and Portuguese tourists on political and security grounds.[82] As a result of these and other measures, the tourist trade was practically wiped out. Between 1964 and 1969, the total number of Southern African visitors to Zambia plummetted from 50,000 to 10,000 with the collapse of tourist traffic proportionately even more devastating. Livingstone, the tourist capital of the country and already suffering from the effects of UDI, was particularly severely hit. Nevertheless, this was a price the Government was prepared to pay to promote economic and social disengagement. In this connection, the increase in East African visitors has served as only a marginal compensating factor. Although numbers have more than doubled, they remain small and, in the case of tourists, almost negligible - totally only 12 in 1968.

Conclusions

Having surveyed the major indicators of Zambian disengagement from Southern Africa and integration with East Africa, it remains to assess their various dimensions in terms of the model previously postulated (Table 2). Inevitably, the process of selecting factors and constructing composite indicators based on simple unweighted arithmetical means is somewhat arbitrary and the resulting indices rather crude. Nevertheless, they are suggestive of trends, even if not precise measures. Wherever possible, comparisons are drawn between Southern Africa and East Africa (Tables 38 and 38) and between Rhodesia and Tanzania (Tables 39 and 40). The conclusions are summarized in Table 41.

Table 37

Dimensions and Degrees of Disengagement from Southern Africa, 1964-1972*

Actor Level	Functional Dimensions: Political System				Society				Economy			
	Table	Indicator	Index	Mean	Table	Indicator	Index	Mean	Table	Indicator	Index	Mean
Governmental	8.	Agreements	57	28	30.	Contract labour	0	0	14.	Trade	62	60
	9.	Government representatives	0			Sports	0		14.	% Trade	32	
									18.	% Energy	28	
									19.	% Transit	88	
									22.	Copper route	75	
									23.	% Trade & transit	73	
Societal: Zambian					28.	Alien Africans	76	68	31.	Southern African business visits	(48?)	-
Societal: European					25.	Air flights	60	31	25.	Air flights	60	70
					27.	% Literature	19		35.	Business visits to SA	81	
					32.	Population	24			Southern African business visitors	(21)	
					34.	Immigrants	4					
					35.	Visits to SA	52					
					36.	Southern African visitors	29					

* Indices in brackets are excluded from calculations of means as they are based on incomplete or unreliable data, or on indicators which are ambiguous or have no suitable basis of comparison with Southern Africa.

Table 38

Dimensions and Degrees of Integration with East Africa, 1962-1972*
(Southern Africa 1964=100)

Actor Level	Functional Dimensions											
	Political System				Society				Economy			
	Table	Indicator	Index	Mean	Table	Indicator	Index	Mean	Table	Indicator	Index	Mean
Governmental	8.	Agreements	87	64		Sports	+	+	14.	Trade	9	23
	9.	Government representatives	60			Telecommunications	+	+	14.	% Trade	5	
	10.	Heads meetings	(44)						18.	% Energy	35	
									20.	% Transit	34	
									23.	% Trade & transit	26	
									29.	Copper route	29	
Societal: Zambian					25.	Air flights	48	26	31.	EA business visitors	+	+
						% Literature	(141)					
					28.	Alien Africans	18					
					36.	EA visitors	12					
Societal: European					25.	Air flights	48	30	25.	Air flights	48	48
						% Literature	(141)					
					32.	Population	(134)					
					36.	EA visitors	12					

* Indices for East Africa are based on Southern Africa 1964=100 (except for Government Representatives and Heads of State Meetings), and therefore do not measure changes within East Africa over time. Indices in brackets are excluded from calculations of means as they are based on incomplete or unreliable data, or on indicators which are ambiguous or have no suitable basis of comparison with Southern Africa.

Table 39

Dimensions and Degrees of Disengagement from Rhodesia, 1964-1972*

Actor Level	Functional Dimensions: Political System: Table	Indicator	Index	Mean	Society: Table	Indicator	Index	Mean	Economy: Table	Indicator	Index	Mean
Governmental		Common services:		21	30.	Contract labour	0	0	14.	Trade	10	29
	4.	Board meetings	34			Sports	0		14.	% Trade	5	
	5.	Bureaucracies	8						17.	Oil	0	
	6.	Scale of operations	27						20.	% Transit	61	
	8.	Agreements	38						22.	Copper route	51	
	9.	Govt. repres.	0						24.	Trade & transit	47	
Societal: Zambian					28.	Alien Africans	110	84	31.	SR business	(65?)	-
					29.	Zambians abroad	58					
Societal: European					25.	Air flights	51	21	25.	Air flights	51	51
					27.	% Literature	0			SR business visits	(15)	
					32.	Population	23					
					34.	Immigrants	1					
					36.	SR visitors	30					
						Visits to SR	(20?)					

* Indices in brackets are excluded from calculations of means as they are based on incomplete or unreliable data, or on indicators which are ambiguous or have no suitable basis of comparison with Rhodesia.

Table 40

Dimensions and Degrees of Integration with Tanzania, 1964-1972*
(Rhodesia 1964=100)

Actor Level	Functional Dimensions											
	Political System				Society				Economy			
	Table	Indicator	Index	Mean	Table	Indicator	Index	Mean	Table	Indicator	Index	Mean
Governmental		Common services:		109		Sports	‡	‡	14.	Trade	7	34
	7.	Scale of operations	79			Telecommunications	‡		14.	% Trade	3	
										Oil	100	
	8.	Agreements	154						20.	% Transit	30	
	9.	Govt. repres.	93						22.	Copper route	29	
	10.	Head meetings	(133)						24.	Trade & transit	37	
Societal: Zambian						% Literature	(1)	23	31.	Tanzanian business visits	‡	‡
					28.	Alien Africans	43					
					36.	Tanzanian visitors	12					
Societal: European					25.	Air flights	18	18	25.	Air flights	18	18
						% Literature	(1)					

* Indices for Tanzania are based on Rhodesia 1964=100 (except for Government Representatives and Heads of State meetings), and therefore do not measure changes within Tanzania over time. Indices in brackets are excluded from calculations of means as they are based on incomplete or unreliable data, or on indicators which are ambiguous or have no suitable basis of comparison with Rhodesia.

Table 41

Dimension and Degrees of Disengagement and Integration, 1964-1972*

Zambian Actor Level	Functional Dimensions: Political System		Society		Economy	
Governmental	Southern Africa	East Africa	Southern Africa	East Africa	Southern Africa	East Africa
	28	64	0	++	60	23
	21	109	0	+	29	34
	Rhodesia	Tanzania	Rhodesia	Tanzania	Rhodesia	Tanzania
Societal: Zambian			Southern Africa	East Africa	Southern Africa	East Africa
			68	26	minus	+
			84	23	minus	++
			Rhodesia	Tanzania	Rhodesia	Tanzania
Societal: European			Southern Africa	East Africa	Southern Africa	East Africa
			31	30	70	48
			21	18	51	18
			Rhodesia	Tanzania	Rhodesia	Tanzania

* See notes below Tables 38 and 40.

Governmental Level

The empirical evidence confirms the conventional wisdom that success in political and administrative disengagement from Rhodesia has been substantial and that progress towards integration with Tanzania has, in relative terms, been considerable In fact, positive Zambian interactions with the Tanzanian political system are now broader and more intense than they were with Rhodesia during the early post-Federal period. Available indicators on collaboration with the Southern African and East African regions are less potent. Yet, they too reveal similar, if less pronounced trends. The momentum towards a closer and more institutionalized relationship with the East African Community, has, however, slackened, with summit meetings of Eastern African heads of state less frequent (Table 10).

In protest against racial practices south of the border, Lusaka has intervened effectively to minimize certain - mainly European - societal contacts across the Zambezi. In addition to terminating the recruitment of contract labour, it has banned sports activities, entertainment functions, and occasional films and publications. Moreover, stricter frontier formalities and restrictions on transportation services, especially with Rhodesia, have been introduced, though no general ban on travel, telecommunications or postal services has been imposed.[83] At the same time, there has been active official encouragement of strengthened social ties with East Africa. No reliable measure of the vitality of these links is available, but it is doubtful if they are yet as strong as past relationships with the South, except in the field of sport.[84]

In the economic sphere, firm government directives have transformed Zambia's traditional trade patterns and transportation routes. On the other hand, the area of greatest disengagement - trade - is paradoxically the one in which the least progress has been made in developing closer economic ties with East Africa. Moreover, by most measures, residual economic dependence on the South in 1972 still appeared to be more significant than the new links being forged with the East. The closure of the Rhodesian border has however, radically altered the relative importance to Zambia of these two regions.

Societal Level

The principal indicators of societal interaction between Zambians and Africans in Southern Africa and East Africa are changes in the size of the respective foreign communities on either side of the borders (Tables 28-36). Although the resulting indices do not inspire great confidence, they do suggest a considerable measure of social disengagement from the South - though rather less in the case of Rhodesia - and a corresponding increase in social integration with East Africa. Nevertheless, on balance, relations at the African societal level still appear to be closer with the South than with the East.

Assessments of private Zambian economic ties with neighbouring countries are even more speculative. The most that can be deduced from the skimpy data available is that contacts between African businessmen are expanding with East Africa and diminishing with Southern Africa, and that the former may now be several times as numerous as the latter.

Indicators of social interaction between the European community in Zambia and the South are more readily available and reliable. These suggest that a remarkable degree of disengagement has already been achieved, especially with respect to Rhodesia. In fact, the weakening of links across the Zambezi appears to have been proportionately greater among Europeans than among Africans, though clearly the cohesiveness of the former community was far more marked at the time of Independence than in the case of the latter - and probably still is. Even European business contacts have diminished significantly. In relations with East Africa, the European factor is less relevant as a measure of integration. Yet, to the extent that the frequency of air flights is a gauge of European commercial involvement, it would appear that despite the growing closeness East Africa still ranks below Southern Africa in importance. Moreover, Nairobi rather than Dar es Salaam is the focal point of business interest in East Africa.

The transaction flow analysis developed in this paper points to the following conclusions:

1. The Zambian Government's determined efforts to disengage from the South and especially from Rhodesia have been remarkably successful, even in the critical economic sphere - so much so that a final break with Rhodesia in January 1973 proved feasible.

2. East Africa, and especially Tanzania have partially succeeded in appropriating Southern Africa's historical role as an outlet to the sea for Zambia. Dependence on East Africa is least apparent in the field of trade - which may help to explain Zambia's caution concerning membership of the East African Community. Political and administrative ties with Tanzania are now closer than with Rhodesia at the time of Independence.

3. Societal contacts are diminishing with Southern Africa and increasing with East Africa, though links with the former still appear to be closer than with the latter, even for Zambian Africans.

4. The reduction in the scope and frequency of European interactions with the South is largely a function of the altered size and composition of the expatriate community in Zambia. Business contacts have suffered least.

5. In general, disengagement and integration have proceeded further at the governmental level than at the societal level, and in the political sphere than in the social and especially the economic spheres.

6. Indices of Zambian interaction with Rhodesia are generally lower than with Southern Africa as a whole, and higher for Tanzania than for East Africa. This supports the view that geographical propinquity accentuates existing behavioural predispositions, whether cooperative or conflictual.

7. Disengagement from Southern Africa has achieved more progress than integration with East Africa, partly no doubt because nationalist pressures reinforce the former but inhibit the latter. This confirms the conventional wisdom that conflict is more "natural" than cooperation.

8. The real turning point in the structural reorientation of Zambia's political

economic and social relations with its neighbours was UDI, not Independence. This suggests that the more sharply the ideological issue is focussed and the greater the threat to the material interests of the nation, the greater the likelihood of foreign policy goals being realized.

NOTES

1. Press Conference, 25 October 1964. Zambia Information Services (ZIS) Background No. 27/64, 18 November 1964. See also Central African Mail 19 June 1964, 5.

2. UNIP Policy (Lusaka: UNIP [1962] 9 and 65. "One of the projects to receive priority will be the railway line from Kapiri Mposhi to Tanganyika." When UNIP Becomes Government (Lusaka: UNIP, 1963) n.p.

3. To Richard Hall 1963. Africa Digest 15(1), February 1968, 6.

4. ZIS Press Release No. 210/65, 11 February 1965; No. 233/65, 16 February 1965; No. 564/65, 12 April 1965; and No. 1600/65, 6 October 1965.

5. Kenneth D. Kaunda A Humanist in Africa: Letters to Colin M. Morris (London: Longmans, 1966) 127.

6. Frank C. Ballance Zambia and the East African Community (Syracuse: Program of Eastern African Studies, Syracuse University, 1971) 1.

7. Economic Report 1971 (Lusaka: Ministry of Finance, 1972) 55.

8. Mindeco Limited, Annual Report 1971 9.

9. Mindeco Mining Yearbook of Zambia 1971 (Kitwe: Copper Industry Service Bureau, 1972) 24.

10. "Business Review" Times of Zambia, 11 February 1972, 8.

11. Ballance Zambia and the East African Community 55-61; "Business Review" Times of Zambia, 25 June 1971, 8.

12. The conscious promotion of cooperation is a much broader definition of integration than many currently in use. Ernst Haas restricts the term to "the process whereby political actors in several distinct national settings are persuaded to shift their loyalties, expectations and political activities to a new centre whose institutions possess or demand jurisdiction over the pre-existing national states." The Uniting of Europe: Political, Social and Economic Forces, 1950-1957 (Stanford: Stanford University Press, 1958) 16 Richard W. Chadwick's formulation of integration as "the intensity of organized, cooperative activities of two or more nation-state systems" is closer to that employed here. "A Brief Critique of 'Transaction Data and Analysis: In Search of Concepts' by Barry B. Hughes" International Organization 26(4), Autumn 1972, 681.

13. President Amin of Uganda represents a partial exception. His emergence has provided a significant brake on the momentum towards integration in Eastern Africa.

14. Hayward Alker and Donald Puchala advance this as a condition for community formation. "Trends in Economic Partnership: The North Atlantic Area, 1928-1963" in J. David Singer (ed) Quantitative Politics: Insights and Evidence (New York: Free Press, 1968) 289.

15. "The Dilemma of the Pan-Africanist" Zambian Papers No. 2, 1967, 4 and 5.

16. Hughes "Transaction Data and Analysis" 672-674.

17. Ibid. 661-62; James A. Caporoso "Theory and Method in the Study of International Integration" International Organization 25, Spring 1971, 239-40; Donald J. Puchala "International Transactions and Regional Integration" International Organization 25, Autumn 1970, 733-40.

18. J. S. Nye Peace in Parts: Integration and Conflict in Regional Organization (Boston: Little, Brown, 1971) 26-27; Donald J. Puchala "Integration and Disintegration in Franco-German Relations, 1954-1965" International Organization 24, Winter 1970, 184; Hughes "Transaction Data and Analysis" 679.

19. Nye Peace in Parts 44.

20. Southern Rhodesia, Prime Minister's Office Report of the Central African Conference Victoria Falls Hotel, July 1963 (Salisbury: Government Printer, 1963) C.S.R. 30-1963, 8-9.

21. Nye Peace in Parts 51 and 54.

22. ZIS Press Release No. 395/63, 5 April 1963.

23. Report of the Central African Conference 9-10.

24. Rhodesia and Nyasaland Federation. The Federation of Rhodesia and Nyasaland (Dissolution) Order in Council 1963. S.I. 1963/2085, 20 December 1963, sec. 70(1).

25. Ibid. sec. 71; "Agreement between the Government of Southern Rhodesia and the Government of Northern Rhodesia relating to the Rhodesia Railways" 10 December 1963, Northern Rhodesia Government Gazette 53(72) 13 December 1963, 847-56.

26. Federation of Rhodesia and Nyasaland (Dissolution) Order in Council, sec. 36; "Agreement between the Government of Southern Rhodesia and the Government of Northern Rhodesia relating to the Central African Power Corporation" 25 November 1963, Northern Rhodesia Government Gazette 53(63), 26 November 1963, 725-29.

27. Federation of Rhodesia and Nyasaland (Dissolution) Order in Council, sec. 50; "Agreement between the Government of Southern Rhodesia, the Government of Northern Rhodesia and the Government of Nyasaland relating to the Central African Airways Corporation" 4 December 1963, Northern Rhodesia Government Gazette 53(67), 5 December 1963, 797-803.

28. Federation of Rhodesia and Nyasaland (Dissolution) Order in Council, sec. 61; "Agreement between the Government of Southern Rhodesia and the Government of Northern Rhodesia and the Government of Nyasaland relating to the Agricultural Research Council of Central Africa" 23 December 1963, Northern Rhodesia Government Gazette 53(79), 27 December 1963, 924-31. Zambia rejected proposals to retain common meterological, statistical, film and tourist services. Subsequently, Zambia withdrew from the Tobacco Research Board (June 1965), the Standards Association (August 1966), and the Central Registry of Patents and Trade Marks (September 1968), all in Salisbury.

29. UN Treaty Series vol. 551, 119-27, and vol. 568, 215-31.

30. Central African Mail 24 January 1964, 4; National Assembly Debates 12 January 1965, col. 17.

31. ZIS Press Release No. 1404/66, 29 July 1966, 3 and No. 2049/66, 14 November 1966, 1. President Kaunda claimed that the British Government had insisted in 1963 on joint operation of the Rhodesia Railways system, "despite the wish expressed by this country and Rhodesia that the railways should not be run on a unitary basis." Ibid.

32. Nye Peace in Parts 23-24.

33. Federation of Rhodesia and Nyasaland (Dissolution) Order in Council, sec. 48. Under the Federation of Rhodesia and Nyasaland (Dissolution) Order in Council (Amendment) Act, 1967, Zambia revoked this power.

34. Rhodesia Railways 17th Annual Report, 1966 3. The Committee of Finance Ministers set up to administer the Bank of Rhodesia and Nyasaland also never met.

35. National Assembly Debates 14 June 1967, col. 108.

36. Rhodesia Railways 17th Annual Report, 1966 2. The Higher Authority for Power has resorted to resolutions five times since UDI.

37. Rhodesia Railways 18th Annual Report, 1967 7. Central African Airways 22nd Annual Report, 1967/1968 2.

38. Zambia Information Services Press Release No. 2049/66, 16 November 1966. British H. C. Deb. 1 November 1966, cols. 56-57; Africa 1965 No. 25, 24 December 1965, 2.

39. National Assembly Debates 23 September 1970, cols. 35-36; "The Southern Rhodesia (Higher Authority for Power) Order 1970" No. 892 Statutory Instruments, 1970 (London: HMSO, 1970); Part II, 2824-25. Two retired colonial officials were appointed: Sir Evelyn Hone, last Governor of Northern Rhodesia, and James C. Morgan.

40. ZIS Press Release No. 2049/66, 14 November 1966.

41. Rhodesia Railways 18th Annual Report, 1967 6.

42. Ibid. 8.

43. Central African Power Corporation Annual Report and Accounts, 1966 2; ibid. 1971, 1. The meetings were in early 1966 and in December 1970. It is not clear if the Rhodesian "members" attended on the latter occasion.

44. Rhodesia Railways 21st Annual Report, 1970 5.

45. A total of 1330 Zambians and 32,250 Tanzanians were employed as general workers on the railway in 1971 (National Assembly Debates 1 December 1971, col. 315). In 1973, estimates of African employees were 30,000 on construction and 8,000 in operational jobs (Africa No. 28, December 1973, 103).

46. Ballance Zambia and the East African Community 31-38 and 51-52. Lusaka and Dar es Salaam were determined to have the Tazara railway administratively independent of both Zambia Railways and East African Railways. In the case of East African Airways Zambia was anxious to ensure that airline facilities

would not be concentrated in Nairobi to the same extent as Central African Airways facilities were centralized in Salisbury.

47. ZIS Press Release No. 88/68, 12 January 1968.

48. Withdrawal from the APU (and ATU) took effect on May 31, 1966, but the concessionary postal rates continued until September 1967. First Report of the Auditor-General on the Public Accounts for the financial year ended 31st December 1967 (Lusaka: Government Printer, 1968) 26.

49. National Assembly Debates 20 January 1965, col. 394, 21 September 1966, col. 2335, 27 August 1968, col. 444; "The Fugitive Offenders (Southern Rhodesia) Order, 1966", Statutory Instrument No. 371 of 1966, 11 October 1966, Supplement to the Republic of Zambia Government Gazette 17 October 1966, 1235.

50. Central African Mail 24 January 1964, 3-4.

51. National Assembly Debates 11 August 1966, col. 582; Ministry of Labour Annual Report of the Department of Labour 1968, 1.

52. Douglas G. Anglin "Confrontation in Southern Africa: Zambia and Portugal" International Journal 25, Summer 1970, 515.

53. Alker and Puchala "Trends in Economic Partnership" 288-89.

54. Dear Mr. Vorster ...: Details of exchanges between President Kaunda of Zambia and Prime Minister Vorster of South Africa (Lusaka: Zambia Information Services, 1971). Contact was resumed in 1974, again on South African initiative.

55. Tanzania and Kenya opened missions in Lusaka in 1969 and 1970 respectively. There has never been any Ugandan representation in Zambia, even on a non-resident basis.

56. ZIS Press Release 1529/65, 23 September 1965, and 1971/76, 6 December 1965; National Assembly Debates 19 January 1965, cols. 314-16.

57. Following the breakup of the Federal common market, imports of Rhodesian goods became subject to Zambian tariffs. For the first six months, duties were suspended, but this suspension was withdrawn for most goods (except foodstuffs) on June 27, 1964 and for the remaining goods on March 24, 1965. However, to offset a rise in the cost of living, a general suspension of duty was introduced for a variety of goods. Two days after UDI, Commonwealth preferences on Rhodesian goods were withdrawn and in December 1965 import controls were introduced. These are now the major instruments for controlling Rhodesian trade. Report of the Controller of Customs and Excise, 1964-65 (Lusaka: Government Printer, 1966) 2; 1965-66, 2.

58. Legislative Assembly Debates 17 March 1964, cols. 161-2. This restored them to a basis of equality with tariffs on Tanganyikan and Ugandan goods.

59. Ballance Zambia and the East African Community 104.

60. Report of the Controller of Customs and Excise 1965-66, 2.

61. Annual Report of the Ministry of Commerce, Industry of Foreign Trade, 1967 (Lusaka: Government Printer, 1968), 5-6; ZIS Press Release 1952-68, 31 October 1968.

62. Marion Bone "Zambia's Relations with Tanzania" May 1968, mimeo, 2.

63. In addition, Zambia has exhibited in Dar es Salaam each year since 1968. The East African governments have also had stands at the Ndola Trade Fair: Kenya since 1965, Tanzania since 1967 and Uganda 1968-70. Rhodesia was represented at Ndola in 1964, and South Africa planned to participate but later withdrew.

64. The pipeline was opened in December 1964 and the refinery in May 1965.

65. ZIS Press Release 638/66, 15 April 1966.

66.

British Airlift: Nairobi/Dar-Lusaka/Ndola (19 December 1965 - 31 October 1966)	5,400,000 gallons
Canadian Airlift: Kinshasa - Lusaka/Ndola (27 December 1965 - 30 April 1966)	1,100,000 gallons
American Airlift: Kinshasa - Lubumbashi (4 January - 30 April 1966)	3,200,000 gallons
	9,700,000 gallons

67. In March 1973, the UN Mission to Zambia estimated annual needs for coke at 80,000 tonnes. Report of the Security Council Special Mission S/10896/Add. 1, 6 March 1973, 16. Coke is needed for the lead mines at Kabwe and the lime works at Ndola.

68. Edwin T. Haefele and Eleanor B. Steinburg Government Controls of Transport: An African Case (Washington: Brookings Institution, 1965) 10-23; Charles Elliott (ed) Constraints on the Economic Development of Zambia (Nairobi: Oxford University Press, 1971) 329-37.

69. R. L. Sklar "Zambia's Response to UDI" Mawazo 1, June 1968, 20-25.

70. African Development October 1974, 269.

71. Vice-President Kapwepwe had argued in 1969 that it was "advisable to maintain some imports from the South for a short period" lest the East Africans "seek to exploit our willingness to divert supply away from the South." Zambia Mail 13 December 1969, 1.

72. ECM/Res. 13 (VI) 5 December 1965; ZIS Press Release 157/66, 25 January 1966.

73. Report of the Fourth Africa-Indian Ocean Regional Air Navigation Meeting, Rome, 23 November-18 December 1964. ICAO Document 8477, AFI/IV, 8-23, Supplement No. 1,5.

74. In Zambian parlance, an alien is normally a non-Zambian African, whereas an expatriate is a non-African, generally a European. Non-African Zambian citizens are also sometimes loosely classified as expatriates.

75. In 1972, the number of "foreign Bantu" from Zambia in South Africa was officially given as only 638. This presumably excluded Zambians who had settled there. South Africa, House of Assembly Questions and Replies Vol. 45, col. 1010, 14 June 1973.

76. Thomas Rasmussen "Political Competition and One-Party Dominance in Zambia" Journal of Modern African Studies 7, October 1969, 26-27.

77. The number of Zambian males employed in Tanzania was as follows:

1962 - 3254
1963 - 2643
1964 - 2524

Tanzania Annual Report of the Labour Division, 1964-1965 (Dar es Salaam: Government Printer, 1969) 17 and 51.

78. Zambia Mail 25 May 1967, 4; Ministry of Home Affairs Annual Report, 1965 (Lusaka: Government Printer, 1967) 17.

79. The Lusaka cell of the notorious Afrikaner Broederbond was reportedly disbanded in 1966. Sunday Times of Zambia 17 December 1972, 11.

80. Migration Statistics 1966, 1968; 1966 statistics available only for August to December.

81. Zambia Information Services Press Release No. 172/67, 9 February 1967, 1.

82. Ministry of Home Affairs Immigration Department Annual Report 1966, 2.

83. Mail bearing rebel stamps was for a time surcharged. Passenger train service across the Victoria Falls Bridge ended in September 1969, but the express bus service between Lusaka and Salisbury was greatly improved. Even when in December 1972 Rhodesian buses were banned from crossing into Zambia, steps were taken by the Government-controlled United Bus Company of Zambia to provide connecting services at the border. These arrangements were overtaken by events. Since January 1973, virtually no one has been allowed to cross the border.

84. Bone "Zambia's Relations with Tanzania" 10-11.

3. Towards a Political Economy of Southern Africa

Chapter Ten

FINANCIAL, COMMUNICATIONS AND LABOUR TRANSACTIONS IN SOUTHERN AFRICA*

Timothy T. Thahane

i. Introduction

Southern Africa consists of approximately 48 million people and contains some of the richest mineral deposits in the world; it is inter-connected by a rail system using the same track gauge and enjoys the best network of roads in Africa. Except for Angola and Mozambique (perhaps Namibia as well) the region shares certain common experiences and, to some extent, similar institutions arising from past political association with Great Britain. Also located in this region are some of the most industrially advanced areas on the African continent, using highly sophisticated technology. Viewed purely from an economic standpoint, Southern Africa should offer the best prospects for intra-regional co-operation in Africa. However, this is not the case. The economic, trade, financial and communications ties of the states in the region are more with Europe than with one another. Why is this so?

One of the major causes for less intra-regional trade in Southern Africa than with Europe is found in the predominence of political issues in the region. The apartheid policy of South Africa, the colonial administration of Portugal in Angola and Mozambique and the attitude of the Smith Regime in Rhodesia all divide Southern Africa along racial lines. This notwithstanding the fact that some of the black independent states have been compelled by their differences in size, economic power and by their geographical situation to undertake a "marriage of convenience" with South Africa and Rhodesia. Zambia's relative success in breaking out of the grip of these two states has been due largely to its much better financial base deriving from its mineral wealth of copper. The situation is more complex for Botswana, Lesotho and Swaziland and to some extent Malawi. Except for Malawi the other three states are in formal Customs Union and informal Monetary Union arrangements with South Africa; we discuss these institutional arrangements below.

If political conditions were to change in Southern Africa in the future, good prospects for increased economic co-operation and intra-regional trade would exist. Their foundation would be South Africa's enormous labour shortages, on the one hand, and its industrial capacity which would make it an exporter of manufactured goods to its neighbours, on the other. However before such change occurs all that we can do is to try and understand the complex problems of the region with a view to identifying and aiding positive elements of change and avoiding those that would lead to a consolidation of the status quo.

My paper concentrates on the financial, communications and labour transactions in the region. Neither time nor availability of data on inter-country transactions permit a detailed and critical analysis; the exploration of inter-country linkages offers a fertile ground for future research. As far as financial transactions are concerned I will briefly sketch developments in a few countries, especially South Africa, just to give an indication of their growth. Indirect references to inter-country flows will be made where appropriate.

ii. Financial Sectors

The development of banking in Southern Africa has been dominated by two British commercial banks: Standard Bank and Barclays Bank D.C.O. In the case of South Africa these banks established themselves between 1838 and 1862. They quickly introduced branch banking in place of the traditional local unit-bank system that they had followed since the beginning of the 19th century. By availing themselves of the facilities of the London money market, Barclays and Standard Bank grew rapidly through mergers and acquisitions. In fact, by 1926 there were only four banks in South Africa: Standard Bank, Barclays Bank D.C.O., the Netherlands Bank and Stellenbosch and District Bank, the last being a left-over from the early unit banks.[1]

The head offices of the three foreign banks were abroad, two in London and one in Amsterdam. The South African Government, concerned that "banking was becoming monopolistic and that South African interests were not always best served by institutions whose head offices were abroad"[2] created a new indigenous bank in 1941, the Volkskas. In this respect South Africa shared the fears that were later raised by Zambia, and Tanzania, with respect to foreign control of the banking sector. The only difference occurred in the policy instruments used to achieve control of the financial sector by these states. In 1973, the South African Minister of Finance gave all foreign banks a warning that they should retain only ten per cent control or less by the end of the decade. Their interests should be sold to South Africans.

Although reliable data on the relative growth of commercial banks in South Africa since the 1860's is unavailable, Table 1 shows the number of commercial banks and their relative shares of liabilities to the public as of August, 1961.

Table 1

Commercial Banking in South Africa, 1961

Name of Bank	Liabilities to the public (R million)	Number of Branches	Number of Sub-Branches	Number of Agencies
Barclays Bank D.C.O.	467.60	340	14	309
Standard Bank	410.10	350	18	272
Volkskas	151.40	160	--	96
Netherlands	63.84	42	2	36
French Bank of SA	8.53	5	--	--
Stellenbosch and District	4.26	1	--	2
First National City	4.19	2	--	--
Chase Manhattan	2.34	3	--	--
SA Bank of Athens	2.09	2	--	--
Totals:	1115.20	905	34	715

Source: Houghton Hobart D., The South African Economy (London: Oxford University Press, 1967. Second Edition) 184

Despite the rapid growth of commercial banking operations in the economy of South Africa, foreign banks continued to take a larger proportion of the increase in liabilities. The two British banks alone held over 78% of all liabilities of the commercial banks; the rest of the foreign banks held another 8%. Given this high control of the financial sector by foreign banks, one can certainly appreciate the recent concern of the South African Government referred to above.

Prior to 1965 the publication of financial statistics by the South African Reserve Bank included those of the commercial banks in Botswana, Lesotho and Swaziland. Thus the residents of these countries may have contributed to the overall growth of commercial banking in South Africa between the 1860's and 1961.

Table 2 shows the increase in the assets of the banking sector in South Africa between 1965 and 1972. These rose from R3430.1 millions to R7728.1 millions, an increase of 125%. The largest growth of 136% occurred in the claims of the banking sector on the government compared to 104% increase in the sector's claim on the private sector. This indicates the important role which commercial banks play in providing internal finance especially for the government.

Although the banking sector provides a high degree of financing to both the private and public sectors, South Africa still remains a net importer of capital especially for the development of its mining and power sectors. Since the beginning of the sixties when the World Bank ceased to provide loans to South Africa for the power development, ESCOM (Electricity Commission) has managed to raise all its funds in Europe. Various consortia of German, Swiss and other European banks have often joined together to provide financing for certain major projects in South Africa. Also, subsidiaries of European companies such as Mercedes, Volkswagen, Leyland, etc. often raise money through their headquarters to finance their plants. Funds for the mining sector are usually provided by the Mining Houses which have close ties with several financing houses in London. It is expected that these consortia of overseas banks will also provide financing for the Saldhana and Richards Bay projects.

Despite its highly developed financial and industrial sectors, South Africa is still underdeveloped in comparison to its potential. Its mineral and other natural resources still offer good prospects for foreign investment. In this regard South Africa may be compared to Canada.

Because of the high demand for external capital South Africa prohibited building societies from making investments in the neighbouring states, even though those societies collected deposits and premiums from all the countries in the region. Following representation by Lesotho and other States in the region the Act was amended in 1967 to permit the societies to invest as much as they collected from the neighbouring states under conditions to be specified by the Registrar of Building Societies. It is important to note that all the financial institutions banks, insurances, building societies, etc., collected surplus funds from the region and invested them only in South Africa. For example, it was estimated in 1969 that Lesotho was exporting annually between R150,000 and R200,000 through the building societies alone.

Before leaving this section reference should be made to the development of the South African Reserve Bank. The Bank was not established until 1920, and at the beginning it did not have as much influence and power as one would have expected of a central bank. Its position vis-à-vis the long established commercial banks was strengthened by two factors: a) the agreement with the Chamber of Mines in 1925 according to which the Bank became the channel for selling all South African gold, and b) the transfer to the Bank of government accounts in 1927. Since then, the Reserve Bank Act has been amended several times to give it complete control over all the activities of the financial institutions. The liabilities of the Reserve Bank grew between 1965 and 1972 from R 616 million to R 1,362 millions.

Until late in the 1940's there was no market in South Africa for short and medium term securities. The government fostered its development by establishing in 1949 (a year after the Nationalist Party came into power) a National Finance Corporation (NFC) with powers to accept deposits, invest in treasury bills and other short-term securities. Other financial institutions such as building societies, insurance companies, etc., could keep their surplus funds with the Corporation and count them as liquid assets for reserve purposes. The Corporation enjoyed very rapid development. It is interesting from the point of view of internal financing and self-reliance to note that in 1972, NFC held 86% of its total assets of R 359 million in Treasury Bills, Land Bank Bills and Government stock.

From this brief description it can be seen that South Africa has made rapid progress in the development of various monetary institutions and other complementary financial institutions such as discount houses, trust banks, land bank, accepting houses, and the Johannesburg stock market which compared favourably with those in London, New York or Zurich. Until recently the governments of BLS could not float any debentures on the South African capital markets even though they shared the same currency. This situation has now changed.

a. Financial Flows Between South Africa, Zambia and Malawi[3]

The preceding section sketched briefly the evolution and rapid development of the South African monetary and banking sectors and reference was made to some of the most important financial institutions which dominate the transactions in the banking system. It may be useful in this section to analyse briefly the links, both formal and informal, between this highly developed system and the other states in Southern Africa. Specifically one would have expected close cooperation between the central bankers of the region in order to establish some kind of a payments arrangement.

Again, because of the political issues that dominate the region, this has not been possible. The result is that Malawian and Zambian kwachas cannot be exchanged in South Africa while Rhodesian dollars and Mozambique and Angolan escudos are acceptable. The South African rand is unacceptable in Zambia. However, despite the lack of formal payments arrangements between Malawi and Zambia, on the one hand, and South Africa, on the other, there is a substantial amount of trade flow among the three countries and Rhodesia. The trade flows imply some financial transactions even though at a higher level since final settlements can be effected in gold or the hard currency of a third country.

Since independence Zambia has gone a long way towards changing its trade patterns with the white Southern Africa. Zambian exports to South Africa decreased from K 26.2 millions in 1964 to K 10.4 in 1971. Nevertheless, imports increased from K 32.4 millions to K 58.6 over the same period. The main explanation for the increase in imports is found in the spare parts for the mines which come largely from South Africa. With Rhodesia on the other hand, Zambia has in the same period decreased both its exports and imports from K 13.8 million to K 0.3 millions and K 61.7 millions to K 21.0 millions respectively. With the completion of Tanzam Railway in 1975-76 the diversion of trade will be complete. The closure of the border with Zambia by Rhodesia in early 1973 has sealed the final break of trade relations with Rhodesia until and unless the Rhodesian constitutional problem is solved. Zambia's trade with Botswana is likely to increase with the completion of the road linking the two countries.

In the case of Malawi, which has less resources than Zambia, the position is different. Malawi is seeking closer ties with South Africa as a matter of political choice. Malawi has received financial assistance from South Africa for the new capital Lilongwe. It also has a large number of its people in South African mines and operates scheduled flights to Johannesburg and Salisbury. These ties are likely to grow rapidly in the future. The same is true of the trade with its neighbours, Mozambique and Rhodesia. As of 1969 Malawi's imports came largely from Rhodesia, M.K. 16 million, and South Africa, M.K. 9 million.

It is important to note that Zambia, as opposed to Malawi, pursues a deliberate policy of economic disengagement from white Southern Africa. Its resources and relative distance from South Africa facilitate pursuit of this policy. Malawi, with limited resources and a large number of its people working in both South Africa and Rhodesia, follows a policy of economic co-operation and seeks closer political ties with South Africa as evidenced by the reciprocal visits at Head of State level. If political changes take place in South Africa and Rhodesia, one could expect an increase in the areas of co-operation among the States of Southern Africa, especially between Zambia and South Africa because of the latter's highly developed financial and capital markets and the former's enormous needs for external capital financing.

b. Monetary and Banking Arrangements Between Botswana, Lesotho and Swaziland (BLS)

BLS do not have their own central banks and participate in a de facto monetary union with South Africa; they use the South African Rand as legal tender in their countries. South African coins and notes are imported as required for circulation into BLS countries. In the same way, surplus funds raised in BLS by the commercial banks, which until very recently were branches of South African banks, are exported for investment in South Africa.

As mentioned earlier, unitl 1967 South African financial institutions such as insurance and building societies, which operate in BLS, were prohibited by law from investing in those states. This gave rise to an interesting dilemma in which BLS countries were in desperate need of capital while at the same time exporting it to South Africa through commercial banks, insurance and building societies. The BLS authorities have jointly studied the operations of the commercial banks in their respective countries under the present informal monetary arrangements with South Africa. The results of their study have led to negotiations with South Africa aimed at concluding a formal monetary agreement. They have also enacted similar legislation for controlling the operations of all financial institutions in their countries.

Shortly after independence BLS engaged South Africa in a renegotiation and formalization of their economic links which until then had worked to their disadvantage. The first of these renegotiations involved the Customs Union Agreement which had been in force since 1910. Landell-Mills[5] has adequately dealt with the various issues raised in the negotiations and the new agreement which was signed in 1969. It is sufficient here to note that although the agreement has not been in operation for a long time, the revenue accruing to BLS has enabled them to balance their recurrent budgets. The consultation mechanism of the Customs Union Commission and its Technical Liaison Committee have so far functioned smoothly. Positions on major policy differences especially with respect to industrializatio have often been discussed frankly in the meetings of the commission even though agreement was not always reached.

The second area which came up for renegotiation in 1971 was the monetary arrangements. The issues under discussion involved

a. foreign exchange control and the right of BLS to authorize transactions and remittances of capital, earnings and profits for foreign investments made in BLS;

b. compensation for the South African currency in circulation in the BLS;

c. access of BLS to the South African capital markets which had until very recently been closed to BLS;

d. the right of BLS to issue coins for local circulation in their respective countries;

e. consultation mechanism similar to the Customs Union Commission; and

f. the valuation of reserves if one of the partners should decide to leave the monetary union.

Although agreement is not expected until the end of 1974, certain developments have already occurred. South Africa sought to impose a low limit on the amount of foreign exchange that each of the BLS can authorize in any year without consultation with the South African Reserve Bank which has to make the foreign exchange available. BLS wanted as high a limit as possible in order to give guarantees to foreign investors. Unfortunately the compromise of a R1 million agreed upon was not satisfactory to Botswana which has huge mineral investments, hence its announced intention to establish its own central bank. Until the bank is established Botswana will probably participate in the Southern African Monetary Union on a de facto basis especially in matters of foreign exchange.

The second significant development that has occurred is the establishment by Swaziland of a monetary authority which not only issues coins but also notes for circulation in Swaziland. The notes are fully backed by the Rand and the South African Reserve Bank is represented on the Swazi Monetary Authority.

It is anticipated that the new agreement will contain institutional arrangements for consultation on monetary matters in general and foreign exchange in particular. Just as the Customs Tarriff Schedule is identical for all the member states, the foreign exchange manual is expected to contain similar provisions.

With regard to access to capital markets, South Africa offered its capital markets to the BLS governments in 1969 by amending its relevant Acts (Unit Trust Control Act, Banking Act, The Building Societies Acts, The Insurance Acts, The Pension Act). Their securities were granted the status of "approved securities" which meant that the BLS governments can raise medium and long-term capital under the same terms and conditions as the South African municipalities and public corporations. Botswana has availed itself of this facility to raise R2 millions once.

With respect to commercial banking there are two British commercial banks, Barclays

Bank International Limited and Standard Bank Limited which operate in each of the BLS countries. These are the same giants that dominate commercial banking in South Africa. Until the reorganization of the banking system in South Africa which, among other things, required foreign banks to be incorporated locally, both Barclays and Standard Bank in BLS were branches of those in South Africa. Although now they are controlled from London, they still have close ties with their offices in South Africa and indeed their Managing Directors "reside" in Johannesburg. Standard Bank acts as a banker for the Government in respect of Botswana and Lesotho while Barclays Bank does the same for Swaziland. Recently Standard Bank has been incorporated in Swaziland with Government having a share of 20%. Other financial institutions such as Post Office Saving Banks and the recently established development banks also provide credit. But because there have only been two commercial banks operating in each country, consolidated financial data on commercial banking could not be published (even though it has been collected since 1967) without breaching the confidential nature of each bank's statistical returns. Only a few general observations will therefore be made.

Since independence total deposits in each of the BLS countries have risen sharply, by upwards of 20% in some years. The bulk of the deposits have come from the private sector. The ratio of loans and advances to deposits which has previously been around 50% has moved towards 60% and 70%. This reflects an increasing use of locally generated funds. Historically, the surplus funds were invested in South Africa or England in the form of head office balances. This is also changing.

The informal or de facto arrangement between BLS and South Africa had advantages and disadvantages for the smaller partners. It is an administrative advantage that BLS do not have to worry about the problems of maintaining the external stability of their currencies. In addition, they could also benefit from access to a large capital market in South Africa. The largest cost of this arrangement, however, is that BLS cannot use monetary policy in any of their instruments of economic policy. Inflation generated in South Africa is transmitted easily and measures adopted by the Reserve Bank to control inflation in South Africa may be applied by the commercial banks in BLS regardless of whether or not conditions warrant them. Lack of internal control of the banking system makes internal financing through treasury bills and other short-term debentures very difficult. BLS countries can only give investors guarantees about repatriation of profits and capital after consultation with South Africa. South Africa has, however, been very co-operative on Exchange Controls as far as BLS countries are concerned.

All the same, beyond a certain point goodwill and gentlemen's agreements need to be embodied in internationally binding agreements and this is the object of the negotiations referred to above.

iii. Transport and Communications

Transport and communications constitute an important aspect of economic infrastructure and perform vital service and developmental functions both within a national economy and between various countries. They enable intra- and inter-country trade and movement of goods and people, thereby bringing about greater economic cohesion. Governments often embark on investment programmes in transport and communications either to open the inaccessible parts of the country, hoping to bring about national consolidation, or expressly to promote intra-country trade; this is especially true if different regions of the same country have different resource bases or comparative advantages.

In Africa, modern means of transport and communications were externally established by the metropolitan colonial powers in order to facilitate administration or to establish extraction routes for the raw materials required by overseas industrial processing centres. Because of the heterogeneity of colonial powers and different territories they administered, a disconnected system of transport and communications evolved. Local traffic routes served only as coast-inland extensions of the international North-South routes.

Southern Africa was no exception to the above pattern of development of transport and communications. The only exception was in South Africa where, even before the formation of the Union in 1910, the need to develop a national transport and communications network was clearly recognized. The justification was perhaps the need to integrate the four colonies which formed the Union. Britain was largely behind the move to foster national unity following the Anglo-Boer war of 1899 to 1902. In the Central African Federation of Rhodesia and Nyasaland, (which included Zambia, Malawi and Rhodesia) a national network developed in Rhodesia only.

Zambia and Malawi had to await independence to start on the construction of road networks and this has absorbed a large percentage of their budgets. The same is true of BLS.

A very serious issue which will loom high in the economic and political developments in Southern Africa, (unless a change takes place in Angola and Mozambique) is the fact that six of the countries of the region are land-locked. By an irony of history countries with access to the sea happen to be South Africa, with its negative racial and political attitudes, and Portugal's territories of Angola and Mozambique. This situation will present complex problems for the transportation of imports and exports from the land-locked states to and from the rest of the world since South Africa has not acceded to the 1965 UN Convention on Transit Rights of Land-locked States. Such transit rights are essential for BLS even though South Africa has guaranteed them transit under the revised Southern Africa Customs Union Agreement signed in 1969.

Notwithstanding the above, let us look at the various modes of communication in the region. In doing so it must be born in mind that rail, air and waterways are complementary modes which make up a transport system. They are prerequisites for any increased intra-regional trade, communications and co-operation. Where a continuous haulage of bulky goods such as minerals, crops and timber are involved, railways have an advantage over road transport. Roads are useful where small local shipments are required quickly. They perform a feeder function for railways or ships. Air transport is useful where speed and perishability of products are involved.

a. <u>Railways</u>

The African sub-continent is not well endowed with a coastline that affords many natural harbours or navigable rivers to carry ocean traffic inland. Goods and people have to be transported by road or railways, or in recent years by air. In South Africa, railway construction began in the 1860's with the discovery of diamonds and later gold. They proved to be the most economic means of transporting minerals and crops. The number of miles of open railway between 1861 and 1951 increased from 2 to 13,346. New railway construction has levelled off in recent times because of increased road and air transport. Today, the monopoly and protection given to the railways by law are proving an obstacle to the development of rapid and comprehensive trucking services in South Africa. This monopoly, among other things, reflects the power of the White Railway Unions which are very powerful especially in such fields as job reservation.

Although goods destined for the BLS are not treated differently from those of South Africa on the railways, they sometimes enjoy lower priority in peak periods. At the same time truckers from BLS cannot carry goods either from port or to any point in South Africa which is thirty miles away from their respective borders. They are subjected to the same licensing laws as the South African operators. The issue has been a subject of lengthy negotiations and dispute between South

Africa and its smaller partners since 1970. No satisfactory solution has been reached yet.

The whole of Southern Africa, including Zaire, is linked by a railway system which uses 1067 mm tracks. The rolling stocks of the various railways are all interchangeable. This is very different from the rest of Africa where different gauge tracks are used even between neighbouring states.

Because of the existence of the rail links, Botswana's imports or exports could go by rail through Cape Town: Lesotho's through Durban; Swaziland's through Lourenço Marques in Mozambique; Rhodesia's through Cape Town, Lourenço Marques or Beira; Zambia's through Beira in Mozambique or via Zaire through Lobito in Angola and Malawi's through Beira or Nacala. But the closure of the border with Zambia by Rhodesia and the near completion of the Tanzam railway has altered the picture as far as that country is concerned. Technically, the track of the new Tanzam railway is the same as that used in the whole of Southern Africa and hence interchangeability of rolling stock is possible, if not likely until change in the minority-ruled states occurs.

Viewed from the development point of view it is fair to say that railway construction has stimulated developments in other sectors of the economy only in South Africa and Rhodesia. In Zambia and Swaziland the railways remain in enclave sector for copper and iron ore extraction. Similarly, in Angola and Mozambique they have not contributed to the development of the rest of the economy. In Botswana the railway line is only passing through to Rhodesia from South Africa. To stimulate other developments Botswana intends to take over this line. This announcement partly made Rhodesia and South Africa accelerate and complete the construction of a rail line linking them directly. Of course, another consideration was the deteriorating security situation on the line through Mozambique.

b. Road Transport

In recent years road transport has proved superior to any other mode of transport in terms of flexibility and adaptability. From the construction standpoint there is a wide choice of routes such as access tracks, gravel, laterite and bitumenous roads. Investment in roads can also be phased in accordance with resource availability and need not involve heavy initial capital outlays as in railways or air transport before utilization can take place. In terms of vehicles the same is true: there is a wide choice among the various types, sizes and their carrying capacity which can be augmented by trailers. As has been demonstrated in the

United States, trucking can play a very important role in meeting the needs of a quickly expanding economy as well as being a lucrative business. Railways, on the other hand, are not easily adaptable to changing needs and all rely on heavy state subsidies for their operations.

In the field of road transport, South Africa still boasts of the largest network of good roads and the highest density of vehicles per 1000 persons (especially if one takes whites only) in the sub-region. Again, according to Houghton[6] there were 47,000 miles of roads in South Africa in 1916 and, 112,000 miles in 1959 with over 10,000 miles bituminized. Today there are over 200,000 miles of roads and in excess of 100,000 miles tarred. A ten year road construction programme has recently been approved by the Government with a view to creating a comprehensive national network of highways.

The total number of vehicles in South Africa increased rapidly from 40,000 in 1920 to over one million in 1960, 1.8 million in 1965 and 2.4 million in 1969. The largest growth occurred in private vehicles and this can be explained in terms of the flexibility which they offer in personal transport as well as the protection afforded the railways by the Statutory Road Transport Boards in so far as trucks and buses are concerned. The Boards have the primary responsibility of reducing traffic diversion from the railway by the control of licences for trucks and buses.

In the BLS countries as well as in Malawi and Zambia, heavy road construction began after Independence. The colonial power which administered them did very little to create an infrastructure that would link the various regions of the countries together. In all five states road construction has been given top priority in the respective development plan. Botswana which has approximately 5,000 miles of roads expects to spend over R 15 millions between 1970 and 1975 on road construction alone; in the same period Lesotho, with its 1200 miles of roads, expects to spend over R 10 millions or 23% of its projected expenditures; in Swaziland's post-independence plan, 1969/70 to 1972/73, 17% of the projected expenditure was allocated to road construction. This shows the priority given to the creation of internal road linkages in the BLS countries, and the extension of road networks in Botswana and Malawi to link up with the Zambian system of hard-top roads.

Viewed from a regional standpoint, Southern Africa has the best railway and road linkages in the whole of Africa. This offers great possibilities for movement of goods and passengers in the sub-region as well as opportunities for inter-country co-operation. Co-operation could take place in setting technical standards, licensing, easing border formalities (which are touchy problems at present) and in general harmonization of transport policies. The greatest barriers to the effective exploitation of these opportunities, of course, are the racial and political policies of South Africa and Rhodesia. These make co-operation a "forced necessity" rather than a question of deliberate choice.

c. Maritime Traffic

Maritime traffic is relevant to South Africa and the two Portuguese-speaking States only. Between 1960 and 1969 goods loaded at all South African ports more than doubled, while goods unloaded nearly tripled; the same trend is found in the goods at Mozambique ports. The substantial increase in goods loaded at Angola ports may be accounted for by the rerouting of Zambian trade as a result of the 1965 UDI by Rhodesia. By and large, these figures reflect all the goods sent to or received from the rest of the world by the sub-continent with the exception of trade that may go through ports in Tanzania, Kenya and Zaire. It also indicates the marriage of convenience between the various partners of the sub-continent.

d. Air Services

In the same way as it does the railways, South Africa dominates air services in the region; it has developed a good internal network of air services. Many South African cities are now linked by air. This mode of transport becomes economic when transactions increase between the cities, and people become relatively rich. Internationally there are, on average, three jumbo jets coming into and leaving Johannesburg daily together with other trans-continental jets. They come and go to different places in Europe, United States, Australia, and South America. The expectations are that by 1980 there will be approximately one million overseas visitors coming to South Africa per annum by air.

Despite the increased North-South flight schedules it is unfortunately still very difficult to travel within the region. The BLS countries are badly served by air connections between their capitals and Johannesburg. A visitor from Europe often has to spend the night only 300 miles from his destination. Similarly, it is very difficult to get from South Africa to Lusaka. One has to travel via Malawi or Botswana and flights are often fully booked despite almost daily flights on both routes. There are a number of flights a day between South Africa on the one hand and Rhodesia and Mozambique. With co-ordination and better time tables, the whole region may be better served by the present airlines. Air cargo has grown rapidly in South Africa and Zambia, for different reasons, but not in other States. This reflects the respective stages of development of these States and the standard of living of their people. As development accelerates, air transport can be expected to play an important role in the different countries of the sub-region.

The issue of overflight rights over South Africa for the BLS countries is going to present them with a formidable difficulty. South Africa will be very reluctant to grant such rights because of its desire to control the people who visit these countries. Various South African commentators see such a possibility as an opening for subversive elements. Of course, these fears are unfounded, but who will convince South Africa of that?

e. Post and Telecommunications

Like transport, the post and telecommunications networks of Southern Africa still reflect the North-South nexus with Europe. The abundance of North-South radio, telegraph and underwater cables with Europe do not help difficult intra-regional communications. From Lesotho, for example, one can get London on the phone without putting the receiver down, while a call to Zambia may take up to two days. This problem reveals a lack of telecommunications infrastructure covering the region. Internally, each of the black states is just formulating its long term development plans. They are besieged by several problems: obsolete transmission equipment, lack of trained personnel with accompanying institutional inadequacies, disparities in tariff structures and rates, and lack of inter-country co-operation in the solution of these problems.

The African states, excluding South Africa and the Portuguese-speaking States, are co-operating in the UNDP/ITU pre-investment Survey for a Pan-African Telecommunications Network. It is expected that the system linking all countries in Africa and the rest of the world will be operational by 1980. Botswana is surveying the route via Lusaka while Lesotho is examining the technical and financial implications of a direct link with Nairobi. Swaziland will probably join the network too. The African Development Bank (ADB) and other multilateral agencies are expected to finance the project. In addition, ADB is now considering telecommunications projects for Botswana, Swaziland, Zambia and Lesotho. These projects involve a large extension of telecommunications into the rural areas. In South Africa the programme for automatization is in full swing.

Postal relations are no different. Letters to any part of the sub-region often take longer than those to Europe. Perhaps this can be expected since letters are carried by railway, and airlines; if there is insufficient intra-regional transport flows, letters will usually go via the former metropolitan cities such as London. To quote but one example, from Lesotho there was no postal bag to any of the African countries until two or three years ago. Letters to Zambia or Malawi went into a bag for London. The situation is different today since there are now two bags, one to East and the other to West Africa. Before the independence of the black states in Southern Africa, an African Postal Union was established between them and South Africa. Unfortunately, this Union never became operational and remains only in the records. It is doubtful whether it will ever be resuscitated.

In general one can say that unlike the railway and transport infra-structural networks, which span the whole of the region, in telecommunications there are disconnected and small national systems which lack qualified personnel and use different equipment. Again, potential exists for co-operation but it cannot be exploited. Nevertheless, the black states in Southern Africa are more likely to establish inter-connected systems sooner than one would have expected. In the field of training they are already co-operating through a UNDP-financed centre in Blantyre which is also linked with one in Nairobi. The same co-operation is extending into other fields such as postal services and soon into aviation. Malawi already has an air agreement with Lesotho and Swaziland. Consultations are underway about the possibility of establishing a regional airline to link the various countries in Southern Africa. With the development of such infrastructural services we will see more inter-country trade and other transactions, including mail, in the region.

iv. Labour Transactions

The difficulties of obtaining data on inter-country financial and communication flows contrast sharply with the relative documentation of labour transactions in Southern Africa. For this we are indebted to a number of scholars, historians, sociologists, and economists. One of the latest to make a very useful study of migrant labour in South Africa is Francis Wilson.[7] The remarks in this section are based largely on his work and those of other authors. Wilson's books may be consulted for a detailed analysis of the magnitude and problems of migrant labour in South Africa.

The labour situation in the African sub-continent has been dominated by an insatiable labour demand by South Africa and to some extent Rhodesia, on the one hand, and the depressed employment conditions in the neighbouring states, on the other. From its early days, South Africa was founded on slave labour whose abolition led to the great trek in 1836. The discovery and subsequent mining of gold and diamonds in the 1860's and the 1880's aggravated the already acute labour shortage annually experienced by the farmers, especially on the sugar plantations of Natal. The sugar growers resorted to the introduction of indentured Indians who were later successfully organized into a non-violent strike in 1913 by Mahatma Ghandi.[8]

The mining companies and the government authorities developed two instruments in order to organize the supply of labour to the mines: the law and recruiting organizations. Numerous acts to control the mobility of black labour were passed in various provinces of South Africa. According to Wilson, the power of mining financiers was demonstrated in the Transvaal in 1895 by the enactment of a pass law drafted by the Chamber of Mines. These restrictive Acts have been amended and tightened over time until the 1969 Bantu Laws Amendment Act which sealed the historical attempts to control and direct black labour without any powers of collective bargaining.

The second and most powerful instrument was the recruitment machinery of the Chamber of Mines established as early as 1893. According to Wilson again: "The Chamber established a Native Labour Department with the two-fold objective of assuring an adequate and regular supply of black labour by opening up sources of supply within Transvaal and by arranging for the recruitment of labourers from Mozambique and taking of '<u>active steps for the gradual reduction of native wages to a reasonable level</u>'" (my underlining).[9] Taking 1936 as 100, the annual real earnings of black miners in 1969 had decreased by 1% while those of white miners increased by 72%.

During the Anglo-Boer war labour shortages become so acute that the mines began to recruit Chinese from North China. As a result, there were 51,000 indentured Chinese in the gold mines in 1906. With strong Liberal government pressure in Britain against "Chinese slavery" they were repatriated and the Chamber of Mines resorted to recruitment from the "Protectorates" of Basutoland, Bechuanaland and Swaziland through the Native Recruiting Corporation (N.R.C.). A sister organization, Witwatersrand Native Labour Association (W.N.L.A.) had long been active in Mozambique, Malawi and Zambia. There was a gentlemen's agreement not to compete for labour in Rhodesia and the plantations of Mozambique.

Employment in the mines or at farms is usually by contract of nine to eighteen months. The miners live under deplorable conditions in mine compounds although better ones have been built lately. They cannot bring their families and at the end of the contract they have to go back to their homes. Wilson and others have called this a system of oscillating migration "whereby unskilled black workers came to the mines for a limited time and then returned to their rural homes",[10] without terminal benefits of any kind. For a detailed analysis of the advantages and disadvantages of the oscillating migration system and its economics, see the two studies by Wilson.

Skilled mine workers, recruited from all over the world, the United States of America, the United Kingdom, Canada, Germany, Australia, streamed into South Africa in such large numbers that migration averaged about 24,000 per annum between 1890 and 1913. The apartheid policy also helped by reserving skilled jobs for the whites. Skilled training was provided only to a few whites and not to the large number of black workers. The policy of training black workers and building homes for them around the mines appears to have paid off in Zambia and Zaire in terms of productivity increase and stabilization of the labour force. Even this started after independence.

For the purposes of this paper the most important thing is to look at the numbers and flows of migrant workers in Southern Africa as a whole. Table 3 gives the percentage distribution of the geographical sources of black labour in the gold mines, between 1906 and 1969. Except for Rhodesia, W.N.L.A. recruited men from Malawi, Tanzania, Zambia, Botswana, Angola, and Namibia north of latitude 22° through its network of recruiting agencies. It concluded agreements with various governments except for Tanzania where men from the Southern province often signed up at the recruiting agencies in Northern Malawi. Of the 31,000 "tropicals" (as they were called) recruited by W.N.L.A. in 1952, 23% came from Malawi, 16% from Tanzania, 10% from Namibia and 6% from Barotseland in Zambia. The rest must have come from Mozambique, Angola and Northern Botswana. The mine authorities constructed roads and used light air services in order to bring the recruits to areas where they were transported onwards by railways, thereby making use of the railway services that span the region.

It was estimated in 1972 that there were approximately 840,000 black migrant workers in Rhodeisa and South Africa, drawn from the various countries of Southern Africa. Malawi contributed about 33%, Lesotho 25%, Zambia 5%, Botswana 7%, and Swaziland 4%. About 75% of these workers were in South Africa, where approximately 300,000 were employed in mining. The rest were in agriculture and transport, especially railways. Table 3 also indicates the degree of dependence of

Table 3

Percentage Distribution of the Geographical Sources of Black Labour Employed by the Chamber of Mines

1906 - 1969

	1906	1916	1926	1936	1946	1956	1966	1969
South Africa	22.9	49.2	41.3	52.1	41.3	34.7	34.0	31.4
Lesotho	2.6	7.9	10.9	14.5	12.5	11.9	16.8	17.5
Botswana	0.4	1.8	1.0	2.3	2.3	3.1	5.0	4.0
Swaziland	0.7	1.9	2.1	2.2	1.8	1.6	1.1	1.4
Mozambique	65.4	38.1	44.5	27.8	31.5	30.8	28.4	26.9
North of Latitude 22°	8.0	1.1	0.2	1.1	10.6	17.9	14.7	18.8
Total labour in absolute numbers ('000)	81	219	203	318	305	334	383	371

Source: Wilson, F. Labour in the South Africa Gold Mines, 1911 - 1969
Cambridge, Cambridge University Press, 1972, page 70

South African mines on foreign labour.

The total number of migrants from Lesotho generally fluctuates between 150,000 and 200,000 depending on the climatic or agricultural conditions at home. The majority of the people are compelled to seek work in South Africa because of the lack of employment opportunities at home. The economic costs of this system for Lesotho far outweigh the benefits and this explains the government's development strategy to create as many jobs as possible and, in any case, no less than the annual increment in the labour force. The Government is also aware of the powerful political leverage South Africa has through this large number of migrant workers since there is no formal agreement covering the employment of these people by South Africa. This is another area for renegotiation of economic links.

The remittances and deferred pay provided by miners go a long way towards providing incomes to many families in Lesotho. These have averaged about R 6 million over the last two years. Unlike Lesotho, Mozambique and Malawi have agreements with South Africa under which workers make varying compulsory remittances to their homes. Mozambique's agreement with South Africa permits the mines to recruit 80,000 to 120,000 men per annum in return for South Africa's routing of a greater part of her Southern Transvaal trade through Lourenco Marques. This provides Mozambique with useful revenue. Botswana and Swaziland have a smaller number of workers in South Africa. The numbers have been decreasing in recent years. Zambia, on the other hand, has now forbidden recruitment of Zambians into South Africa. Malawi suspended recruitment in 1974, following a crash of a W.N.L.A. plane carrying 75 Malawians back via Botswana. Although the ban may be lifted later, for the time being it strengthens Malawi's hand in negotiating better conditions for its people.

A great potential for co-operation between the countries with migrants in South Africa exists. They can negotiate jointly with South Africa to ensure that their people enjoy pensions and other social benefits. At present these migrant workers spend their economic life contributing to the development of South Africa, but in old age their home countries have to care for them and provide medical facilities. efore they join this process of oscillating migration, their home countries lso provide initial basic education for them and the benefiting employers do ot contribute in either taxes or other means to the costs of financing education n these countries.

ne system of oscillating migration and colour discrimination are endemic to the hole social, economic and political life of South Africa. The wealth and economic power of South Africa are based on it. But it can be changed or be made somewhat more civilized by permitting migrants to bring their wives or have frequent and regular visits from them. Its present inhumanity is worse than the penal systems of the United Kingdom and the United States of America, which do permit such visits. It is "an evil canker at the heart of a whole society, wasteful of labour, destructive of ambition, a wrecker of homes and a symptom of our fundamental failure to create a coherent and progressive society."[11]

From another point of view, the labour exporting countries have a powerful tool for co-operation with their politically difficult neighbour. Without actually withholding labour, important improvements and concessions can be jointly negotiated, especially in the mining sector which depends almost entirely on foreign workers. This is, however, a two-edged sword which may force the mines to mechanize quickly and to employ local black labour by substantially increasing wages.

v. Conclusion

From the above brief observations, it is clear that a valuable economic and institutional infrastructure at varying stages of development exists in Southern Africa. The railway and transport networks are the most interconnected of this infrastructure. The land-locked position of some states in the sub-region will require special attention from their transit neighbours. High opportunities for inter-country co-operation exist, but they cannot be exploited with ease because of political and racial issues that dominate the area. The treatment of migrant workers by South Africa is going to become more and more sensitive in the future since the migrants enjoy freedom and equality in their home countries, while they have to abide by the apartheid laws in South Africa. At the same time the field of migrant labour offers immediate possibilities for co-operation among the various labour exporting countries and their importer in order to ease the personal difficulties of the workers. With expected political changes in the Portuguese territories and Rhodesia, more avenues for co-operation will be created among the black states in Southern Africa. In time change may also occur in South Africa which will advance intra-regional co-operation in such fields as finance, trade, and communications.

NOTES

* The views expressed in this essay are those of the author and should not be taken to represent the policies of the agencies for which he has worked.

1. D. Hobart Houghton *The South African Economy* (London: Oxford University Press, 1967. Second Edition) 183

2. *Ibid.*, 183

3. See International Monetary Fund *Surveys of African Economies*, Vol. 4 (Washington, 1973) for discussion of Zambia's and Malawi's economies and finances.

4. See *ibid.*, Vol. 5 for discussion of the economies and finances of Botswana, Lesotho and Swaziland.

5. P. M. Landell-Mills "The 1969 Southern African Customs Union" *Journal of Modern African Studies* 9 (2) 1971, 263-81

6. Houghton *The South African Economy*, 191

7. See Francis Wilson *Labour in the South African Gold Mines 1911 - 1969* (Cambridge: Cambridge University Press, 1972) and *Migrant Labour in South Africa* (Johannesburg: South African Council of Churches and SPRO-CAS, 1972)

8. Houghton *The South African Economy*, 143

9. Wilson *Labour in the South African Gold Mines*, 3

10. Wilson *Migrant Labour in South Africa*, 5

11. Houghton *The South African Economy*, 95

Chapter Eleven

EXPANDING BOTSWANA'S POLICY OPTIONS

Donald Rothchild and Robert L. Curry, Jr.*

No African leadership is more poignantly aware of its limited international and domestic policy options and their consequences than Botswana's. In an address to the Botswana Democratic Party Conference at Molepolole on March 28, 1970, the President, Sir Seretse Khama, was most explicit in emphasizing that his country's "options are limited by circumstances." He explained as follows:

> But first let us make it clear that we are free from illusions. We are well aware that we are still a largely undeveloped, sparsely populated country, whose first concern must be our own development. We must put the highest priority on our development effort if independence is to have real meaning for our people. We recognize that we are not a world power, to be reckoned with in the highest international circles. No other country trembles when we speak. We have no army. The machinery through which we conduct our diplomatic affairs is fairly rudimentary. Because of financial and manpower limitations we have at present only four foreign missions, and these together with the external affairs section of my own Office, have small staffs. So we are not unaware of our limitations.[1]

For President Khama, the four key objectives of democracy, development, self-reliance and unity will be difficult to achieve primarily due to geographic, economic and political constraints that limit policy options. The main geographic constraint involves the country's land-locked position and its limited access to the "outside" world. But this constraint of nature can be coped with. An example of this enlargement of man's capacity to control nature[2] is the road to its northern neighbor, Zambia, which is currently under construction. The President noted that "despite the difficulties which Botswana faces in such co-operation with independent Africa we are determined to extend trading and other links. This is why we are seeking to build a road from Nata to Kazungulu, because it will open up new possibilities of trade with Zambia as well as contributing to the development of Northern Botswana."[3] The road, then, is a substantive effort to modify the geographic constraint against external political and economic relations.

Diversifying these relations means coping with the economic and political constraints that limit policy - choice. In light of this situation of limited choice, this essay seeks to raise a basic issue, applicable to other African states besides Botswana: is it possible that policymakers might expand economic resources and political ties that would permit a greater scope for developing and implementing policies directed toward attaining the four key objectives? In effect, to what extent can resources be expanded to increase choice under current circumstances? Our focus is three-fold: first, on Botswana's post-economic performance in regard to its current options; second, on the environment of limited economic prospects for facilitating expanded options; and third, on those political and economic factors threatening the country's capacity to generate growth and developmental policy options. Although only tentative conclusions can be drawn from an analysis based on the Botswana predicament alone, we hope that this policy-oriented line of analysis will further the examination of what problem-solving initiatives may be available to statesmen in late developing countries.

I. An Environment of Limited Options

Botswana's limited policy options are in large measure related to economic factors. But before discussing their constraints on policymaking in Botswana, it is useful to outline briefly other key factors: the country's demographic and political situation, and its administrative machinery. Demographically, Botswana, a spacious, largely arid, and sparsely populated land of some 648,000 people,[4] is intermeshed, for the present at least, in what has been referred to as a subordinate state system.[5] A calm center in the midst of subregional racial conflict, this landlocked country comprising 570,000 sq. kilometers borders upon the Republic of South Africa on the south and southeast, South West Africa (Namibia) and the Caprivi Strip on the north and west, Rhodesia (Zimbabwe) on the northeast, and Zambia on the north. Although committed to pan-African ideals and objectives, Botswana's geographical position reduces the options open to its leadership and tends to induce it to follow a cautious and pragmatic policy toward the white-dominated regimes along its borders.

Politically, Botswana's options are indeed limited. Its government, possessing no army and only a small police force, has necessarily pursued a course of prudence by ruling out guerrilla operations from its territory against Rhodesia and South Africa.[6] Even so, President Khama's regime has firmly aligned itself with majority African opinion to its north; it has taken a consistently strong stand on the appropriate conditions under which "dialogue" might be productive and, to the extent possible, applied sanctions against the rebel regime in Rhodesia.[7] Nevertheless, such economic ties as labor migration and the sale of products to rich markets in the south (reinforced by a longstanding customs union arrangement and full currency exchange) act, temporarily, as powerful restraints upon an overly vigorous northward orientation.

Botswana, then, operates in an environment of strikingly limited options. These demographic and political limitations are interrelated and overlapping; yet, when taken as a whole, they represent a pattern of constraints upon policymakers which is one of the most inhibiting on the African continent. It should be emphasized at this time that if stress is placed in this chapter upon such factors as administrative and economic frailty, geographic isolation, and dependence upon the white-dominated regimes of Southern Africa, we are not unmindful of other important constraints (such as inadequate mechanisms of distribution; insufficient communications and transportation facilities; the persistence of racial, ethnic and class cleavages; and low levels of public participation). However, the particular restrictions on policymakers dealt with here are selected on the basis of their immediate relevance to Southern Africa. One such restrictive tie is the Southern African Customs Union, as we have noted. The agreement not only affords access to revenues on the parts of Botswana, Lesotho and Swaziland, but it also permits them, after consultation with their partners, to protect infant industries through the establishment of tariffs (for a minimum of eight years), and to regularize transactions among the partner states by bringing a Customs Union Commission into being, and to provide for fuller BLS participation in the agricultural marketing arrangements administered externally in South Africa. Even so, these concessions underline the enduring nature of South African superiority in the regional system. For all the inequities remaining in this assymetrical connection, Botswana is still compelled, short of a quantum leap in the form of additional options, to find an accommodation to the realities of the regional power situation. From the South African perspective, the 1969 customs union pact can therefore be viewed "as another example of the success of the 'outward policy' ".[8] From Botswana's perspective, however, the necessity to interact with a dominant white-minority regime within the arrangement is as anxiety-provoking as it is constraining.

Interconnected with the issue of dependence upon the white dominated regimes discussed above is another major constraint - Botswana's land-locked position. For a state to be both interconnected with a dominant neighbor and landlocked is to be vulnerable in the extreme. Not only are its linkages to the Southern African subordinate state system reinforced by the limitations of geography but its lack of easy access to ocean ports involves a series of burdens which complicate the tasks of economic development. For one thing, the costs of transportation, handling and storage are greater for hinterland than coastal countries. For another, transportation delays are frequently encountered by customers distant from port cities. For still another, the reliance upon other states for transit rights puts a heavy premium upon continued goodwill. And finally, security and customs costs tend to be higher for landlocked countries. Consequently, distasteful as is the prospect of close relations with white dominated regimes in the vicinity, Botswana's policymakers are drawn by the realities imposed by geography to accept the basic economic unity of the Southern African region and to try as best as possible to cope with the inescapable economic and political costs arising from its hinterland position.

The gravity of the situation arising from Botswana's isolation cannot be fully appreciated without a look at the distances its exporters and importers must cope with in pursuing their business activities. All of the rail routes through white-ruled Southern Africa run for a distance of more than 1,000 km., the major route (Gaborone-Mafeking-Johannesburg-Durban) being 1,240 km.[9] The road distances through these territories are only marginally smaller; nevertheless, a minor road from Gaborone to Pretoria to Lourenco Marques does cover a distance of 930 km.[10] Projected routes through African-controlled lands offer an alternative to these subsystem constraints, but at a high cost in terms of transportation, handling, delays, and so forth. The proposed road and rail system from Francistown to Kasungula to Kapiri Mposhi to Dar es Salaam covers an estimated distance of 3,100 km. - a stretch over 1,000 km. greater than the Tanzam railway now under construction from Ndola to Dar es Salaam.[11] In brief, although Botswana can undeniably break the stranglehold imposed by integration with its neighbors in the south, the fiscal costs in pursuing such a policy on an extensive scale will come high.

An ancillary constraint upon policymakers is Botswana's <u>administrative frailty</u>, an outgrowth of the political and geographic factors already noted as well as the economic consequences of a colonial heritage of neglect. In fact, human, fiscal and material resources for administrative purposes are in short supply substantially as a result of the former administering authority's inactivity. British officials did little to recruit and train their Botswana colleagues for the responsibilities of independence and spent only small amounts upon constructing an administrative structure capable of dealing forcefully and effectively with post-independence developmental needs. No doubt this is partly due to the brief interlude between self-government and independence and to the expectation that Botswana's political future lay in some form of incorporation into South Africa. Nevertheless, it has given rise to problems of administrative transition which are summarized well in the <u>National Development Plan 1970-75:</u>

> The move to Gaborone, coinciding with the acquisition of self-governing status, triggered a sudden expansion of the Central Government. Where the central administration in Mafeking had consisted of no more than 25 officers under the Resident Commissioner, there were, by 1967, some 275 equivalent Ministerial posts in the seven Ministries which were created. The initial unfamiliarity of the Public Service with the new organizational structure caused transitional problems which were exacerbated by the death of qualified local officers and the departure of a number of

> expatriates after independence. These difficulties were in turn heightened, by the intensification of emphasis on economic and social advancement, by a rapid expansion of the development programme and by the fact that reforms were simultaneously introduced in the system of local administration.[12]

Moreover, with a mere R12m. at its disposal in the 1969-70 fiscal year for ordinary recurrent expenditures purposes, Botswana's bureaucracy was hardly in a position to expand its services much less to push ahead on projects such as basic infrastructure development, rural development or programmes designed to provide social services broadly.

Some insight into the fiscal constraints under which Botswana authorities operate comes from an examination of Government revenue and expenditures. In the 1969-70 year, for example, provisional government revenue was R22.5 m. and expenditure R18.9m.[13] The provisional expenditures for that year were grouped as follows: ordinary recurrent expenditures (including Parliament; the Office of the President; the Ministries of Finance; Home Affairs, Agriculture; Education, Health and Labour; Education; Commerce, Industry and Water Affairs; Local Government and Lands; Works and Communications; and Development Planning; and the Administration of Justice; the Attorney-General; Audit; and the Public Service Commission) came altogether to R12m.; recurrent expenditure arising from capital development, R0.001m.; statutory expenditure (including public debt; pension, gratuities and compensation; Overseas Service Aid Scheme), R2m; and expenditure from the Development Fund (in particular, for the Ministries of Finance; Agriculture; Commerce, Industry and Water Affairs; and Works and Communications), R4.9m.[14] Such fiscal restraints have an enormous impact upon overall organization capabilities, for they restrict administrative officials in their attempts to undertake active and sustained efforts at problem solving.[15] They also limit the ability of the public sector to provide employment and income-earning opportunities for Botswana's people.

One major point emerges from their geographic and political constraints, Botswana despite all preferences to the contrary, is for the present intertwined with the fate of the Southern African subordinate state system. The indivisibility of this state system - geographically and politically - is underscored by economic considerations; e.g. the migration of some 40,000 Batswana each year for work in the mines and on the farms of South Africa;[16] the remittances taken from the wages of Botswana miners; the critical importance of the South African market for Botswana's exports and imports; the dependence upon South African capital, personnel, equipment and enterprise in the local mining industry; the heavy reliance upon South African tourism; the free and unrestricted currency exchange system; the extensive railroad, air, road and communications linkages with Rhodesia and South Africa; and the customs union arrangement. The latter thus far has been an exceptionally important feature of Botswana's subdominant linkage to South Africa. It is through this agreement that the country earns most of its export earnings and that the Government collects public revenues to finance administration and other projects and programmes. The country's earnings recently increased due to the implementation of a modification in the customs union agreement which came into effect in 1970. It carried with it a new revenue sharing formula expressed as follows:

$$(1) \left[\frac{A + B + C}{D + E + F + G} (H) \right] 1.42$$

where, A = c.i.f. value of a country's imports,

B = before tax value of production and consumer goods subject to excise (or sales) taxes,

C = excise and sales taxes paid on (B) above,

D = c.i.f. value of common customs area imports,

E = customs duties and sales taxes paid on D,

F = before tax value of goods produced and consumed in the area which, in turn, are subject to excise (or sales) taxes,

B = excise and sales taxes paid on (F) above, and

H = the value of the common revenue pool.[17]

The most notable new feature is the 1.42 multiplier which, in effect, increases the proportional share distributed to the smaller countries by 42 per cent. This has meant increased revenue for Botswana; in 1969/1970, under the old formula, the country's revenue was R4.6m; it rose to R5.1m. in 1970/1971, and to R8.3m. in 1971/1972. Despite the increase, the negotiated figure of 1.42 has not, however, resulted in enlarged export earnings in a fashion matching the rise in imports.

Botswana's experience with the customs union points to the nature of South African hegemony in the region. To be sure, customs union agreements do in theory offer underdeveloped countries a potential option for the pursuit of productionist objectives; such advantages as economies of scale, increased diversification, coordinated planning, and enhanced international leverage have received extensive treatment in the literature on interstate integration.[18] In this particular instance, however, economic integration has done little if anything to encourage the creation of industries in Botswana, Lesotho or Swaziland and has undoubtedly had the effect of reinforcing the indivisibility of the Southern African subordinate state system. Assessing the costs and benefits of Southern African regionalism, Peter Robson concludes as follows:

In the absence of empirical data it is impossible to determine the balance

> of advantage to the territories in respect of their access to the South African domestic and overseas market for primary products, but they may have been quite favourable in terms of savings in marketing costs, and prices obtained. But the quotas imposed (as with livestock) limit the gains. Moreover, for some products not marketed through boards, such as timber, there appears to have been a tendency for the South African government to discourage the purchase of the products of BLS by administrative means when the interest of South African producer has demanded this.[19]

And another observer, giving the last point an added dimension, has remarked that the customs union arrangement has afforded South Africa an opportunity "for political manipulation" in its relations with these states along its borders.[20] It is a political manipulation based upon economic poverty in the BLS countries. Botswana, for example, cannot significantly expand administrative services or other projects or programmes in an environment of extremely scarce economic resources. And until quite recently, not only were the country's economic resources obviously scarce, but there was no real hope of expanding the existing resource endowment. Resource scarcity meant, and will continue to mean, dependence and limited policy options.

II. Poor Economic Performance and Limited Options

Botswana's main economic difficulties, then, are derived from the country's limited, utilizable resources and productive technology. This economic frailty gives rise to such problems as low per capita income and low levels of productivity for domestic goods and exportables, and few formal employment opportunities. The country's generally disappointing performance has further resulted in substantial annual balance of trade deficits that require transfers of funds from abroad to finance them. Such transfers have been in the form of government external finance (primarily borrowing and secondarily grants), and direct private investment by foreign companies.

The country's <u>per capita income</u> is so low that the United Nations classifies Botswana as one of the least developed of the developing countries.[21] Only the crudest of estimates exist on recent national income and gross domestic product levels. These show that in 1970, national income appeared to be approximately \$50m. and gross domest product \$55m.; between 1970 and 1973, each has likely grown by about \$5m.[22] On the basis of current population estimates, this level of GNP would indicate a per capita income of some \$85 annually.[23] Data are also available regarding employment and wages by sector, and we have presented these in Table 1. It reveals in detail the striking shift in employment and income from the agricultural sector toward central administration, service and mining.

Table 1

Botswana: Employment and Wages by Sector, 1967/1968 and 1970/1971

	Wage Earners		Annual Wage Bill			
	Number	Per cent of total	Amount (thousand rand)	Per cent of total	Average Yearly Wage (rand)	Number of Establishments
1967-1968						
Agriculture	7,750	27.6	588.6	4.9	78.0	284
Mining and quarrying	814	3.0	362.3	3.0	445.0	4
Manufacturing	1,358	5.0	702.0	5.8	517.0	19
Construction	1,566	5.7	518.1	4.2	330.8	14
Commerce	5.508	20.0	1,743.0	14.4	316.4	612
Transport and communications	1,135	4.2	953.3	7.9	840.0	12
Finance	134	0.5	237.2	2.0	1,770.1	9
Central Government	5,289	19.3	5,185.8	42.7	980.3	(42)[a]
Other services	4,014	14.7	1,835.6	15.1	457.3	307
Total	27,388	100.0	12,124.9	100.0	442.7	1,261
1970/1971						
Agriculture	4,302	11.5	756.2	3.7	175.7	295
Mining and quarrying	3,468	9.2	2,773.7	13.6	799.8	36
Manufacturing	2,315	6.2	1,450.6	7.1	626.6	39
Construction	2,236	5.9	1,066.3	5.2	476.8	56
Commerce	7,341	19.6	2,370.2	11.7	322.8	733
Transport and communications	1,640	4.4	1,808.2	9.0	1,102.5	20
Finance	1,342	3.6	1,152.9	5.7	889.1	42
Central Government	9.645	25.7	6,684.6	33.0	693.0	(56)[a]
Other services	5,231	13.9	2,252.6	11.0	430.6	93
Total	37,250	100.0	20,315.3	100.0	541.4	1,314

[a] Not included in total Number of Establishments.

Source: International Monetary Fund *Surveys of African Economies* 5 (Washington, D.C.: 1973) 60.

Data on productivity is also scarce; nevertheless, from what can be pieced together, low productivity levels are clearly suggested. The economy's recent performance in two commodities, beef and milk, was especially distressing. The United Nations estimates that for the 1952-55 period, the country produced 18,000 metric tons of beef annually; this climbed to 21,000 tons yearly during the 1961-65 period. By 1969-71, annual production rose to 23,000 metric tons. Beef production increased by no more than 1.5 per cent annually during this nineteen-year time span, and the metric ton production of milk declined from thirty-two metric tons annually in the 1952-56 period to twenty-eight tons annually in the 1968-70 period.[24] The number of grazing cattle increased only marginally from 1,129,000 head in 1952 to 1,320,000 annually in 1968 and 1969, and rose to 1,481,000 in 1970.[25] This amounts to an annual increase of about 1.5 per cent. A major factor contributing to the economy's work performance during the 1960s has been a serious drought. "The cattle population was reduced by about 30 per cent by the droughts of the mid 1960's, but by 1971 it had risen again to 1,700,000."[26] Botswana's crops have been affected similarly by the unseasonally low rainfalls. The country's " . . . main food crops are sorghum, maize, millet, beans and cowpeas (and) . . . available estimates show that total production of sorghum, maize and millet increased sharply in 1968/1969 but dropped again in 1969/1970 as a result of scattered droughts."[27] However, "The rainfall was good in 1970/1971 . . . and output was higher."[28]

Prior to 1970, only rather small scale mining of gold, asbestos, kyanite, manganese and other minerals took place. The turnabout in mining production came that year and is now an important aspect of the country's future economic growth and development.[29] Thus by the early 1970s, mining accounted for nearly ten per cent of domestic employment (up from three per cent in the 1960s). In the 1970-71 period, this sector accounted for nearly fifteen per cent of wages earned by residents (an increase from three per cent during the 1960s). We shall leave a fuller discussion of the contribution of mining activities to development until later. In brief, then, Botswana's poor performance affected not only domestic consumption but the ability of the country to generate export products, and therefore, export earnings; in addition, it generated insufficient employment opportunities for Botswana's citizens. As a consequence, approximately twelve per cent of the work force has been employed in neighboring countries in recent years, and a larger percentage can be said to be underemployed.

The country's balance of trade deficits have been extensive and increasing annually; this is significant because Botswana's money economy is tied closely to the external sector. In 1970, export earnings accounted for forty per cent of state income and spending on imports was the largest category of state expenditures. The gap between export earnings and spending on imports has been significant, and has been widening: in 1966, export value lagged behind the value of imports by R8.1m.; by 1971, it had risen to R27m.[30] The country's main exports, meat carcasses and livestock products, are ones whose market prices either decline, or do not rise. Principal markets are the United Kingdom, South Africa and, lately, Hong Kong; the remaining export customer-countries are Zambia and Rhodesia.[31] Since 1970, however, favorable income growth conditions in the export-destination countries, as well as recent expansions in Botswana's productivity, has meant a rapid increase in sales. Such sales had been in a state of stagnation during the 1960s. Table 2 shows external trade data from 1960 to 1971, noting particularly the expansion in exports from 1969 to 1971 and, the tremendous expansion in imports during this more recent period leading to an enormous annual trade deficit.

Table 2

Botswana: Exports and Imports, 1966-71
(In millions of Rand)

	1960	1966	1967	1968	1969	1970	1971
Exports	5.49	10.72	9.22	7.49	13.06	15.82	20.70
Livestock and products	5.00	10.40	8.74	7.19	10.15	13.79	16.00
Minerals	.00	.02	.02	.22	.58	.40	.50
Other	.49	.30	.46	.08	2.33	1.63	4.20
Imports	14.00	18.82	22.37	23.23	30.80	35.30	48.40
Trade deficit	-8.51	-8.10	-13.15	-15.74	-17.74	-19.48	-27.70

Source: Surveys of African Economies 5, 92.

As shown in Table 2, from 1970 to 1971, imports climbed thirty-seven per cent; the jump is explained by the rapid expansion in capital good inflows destined for the mining sector. This rapid rise is likely to continue in light of the continued expansion of the country's mining sector. ". . . future rates of increases" comments a recent International Monetary Fund survey, "will depend mostly on imports necessary for the construction of the copper-nickel complex at Shashe [and] projections indicated that imports would reach a value of about R80 million in 1972."[32] If future data prove this projection to be accurate, it would mean a massive seventy-five per cent increase in imports. Such an amount could hardly be matched by increased export earnings. Consequently, the country would have to borrow extensively from internal and, to an even larger extent, from external sources. This external aspect of the borrowing problem could pose immense difficulties for the Government in the future, as external borrowing eventually entails increased debt servicing payments - possibly at the expense of public revenues available to finance much-needed domestic programs. Reliance on external borrowing will persist until an adequate internal financial and banking structure is developed.

When extensive and increasing balance of trade deficits persist, other elements of the country's balance of payments must compensate for these deficits. In this regard the International Monetary Fund reported the following:

> In 1970 Government received transfer payments from abroad of R11.5 million and official capital imports amounted to R3.5 million. In the same year, the Government increased its foreign accounts by R0.4 million and the banking system's consolidated accounts indicated a net inflow of approximately R3.6 million. The private sector's net transactions incurred on transfer and capital account are thus estimated on a residual basis to have amounted to R14.7 million [$20.6 million]. This latter total is made up of net payments of factor income (migrant workers) and property income from abroad, as well as transfers connected with development of the country's mining sector, which is largely financed by foreign long-term capital.[33]

At this point we can integrate our observations about the country's balance of trade and payments with the Government's budget. The Government has borrowed externally to pay for imports that could not be covered by current earnings. It receives customs union revenues included both as export earnings for the country and as governmental public revenues. In addition, Government expenditures on goods imported from abroad are counted both as country import spending and as public expenditures. The Botswana Government's customs union receipts are a form of indirect revenue collection and, when added to direct taxes on personal income, duties, licenses and non-tax revenue (primarily receipts from services), they provide the Government with the wherewithal to purchase both domestic goods and importables. But during the 1960s in order to maintain budgetary operations at desired levels, the Government had to supplement these limited means by external borrowing. For example, in 1970, the Government received foreign transfer payments on the order of R11.5m. In that year, official capital imports amounted to R3.5m., and these imports were mainly road construction equipment relating to the newly expanded economic activity in the mining sector.

III. Economic Possibilities and Potentials for Expanded Options

Economically and politically, the environment seems ripe for change. In recent years, important discoveries of various minerals and ores have been made in Botswana's north-east region. Thus the Director of Geographical Survey reported the following summary statement in 1969:

Table 3

Botswana: Mineral Production, 1965-1971

	1965	1966	1967	1968	1969	1970	1971
			Value (thousand rands)				
Diamonds	-	-	-	-	211.6	1,980.3	-
Asbestos	185.3	15.1	-	-	-	-	-
Manganese	32.0	10.0	22.8	215.3	365.2	752.4	-
Talc	-	-	0.8	1.4	0.4	0.4	-
Semiprecious stones	-	-	-	-	3.5	4.9	-
			Volume				
Diamonds (carats)	-	-	-	-	31,453	463,595	871,765
Asbestos (short tons)	1,369	114	-	-	-	-	-
Manganese (short tons)	4,374	964	4,688	11,021	24,520	53,254	39,228
Talc (short tons)	-	-	80	127	56	40	44
Semiprecious stones (short tons)	-	-	-	-	7	15	120

Source: Surveys of African Economies 5, 47.

> The presence of deposits of asbestos, coal, copper, diamonds, gold and silver, kyanite, manganese and nickel has been noted. Other minerals recorded include ores of antimony, arsenic, lithium, bismuth and tungsten. Amongst others, chromite, fluorspar, graphite, gypsum, iron ore, lead, pyrites, sodium carbonate and sodium bicarbonate-bearing brines, talc and zinc are known, in addition to limestone, fireclays and industrial ceramic materials, semi-precious stones and potential ornamental building stone.[34]

Such wide-ranging discoveries offer hope of significantly improving what has heretofore seemed a grim picture of this country's growth and developmental potential. Botswana's leaders have been quick to seize the opportunity. By 1973, Bamangwato Concessions Ltd. had invested R110m. (1 Rand = $1.49), with the Botswana Government raising another R60m. In grants, loans and credits to finance the building of a new town and supporting facilities, in a promising copper-nickel ore as well as provide employment for 2,000 people a year beginning in 1973. In addition, a major discovery of diamonds at Orapa has been

Table 4

Size and Grade of Copper and Nickel Deposits

	Million short tons	Per cent Copper	Per cent Nickel
Phikwe			
Proven	20.90	1.16	1.49
Probable	6.77	1.16	1.21
Selibe			
Proven	10.50	1.57	0.66
Probable	3.00	1.32	0.92

Note: Botswana Roan Selection Trust Ltd. has also carried out work in the Matsitama area and the proven and probable tonnages are 4.7 million tons and 1.72 million tons, with average grades of 2.24 per cent and 2.15 per cent of copper respectively. The exploration for other mineral deposits continued throughout some 2,000 square miles of the R.S.T. concession area.

Source: Standard Bank Group, Annual Economic Review: Botswana (October 1969) 7.

developed by De Beers; this mine, which operated at full capacity in 1971, produces over two million carats of diamonds as well as government revenues of R4m. per annum.[36] Although such mineral-based assets must not be allowed to obscure what remains a picture of overall underdevelopment, they nevertheless do provide an important multiplier effect. The gross national product of Botswana is predicted to increase as much as fifteen per cent annually in the 1970s and investment in a variety of light industries and improved infrastructure can be anticipated.[37]

Botswana's potential for economic improvement, then, is based upon the potential for earning and employment generated by the extraction of minerals and ores. Manganese, which has been mined in southeastern Botswana for some time, became increasingly important as an export earner by 1970. Other mining ores certain to become major exports for Botswana are diamonds, copper and nickel (see Tables 3 and 4).

In addition to mining, economic growth and development it would be helpful if the total volume and value of traditional exports could be expanded both through increased production and through favorable market conditions abroad. The former entails growth primarily in the cattle industry. Data from 1970 to the present suggest expanded production of cattle and dressed meat items, with future increases in these exports to customer countries in the subordinate state system a likely possibility. Moreover, crop yields per acre in non-drought areas are increasing as a result of better methods of land use, and total crop yields are rising as more land is cultivated. Both of these factors are in part attributable to mechanization. In this regard, it instructive to note that while there were only fifteen tractors available for use in Botswana's agricultural sector in 1952, there were 98 as of 1961, and 170 as of 1969.[38] Thus economic factors appear to be looking up in Botswana. But after long years of colonial neglect and political dominance, the question of whether economic potentials can be realized is another question. This is especially true if realizing its economic potentials means that Botswana can break, or at least lessen, its political ties.

IV. The Political Potential for Facilitating Economic Expansion

Certainly in the changing political environment of the late 1960s and early 1970s, a dynamic process has been unleashed which to some extent at least enlarges Botswana's options. For one thing, in 1968 Botswana achieved independent statehood under international law. Statehood entitles the country to membership in a variety of international organizations and involves a recognition of its freedom and autonomy in a world of states. Negatively, such statehood implies security from the long-standing anxiety over Botswana's direct incorporation into the South African polity; positively it means access to diplomatic agencies around the globe. Such access to powerful international actors creates a potential for independent maneuver imprudently dismissed by cynical observers. Power is normally relational not undirectional;[39] the weak, particularly when butteressed by external political support, can at times influence the strong in a manner disproportionate to their measurable economic or military strength. As one author astutely observes, commentators should be careful not to "underestimate the reinforcement of statehood which a small country can derive from the international political system ...."[40] By making frequent appearances on the international stage, Botswana's leaders assure an important political resource of sympathy and support for their country. In doing so, they increase their ability to extract concessions, minor as they may sometimes be, from powerful neighbors in the subordinate state system.

Directly related to the above point on initiatives fostered by statehood is another on the adoption of a liberal and pan-African doctrine. In this respect, President Khama's endorsement of such principles as non-interference, self-determination, self-reliance, non-alignment, non-racialism and pan-Africanism are not to be taken lightly.[41] They are of substantive importance in this instance partly as they enable Botswana's leaders to identify with the great majority of the world community. This proposition is advanced effectively by Richard Dale when he observes that,

> ... the norm of non-racialism allows the Republic of Botswana to relate to universal values such as those articulated in the numerous, authoritative pronouncements of the United Nations ... Through these shared values Botswana can participate as vigorously as its resources permit in the activities of the international community. This is all the more important because this new nation, for much of its existence, has led a sheltered life. As one of the three British High Commission Territories in southern Africa, it was off the beaten track of world and colonial politics.[42]

Thus Botswana's ideologically liberal "outward policy" has created additional options for its policymakers. They have been able to forge new symbolic and material links with countries directly to the north, particularly Zambia, as well as with other countries in Africa and the world at large.

The reference to material benefits from a northward-oriented policy leads logically to a discussion of efforts to expand trade opportunities. For its part, Zambia's attempts to diversify its trade have the twin objectives of increasing business activities while at the same time attracting border states such as Botswana into its orbit. President Kenneth Kaunda puts the matter succinctly as follows: "politically and economically, it [the diversification of trade and trade routes] has been and still is a matter of life and death."[43] In seeking an enlargement of politico-economic options through trade contacts, then, Zambia and Botswana both exhibit convergent interests.

Such similarity of purpose has naturally led to a search for means to promote inter-unit commercial ties. These ambitions were given a boost in 1970 by the announcement of an intention to construct an all-weather highway linking Botswana and Zambia.[44] This Botzam highway (sponsored by a $15m. grant from the United States Agency for International Development) will, when completed in 1975, facilitate the interchange of goods between the two landlocked states;[45] Zambia will find new markets for its manufactured goods (in particular, mining equipment) while importing more meat products from Botswana. Although it is too much to contend that such trade will bring about a major attenuation in Botswana's current linkage to the Southern African subordinate state system, it nonetheless is an initiative of far reaching significance. In this vein, when speaking of the Botzam highway, Sir Seretse Khama declared:

> Botswana-Zambia relations, which are at present based mainly on common

> aspirations, will then take on economic muscle. Our efforts to expand trade will be greatly stimulated and we shall be able to consult together and plan for further regional development.[46]

Yet despite such hopes for benefits resulting from increased contacts with states to the north, other Botswana officials are quick to add a note of caution. As one Botswana economist employed by the Government views the matter: "We certainly don't intend committing economic suicide by severing all our ties with the south as soon as the road is completed."[47]

There are signs that emerging economic opportunities will expand the country's chances for broader world contacts. Of major importance in this regard is the discovery of mineral and ore wealth; as a consequence of these finds the composition of exports will from this time forward reflect substantial diversification. This will lessen reliance upon traditional and inadequate export bases - primarily cattle, dressed meat and meat products. And the interaction of political and economic change could have profound effects on the well-being of Botswana's people. But one potential constraint - one largely unforeseen thus far, appears to be surfacing. It is this: can Botswana gain adequate access to the financial wealth generated by mining? Basically it is a matter of whether the Government can gain benefits that substantially outweigh the costs of having foreign companies become instrumental in Botswana's emerging mining sector. Therefore, it is to this matter that we now turn.

V. Realizing the Potential for Expanding Policing Options

One of the Government's economic costs is its responsibility to develop the infrastructure required to support mining. The Government, for example, is obliged to undertake road construction related to mining activities. The Government is to repay the De Beers Prospecting, Botswana, Ltd. loan for these construction activities out of the dividends derived from its ownership in mining ventures. In regard to the Government's revenue collections, the International Monetary Fund estimates that, ". . . in each of the years 1972-73 and 1973-74 the mine will contribute R1.7 million and in 1974-75, R2.9 million; subsequently, it will contribute about R6 million a year."[48]

The mining of nickel and copper requires complicated procedures on the transfer of capital and the financing of development. For example,

> The development of the mining portion of this project, known as the Shashe Complex, is being carried out by Bamangwato Concessions, Ltd. (in which American Metal Climax, Inc. and Anglo American Corporation hold 29.4 per cent each of the shares). The Botswana Government is developing the necessary infrastructure at an estimated cost of $54.4 million, and private capital will provide R106.4 million to develop the mining facilities. Of

> the latter sum, R38.6 million is to be equity financed, the Kreditanstalt fur Wideraufau of Germany will provide R43 million, in the form of suppliers' credits, and the rest will come from subordinated loans from shareholders. Botswana Roan Selection Trust owns 85 per cent of Bamangwato Concessions and the Botswana Government owns the remainder.[49]

But will the Government's collections cover those costs and finance development programmes and projects as well as enable it to expand administrative services? In this regard, a number of elements would appear to make the benefits to Botswana appear auspicious: new resources have been discovered while at the same time traditional export production is increasing; private and public capital is flowing into the country to develop the newly discovered natural wealth; and additional public capital is coming in to finance the growth of an infrastructure. The upshot of all this enterprise will likely be more export earnings, resulting in some rise in employment and incomes for residents and some added revenue for Government. But three critical threats to this seemingly bright picture deserve mention: first, private capital is entering Botswana in search of profit maximization, and the power of these companies to achieve their interests is manifold; second, the Government appears impatient to attract foreign capital and, in doing so, might permit extraordinary profit taking at the expense of tax and royalty revenue otherwise availing; and third, the Government's actual expenditures on infrastructure development exceed expected costs due to import inflation. And we are particularly concerned that these factors will combine to put Botswana in a serious external debt situation - a position so well known to many developing countries that rely on private investment from abroad to finance local mining ventures.

VI. Generating Future Constraints

On the surface, debt-servicing does not appear to be an imposing problem for Botswana, at least for the time being. In recent years, debt-servicing has remained at about six per cent of total Government expenditures (and total revenue collections). This is not an especially high proportion in comparison to other countries.[50] Nevertheless, the funds spent on the servicing of debts cannot be used for financing growth and development projects, and this is particularly distressing to a poor state such as Botswana. "As a proportion of domestic revenue," notes one study, "outlays on this item have increased from 8 per cent in 1964/1965 to almost 13 per cent for 1969/1970."[51] (Note that total Government expenditures are equal to total revenue collections which, in turn, are the additive of domestic revenue plus net foreign transfers. Usually these transfers are public and derive from loans and grants made by individual donor countries or public agencies such as the International Monetary Fund and the World Bank Group.)

Clearly the Government must also be careful to ensure that its share of the earnings of foreign companies will be sufficient to cover budgetary expenditures. For example, will the current arrangement with De Beers secure sufficient public revenue to provide for directly-related expenditures? From its limited profit share, the Government must not only pay off the loan made to it by the company for infrastructure development, but it must, in addition, have adequate revenue left to provide needed social services and to undertake other infrastructure development projects. Thus fiscal adequacy depends upon whether there is a large enough revenue collection base (i.e., company profits) and whether domestic revenue collections are fiscally adequate. Inadequacy means that the Government must find an option - usually public transfers from abroad. In this regard, we feel it instructive to examine the experience of another African ore-dependent country, Liberia, which, in the late 1950s and early 1960s, faced a situation similary to that now confronting Botswana. Quite possibly, Botswana's decision-makers could profit by examining the Liberian precedent in this respect.

Because of downward pressure on mining profits and hence on the tax base in Liberia and inadequate rate schedules, concession contributions from 1958-1970 decreased as a proportion of the collected public revenue, falling roughly from one-half to one-third. The Liberian Government's inability to collect sufficient public revenue caused supplementary external borrowing, and loans and grants therefore became important sources of national finance. The Government, concerned over the rising costs of servicing these debts, required that nineteen per cent of the total revenue and twenty-nine per cent of the public revenue be used to cover these servicing costs; these figures rose to twenty-four per cent and thirty-three per cent respectively during the 1968-1970 period, when debt-servicing payments exceeded foreign transfers to Liberia by more than $1m. Just one of the effects of this situation has been a sharp relative decline in expenditures on essential public services.[52]

In order to head off a similar situation in Botswana, we feel that the Government might well consider using a tax base other than company profits to a greater degree. We suggest consideration of increased use of unit export tax based on units of output export (royalties). Such a tax "relates directly to . . . expanding capacity to produce and export."[53] It avoids machinations of the international pricing mechanism - particularly the matter of transfer pricing.

An ancillary problem limiting Botswana's economic benefits has to do with employment. Because of the capital-intensive nature of Botswana's mineral and ore mining industries, limited employment opportunities are accruing to the people. The industry's technology is transferred to the country through direct foreign investment from companies with strong preferences for labor-saving devices. The Botswana Government, anxious to develop an industrial base as well as to attract investors from abroad, accepted the priorities set out by the British-based Economic Survey Mission in 1964. To be sure, industrial technology's potential contribution to the process of economic growth and development in Botswana, as well as in other developing countries, is manifest. Even so, the obtaining of technology through transfers from multinational firms based in rich industrialized countries comes at a price. Three critical aspects come to mind. The _first_ is whether the industrial technology transferred is useful in increasing employment and per capita real incomes as well as in decreasing unemployment rates in developing countries. Hans Singer, among others, has noted that African and other developing countries tend not to receive industrial technology that is appropriate to attaining these objectives. He concludes that the industrial technology these countries receive from abroad ". . . is not sufficiently different from that of rich countries, not sufficiently (labour) employment intensive to prevent spreading unemployment, poverty and inequality."[54] The _second_ is whether, upon attaining economic growth objectives, the benefits are widely shared by the people of the country. Singer notes that an insufficient difference in industrial technology tends to increase the incomes of a small elite associated with the "modern industrial" sectors, thereby promoting further income inequalities in the process.[55] The _third_ is the extent to which the industrialization accompanying the new technology is free from unwanted external (or side) effects. Obviously in Africa as elsewhere, growth tends to be accompanied by such unwelcome side-effects as environmental degradation and rural-urban and agricultural-industrial disruptions and imbalances. A prudent government must take steps in advance of a full transfer of modern technology to reduce harmful externalities to a minimum.[56]

VII. Conclusion: Coping with Future Constraints

The Government of Botswana is not without its own options. First, in the ancillary matter of employment, it might encourage greater employment of local labor in the construction of housing and other infrastructure elements as well as in mining directly. With regard to the latter, a bargaining dimension is present in its relations with the multinationals which could be exploited to its advantage: it could negotiate with the companies for a commitment to modify technology to suit local resource endowments, _i.e._, shifting toward more labor-intensive production techniques so far as practicable under current circumstances. For another thing, the Government might rapidly step up training and education in the labor skills that are required by the advanced technology being transferred to the country.

In the matter of avoiding debt-servicing problems - our primary focus here - it is useful to observe the case of Liberia where nearly one-third of the value of national income has been transferred abroad in recent years. This rose from sixteen per cent in the late 1950s to thirty-two per cent by the late 1960s. The recent transfers not only involved debt-servicing expenditures to foreign lenders but also included expatriated profits by foreign companies and expatriated wages (and monies spent vacationing in South Africa) by their foreign workers.[57] It might be helpful for Botswana to consider imposing reasonable restraints upon the transfer of profits (and wages) abroad - particulary should the transfers lead to critical foreign exchange losses for the country. Alternatively, this objective might be achieved through a more vigorous policy designed to gain additional public revenues from the profits of foreign-based companies; i.e., increasing the tax rate schedule and/or expanding the tax base through bargaining to reduce tax avoidance and tax evasion. This policy would focus on reducing the profit base prior to repatriation.

We feel that Botswana's current economic planning exercises do not focus adequately on the points raised above. The current development plan, published in September 1970, centers on advancing the mining sector, diversifying the economy, and allowing ample opportunity for private investment (domestic and foreign). Our concern is that attention also be paid to other short and long term goals: i.e., coping with external debts, dealing with external demands for the expatriation of wealth, and modifying transferred technology to suit local resource endowments.

Two planning institutions which also tend to ignore these goals are the National Development Bank and the Botswana Development Corporation. The bank, established in 1964, operates to further economic development by making long and medium term loans and by making share capital available to local ventures. The National Development Bank's policy "aims at intensifying efforts to promote assistance to small farmers and to lend funds to promote the development of livestock and to foster the Karakul sheep industry."[58] The Botswana Development Corporation, established in 1970, identifies ". . . business opportunities in industry, commerce and agriculture, undertake[s] the related feasibility studies, and interest[s] potential investors in specific projects."[59] It also participates ". . . in the equity of new ventures, the management of the Government's investment in industry and commerce, the promotion of indigenous industrial and commercial entrepreneurs, and lending to private enterprises."[60] The two institutions are intent upon encouraging domestic industrial investment. although the mining sector, where the country's natural wealth is concentrated, is largely by default left to foreign capital and technology. In effect, the Government has relied on fiscal policy applied to, rather than advancing domestic financial participation in, the mining sector.

In addition it must be noted that the Government's modest shareholder participation is augmented by revenue raised through direct taxation of mining company profits. But some dissatisfaction with current tax laws has become manifest.

> A growing need has been felt to revise the existing income tax laws to make them applicable to the mining enterprises and provide incentives for speedier economic development. Preliminary work on the restructuring of direct taxation has been completed by a team of experts from the Commonwealth Secretariat, and the International Monetary Fund has sent a legal expert to Botswana for six months under its technical assistance program to assist in revising the law.[61]

This could be disturbing if the Government's impatience for speedier "development" leads to a lenient tax policy geared to provide an incentive to potential foreign investors. Surely fiscal adequacy cannot be sacrificed to attract foreign investment, particularly if there are not broad benefits to the country's people in terms of employment and income and if revenues are needed to cover expenditures on desperately needed public goods and services.

In conclusion, the Botswana Government function within an environment where political, geographic and economic factors have limited policy options. But recent economic resource discoveries and political initiatives could facilitate the expansion of policy options to Botswana's decision-makers.[62] The most notable aspect is the discovery of a range of highly marketable minerals and ores. Considering these possibilities by themselves, the prospects might appear bright. But such a view is incomplete and inadequate because future constraints on policy options are being generated. These constraints have to do with such matters as potential debt-servicing costs and the inappropriate capital-intensive technology in mining that limits employment and income earned by local workers in the mining sector. These factors do not seem to receive sufficient attention in current analyses of Botswana's economic reorganization and modernization. Therefore we urge that if Botswana's full potential for economic growth and development is to be optimized, its policy-makers must learn from experiences of others - particularly in Africa. We suggest Liberia as an example to be avoided - for Liberian policy-makers are only now undoing past bargaining failures. We hope that without being presumptuous, we can suggest that Botswana's policy-makers curb impatience to attract foreign capital because this tends to shift more benefits and fewer costs to the companies; and it leaves fewer benefits and/or more costs to Botswana. A more favorable bargaining posture by the Government of Botswana will mean that it will have a better chance of avoiding debt problems as well as bringing more employment and income earning opportunities to its people.

NOTES

* The authors wish to express their appreciation to Professors Richard Dale, Robert Lieber, Sheridan Johns and Timothy Shaw for valuable suggestions on organization and presentation.

1. Republic of Botswana, Botswana's Foreign Policy (Gaborone: Government Printer, 1970), 2.

2. See David E. Apter Choice and the Politics of Allocation: A Developmental Theory (New Haven: Yale University Press, 1971) 18.

3. Botswana's Foreign Policy, 4.

4. Republic of Botswana, Statistical Abstracts 1970 (Gaborone: Central Statistics Office, 1972) Table 7.

5. See Larry W. Bowman "The Subordinate State System of Southern Africa", International Studies Quarterly 12(3), September 1968, 231-261, reprinted in this volume; Richard Dale "Southern Africa: Research Frontiers in Political Science" in Christian P. Potholm and Richard Dale (eds.) Southern Africa in Perspective (New York: Free Press, 1972) 11-15; Kark Kaiser "The Interaction of Regional Subsystems", World Politics 21(1), October 1968, 84-107, and I. William Zartman "Africa as a Subordinate State System in International Relations", International Organization 21(23), Summer 1967, 545-564.

6. "This [caution on guerrilla activities] is not just a question of being nice," a Botswana Government official declared. "Botswana just cannot afford to allow itself to be used for armed forays against the South." John Borrell "Freedom Highway", Daily Nation (Nairobi) June 11, 1973, 6. Also, see Southern Africa 6(4), April 1973, 11, and James Barber South Africa's Foreign Policy (London: Oxford: Oxford University Press, 1973) 246.

7. See Colin Legum "The problems of the land-locked countries of Southern Africa in the confrontation between independent Africa and South Africa, Rhodesia and Portugal" and H.C.L. Hermans "Botswana's options for independent existence" in Zdenek Cervenka (ed.) Land-locked Countries of Africa (Uppsala: Scandinavian Institute of African Studies, 1973), 165-187 and 197-211.

8. Richard Dale "Botswana" in Christian P. Potholm and Richard Dale (eds.) Southern Africa in Perspective, 115. "Despite the differences in political and social systems, and the disparity of wealth and resources between the two countries, and given the close economic links," observes the National Development Plan 1970-75, "Botswana and the South Africa have achieved, and wish to maintain, a stable relationship based on interdependence, coexistence and mutual non-interference." Republic of Botswana National Development Plan 1970-75 (Gaborone: Government Printer, 1970) 18.

9. Douglas Anglin "The politics of transit routes in land-locked Southern Africa" in Cervenka (ed.) Land-locked Countries of Africa, 121.

10. Ibid., 10.

11. Ibid., 7, 10.

12. National Development Plan 1970-75, 121.

13. Statistical Abstracts 1970, Table 58.

14. Ibid.

15. For a discussion of this phenomen in relation to the foreign affairs field, see Maurice A. East "Size and Foreign Policy Behavior: A Test of Two Models", World Politics 25(4), July 1973, 558-559, 567-568.

16. Leonard M. Thompson "South Africa's Relations with Lesotho, Botswana and Swaziland", African Forum 2(2), Fall 1966, 73 and Kenneth W. Grundy Confrontation and Accommodation in Southern Africa (Berkeley: University of California Press, 1973) 62-63.

17. Martin Legassick "The Southern African Bloc: Integration for Defense or Expansion?", Africa Today 15(5), October-November 1968, 14-15. Also see Customs Union Agreement Between the Governments of Botswana, Lesotho and South Africa, December 11, 1969, Art. 14(2).

18. For example, see Donald Rothchild "A Hope Deferred: East African Federation, 1963-64" in Gwendolen M. Carter (ed.) Politics in Africa: 7 Cases (New York: Harcourt, Brace and World, 1966) 219-223, and his Politics of Integration: An East African Documentary (Nairobi: East African Publishing House, 1968) Part IV; and Arthur Hazlewood "Problems of Integration Among African States" in Arthur Hazlewood (ed.) African Integration and Disintegration (London: Oxford University Press, 1967), Chapter 1.

19. Peter Robson Economic Integration in Africa (London: George Allen and Unwin, 1968) 262.

20. Martin Legassick "The Southern African Bloc: Integration for Defense or Expansion?" 10. For an example of political manipulation in colonial times (involving a threat to restrict cattle imports unless Britain agreed to transfer Bechuanaland to the Union), see Ronald Hyam The Failure of South African Expansion 1908-1948 (London: Macmillan, 1972) 106.

21. United Nations Survey of International Development 8(9), November 1971. The classification is based on the United Nations General Assembly Resolution No. 2768 (XXVI). Other African countries similarly classified are Burundi, Chad, Dahomey, Ethiopia, Guinea, Lesotho, Malawi, Mali, Rwanda, Somalia, Sudan, Tanzania and Upper Volta. The United Nations Committee for Planned Development places these and 10 other developing countries in a "hardcore" least-developed group.

22. Lamberto Dini, Brian Quinn and Lennart Wohlgemuth "The Economy of Botswana", International Monetary Fund Staff Papers 17(1), March 1970, 129.

23. Statistical Abstracts 1970, Table 7.

24. United Nations Statistical Yearbook (New York: 1971) 207.

25. Ibid., 106.

26. International Monetary Fund Surveys of African Economies, 5, (Washington, D.C.: 1973) 33.

27. Ibid., 37.

28. Ibid.

29. Ibid., 40

30. Ibid., 92.

31. Standard Bank Economic Review of Botswana, Lesotho and Swaziland (London: November 1971) 4.

32. Surveys of African Economies, 5, 94.

33. Ibid., 94-95.

34. P. Smit Botswana: Resources and Development (Pretoria: African Institute, 1970) 13-14. Also see Dini, et al. "The Economy of Botswana", 153-173.

35. On the heavy input of Government investment in these mining-related initiatives, see Dudley Jackson "Income Differentials and Unbalanced Planning - The Case of Botswana", Journal of Modern African Studies 8(4), December 1970, 556.

36. Christopher Joubert "Still awaiting the real impact from copper", African Development, February 1973, BLS 5.

37. Martin Curwen "BDC encourages private investors", African Development, February 1973, BLS 9.

38. United Nations Statistical Yearbook (New York: 1971) 118.

39. For a discussion of the relational nature of power (with special reference to interethnic encounters), see Donald Rothchild "Changing Racial Stratifications and Bargaining Styles: The Kenya Experience", Canadian Journal of African Studies 7(3), 1973, 419-431.

40. Willie Henderson, review of three works on Botswana, in Journal of Modern African Studies 11(1), March 1973, 174.

41. Botswana's Foreign Policy, passim. Also see Willie Henderson "Independent Botswana: A Reappraisal of Foreign Policy Options", African Affairs 73 (290), January 1974, 40-41.

42. The Racial Component of Botswana's Foreign Policy (Denver: University of Denver Center on International Race Relations, 1971) Studies in Race and Relations 2(4), 7. Also see Sheridan Johns "Botswana's Strategy for Development: An Assessment of Dependence in the Southern African Context", Journal of Commonwealth Political Studies 11(3), 1973, 214-216.

43. Dr. Kenneth Kaunda A Path for the Future, an address presented at the opening of the Sixth General Conference of the United National Independence Party, Mulungushi, May 8, 1971, 18. (Mimeo.; italics added.)

44. For a discussion of the intricate boundary issues surrounding this announcement, see James Craig "Zambia-Botswana Road Link: Some Border Problems" in Zambia and the World: Essays on Problems Relating to Zambia's Foreign Policy (Lusaka: University of Zambia, 1970) 25-32.

45. Paradoxically, it may also act as a conduit for the flow of South African manufactured goods northward.

46. John Borrell "Freedom Highway", Daily Nation(Nairobi), 11. On the limitations of this alternative, an economist writes that "for the foreseeable future, exports of industrial goods will have to play a small role in Zambian industrial development, if only because Zambia is a high-cost

producer by comparison with its main rivals in its potential export markets." James Fry "Is the Industrial Boom Running Out of Steam?", African Development, October 1973, 239.

47. James Fry "Is the Industrial Boom Running Out of Steam?", 239.

48. Surveys of African Economies 5, 41.

49. Ibid., 42. Also see National Development Plan, 1970-75 for an outline of infrastructure development and the expected financial and developmental benefits that are predicted to accrue to the Government and the people of Botswana.

50. For example, Liberia's proportions of debt-servicing to total expenditure is much greater than Botswana's. This factor is an extremely serious impediment to the Liberian Government's capacity to expand its financing of growth and development projects.

Liberia was in the same position as Botswana just prior to that West African country's rapid development of iron ore exports from 1958 to the present. Liberia's debt-servicing problems came about because of the Government's international borrowing to finance its infrastructure development during the period witnessing the iron ore industry's meteoric rise. The Liberian Government simply could not collect public revenues from iron ore concessions, and elsewhere, to finance its efforts. This required supplementary external borrowing, and eventual debt-servicing problems. See Robert L. Curry, Jr. "Liberia's External Debts and Their Servicing", Journal of Modern African Studies 10(3), December 1972, 621-626.

51. Dini, et al. "The Economy of Botswana", 153.

52. These findings are drawn from Robert L. Curry, Jr. "Liberia's External Debts and Their Servicing", 621-626.

53. Ibid., 626. For a more complete examination of the unit report tax base, see Carl Shoup, et al. The Tax System of Liberia (New York: Columbia University Press, 1971) 70-74.

54. Hans Singer "The Development Outlook for Poor Countries: Technology is the Key", Challenge 16, May-June 1973, 44.

55. Ibid., 45. Professor Singer's remarks are based on the findings of a study that he and Professor Richard Jolly conducted. See International Labor Organization, Employment, Incomes and Equality: A Strategy for Increase Productive Employment in Kenya (New York: United Nations, 1972). Also see two articles by J.R. Harris and M.P. Todaro: "Urban Unemployment in East Africa," Eastern African Economic Review 4, December 1968; and "Wages, Industrial Employment and Labor Productivity: The Kenya Experience," Eastern African Economic Review 5, June 1969.

56. William Eastlake "Environmental Economics", Journal of the University of Liberia 1, December 1972.

57. Curry "Liberia's External Debts", 621-26.

58. Surveys of African Economies 5, 87. Also see National Bank, Annual Report (Gaborone: various years).

59. Surveys of African Economies 5, 89. Also see Botswana Development Corporation, Annual Report (Gaborone: various years).

60. *Surveys of African Economies* 5, 90.

61. *Ibid.*, 68. The tax system allows companies to deduct for tax purposes 125 per cent of the cost of such training. Other tax reliefs are possible for companies that build physical structures that become a "permanent" part of the country's infrastructure. The Government has also made separate tax agreements with a half dozen companies in lieu of enforcing the generally applicable tax laws. It continues to explore the possibility of new initiatives, including the imposition of a royalty on production to supplement the tax levy and the establishment of a joint-venture partnership (through the acquisition of a 51 per cent holding in the mining enterprises). Much of this emerging policy is similar to Zambia's measures of 1970 which gave that government 51 per cent ownership of the Zambian mining firms.

62. The fast moving political events now occurring Southern Africa continue to hold the promise of broader options for Botswana. A conference recently held in Lusaka, which included the Heads of State of Tanzania, Zambia, Botswana and the leaders of FRELIMO of Mozambique, dealt with common aims, objectives and strategies to cope with Rhodesia and Southern Africa; and with the development of a more united policy toward Namibia and Angola. These rapidly unfolding events, including moves towards change in Rhodesia, could have a profound impact on Botswana as a country identified with its northern Black African neighbors. This promises new political and economic ties, offering the potential for significant contact between Botswana and the "outwide" world, that is, the world outside the Southern African subordinate state system.

Chapter Twelve

BOTSWANA AND THE BANTUSTANS

Christopher R. Hill

In the past Botswana, Lesotho and Swaziland have frequently been discussed together as "the three ex-High Commission Territories" or, more recently, Boleswa. It is, of course, true that the Boleswa states still have much in common, but their most striking shared characteristic, dependence on Britain, is now a thing of the past. Since independence and particularly in the past few years, a growing body of scholarly writing has been concerned with the three individual states, though this is not to say that the common factors which result from their history and geography have been lost to sight. It is worth adding that in the Boleswa states themselves little emphasis is placed on their common characteristics. Indeed in Botswana's very comprehensive National Development Plan 1970-75 reference is made to the other two in only two contexts - the University of Botswana Lesotho and Swaziland (UBLS) and the Customs Union.[1]

In this chapter I am dealing only with Botswana, I consider first its internal problems, most of which are very familiar to anyone interested in developing Africa, and the methods employed by the Botswana Government to tackle them, some of which have a stronger flavour of pragmatic commonsense than is discernible elsewhere. I shall then discuss Botswana's foreign relations, both in southern Africa and in the international system, and shall offer some observations on whether, and to what extent, Botswana's situation may be considered 'neo-colonial'.[2] Finally, I shall suggest some comparisons between Botswana and the South African Bantustans, using the Transkei as prime example, because it is the longest established of these potential states.

Some of the internal problems which most pre-occupy the Botswana Government are: population control, education, the lack of skilled manpower, the lack of jobs for the growing population, the need to increase the national herd and the annual offtake from it, and the need to extend arable farming. Related to these such issues as the continuing movement towards democratic local government and reduction of the chiefs' powers and privileges, without however totally undermining their authority or destroying their traditional standing.[3] This in turn is linked with the reform of land tenure and Government's intention to bring about greater equality among cattle owners. Another objective which is constantly reiterated is to prevent the development of structural imbalances of incomes and opportunities between the towns and the rural areas, to the detriment of the latter.[4]

To deal with these problems the Government has formulated a development strategy which is remarkably pragmatic and which, I think it is fair to say, rests upon a liberal orientation or ideology.[5] Certainly it is a view of the world which accepts capitalism, both national and international, as necessary and beneficial. Nor do my own observations of Botswana's governing elite lead me to suppose that such acceptance is expressed merely because there is thought to be no alternative. There is not, in other words, any suggestion in governing circles that capitalism is a second best to be adopted unwillingly, though it must be added that so far not much thought seems to have been given to the problems which will almost certainly appear with the emergence of an indigenous entrepreneurial elite.

With liberal values and capitalist intentions there does, however, go the belief that development cannot be achieved without popular participation.

> The planning system is one of participatory democracy reaching down to the grass roots. The objective is to involve villages actively in the development process. The policy is one of self-help and self-reliance, backed by financial incentives and technical assistance.[6]

The assumption being made here is the (to me) unexceptionable one that participation is good in itself. I think it is also implied that grass roots involvement in the planning process is more efficient than development whose origin and direction lie in the hands of some remote central body.

Similar thinking is elaborated in a section on community development:

> Community development is a method of improving the standard of living in a country through the active participation of the people. Through Community Development the people learn to analyse the needs in their Communities and, to put their plans into action. The Government recognises that the economic and social development of Botswana greatly depends on the extent to which the majority of the population are prepared to change their traditional attitudes and practices for a more modern and scientific mode of life. In a country such as Botswana, where the life of the majority of the people is determined by tradition, all development means change, change not only in their way of life but also in the attitudes and values which underlie this way of life. In order to be successful, plans for development in areas which affect the people - such as new methods of cultivation, the introduction of new types of crops, changes in attitudes to health and nutrition - must be understood by the people and the reasons for these developments appreciated. Community development is concerned with teaching the people in the villages and townships to prepare themselves for change, to welcome it and benefit from it.[7]

Words like 'scientific', 'modern' and 'development' itself are left undefined. I take this to be because, in Botswana's situation, national leaders hold their meanings to be more or less self-evident. 'Scientific' and 'modern' refer to Western scientific rationality and the modernity of advanced capitalist economies. 'Development' refers to the process whose end-product is a higher standard of living, provided that the process includes popular participation and does something to remedy present inequalities and to prevent new ones becoming entrenched.

That inequalities are great is illustrated by the March 1972 estimate that, of a total population of 626,000 "100,000 people are resident on holdings which possess no cattle whatsoever, whilst on the other hand 4% of the holdings claim some 30% of the cattle."[8] In September 1970 average per capita rural income was about R 35 p.a., though the modal rural income was well below this, owing to the concentration of cattle wealth in few hands. Unskilled labour in the modern sector earned between R6 and R20 per month, whilst wages in the rural areas were about R5.[9] Government is concerned to prevent the emergence, as a result of mining development, of a new rich class of unskilled employees in the modern sector.

> If Botswana is to avoid the social unrest caused by gross inequalities of wealth between the rural and the urban sectors experienced in other African countries, wages levels on the mines and in Government (the other major employer) must be restrained, and the surplus resources thus liberated used to promote rural development.[10]

Against this background Government's strategy for dealing with the country's development may be summed up quite briefly.

The population is growing so rapidly that "the net increase in the adult [ages 15-65] labour force is expected to be 10,000 per annum, whilst the average annual net increase in employment opportunities will only be 2,000."[11] The Brigades, which provide post-school training for young people who would otherwise be unemployed, will mop up some of the surplus and provide artisans for the rural areas. Otherwise the solution lies in increased cottage industry (but only if the products can be marketed competitively with those from South Africa), increased opportunities for rural employment (with associated land tenure reforms), the growth of 'link industries' stemming from development of the mining complexes and, as a last resort, mining and other employment in South Africa. However, it is noted in the plan that mining employment in South Africa will not continue indefinitely, though no elucidation of this remark is given.[12]

Other possible sources of employment are self-help and 'food for work' schemes. These tend to be disliked, but they do at least keep people alive. Ultimately, though, the solution to the population problem is family planning and it is noteworthy that, unlike so many Governments, Botswana has recognised the fact and is taking action.

In the field of education agonising decisions have had to be taken. The choice was between providing a little education for all or most children, or a longer period at school for only half the age-group. The value attached to education, as a means of escape from rural poverty, is very high and the political pressure for its expansion is intense, as is demonstrated by the very high proportion of District Council budgets devoted to it. Nevertheless, the Government has taken the second course and is concentrating on establishing more schools going up to sixth form equivalent, though of course only a fraction of the primary school population will reach secondary school and the rest will have to be prepared at primary school for the agricultural way of life that lies ahead.

In view of the extreme shortage of manpower such a decision, though painful, must have seemed the only one possible; in consequence it is hoped that Botswana will be able to meet its manpower needs by the 1990s. This seems somewhat optimistic, given the overwhelming preference of students for Arts degrees, though this trend may to some extent be reversed by tied bursaries.[13] Nor has much thought yet been given to the situation which will arise when the schools and U.B.L.S. have filled all vacancies for high-level manpower. It seems unlikely that job opportunities will have expanded to the point where they can annually absorb the new crop of university graduates and school-leavers, which suggests that in a quarter of a century or less the problem of unemployed graduates may have reached Botswana.

Enough has been said to illustrate the temper of the Botswana Government. But domestic and foreign affairs cannot be separated and it is in the latter that Botswana's dependence is most amply illustrated as well as her President's skills in projecting an attractive image of Botswana internationally. As Willie Henderson says:

> The international community has developed a set of institutions and procedures which can be manipulated by these small states to achieve some of their own ends. Botswana is undoubtedly beginning to make full use of such potential support from the wider political system.[14]

Botswana must depend on the outside world in a number of obvious ways. Although she no longer requires a British grant-in-aid to balance the budget, she cannot do without project aid for development and this is obtained from several countries (e.g. Sweden) as well as Britain. She must also seek private investment in manufacturing industry to generate employment, but here she is in competition with South Africa. In this situation image-making and image-maintenance are vital, for without Botswana's reputation as a peaceful, non-racial democratic and above all, stable state the flow of aid might dry up with disastrous consequences. As the Vice-President said, when referring to Canadian and American loan contributions to the Shashe project infrastructure: "This is a most welcome indication of the confidence which major nations have in the stability of this Government and its ability to execute and administer a very large development programme."[15]

The two most important facts of Botswana's international life are the discoveries of diamonds and copper and the country's geographical location alongside South Africa and Rhodesia. Her agreements with the mining companies, though not disadvantageous in themselves, tie her firmly into the international capitalist system and her multifarious links with her powerful neighbours require no repetition here. It may be thought that, if any situation deserves the neo-colonial label, Botswana's does.

Michael Barratt Brown gives a most lucid analysis of the dangers attendant upon close relations with international corporations:

> The problem for the underdeveloped nations is that underdevelopment is not non-development, but a distortion of development. Their economies are unbalanced both in the concentration upon production of one or two primary products for an export market and in the outward orientation of capital and enterprise.[16]

The result is a double distortion; at the national level a dualism occurs between "..a foreign industrial capitalist sector with its base in the advanced capitalist countries and an indigenous backward, even feudal, agricultural sector."[17] At the international level there occurs an "...artificial world division of labour between manufacturing and primary production" whose result is "...not only to hold back the economic development of the countries thus rendered underdeveloped but to hold back their political development through the support given to feudal and comprador client ruling classes."[18]

Botswana's governing elite, who are well aware of the dangers of distorted development, might well reply that they had had no choice but to encourage and co-operate with mining development. Strictly speaking this would not be true, for in principle at least it <u>was</u> open to them to refuse to develop the mineral deposits at all. From the point of view of practical common sense, however, there was no choice if any approach to economic independence was to be made, though it is a legitimate point that practicality and common sense are, in this context, notions relating to the capitalist market place; to employ such notions provides a further indication of adherence to the dominant ideology of Western Europe.

President Khama and his colleagues might accept the neo-colonial label, if by neo-colonialism is meant the domination of an economy by foreign-based capitalist enterprise, but they would see that state of affairs as inevitable, something to be regretted perhaps, but not altered. It goes almost without saying that they would therefore reject the derogatory overtones usually associated with the expression 'neo-colonialism' and point instead to the great efforts they are making to ameliorate their quasi-colonial relationship with South Africa - for example by establishing a separate currency.

It might of course be argued that to exchange the embrace of South Africa for a relationship with mining companies is like a deal in whips and scorpions, but that is not how Botswana sees it. On the contrary, I suspect that Botswana's leaders would adopt a view of neo-colonialism somewhat different from the one given above, and would see it as a situation in which the wishes and interests of a people are actively frustrated by the interests and wishes of a former Colonial power. Such a situation does not exist in Botswana, where the different sets of interests are perceived by Government as complementary.

Nobody would suggest that dependence on South Africa can be destroyed: it can only be lessened. In some areas of public life collaboration with the Republic is positively desirable: it would for example be madness not to work together on the control of foot and mouth disease or tsetse fly. Similarly, if there are to be regular flights between Gaborone and Salisbury and Johannesgurg, flight information and weather forecasts must be pooled. If package tours are to fly direct from Johannesburg to Maun, officials concerned with tourism must be in close touch.

The list could be extended. The point is that transnational (as opposed to international) relations operate smoothly in the worlds of commerce, finance, transport, and so on and the absence of full diplomatic relations does not inhibit effective and regular contact at official level. Even the improved road and ferry links with Zambia will do little to alter, except psychologically, the symbiotic relationship between Botswana and South Africa. Indeed the South African Minister of Foreign Affairs, Dr. Hilgard Muller announced the Republic's intention of using the new road: "In fact, if such a road were built by Botswana, we would be able to make use of it, just as Botswana and other neighbouring states are also making use of our roads."[19]

The mines will not only produce wealth, (though relatively few jobs) but the companies' presence provides the Botswana Government with a powerful alliance, since they would react most strongly to any attempt or threat by South Africa or

Rhodesia to cut Botswana's main artery by impeding free traffic on the railway. It may also be assumed that any incursion into Botswana by foreign troops or para-military police would excite the companies' displeasure because it would work against stability. (Of course a complete territorial incorporation, provided it were peaceful, would be another matter, but that is no longer on the cards - except in nightmares).

Botswana's main weapons, though, are diplomatic, and President Khama has displayed great skill in delineating over the years a position which is balanced but without ambiguity. He has succeeded both in persuading other African states that it is impossible to defy the constraints imposed upon Botswana's freedom of action, and in establishing progressively closer relations with those states. The links are not only between the President and other Heads of State, but between the Botswana Democratic Party and other ruling parties. At official level civil service training in other African states has done something to break the feeling of psychological isolation.

In an important speech in March 1971 the President spoke of "..the unique character of the moral issue with which Southern Africa confronts the world." He said "...we must question the effectiveness of the great expenditure of words devoted in the United Nations and elsewhere to the problems of Southern Africa." He stated his own belief that it was still possible to work for peaceful change and that he agreed with President Nixon that wholesale violence would 'hurt the very people it would purport to serve'. But he also said: "...we can no more condemn those who resort to violence to gain freedom in such situations than we could condemn the violence of European resistance movements against German occupation or the violence of the Hungarians against the Rumanians in 1956." Nor did he condemn violence in the special circumstances of the Portuguese African territories, because there it had achieved change.

He regarded South Africa's outward-looking policy as "...for export only - it has nothing to do with internal liberalisation" and went on to reflect on the "interesting condition" of white policies in South Africa, created partly by the urbanisation of Afrikanerdom. He touched, too, on a subject much discussed in academic circles[20] when he said:

> White opinion is becoming increasingly aware of the contradictions within South African society - the most notable of which is the contradiction between economic growth and separate development. It still remains to be seen whether there is a contradiction between economic growth and straightforward white supremacy.[21]

None of these are a stooge's world, nor is Botswana a stooge state. But it is a satellite state. What I have tried to do is give an indication of what diplomatic, political and economic options remain open and which ones are closed off by contiguity with South Africa and Rhodesia.

It may be useful to introduce the comparison with the Bantustans with another passage from the speech quoted above.

> Black politics [in South Africa] are changing too, although the limitations on self-expression make these changes hard to interpret. There are leaders emerging, some of whom are genuine and who, while working for their people within the framework of separate development, have lost no opportunity of pointing out the vast credibility gap between theory and practice. I reject sovereign political units based on ethnic criteria, but the potential significance of the Bantustan experiment should not be overlooked. Its consequences are feared by the white public, but increasingly politicians from the largely English-speaking United Party and the more liberal 'Progressives' are accepting that the consolidation of the Bantustans and the development of quasi-democratic institutions in them is a policy which would be difficult to reverse completely. Much remains to be done, however, before these fragmented and over-populated areas could begin to look like even remotely credible mini-states. Botswana, Lesotho and Swaziland are a constant challenge to their credibility. Bantustan development cannot be condoned but its implications deserve careful analysis.[22]

This important quotation could be analysed at length but I think the essence of what the President is saying in this passage is that the Bantustans are here to stay. My own view is that the South African Government will eventually be prepared to give at least some of the Bantustans independence, though how independence is to be presented in such a way as to be acceptable to Mr. Buthelezi of KwaZulu and Mr. Mangope of Bophuthatswana or indeed Chief Kaiser Matanzima of the Transkei must be a matter for nice judgement in Pretoria. Furthermore, as Mrs. Lipton has pointed out in a most useful article,[23] the United Nations may take some persuading when the first Bantustan applies for its seat. However, despite all these difficulties Mr. Vorster said in the House of Assembly on April 19th, 1972:

> If there is a Bantu people that believes the time has arrived for it to become independent, it can come and discuss the matter with me... When I speak of independence, I mean independence which Botswana or any other country has. [24]

It is obvious that Botswana's present situation differs greatly from the Bantustans' in certain respects, though in others they are not very dissimilar. I shall now, in concluding this paper, look briefly at some of the similarities and differences.

They are alike in respect of poverty, overcrowding, overgrazed land, inadequate secondary school facilities and therefore an insufficient supply of high level manpower. However, whilst an absolute limit is imposed on the supply of African land in the Republic by the provisions of the Bantu Trust and Land Act, 1936, in

Botswana it should be possible substantially to extend the areas devoted to dry-land farming and, if the waters of the Okavango are eventually harnessed, much at present unusable land would come under cultivation. In Botswana, as in the Bantustans, Chiefs' powers are a central political issue, though in Botswana they have been gradually reduced, whilst in the Bantustans they are sustained by the Republican Government. If, however, in the Transkei a Democratic Party Government were to replace the Transkei National Independence Party the Chiefs might well be removed to an upper house, as in Botswana.

Clearly, Botswana is free in a number of ways in which the Transkei is not. Botswana can raise loans internationally, may solicit aid from any source, intends to run its section of the railway itself, and has even been able to press ahead with withdrawal from the rand monetary area. Similarly, Botswana encourages foreign investment without hindrance, promotes tourism and produces comprehensive development plans. She is free now of British budgetary aid, whereas in 1972-3 the Department of Bantu Administration and Development spent over R28m. in the Transkei.[25] Above all, from the material point of view, Botswana's rich mineral deposits provide an assured base for growth. The Transkei's only significant export is labour; Botswana has copper, nickel and diamonds as well.

Most important of all to the Batswana may be the psychological freedom which people, black or white, cannot enjoy in South Africa. Race relations are not perfect in Botswana and may deteriorate as mining development proceeds, but at least the official 'line' is entirely clear and non-racial. In so far as Botswana's policy is successful it must be a constant source of irritation to white South Africans.

The list of differences could be prolonged. My point, however, now that the gaps between Botswana and the more convincing Bantustans have been indicated, is to argue that it is perfectly possible that most of those gaps will be closed, provided certain assumptions are made. Those assumptions are that independence will be negotiated on terms acceptable to the Bantustan leaders, the South Africa Government, and the South African electorate, and that independent Bantustans will be recognised as such internationally and allowed to take their seats in the United Nations.

It would be foolish to suggest that Bantustan independence will solve any racial problems in White South Africa itself. But the Pretoria Government may well be finding "the politics of domestic colonialism",[26] more trying than had been foreseen and there seems little reason to prolong unnecessarily the present somewhat uneasy relations between Bantustans and mother state. South Africa's policy makers presumably realise that independence will pose no significant threat and they probably believe that the policy of separate development is not now reversible. It will still be possible to control physical access to and egress from the new states, they will remain dependent on the Republic for jobs and in so far as they diversify sources of aid, South Africa will be able to reduce its grants.

The independent Bantustans would, on the other hand, gain the advantages, psychological and material, which independence brings. Lack of natural resources and rapidly increasing unemployment make KwaZulu and the Transkei even less likely than Botswana to escape from poverty, even if they eventually develop outlets to the sea. Nevertheless the experience of the Boleswa states shows that independence is valued and that even the smallest states can play a part in world affairs. I see no reason why the Transkei, at least, should not enjoy the satisfactions associated with political independence, within the limits imposed by economics, geography and history.

In conclusion I suggest that the sensitivity one meets in Boleswa when Bantustans are discussed is misplaced. It is not the case that the Boleswa states are "indistinguishable from Bantustans." It may be that some Bantustans will take the Boleswa states as their models and become, in a number of important respects, indistinguishable from Boleswa. If so some improvement will have occurred in the Southern African situation.

NOTES

1. National Development Plan 1970-75 (Gaborone, Government Printer, September 1970), hereafter referred to as The Plan.

2. Sheridan Johns discusses some of these points, and takes a somewhat similar line to my own in his valuable paper "Botswana's Strategy for Development: An Assessment of Dependence in the Southern African Context" in Journal of Commonwealth Political Studies 11(3), November 1973, 214-230. I had, regrettably, not read Dr. John's article before my own was first written.

3. For the beginning of this process see Local Government in the Bechuanaland Protectorate (Legislative Council Paper, no. 21 of 1964), supporting proposals for the establishment of District Councils. In para 21 the bland observation is made: "Their direct personal power will necessarily be reduced but it is believed that the Chiefs will not wish to oppose liberal principles which are embraced everywhere in the free world."

4. See, for example, The Plan, ch. 2, para 19.

5. I am here agreeing with Willie Henderson in his note on some recent Botswana monographs, Journal of Modern African Studies 11(1), March 1973, 172-175.

6. The Plan, ch. 11, para 15.

7. Ibid., ch. 9, para 64.

8. Government Paper No. 1 "Rural Development in Botswana" (Ministry of Finance and Development Planning, Gaborone, March 1972). In Employment Survey (August 1973) (Gaborone: Government Printer, June 1974), the mean monthly wage of citizens in the modern sector of agriculture is estimated at R25. The estimated number of citizens so employed is only 5643.

9. The Plan, ch. 2, para 20. See also ch. 1, para 23, where the average non-agriculture wage is given as R509.

10. Ibid., ch. 2, para 19.

11. "Speech presenting National Development Plan 1970-1975 to the National Assembly" by His Honour the Vice-President Dr. Q. K. J. Masire, M.P., para 20. (Government Printer: Gaborone, November 1970).

12. The Plan, ch. 2, para 13.

13. See: "Planning with a Purpose", speech by His Excellency the President, Sir Seretse Khama, opening the fourth session of the second Parliament of Botswana, Gaborone, 11 December 1972, paras 44-46. (Gaborone: Government Printer).

14. Henderson, op.cit., 174.

15. Masire, op.cit., para 16.

16. Michael Barratt Brown, "Marxist Theories of Imperialism" in Essays on Imperialism (Nottingham, England: Spokesman Books 1972), 50.

17. "The Stages of Imperialism" in ibid., 71.

18. "Imperialism and Working Class Interests" in *ibid.*, 84-5.

19. House of Assembly, *Debates*, 3 September 1970, col. 3279.

20. See especially Adrian Leftwich (ed.) *South Africa, Economic Growth and Political Change* (London: Allison and Busby, 1974).

21. *Africa and America in the Seventies*. Address by His Excellency the President of the Republic of Botswana, Sir Seretse Khama, to the Third Annual Conference of the African-American Dialogue, Lagos, March 1971. (Government Printer: Gaborone), passim.

22. *Ibid.*, para 25.

23. "Independent Bantustans?" by Merle Lipton, *International Affairs* 48(1), 1-19.

24. House of Assembly, *Debates*, cols. 5280-2. Quoted in *A Survey of Race Relations in South Africa 1972*. Compiled by Muriel Horrell *et al.* (Johannesburg, South African Institute of Race Relations, January 1973) 32.

25. *Ibid.*, 186. The figure includes project aid.

26. The subtitle of *South Africa's Transkei* by Gwendolen M. Carter *et al.* (Evanston: Northwestern University Press, 1967).

Chapter Thirteen

ANTI-NEO-COLONIALISM IN SOUTH AFRICA'S FOREIGN POLICY RHETORIC*

Kenneth W. Grundy

This paper is designed to discuss and to stimulate discussion about the present and future international role of the Republic of South Africa and especially of South Africa's role in the global capitalist order.

There is a tendency among students of international relations in Southern Africa to regard, usually implicitly although often explicitly, the foreign policy goals of the Republic of South Africa as virtually in harmony with those of the major European and North American capitalist states. Some would subscribe to a kind of conspiratorial theory of United States or British-South African relations. Others would contend that the nature of stratification in the global imperialist system necessitates that South Africa serve as a regional agent of the core imperialist states. It has been argued that the reverse relationship, Great Britain doing the bidding of South Africa, prevails. Still others view the interactions as fortuitous rather than calculated. They would maintain that given the prevailing socio-economic and strategic balances, foreign policy similarities are simply a function of a genuine co-terminality of interests, objective and subjective.

The relationships between colonial-settlers and their former metropolitan centers and other periphery states have been variously described, especially regarding the case of South Africa. Often a single writer or team of writers will utilize more than one set of phrases and metaphors. South Africa has been called a "colony", it displays "features of a colony", and is "no longer a colony" of Great Britain. It has been stated that British policy in Southern Africa has been abandoned to the dictates of South Africa. It is also argued that foreign investments (including British) are using South Africa as a "launching pad" to penetrate the rest of the continent.[1] "South African capital," we are told, "participates as a junior partner in the exploitation of the less developed regions on its periphery."[2] Elsewhere we can read that "Britain has ceded her 'sphere of influence' [in Southern Africa] to apartheid, only to join this aggressive scheme as an accomplice." Yet it is also contended that without these vital economic, political, and strategic links, the entire apartheid structure would crumble or at least be so weakened as to be mortally vulnerable.[3] It is suggested that the minority government now makes decisions that dictate patterns of investment and trade,[4] that South Africa has fostered an "imperialism" of its own,[5] and yet it is still highly dependent on capital, technology, weapons and political support from abroad. Others have argued that Great Britain is no longer the principal mentor of South Africa. Rather South Africa is still "dependent" on the influx of foreign capital, but the source of that capital is now the United States. Thus South Africa is "a satellite to the leader capitalist nations" at the same time that it has "assumed the role . . . of a national metropolis" toward regions within and on its borders."[6] No doubt foreign interests that invest in South Africa do so because, inter alia, they are impressed by the growth possibilities, not only of the domestic South African market, but of the regional external market as well.

Whatever the phrases used, the relationships between South Africa's brand of imperialism and that of the total system, and which global powers are the principal intrusive actors in the region are hotly debated.

But the fact remains that in the context of many such analyses, it becomes difficult to explain and understand the continuing pull and tug of international relations between the Republic and its former metropolitan and neo-metropolitan "partners", especially when ambiguities crop up, as they invariably do. When the Republic appears to act in anti-British or in anti-colonial ways, analysts are often drawn then to three possible responses. First, the ostensible discrepancy may be ignored, disbelieved, or repressed. Second, it may be explained as hypocrisy, miscalculation (i.e., a "foolish" policy for one or the other actors), or duplicity (i.e., designed to mask the "real", underlying orchestration of relations). Or, third, it may be written off as an emotional reversion to historical, introspective and defensive ethnic (Afrikaner) isolationism: the laager complex or laager mentality manifesting itself in foreign affairs. Invariably an effort is made to explain away differences. Seldom are differences analyzed as if they might be valid expressions of conflicts of interest between White and capitalist South Africa on the one hand and White and capitalist Great Britain or the United States, on the other.

A crucial intermediary force in the imperialist system has been colonial-settlers, especially when they are able to establish their own minority regimes. The term colonial-settler must include not only settlers, but the entire administrative baggage associated with the expatriate mercantile-extractive complex - the local staffs of metropolitan-based companies, the colonial civil service at the lower (less mobile) grades, and the agents and backers of these interests in the metropolitan country.[7] It is this constellation of interests that has emerged as what Arghiri Emmanuel has referred to as a "third factor", "a third element", and an "independent factor" insinuating itself between imperialist capitalism and the indigenous peoples of periphery states.[8] They are vital chiefly because they display features of independence from the government of their "mother country." In Emmanuel's estimation there is an important deficiency in Marxist schemas of imperialism and colonialism insofar as they apply to the process of decolonization and the phenomena of neo-colonialism and neo-imperialism, and particularly insofar as colonial-settlers have baffled Marxist analysts. Colonial-settler governments can both strengthen and challenge the established imperialist order. They are a go-between and an irritant in the system. It is not necessarily inconsistent to see them thus at one and the same time. But they have, nevertheless, proven resistant to easy categorization.

The fact is that anti-colonialism, because of the above-mentioned factors, is strongly entrenched in the heritage of dominant sections of South Africa's White population. Afrikaner nationalists and English-speaking business interests both have reasons for appearing to be anti-imperialist or anti-neo-imperialist. These themes find contemporary echo in specific South African pronouncements, manifestations of anti-neo-colonialist rhetoric that are both genuine and also self-serving.

A couple of examples should convey the tone of this theme. In a 1959 address to the South African Bureau of Racial Affairs, Foreign Minister Eric Louw asked rhetorically about the emergent Black states of Africa: "Do they realize that the so-called concern for their progress and welfare, shown by 'outside' states, is not always altruistic?" Thus, he went on, "our fellow-states in Africa" must bear in mind that "as regards offers of financial assistance, they might also do well to take heed of Laocoon's advice, viz. 'Timeo Danaos et dona ferentes.'"[9] In another passage, Louw warned of "self-appointed advisers from outside" who seek private gain or the promotion of the political and economic interests of the countries that sent them. Thus, "if assistance is granted by a foreign government, a political quid pro quo will be demanded (or at least be expected)."[10]

Louw's successor as Foreign Minister, Dr. Hilgard Muller, repeatedly denies that South Africa's "outward policy" is imperialistic. In a 1970 statement he opined, "There is no old-fashioned imperialism or neo-colonialism in this."[11] And to two separate university audiences, almost three years apart, he delivered precisely the same message, with only one word changed: "South Africa is strongly opposed to any form of neo-Colonialism or economic Imperialism. We consistently refuse to interfere in the affairs of others and resist attempts by others to interfere in our affairs."[12] Are these expressions a product of a belated and humane concern for the freedom and independence of peoples in neighboring states? Not likely! But it is also unfair to regard them as purely hypocritical rhetoric, fashioned to mislead and disarm South Africa's opponents. For, these attitudes are consistent with some features of Afrikaner political thought, and they are, in addition, self-serving in the present context of South Africa's global and regional relations.

To begin with it is necessary to trace broadly the evolution of this sort of thinking in South Africa. This will be followed by an analysis of the component themes that have been developed. And finally an effort will be made to place contemporary South African expressions of anti-neo-colonialism in their proper context.

With the flowering of Boer-Afrikaner identity during the institution of the Afrikaner republics and during the Anglo-Boer Wars (1880-1881 and 1899-1902) the ideological line was direct and uncomplicated. Boers yearn for self-government and autonomy. The British government has been the oppressor of the Afrikaner people. British settlers in South Africa have been their agents. The Imperial British should allow the Boers to control their own destinies. Imperialism and colonialism were wrong.[13] Yet as with many other facets of political thought, the Boer conception of imperialism and self-rule was riddled with inconsistencies. While Boers bristled under laws and constraints imposed by the Crown, they in turn laid claim to land belonging to the indigenous inhabitants and evolved a master-serf relationship with the Blacks they encountered, a relationship that continues in its fundamentals to this day. Likewise, in affairs beyond its borders, South Africa sought to extend its hegemony.[14] In defense of their socio-political order they erected an ideology as grotesque as it was ingenious.[15]

Thus, theirs was a myopic rendering of what purported to be universal principles, a product as much of the Boer hatred of and competition with Great Britain as of a distaste for imperialism per se. Nonetheless the legacy of anti-imperialism remained to deposit a residue of distrust for Great Power machinations in South Africa's political rhetoric. It surfaced, for example, in General Smuts championing the cause of small states at Versailles and in the League of Nations.

The 1939 decision to join Great Britain in her war against Germany unleashed, once more, the reservoir of anti-British and anti-imperialist sentiment. South African entry into the war signified to Afrikaner nationalists a denial of their independence and a reassertion of British imperialism.[16] The Second World War contributed to the growth and unity of Afrikaner nationalism. It was also the catalyst in the rise of the Nationalist Party, which became increasingly determined to take over the government (it did in 1948) and to make South Africa a republic (it did in 1961). The latter act was the symbolic gesture of defiance and independence aimed at Great Britain and English-speaking South Africans, although the latter were not of one mind on the republican issue.

Accompanying the renewed expression of anti-British sentiment among Afrikaners in the 1940's and 1950's came a strange new appreciation and support for colonialism by European Powers elsewhere in Africa. As Rhoodie and Venter argue:

> the Second World War brought about the permanent disappearance of the 'walls' which isolated the Whites in South Africa from the rest of the continent. The previous detached approach to external affairs had at the same time to make way for a reappraisal of South Africa's place in the geo-political and socio-economic structure of the African continent.[17]

In this mode Prime Minister J. D. Strydom, in 1956, could maintain that:

> after the Second World War we suddenly realized that 160,000,000 or more non-Europeans of Africa, who through the ages have slept, have awakened; . . . through correct guidance and management we can preserve the good relationship between one another (Europeans and Natives) and build it up further so that the majority at least realize that both White and Black have the right of existence in Africa, _everyone in his own sphere and territory_.[18]

The first serious policy proposals in reaction to the weakening of colonial control were manifested in 1945 in Dr. D. F. Malan's various proposals for a Charter of Africa, and in their continued reintroduction as late as 1954. Malan's proposed Charter was to be a pronouncement by all the powers possessing territories or with interests in Africa. In it, they were to declare that the continent be preserved in its development for the Western, European, Christian civilization. The Charter proposal also included a desire to "protect" the indigenous Africans from penetration by the peoples of Asia, the suppression of Communist activities in Africa, and the prevention of the militarization of Africa, by which he meant the arming of the "natives." Although nothing formal came of this suggested bloc, South African policy makers continued to support and justify colonial rule in Africa.

Later this call was refined to involve a South African arrangement with British imperialism, heritage and rhetoric notwithstanding. The old ambiguities, the old "love-hate" relationship with Britain was rekindled. "South Africa," said Prime Minister Malan in 1950, "has during her history come to know . . . two Englands.

The one is England at her worst. The other is England at her best. South Africans this side of the House and the Afrikaner-speaking sections of our people know them both."[19] By this he seemed to mean that England at her worst was England governing South Africa, and England at her best was England governing the rest of Africa.

By the time of the impending independence of French and English-speaking colonies in the late 1950's, the South African government had become convinced that colonialism must resist and delay the inevitable. In the same 1959 address in which he denied that South Africa was a colonial force and in which he warned Africans to beware of "altruists" bearing financial assistance, Foreign Minister Louw defended colonial rule to the north. "[I]t is unwise for a colonial power to withdraw its guiding hand, and to grant full independence to a country where the people are not yet sufficiently matured and ripe for independence . . . ."[20] South African regimes were beginning to appreciate the strategic advantage of buffer colonial regimes on their borders and to feel the icy blasts of the "Winds of Change". Thus South African statesmen could excoriate the European colonial powers for what they regarded as a too hasty liquidation of their empires, at the same time that they, themselves, were seeking to sever the vestiges of British overrule by urging the establishment of a Republic and the end of South African involvement in an increasingly hostile British Commonwealth.

It took the South Africans some years to realize that you don't have to own the cow in order to milk her. Just as independence did not signal an abandonment or withdrawal of British influence and interest in Africa, so South Africa learned that she need not occupy territory in order to profit from various forms of unequa association. The evolution of apartheid thinking, the development of the idea of Bantu Homelands, the progressive movement toward "self-government" in these territories, the acquiescence in the ultimate juridical independence of the former High Commission Territories, and the effort toward an "outward looking" foreign policy were all part of this maturation in South African control mechanisms and the ideology associated with them.

With these more subtle and sophisticated forms of domestic and foreign policy came a realization, perhaps long festering in the viscera of true Afrikaner nationalist that at heart South Africa and Great Britain were competitors in Southern Africa. It must be emphasized that Great Britain and South Africa were, from the time of the Greak Trek of the 1830's, in a direct and spasmodic contest for control over the interior of Southern Africa. The Boer Wars, correctly interpreted, were not fought over the various conflicting native policies but over who would dominate t hinterland. General Smuts for years labored in the belief that Great Britain and South Africa could reach accommodation on this issue, thereby permitting the expansion of South Africa northward. As nationalist Afrikaners came to dominate political thinking in white South Africa, British governments became more defensive about its territories in the region. In this light, the establishment of the Central African Federation was designed to paralyze and resist the expansion of efflorescent Afrikaner nationalism. If, as Professor W. M. Macmillan wrote in 1949, "South Africans express at times an almost proprietary interest in the Africa beyond,"[21] the British took it upon themselves to obstruct that proprietary interest. The British dilemma over Rhodesia is still preoccupied by this fear. Foreign Secretary Sir Alec Douglas-Home expressed it with clarity: "I always have very much in mind that if we are unable to make a settlement, Rhodesia would become virtually a part of South Africa."[22] Many in South Africa and elsewhere already regard this as an accomplished fact.[23] It is this distrust and dislike that apparently led one Nationalist to tell Prime Minister Vorster at a Party congress: "the Union Jack is the flag of the only and the greatest enemy the Afrikaner has had . . . ."[24] Anti-British imperialism strikes sympathetic chords in Afrikanerdom, at the emotional-personal level and at the broader power-interest level.

As South Africa industrializes and her economy booms, she increasingly sees herself displacing (as she is at once cooperating with) Great Britain as the dominant European-Capitalist force in the region. She sees herself as a regional core, powerful and confident within her realm. It may be premature, given the balance of politico-economic forces in the world, but it certainly is not out of the question for South African zealots. And it has given rise to a subtle undercurrent of anti-imperialism finding its way into South African foreign ideology. It is reminiscent of pre-1890 British anti-imperialism, backed by the industrial and financial might of the U.K., and reinforced by her desire for free-trade and open competition. It was a policy based on sound economic advantage and hardly a commitment to self-government for the world's underdeveloped peoples. It is reminiscent, too, of American anti-imperialism at the turn of the century and anti-colonialism in the late 1940's and 1950's as the new industrial giant insisted on "open doors" and "self-determination". These norms could be universally trumpeted. They fit well with a liberal posture. But they were also self-serving to the United States at crucial stages of her economic and political life.

With South Africa, anti-neo-imperialism in the general is not a dominant theme. How could it be? It is just beginning to be tested by the more optimistic South

Africans. But it is one that fits well into the "official" heritage of South Africa. It is also pro-South African in that it rationalizes South African economic growth and strategic considerations, and moreover, contributes to elbowing Great Britain out of Southern Africa. For imperialism and colonialism are always more apparent when they cross the sea, and less obvious when they merely represent the geographical and economic expansion of interests of a flourishing neighbor. The 18th and 19th century westward expansion of the United States and 19th century eastward movement of Czarist Russia somehow, at the time, seemed less conscious and less pernicious than French or British imperial expansion. In the constellation of power in Southern Africa, many white South Africans see their country on the threshold of economic growth and regional dominance. South Africa strives to replace Great Britain as the paramount economic force in Lesotho, Botswana, Swaziland, Rhodesia, and Malawi. She would like to displace the Portuguese in Mozambique and to a lesser degree in Angola. South African businessmen cannot help but be buoyed by their successes. It is no accident that the "outward policy" and South African economic and political activity throughout Southern Africa came after and coincidental with British imperial withdrawal from Southern Africa.

But one cannot help but see South Africa's confident rhetoric and measured anti-neo-colonialism as a passing phase in her foreign policy. In the short run she welcomes the opportunity to displace British power in Southern Africa. She sees South Africa as gaining economically from expanded ties with Black Africa. She even, from time to time, hints that she would prefer stable Black governments in her zone of interest to unstable settler regimes. South Africans are approaching the transition in Mozambique within this sort of framework, although they await the changes with trepidation. They also seem to be, once again, rethinking their ties with the Smith regime, largely because they see Smith as unbending and unreliable. South Africa defends Rhodesia as long as Rhodesia buffers the Republic. Recent events call this into question.[25] This does not mean that South Africa would abandon her white settler neighbors for just any Black government. But an indigenous, bourgeois elite, willing to compromise and live with South Africa's white regime might be given encouragement.

Britain, with global imperial interests, saw South Africa as provincial, narrow, too parochial to be able to make sacrifices to save the greater British empire. Verwoerd as much as said this when he argued that Britain with her world-wide responsibilities had subordinated the interest of all the inhabitants of Southern Africa to Britain's global interests. But now South Africa is using the same sorts of arguments with the other white settlers in Rhodesia, Mozambique and Angola. South Africa, with wide-ranging regional interests, accuses the settlers of being too provincial and thereby threatening the stability of the total region, South Africa, her leaders insist, has a broader perspective. It is ironic that South Africa should, having become a limited imperial force in her own right, employ the reasoning that had once been and still is employed against her.

The facts remain, however, that there are not only absolute limits to the hegemonic potentialities of a White-ruled South Africa, but there are built-in factors that will bring about a steady shrinkage in South Africa's relative power - chief among them African nationalism, continental Pan-Africanism, and global anti-imperialism. South Africa's anti-neo-imperialism, be it self-delusion, conscious ideological obfuscation, or a long-range desire to undermine the U.K. and supplant British power regionally, represents the high-point in South African optimism about her possible role in world affairs. Present-day South Africans have allowed their imaginations to soar. The present Director of Information once wrote that "if allowed to proceed unhindered developments could lead to the creation of a new multi-national giant, the Europe of Africa, which will one day exercise a profound influence on developments in Africa, if not in the world."[26] But this sort of euphoria may be a pose, not really believed. Realists sense that the prefatory clause, "if allowed to proceed unhindered," will never prevail. What South Africa's leaders really hope for, one suspects, is an endorsement by the capitalist giants of her own brand of imperialism or subimperialism as it has been called. But capitalism is still competitive in essence, and actors dream of improving their own situations within the total system. Hence the ambiguities. But once South Africa's regional hegemony is acknowledged and once South African officials realize the inherent limits to their continental dreams, they will probably be content to collaborate (as they are now in many respects) with capitalist powers in order to reap maximum gain from her geo-political advantages and her intermediary status in the economic hierarchy of global capitalism. Under such an arrangement a conflicting yet complimentary economic partnership and a positive community of security interests emerge. The global capitalists supply the money, technology, trade, and long-term "protection" and strategic support, and the ideological legitimization in the capitalist world. Those who rule South Africa provide the political structure for controlling and exploiting indigenous labor, access to key raw materials, and the ruthlessness and muscle to maintain local order. They need one another, but they still don't trust one another, since each can conceive of arrangements that might be even more profitable to itself.

In this regard, one cannot help but be impressed by the prescience of J. A. Hobson. In 1902 he wrote that the "new Imperialism" of Great Britain antagonizes "colonial self-government" in South Africa, and furnishes a "disruptive force" in relations between Britain and the "self-governing colonies."[27] As he saw it then, British policy in South Africa had unleashed "a lasting antagonism of economic interests," which would arouse a demand for complete severance from British control as the "only alternative" to a control that the settlers will regard as an "intolerable interference with their legitimate rights of self-government."[28] The "parasitism" of colonial settler rule, he argued, is first and foremost operating to further the interests of a small class of traders, mine-owners, farmers and investors who wish to dispose of the land and labor of the indigenous peoples for their own private gain. This "private management for private immediate gain is the chief operative force" in the community, and is "unchecked, or inadequately checked by imperial or other governmental control." Since these patterns are established "primarily" for the benefit of white traders and investors, the interests of "the world of white Western consumers," i.e., the imperial nation, are only secondary, and herein lies the inherent conflict of interest between colonial settlers and the metropolitan Core.[29] Thus:

> A distinctively colonial or South African expansion was the policy of the politicians, financiers and adventurers up to the failure of the Jameson Raid; reluctantly they sought the cooperation of British imperialism to aid them in a definite work for which they were too weak, the seizure of the Transvaal mineral estates; their absorbing aim hereafter will be to relegate British imperialism to what they conceive to be its proper place, that of an _ultima ratio_ to stand in the far background while colonial Imperialism manages the business and takes the profits. A South African federation of self-governing States will demand a political career of its own, and will insist upon its own brand of empire, not that of the British Government, in the control of the lower races of South Africa. Such a federal State will not only develop an internal policy regarding the native territories different from, perhaps antagonistic to, that of British Imperialism, but its position as the "predominant" State of South Africa will develop an ambition and a destiny of expansion which may bring it into world politics on its own account.[30]

Now, over seventy years later, that pattern has been nearly realized. As South African economic groups display aggressiveness and imagination to move outward, metropolitan interests generally follow in their wake, content to play a supportive role, to let the international onus of "expansionism" fall on South Africa, as long as the profits flow to them, too. They are willing to supply those components of expansion that they can best provide - technology, capital, advice, encouragement and political-strategic protection. At other times the metropole may actually initiate the outward movement, for the relationship involves cross-fertilization and mutual support.

Even though the control mechanisms may be slipping from the hands of the ruling elements in the metropolitan state, or perhaps more accurately those ruling elites are more selective in applying the leverage they still possess, the new relationships are so lucrative as to neutralize protest and resistance in the various elites, notwithstanding sporadic public outcries of righteous indignation. But the structural changes are central.

Much current discussion of imperialism flows from the common sense proposition that whoever pays the piper calls the tune. Things are not that simple in practice. Although the strength of a state's capital and its political autonomy are related, there is no one-to-one correlation between the two. We have arrived at a situation in Southern Africa (and elsewhere, too) where there is a widening "non-correspondence between the nationality of capital and the nationality of effective state power."[31] For example, the imperialist core may be prevented, by virtue of domestic political problems or external pressures and risks, from applying their full military and financial power elsewhere. Even should they attempt to do so, various factors do not guarantee their success. Hence, in regional affairs they may, by necessity, defer to governments that on one hand may appear to be junior partners but on some questions effectively become equal or even senior partners. It may well be that South Africa will force important revisions in the terms of its relationship to the wider imperial system on issues especially vital to its interests.

NOTES

* An earlier version of this paper was read at the Seventeenth Annual Meeting of the African Studies Association, November 1, 1974, Chicago, Illinois. It benefits from the comments and criticisms of George W. Shepherd, Jr., James Mittelman, and Timothy Shaw. Many of the ideas and background data were developed with the assistance of a grant awarded by the Joint Committee on African Studies of the Social Science Research Council and the American Council of Learned Societies. The author would like to thank these individuals and organizations and to indicate that they have absolutely no responsibility for the defects of this paper.

1. Abdul S. Minty *South Africa's Defence Strategy* (London: Anti-Apartheid Movement, October 1969) 9 and 15. See also *NUS - AAM: Free Southern Africa* (London: National Union of Students - Anti-Apartheid Movement, 1971) 19. Similar arguments with regard to the United States using Brazil as its advance agent in Africa are propounded in: L. T. "What is Brazil up to [in] Black Africa?", *World Youth* (Budapest) 1, 1973, 14-15; and as the U.S. Agent in South America in Ruy Mauro Marine, "Brazilian Subimperialism", *Monthly Review* 23(9), February 1972, 14-24.

2. Bernard Magubane "Imperialism and the South African Problem", paper presented at the Annual Meeting of the American Sociological Association, Denver, Colorado, September 1971, 15. My italics.

3. Ruth First, Jonathan Steele, and Christabel Gurney *The South African Connection: Western Investment in Apartheid* (London: Temple Smith, 1972) 294 *et passim*.

4. *Ibid*., Chapter 12, "Western Trade Follows the South African Flag".

5. Anthony Atmore and Nancy Westlake "A Liberal Dilemma: A Critique of the Oxford History of South Africa", *Race* 14(2), October 1972, 130; and Sean Gervasi, "The Significance of South Africa's Economic Relations with the Western Powers" (London: Anti-Apartheid Movement, mimeo.), a paper prepared for a conference to commemorate South Africa Freedom Day, Round House, London, 4 July 1971, esp. 8-9.

6. Magubane "Imperialism and the South African Problem", 5 and 7-15.

7. Arghiri Emmanuel "White-Settler Colonialism and the Myth of Investment Imperialism", *New Left Review* 73, May-June 1972, 38. A general critique of Emmanuel's work, especially of his basic thesis that imperialism is not solely a function of capitalism but of unequal exchange that presumably all industrialized countries can engage in, is Geoffrey Pilling "Imperialism, Trade, and 'Unequal Exchange': The Work of Aghiri [sic] Emmanuel", *Economy and Society* 2(2), May 1973, 164-185.

8. Emmanuel "White-Settler Colonialism", 36, 40 and 38.

9. Louw in *South Africa in the African Continent: Papers Read at the Tenth Annual Conference of the South African Bureau of Racial Affairs* (Stellenbosch SABRA, 1959) 18.

10. Ibid., 12.

11. The Star (Johannesburg), Weekly Air Edition, 4 April 1970, 3.

12. Muller "The Republic of South Africa in a Changed World" (Pretoria: Department of Information, Fact Paper Series, 1968) 5; and Muller "South Africa's Africa Policy", Bulletin (of the Africa Institute, Pretoria) 8(6), July 1970, 256; speeches of 31 August 1967 and 25 April 1970, respectively.

13. F. A. van Jaarsveld The Awakening of Afrikaner Nationalism, 1868-1881 (Cape Town: Human and Rousseau, 1961).

14. Ronald Hyam The Failure of South African Expansion, 1908-1948 (New York: Africana Publishing, 1972).

15. John Laurence The Seeds of Disaster (London: Victor Gollancz, 1968); and Leonard Thompson "Afrikaner Nationalist Historiography and the Policy of Apartheid", Journal of African History 3(1), 1962, 125-41.

16. Michael Roberts and A. E. G. Trollip The South African Opposition, 1939-1945 (London: Longmans, Green, 1947).

17. N. J. Rhoodie and H. J. Venter Apartheid (Cape Town: National Commercial Printers, 1961) 199-200, as quoted in J. E. Spence Republic Under Pressure: A Study of South African Foreign Policy (London: Oxford University Press, 1965) 15.

18. Ibid., 200.

19. House of Assembly, 27 January 1950, vol. 242, as quoted in James Barber South Africa's Foreign Policy: 1945-1970 (London: Oxford University Press, 1973) 62.

20. Louw in SABRA Papers, 12.

21. W. M. Macmillan An Africa Beyond the Union (Johannesburg: 1949) 6; as quoted in Spence Republic Under Pressure, 2.

22. New York Times, 10 November 1971, 3.

23. See, for example, Eschel Rhoodie The Third Africa (Cape Town: Nasionale Boekhandel, 1968) 58.

24. The Star, Weekly Air Edition, 22 September 1973, 5.

25. Kenneth Good "Settler Colonialism in Rhodesia", African Affairs 73(290), January 1974, 10-36.

26. Rhoodie The Third Africa, 3.

27. J. A. Hobson Imperialism: A Study (London: George Allen and Unwin, 1902), 355.

28. Ibid., 354.

29. Ibid., 280-284.

30. Ibid., 346.

31. Editorial "Imperialism in the Seventies: Problems and Perspectives", Monthly Review 23(10), March 1972, 1-8.

Chapter Fourteen

THE POLITICAL ECONOMY OF TECHNOLOGY IN SOUTHERN AFRICA*

Timothy M. Shaw

This essay suggests that the hegemony of South Africa in Southern Africa is a function of its dependence on the international capitalist economy. Its role as a "middle power" in the regional politics of Southern Africa advances the interests of western countries and corporations. However, the perpetuation of its regional dominance is related not only to the indulgence of the great powers and to the lack of choice of subordinate states in the region; its regional power is also dependent on its economic growth and world demand for its resources. The focus of this paper, on the political economy of technology in Southern Africa, is a preliminary attempt to analyse the impact of technological change on the politics of the region. Control over capital, research and distribution is never a purely technical issue; this is particularly so in Southern Africa where economic dominance is a vital factor in the perpetuation of racial and social inequalities. However, in this region the logic of production clashes with the demand for racial differentiation and separation. Technological advance in Southern Africa is perverted, therefore, to perpetuate the racial oligarchy. The development of capital-intensive industries may reduce the dependence of white entrepreneurs on black labour, but it also condemns the labour reserves to a superfluous status. Conversely, cheap labour may reduce interest in technological change until its demands for improved conditions and pay erodes its profitability. With the present access of white Southern Africa to western technology, the region may become a distinctive dual economy[1] in which differential access to technology reinforces racial, class and regional inequalities.

The prospects of a partial superpower withdrawal from direct global hegemony increases the foreign policy choices of South Africa. Although its status as a middle power in a feudal international system cannot be changed rapidly,[2] it might adopt a rebellious rather than loyalist stance.[3] It may advance western interests by proxy or raise the price of cooperation by associating with less compliant industrial states like France or Japan. However, its choices are also limited by the unwillingness of most non-western states to associate with the Republic; its 'counterdependence' strategies[4] are constrained by its international acceptability. Conversely, its effectiveness as a regional power is undermined by opposition in Southern Africa to its racism. Nevertheless, minority or majority rule in South Africa would not change its regional hegemony, although they might affect its scope.

South Africa's quest for respectability is advanced by its status as a branch-plant economy in the structure of multinational corporations. South Africa pays the price of high profitability for this association, to overcome misgivings about its racial structures. Its participation in the global organisations of the multinationals is one method of securing status and acceptability; white nationalism in Southern Africa is thus ambivalent about openness to foreign investment and procedures. Its middle power role in global politics is comparable to its middle level role in the capitalist world economy. Hymer suggests that the vertical division of labour within the firm is being replicated by an hierarchial division of labour between geographical regions. This "would tend to centralize high-level decision-making occupations in a few key cities in the advanced countries surrounded by a number of regional sub-capitals, and confine the rest of the world to lower levels of activity and income, i.e. to the status of farms and villages in a new imperial system".[5] The Witwatersrand is clearly eligible for the status of 'regional sub-capital' for Africa, both for a fragmented Republic and for the 'coprosperity sphere'. The Bantustan system duplicates global uneven development on a local scale, with reserves being concentrated at the centre at the expense of the underdevelopment of the periphery. South Africa's dominance of the Rand Customs and Currency Area reveals its capacity for intervention in the regional economy in the interests of industrial concentration around Johannesburg; the inherited inequalities in the region reduce the bargaining power of BLS in their quest for a redistribution of resources and a reversal of their underdevelopment.[6] Their dependence on South Africa is the third level of interaction in a global hierarchy in which the Republic itself is subordinate to corporate and diplomatic decision-making in the capitals of rich states.[7] South Africa may lose this status either if it becomes internationally more isolated or if it cannot duplicate technological changes in Southern Africa. Post-industrial society is dependent on development in a few advanced sectors; if Europe cannot compete with American multinationals, then clearly Southern Africa will remain dependent on external research and development.[8] South Africa cannot become one of the new industrial states without access to western technology; its mineral resources encourage but do not guarantee a positive response to its demands. Anglo-American sells gold, diamonds,uranium, copper and coal to western states and invests in Zambia, Botswana, Canada, Rhodesia, Swaziland, Mauritania, Zaire, England and Australasia; its integration in the world capitalist economy enables it to buy patents, rights and technology from a wide variety of countries and companies.[9] The mutual interests of regional and global corporations encourage such exchanges and interdependence. South Africa has diversified its relations in technological exchange to enhance its access and deter sanctions on knowledge. It builds jet fighters from Italy and France, missiles from France, computers from IBM and ICL, uses nuclear technology from West Germany and France, microwave circuits from Japan, and chemical engineering from Britain and the US. The case studies of railways and energy presented below are illustrative of the importance and limitations of a technological focus on South Africa's international relations.

1. The Political Economy of Regional Politics

Although studies of regional cooperation and conflict have corrected our preoccupation with bipolarity, they have paid insufficient attention to the political economy of integration and confrontation. In Southern Africa, the advocates of regional cooperation are in opposition to advocates of liberation.[10] The coalition between the UN, OAU, liberation movements and support groups advocates independence for the black majorities in Southern Africa before the advent of regional or continental unity. By contrast, multinational corporations, ruling elites, and settlers prefer regional co-ordination to political change; regional communication and power projects, military cooperation and coprosperity diplomacy advance economic growth without disturbing the basic characteristics of the subsystem.[11] The process of labour migration widens involvement in regional transactions and encourages interdependence. However, orthodox approaches to regional institutions is suggestive of the need to pay increased attention to the political economy of redistribution, especially if integration leads to new concentrations of power and growth rather than to a more egalitarian distribution of resources.[12] We must extract patterns of interdependence and dependence in Southern Africa to evaluate the impact of regionalism on the independence of states in the subsystem and to analyse the foreign policy choices of these actors.[13] In particular, we should examine the impact of transnational actors on both regional politics and state sovereignty; the flow of investment, profit and technology is a constraint both on independence and on regional development.

Multinational corporations have been important advocates of regional integration. They advance the rationalisation of production and distribution in the European and East African Communities and contribute to industrial concentration in countries with advanced economies and permissive attitudes towards their operations, like West Germany and Kenya. South Africa is the appropriate center for Southern Africa and can advance its own interests in the "second scramble" providing association with apartheid has no great costs in other regions for multinationals. "The 'internationalization' of Southern Africa and the growing strength of South African corporation interests coincide with the striking change in South African foreign policy from islationism to expanionism and, at the same time, with the closer integration of South African, British and European economic interests and political strategy".[14]

Western governments and corporations want to perpetuate their access to Southern Africa's mineral resources, especially to South African gold, diamonds, chromium and platinum, Rhodesian copper, chrome and asbestos, South West African uranium and Angolan oil, diamonds and copper.[15] However, new technologies and sources of minerals, including the ocean floors, have reduced dependence on the flow from Southern Africa and so eroded the region's ability to bargain for diplomatic acceptability. Nevertheless, corporate Research and Development (R&D) is dependent on sale of patents, processes, equipment and personnel and the small size of the scientific community in Southern Africa makes it a good market for such goods. The mining companies have themselves diversified into manufacturing, finance and property in association with external technology. This includes investment by Southern African corporations like Anglo-American and Rembrandt in Europe, North America and Australasia.[16] Such interdependence is a deterrent to governments and companies in the west to stop either investment or technology going to Southern Africa. However, the prospect of a choice between investment in Southern Africa or in Black Africa is unwelcome to corporate officials and they have attempted to justify relations with all states on grounds of their apolitical interests. However, their ability to manipulate their relations in Black Africa is indicative of their political impact. They play a critical role in the political economy of linkage politics in states like Zambia,[17] Kenya, Nigeria and the Ivory Coast; we have paid insufficient attention to their ability to advance change in Southern Africa. Their capital and technological resources could be employed to confront rather than support racist rule if the costs of collaboration were raised by Black Africa or western governments.

Concern in the west about the exploitation of black labour in Southern Africa coincided with attempts by regional multinational corporations to improve their image. Both are responses to radical demands for both racial equality and majority rule. Oppenheimer has revived and popularised the thesis that higher wages for black workers will lead to economic development and political advancement; foreign investors are anxious to perpetuate their interests by mollifying critics of excessively low salaries. Both groups are concerned about radical criticism in Europe and North America and activities of the liberation movements. Their liberal response may deflate or deflect comment, but it does not undermine the regional structures. Although the 'poor' whites and trade unions may feel insecure, the advocacy of a neocolonial solution by multinationals serves their interests. Moreover, improved incomes and status for some black workers have been accompanied by police measures against black trade union, student and church leaders and the relentless moving of the black population into Bantustans. Nevertheless, experience of multinationals with African regimes and regional integration may encourage them to abandon their collaboration with apartheid and advance moderate groups in Southern Africa. Political change in South Africa is a precondition for effective South African hegemony in the region and for a reduction of criticism against the role of multinationals. Further, any delay in such change increases the likelihood of more radical governments in the liberated areas and states which would be less cooperative with external entrepreneurs. The importance of foreign investment and technology in Southern Africa increases their leverage in advancing neocolonialism as a solution to regional conflict.

Apartheid has circumscribed South Africa's sphere of influence. Dialogue and the outward-looking policy were designed to widen it and to challenge the liberation movements. The rejection of dialogue and the Waldheim initiative have limited the scope of South Africa's coprosperity sphere and encouraged radical opposition to white regimes. South Africa's trade with Africa has declined as markets in Congo, East Africa and the Central African Federation have been lost; trade and investment is now concentrated in a group of "least developed" and landlocked black states (BLS and Malawi)[18] and in Angola, Mozambique, Rhodesia and South West Africa.[19] South Africa needs to win international respectability before it can widen its regional hegemony, either through decolonisation for Namibia or the Bantustans, or majority rule in the Republic. However, the rise of white nationalism and settler economic power complicates the process of change in the region. Multinationals have been able to coopt new ruling elites in the Third World; they may be less able to influence settler communities towards cooperation with transnational society. The development of state capitalism in Southern Africa parallels and even exceeds that in Black Africa.

2. White Nationalism and Dependence

Settler communities have a characteristically ambivalent relationship with the metropole; they accept imperial protection and preference but resent any intervention or control. They were able to exploit close ethnic relationships while avoiding direct imperial rule; they attracted finance from the centre but escaped colonial administration. So the settlers in South Africa and Rhodesia were able to develop a sophisticated industrial base built on their control over mineral reserves and to prevent the underdevelopment of the Witwatersrand and Wankie as extractive centres only. The "national bourgeoisie (the settlers) (was) sufficiently strong to uphold a 'national' interest vis-a-vis the metropolitan countries".[20] The ability of settlers in Southern Africa to control the export of economic surplus and to develop a relatively integrated industrial structure enabled them to resist decolonisation. Further, Southern Africa was not an appropriate area for a neocolonial solution as the minority regimes were unprepared to encourage further dependence on external capital. The settlers were unconcerned about the damage to metropolitan interests done by their resistance to majority rule. African nationalism has generally been more accommodative to metropolitan concerns than Afrikaner nationalism.[21] Party politics in white Southern Africa are divided over the acceptability of linkages with metropolitan governments and companies--the Rhodesia Party, like the United Party in South Africa, is more accommodative towards foreign capital whereas the Rhodesian Front, along with South Africa's Nationalist Party, is primarily concerned with domestic wealth.[22] The association between the Progressive Party and the Oppenheimer family is well known and is compatible with the enhanced prospects of a "neo-colonial solution" advanced by the Progressives. The Smith regime has encouraged Rhodesian companies as one response to the impact of sanctions; the Nationalist governments since 1948 have supported Afrikaner economic nationalism. The development of the Afrikaner 'nation' under Verwoerd and Vorster led from political and cultural superiority to demands for economic equality with English-speaking South Africans. The state encouraged both an extension of national ownership and a redistribution of resources in favour of Afrikanerdom. The exclusiveness of Afrikaner culture was enlarged by state aid for the Afrikaner economy. Afrikaner finance houses were developed to provide capital for Afrikaner industrial growth. The successful Afrikanerisation of the economy has led away from non-profit ethnic motives for enterpreneurship towards more orthodox criteria.[23] It has also disturbed traditional Afrikaner values and encouraged a modernisation of Afrikaner society which may upset its advocates. State corporations include the South African Railways and Harbours Corporation (SAR), Industrial Development Corporation (IDC), Electricity Supply Commission (ESCOM), the Iron and Steel Corporation (ISCOR), African Explosives and Chemical Industries

(AE & CI), Armaments Corporation (ARMSCOR), South African Marine, and South African Airways (SAA). Among the more powerful Afrikaner corporations are: Rembrandt (tobacco), Nedbank, Volkskas, and Trust Bank (finance) and General Mining (mining and engineering). The size and scope of Afrikaner finance and industry reduces the potential impact of economic disengagement.

In Southern Africa, settlers have felt betrayed and alienated by changes of opinion in the rest of the world. The development of an embattled laager mentality has been expressed not only by an intensification of segregation and order but also by the extension of state or local control over the economy. Sanctions against Rhodesia and embargoes against South Africa have encouraged the development of state capitalism in Southern Africa. The structure of dependence in the region has evolved, therefore, away from direct imperial economic control through local subsidiaries and administration to local ownership and a more balanced relationship with multinational corporations. The local "compradour" class has been transformed from an expatriate colonial group into an indigenous white elite. This is not only a critique of the assumptions of _dependencia_ theorists; it also complicates imperial withdrawal. The inheritors of state power in Southern Africa have not been the black leaders but rather white nationalists. They have followed similar strategies to "radical" African regimes, especially strategies favouring state capitalist structures. In South Africa the Afrikaner financial oligopoly has advanced Afrikaner interests in industry, commerce and agriculture. The growth of state industries and the related development of an Afrikaner financial infrastructure has challenged the dominance of English-speaking entrepreneurs in South Africa. Similarly, in Rhodesia, Angola and Mozambique, territorial interests have replaced the dominance of imperial corporations and concerns.

Rules for increasing "South African content" and related measures advancing settler autonomy in Southern Africa have undermined assumptions about the efficacy of withdrawal as a means to undermine white power. Barclays National Bank and Standard Bank are now incorporated in South Africa and are to be owned in a majority by South African investors;[24] this organisational decentralisation reduces critical pressure on the banks from both white and black critics. Southern Africa is now less interested in capital flows than in access to technology. Regional capital can often finance substantial regional projects without significant external financial support. However, because of the small regional research base, local companies and branches depend on access to technological change, skilled labour and inputs from extra-regional sources, in crucial advanced fields like electronics, nuclear power, aircraft and chemicals, the region relies on external inputs of technology. Except for formal agreements and local assembly arrangements, this flow of ideas is difficult to assess. However, the emphasis placed by the South African government on continued access to such functional and scientific developments is one indication of its importance.

Advocates of change in Southern Africa should focus on technological linkages as well as on capital inflows and interlocking directorates. Withdrawal of western capital would over time advance settler interests but might retard regional integration. Sanctions against technical information might undermine the progress of state capitalism in Southern Africa. International organisations concerned with colonialism and racism might focus on this relationship rather than on the structures of South Africa's financial dependence on the west. The region can more readily do without western capital than without western technology. The development of railways and nuclear power in southern Africa are also suggestive of the politicisation of economic and technological change and are presented as case studies of South Africa's simultaneous dominance and dependence.

3. The Politics of Railways in Southern Africa

Railways are intimately concerned with the political economy of Africa; they contributed to the early imperial administration and exploitation of the continent and continue to have strategic and symbolic significance. Development is still closely associated with railway projects in Africa. UDI encouraged Zambia to accept an offer from China to build the TAZARA railway from Dar es Salaam to Kapiri Mposhi, south of the copperbelt. South Africa financed the extension of Malawi Railways to join the Mozambique railway to Nacala port, thus reducing Malawi's dependence on Beira; Canada is now providing aid to build the system from Salima on Lake Malawi to the new capital, Lilongwe. This is a potential contribution to an improved regional infrastructure as Malawi could extend the line further to either the main Zambia Railways or to TAZARA. Rhodesia has been dependent on rail routes to Beira, Lourenco Marques and through Botswana to South Africa; with the advent of Frelimo disruption to the Beira line and political change in Mozambique, a new line between Rhodesia and South Africa was rapidly constructed. This Rutenga-Beit Bridge connection may soon be duplicated by a further direct Rhodesia Railways-South African Railways link from West Nicolson. In addition to smaller lines like Swaziland Railways, the Richards Bay line and the Selebi-Pikwe extension, a line has been proposed to link Rhodesia with South West Africa across Botswana. This contribution to Southern Africa's regional infrastructure is now unlikely to be built despite its possible contribution to Botswana's development. Zambia continues to use the Benguela Railway through Angola as well as the Great North Road to Dar es Salaam and Mombasa. A Frelimo government in Mozambique may encourage it to use the Malawi route more intensively and so to increase its options including Tazara. Although railways in Africa are not yet technologically advanced, they are indicative of the political process of economic decision-making.

4. The Politics of Energy in Southern Africa

Industrial development in Southern Africa has increased the region's dependence on the flow of oil. UDI and UN sanctions against Rhodesia indicated the impact of an oil embargo on one state in the subsystem. The 1973 Arab oil embargo on the region revealed its vulnerability despite the development of alternative energy sources such as thermal power, hydro-electricity and nuclear energy. The revival of Arab interest in African issues led to a collective OAU stand against diplomatic ties with Israel and a positive response by the Arab states to use the "oil weapon" in Southern Africa as well as in the Middle East conflict. Oil imports provide 24% of South Africa's energy demands; the rest comes from coal-fired electricity power stations (32%), coal and coke (32%) and gas (12%). Most of the imports of R200 million each year before 1973 came from Iran, with some from Saudi Arabia, Venezuela and re-exports from the UK and US. Most of the more modest imports for the rest of the region also come from Iran and Saudi Arabia. South Africa had prepared for an oil embargo by stockpiling oil, converting coal into oil and diversifying its energy sources. Its shortage of water led to development of the Cabora Bassa, Cunene and Ox-Box schemes in Mozambique, Angola and Lesotho respectively, to supply both power and irrigation.

Despite South Africa's massive stockpile and the supply of unsuitable Cabinda oil, a decline in oil threatened the development of the regional economy. Although South Africa depends more on thermal power than most states its transport and chemical industries are particularly vulnerable. Iran supplies a significant proportion of South Africa's oil and is a partial owner of related chemical industries in the Republic.[25] The oil embargo also affects BLS and Malawi and there were indications that their supplies through South Africa were cut more drastically than imports into the region because of the Republic's control of most of the region's refining capacity. Diplomats from these black states have appealed for a lifting of the boycott and both Malawi and Botswana hope to import oil through Zambia as soon as hard-top roads are complete; political change in

Mozambique may help the supply situation in Malawi. A reduction in oil supplies will not only reduce the rate of growth in South Africa and hence generate problems of underemployment and decline in incomes; it also threatens South Africa's strategic position as its sophisticated arsenal of fighters, tanks and navy are all dependent on oil. But in bargaining for oil, and hence for its economic development and military security, South Africa still has its mineral reserves. In times of high inflation, in part caused by the high price of oil, South African gold and diamonds are in especially high demand. And its uranium is a vital ingredient in alternative energy supplies. Moreover, the links between France, Iran and South Africa in exchanging technology and capital for oil have reinforced South Africa's ability to buy oil from Iran. Also, multinational oil corporations have not lost all their power through the growth of nationalisation in the Arab states. They have manipulated oil flows to circumvent official embargoes against Holland and Southern Africa. Deliveries to South Africa have returned to pre-embargo levels but Rhodesia's supply now comes through the Republic, rather than from the Sonarep refinery in Lourenco Marques. The cost of the embargo to the Arab states was minimal given the high price of oil, but manipulation by the multinationals has eroded its impact. South Africa re-exports a third of its oil imports, mainly for aircraft refueling and for ship's stores. Even when the Suez Canal reopens, the Cape Route will remain important for supertankers and container ships; western economic interests encourage a regular flow of crude to the region. The frequency of tanker traffic past oil refineries in South Africa indicates the problems of effectively monitoring oil sanctions until multinational control of distribution is reduced.

One alternative source of energy, with profound military implications, is nuclear power. South Africa and South West Africa have significant uranium reserves and the South African Atomic Energy Board has developed its own, relatively inexpensive, uranium enrichment process at its Pelindaba research complex. Its first research reactor, Safari 1, went critical in 1965 and South Africa has offered to share its enrichment technology with the world on appropriate terms. Its nuclear capacity was developed initially in cooperation with Britain and America; their Combined Development Agency allowed South Africa to mine, process and sell uranium from 1952. Apart from the provision of technology and buying the output, Britain and the United States financed the whole programme which in its first twenty years added R1,000 million to South Africa's national income. In 1969 sales agreements were extended to West Germany, Japan and Switzerland. In 1970, the Nuclear Fuels Corporation of South Africa (NUFCOR) announced that it was now able to process and sell enriched uranium from its pilot plant; in 1973 it decide to build a R500 million full-scale prototype plant. South Africa's enrichment technology has been developed in association with West Germany and 50% of the uranium to be processed comes from the Rossing uranium mine in Namibia. South Africa needs western technology and markets to develop nuclear power capability. It is to build its first nuclear power station, the Koeberg A, near Cape Town and has invited tenders for its construction; it is likely that a French consortium will build the power station, although South Africa uses West European and not French techniques to enrich uranium. South Africa is short of energy and most of its nuclear research has gone into peaceful, rather than military, uses. Power from the nuclear Cape Town generator will be fed into the ESCOM system. Plans for a second nuclear station are in process. Nuclear power will permit continued industrial growth and increase South Africa's self-sufficiency in energy.[26]

South Africa has the capacity to develop nuclear weapons from this nuclear industry. However, such nuclear capability might be counter-productive in terms of the guerrila threat and the displeasure of the African and global community. South Africa's concern for respectability and contact with the western alliance may deter the development of such weapons; conversely, rejection by NATO states might lead to less rational policies and to its own unilateral action against the alleged communist threat to the Cape Route. A collapse of the nuclear nonproliferation system may encourage the development of an independent deterrent by South Africa as one symbol of its aspirations to middle power status.[27] But it depends on western technology both for uranium enrichment, nuclear capacity, and delivery systems; the cooperativeness of NATO states would depend on a range of factors, including the security situation in Southern Africa and the development of western links with Black Africa. South Africa might acquire a nuclear capability at the same time as it withdrew its forces from Zimbabwe and Namibia; defence in the *laager* might be more credible, at least to the white electorate, if it included a nuclear deterrent.

5. The Political Economy of Fragmentation: The Prospects for a Neocolonial Subsystem

The regional subsystem of Southern Africa may be transformed by either political change in each of its units or by the process of Bantustanisation. The coup in Portugal and the advent of a transitional FRELIMO government in Mozambique provides a test of resilience of regional linkages. Political change in Malagasy and Ghana undermined South Africa's 'outward-looking policy'. The end of colonial rule in Mozambique has brought new problems and prospects not only for South Africa and Rhodesia but also for Malawi and Swaziland. A socialist government in Mozambique challenges not only white rule but also capitalist black regimes. However, the interim Chissano cabinet in Lourenco Marques operates under certain constraints - the need for foreign exchange by providing transit and port facilities, the desire to keep white artisans and capital in Mozambique, and the tradition of labour export to South Africa. The transitional government is likely to be selective in its response to this inheritance of ties with the region and impose sanctions on Rhodesia while continuing the development of Cabora Bassa Dam. The readiness of Southern African entrepreneurs to cooperate with the new government (with the notable exception of the ubiquitous Jorge Jadim) suggests that they adopt a pragmatic response to political change. Anglo-American, the main shareholders in the ZAMCO consortium, has experience of working with black governments in Zambia and Botswana, Mauritania and Zaire. With a rearrangement of its impact, Cabora Bassa offers important development prospects for the new Mozambique; its power could be partially redirected away from the Transvaal. Clearly military cooperation between Portugal and South Africa will now be terminated, but economic exchange is likely to continue, depending on FRELIMO's response to the problems of finance, race and order in Mozambique.

The development of Bantustans in South Africa is a different rationalisation of the present subsystem. The designs for a "multi-national" state advance a "neocolonial" solution for the Republic's problems of inequalities based on the development of white industrial cores and black labour reserves. The attempt to relocate blacks without reducing South Africa's rate of growth is a function of technological advance. Access to nuclear, computer and communications advances permits some industries to reduce their labour intensities. Mining and agriculture may be least responsive to such change but the consumer and service sectors in South Africa are increasingly automated and capital-intensive. Industry is able, therefore, to maintain profitability despite black wage demands not only by inflation but also by reducing its work force. This process will lead not only to unemployment and underemployment in the Bantustans but also to a black labour aristocracy in the Republic. This may support the Bantustan leadership and so advance the fragmentation, but not the liberation, of South Africa.

South Africa's advocacy of regional integration has met with political resistance because of its apartheid structure. Moreover, the prospect of a regional defence of white supremacy is undermined by the advent of new governments in the ex-Portuguese territories. The political and strategic vulnerability of Rhodesia and Namibia, combined with demographic trends in the Republic, have led to advocacy of an essentially neocolonial solution to regional conflict. Multinational corporations advance not only liberal pay and job reservation policies in the Republic but also acceptance of black rule throughout the region outside South Africa. The experience of collaboration with ruling elites in black Africa has enhanced their confidence in parastatal arrangements. They might prefer partial state ownership with security to private ownership with insecurity. Continued guerrilla conflict will lead to declining profits and worsening race relations; protracted warfare reduces the prospects of cooperation between white capital and black government.

Political change in Portugal raises the prospect of a significant evolution of regional politics. South African hegemony cannot be maintained by military supremacy alone. Rather, its long-term interests may be best advanced by economic exchange. A withdrawal of South African troops from Zimbabwe and Namibia may encourage other forms of cooperation. The ability of the Republic to perpetuate its regional dominance by economic rather than military strategies increases its dependence on western technology and trade; its encouragement of, or permissiveness towards, formal decolonisation in the region may improve its external image and reduce foreign demands for change. The possibility of a switch from a military defence of the *laager* to disarming opposition by the logic of a regional economy may depend on the acceptability of such a strategy to the white electorate. However, the demise of dialogue suggests that South Africa's economic prospects would be advanced by political change; the structure of the region is less readily changed than any of the regimes in its parts. Separate development conflicts with economic growth; industrial decentralisation is a political choice of retarded growth but with social advantages for Afrikanerdom.[28] White affluence in Southern Africa might afford a reduced rate of growth in the interests of political survival. Moreover, South Africa's economic development requires markets for its manufactured goods and capital equipment. Regional military withdrawal might encourage regional integration and secure South Africa's regional economic hegemony. The dependence of other states in Southern Africa on South Africa might increase after rather than before liberation, and so perpetuate the interest of western states and corporations in the subsystem.

NOTES

* An earlier version of this paper was presented at the African Studies Association Conference, Chicago, November 1974. Support from Dalhousie University is gratefully acknowledged.

1. See Percy Selwyn "The Dual Economy Transcending National Frontiers: The Case of Industrial Development in Lesotho", Institute of Development Studies at the University of Sussex, March 1972, and Roger Leys "Lesotho: Non-development or Under-development - Towards an Analysis of the Political Economy of a Labour Reserve", Canadian Association of African Studies Conference, Halifax, February 1974.

2. See Robin Jenkins Exploitation: The World Power Structure and the Inequality of Nations (London: MacGibbon & Kee, 1970) 83-85, and Immanuel Wallerstein "Dependence in an Interdependent World: The Limited Possibilities of Transformation Within the Capitalist World Economy", African Studies Review 17(1), April 1974, 1-26.

3. On the prospects of 'Heterocentricity' and a 'Multi-tier Balance' Between Super- and Middle-powers, see George Liska States in Evolution: Changing Societies and Traditional Systems in World Politics (Baltimore: John Hopkins, 1973) especially 124-151.

4. See Marshal R. Singer Weak States in a World of Powers: The Dynamics of International Relationships (New York: Free Press, 1972) 41-44 only.

5. Stephen Hymer "The Multinational Corporation and the Law of Uneven Development" in Jagdish N. Bhagwati (ed.) Economics and World Order (New York: MacMillan, 1972) 114.

6. See Percy Selwyn "Core and Periphery: A Study of Industrial Development in the Small Countries of Southern Africa", Institute of Development Studies at the University of Sussex, November 1973. Discussion Paper Number 36.

7. For an application of Hymer's Model of Corporate Control in the Cases of Charter Consolidated and Anglo-American, see Nathan Shamuyarira "Interpenetration of the Southern African State System", IPSA Ninth World Congress, Montreal, August 1973.

8. See Jean-Jacques Servan-Schreiber The American Challenge (Harmondsworth: Pelican, 1969).

9. See Anglo American Corporation of South Africa 57th Annual Report 1973 (Johannesburg, 1974).

10. See Timothy M. Shaw "The Military Situation and the Future of Race Relations in Southern Africa" in Ali A. Mazrui and Hasu H. Patel (eds.) Africa in World Affairs: The Next Thirty Years (New York: Third Press, 1973) 37-61.

11. See Timothy M. Shaw "Review Article - Southern Africa: Cooperation and Conflict in an International Subsystem", Journal of Modern African Studies 12(4), December 1974, 633-655.

12. See Lynn Krieger Mytelka "The Salience of Gains in Third World Integrative Systems", World Politics 25(2), January 1973, 236-250.

13. See Chapter Three.

14. Ruth First, Jonathan Steele, Christobel Gurney The South African Connection: Western Investment in Apartheid (London: Temple Smith, 1972) 292.

15. See, for instance, Ian Mackler Pattern for Profit in Southern Africa (Lexington: Lexington, 1972).

16. See Ben Turok "The Gold Industry in the South African Economy", UN Unit on Apartheid Notes and Documents 26/74, September 1974.

17. See Timothy M. Shaw "Zambia: Dependence and Underdevelopment", University of Zambia Seminar, July 1974.

18. See Timothy M. Shaw "The International Subsystem of Southern Africa: Introduction" in Zdenek Cervenka (ed.) Landlocked Countries of Africa (Uppsala: Scandinavian Institute of African Studies, 1963) 161-164.

19. Cf. Adrian Guelke "Africa as a Market for South African Goods", Journal of Modern African Studies 12(1), March 1974, 69-88, and Robert Molteno Africa and South Africa (London: Africa Bureau, 1971).

20. Giovanni Arrighi and John S. Saul "Nationalism and Revolution in Sub-Saharan Africa" in their Essays on the Political Economy of Africa (New York: Monthly Review, 1973) 55.

21. See Arghiri Emmanuel "White Settler Colonialism and the Myth of Investment Imperialism", New Left Review 73, May/June 1972, 35-37.

22. See Kenneth Good "Settler Colonialism in Rhodesia", African Affairs 73 (290), January 1974, 22.

23. See Randall G. Stokes "The Afrikaner Industrial Enterpreneur and Afrikaner Nationalism", Economic Development and Cultural Change 22(4), July 1974, 557-579.

24. An invaluable source of data on companies and directors in South Africa is Beerman's Financial Yearbook of Southern Africa (Johannesburg: Combined Publishers, annual in two volumes).

25. See Barbara Rogers "Southern Africa and the Oil Embargo", Africa Today 21(2), Spring 1974, 3-8.

26. See "South Africa's Growing Nuclear Capacity and Potential" Africa Bureau Fact Sheet 39, October 1974.

27. See Chapter Seventeen by Spence [illegible] do Cassuto "Can Uranium Enrichment Enrich South Africa?". [illegible] World [illegible] 26(1), October 1970, 419-427.

28. See Ralph Horwitz [illegible] ical [illegible]onomy of Sou[illegible] Africa (London: Weidenfeld & Nicolson, 1967) [illegible] or Bell Industrial [illegible]tralisation in South Africa (Cape Town: OUP, [illegible]

4. Southern Africa in World Politics

Chapter Fifteen

PORTUGAL IN AFRICA: THE ECONOMICS OF THE DECLINE AND FALL

Zbigniew A. Konczacki

The Burden of History

After the establishment of the republic in Portugal in 1910 the attitude of the metropolitan government towards the colonies became more liberal. Angola and Mozambique pursued new development projects and began to borrow heavily during the decade of semi-autonomy which followed, resulting in serious trade deficits. The financial plight had to be remedied through considerable loans from the metropolitan government which, at that time, could ill-afford such assistance.

Political and economic difficulties within Portugal itself led to a coup in 1926. The dictatorship which emerged relied on the advice of Antonio de Oliveira Salazar who became first the Minister of Finance and in 1932 Prime Minister. The need for stringent economic policies forced the new government to cancel most of the autonomy enjoyed so far by the colonies. The Colonial Act of 1930 became a framework of the policy of the 'New State'.

It is not the intention of this paper to dwell on the ideology that lay behind that policy. However, a few explanatory remarks are necessary. Portugal's serious economic position, which was of her own making, deteriorated during the Great Depression and consequently no resources were available for economic development in Africa. A substitute was found readily in a vague, mystical idea of a 'mission'. This idea was based on the subconscious beliefs of the oldest European colonial power. To an average European or American, not to mention a modern African, that concept was so alien that few attempts have been made to interpret it. The new rulers of Portugal tried to create a colonial mentality out of the traditions of the golden age of Portuguese expansion, the heroic elements of Lusitanian overseas policy and the material realities of the present.[1] It was a source of pride to the Portuguese that their small nation ranked among the largest colonial powers.

The Constitution of 1933 embodied strong feelings regarding territorial integrity. Some thirty years earlier the inalienability of African possessions was hardly a dogma for some of the leading Portuguese statesmen. At that time many Portuguese doubted their country's ability to stay in Africa.[2] In 1891 Minister Ferreira d'Almeida went even so far as to propose in the Cortes that Mozambique and Goa be sold and the proceeds used to develop Angola.[3] This suggestion would have been anathema to a man like Salazar, who framed the Constitution of 1933, and in terms of which the State could not alienate any part of its colonial lands. The Portuguese controlled territories in Africa and Asia ceased to be regarded as colonies and were granted a status of provinces subject to direct rule from the central government.

There is no point in trying to analyse the question whether members of the now defunct government genuinely believed in Portugal's special mission in Africa or whether the concept was merely a smoke screen for other policy goals that were never officially disclosed.[4] What is striking, however, is the obvious discrepancy between the declared ideology of action and the actual results of it.

Internal pressures and foreign criticisms led to policy re-evaluations. In James Duffy's words, the Angolan uprising which started in 1961 meant 'the death of the dream',[5] and since then the reality became a nightmare. Under these conditions revisions of the old legislation became inevitable. Adriano Moreira, who was appointed Minister for Overseas Affairs in 1961, carried out these revisions which aimed at administrative and economic decentralisation. Realising that the policy of assimilation was a failure the government abolished the native statute thereby ending the legal distinction between 'natives' and 'assimilados'. A free movement of goods among the various national territories was to be permitted. In 1962 Moreira was dismissed due to strong opposition from within the government. His reformist policies, challenging the old order, failed as under the existing dictatorial system their implementation was an impossibility. The new legal status of Africans remained a dead letter of the law.[6]

It seems now highly anachronistic, that throughout the 1960s right up to mid-1970s Portugal held on to her African territories while the other colonial powers divested themselves of theirs.

Salazar gave reasons for this policy in his speech 'The decision to stay', delivered in 1966.[7] 'The African peoples' he said 'sought to de-colonise themselves either by liberally receiving their independence from the nations that held sovereignty over them, or by claiming it until they got it', and he pointed out that in reality due to conditions existing in most African territories neo-colonialism merely replaced colonialism.

In Salazar's mind there seemed to be no other alternative. Consequently it was better for Portugal to continue its presence in Africa as the latter could only benefit through the Portuguese civilising mission within the framework of the multi-racial approach.[8]

Marxists of all denominations were ready to agree with Salazar that the only alternative to colonialism was neo-colonialism, but in contrast to the dictator and his followers they could not agree with the conclusions that he drew from this assertion. Apart from being a politician Salazar was also an economist. He began his career as a professor of political economy at Coimbra and no matter how outmoded his economics may have been, he certainly took economic factors into account when he decided to keep Portugal in Africa as a fully-fledged colonial power.

The Rationale of Portuguese Colonialism

An analysis has now to be made of the economic factors governing the relations of Portugal and her African possessions Angola and Mozambique. Although economic factors were of great importance political considerations cannot be minimised or overlooked. But they are outside of the scope of this paper.

The historical patterns of the economic development of Portugal and her colonies and the resulting structural characteristics indicate quite clearly that the relationship between these economies was not typically colonial in the accepted sense. It differed significantly from the mature colonialism evolved by Britain, France, and even Belgium. Mature colonialism possesses three distinctive features which relate to trade, capital investment and labour relations.

With regard to trade generally two features emerge: firstly, in a given colony's foreign trade imports from and exports to the mother country predominate; secondly, imports consist mainly of manufactures and capital goods and exports chiefly of raw materials the demand for which is often inelastic. The conditions of dependence are usually strengthened by various institutions controlling the exchange. Their activities center on production, marketing, transportation and finance. Monopolistic or oligopolistic market structures are often created. Most of these characteristics of external trade are likely to continue after political independence is achieved.

Capital investment in a colony is, as a rule, determined by the trading interests of the mother country. Investment funds originate primarily in the metropole and are used to finance productive activities which concentrate in the industrial enclaves producing for export. Output of such enclaves seldom includes manufactured commodities. [illegible] capital investment is mostly in the hands of large companies whose activities are spread over a number of different countries. Frequently they form interlocking groups. The degree of dependence created by this form of investment is related to the proportion of the economy subject to the continuing control of the investor.

Independent countries defend themselves against exploitation by foreign capital by nationalising the expatriate assets. The real issue at stake is not the ownership of the assets but the control over them. In the context of a neo-colonial relationship foreign control is likely to continue for a considerable time. The shortage of local managerial and technical skills makes the reliance on foreign assistance inevitable even if the expatriate assets are nationalized. Hence the new type of dependence assumes the form of 'technological' dependence based on 'intellectual' imports. It often overlaps with particular forms of trade or direct investment dependence but it may be present even when other forms of dependence are relatively low.[9]

Native labour is exploited in a more subtle way. Labour market is determined, among other things, by some inherited factors beyond the control of the legal system. Low wages (in a relative sense) are not only a reflection of low productivity but also of prevalently monopsonistic powers by employers. There is usually an ample supply of labour which far exceeds the demand. Low productivity is mainly the result of the lack of training and this, in turn, is largely due to discrimination. As a rule, skilled jobs are reserved for the people from the mother country.

Metropolitan countries which were in the stage of mature colonialism viewed the transition to neo-colonialism without apprehension. A crude cost-benefit analysis, based on both economic and political data, indicated that the future gains would exceed losses. This relationship is typical of the economically more developed countries, on the one hand, and the less developed ones, on the other. Portugal did not fit that mould. Till recently she displayed numerous characteristics of a less developed economy vis-a-vis her underdeveloped colonies and, to this day, she remains one of the least developed countries of Europe. Her own position in the world economy determined the manner in which she exploited her colonial territories.

Let us consider the most essential features of Portugal's underdeveloped economy. Portugal still has a relatively low per capita income, placing her merely on the threshold of the more developed world. In 1970 with U.S. $660 per annum, she was ahead of only two countries in Europe: Yugoslavia and Albania. Furthermore, Portugal's income distribution is far more uneven than that of many European countries. This is not an unequivocal indicator of lagging development,[11] but it gives some support to the hypothesis that the Portuguese colonial policy was dominated by the vested interests of the powerful upper income group. It was achieved at the expense of a large segment of low-income population.

A study of income distribution in selected fourteen European countries, in the early 1950s, carried out by Professor S. Kuznets, shows that Portugal's income distribution was far more unequal than was the case of most other countries dealt with in the survey.[12]

The proportion of economically active population in agriculture tends to be high in the less developed countries and in the case of Portugal it is one of the highest in western Europe. In terms of percentages Portugal's economically active population in agriculture was 43.9 per cent in 1959, 33.6 per cent in 1965, and 27.6 per cent in 1972. Comparable percentages for 1972 for Germany, Canada, the U.S.A. and the U.K. were 7.5, 6.9, 4.2 and 3.1 respectively.[13]

Agriculture's contribution to Gross Domestic Product in 1960, 1965 and 1971 amounted to 23.4, 19.4 and 15.0 per cent respectively.[14] This shows that in mid-1960s roughly one-third of the economically active population was needed in the agricultural sector to produce about one-fifth of the GDP. As the result of primitive agricultural methods and low productivity of labour in that sector Portugal was forced to import substantial quantities of foodstuffs.

The relative underdevelopment of Portuguese economy is also revealed in her relationship with England showing a classic example of semi-colonial dependence.[15] This commercial dependence began in the seventeenth century and the Methuen Treaty, concluded with Britain in 1703, had far-reaching consequences. During the nineteenth century Portugal failed to create an industrial economy and was unable to establish a complementarity between the metropole and her colonies in the absence of exportable manufactures and capital for overseas investment.[16] Since the middle of the nineteenth century a rapidly growing external debt was a striking feature of Portuguese dependence. In recent years Portugal continued to rely heavily on foreign sources of capital and her external trade consisted largely of imports of manufactures and exports of primary products. Her commercial relations continue to be dominated by Great Britain.

Being herself economically dependent on other countries Portugal exerted an even more direct control over her overseas territories. A more thorough study of the economic aspects of Portugal's colonialism was seriously thwarted by the paucity of information. Probably only a fraction of the data known to the previous regime was made available to the public. Even these statistics were edited and presented in such a way that no meaningful conclusions could be arrived at on their basis. The tendency to camouflage goes back to the 1930s, when all goods brought to Africa on Portuguese ships were listed as Portuguese exports, irrespective of place of their manufacutre. Since such imports were subject to comparatively low customs duties, foreign exports were encouraged to trans-ship them via Lisbon.

The existence of the escudo zone payments system offered another opportunity to camouflage the true financial picture. This zone covered both Portugal and her overseas territories making it difficult to distinguish between the separate monetary flows. One could cite many more such instances.

Some light must now be thrown on the crucial elements of Portugal's colonial relationship with her African possessions in the fields of trade, capital investment and labour.

Trade Relations

Portugal's position in the overseas trade of Angola and Mozambique was predominant.

Table 1

Angola and Mozambique: Percentage of Trade Accounted for by Portugal, 1938-1970

Year	Imports (C.I.F.)		Exports (F.O.B.)	
	Angola	Mozambique	Angola	Mozambique
1938	41	20	43	41
1948	47	29	24	39
1955	47	29	22	44
1960	47	28	24	48
1965	39	36	35	37
1970	35	28	34	38

Source: United Nations *Yearbooks of International Trade Statistics.*

Table 1 indicates that in 1938 roughly two-fifths of Angola's imports came from Portugal and a similar proportion of her exports was absorbed by the metropolitan market. In the case of Mozambique the corresponding proportions were about one-fifth and two-fifths respectively. The proportion of imports from Portugal rose considerably during the war years, as most other trade outlets were blocked. In 1943 it reached nearly three-quarters of Angola's total import value.[17] In the post-war years, Angola's imports from Portugal continued to be proportionately higher than her exports to the metropole. The opposite trend was discernible in the case of Mozambique. In 1970 Portugal's position in the trade of Angola and Mozambique was still predominant. In the same year Angola's total imports from the metropole were in the region of 35 per cent and her exports amounted to 34 per cent. In the case of Mozambique the percentages were 28 and 38 respectively.

Exports from Portugal to her African territories included a large proportion of re-exports of manufactures and capital equipment from other countries. The origin of these goods was disguised by official statistics. Consequently the foreign trade pattern could not be considered as typical of a more developed country which would be in a position to produce most of these exports.

On the other hand, neither Angola nor Mozambique held a predominant position in Portugal's distribution of trade. (see Table 2)

Table 2

Portugal: Percentage of Trade Accounted for by Angola and Mozambique, 1938-1970

Year	Imports (C.I.F.)		Exports (F.O.B.)	
	Angola	Mozambique	Angola	Mozambique
1938	4.9	3.3	5.4	5.0
1948	2.6	4.4	11.7	10.1
1955	5.6	7.4	13.3	7.4
1960	5.4	7.0	13.1	8.9
1965	7.7	5.0	14.1	8.8
1970	9.6	4.2	12.5	9.0

Source: United Nations *Yearbooks of International Trade Statistics*.

Prior to the war the Portuguese imports from and exports to the two African territories were even less significant than they were in more recent years. In 1938 Angola and Mozambique accounted for only 8.2 per cent of the total value of Portugal's imports and 10.4 per cent of her exports, whereas in 1970 the corresponding percentages were 13.8 and 21.5.

If a distinction is made between the two African territories it would become apparent that in the 1960s the percentage of Portuguese imports accounted for by Angola showed a rising trend and in the case of Mozambique a falling trend. On the other hand, throughout the period under review, the proportion of exports from both territories was far more stable.

It can be assumed that trade transactions have been used by the metropolitan country to exploit her privileged position. This is known to have happened in the case of rough diamonds imported from Angola and in the case of sugar from Mozambique. But the total effect on the Portuguese economy of the subsidies hidden in such transactions, was limited by the insignificant proportion which the colonial trade occupied in the total value of Portugal's foreign trade.

Capital Investment

Substantial foreign investment helped neo-colonialism. Portugal's position in Africa differed from that of the other colonial powers. Portuguese territories in Africa were always grossly undercapitalised and a considerable proportion of investment was made by foreign countries.

Professor S.H. Frankel estimated in 1936 that a large part of capital invested in the Portuguese colonies was supplied by the British investors.[18] For example, the Benguela Railway, completed in 1936-37 was largely built with British capital with some participation of German and Portuguese investors. This railroad was intended to serve the copper belts of the then Belgian Congo and Northern Rhodesia. Another early example of foreign investment based on the British and French capital was the Mozambique Company, active in the districts of Manica and Sofala.[19]

Prior to the second World War the Portuguese methods of stimulating exports from the metropole to the colonies were in direct conflict with the industrial development of the latter. For many years Portugal's economic policy was overly mercantilist. For example a regulation of 1936 prohibited the existence of identical industries in the metropole and in the colonies. This led to a paradoxical situation. Angola, which at that time was producing considerable quantities of wheat, had to export her grain to Portugal and to import wheat flour. She was prevented from operating flour mills. Mercantilism was practised, in its various forms, until recently.

It is still true that Angola and Mozambique are largely undercapitalised and that a considerable proportion of investment capital is of foreign origin. Today, in addition to the British investments a considerable amount of capital comes from the U.S.A., South Africa and some European countries.

Prior to 1962 Portuguese government was suspicious of and opposed to foreign investment. The change in policy was prompted by the heavy costs of counterinsurgency which Portugal had to bear. At the same time Portugal was experiencing a deterioration in the long-standing pattern of trade deficits with countries outside the escudo zone. Added to that she experienced a serious lag in productive capacity of her economy.[20] In 1964-65 investment laws were modified in order to create conditions favourable to foreign investors.[21] Foreign firms were allowed to transfer full profits abroad, whereas Portuguese firms could only remit one-fifth of their profits to the mother country. Soon the results became visible. Foreign capital investment rose from 10.5 per cent in 1962 to 26.7 per cent in 1966 of the total annual investment in Portugal alone. In 1969 out of 1.8 billion escudos invested in the escudo zone by foreign firms 60 per cent of that amount went to the colonial territories.[22]

The Gulf Oil Corporation is the best example of massive American investment. Gulf Oil developed a major new field in Cabinda with a capital of some $150 to $250 million. Other American investors moved into extractive, capital-intensive exploitation of Angolan diamonds, sulphur and phosphates.[23]

On the other hand, American capital stayed out of the huge Cabora Bassa Dam project in Mozambique which is financed by the West German, French, British and South African investors. There is also a very sizeable South African investment in the Kunene River Development project on the border of Angola and Namibia.[24]

As a result of the national emergency Portugal was forced to accept foreign neo-colonialism in the form of heavy capital investments not only in the metropole itself but also within the borders of her African possessions. It is clear that the foreign capitalist is the main beneficiary of this neo-colonialism as he is in a better position to survive the surgery of independence. Portugal has to pay a price for her state of relative economic underdevelopment.

The Question of Labour

One of the pillars of the Portuguese colonial system was the exploitation of labour. Portugal relied partly on the direct method of forced labour, and partly on the indirect method of taxation in order to obtain supply of cheap labour. The most effective means, in the latter case, was the collection of the head tax in Angola, and the hut tax in Mozambique.[25]

Forced labour was used to provide manpower to plantation owners. A circular letter issued by the Governor of Angola in 1921 recommended that at least 15 per cent of men perform work on plantations. The employers had to pay contractual wages.

Although the other colonial powers abandoned widespread use of forced labour, Portugal continued to take advantage of this form of modern slavery. The Forced Labour Convention of 1930 was ratified by Portugal only in 1956. But even then the Portuguese legislation preserved certain provisos which in fact violate the terms of the Convention. Forced labour was allowed to be used in both governmental and municipal public works.[26]

In 1954, in the Department of Native Affairs in Luanda(Angola) the number of 'contract labourers' was 379,000. A labourer had to work for three to four months each year for the colonial administration.[27]

The existing legislation did not permit private employers to use forced labour. In practice, the authorities often went beyond these legal limits. Compulsory cultivation schemes of cotton and castor oil plants served as a pretext to use this kind of labour. These schemes were undertaken by European planters who held concessions from the government.[28]

The institution of forced labour had a great impact on the African. It meant a separation from his family as well as a certain stigma. Consequently the acceptance of low wage rates offered by private employers was preferable. It is, therefore, wrong to presume that these workers responded to the normal economic incentives; they were rather victims of reckless recruiters.[29]

In the post-war years the practice of recruitment was still widespread. Restrictions were placed on the movements of the Africans who could not leave the areas of their domicile unless they concluded a contract of service through a recruiter. In Angola these restrictions were in operation till the end of 1956. In Mozambique recruiting was done on a large scale to satisfy the South African and Rhodesian demand for labour.[30]

The system, as outlined above, permitted widespread exploitation of labour giving rise to either additional tax revenue accruing to the government through the extensive use of forced labour,[31] or to abnormal profit rates in the case of private entrepreneurs through the various forms of illegal employment.

Recent Developments

Until fairly recently Portugal and her colonies created the impression of a closed system, impervious to the impact of the 'winds of change' blowing from outside with an increasing force. But this image of colonial exploitation of underdeveloped Angola and Mozambique by their economically and politically backward 'master' had to change drastically when the liberation wars started. The acceleration of economic growth in the African territories in the 1960s can be attributed to a number of factors. By far the most important were major mineral discoveries in Angola which by the mid-1960s began to contribute greatly to the Angolan economy. Needless to say, the opportunities created by these discoveries, coupled with the new investment laws, encouraged the inflow of capital on an unprecedented scale.

Under the impact of the unleashed economic forces some of the most anachronistic mercantilist restrictions had to be modified, a move which formed part of Moreira's reforms initiated in 1961. Angola and Mozambique were permitted to industrialise even in the areas where Portugal herself was developing, namely in the fields of light engineering, textile, clothing and footwear industries.

In the post-World War II years Portugal encouraged a policy of assimilation in her African possessions, the failure of which provoked criticisms from abroad. Portugal decided, instead, on a new policy of intensified colonisation of white settlers from the mother country. Due to this policy, by 1970, the permanently settled white population of Angola reached the mark of 350,000, while total population of the Africans was over 5 million.[32] In Mozambique the ratio between the whites and the blacks was 150,000 to 8 million.

All these events, involving resource discoveries, influx of capital, and immigration, point to an unprecedented acceleration of the development process in the African territories with Angola in the forefront. Between 1969 and 1972 Angola's industrial production doubled, rising from just over 6,000 million to 12,000 million escudos.[33]

In Portugal, meanwhile, priority was given to war effort and the development in Africa.

In the late 1960s the cost of defence and security reached 45 per cent of total government expenditure or 9 per cent of national income.[34] The need for new sources of revenue led to substantial tax increases and heavy reliance on foreign credit: Portugal's foreign debt rose from 1,839 million escudos in 1961 to 8,665 million escudos in 1969.[35]

Another factor which adversely affected the economy was an increase in emigration. Yearly over 170,000 migrants were leaving for France, Holland, Belgium, Switzerland, West Germany etc., in search of employment.[36] Thousands of families emigrated not only to escape poverty but also to protect their sons from a lengthy military service.[37]

A prolonged war was fought at the expense of the nation's social services, development and the depopulation of the country which already had a low natural rate of population growth.

Even General Spinola, whose book Portugal and the Future was published in February 1974, expressed fear that Portuguese dictatorship and its policies propelled the nation towards inevitable disaster.[38]

Conclusions

There are few people in today's Portugal who do not agree that the country was bled white for the sake of colonial interests. The general feeling is that the ruling group failed to redistribute economic gains more equitably and to improve the welfare of the people both in the metropole and in Africa. In light of recent events it is becoming more and more apparent to all that Portugal's African possessions were not profitable to the nation as a whole.[39] Gains from African territories benefited merely fractional interests such as businessmen and settlers. Ending the wars and granting independence to the colonies became a logical necessity. Even if a complete economic break with the African territories takes place the long term benefits will outweigh the losses. The diversion of material and human resources from the war effort to the development of the domestic economy will now become possible. On the other hand, Angola and Mozambique will undoubtedly avail themselves of international aid from which they were previously excluded.

Portugal's prolonged colonial presence in Africa served merely the fractional interests. The nation itself was a pawn in the hands of the dictatorial regime which identified its own interests with those of the small group of exploiters.

This situation explains Portugal's reluctance to relinquish her African territories. Having never reached the stage of a 'mature colonial power' she was unable to adopt a more sophisticated neo-colonial method of economic and political control over the 'liberated' territories. This anachronistic approach could not continue indefinitely. The untenable position in which the regime found itself, hastened its demise in April 1974. What may have appeared rational to the ruling elite became obviously irrational in the eyes of the majority of the nation.

Notes

1. James Duffy Portuguese Africa (Cambridge, Mass.: Harvard University Press, 1961) 270.

2. R.J. Hammond Portugal and Africa 1815-1910 (Stanford, Calif.: Stanford University Press, 1966) 202.

3. Ibid., 185.

4. It is possible that a large fraction of the Portuguese society genuinely believed in that 'myth'.

5. James Duffy Portugal in Africa (Harmondsworth, Middlesex: Penguin Books Ltd., 1962) 210.

6. R.H. Chilcote Portuguese Africa (Englewood Cliffs, N.J.: Prentice-Hall, Inc., 1967) 17-18.

7. Antonio de Oliveira Salazar The Decision to Stay (Lisbon: Secretariado Nacional da Informacao, 1966).

8. Ibid.

9. W. Minter Imperial Network and External Dependency: The Case of Angola (Beverly Hills/London: Sage Publications, 1972) 21.

10. World Bank Atlas, 1972.

11. Professor Kuznets' opinion that the size distribution of income remains more unequal in the less developed than in the more developed countries has been challenged but not convincingly refuted. (See: S. Kuznets Modern Economic Growth, London: Yale University Press, 1966, 424-25). Kuznets' hypothesis has been based on overall measures of inequality but a recent analysis of the trends in the income shares of the different deciles seems to put in doubt the evidence provided by overall coefficients.(See: P. Roberti "Income Distribution: A Time-Series and a Cross-Section Study" The Economic Journal 84/335/ September 1974, 629-35).

12. The overall measures used by Kuznets include a measure of inequality and concentration ratio . (See: S. Kuznets 'Quantitative Aspects of the Economic Growth of Nations: VIII Distribution of Income by Size' Economic Development and Cultural Change 11/2/, Part II, 1963).

13. OECD Labour Force Statistics 1961-1972 (Paris, 1974).

14. OECD National Accounts Statistics 1960-1971.

15. W. Minter op.cit., 6.

16. J. O'Brian 'Portugal in Africa: A Dying Imperialism' Monthly Review May 1974, 21.

17. The war period data is excluded from the tables as being abnormal.

18. S.H. Frankel Capital Investment in Africa (London: Oxford University Press, 1938) 204.

19. Portugal held only ten per cent of the shares. The Company's charter expired in 1942.

20. M.A. El-Khawas 'Foreign Economic Involvement in Angola and Mozambique' Issue 4(2), Summer 1974, 21.

21. J.A. Marcum Portugal and Africa: The Politics of Indifference (Syracuse: Syracuse University, 1972) 10.

22. Eduardo de Sousa Ferreira Portuguese Colonialism from South Africa to Europe (Freiburg: Aktion Dritte Welt, 1972) 55.

23. J.A. Marcum op.cit., 10-11.

24. Ibid., 36-37.

25. The imposition of a tax creates a need for money income which has to be earned.

26. International Labour Office African Labour Survey (Geneva, 1962) 299-300.

27. Americo Boavida Angola: Five centuries of Portuguese exploitation (Richmond, B.C.: LSM Information Center, 1972) 50.

28. ILO op.cit., 300.

29. J. O'Brian loc. cit., 28.

30. ILO op.cit., 312-13.

31. The obligation to supply personal services in the form of labour can be considered as a tax.

32. Sources of information on the size of the white population of Angola are not consistent. The figure varies from 350,000 to 500,000.

33. Colin Legum Africa Contemporary Record (London: Rex Collings, 1973) B480.

34. Africa South of the Sahara (London: Europa Publications Ltd., 1974) 139.

35. Eduardo de Sousa Ferreira op.cit., 51.

36. J.A. Marcum op.cit., 36.

37. 'Change in Portugal' The Economist May 4, 1974, 35.

38. Ibid.

39. An analysis based on Portugal's Balance of Payments Statements with the African territories in recent years shows that the total surplus of the metropole ranged between 1 and 3 per cent of national income, an insignificant proportion if compared with the magnitude of the metropolitan war expenditure alone.

Chapter Sixteen

THE EFFECT OF EXTERNAL PRESSURE ON BRITISH FIRMS INVESTING IN SOUTH AFRICA[1]

Charles Harvey

1. Introduction

This paper is mainly an analysis of recent efforts in the UK to get British firms to raise the wages of their black employees in South Africa. A number of firms have been subject to public pressure for some years, but mainly from the withdrawal lobby so that any raising of black wages which may have taken place before, say, 1973, was as a justification for not withdrawing rather than in response to pressure on wages as such. The selection of firms for this type of pressure was rather arbitrary - for example Barclays Bank received a great deal of attention and Standard Bank almost none, probably because Barclays has a network of branches in the UK whereas Standard does not. In any case, the number of firms subject to pressure was very small.

In late 1972 and early 1973 a number of events took place which had an influence on black wages. Firstly, a large number of strikes by black workers took place in Durban.[2] Secondly, in March 1973 the Guardian published as a front page lead story the findings of a reporter that British firms were paying "starvation wages".[3] The matter was taken up by other newspapers and by the House of Commons and, despite the pressure coming mainly from Labour members on a Conservative government, the Trade and Industry Sub-Committee of the Expenditure Committee (under a Labour chairman) began an enquiry in May.[4]

It is a little difficult at first to explain why the Guardian's "revelations" should have caused such a stir. The basic facts were well enough known to anyone making even a very short study of the subject. The average wage for Africans in manufacturing in 1972 was R60 per month. Poverty Datum Line (PDL) estimates varied from one area of the country to another but were invariably above R70, and over R80 per month in the biggest industrial area, centred on Johannesburg. There was no indication that British firms were paying better wages than South African or other foreign firms. It was therefore simple to deduce that British firms were paying most of their workers below the PDL and some of them (those below the average wage very substantially below the PDL.[5] Probably the Guardian caused such a stir because the article was run as a news story on the front page, rather than as a feature article on an inside page, and because it named well known names.[6] In addition there was no particularly striking rival news story that day. Nevertheless, even when this acknowledgement has been made to a brilliant piece of publicity, it is also probably true that in some mysterious way the timing was precisely right in a broader sense - come the hour, come the right story.

Before examining the impact of the Guardian publicity and the Parliamentary enquiry, and their longer term implications, it is worth looking quickly at the situation before these events, to see what possible reasons firms had at that time for paying more than the going rate for their black labour, and what effect it had on their operations.

2. The Pre-Enquiry Situation

There are a number of reasons why a firm might find it easy to pay high wages to black workers. Most obviously, if black wages are a small proportion of total costs, increasing them has a commensurately small effect on costs. So firms using very capital intensive techniques, with very low total (black and white) labour costs, and firms with a low black to white labour ratio (even if labour intensive) might be expected to be less unwilling to raise black wages. There would be no particular reason for them to do so, however, even if the cost were small, in normal circumstances.

My own research into this subject[7] was completed just before the Guardian revelations (and before the Durban strikes had affected any of the sample firms) and so is able to throw some light on the subject. My sample consisted of 11 firms who had agreed in the UK to co-operate to the extent of answering questions in London and in South Africa. The sample was of course biased by the very fact that the firms had agreed to co-operate; the sole advantage of this bias was that the sample probably contained a disproportionate number of firms which thought they had a good record in South Africa - this enabled the research to discover rather more about the "better" firms than would have been possible from a random sample.

Of the firms for which it was relatively cheap to pay more than the going rate to black workers, only those which had been subject to public attack in the UK were in fact doing so. Others were not. It thus appears that it is relatively easy to push firms into paying better wages if it is not going to raise their costs significantly; equally, firms will not pay higher wages if they escape publicity.

More interesting were the four firms with a high ratio of black to white workers and above average wage rates for blacks. One of these was exceptionally profitable and had received some publicity in the UK; two had important (and concentrate interests in raw materials in black Africa and sufficiently dominant marketing positions in South Africa to be able to afford higher wages; the fourth of these firms had brought in better management to raise productivity and wages had gone up as well.

What was also clear from the sample (and from the information provided later by the parliamentary enquiry) was that firms for whom it was not cheap to raise black wages would not necessarily do so as a result of pressure.

Firms that had increased wages for "external" reasons had found that productivity increased, or expected it to do so. The principal reasons for this were reduced labour turnover and improved management - as one manager put it, the firm stopped treating its black workforce as an undifferentiated black mass of unskilled units. Productivity is further discussed in section 5 below.

Table 1

Salaries and Wages: Non-Agricultural Sectors Only

Year Ended 30 June	Whites: Increases in current prices	Whites: Increases in constant prices	Non-Whites: Increases in current prices	Non-Whites: Increases in constant prices
1971	+12.2	+7.3	+14.7	+ 9.8
1972	+ 8.7	+2.1	+ 9.1	+ 2.5
1973	+ 7.6	-0.5	+11.1	+ 2.7
1974	+10.8	+1.1	+21.0	+10.4

* to end-March 1974 compared with end-March 197[illegible]

Source: [illegible]uth African Reserve Bank, Annual Rep[illegible] [illegible]974

3. The Effects of Publicity

Strictly speaking, it is not possible to distinguish between the wage rises that would have occurred anyway and those that were induced by publicity in the UK. In particular, the strikes in Durban in late 1972 and early 1973 not only had an important effect on the firms involved, but also caused other firms to raise wages in order to prevent trouble and, no doubt, in order to maintain a competitive position in the labour market.

Furthermore, black wages in South Africa were beginning to rise faster than white wages, before any of the events which are discussed here took place, as is shown in Table 1.

Because black wages are so much lower than white, the absolute increases in white wages are still higher than those in black wages; nevertheless, there has been a definite change in the trend since 1970 - in the previous five years the ratio of white to black wages increased.

The publicity in the UK following the Guardian articles and during the Sub-Committee enquiry, occurred, therefore, against a background of black wages rising faster than for some time and of an unprecedented series of strikes. Nevertheless, the rises that occurred immediately before the Sub-Committee enquiry (or were promised for the near future) were so large, and so precisely timed, that they must have been caused at least partially, and in many cases wholly, by the enquiry itself. Thus company after company came to the enquiry armed with memoranda showing (as they thought) that they were paying their workers above PDL levels - but also showing that they had granted increases, in some cases very large increases, in March and April. Thus of the 32 firms giving oral evidence, no less than 25 are listed in the Report as having given recent increases.[8]

This series of wage increases was in itself a fairly remarkable result of the institution of the enquiry, even before the Sub-Committee produced its report. It also demonstrated the power of information. Whereas it had taken a private researcher (myself) a year to extract information from a biased sample of 11 firms, parliament, backed by the implied threat of subpoena (which is available to parliamentary committees), was able to extract evidence from some 140 firms in a matter of weeks, with a more or less 100% response - and to subject the senior executives of 32 of them to public questioning. This degree of public exposure - the Guardian devoted a full page to each day's hearings, and the other newspapers gave a fair amount of coverage as the household names appeared - had, for whatever reason, a quite different degree of impact to previous bouts of publicity.

Nevertheless, even among the firms called to give oral evidence, many workers were still below the PDL after the pre-enquiry increases. The basic attitude of many firms was revealed by their tendency to compare wages with inappropriate PDL's, to assume more than one wage-earner per family thus "permitting" the payment of less than the PDL to employees, to include holiday bonuses in average monthly wages[9], and to assume the working of quite substantial amounts of overtime in the earnings figures presented. A great deal of the Sub-Committee's questioning of company witnesses was taken up with such points and with trying to establish how many workers were still below the relevant PDL. From one point of view this seemed trivial when it was clear from aggregate figures that very few firms in South Africa paid average wages at or above the PDL, let alone minimum wages. From another point of view, it was precisely this concentration on one easily understood issue that had provided the impetus necessary to get the enquiry set up and for it to continue with such effect.

The Report lists 63 firms with some employees below the relevant PDLs (Tables 7.3 and 7.4). A summary of these by sector is given in Table 2.

Table 2

African Workers Paid Below the Relevant PDL in British Firms, 1973

Sector	No. of firms	No. of workers	% of labour force
Manufacturing	50	19,510	17.4
Construction	2	894	58.0
Mining	6	56,213	62.8
Agriculture	3	713	not meaningful
Commercial	5	655	6.1

Source: Evidence, passim, as analysed by Davies, op. cit., Table IV. Some firms appear in more than one sector.

Davies also compared the proportion of the labour force paid below the PDL with black to white labour ratios and capital employed per black worker, in the sectors shown in Table 2 and in subsectors of manufacturing. Broadly, the British firms confirmed the expectation that those for whom black wages were less important as a component of costs would pay better black wages. The two sectors which appear to pay better wages (i.e. fewer workers below the PDL) than would be expected from this argument were textiles and heavy engineering. Suggested reasons for this deviation are the strength of black unions in the textile industry and the fact that both sectors were particularly affected by strikes in early 1973.[10]

It thus seems likely that British firms are considerably influenced by the logic of the market even though, to me and to the Sub-Committee, there was a very considerable tendency to claim humanitarian reasons for paying higher wages. Put differently, resistance to external pressure on black wages depends not only on the character of the management, in the UK as well as in South Africa, but also on the cost of concessions.

4. Lasting Effects

It is clearly not likely that parliament will mount a major enquiry into the practices of British firms in South Africa at frequent intervals. Yet information of the type provided by the parliamentary enquiry is extremely expensive and difficult to obtain by private research and indeed may not in large part be obtainable at all. It is equally clear that information in this context gives a great deal of additional power to external pressure groups, although the impact of successive sets of "revelations" is likely to diminish over time.

The parliamentary Report included a recommendation "that companies be invited to submit reports on their practices and on progress concerning African wages and conditions".[11] This seemed at the time an extremely weak recommendation - more effective would have been a compulsory annual submission on the key issues to the relevant ministry (the Department of Trade and Industry, DTI). The subsequent election of a Labour government has meant some considerable tightening of this requirement. Although the government's request for information is still not mandatory, both the minister and his deputy have been reported as saying that if the information is not forthcoming it will be induced by legislation. In addition a First Secretary (Labour) has been appointed to the staff of the British Embassy in Pretoria - with, as the minister has pointed out in a letter to the relevant firms in the UK, the clear intention of discouraging firms from trying to provide inaccurate or misleading information.[12]

All this is a major change from the pre-enquiry situation when, as was made clear in the DTI's evidence, the government simply gave help to British investors (and exporters) in much the same way as elsewhere in the world. There was an ambiguous request that firms operating in South Africa "keep abreast of the best current standards of employment in South Africa" which DTI officials claimed they stressed in their "day-to-day contacts with firms".[13] It certainly had no perceptible effect on British practice as was shown by part of a survey conducted in 1972, at the request of the UK South Africa Trade Association (UKSATA) - British firms paid almost identical wages to those paid by South African firms.[14]

Several writers have pointed out that even if external pressure to raise wages can be sustained, a point on which it is easy to be sceptical, it is no substitute for proper bargaining through trade unions or their equivalent. It was perfectly clear from the parliamentary enquiry that British firms were on the whole even more reluctant on this issue than on wages. It may well be that the next major effort by external pressure groups should be on this issue, hoping no doubt that concentration of effort on a single important issue will be as effective (or more so) as the campaign on wages and absolute poverty levels.

The point to make here is a rather different one. The raising of wages in itself may increase the possibility of less unequal bargaining between management and black workers. Some of the effect of higher wages is to increase the productivity of the workers, reduce their rate of turnover, improve the quality of management applied to them and thus to increase the workers' bargaining strength. Put differently, the payment of higher wages sharply reduces the willingnes of management to contemplate the dismissal of workers in the event of a strike, as the extreme example, and increases the need for better communication between management and workers in a whole range of less dramatic circumstances.

Furthermore, it would appear that a breaking of the old pattern of very low wages, high turnover, extreme authoritarianism in management, etc., may create social and industrial unrest among workers. For example, there would seem to be some connection between rapid increases in mining wages and the series of incidents at mining locations in 1973 and 1974. At the very least, higher pay enables workers to contemplate striking without immediately going hungry, at the same time as it raises the possibility of even higher pay. It may also be relevant to this line of argument that the Natal Employers' Federation voted for "Trade Union rights" for workers before the Durban strikes,[15] but after African wages had begun to rise faster than for a long time.

The other lasting effect of the UK campaign on wages should be on the UK management of the companies involved. With the partial exception of the small number of managements which had already been in the public eye because of their involvement in South Africa, it is clear that a very great degree of ignorance existed and was allowed, by the absence of any pressure, to continue. It was clear to me, for example, in interviewing company executives in the UK, that in many cases the subject of South Africa was not of regular concern - ignorance both of facts and arguments was considerable, only the most superficial of rebuttals or justifications were available (as it were) in well-practised phrases.

The Sub-Committee hearings also revealed that the chairmen even of large and well-known companies were extremely ill-informed about South Africa and, in some cases, had swallowed whole the myths and misconceptions about Africans that they had heard from the white South African establishment. For example, the ICI gave his version of the backward-bending supply curve of labour thus: "... some of these men (meaning African employees) have a very low standard of comparison and so ... when they get above a certain earning they have no wish to go any higher and so maybe take the day off." He was interrupted by one of his fellow ICI witnesses who explained that in 1971 ICI (South Africa) had African employees fill in a questionnaire, with illiterates receiving help, to find out what they wanted most. "The answers were very clear: what they wanted most was more money and what they wanted second was more education for their children."[16]

The second example reveals how even those professionally involved with South Africa can continue to believe, or at least propagate, myths - even when the myths are themselves contradictory. Thus Mr. W. Luke, Chairman of UKSATA, managed to say within the same answer (while giving oral evidence), firstly that those living in the homeland areas "live on the land and do not starve", secondly that investment in the homelands must be allowed at less than PDL wages because otherwise: "Are we to send this man back and say we are not interested in investing in the Transkei at all, just go home? If we do, the answer to that one is starvation."[17] Mr. Luke revealed in many other ways his appalling attitude to Africans, yet he was the main institutional representative of British firms with interests in South Africa.

A third example demonstrates that visits to South Africa do not necessarily result in greater enlightment. The physical separation of the races in housing, and especially the migrant labour system which separates a worker from his family by hundreds of miles, make it difficult (and sometimes impossible) for any but the most determined enquirer to see the real effects of low wages. This does not prevent visitors to South Africa using very partial and prejudiced sources to bolster their beliefs; thus Lord Stokes (Chairman of British Leyland): "I go round our factories there a lot and one is well received by the coloured an. Bantu workers ...".[18] This nonsense should be compared with the extremely fun description of a visit by the chairman of Ford, from the worker's point of view in "Siswe Bansi is Dead".[19]

It is obviously possible that greater awareness among British bu en, of the issues involved in investing in South Africa, can lead to greater sophistication in meeting criticism, as well as to greater knowledge (which is presumably desirable) of South African working conditions. However, a principal argument of those advocating disengagement of British business from South Africa has been that a disengagement campaign "can make a major contribution towards raising the political consciousness of Western public opinion and that this will itself be an important contribution towards the struggle of the liberation movement in South Africa".[20] It would seem that the campaign on the treatment of black workers has contributed to this raising of political consciousness: partly because it was something different, and old campaigns (however well mounted) lose some impact over time; partly because the disengagement lobby had forced British firms into saying they were "good" employers, so that public exposure forced some of them into a public reaction.

There has been some criticism of the wages campaign on the grounds that it would allow firms to feel that, having raised wages, there is no need for further action. That could happen, but only if it is allowed to happen - future campaigns could concentrate on some of the issues that were comparatively neglected by the Sub-Committee, such as worker organisation (as already suggested), migrant workers, training, the industrial colour bar, etc. Meanwhile the disengagement lobby has not been diminished by the activities of the wages lobby, since the latter was largely an additional resource.

5. Effect on Employment

Several firms giving evidence to the Sub-Committee said they were worried about the effect on employment of increased wages. The point has been taken up by others, including myself.[21] Clearly, higher wages *ceteris paribus* increase the cost of labour compared with other inputs; equally clearly there is a paradox to be explained in that economists appear to be recommending wage restraint in Kenya, Zambia and elsewhere, but increased wages in South Africa. The question of higher wages for the lowest paid is, as it turns out, a good deal more complex in its total impact on the economy than the immediate impact on the cost of labour relative to the cost of other inputs.

Firstly, and most fundamentally, it is surely clear that if one group (the whites) have great economic and political bargaining strength and the others (the blacks) have almost none, then pushing up black incomes by whatever means will be partly at the expense of white incomes - whites will no longer have the field to themselves.

Secondly, if blacks are initially paid very low incomes indeed then it is possible for productivity to increase very sharply indeed as a result of higher wages - through reduced labour turnover, better nutrition and health, better management and organisation, without any mechanisation. If a man earning R20 a week produces more than twice as much as he did at R10 a week then the cost of labour (as opposed to wage rates) goes down in relation to the cost of other inputs. It may even be that an external impetus is the only way of escaping from the "60 cents -a-day syndrome" of low wages and low productivity.

Thirdly, if the old system of white wages increasing at faster rates than black wages were to continue then the economy would continue to expand by providing more and more luxuries for whites. A shift in the growth of income to the lowest paid would shift the structure of demand to the goods bought by the lowest paid - which are arguably more labour and local content intensive and thus are employment-creating. In addition, such a redistribution of income is, by almost any standard, a desirable thing in itself.

Fourthly, if profits are reduced because of higher black wages (they might not be if productivity rose sufficiently) it does not necessarily follow that savings and investment would fall pro rata. The firms in my sample could nearly all well afford a higher black wage - the majority had a ratio of black wages to sales revenue of 5% or less and none had a ratio of more than 15%. The ratio of the white to the black wage bill ranged as high as 30:1 (in which case a 1% increase in white wages costs the same as a 30% increase in black wages). The firms giving evidence to parliament presented the same picture. The average return on British investment in South Africa is more profitable than in any other major area of overseas investment. In short, investment would probably continue at lower levels of profitability.

Fifthly, it is widely assumed that there is widespread unemployment in South Africa among black people. The evidence is very ambiguous, however. It is hard to believe that the poverty lobby, external and internal, on its own has succeeded in causing black wages to rise faster than white for four years. Secondly, the mines find it very hard to get enough labour; only about 20% of their black workers are South African (nearly 40% if Lesotho is included). Indeed, threatened with the withdrawal of Malawians, Rhodesians, Mozambicans and Angolans (another 55%) the mines have recently increased their wage rates for Africans by very large percentages, in the hope of becoming less dependent on foreign labour. A shortage of labour for mining is consistent with unemployment among women and those too old or unfit to work underground; but it is not consistent with widespread male unemployment. In short, concern about unemployment may be to some extent an excuse for not paying a better wage.

To return, then, to the apparent paradox of advocating wage restraint in order to combat unemployment: the point is the need to have wage restraint among the "working poor". The ILO employment mission to Kenya, for example, in advocating an incomes policy recommended no increase in incomes for those earnings above £700 a year, but did not recommend wage restraint for the very low paid.[22] Analogies between South Africa and developing countries usually turn out, in fact, to be false. For example, supporters of the South African white polity point out that black wages in South Africa are higher than in many poor countries including most of black Africa.[23] This is a false comparison. Unskilled workers in Britain are paid more than unskilled workers in underdeveloped countries because Britain can afford higher wages. So can South Africa.

6. Wages and Fundamental Change

Proponents of different tactics, notably disengagement, object to the wage lobby on the grounds that higher wages do not amount to fundamental change, that the South African white polity can adjust to marginal change - in black bargaining power, in the industrial colour bar, in black income - without reducing its stranglehold on power.

The argument at this stage tends to become hypothetical, since it is about possible ways in which South Africa might change in the future and about the sort of society that might emerge after a "fundamental" change, that is presumably the emergence of a political order in which whites no longer had control (whether power-sharing with black hegemony or the exclusion of whites from political power).

It is indeed very likely that higher black wages will not in themselves cause fundamental change; it is equally likely, though, that they will not hinder such change. On the contrary, successful revolutions peaceful or violent, require leaders, who in turn require the backing of real economic strength. When "fundamental change" does take place, a black-led government would still have to live with more than 4 million whites - they can hardly all go away since for one thing it is difficult to think where they could go - and will have to try and redistribute income in some way or other from the whites (mainly) to the poor, who will also still exist. That redistribution will be easier to the extent that black labour possesses relative economic bargaining strength.

One final point: the existence of large British investment in South Africa undoubtedly creates a belief that Britain has an interest in the status quo and thus frequently puts the British government on the "wrong" side (if Conservative) or at best in a dilemma (if Labour). The economic interest is in fact exaggerated - the nominal "value" of the investment, usually put at something of the order of £1 1/2 billion, cannot be realised because the investments cannot all be sold at once, nor, if they *were* sold, would foreign exchange be made available. The value of the investment is just the 1% or so of Britain's foreign exchange earnings that accrues in profits from South Africa, the £1 1/2 billion being an accounting figure, not something realisable in cash.

Nevertheless, it appears important to many people, not least to governments; and the international politics of isolating the present South African regime would be much easier to pursue if it did not exist. Making life uncomfortable for foreign investors, whether by abusing them for paying low wages, or reducing their profitability by inducing them to pay higher wages, or increasing the bargaining power of their workers if higher wages lead to higher productivity, might eventually lead to a reduced investment, if not in absolute terms then at least relative to other yardsticks, such as total British foreign investment. Only if one believes that the paying of better black wages will in some way strengthen the cause of white South African supremacy or in some way reduce external hostility to it, does it seem reasonable to oppose external pressure in that direction. It is however, still too soon to do more than argue about this point. In any case change, fundamental or otherwise, is going to arise much more from action within South Africa and in the immediately surrounding countries than as a result of any thing that happens in Britain.

NOTES

1. This paper draws heavily on Robert Davies "British Capital in South Africa: A Study of British Affiliated Companies as Employers of African Labour in the Early 1970's", a study commissioned by the Study Project on External Investments in South Africa and Namibia and to be published in 1975 as an IDS Communication (with a short introduction by myself). I am very grateful to Robert Davies for allowing me to use his manuscript. Neither the Study Project nor the IDS has endorsed any of the views expressed in this paper.

2. January-March 1973; there were 160 work stoppages in 146 firms, involving 61,410 Africans. Duration of stoppages: less than one day - 32; one day - 38; one to two days - 24; two to three days - 32; three to seven days - 38. Wage increases - 118; no change - 28; dismissal of strikers - 7 cases. Wage increase less than R1 per week - 3 cases; R1 to R2 - 71 cases; more than R2 - 36 cases.

3. The Guardian March 12, 1973

4. See Fifth Report from the Expenditure Committee Session 1973-74 "Wages and Conditions of African Workers Employed by British Firms in South Africa", HMSO, 1973 (henceforward: Report); and Expenditure Committee (Trade and Industry Sub-Committee) "Wages and Conditions ... ", Minutes of Evidence Volumes I to IV (henceforward: Evidence I, II, etc.).

5. The London Sunday Times had carried a long feature by Dennis Herbstein in 1971 (April 18, 1971) giving details on a dozen or so companies.

6. The Guardian also ran one, two and sometimes three different stories on the subject every day for several weeks afterwards.

7. Evidence I, 310-328 and oral evidence, 328-337; and Charles Harvey "British Investment in Southern Africa", Journal of Southern African Studies 1 (1), October 1974.

8. Report, Table 6.1 "Some recent increases made in African wages by affiliated companies of firms giving oral evidence", 32, 33.

9. The averaging out over the year of holiday bonuses paid in a lump sum annuall not only ignores the month-to-month problems of survival on very low wages, but the high cost of travel for migrant workers returning to distant "homelands" to see their families.

10. Davies, "British Capital in South Africa", Section III, 3.

11. Report, 97.

12. "Shore Tightens Up On African Pay", The Guardian February 2, 1975.

13. Evidence I, 342.

14. Report, 31. UKSATA's own attitude was equally soft - the full flavour can only be obtained by reading the evidence, but in answer to the very first

question the UKSATA Chairman, Mr. W. Luke, remarked inter alia: " ... our principal aim is to maintain friendly relations with South Africa". Evidence I, 2.

15. See Financial Mail (Johannesburg) December 12, 1975.

16. Evidence I, 309.

17. Evidence I, 6.

18. Evidence I, 149. A similar piece of evidence was given to me privately by the chairman of one of my sample firms.

19. See Athol Fugard Three Port Elizabeth Plays (London: Oxford University Press 1974).

20. Last sentence in Colin Legum "The Case for Economic, Political and Military Disengagement from South Africa", Study Project Paper Number 17. The same argument is used in Immanuel Wallerstein "Disengagement as a Tactic in the Liberation of South Africa", Study Project Paper Number 16.

21. Evidence I, 315-319; Harvey "British Investment in Southern Africa", 58-62. The paragraphs that follow repeat many of the same points.

22. ILO "Employment, Incomes and Inequality: A Strategy for Increasing Productive Employment in Kenya" Geneva 1972, Chapter 16.

23. See the Club of Ten advertisements specifically attacking The Guardian's South African wages campaign - The Times June 10, 1974, and subsequent editions.

Chapter Seventeen

NUCLEAR WEAPONS AND SOUTH AFRICA - THE INCENTIVES AND CONSTRAINTS ON POLICY*

J. E. Spence

1. Introduction

The last decade has witnessed a growing concern with the question of nuclear proliferation reflected in a large volume of literature devoted to both the technical and political considerations involved in trying to devise means to discourage the spread of nuclear weapons to Nth powers. The Republic of South Africa has, however, rarely been the subject of any detailed discussion in this context: at best, it has merited a passing reference or footnote as compared with the attention lavished on India, Israel, West Germany and Japan - the prime contenders for nuclear power status. This indifference to South Africa's nuclear pretentions is explicable if we bear in mind that until quite recently its potential capability has been relegated to the second rank of those powers deemed likely to have the capacity, and more important, the will to develop nuclear weapons, that is, powers such as Argentina, Australia, Belgium and Pakistan. This group has been traditionally regarded as requiring up to 15 years to produce a weapon system once the initial decision to do so has been taken.

However, this estimate as it applies to the Republic has been substantially revised during the last three years. It is now suggested that its government could test a crude nuclear device within four years of embarking on a military programme and that a small number of U235 weapons could be produced within a further four year period. It should be stressed, however, that there is no clear evidence of any such intention at the present time. (There also remains the question of a delivery system: at present only the Canberra B112 aircraft would be suitable. Possibly, South Africa might be able to count on French assistance for a more advanced aircraft of the kind that would be required towards the end of this decade. How likely this will be must remain a matter of speculation: it is one thing to supply conventional weapons to the Republic; quite another to be seen as actively contributing to the development of a South African nuclear capability - especially in view of French interests in Africa and the proclaimed intention not to encourage proliferation).

The more favourable forecast of the government's nuclear capacity is largely based on the announcement in July 1970 that scientists employed by the South

African Atomic Energy Board had been successful in pioneering a new process - "unique in its concept" for uranium enrichment.[1] South Africa is, of course, a major producer of uranium in its natural state, but up to 1970 had lacked the means to enrich it and thus make possible the efficient production of weapons-grade material.

There are in addition other reasons why South Africa's position deserves re-assessment: (1) the government has not signed the non-proliferation treaty; (ii) the heavy defence expenditure of the last 13 years coupled with the increasing concern manifested over matters of internal and external security has aroused speculation over the Republic's ultimate intentions in the nuclear field;[2] (iii) the fact that South Africa, unlike powers such as Italy or Belgium, has never enjoyed the benefit of protection conferred by alliance with a super power; moreover the ambiguity of its military relations with the Western powers and the persistent efforts made to transform this ambiguity into a degree of formal incorporation within the alliance structure of Western defence suggests an incentive to acquire nuclear weapons as both a symbol and a practical demonstration of the state's capacity to stand alone against the strictures and, if need be, intervention of the outside world; (iv) in a related context, we must consider the South African perception of the significance to be attached to the presence of Soviet warships in the Indian Ocean, and (v) the extent to which policy makers might regard nuclear status as enhancing the claim to be a hegemonic power in Southern and Central Africa.

It is considerations of this kind that suggest that a decision to opt for the development of a nuclear weapons programme is bound to involve a delicate balance of constraints and incentives of a kind not present in anything like the same degree for the smaller powers of Eastern and Western Europe, the majority of which have signed the N.P.T. - nor, for that matter, for powers such as Brazil and Spain which to date have not done so.

2. The Development of South Africa's Nuclear Programme

The South African Atomic Energy Board was established in 1949 and the first uranium plant opened in 1952. The Republic is the world's third largest supplier of uranium and its resources are estimated to be "three million tons in the economically exploitable price range".[3] The United States and Britain are the major export markets for uranium concentrate and by 1966 sales abroad had earned South Africa some R1,000 million. During the early '60s these exports began to fluctuate, however (from 6,400 tons in 1959 to 2,900 tons by 1965). This was due to a "fall back in constructing nuclear power stations",[4] but by the 1970s demand had begun to rise, although not sufficiently to prevent stock-piling taking place in considerable quantities.

By 1965 South Africa's first research reactor (Safari I) had gone critical. During the next five years the government was at pains to deny any suggestion that its nuclear research had military implications.[5] Instead, emphasis was placed on the following objectives of policy: (i) the development and exploitation of the country's uranium resources; (ii) research into the use of atomic energy as a cheap method of producing electricity; (iii) production of radio-active isotypes and the development of new uses for them.

The marginal interest shown by scientific and strategic experts in the Republic's potential as a nuclear power sharpened with the announcement by Mr. B.J. Vorster, the Prime Minister, that the S.A.A.E.B. had devised a new process for uranium enrichment. Describing this process in rather extravagant terms as "unequalled in the history of our country", Mr. Vorster asserted that

> South Africa does not intend to withhold the considerable advantages inherent in this development from the world community. We are therefore prepared to collaborate in the exploitation of this process with any non-Communist country willing to do so, but subject to the conclusion of an agreement safeguarding our interests.[6]

The utility of the project was justified in economic terms[7]: by 1980 annual production of enriched uranium would reach 6,000 tons, constituting 14% of the West's output and worth about 290 million dollars in export value. Secondly, the Republic's efforts to establish a substantial nuclear programme would prove less expensive if enriched uranium was available.[8] Despite the officials emphasis on the economic rather than the military potential of the project, it is plausible to interpret this development as having a strategic significance in the more general sense of the means required to maintain and enhance the political and economic viability of the Republic in relation to the external world.

If, for example, we assume that a major objective of South Africa's foreign policy in the post war period has been the consolidation and further integration of its economic and military links with Western powers, then the prospect of making an important contribution to the West's stock of nuclear technology becomes attractive to the extent that these ties are thereby strengthened. This view is not inconsistent with a parallel determination to become self sufficient in key raw materials (oil and rubber are obvious examples in this context) and thus reduce the Republic's vulnerability to external sanctions or cut-offs in supply. Thus in the case of uranium,

> The reason for Pretoria's willingness to take the costly route was plain: South Africa could not depend on the co-operation of those very few countries - United States, Britain, France, Russia, China - equipped to enrich

> the fissile component of uranium, the key to smaller, more highly rated hence cheaper nuclear stations.[9]

The claim to have a novel and relatively cheap enrichment process has generated a degree of scepticism among informed commentators.[10] Their criticisms stress the fact that the project has only reached the pilot stage while there is considerable doubt about South Africa's capacity to achieve at substantially lower cost a goal which has required extensive governmental financial support, a sophisticated technology and a highly trained management and scientific elite both in the United States and Western Europe. (In the latter case it is interesting that Britain, Holland and West Germany have felt obliged to combine their resources in pursuit of enrichment technology).

These criticisms are not necessarily as damning as might appear at first sight. We should bear in mind Mr. Vorster's offer to collaborate with other countries in the exploitation of the process - an ambition which might be interpreted as an attempt to make a virtue out of necessity. The explanation for this lies in the fact that for many years before 1970 South Africa's scientists concentrated their research on nuclear power generation by means of reactors using uranium in its natural state. This was regarded as a cheaper method and not dependent on external technological and capital inputs to the same extent that would be the case if a commitment were made to the production and subsequent use of the enriched variety. What presumably led to the decision to concentrate on enrichment technology was, as David Fishlock stresses, the danger implicit in relying on the continued goodwill of those powers who alone possess the facilities to enrich natural uranium. By contrast the development of a home grown enrichment process would eliminate this crude dependence on outside assistance; collaboration with one or more of the Western powers might still be necessary to make the process viable in economic terms, but the relationship would be akin to a partnership concerned to exploit jointly South Africa's new process, rather than reflecting a vulnerable dependence on a technologically more advanced state.

Thus tentative approaches to the 'European club'[11] (Britain, Holland and West Germany) have been made, presumably in the hope that one or all of these powers would be willing to place their expertise, and more important, their financial backing behind South Africa's aspiration to exploit the new process. These overtures, however, have not so far evoked any positive response; on the other hand, it is worth noting that the United States has offered to share its enrichment technology with states regarded as good security risks and South Africa might well qualify under this heading.[12]

The government's strategy seems reasonably clear: to turn the new process to commercial advantage and involve South Africa in the business of advanced nuclear technology at the international level. There are difficulties, however, in the way of achieving this objective and these serve to complicate the choices before the government.

In 1965 Britain won orders from Germany to the value of £500,000 for conversion of South Africa's uranium to uranium fluoride and the British have been disturbed at the possibility that the Republic might now be in a position to make 'hex'. The resulting loss of contracts could only be countered by licensing the use of British technology in South Africa itself and although this technology is unclassified, such a step would be of major assistance to South Africa if her leaders opted to manufacture nuclear explosives as distinct from fuel[13]. Moreover Britain is already committed to buying substantial quantities (7,500 tons) of the natural uranium deposits discovered in South-West Africa for delivery in the years 1975-82 and this might well compete with the demands of any large scale enrichment plant established in South Africa.[14]

There are also clearly obstacles in the way of raising abroad the capital required to make the new process viable. As Aldo Cassuto has argued

> Mr. Vorster's offer of participation in the advantages of a technically unspecified and economically unassessable discovery by South African scientists would imply the contribution of foreign capital to an extent that not even the best informed experts of Pelindaba ... are in a position to forecast[15].

The question of whether South Africa would in time be able to offer a competitive enrichment service is further complicated by the slow progress of uranium production. According to Cassuto, the 1969 figure of just under 4,000 tons was one-third less than the high figures achieved during the 1950's. Moreover the uranium consortium (NUECOR) has failed to secure valuable contracts in the international market against Canadian competition in particular, and several lucrative contracts with the Japanese concerns have gone to the latter. (The latter have apparently had doubts about the limited extraction capacity of the South African industry). Nor does there appear to have been any significant expansion of the uranium mining industry, although two new extraction plants have recently been built. If South Africa is to compete effectively with other uranium producers for a share in an expanding world market, then it is argued that much has to be done to increase local production and this becomes all the more necessary in view of the recent discovery of extensive resources in Australia which some claim can be exploited at a fraction of the cost incurred by South African mining interests. The pessimistic interpretation of South Africa's prospects is well summed up by Cassuto's statement that

> Entering the competition to supply European requirements of uranium, whether

> enriched or not, in the late 1970's and the early 1980's seems to be out of the question in the light of the information now available ... Such priorities as fueling domestic nuclear stations and the feeding of a large enrichment plant would further reduce the availability of commercial uranium for export and... make it necessary to increase productive capacity by at least 100 or 200% to allow substantial exports at competitive prices for long term contracts as generally required by the electricity industries.[16]

Admittedly views of this kind must be qualified by the knowledge that information about South Africa's uranium production and its long term nuclear potential is heavily circumscribed by the demands of security legislation such as Act. No. 90 of 1967 which imposes severe sanctions on anyone guilty of publishing material relating to the prospecting, production and pricing of uranium.

3. Attitudes to the Non-Proliferation Treaty

The claim to have developed facilities for uranium enrichment coupled with South Africa's unwillingness to sign the NPT might suggest that its government is intent on maintaining the option to develop nuclear weapons for as long as possible. Yet, as has been argued earlier, current policy appears designed to impress upon the Western powers the positive contribution South Africa's scientists can make to advanced nuclear technology in the civil field in the hope that new economic and technological links can be forged with those states whose good-will and support the Republic has traditionally attempted to win. Thus over the long term the choice might be construed as lying between a decision to opt for nuclear power status in a military sense (regardless of the political consequences) or, signing the Treaty following the conclusion of some mutually advantageous agreement with those powers willing to work with the Republic as a partner in pioneering and developing new skills in nuclear technology. In the short-term, the government's strategy could be directed at creating an impression that its refusal to sign the NPT implies a threat to develop nuclear weapons at some unspecified time in the future and providing at the same time a bargaining counter to persuade Western governments to take seriously South Africa's offer of collaboration in the nuclear field. For the time being, however, politico-economic objectives do not necessarily clash with military aspirations in so far as the South African government does not as yet feel obliged to make the choice between them.[17] (In passing it should be stressed that it is difficult to see what possible advantages South Africa might gain if its government signed the Treaty 'blind' i.e. without some significant quid pro quo of the kind described above. Signature would not especially enhance the government's standing in the world unlike the case of states such as Canada or Sweden whose decision to do so was in a sense confirmation - both internally and externally - of a diplomatic image of 'liberal' concern with the evils of world politics. By contrast South Africa's policies arouse no such expectation on the part of its critics).

Yet if this policy of waiting upon events is to remain viable, much will depend upon the West's assessment of the likelihood of the Republic becoming a nuclear power should the former decline to enter into any agreement on nuclear cooperation in the civil field. And here the evidence of South Africa's role in the International Atomic Energy Authority is instructive in so far as delegates have continually stressed their government's unwillingness to do anything that might contribute towards an increase in the number of nuclear-armed states. What in fact the delegates have been at pains to deny is any suggestion that South Africa was selling uranium to buyers who might conceivably be diverting it to clandestine military purposes.[18] What is significant in the context of a discussion on the constraints militating against the Republic becoming a nuclear power is the concern of the South African government to demonstrate its commitment to observe the rule of law and in general maintain the proprieties of international behaviour - if only to point a contrast to the 'illegal' demands made upon the Republic by its enemies at the United Nations and elsewhere. This emphasis on a 'correct' posture is especially noticeable at the I.A.E.A. and is combined with an insistence that the Agency concentrates on technical issues rather than become an organ of political and ideological debate. There can be no doubt that the government attaches considerable importance to its standing within the Agency welcoming the opportunity to make a valuable contribution in terms which have not been available in other international organizations.

An analysis of the reservations ruling out for the time being the signature and ratification of the NPT and listed by South African spokesmen during the General Assembly Debate on the NPT in May 1968[19] supports the view that the Republic is at this stage more concerned with gaining tangible benefits in the political and economic sphere rather than committing itself irrevocably to the achievement of nuclear power status - an option which as we have already noted it can afford to keep open as a last resort.

South Africa specifically objected to the NPT on the following grounds:

i) The Treaty is one-sided and discriminatory in so far as it does not effectively commit the existing nuclear powers to take active measures to reduce and ultimately eliminate their own stock-piles of weapons. This objection was hardly the core of the South African case against the Treaty. It was cited by many other powers, but it is by no means self-evident that the Republic shares the general interest of many small and medium-sized states in a deceleration of vertical proliferation. It is at least plausible that the resulting detente between nuclear powers embarking on massive measures of arms control would seriously weaken the validity of the South African claim to be indispensable to the security of the west.[20]

ii) The Treaty is guilty of technological discrimination against the 'have not' powers who cannot be sure that the "potential benefits from any peaceful applications of nuclear explosions" would be passed on. As the South African delegate remarked:

> In return for the restrictions and impositions which would be non-nuclear-weapon States are required to accept and which we would normally accept willingly, we are offered promises by the nuclear-weapon States of technical cooperation in the further development of the applications of nuclear energy for peaceful purposes. Promises seem hardly adequate. Experience has shown that technical information and material required for peaceful purposes are sometimes withheld, even when specific agreements make their provision contractually obligatory.[21]

This statement must be read in the context of the earlier discussion about South African aspirations for closer nuclear ties with the West in terms of its position as a major uranium producer and the expertise it has laboriously built up in the field of nuclear technology. It indicates the government's concern to enjoy partnership status through the pooling of nuclear resources rather than take on trust the promises of the nuclear club and risk relegation to the ranks of those powers which have little option but to accept the uncertain benefits accorded to non-nuclear signatories of the Treaty. Moreover, the Republic's experience of discrimination in other fields (the sale of arms, for example) serves to strengthen this mood of scepticism.

iii) Yet another and perhaps the most important objection is related to the question of safeguards. As Mr. Botha, the South African delegate, explained, his government was not prepared to put its mines and ore-processing plants under international inspection - a potential requirement, he argued, implicit in the wording of Article III, paragraph 1 of the Treaty. This was cited as a threat to sovereignty on the grounds that "the greater the production of uranium by non-nuclear weapon states, the more extensive and stringent the safe-guards to which they become subjected." Furthermore, some controls would hamper the development of peaceful uses of nuclear energy while inspection procedures would encourage industrial espionage and put at risk the technical advances pioneered by non-nuclear states. Nevertheless, his government was prepared to delay its final decision until the precise nature of the safeguard's provisions were decided upon by the I.A.E.A.[22]

This objection is partly explained in terms of the strong attachment the South African government has always exhibited to the sanctity of domestic jurisdiction and its deep antagonism to any attempt at external interference with its domestic arrangements. No doubt the desire to protect commercial advantage is the strongest motive in this particular context, but it is hardly surprising to find traces of its traditional 'legalistic' attitude in forming its position on nuclear matters.

iv) Finally, the Republic's spokesmen have expressed doubts about the security guarantees associated with the Treaty for non-nuclear power signatories.[23] Here again there is evidence that South Africa interpreted its present needs in terms of past experience. Given the hostility generated against its policies at the United Nations, given the isolation that has been a striking feature of its role within that organization, the government has ample cause to be sceptical about the efficacy of any guarantees eminating from that quarter. The lack of any real guarantee deriving from United Nations declarations, together with the fact that the Republic has never enjoyed the benefits of protection conferred by membership of the Western alliance structure, might at first sight suggest an incentive to acquire nuclear weapons to compensate for the status of being an outcast. Ironically, this argument might have been more compelling in the late 1950's and early 1960s when the Republic's unpopularity was at its height and the government seemed menaced by a combination of factors - the threat of sanctions by the U.N., internal unrest as symbolized by the events of the Sharpeville crisis and the prospect of defeat in the legal battle over South West Africa. At the time, however, a rapid acquisition of nuclear weapons was out of the question for technological reasons; paradoxically, however, these threats have receded as coincidently the time-lag for the development of nuclear weapons has shortened dramatically.

One must be wary of exaggerating the importance of such guarantees for South Africa. At present, no power aspires to threaten the Republic with nuclear weapons; nor is it likely that any of its enemies on the African continent will be in a position to do so for a long time to come, if at all. Therefore the question of formal guarantees from the great powers against such an eventuality remains a theoretical issue in a way which is presumably not the case with say Australia, which - it might be argued - has otherwise a greater incentive to acquire weapons to the extent that it has reason to fear Chinese nuclear aspirations.

4. Political and Strategic Considerations

It would be foolish to accept uncritically the cluster of arguments put forward by South Africa in defence of its decisions to delay signature to the NPT. The emphasis on discrimination whether military or commercial, the fear that an extension of the safeguard system will erode the principle of domestic jurisdiction, the scepticism about guarantees - all these assertions might be taken as so much rhetoric disguising nuclear power status at a time conducive to the achievement of maximum benefit both in a military and political sense. On the other hand, the outside observer must guard against the temptation to impute 'wicked' motives simply because in all other respects the policy of the state in question appears reprehensible. Thus by curious logic South Africa is seen as an 'obvious' candidate for nuclear power status on the grounds that this is an inevitable course of action for a state which in the past has not shown a decent respect for enlightened opinion. This is not to deny - as we have argued earlier - that the government might well be interested in using its reluctance to sign the Treaty as a bargaining counter to intangible economic and political gains. What must be stressed, however, is that in this respect at least, South Africa is not unique in having to calculate the advantages and disadvantages in developing nuclear weapons. If it decides against so doing, it will be because a higher priority is assigned to using its technological achievements as a means of strengthening ties with the West. If this view is accepted as the dominant strain in current policy, then some credence at least must be attached to the reservations voiced during the debate on the NPT, which relate to the dangers of technological discrimination. Thus, there is nothing 'inevitable' about the Republic getting the bomb. This view is strengthened if we examine the purely strategic arguments for and against the acquisition of a nuclear capability. Obviously these cannot be separated from a consideration of the political implications stemming its present status as a non nuclear power.

The first question to be asked is whether the addition of nuclear weapons to the South African armoury will enhance its security in a military sense.

The government's fierce anti-communist posture in the external realm derives from a variety of sources, not the least of which is the conviction that any attempt to employ the weapons of subversion and terrorism against the Republic is likely to be communist inspired and actively supported by the Soviet Union and/or China. In the Government's view, this threat would still remain, however amicable American-Soviet relations were to become, and there would be the added disadvantage implicit in the development - remote as this may seem at present - of a coincidence of interest between the super powers in bringing pressure to bear upon South Africa if only to forestall massive Chinese support for an accelerated campaign of insurgency by the African states. The need to cope with this contingency might constitute a strong incentive to acquire nuclear weapons, although it is doubtful whether in these circumstances the Republic could deter both a United States/Soviet 'pre-emptive' intervention and the prosecution of a major insurgency by its enemies. Threats to destroy Lusaka and Dar-es-Salaam with nuclear weapons might well provoke a crisis that would rapidly spread beyond the confines of the African continent and South Africa's survival in its present form would not, therefore, be automatically guaranteed. In any event, this scenario assures a pattern of world order radically different from that which prevails at present and there are - as we shall see presently - countervailing forces working against the immediate acquisition of nuclear weapons by South Africa in the short term. This of course is not to deny the possibility that South Africa might deem it a wise precaution to stockpile both scientific expertise and material resources for the production of nuclear weapons at relatively short notice.

By the same token, the military utility of nuclear weapons seems dubious given the government's perception of a threat confronting the regime. The latter has concentrated on developing an effective counter-insurgency capability and it is difficult to see how nuclear weapons could usefully add to it.[24] It is unlikely that such weapons would deter the promotion of wars of liberation by South Africa's enemies abroad and any attempt to use them in response to a conventional invasion by the combined forces of the O.A.U. would run the risk of involving the great powers in the conflict and this, as we have seen, is the one eventuality the South African government is most anxious to avoid.[25] Nor can there be any doubt that for the present the Republic has managed to contain successfully any threat of insurgency within its own borders, and has replaced reliance on Portuguese and Rhodesian forces to keep the external threat distant from its borders by active diplomacy to minimise such threats. Thus the case for developing a nuclear capability diminishes in importance in view of Africa's inability seriously to threaten the Republic's security and the latter's perception of what is required to deal with any further escalation of the present level of insurgent activity.

In this context we should note Mr. Vorster's periodic threats to strike directly at the homeland of those states providing sanctuary for African insurgence. This, however, would literally be a weapon of last resort to be employed only if the insurgents began to make significant inroads into the South African security network. At present, however, the Zambian government shows no sign of being deterred from its supportive role and one wonders how far it would reconsider its commitment if and when the insurgents began to make sizeable gains. This would presumably depend upon a range of factors such as the costs the Republic would incur in terms of heightening the likelihood of external intervention if retaliation was offered against Zambian targets. There is also the <u>strategic</u> utility of such bombing to be considered and here the parallel of American airpower in North and South Vietnam springs readily to mind. This is to speculate, however, beyond the confines of this paper, but it is perhaps worth considering how far both Zambia and South African calculations would be effected by the substitution of nuclear weapons for the conventional strength already possessed by the former. My guess - and it cannot be more than that in so speculative an area - is that a nuclear capability might well be less credible if only because of the opprobrium that attaches to any state (and South Africa is not just any state) brandishing nuclear weapons over the defenceless heads of its weaker neighbours.

It seems improbable that either the Soviet Union or China would be willing to back their present degree of support for wars of liberation directed against South Africa with nuclear threats. At this stage the interest of both the major communist powers in the conflict between black and white Africa is peripheral as compared with their respective commitments in the Middle East and South East Asian regions. Furthermore, the attempts by a variety of freedom movements to provoke insurgency in South Africa squares with the emphasis in Chinese revolutionary theory on the idea of the protracted struggle using the classic techniques of guerrilla warfare. It is difficult to see how the threat of nuclear attack could be accommodated satisfactorily within this theory and what advantages would be forth coming as a result for those engaged in wars of this kind against the white South.

Given the efforts made by the Great Powers to prevent existing conflict escalating to the nuclear level, it is not unreasonable to assume a tacit degree of common interest in avoiding unilateral intervention with nuclear means in areas which so far have ostensibly remained free of Great Power confrontation. This could be true of Southern Africa where, it might be argued, both the Soviet Union and China have good reason to believe that the ultimate resolution of the conflict in that region can be left to the more orthodox instrument of revolutionary warfare, however long this may take. Moreover, even if we assume the worst possibility, any major intrusion by the Soviets or Chinese in the Southern African region involving the use of either conventional or nuclear weapons could be construed by the West as a major threat to the precarious stability of the _global_ balance of power requiring, therefore, an appropriate and meaningful response.

Yet another interpretation competes for our attention, however: it may be that Soviet interests in the area as manifested, for example, by the deployment of warships in the Indian Ocean since 1968 is motivated by _political_ rather than military considerations and designed to gain influence on the littoral states and to exert leverage in situations of internal crisis. If this proposition is accepted, then it constitutes a further argument against the Republic's deriving any advantage from the acquisition of nuclear weapons. Such action would probably serve to enhance Soviet influence in East and Central Africa if only on the grounds that the leaders of states in those areas would constitute a receptive audience to Soviet propaganda that stressed the aggressive ambitions of a

Republic armed with weapons of mass destruction.

Thus it is difficult to take seriously the argument that South Africa's exclusion from the formal structure of Western alliance arrangements necessitates the creation of a nuclear weapons capability to deter or at least complicate the calculations of those powers which might wish to intervene more directly in the confrontation between independent Africa and the white dominated states in the South. We have tried to show that the incentive to interfere at a level above the present one of arming and training guerrillas is lacking: further, even if such incentives were present, and accepting that South Africa has good reason to doubt the efficacy of any guarantee offered by the United Nations, the fact remains that the Western powers could hardly be indifferent to a situation which threatened the continued stability of the Indian Ocean region on a scale in which the Communist powers were actively damaging their extensive political and economic interests in maintaining the safety of the sea routes round the Cape.

Moreover, a decision to take up the nuclear option might have adverse diplomatic effects on South Africa's relations with the Western powers: not only because of the latter's hostility to the proliferation of nuclear weapons in general, but because of the effect this would have on a relationship which is already sufficiently ambiguous and subject to periodic strains and criticism from third parties. The spectacle of a nuclear armed South Africa would inevitably call into question still further the morality of dealing with a country, the domestic policies of which arouse such widespread hostility. It may be that in the last analysis criticisms of this kind could be ignored with impunity in the knowledge that there are few if any effective sanctions that can be brought to bear on the Western powers to alter their policies towards the Republic. On the other hand, both Britain and the United States would come under severe pressure from the more militant of the African states and make more difficult the traditional justification of British Conservative leaders that the best way of achieving racial harmony in South Africa lies in a policy of conciliation and cooperation with Afrikaner Nationalism.

Given that Britain and South Africa have an interest in maintaining existing political and economic links, it is obviously to their mutual advantage that this relationship remains free - as far as possible - for any stress caused by external or internal criticism by those who aspire to embarrass both countries and to cast doubt on the legitimacy of British economic involvement in South Africa. Nor can the question of sanctions be summarily dismissed: British interests in independent Africa are considerable and from time to time they are subject to threat by African leaders impatient with British unwillingness to take active steps to induce change in the Republic[27]. Clear evidence that South Africa was developing nuclear weapons would thus strain British relations still further with independent states on the continent and at the very least obstruct the attempt by both governments to keep their relations with each other on a footing of quiet, relatively undisturbed normality.[28]

The attempt by South Africa to establish political and economic links with independent African states would also be inhibited rather than enhanced by the adoption of a nuclear posture. Such a policy would only serve to deepen the hostility of the militant wing of the O.A.U. represented by Zambia and Tanzania and nullify still further the efforts of states such as the Ivory Coast and Malawi to promote "dialogue" between the Republic and black Africa. That the Nationalist Government attaches great importance to the cultivation of good relations with its northern neighbours is not in dispute: the purely economic advantages of obtaining a wider market for South African manufactured goods and the surplus investment generated by a rapidly developing economy are clearly appreciated. The economic penetration of Southern and Central Africa is also seen as helping to create conditions of political stability in societies which might otherwise become subject to internal dissension and the effects of which might spill over into the Republic itself. Coupled with these economic motives is a deeply felt aspiration to become a regional power recognized by the West as responsible for the security of the region as a whole and prepared to play its part as a bastion of Western influence in Southern and Central Africa. As Larry Bowman has rightly observed, the ultimate goal is to establish "an economically and militarily strong South Africa, surrounded by client states, befriended by the Great Powers, and geographically isolated from any significant political enemy"[29]

No doubt it could be argued that developing a nuclear capability would add substance to these aspirations in so far as it would symbolise in a meaningful way South Africa's capacity to play an independent and creative role in an area to which the Western Powers seem to be assigning an increasingly low priority in their foreign policy calculations. It would also have the added advantage of demonstrating South Africa's commitment to maintaining the peace, in terms of the Nixon Doctrine's emphasis on self-reliance and the shouldering of local responsibility in areas which had hitherto fallen under the wing of American omnipotence.

There are, however, a number of objections to this view. First, the success of South Africa's "outward movement" requires at the very least that those at whom it is directed can be persuaded to accept that its motives are essentially peaceful and cooperative in nature. Secondly, that the practice of apartheid at home is in no way a threat to peace and security abroad;[30] and thirdly, that hegemonic ambitions can be reconciled in the eyes of the outside world with the claims of the official ideology of "peaceful coexistence" on the basis of "tolerance and mutual respect, the recognition of the sovereign independence of all states and non-interference in each other's domestic affairs"[31].

It is difficult to see how the acquisition of nuclear weapons would help promote these objectives; a nuclear posture would be open to misinterpretation - however much the government stressed its defensive nature - on the grounds that its adoption signified an intent to follow a more aggressive and bellicose policy toward its weaker neighbours. And here it must be stressed that South African leaders are very sensitive to accusations that their policy towards independent Africa constitutes a variety of latter-day great power imperialism.[32] What is crucial in this context is the interaction between its policies towards black Africa and relations with traditional allies in the Western camp. As Dr. Hilgard Muller, the Republic's Foreign Minister stated in August 1968:

> As the West becomes aware of our fruitful cooperation with the African states, their attitude towards us improves. I believe that it will happen to an increasing degree because we *must simply accept our relations with the rest of the world are largely determined by our relations with* the African states (authors italics)[33]

Thus opting for a nuclear weapons capability might well undo the work that has been put into the task of maintaining this network of relations in good repair. The fears aroused in Africa about the Republic's ultimate intentions would combine with Western doubts about the wisdom of too close an association with a power bent on nuclear independence (and with whom relations have always presented problems because of unpalatable domestic policies). The end-result might be a return to the isolation of the fifties and early sixties, which the present government has made a major objective of foreign policy to end.

Thus, on balance, there exists a number of political restraints which appear to preclude South Africa's becoming a nuclear power in the near future. The belief that a nuclear capability will enhance prestige may well be a factor influencing a decision of other would-be nuclear powers, but it is very doubtful whether this would be true of the Republic. The status which allegedly comes from acquiring nuclear weapons may well serve as an integrating factor in developing societies, but in South Africa's case the effect of such a development on the Black majority would hardly be similar. As far as the two white communities are concerned, their cohesion into a single white community has been helped by the criticisms launched against the Republic from abroad. Nuclear weapons might help consolidate this sense of white South African identity, but this would only occur as a by-product of a decision to go nuclear on the quite different grounds of national security and the needs of external defence. The aspiration to acquire 'respectability' in the eyes of its traditional associates in the Western camp is deep-rooted and foreign policy throughout the post-war period has concentrated on attempts to persuade these powers that South Africa is indeed indispensable to their security needs in the South Atlantic-Indian Ocean region. Adoption of a nuclear posture would cut across these efforts to tie the Republic more closely into the structure of Western defence and equally run counter to a policy based on strengthening economic and political links with a view to enhancing the Republic's value as a trading partner and reliable ally.

Finally we should bear in mind that a defence policy of the Republic has always been seen as securing certain foreign policy objectives, apart from the obvious one of insuring the survival of the white minority. This is well summed up in the following quotation from an influential newspaper:

> The world respects the country that is militarily powerful ... in addition ... (a powerful defence force) ... is a useful instrument for the creation of good relations outside the country. Friendly approaches are usually made towards a country with a powerful military fist, because such a country can be a valuable ally in war-time, and in time of peace again it can be a valuable market or a seller of armament and strategic material. The resulting trade helps to build bridges of friendship, even on the diplomatic level.[34]

As this extract clearly implies, defence policy is seen as having a direct bearing on the Republic's capacity to gain support abroad and win friends and allies. Given the absence of any immediate threat to its security, it is not surprising that foreign and defence policy objectives have been seen as interacting with each other to produce an image of a society determined to win legitimacy abroad and establish its credentials as a trustworthy and reliable partner of the Western Powers.

In conclusion, it would seem that political, strategic and economic considerations militate against South Africa's becoming a nuclear power in the next five years: politically, such a step would damage long-standing aspirations to enjoy increasingly cooperative relationships with traditional allies; in strategic terms, the potential increment to the Republic's security represented by a nuclear weapons capability would seem to be outweighed by the inevitable distrust that would surround its intentions especially in those regions of Africa where it is at present attempting to maximise political and economic influence. In the economic context, South Africa would appear to have more to gain from using its nuclear resources to strengthen its commercial and technological ties with the advanced nations of the West, than from branding itself as a nuclear outsider and adding considerably to the opprobrium which in the past has surrounded its role in international politics.[35]

One major qualification remains to be made: the constraints discussed in the preceding analysis assume a world in which the pressures against non-proliferation come to outweigh the incentives to join the nuclear club. In other words, South Africa is unlikely to be the seventh nuclear power; on the other hand, if gross proliferation[36] were to take place South Africa might have relatively little to lose in prestige terms by becoming for example the twelfth nuclear power. It remains the writer's conviction, however, that even if proliferation does take place at a rapid rate during the next decade, the constraints on South African policy will still remain important and probably dominant in the context of the choice as it might present itself at that time.

Conversely, if there is a gadarene rush to sign the Treaty on the part of those who so far have refrained from doing so, South Africa might find the status of a solitary non-signatory somewhat uncomfortable especially if critics use this as a means for sharpening hostility against its government on general grounds. At present, however, given the becalmed state into which discussion of non-proliferation seems to have drifted, this is hardly a significant constraint. As a consequence of this slackening of interest in halting the non-proliferation of nuclear weapons, it may be that little pressure is currently being exerted on the Republic to sign the NPT. However, an additional reason, more disturbing from South Africa's point of view, may well be a calculation by the Western powers that the Republic has little to gain in either political or military terms from opting for nuclear power status. And if this means a dimunition in its bargaining power with the West, South Africa will probably have little choice but to maintain its present noncommital policy if only on the grounds that a bird in the hand may be of some yet unforeseen advantage when all the others have flown!

NOTES

* An abridged version of this essay was included in the author's monograph on The Political and Military Framework (London: Study Project on External Investment in South Africa and Namibia, 1975) and is printed here with the permission of the author and the Study Project.

1. See Prime Minister's speech, South Africa Parliament. House of Assembly, Debates, Vol. 25, cols. 57/8.

2. Public speculation that South Africa is about to embark on a weapons programme has by and large been confined to the press (both local and overseas); see, for example, the view expressed by Rude Pravo (a Czech Journal) in August 1967 that South Africa and West Germany were collaborating in the production of nuclear weapons. Official opinion in the Republic has always emphasized the peaceful nature of the government's nuclear programme and has been careful not to encourage expectations to the contrary. Certainly there has been very little in the way of informed discussion about the options available to South Africa in either the press, parliament, or, for that matter, among the tiny elite of intellectuals who might have been expected to concern themselves with these matters. One major inhibition is the government's act of discouragement of any significant discussion of defence and security issues in general.

3. The Near-nuclear Countries and the N.P.T. (New York: Humanities Press for the Stockholm International Peace Research Institute, 1972) 32.

4. See Abdul S. Minty "Apartheid Atomic Bomb?", Sechaba 5(7), July 1971.

5. See, for example, the statements made by Dr. A. J. A. Roux, Director-General of the Atomic Energy Board, and Mr. P. Botha, Minister of Defence and quoted in the Daily Telegraph (London), 20 April 1965 and Sunday Express (Johannesburg), 22 December 1968, respectively.

6. House of Assembly, Debates, op.cit., cols. 57/8.

7. Dr. Roux, did, however, claim that South Africa was by virtue of the new process in a position to manufacture nuclear weapons and some elements of the Afrikaner Press were quick to emphasize the possible military and political implications: "Mr. Vorster has not yet said categorically that South Africa will never make an atom bomb. In view of this fact, people will have to look at us in a new light. South Africa now becomes an altogether different proposition if you want to tackle it. This bargaining power can be used in various fields in the difficult years that lie ahead. America, for example, would have to revise its strategy toward us". Die Beeld (Pretoria), 26 July 1970.

8. The government had already decided to build a 350 Mwe nuclear power station at Melkbosstruit in the Cape Province, completion of which was scheduled for 1977.

9. David Fishlock, "Pretoria Pursues the Atom", Financial Times (London), 18 February 1971.

10. See in particular the writings of David Fishlock in the Financial Times (London) and Aldo Cassuto, "Can Uranium Enrichment Enrich South Africa?", The World Today 26(10), October 1970, 419-427. Thus according to the latter, "the R50 million set aside for the pilot stage is significant as an act of faith in the results of research at the laboratory stage, as it cannot bear comparison with the investment capital required for the ultimate building of a production plant of 'large proportions'". He further cites the high cost involved in building enrichment plants in the United States and Western

Europe - "requiring investments of an order of magnitude that no State budget of the size of the South African one can possible afford", 420.

11. So called in view of the member states joint commitment as signatories of the 1970 Tripartite Agreement to develop the Centrifuge process for making enriched uranium.

12. See Robin Neesham, "Nuclear Power: South Africa's Big Stake," the South African Financial Gazette, 30 March 1972.

13. I am indebted to David Fishlock's articles op.cit., for the information in this section.

14. The exploitation of the South West African deposits is the responsibility of the Rio Tinto Zinc Corporation undertaken in terms of the contractual arrangements with the United Kingdom and South Africa Atomic Energy Boards. Production began at the Rossing mine in 1973.

15. Cassuto, "Can uranium enrichment enrich South Africa?", 420.

16. Ibid., 421 and 425.

17. It is interesting, although perhaps no more than coincidental, that the announcement of the new process in July 1970 occurred at the height of the controversy over the British Conservative's announcement that it proposed to sell arms to the Republic. Was this perhaps an attempt by Mr. Vorster to influence British thinking on the subject of military cooperation with South Africa? If we accept that the timing of the announcement was deliberate, might it not be plausible to argue that Mr. Vorster was in effect stressing South Africa's capacity to act independently, if need be, in the defence field in general and in nuclear matters in particular? Alternatively (and the positions are not mutually exclusive), the Prime Minister's statement might have been calculated to suggest to the Western powers that his government had a positive contribution to make in the scientific and technological realm and that the price of South African cooperation (and its signing of the N.P.T.) was a greater degree of receptiveness to its aspirations on the part of London and Washington.

18. The United Nations. General Assembly. A/C 1/PV.1571, 20 May 1968.

19. Ibid.

20. Indeed, it could be plausible argued that the South African government has always had an interest in the maintenance of Cold War tensions and there are few signs that the present level of detente between the West and the Soviet Union is taken at face value. N.B. The reaction of the South African government to the invasion of Czechoslovakia in 1968: this was construed as evidence that the 'leopard had not changed his spots' (Mr. Botha's phrase in a parliamentary debate on foreign policy in 1968).

21. United Nations. General Assembly. A/C. 1/PV. 1571, op.cit., 53-55

22. Ibid. See also House of Assembly Parliament. Debates, op.cit., col. 57.

23. These are contained in the Security Council Resolution of June 1968 and the Declarations of the United States, The United Kingdom and the Soviet Union associated with this resolution. These oblige the great powers to seek immediate Security Council action to assist a non-nuclear signatory of the treaty that is subject to aggression or the threat of aggression by a nuclear armed power.

24. This assumption has received substantial confirmation in a closely-argued analysis by Geoffrey Kemp. His interpretation of South Africa's defence expenditure between 1948 and 1971 reveals that apparently "at least eighty per cent of the . . . defence programme budget is allocated for the landward threat," G. Kemp, "South Africa's Defence Programme", Survival 14, 1972, 159.

25. See P. Alden Williams, "Republic of South Africa and Sub-Saharan Africa" in Edgar S. Furniss Jnr. and Alden Williams, Political Problems of Nth Country Nuclear Arms Choices, 1966/1980 (Columbus: Ohio State University for the Mershon Centre for Education in National Security, 1965) 77.

26. A scenario often cited in this context by Western supports of arms sales to the Republic assumes an attack on Western merchant ships and oil tankers by Soviet warships in the Indian Ocean. For a discussion of this issue see J.E. Spence, The Strategic Significance of Southern Africa (London: Royal United Services Institution, 1970).

27. N.B. Britain has extensive trading interests in both black and white Africa.

	U.K. exports (f.o.b.)			U.K. imports (c.i.f.)	
	1964	1969		1964	1969
To South Africa	£228m	£291m	From South Africa	£147m	£301m
To Black Africa	£289m	£359m	From Black Africa	£280m	£515m

Quoted from Merle Lipton, "British Arms for South Africa", The World Today 26(10), October 1970, 431.

28. An illustration of the way in which individual African states can exert pressure on Britain arises is the reported hostility of President Gowan of Nigeria to the Smith regime in Rhodesia and any suggestion of a settlement between Whitehall and Salisbury over the heads of the Rhodesian Africans. The British interest in the exploitation of Nigerian oil deposits is certainly one reason why sanctions against Rhodesia have been maintained by the present Conservative government. See Patrick Cosgrove, "Last Year of Rhodesian Sanctions", The Spectator, 7534, November 1972, 786.

29. Larry Bowman, "The Subordinate State System of Southern Africa", International Studies Quarterly 12(3), September 1968, 259, and reprinted in this volume as Chapter One. The ideological version of this policy has been described by the Prime Minister as demonstrating "to the world that race groups with different views and . . . nations following different policies . . . (can) live in peace alongside one another in the same geographic area". South Africa. Parliament. House of Assembly, Debates (speech of the Prime Minister) Vol. 17, col. 2606, 21 September 1966.

30. This is a standard defence by South Africa at the United Nations against the accusations of those who claim that apartheid by definition is a threat to the peace and security of the African continent.

31. Hilgard Muller (Foreign Minister), "South Africa and the World", Report from South Africa, December 1969, 8.

32. N.B. Mr. Vorster's statement that "We wish to avoid the dangers of neo-colonialism in any pattern of assistance which may be agreed upon, but we expect in return a recognition of our own sovereignty within our borders".

33. Quoted in Abdul S. Minty, South Africa's Defence Strategy (London: Anti-Apartheid Movement, 1969), 15.

34. Editorial comment in Die Volksblad, 6 May, 1969.

35. For a detailed analysis of United States - South Africa scientific co-operation, see D.S. Greenberg, "South Africa - Booming Nations Research and Industry Benefit from Close Ties with the United States", Science, 10 July 1970, 157-163.

36. See R. H. Rosecrance, Problems of Nuclear Proliferation (University of California, Los Angeles, 1966), 42 44. Security Paper No. 7.

Chapter Eighteen

THE ORGANISATION OF AFRICAN UNITY AND THE CONFRONTATION OF INDEPENDENT AFRICA WITH THE WHITE SOUTH

Zdenek Cervenka

Introduction

The Organization of African Unity (OAU) is so much a part of the continent's landscape that it is difficult to think back to only eleven years ago when it was not there: a flinty, resilient, gnarled and blackened ebony tree on the African Highlands, which draws the lightning wherever it happens to strike on the continent and which, at other times, provides the shade and shelter for palaver, indaba or baraza. The OAU has never been without its troubles since its birth in 1963, nor was it without them in 1974 - but, unusually, it was also a year of signal triumphs. The unfinished African revolution took a decisive step forward with the abandonment by Portugal of its centuries of colonial rule and the consequent change in the balance of power in Southern Africa which produced the prospect of dramatic changes in Rhodesia and Namibia, if not yet in South Africa itself.

This historic breakthrough came as a result of the success of two arms of OAU policy: its commitment to armed struggle in Southern Africa in the absence of meaningful negotiations, and its diplomatic role in the UN and the Third World.

Foundations of the OAU Policy on Southern Africa

The importance of the OAU within the context of the confrontation between independent Africa and the white supremacy regimes in Southern Africa stems from the fact that it was the common stand of African States on racial discrimination and colonialism which gave birth to the OAU Charter ten years ago on May 25, 1963 in Addis Ababa. Whatever else Africa has been divided about, it has always been virtually unanimous in its determination to eradicate all forms of colonialism from Africa, and to put an end to the South African Government's policy of apartheid.

This sense of unity, which originates in common historical experience of colonialism and the indignity of racial discrimination also sustained the Organisation throughout the first ten years of its existence. In 1963 the OAU policy on

Southern Africa was largely identified with the policy on colonialism and apartheid as Southern Africa encompassed the largest remaining colonial empire of Portugal in Africa and the white regimes practising policies of racial discrimination. Its foundations were laid both by the Charter which declares as one of its purposes "to eradicate all forms of colonialism in Africa" and by the two principal resolutions adopted at the same meeting: Resolution on Decolonization and the Resolution on Apartheid and Racial Discrimination.[1] The Resolution on Decolonization is the more important of the two. In its declaratory part the member States reaffirm their duties to support dependent people in Africa in their struggle for freedom and independence. They describe colonialism as "the forcible imposition of the colonial powers of the settlers to control the governments and administrations of the dependent territories which is a flagrant violation of the inalienable rights of the legitimate inhabitants of the territories concerned." In the operative part the African States agreed on the following measures:

1. To send an OAU delegation to the United Nations to plead the case of dependent territories with the Security Council.
2. To break off diplomatic and consular relations between all African States and South Africa and Portugal.
3. To institute a boycott of the foreign trade of Portugal and South Africa by
   (a) prohibiting the import of goods from those two countries;
   (b) closing African ports and air ports to their ships and planes; and
   (c) forbidding the planes of those two countries to overfly the territories of all African States.
4. To establish a Liberation Committee (officially called the Co-ordinating Committee, responsible for harmonizing the assistance from African States and for managing the Special Fund to be set up for that purpose) with headquarters in Dar es Salaam.
5. To provide liberation movements free transit, material aid and assistance in various fields by bodies of volunteers established in each country.

The Resolution on Apartheid and Racial Discrimination is largely complementary to that on colonialism. This is because the white regimes in South Africa, Rhodesia and Namibia have always been viewed by independent Africa as an alien rule imposed on the African population. The OAU stand in 1963 was one of non-recognition of their white minority regimes until majority rule prevailed. However, in the Lusaka Manifesto of 1969 the Africans conceded that South Africa was an independent sovereign State. This view was reaffirmed by Vernon V. Mwaanga, Foreign Minister of Zambia in his speech at the emergency session of the OAU Council of Ministers in Dar es Salaam in April 1975. But the firm opposition of OAU members against apartheid remained unaffected.

For Africans throughout the continent, apartheid became a symbol of "a crime against humanity, a flagrant violation of the principles of the United Nations and a massive and ruthless denial of human rights constituting a threat to peace".[2] Concurrently, the rule of the white minority of less than four million over fifteen million Africans has all the characteristics of colonial rule.

South Africa is despised by independent Africa. It helps to maintain the illegal rule of the white minority in Rhodesia by defying international mandatory sanctions. It allegedly provided military assistance to the Portuguese colonial armies in Angola and Mozambique, and certainly did so in Rhodesia. Its own military build-up is regarded as a threat to independent African states. It has committed acts of aggression against Zambia. Its occupation of Namibia (South West Africa) is contrary to the United Nations decision to terminate the South African mandate and proclaim Namibia to be an international territory under UN administration. For the OAU, the task of the elimination of apartheid is regarded as an integral part of the task of the liberation of the African continent.[3]

The OAU's policy on apartheid has been threefold:

1. Adoption of measures by the African states themselves; the severence of diplomatic relations with South Africa, the imposition of an economic blockade, the accommodation of refugees from South Africa, and support for the liberation movements within South Africa.
2. Diplomatic pressure on non-African states, and on the United Nations Organisation, which has been repeatedly requested to impose economic sanctions on South Africa.
3. A world-wide campaign "to explain and provide information on the true nature and terrible effects of the policy of apartheid."[4]

The OAU regarded the continuing deterioration of the situation in South Africa as representing a serious threat to peace and international security, a view endorsed by the General Assembly of the United Nations but not by the Security Council.

The OAU's view of apartheid was, however, endorsed by a number of important international conferences. For example, the policy of apartheid was strongly condemned by the International Conference on Human Rights, held under the auspices of the UN at Teheran in May 1968,[5] and a detailed programme of action was formulated by the Oslo Conference on Southern Africa in 1973.[6] [illegible] Draft Convention on the Suppression and Punishment of the [illegible]me of Apartheid, adopted by the 28th General Assembly of the United Nations in 1973, highlights the success of the OAU campaign to outlaw apartheid. The African states, encouraged by the conclusions of the International Conference on Economic Sanctions Against South Africa held in London in 1964 which stated that "the adverse effects of a policy of collective sanctions on world trade, f[illegible]e and on the economies of individual countries having a significant share in the South African economy would be small and marginal, and arguments that vital economic interests are at stake are highly exaggerated",[7] demanded the imposition of economic sanctions. But France, Great Britain and the United States would not even consider it. Gradually, the OAU's appeals gave way to expressions of concern, regret, and finally to strong condemnation. During 1964, the OAU appealed to the major trading partners of South Africa "to discontinue the encouragement they are giving to the maintenance of apartheid by their investments and commercial relations with the Pretoria Government." One year later, at the OAU Summit in Accra, the Heads of State urged all states to institute a strict embargo on the supply of arms to South Africa, and asked France in particular to cease forthwith the supply of military equipment to South Africa. In 1965 the Accra OAU Summit launched a special appeal "to the major trading partners of the Republic of South Africa - particularly the United Kingdom, the United States, Japan, the Federal Republic of Germany, Italy and France - to discontinue their growing economic collaboration with the South African Government, since such collaboration encourages it to defy world opinion and to accelerate the implementation of the policy of apartheid."

During 1967, the OAU concluded that the direct responsibility for the aggravation of the situation in South Africa lay with the principal trading partners of South Africa - especially three of the permanent members of the Security Council - for their refusal to comply with the recommendations of the UN General Assembly and the OAU.[8]

The 1968 OAU Summit "condemned unreservedly" Great Britain, the United States, France, West Germany and Japan for their "continued political and military collaboration with the South African regime" which made it possible for South Africa to persist with its racial policies. West Germany, Italy and France were also condemned for selling military equipment to South Africa and assisting South Africa in the production of ammunition and poisonous gas. Two years later, the OAU warned these states that "any form of military or other co-operation with South Africa, Rhodesia and Portugal constitutes a hostile act against all African States and their peoples."

An important African initiative on decolonisation came in 1969 with the Lusaka Manifesto. The Manifesto on Southern Africa is a joint statement agreed upon by representatives of Burundi, the Central African Republic, Chad, Congo, Ethiopia, Kenya, Rwanda, Somalia, Sudan, Tanzania, Uganda, Zaire, and Zambia at the Conference of East and Central African States in April 1969. It was endorsed by the Assembly of Heads of State and Government of the OAU in the same year and by the General Assembly of the United Nations.[9] The Manifesto makes clear that Africa's objective is human equality and human dignity regardless of race and the implementation of the principle of national self-determination. It calls the regime in South Africa "an open and continual denial of the principles of human equality and national self-determination" and identifies it with "a position of privilege or the experience of oppression depending on one thing which is beyond the power of any man to change - his colour, his parentage and his ancestors." It resolves that Africa must act to bring this racial oppression to an end.

The Lusaka Manifesto goes on to say that, for this purpose, "we would prefer to negotiate rather than destroy, to talk rather than kill." But after briefly reviewing the situation in each area, it regretfully acknowledges that there is nothing to talk about, until the fundamental principles of human equality and self-determination have been accepted by those who now deny them. At present the road of peaceful progress towards their implementation is blocked by those presently in power. The signatories of the Manifesto therefore accept that the peoples of Southern Africa have no choice but to fight for their freedom - to fight for the acceptance of a principle on the basis of which - and only on the basis of which - meaningful discussion could then take place between these peoples and those in power.

Thus, the Lusaka Manifesto makes it clear that the strategy of armed resistance has been accepted by Africa with reluctance. It points out that peaceful progress towards the implementation of the principles of human equality and self-determination is not possible if those in power reject those principles and relentlessly suppress any attempt to further them by peaceful means. The Lusaka Manifesto concludes that "armed resistance is thus the only way through which a climate of change can be created in Southern Africa."

The Lusaka Manifesto was reviewed by the 7th Summit Conference of East and Central African States in October 1971 which adopted the "Mogadishu Declaration". The assembled African leaders reiterated their view that "there is no way left to the liberation of Southern Africa except armed struggle to which we already give and will increasingly give our fullest support." As in case of the "Lusaka Manifesto" the Declaration was adopted by the OAU as its official policy on Southern Africa.[10]

However, the success of any international campaign against South Africa (as well as international efforts on any other issue) whether within or outside the United Nations Organisation depends primarily on the attitude of the permanent members of the Security Council - the United States, the Soviet Union, China, Great Britain and France. Three of them - France, Great Britain and the United States - are the main trading partners of South Africa and the principal investors in South African business.

In 1971, 22% of South Africa's industry was foreign-controlled, chiefly by US and British financial interests in the form of multinational companies. Four major concerns representing mainly US and British capital are in control of the majority of investments throughout the area: the Anglo-American Corporation of South Africa (multinational), Charter Consolidated (UK), which is a merger of two concerns; and the Rhoan Selection Trust and Lonrho (UK). In addition, six large mining companies are a major force in the economy. Among these are De Beers Consolidated Mines, owned by the Oppenheimer concern, which controls 80% of the world's diamond trade, and the related Anglo-American Corporation which controls 40% of South Africa's gold products.[11]

The Western concern for South Africa also has strategic motivations. Ever since the closure of the Suez Canal in 1967, the sea-route around the Cape of Good Hope has assumed a vital importance to the West, both for oil supplies and for Western military strategy in the Indian Ocean. South Africa has for many years tried to draw Western attention to the strategic importance of Southern Africa. In this context, Portugal's former premier Marcello Caetano in 1969 deplored the fact that the major Western powers did not seem to understand that "Africa is more important than Asia to the West."

The October War in 1973 between Israel, Syria and Egypt, and the ensuing Arab oil boycott against the United States, Western Europe and South Africa, suddenly highlighted the strategic position of the contested African territories. At the same time, it became obvious to a large part of the Western world that their societies were dependent on one single source of energy, oil, and that a sudden cut of oil supplies could cause severe economic disruption.

Before the oil crisis in 1973, the monthly total volume of oil shipped around the cape amounted to some 20 million tons, of which about 90% was destined for European ports. [illegible] 20,000 ships a year call at the Cape, and another 14,000 pass without [illegible] [illegible]e larger [illegible]nkers of up to 350,000 tons will have to continue to [illegible] route a[illegible] reopening of the Suez Canal, as the Canal is li[illegible]s in the [illegible] ton class at [illegible]st.[12]

[illegible]th Afric[illegible]bitions to [illegible] recogni[illegible] [illegible]portant ally of the West are [illegible]rther enha[illegible] by the Soviet Navy presence in the Indian Ocean. South Africa has consistently warned of the possibility that the "vacuum" in the Indian Ocean after British withdrawal from east of Suez might be filled by the Soviet Union, as expressed, for example by Admiral H. H. Biermann, the Commander-in-Chief of the South African Defence Force:

> Communist penetration into the Southern Hemisphere, and the threats that this portends, have caused the Southern Hemisphere, and particularly the Indian Ocean to emerge dramatically from a position of relative obscurity and to assume a conspicuous position in the East-West power struggle. The focal point in this changed perspective is occupied by Southern Africa - and the Republic of South Africa.[13]

Since 1968 the question of the strategic importance of the Indian Ocean has become a highly controversial issue which has not yet been resolved.

South African diplomacy which for years was trying to present the African opposition against the white minority rule as "communist inspired" and the Soviet and Chinese presence in Africa as a preparation for "conquest of strategic countries" provided plausible arguments for NATO military thinkers to solve. But this position was weakened by the continual attacks on its policy of apartheid and by its intransigency over Namibia.

Thus it became increasingly difficult for the Western Powers to justify their continuing support for the Pretoria regime. The collapse of the Portuguese colonial empire coupled with the growing economic dependency of Western industries on the raw materials of South Africa's adversaries created a new situation which the Western powers simply could not afford to ignore.

The turning point came on October 25, 1974, when three African members of the Security Council - Cameroon, Kenya and Mauritania - tabled a resolution calling for the immediate expulsion of South Africa from the United Nations. Although the move was blocked by the triple veto of the United States, Great Britain and France (the first time ever the three countries had cast their veto together), it was made clear that in exchange for their veto they would expect a tangible proof that South Africa would begin to eradicate its racial injustices and withdraw from Namibia; otherwise it may not count their veto in the future.[14]

South Africa's appraisal of the new situation was reflected in the speech by the South African Prime Minister John Vorster on October 23, 1974 in his address to the Senate.

> South Africa has come to the crossroad and must now choose between peace and an escalation of violence. If the subcontinent chooses violence it

> would find that the price to be paid was too high. Africa, especially South Africa, would guard against taking a road that would lead to disaster.[15]

The only sure way he could see of avoiding such violent confrontation in Southern African was to seek a new accommodation with his neighbours. This, if successful, would have the added advantage for South Africa of avoiding the loss of much needed Western support that would be jeopardized if South Africa got drawn into a military conflict.

President Kaunda of Zambia in a significant speech in Lusaka on October 26, 1974 welcomed the South African Premier's statement, describing it as "the voice of reason for which Africa and the rest of the world have been waiting." He expressed his willingness to co-operate with South Africa in order to create conditions of peaceful change but he made it clear that such co-operation is possible only in accordance with the principles laid down in the Lusaka Manifesto. This has also been the basis of Zambia's diplomatic initiative to bring about detente in the area. The details of the proposal were revealed by President Kaunda in an interview with the editor-in-chief of Africa in February 1975.[17] Vorster's energetic diplomatic pursuit of this peaceful option, which included a trip to Monrovia in February 1975 to discuss the situation in Southern Africa with President Tolbert of Liberia, brought early promise of success.

Premier Vorster sees detente in Southern Africa as offering three valuable alternatives:

1. It will reduce the dangers of guerilla warfare.
2. It will help to buy the time he needs to "give apartheid a human face" by promoting "independence for his own eight Bantustan Homelands and Namibia" in order to create what he likes to describe as a "United Nations in Southern Africa."
3. It will bring nearer his dream of a Southern African Economic Community with Pretoria as its centre.[18]

His African partners in the detente, namely Presidents Kaunda, Nyerere and Seretse Khama, do not see the future in quite the same way. They insist on the independence of Rhodesia under black majority rule as a prerequisite for peace and a test of South Africa's true intentions. They see a chance of achieving this goal without the dangers of armed struggle and regard Namibia as the next issue while leaving South Africa's future to be settled at a later stage. At the emergency meeting of the Council of Ministers of the OAU at Dar es Salaam in April 1975 they made it clear that there can be no detente without first taking a step in Rhodesia which Vorster, despite the great publicity given to his alleged "pushing of Ian Smith towards settlement with his Africans", has not yet taken.

In his speech to the OAU Foreign Ministers on April 8, 1975 President Nyerere said:

> This conference will have succeeded if it leaves South Africa in no doubt at all that we are still ready to use peaceful means to achieve independence in Rhodesia and Namibia but if this is made impossible, we shall resume and intensify the armed struggle. It is important that both our friends and our enemies should know that we mean what we say.[19]

In a document submitted to the OAU Conference by Tanzania called "African Strategy in Southern Africa"[20] Tanzania made a number of recommendations which were subsequently adopted by the Conference. They included the intensification of the oil embargo against South Africa, the banning of South African ships, aircraft and tourists and phasing out of the African migrant labour in South African mines. The "Declaration" adopted by the conference emphasised that actions leading to the expulsion of South Africa from the United Nations and other international organisations would continue and that South African liberation movements would receive increased support. Although the meeting agreed to give negotiations with Rhodesia and South Africa a further chance to produce a settlement in Rhodesia, at the same time it also recommended preparation for reversion to guerilla war in case they do not. After the Dar es Salaam Conference the next move was left to the South African Premier who would have to make radical domestic changes in apartheid and more convincing moves abroad - such as the withdrawal of South Africa's 2,000 man semi-military police contingent from Rhodesia. At the time of writing he has failed to do so and thus it is difficult to predict the future course of events in Southern Africa. However, one thing is certain: if the opportunity for securing peaceful change in Rhodesia and Namibia offered by the "detente" in 1975 is lost, the escalation of violence will inevitably follow.

The Military Approach to Decolonization

The military strategy contemplated by the OAU throughout its existence is based on the following principles:

1. Support of the armed struggle by the liberation movements in the dependent territories by providing them with material aid.
2. The possibility of direct intervention by the armed forces of the African states.

The verbatim records of the Addis Ababa Summit in 1963 clearly show that some of the African leaders were then seriously proposing the intervention by armies of independent African States. Ahmed Ben Bella, then the President of Algeria, offered an army of 10,000 Algerian volunteers ready to go to Angola "to assist their brothers in arms." President Kwame Nkrumah proposed the creation of an African High Command which would meet the colonial aggression against Africa "by the full weight of our united strength."

President Sekou Toure of Guinea went as far as demanding "that this Conference lays down a deadline for foreign domination of Africa, after which date our armed forces should intervene directly in the legitimate defence of the African continent against aggressors." He also proposed that each independent African State contribute one per cent of its national budget to a national liberation fund. President Obote offered Uganda as a training ground "for the land forces that are necessary for the liberation forces which are needed in the struggle against colonialism."

Despite the advocacy of some African leaders, notably Ben Bella of Algeria and the late Dr. Kwame Nkrumah of Ghana, to assist the liberation movements with armies of independent African States, the majority of the OAU maintained the view that the military struggle should be carried out by the liberation movements in the dependent territories and that the support of the independent African States should be limited to moral and material help only. An attempt to change this policy took place only at the 9th OAU Summit Meeting in Rabat in June 1972, where the following decisions were made:

1. In the "recommendation of special measures to be adopted on decolonisation and the struggle against apartheid and racial discrimination", OAU members were asked to provide transit facilities for all arms and war material destined to the African liberation movements.
2. Member States of the OAU were asked to make available both arms and men, and to place them at the disposal of the proposed Executive Secretariat of Defence.

But in general, the Rabat Summit reaffirmed that the OAU priorities remained the same as in 1963. The appeals for direct involvement of independent African States in the armed struggle for liberation which were heard in Rabat had been heard nine years ago in Addis Ababa. The difference between the Addis Ababa and the Rabat meetings was that in 1963 the consensus of opinion was that national liberation movements should wage their own guerrilla wars with only the support of the independent African States. The consensus at Rabat was to involve armies of the independent African States directly in the liberation struggle in order to liquidate Portuguese colonialism. Although Guinea-Bissau was chosen as the first target, the new policy fully applied to the Portuguese colonies in Southern Africa as well.

The task to elaborate the military strategy fell on the Defence Commission of the Organisation which was asked to prepare detailed military plans of regional defence to ensure that if any country were attacked it would be able to rely on immediate military support from its neighbours. In this connection it should be pointed out that when the African States talk about defence they have in mind defence against colonialism which they regard as "aggression" in terms of Article 51 of the United Nations Charter authorizing member States the right to individual or collective self-defence. This view had been upheld by the United Nations itself.

On November 2, 1972, the Assembly adopted four resolutions which reflected the substantive growth of the UN decolonization ideology. The first of these resolutions (Resolution 2908 (XXVII)) on the implementation of the Declaration on Decolonization reaffirmed that "the continuation of colonialism in all its forms and manifestations including racism, apartheid...as well as the waging of colonial wars to suppress the national liberation movements of the colonial territories in Africa is incompatible with the Charter, the Universal Declaration of Human Rights, and the Declaration (on decolonization)." More important, the Assembly considered the situation "a threat to international peace and security" and reaffirmed its recognition of "the legitimacy of the struggle of the colonial peoples...to exercise their right to self-determination and independence by all the necessary means at their disposal."[21]

Since 1970 the Defence Commission of the OAU has been working on the proposal for a regional defence system which was submitted to the OAU Summit in 1971 and its revised draft again in 1971 and its revised draft again in 1972.[22] But the OAU Defence Committee's aim to establish a joint Military command for Africa has not prospered beyond the levels of aspiration and rhetoric.

The last (fifth) session of the Defence Committee held in Conakry in January 1974 was more preoccupied with pleas to make more effective the support given by African States to the liberation movements to bring about the defeat of Portuguese colonialism, which fell apart four months later through the working of the revolutionary forces in Portugal.

The Role of the OAU Liberation Committee

The very nature of the OAU Liberation Committee, charged with the implementation of the principal aim of OAU - the liquidation of colonialism - has made it one of the most controversial organs of the Organisation. The little publicity allowed by the OAU and its host country Tanzania for explaining its true function left plenty of room for speculation which some journalists often use as a substitute for speculation which some journalists often use as a substitute for facts. From its onset the Committee acquired the reputation for being a headquarter of clandestine subversive operations of a Military High Command conducting the military operations of the liberation movements. Rumours about massive purchases of Soviet, Chinese and Czech arms emanating largely from the South African sources were designed to label the Committee as a centre of Communist conspiracy against Africa. Contrary to the general belief that the Committee is engaged mostly in arm deals and military strategy its function has always been primarily diplomatic.[23]

It is not generally known that the Committee, as a body of the OAU, is closely co-operating with the United Nations and its specified agency providing humanitarian assistance to liberation movements. Diplomatic negotiations are also carried out by the Executive Secretariat with African Studies and "friendly" non-African states - a description used for the Scandinavian countries, the Soviet Union, China and Eastern European countries. But it is the dealing with the liberation movements which dominates the activities of the Liberation Committee and its Secretariat.

Throughout its history the Liberation Committee reflected the turbulent changes in Africa and within the OAU; the succession of coups d'etat; the overthrow of African militant leaders, notably Kwame Nkrumah of Ghana; the Nigerian Civil War; the debate about "the dialogue with South Africa", all of which diverted the attention of the OAU members from their obligations towards the Liberation Committee.

Within the framework of the OAU the controversies over the Committee were mainly a result of the conflict between the States advocating armed struggle against colonial and white minority regimes and those professing "a peaceful approach to decolonization". As often is the case, the States with the largest arrears in contribution to the Special Fund administered by the Liberation Committee were its noisiest critics. The constant criticism of the Liberation Committee made it subject to never ending scrutiny by the Assembly of Heads of State and Government which continuously changed the scope of its competence, its structure and its composition.

There has also always been a problem of guarding the Committee's secrets. An essential condition for the success of any organisation dealing with movements engaged in guerilla warfare is that its communications, reports and recommendations must be kept in absolute secrecy. This was one of the main reasons why the African leaders in Addis Ababa in 1963 granted the Liberation Committee an autonomous status. The Committee was directly responsible only to the Assembly of Heads of State and Government. Meetings were closed to non-members and the powers of the Executive Secretary of the Liberation Committee exceeded even those of the Administrative Secretary-General of the OAU. Needless to say this arrangement was resented very much by both the General Secretariat and the non-members of the Committee. The process through which the Committee began to be stripped of most of its powers is described further on. When in 1966 the Assembly of Heads of State and Government decided that all the reports of the Liberation Committee were to be distributed to all members States of the OAU (with the exception of Malawi) it could have been safely assumed that these reports would find their way to the files of Embassies of non-African powers interested in the progress of the armed struggle against their allies. A turn for the better came after the 1970 OAU Summit at Rabat whose militant spirit, comparable to the "spirit of Addis Ababa" in 1963, gave the Committee a new lease on life.

The OAU Assembly established a committee entrusted with the task of conducting a study, after consultations with the liberation movements and all Member States of the OAU, of the mandate, the structure and the composition of the Liberation Committee. The report of the Committee, composed of representatives from Algeria, the Central African Republic, Ethiopia, Kenya, Morocco, Senegal and Sierra Leone was debated at the 21st session of the Liberation Committee held in Accra in January 1973. It produced a major breakthrough in the search for a new policy on African liberation.

The recommendations contained in the report were embodied into "The Accra Declaration on the New Strategy for the Liberation of Africa".[24] The following are the main points of the new strategy adopted by the OAU Liberation Committee:

1. The liberation of Africa is a collective responsibility of all African States. While the responsibilities of carrying on the armed struggle rest with the liberation movements its intensification presupposes the availability of appropriate resources at their disposal.
2. The "collective responsibility" of the OAU Member States was specified as follows:
   a) To pay immediately their outstanding dues to the Special Fund;
   b) To make additional voluntary material and financial assistance to the liberation movements which is a must in the current situation;
   c) To provide training facilities for the cadres of the liberation movements; and
   d) To be ready for collective military and economic assistance to any OAU state in case it becomes a victim of an aggression committed by Portugal, Rhodesia or South Africa.

3. The policy regarding the liberation movements was specified as follows:
   a) Granting of recognition and assistance will be given only to the "Fronts" which are politically and militarily united and which can provide evidence of effective operation within the country; and
   b) The largest part of the assistance will be given to the liberation movements in the Portuguese territories.
4. The Declaration stressed the need to strengthen the institutional structure of the Executive Secretariat in order to enhance its capacity to respond effectively to the urgent needs of the next stage of the liberation struggle.

The Liberation Committee played a major role in the diplomatic offensive aimed at the swift solution of the Rhodesian situation. As early as August 1974 when none of the later revelations about the contacts between Zambia and South Africa and the meetings in Lusaka attended by the representatives of the Rhodesian government had been made, the Acting Executive Secretary of the OAU Liberation Committee, Ahmed Sidky, told the author of the offer made to the British Government "to offer full guarantee of personal safety and property of Rhodesia's European population and a participation in the political life of the country provided that the Rhodesian government would agree to the complete transfer of power to the African majority."

The plan was put to the British Labour Government by the Zambian Foreign Minister Vernon Mwaanga after consulting the current OAU Chairman President Siad Barre of Somalia and the Heads of State of Kenya, Nigeria, Ghana, Ivory Coast, Liberia, Sierra Leone, Guinea-Bissau, Senegal, Mauritania, Zaire and Gambia. These moves prepared the ground for the historical December 1974 meeting in Lusaka of the Presidents of Tanzania, Zambia and Botswana and of the President of FRELIMO with representatives of African National Congress (ANC), ZAPU, ZANU and FROLIZI. The active part of the OAU Liberation Committee in these negotiations considerably strengthened the hands of the Presidents in their negotiations with the liberation movements.

The increase in the diplomatic activity of the OAU Liberation Committee in the final stage of decolonization of Africa became evident from the fact that the Committee met four times between May 1974 and January 1975; in Yaoundé from May 13-18, 1974; in Magodishu from June 12-15, 1974 (before the annual OAU Summit), in Dar es Salaam from November 24-29, 1974; and again from January 8-14, 1975.

The Yaoundé meeting was important for its 19 point Yaoundé Declaration subsequently endorsed by the Mogadishu Summit. It welcomed the ending of Portugal's fascist regime as being in the interests of both the long-suffering Portuguese people and of Lisbon's colonial subjects; it stressed the importance of the liberation struggle in achieving this change; repeated the importance of the Lusaka Manifesto as offering a possible alternative for peaceful negotiations; reaffirmed the vital importance of the complete independence of all Portugal's colonial territories; opposed separate negotiations between various liberation movements and Lisbon; and recognized the sole right of PAIGC to negotiate on behalf of Guinea-Bissau and of FRELIMO on behalf of Mozambique. It did not designate any of the Angolan liberation movements for negotiations with Portugal; this was done at its meeting in Dar es Salaam in November of the same year. The new strategy for liberation based on the model of peaceful transition achieved in Mozambique was endorsed by the meeting of the Committee in Dar es Salaam in January 1975 where Rhodesia and Namibia were given top priority in the Committee's schedule for 1975.

Conclusions

African objectives in Southern Africa are independence for Rhodesia and Namibia on the basis of majority rule and an end to apartheid and racial discrimination in South Africa.

Africa's strategy outlined at the meeting of the OAU Council of Ministers at Dar es Salaam in April 1975 (see Appendix I for text of Dar es Salaam Declaration) separates the two issues by giving priority to ending the colonial situation in Rhodesia and Namibia. On both issues the OAU is willing to talk with South Africa as well as with the regime of Ian Smith in Rhodesia about the mechanics of a transfer of power as soon as there is any evidence of a willingness to accept these objectives in principle. The task of the OAU is to facilitate the war of African National Council (ANC) in Rhodesia and of SWAPO in Namibia by providing contact through diplomatic channels of the OAU members. The OAU fully recognizes the primary responsibility and authority of the liberation movements in both territories and makes it clear that none of the OAU members assisting these movements should make any commitment on their behalf except at their request. But whatever progress may or may not be made in talks about the transfer of power in Rhodesia and Namibia preparations are being made for continuing the armed struggle if the peaceful transfer is rejected.

While the OAU is prepared to talk with South Africa about Rhodesia and Namibia it refuses to do so on apartheid. The OAU's stand was put clearly in the memorandum of Tanzania submitted to the OAU Council of Ministers' meeting in Dar es Salaam in the following words:

> Talking with the South African government on apartheid is worse than irrelevant. We know what Vorster means by it, we know what it means to the African people of South Africa, as well as to the whole concept of human equality and dignity. Vorster knows what Africa thinks of apartheid. There is no need for any discussion. Further, if and when a South African government decides to change its policies and wants to discuss the new directions with African people, it has no need to use free Africa. Nelson Mandela, Robert Sobukwe and hundreds of other non-white South African leaders are either rotting away physically on Robben Island or in other prisons and places of restriction.
>
> When Vorster decides to release these men and women, to allow peaceful African political activity, and to listen to what they say, we shall know that justice might well triumph in South Africa without the bloodshed we fear. Until those signs are evident we must treat South Africa as an outlaw.[25]

The OAU's strategy thus makes it clear that the fate of Southern Africa will be decided upon from within, rather than from the outside. But the two thrusts of pressure - one exercised by the 40 million Africans of Southern Africa, and the other by the Organisation of African Unity are closely interrelated and one cannot succeed without the other. The resolutions adopted by the OAU on these issues should not be judged only as high sounding phrases which to many Western observers sound hollow. The resolutions are important political decisions, the unanimous acceptance of which demonstrates the united stand of Africans on decolonisation and apartheid. They provide not only political guidance for the foreign policies of the OAU members but are also instruments of diplomatic pressure on the allies of the colonial and white minority regimes in the area. That the Western Powers still refuse to yield to these pressures is certainly not an argument for abandoning the militant stand. Although the West tends to take the OAU warnings very lightly, they are at least forced to explain their policies of partnership with South Africa to their own people, and are even, to a rather limited degree, inhibited from more open support for the regimes that Africa is fighting against. Had it not been for the OAU, pressure on Britain and the United Nations - in the case of Rhodesia - the Ian Smith regime would have long enjoyed recognition and uninhibited, prosperous trade with the West. Had the OAU resigned itself to the policy of dialogue, the South African economic empire would have by now already embraced both southern and central Africa and would be aiming at the north.

The impact of the OAU policy can best be demonstrated on the foreign policies of South Africa's hostages - Botswana, Lesotho and Swaziland. Only 10 years ago, at the OAU Summit in Accra in 1965, they had to answer to criticisms of their close ties with South Africa by a joint memorandum.[26] Today they are winning praise from the OAU for their firm stand an apartheid and for their brave attempts to extricate themselves from the dependence of South Africa. While their geographic position and economic structure precludes them from terminating their economic ties with South Africa, they are certainly trying to reduce these ties and thus gain more room for political independence which they reassert at every available opportunity.[27]

The growing recognition of the usefulness of the OAU leaves no doubt that the Organization is to play a much more significant role in the next decade. The final test of its political and diplomatic strength will come when the liberation of Africa is reduced to a confrontation between the OAU and its last and most powerful adversary: The Republic of South Africa.

NOTES

1. For the text of both resolutions, see Ethiopia Addis Ababa Summit: 1963 (Addis Ababa: Ministry of Information, 1963) 100-101.

2. This is how apartheid was described by the International Conference of Experts for the Support of Victims of Colonialism and Apartheid in Southern Africa, held in Oslo in April 1973. For the proceedings see O. Stokke and C. Widstrand (eds) Southern Africa: The UN-OAU Conference, Oslo, April 9-14, 1973 Vol. I and II (Uppsala: The Scandinavian Institute of African Studies, 1973).

3. In the resolution adopted at the same time as the OAU Charter in 1963, the African leaders were "unanimously convinced of the imperious and urgent necessity of co-ordinating and intensifying their efforts to put an end to the South African Government's criminal policy of apartheid and wipe out racial discrimination in all its forms." One year later, at the Cairo OAU Summit, President Milton Obote of Uganda said that "our own independence and self-respect have no strong image so long as blackmen elsewhere in Africa, indeed anywhere in the world, are still held in bondage solely on the grounds of their colour and are prevented by restrictive laws from holding their heads up as full citizens of a world in which civilisation and entitlement to a good life have never been at any time in the history of mankind the exclusive monopoly of any one race."

4. OAU Council of Ministers Resolution CM/Res. 102(IX), September 1967.

5. The Proclamation of Teheran adopted on May 13, 1968 stated the following:

   > Gross denials of human rights under the repugnant policy of apartheid is a matter of the gravest concern to the international community. This policy of apartheid, condemned as a crime against humanity, continues seriously to disturb international peace and security. It is therefore imperative for the international community to use every possible means to eradicate this evil. The struggle against apartheid is recognized as legitimate.

   For the text of the Teheran Declaration, see UN publication issued on the 25th Anniversary of the Universal Declaration of Human Rights entitled Human Rights (New York: United Nations, 1973).

6. The proposals for action against South Africa include:

   1. International economic and other mandatory sanctions, to be imposed by the United Nations;
   2. the withdrawal of all investments from South Africa;
   3. the termination of all economic and scientific support, in particular nuclear co-operation;
   4. the termination of the purchase of South Africa's gold, platinum, and other minerals;
   5. a halt to immigration;
   6. the termination of all special terms and concessions by the European Economic Community

7. the termination of all military agreements and the imposition of an effective arms embargo;

8. the exclusion of South Africa from all international cultural and sports organizations;

9. the adoption of a "Convention on the Suppression and Punishment of the Crime of Apartheid" by all states.

7. For the proceedings of the Conference, see Ronald Segal (ed) Sanctions Against South Africa (Harmondsworth: Penguin, 1964).

8. CM/Res. 102 (IX) 1967.

9. Resolution 2505 (XXIV) of 20 November 1969.

10. The text of the Mogadishu Declaration was circulated among the UN Members at the request of the Permanent Mission of the Somali Democratic Republic to the United Nations (UN document UN/93(137) of 23 February 1972).

11. Signe Landgren Southern Africa: The Escalation of a Conflict (SIPRI: Stockholm, 1975). See also J. E. Spence "The Political and Military Framework" Study Project on External Investment in South Africa and Namibia (London: Africa Publication Trust, 1975).

12. Landgren, Southern Africa.

13. Quoted by S. Landgren

> Divergent judgements of the situation from and within the Western powers were clearly discernible, following at least three major lines. The first question to consider was whether the growing Soviet naval presence in the Indian Ocean really ought to be interpreted as militarily significant or not. The relevance of the UK and NATO Indian Ocean strategy was closely connected with their perception of the meaning of the Soviet naval presence. Thirdly, there was the position of many of the coastal states around the Indian Ocean, supporting the idea of an Indian Ocean "nuclear-free zone of peace" and opposing all foreign attempts to fill any "vacuum" in the region. This proposal was clearly irreconcilable with the US and NATO point of view, which in 1974 was often summarized as expecting that the Soviet and Chinese threat in the Indian Ocean would lead to a new round of the East-West arms race in this part of the world.
>
> In the discussion of a Soviet threat to the Cape route, furthermore, one crucial question seems largely neglected, namely why the Soviet Union should attempt a direct military attack on Western energy supply routes in the Indian Ocean, and if there really is any Soviet political influence in the littoral states of the ocean.

Ibid.

14. In their own draft resolution the Western powers called on South Africa to make immediate and broad concessions along three lines:

a) Withdrawal of all South African military forces from Rhodesia;

b) Progress on the negotiations for self-determination of South West Africa; and

c) The repeal of certain domestic legislation involving apartheid.

15. Rand Daily Mail (Johannesburg) October 24, 1974.

16. See the address by President Kenneth Kaunda entitled Southern Africa: A Time for Change (Lusaka: Ministry of Information, 1974) delivered on the occasion of the conferment of the degree of LL.D. (Honoris Causa) at the University of Zambia, October 26, 1974.

17. Exclusive interview by Raph Uwechue Africa (London) 42, February 1975, 10-12.

18. Colin Legum in his article "Why Vorster is Turning the Heat on his Own Ally" Observer (London) March 23, 1975.

19. Daily News (Dar es Salaam) April 9, 1975.

20. The full text of the document which contains probably the best analysis of the situation in Southern Africa from the African point of view was reproduced by the Daily News, April 10, 1975.

21. For a detailed study of the problem see Yassin El Ayouty Legitimization of National Liberation: The United Nations and Southern African (New York: IMAS, 1973).

22. The main features of the proposal are the following:

    1. The creation of Regional Defence Systems comprising one or several units of national armed forces from States in the various regional sectors and linked by bilateral or multilateral defence agreements.
    2. A military commander of each of these Defence Systems who would be subordinate to a Chief of Staff, a deputy, and representatives of the national armies of the States concerned.
    3. An office of Military Defence Advisers within the OAU General Secretariat, which would not only co-ordinate all matters concerning the security of member States but also gather military information and intelligence likely to interest the OAU Liberation Committee. This office would comprise a military adviser with the rank of brigadier appointed for two and a half years; and three officers with the rank of major appointed for two years. The latter would represent the three armed forces - land, sea, and air. Members of the office would be appointed by the OAU Summit on recommendations from the Defence Commission Bureau which at present consists of representatives from Ethiopia, Equatorial Guinea and Zambia.
    4. The creation of a permanent Defence Committee which would meet every six months or when called into session by the Chairman of the Bureau. This Permanent Committee would comprise of Bureau members, the Military Adviser in the OAU Secretariat, representatives of the regional or sector Executive Secretariats, the OAU Secretary-General, and the Executive Secretary of the Liberation Committee.

23. During the author's visit to the Committee's Headquarters in Dar es Salaam in August 1974 the Deputy Executive Secretary for Defence Ahmed Sidky firmly refuted the rumours surrounding the activities of the Committee and said that in the last two years the Committee did not itself purchase one single gun or round of ammunition.

24. Only excerpts of the Declaration were published in the press. The full text is in the Library of the Scandinavian Institute of African Studies, Uppsala.

25. For the full text of the memorandum, see article entitled "African Strategy in Southern Africa" Daily News, April 10, 1975.

26. Joint Memorandum by the Leaders of the Elected Governments of Basutoland, Bechuanaland Protectorate and Swaziland to the Heads of African States (Accra, October 25, 1965) quoted by Christian Potholm in "Swaziland" in Potholm and Dale (eds) Southern Africa in Perspective, 151.

27. The policy of Sir Seretse Khama, President of Botswana, was summed up in his speech to the Foreign Policy Society in Copenhagen, Denmark, in November 1970 in the following way:

> We have sought to safeguard our political independence, to ensure our survival as a nation, but to do so with honour and dignity and without sacrificing any of our fundamental principles. We decided never to ignore the harsh realities of our situation as an integral part of Southern Africa. We cannot pick up our vast country and replace it on some more comfortable portion of the map. But we decided at the same time never to condone the racialist policies of our neighbours.

The independent stand of both Lesotho and Swaziland took several years to evolve, but it eventually came close to Botswana's policy as illustrated by the following quote from Chief Leabua Jonathan's address marking the International Day for the Elimination of Racial Discrimination at Maseru on March 21, 1972.

> Lesotho's opposition to racism is part of a national history and goes back to pre-1910 days. It is the abhorrence of racism that led the people of this country to oppose incorporation of the territory into the Union of South Africa in 1910. When, on the attainment of independence in 1966, Lesotho embarked on a policy of peaceful co-existence, this was by no means an indication that she had abandoned her opposition to racism and racial discrimination.

The Government of Swaziland, though considerably more restrained in its pronouncements against South Africa has made it clear on a number of occasions that it does not subscribe to the policy of apartheid. In a joint communique on the talks between the Prime Minister of Swaziland and the President of Zambia in Lusaka in May 1971 both the leaders reaffirmed "their common commitment to non-racial society" and agreed on the need for each country" to make its own contribution to the eventual triumph of self-determination, human dignity and equality throughout Southern Africa".

Appendix I

The following is the text of the Dar es Salaam Declaration on Southern Africa adopted by the Ninth Extraordinary Session of the OAU Council of Ministers held in Dar es Salaam from April 7-10, 1975.

THE COUNCIL of Ministers of the Organization of African Unity Meeting in Dar es Salaam from April 7-10, 1975 in an Extraordinary Session has made an in-depth study of the developments in Southern Africa in general and the situation in South Africa in particular. This evaluation was made with the specific objective of devising ways and means of realising Africa's long cherished objective in the region, namely the total liquidation of the twin evils of colonialism and racism.

COLONIALISM. In recent years Africa has adopted and carried out several strategies against colonialism. When in 1969, the racist and colonial regimes ignored the Lusaka Manifesto, the African States adopted the Mogadishu Declaration in 1971 calling for the intensification of the armed struggle. This was followed by the Accra Strategy of 1973 concentrating on the liberation of the Portuguese colonies.

The victory over Portuguese colonialism which vindicated the Accra Strategy led Africa, this, year, to adopt the Dar es Salaam Declaration by which the OAU has resolved to make use of the victories achieved by the freedom fighters of Mozambique, Angola, Guines Bissau and Cape Verde, Sao Tome and Principe for the advance of the freedom march further south with particular emphasis on the liberation of Zimbabwe and Namibia. The Extraordinary Session of the Council of Ministers while unequivocally reaffirming this Declaration, wishes to highlight the following:

ZIMBABWE. Africa's objective in Zimbabwe is independence on the basis of majority rule. This can be achieved either peacefully or by violent means. Either way, Africa will give its unqualified support to the freedom fighters led by their nationalist movement - the African National Council (ANC).

As long as the objective of Majority Rule before Independence is not compromised, Africa would support all efforts made by the Zimbabwe nationalists to win independence by peaceful means. This may mean a holding of a Constitutional Conference where the nationalist forces will negotiate with the Smith regime. If that takes place, free Africa has the duty to do everything possible to assist the success of such negotiations, until and unless the Rhodesian nationalists themselves are convinced that talks with Smith have irretrievably failed.

In the consideration of Africa's objectives in Rhodesia, it is important to properly evaluate the role of South Africa in that territory. South Africa has troops in Rhodesia which help to maintain the white minority rule. South Africa has frustrated the efforts of the international community by being the major sanctions buster. Both in its military and economic support of the Smith regime, South Africa continues to defy Africa's and the United Nations' opposition. The apartheid regime must put an end to the military and economic support.

While Africa accepts helping in genuine negotiations in order to facilitate the transfer of power to the African majority it must remain absolutely vigilant and undertake the necessary preparations for the intensification of the armed struggle should peaceful solution to the Rhodesia conflict be blocked.

NAMIBIA. Africa's and the United Nations' position on the question of Namibia is unequivocal. South Africa's continued occupation of that land is illegal and all member states of the United Nations are under obligation to refrain from doing anything which implies the legality of its administration. Africa must fulfill strictly this obligation to abstain from any action which may be construed as recognition or acceptance of South Africa's right to be in Namibia.

Africa and the United Nations hold the unity and territorial integrity of Namibia sacrosanct. They are working for the independence of the territory as a whole and are totally opposed to its fragmentation. Africa and the United Nations recognise SWAPO as the legitimate and authentic representative of the whole of Namibia. Despite the specific and unanimous demand of the Security Council, South Africa has not yet agreed to undertake withdrawing from Namibia. In fact the apartheid regime has consolidated its repressive rule in the territory and proceeded with its bantustanization.

The Council of Ministers reiterate their conviction that the only possible solution to the problem of Namibia lies in the implementation by South Africa of Security Council Resolution of December 17, 1974. The African States considering that the Security Council by its own decision is scheduled to convene on or about the 30 May, 1975 to consider the question of Namibia, call upon the Council to take the necessary measures including those envisaged under chapter VII of the United Nations' Charter with a view to effectively overcome South Africa's defiance and contempt of the United Nations decisions.

In the absence of South Africa's willingness to terminate its illegal occupation of Namibia, Africa must assist the national liberation movement of Namibia, SWAPO, to intensify the armed struggle in Namibia. SWAPO should also be supported in every way possible.

APARTHEID. As regards South Africa, both the OAU and the United Nations are dedicated to the principle of full equality for all the people of the country, irrespective of race or colour. It is impossible for free Africa to acquiesce in the denial of human equality and human dignity which is represented by the philosophy and system of apartheid. Thus the OAU like the United Nations, opposes the regime in South Africa, not because it is white, but because it rejects and fights against the principles of human equality and national self-determination.

Africa has repeatedly warned that the apartheid regime constitutes a serious threat to international peace and security. This threat assumes graver proportions as the apartheid regime feels insecure. Despite Vorster's claims at the end of last year that given six months or so the world would be surprised by the changes that would be initiated from within the apartheid republic, the situation has taken a turn for the worst as evidenced by the mass trial of students, the consolidation and strengthening of the "Bantustans" and the vast increase of South Africa's military budget. Clearly, Vorster's Government is not about to depart from the doctrine of apartheid. Indeed, if anything, Vorster's measures have been designed to strengthen the security of the system of apartheid within South Africa.

Confronted with this unabashed determination of the apartheid regime to maintain its white supremacist system, Africa's responsibility is clear. We must ostracise, and urge the rest of the world to ostracise, the South African regime as at present organized.

Africa must maintain the economic, political and cultural boycott of South Africa. The OAU and the United Nations must work in concert for the extension of the boycott. We must, in brief, work for the total isolation of the apartheid regime.

There is no justification at all for changing this policy. Nor is there anything for free Africa to talk to the leaders of the apartheid regime in connection with their policies in South Africa. If current or future leaders of the apartheid regime should desire to begin to move away from the policy of racism in South Africa and to seek the cooperation of the Africans to that end, they could initiate the necessary contacts and negotiations from within.

They would find the oppressed of South Africa and other opponents of racism led by their national liberation movement, ready for such negotiations which should enable the people of South Africa as a whole to determine the destiny of their country. The apartheid regime could initiate such a dialogue by the release of Nelson Mandella and derestriction of Robert Sobukwe, as well as hundreds of other nationalist leaders who are now languishing in South Africa's jails or under Restriction orders.

The Council of Ministers of the Organisation of African Unity resolutely reaffirms free Africa's total rejection of apartheid and all its ramifications, including any so called independent homelands within South Africa.

SOLIDARITY. The Council underscores the importance of all independent African States to remain firmly united in the policy of isolating South Africa and ostracizing its apartheid regime. The Council reiterates its support to the national liberation movements of South Africa in their struggle in all its forms. It also calls for the intensification of international efforts - with the co-operation of Governments, Inter-Governmental and non-Governmental organisations for the eradication of apartheid.

Unprecedented opportunities and challenges prevail in southern Africa subsequent to the collapse of the 500-year-old Portuguese colonialism. Free Africa is determined to capitalise on the opportunities in order to bring closer the day when every inch of African soil will be free from colonial and racist domination. While being cognizant of the fact that South Africa stands as the final major obstacle to Africa's march to liberation, the Council of Ministers reaffirm their unflinching determination to realise the freedom and independence of Rhodesia and Namibia and the total destruction of apartheid and racial discrimination in South Africa.

The Council of Ministers, conscious of the important contribution made by African friends and supporters all over the world in its quest for the liberation of the continent, launches a fervent appeal to them by urging them to continue and intensify their support for solidarity with the liberation of Zimbabwe and Namibia as well as for the ending of the inhuman system of apartheid in South Africa.

CONTRIBUTORS

DOUGLAS G. ANGLIN is Professor of Political Science at Carleton University, Ottawa. He was Vice-Chancellor at the University of Zambia from 1965 to 1969 and has done research at Ibadan and Princeton Universities. He has written extensively on the foreign policy of Zambia and the politics of Southern Africa; his recent articles include "Confrontation in Southern Africa: Zambia and Portugal" International Journal (1970), "Zambia and the Recognition of Biafra" African Review (1971), "The Politics of Transit Routes in Land-locked Southern Africa" in Zdenek Cervenka (ed) Land-locked Countries of Africa (1973) and "Zambia and Southern African 'detente'" International Journal (1975).

JOHN BARRATT is Director of the South African Institute of International Affairs in Johannesburg. He is an editor of International Aspects of Over-population (1972) and Accelerated Development in Southern Africa (1974) and the author of a set of essays on South Africa including "The Department of Foreign Affairs" in Denis Worrall (ed) South Africa: Government and Politics (1971) "South Africa's Outward Policy: From Isolation to Dialogue" in Nic Rhoodie (ed) South African Dialogue (1972) and "Detente in Southern Africa" World Today (1975).

LARRY W. BOWMAN is Associate Professor of Political Science at the University of Connecticut, Storrs. In addition to the seminal article reprinted here he has written Politics in Rhodesia: White Power in an African State (1974) and a series of articles on Southern Africa including "South Africa's Southern Strategy and its Implications for the United States" International Affairs (1971), and "Portugal and South Africa" in Steven L. Spiegel and Kenneth N. Waltz (eds) Conflict in World Politics (1971).

J. BARRON BOYD is Assistant Professor of Political Science at LeMoyne College, Syracuse, New York, and holds a doctorate from the University of South Carolina. His essay on "The Subsystem of Southern Africa: A Structural Analysis" was placed second in the 1973 U.S. student paper competition organised by the International Studies Association.

ZDENEK CERVENKA is Research Director at the Scandinavian Institute of African Studies, Uppsala, Sweden; he previously worked in the Ministry of Justice, Ghana, and the Czechoslovakia Academy of Sciences. He is editor of Land-locked Countries of Africa (1973), a correspondent for Africa and author of The Organisation of African Unity and its Charter (1969) and "Major Policy Shifts in the Organisation of African Unity, 1963-1973" in Kenneth Ingham (ed) The Foreign Relations of African States (1974).

ROBERT L. CURRY, JR. is Professor of Economics at California State University, Sacramento, and has taught at the Universities of Liberia and Zambia. He is author of several books and articles on international exchange and bargaining including A Theory of Political Exchange: Economic Reasoning in Political Analysis (1968) and A Logic of Public Policy: Aspects of Political Economy (1970), both with Larry L. Wade,"Liberia's External Debts and Their Servicing" Journal of Modern African Studies (1972) and "On Economic Bargaining Between African Governments and Multinational Companies" Journal of Modern African Studies (1974) with Donald Rothchild.

KENNETH W. GRUNDY is Professor and Chairman of Political Science at Case Western Reserve University, Cleveland, and has taught at Makerere University, Uganda. He is author of Guerrilla Struggle in Africa (1971) and Confrontation and Accomodation in Southern Africa (1973) and co-author of The Ideologies of Violence (1974). Among his many articles on African politics are "African Explanations of Underdevelopment: The Theoretical Basis for Political Action" Review of Politics (1966), "Host Countries and the Southern African Liberation Struggle" Africa Quarterly (1970) and "The 'Southern Border' of Africa" in Carl Widstrand (ed) African Boundary Problems (1969).

CHARLES HARVEY is a Fellow in the Institute of Development Studies at the University of Sussex, having previously lectured at the University of Zambia. He is co-editor of Economic Independence and Zambian Copper: A Case Study of Foreign Investment (1972) and author of "Financial Constraints on Zambian Development" and "The Fiscal System" in Charles Elliott (ed) Constraints on the Economic Development of Zambia (1971), "The Control of Credit in Zambia" Journal of Modern African Studies (1973), "British Investment in Southern Africa" Journal of Southern African Studies (1974) and "The Economics of Withdrawal" in Foreign Investment in South Africa: The Policy Debate (1975).

KENNETH A. HEARD is Professor and Past-Chairman, Department of Political Science, Dalhousie University, Halifax, Nova Scotia. He taught previously at Rhodes and Natal Universities and has written extensively on the politics of Southern Africa. His publications include Political Systems in Multi-racial Societies (1961) and

General Elections in South Africa 1943-1970 (1974). He is co-editor of Politics of Africa: Dependence and Development (forthcoming).

CHRISTOPHER R. HILL is Director of the Centre for Southern African Studies at the University of York, England, and previously lectured at the University College of Rhodesia. He is author of Bantustans: The Fragmentation of South Africa (1964), editor of Rights and Wrongs: Some Essays on Human Rights (1969), and several articles including "UDI and South African Foreign Policy" Journal of Commonwealth Political Studies (1969), "Independent Botswana: Myth or Reality?" Round Table (1972) and "The Botswana-Zambia Boundary Question: A Note of Warning" Round Table (1973).

SHERIDAN W. JOHNS is Associate Professor of Political Science at Duke University, North Carolina, and has taught at the University of Zambia. Among his essays on Southern Africa are "The Birth of Non-white Trade Unionism in South Africa" Race (1967), "Parastatal Bodies in Zambia: Problems and Prospects" in Heide and Udo Simonis (eds) Socio-economic Development in Dual Economies: The Example of Zambia (1971), "Obstacles to Guerrilla Warfare - A South African Case Study" Journal of Modern African Studies (1973) and "Botswana's Strategy for Development: An Assessment of Dependence in the Southern African Context" Journal of Commonwealth Political Studies (1974).

ARTHUR M. KEPPEL-JONES is Professor of History at Queen's University, Kingston, Ontario, and was formerly Head of the Department of History at the University of Natal, Durban. Among his publications on South Africa are Human Relations in South Africa, Political and Historical (1953), South Africa: A Short History (1966) and "South Africa in 1998: Trends and Developments During the Next Twenty-five Years" Issue (1974).

ZBIGNIEW A. KONCZACKI is Professor of Economics at Dalhousie University, Halifax, Nova Scotia; he previously taught at the Universities of Natal and Alberta. Among his many publications on African economies are Public Finance and Economic Development of Natal 1893-1910 (1967), "Currency and Banking in Ethiopia" The South African Journal of Economics (1962), "Nomadism and Economic Development in Somalia" Canadian Journal of African Studies (1968), and "Infant Malnutrition in Sub-Saharan Africa: A Problem in Socio-economic Development" Canadian Journal of African Studies (1972). He is co-editor of Pre-colonial Economic History of Africa South of the Sahara (1976) and Economic History of Tropical Africa: Colonial Period (forthcoming).

CHRISTIAN P. POTHOLM is Associate Professor of Government at Bowdoin College in Brunswick, Maine, having previously taught at Dartmouth and Vassar Colleges. He is author of Four African Political Systems (1970) and Swaziland: The Dynamics of Political Modernization (1972). He is co-editor of Southern Africa in Perspective: Essays in Regional Politics (1972) and among his many articles on the region are "After Many a Summer? The Possibilities of Political Change in South Africa" World Politics (1972) "The International Transfer of Insurgency Techniques: Sub-Saharan Pathologies" Plural Societies (1972) and "Wanderers on the Face of Africa: Refugees in Kenya, Tanzania, Zambia and Botswana" Round Table (1976).

DONALD ROTHCHILD is Professor of Political Science at the University of California, Davis. He has taught at the Universities of Nairobi, Zambia and Ibadan and has published widely in the field of African politics. He is editor of Politics of Integration: An East African Documentary (1968) and author of Toward Unity in Africa (1960) and Racial Bargaining in Independent Kenya (1973); among his recent articles are "Ethnicity and Conflict Regulation" World Politics (1970), "Rural-Urban Inequities and Resource Allocation in Zambia" Journal of Commonwealth Political Studies (1972), "Changing Racial Stratifications and Bargaining Styles: The Kenya Experience" Canadian Journal of African Studies (1973) and "From Hegemony to Bargaining in East African Relations" Journal of African Studies (1974).

LAWRENCE SCHLEMMER is Professor in the Faculty of Social Science and Director of the Institute for Social Research at the University of Natal, Durban. His writings on the sociology of South Africa include Political Policy and Social Change in South Africa: An Assessment of the Future of Separate Development and of Possible Alternatives to the Policy (1970), "Future Political Implications of Present Trends" in Directions of Change in Southern African Politics (1971), "White Attitudes to the Bantustans" Third World (1973) and "Employment Opportunity and Race in South Africa" Studies in Race and Nations (1973).

TIMOTHY M. SHAW is Assistant Professor of Political Science in the Centre for Foreign Policy Studies at Dalhousie University, Halifax, Nova Scotia; he has taught at Makerere University, Kampala, and the University of Zambia. His publications on Southern Africa include "South Africa's Military Capability and the Future of Race Relations" in Ali A. Mazrui and Hasu H. Patel (eds) Africa in World Affairs (1973), "The International Sub-system of Southern Africa: Introduction" in Zdenek Cervenka (ed) Land-locked Countries of Africa (1973),"Southern Africa: Cooperation and Conflict in an International Subsystem", Journal of Modern African Studies (1974) and "International Organisations and the Politics of

Southern Africa: Towards Regional Integration or Liberation?" *Journal of Southern African Studies* (1976).

J. E. SPENCE is Professor of Politics at the University of Leicester; he previously taught at the University of Natal and University College, Swansea. He is author of *Republic Under Pressure: A Study of South African Foreign Policy* (1965) and *Lesotho: The Politics of Dependence* (1968). Among his many essays on Southern Africa are chapters on "South Africa and the Modern World" in Monica Wilson and Leonard Thompson (eds) *The Oxford History of South Africa, Volume II* (1971) and on "South African Foreign Policy: The 'Outward Movement'" in Christian P. Potholm and Richard Dale (eds) *Southern Africa in Perspective: Essays in Regional Politics* (1972). His most recent article is "Southern Africa's Uncertain Future: Adjusting to a New Balance of Power" *Round Table* 258, April 1975, 159-165.

TIMOTHY T. THAHANE is a member of the Executive Board of the World Bank. He was previously Director of Planning in Lesotho and the Ambassador of Lesotho to the European Economic Community. He has contributed an essay on "Lesotho: The Realities of Land-lockedness" to Zdenek Cervenka (ed) *Land-locked Countries of Africa* which was reprinted as "Lesotho, an Island Country: The Problems of Being Land-locked" *African Review* (1974).

PARTICIPANTS IN WORKSHOP ON SOUTHERN AFRICA, DALHOUSIE UNIVERSITY

(August 1973)

DOUGLAS G. ANGLIN	Professor of Political Science, Carleton University, Ottawa K1S 5B6, Ontario, Canada; Past-President, Canadian Association of African Studies
ROBERT BOARDMAN	Assistant Professor, Centre for Foreign Policy Studies, Dalhousie University
BARBARA BROWN	Graduate Student, Department of Political Science, Boston University, Boston, Massachusetts 02215, USA
LARRY W. BOWMAN	Associate Professor of Political Science, University of Connecticut, Storrs, Connecticut 06268, USA
J. BARRON BOYD	Assistant Professor of Political Science, LeMoyne College, Le Moyne Heights, Syracuse, New York 13214, USA
ZDENEK CERVENKA	Research Director, Scandinavian Institute of African Studies, P.O. Box 2126, S-750 02, Uppsala 2, Sweden
JOHN E. FLINT	Professor of History, Dalhousie University
HERMAN GILIOMEE	Visiting Fellow, Department of History, Yale University, New Haven, Connecticut 16520, USA
KENNETH W. GRUNDY	Professor and Chairman, Department of Political Science, Case Western Reserve University, Cleveland, Ohio 44106, USA
CHARLES HARVEY	Fellow, Institute of Development Studies at the University of Sussex, Falmer, Brighton BN1 9RE, England
GORDON R. S. HAWKINS	Director of Training, UNITAR, 801 United Nations Plaza, New York, N.Y. 10017, USA
KENNETH A. HEARD	Professor and Past-Chairman, Department of Political Science, Dalhousie University
CHRISTOPHER R. HILL	Director, Centre for Southern African Studies and Lecturer in Political Science, University of York, Heslington, York YO1 5DD, England
SHERIDAN W. JOHNS	Associate Professor of Political Science, Duke University, Durham, North Carolina 27706, USA
A. M. KEPPEL-JONES	Professor of History, Queen's University, Kingston, Ontario, Canada
Z. A. KONCZACKI	Professor of Economics, Dalhousie University

ROBERT T. McKINNELL	Policy Branch, Canadian International Development Agency, 122 Bank Street, Ottawa K1A OG2, Ontario, Canada
AKE MAGNUSSON	Director, Scandinavian Research Project on South Africa and Lecturer in Political Science, University of Goteberg, Fack, S-400 25, Goteberg 52, Sweden
P. D. PILLAY	Associate Professor and Chairman, Department of History, Dalhousie University
CHRISTIAN P. POTHOLM	Associate Professor of Government, Bowdoin College, Brunswick, Maine 14011, USA
LAWRENCE SCHLEMMER	Director, Institute for Social Research and Professor of Sociology, University of Natal, King George V Avenue, Durban 4001, South Africa
TIMOTHY M. SHAW	Assistant Professor, Centre for Foreign Policy Studies, Dalhousie University
ROWLAND J. SMITH	Associate Professor of English and Director, Centre for African Studies, Dalhousie University
J. E. SPENCE	Professor of Politics, University of Leicester, Leicester, England
DENIS W. STAIRS	Professor, Centre for Foreign Policy Studies, Dalhousie University
LEONARD THOMPSON	Professor of History, Yale University, New Haven, Connecticut 16520, USA
ABSOLOM VILAKAZI	Professor of Anthropology, The American University, Washington, D.C. 20016, USA; Past-President, African Studies Association (USA)
IMMANUEL WALLERSTEIN	Professor of Sociology, State University of New York, Binghampton, Binghampton, N.Y., USA; Past-President, African Studies Association (USA)
J. BERTIN WEBSTER	Professor of History, Dalhousie University
BRIAN WINCHESTER	Assistant Professor of Political Science, University of Lethbridge, Alberta, Canada
JONATHAN WOUK	Assistant Professor, Centre for Foreign Policy Studies, Dalhousie University
CHARLES J. WOODSWORTH	Department of External Affairs, Ottawa, Canada

SELECTED BIBLIOGRAPHY ON SOUTHERN AFRICA*

Adam, Heribert. "The South African Power Elite: A Survey of Ideological Commitment," Canadian Journal of Political Science 4(1), March 1971, 76-96.

________ (ed). South Africa: Sociological Perspectives. London: Oxford University Press, 1971.

________. Modernizing Racial Domination: The Dynamics of South African Politics. Berkeley: University of California Press, 1971.

________. "Conquest and Conflict in South Africa," Journal of Modern African Studies 13(4), December 1975, 621-640.

Akpan, Moses E. "African Goals and Strategies Toward Southern Africa," African Studies Review 14(2), September 1971, 243-263.

Alpers, Edward A. "Ethnicity, Politics and History in Mozambique," Africa Today 21(4), Fall 1974, 39-52.

Aluko, Olajide. "The OAU Liberation Committee After a Decade: An Appraisal," Quarterly Journal of Administration 8(1), October 1973, 59-68.

Andemicael, Berhanykun. The OAU and the UN: Relations Between the Organization of African Unity and the United Nations. New York: Africana for UNITAR, 1976.

Anglin, Douglas G. "The Politics of Alternative Routes in Land-locked Southern Africa," in Zdenek Cervenka (ed) Land-locked Countries of Africa. Uppsala: Scandinavian Institute of African Studies, 1973, 98-133.

________. "Britain and the Use of Force in Rhodesia," in Michael G. Fry (ed) Freedom and Change: Essays in Honour of Lester B. Pearson. Toronto: McClelland and Stewart, 1975, 43-75.

________. "Zambia and Southern African 'detente'," International Journal 30(3), Summer 1975, 471-503.

________. "Zambia and the Southern African Liberation Movements," in Timothy M. Shaw and Kenneth A. Heard (eds) Politics in Africa: Dependence and Development. London: Longman and Dalhousie University Press, 1977.

Arrighi, Giovanni and John S. Saul. Essays on the Political Economy of Africa. New York: Monthly Review, 1973.

Barber, James. South Africa's Foreign Policy, 1947-1970. London: Oxford University Press, 1973.

Barnett, Don and Roy Harvey. The Revolution in Angola: MPLA, Life Histories and Documents. Indianapolis: Bobbs-Merrill, 1972.

---

* This list is largely supplementary to bibliographies in Heribert Adam (ed) South Africa: Sociological Perspectives (London: OUP, 1971) 301-332 and in Leonard Thompson and Jeffrey Butler (eds) Change in Contemporary South Africa (Berkeley: University of California Press, 1975) 415-431.

Baron, Barnett F. "Southern African Student Exiles in the United States," Journal of Modern African Studies 10(1), May 1972, 73-91.

Barratt, John. "The Department of Foreign Affairs," in Dennis Worrall (ed) South Africa: Government and Politics. Pretoria: Van Schaik, 1971, 332-347.

________. "Dialogue in Africa: A New Approach," South Africa International 2(2), October 1971.

________. "South Africa's Outward Policy: From Isolation to Dialogue," in N. J. Rhoodie (ed) South African Dialogue. Johannesburg: McGraw-Hill, 1972, 543-561.

________, et.al.(eds). Accelerated Development in Southern Africa. Johannesburg: MacMillan for the South African Institute of International Affairs, 1974.

________. "Detente in Southern Africa," World Today 33(3), March 1975, 120-130.

Bates, Robert H. "A Simulation Study of a Crisis in Southern Africa," African Studies Review 13(2), September 1970, 253-264.

Bell, Trevor. Industrial Decentralization in South Africa. Cape Town: Oxford University Press, 1973.

Bender, Gerald J. "The Limits of Counterinsurgency: An African Case," Comparative Politics 4(3), April 1972, 331-360.

Bender, Gerald J. and P. Stanley Yoder. "Whites in Angola on the Eve of Independence: The Politics of Numbers," Africa Today 21(4), Fall 1974, 23-37.

Best, Alan C. G. and Bruce Young. "Consolidation for Independence: The Case of Kwazulu," in Timothy M. Shaw and Kenneth A. Heard (eds) Politics of Africa: Dependence and Development. London: Longman and Dalhousie University Press, 1977.

Bone, Marion. "The Foreign Policy of Zambia," in Ronald P. Barston (ed) The Other Powers: Studies in the Foreign Policies of Small States. London: George Allen and Unwin, 1973, 121-153.

Bowman, Larry W. "South Africa's Southern Strategy and Its Implications for the United States," International Affairs 47(1), January 1971, 19-30.

________. "International Cooperation and Potential Conflict: Portugal and South Africa," in Steven L. Spiegel and Kenneth N. Waltz (eds) Conflict in World Politics. Cambridge, Massachusetts: Winthrop, 1971, 343-356.

________. South Africa's Outward Strategy: A Foreign Policy Dilemma for the United States. Athens, Ohio: Ohio University, 1971. Papers in International Studies, Africa Series Number 3.

________. "Southern Africa and the Indian Ocean," in Alvin J. Cottrell and R. M. Burrell (eds) The Indian Ocean: Its Political, Economic and Military Importance. New York: Praeger, 1972, 293-306.

________. "The Politics of Dependency and Racism in Rhodesia," and "Labour Immigration of Land-locked Countries in Southern Africa," in Zdenek Cervenka (ed) Land-locked Countries of Africa. Uppsala: Scandinavian Institute of African Studies, 1973, 182-187 and 233-235.

________. Politics in Rhodesia: White Power in an African State. New Haven: Yale University Press, 1974.

Bromberger, Norman. "Economic Growth and Political Change in South Africa," in Adrian Leftwich (ed) South Africa: Economic Growth and Political Change. New York: St. Martin's, 1974, 61-123.

Buthelezi, Gatsha. "The Past and Future of the Zulu People," Munger Africana Library Notes 2(10), January 1972.

Caradon, Lord. Southern Africa in International Relations. London: Africa Bureau, December 1970.

Carlson, Joel. No Neutral Ground. London: Davis-Poynter, 1973.

Carter, Gwendolen M. "Challenges to Minority Rule in Southern Africa," International Journal 25(3), Summer 1970, 486-496.

Cassuto, Aldo. "Can Uranium Enrichment Enrich South Africa?," World Today 26(10), October 1970, 419-427.

Cervenka, Zdenek (ed). Land-locked Countries of Africa. Uppsala: Scandinavian Institute of African Studies, 1973.

________. "Major Policy Shifts in the OAU, 1963-1973," in K. Ingham (ed) The Foreign Relations of African States. London: Butterworth, 1974, 323-342.

Chartrand, Philip E. "Political Change in Rhodesia: The South Africa Factor," Issue 5(4), Winter 1975, 13-20.

Chipembere, Henry B. M. "Malawi's Growing Links with South Africa - A Necessity or a Virtue?," Africa Today 18(2), 1971, 27-47.

Christie, Michael. The Simonstown Agreements. London: Africa Bureau, September 1970.

________. Rhodesia: Proposals for a Sell-out. London: Southern African Research Office, February 1972.

Cockram, Gail-Maryse. Vorster's Foreign Policy Pretoria: Academica, 1970.

Cornwall, Barbara. The Bush Rebels. New York: Holt, Rinehart and Winston, 1972.

Crocker, Chester A. (ed). The International Relations of Southern Africa. Washington: Georgetown University, 1975.

Curtis, Neville. "South Africa: The Politics of Fragmentation," Foreign Affairs 50(2), January 1972, 283-296.

Dalcanton, David. "Vorster and the Politics of Confidence 1966-1974," African Affairs 75(299), April 1976, 163-181.

Dale, Richard. Botswana and Its Southern Neighbour: The Patterns of Linkage and the Options in Statecraft. Athens, Ohio: Ohio University, 1970. Papers in International Studies Africa Series Number 6.

________. The Racial Component of Botswana Foreign Policy. Denver: Center of International Race Relations, 1970-71.

Davidson, Basil. "In the Portuguese Context," in Christopher Allen and R. W. Johnson (eds) African Perspectives: Papers in the History, Politics and Economics of Africa presented to Thomas Hodgkin. Cambridge: University Press, 1970, 329-345.

________. "An Inside Look at Angola's Fight for Freedom," Africa Report 15(9), December 1970, 16-18.

________. "Angola in the Tenth Year: A Report and an Analysis, May-June 1970," African Affairs 70(278), January 1971, 37-47.

________. Walking 300 Miles with Guerrillas Through the Bush of Eastern Angola. California: Munger Africana Library Notes, April 1971.

________. "Cabora Bassa," Presence Africaine 82(2), 1972, 39-51.

________. In the Eye of the Storm: Angola's People. London: Longman, 1972.

Day, John. "A Failure of Foreign Policy: The Case of Rhodesia," in Michael Leifer (ed) Constraints and Adjustments in British Foreign Policy. London: George Allen and Unwin, 1972, 150-171.

Delius, Anthony. "International Argument and External Policy in South Africa," African Affairs 69(277), 1970, 371-374.

Denoon, Donald. "Participation in the 'Boer War': People's War, People's Non-war or Non-people's War?," in Bethwell A. Ogot (ed) War and Society in Africa: Ten Studies. London: Frank Cass, 1972, 109-122.

________ with Balam Nyeko and the advice of J. B. Webster. Southern Africa Since 1800. London: Longman, 1972.

________. A Grand Illusion: The Failure of Imperial Policy in the Transvaal Colony During the Period of Reconstruction 1900-1905. London: Longman, 1973.

Desmond, Cosmas. The Discarded People: An Account of African Resettlement in South Africa. Harmondsworth, Penguin, 1972.

Doxey, Margaret. "International Sanctions: A Framework for Analysis with Special Reference to the UN and Southern Africa," International Organization 26(3), Summer 1972, 527-550.

________. "Alignments and Coalitions in Southern Africa," International Journal 30(3), Summer 1975, 518-535.

Dube, Emmanuel M. "Relations Between Liberation Movements and the OAU," in N. M. Shamuyarira (ed) Essays on the Liberation of Southern Africa. Dar es Salaam: Tanzania Publishing House, 1971, 25-68. Studies in Political Science Number 3.

Dugard, John. The South West Africa/Namibia Dispute: Documents and Scholarly Writings on the Controversy Between South Africa and the United Nations. Berkeley: University of California Press, 1973.

Duggan, William R. A Socio-economic Profile of South Africa. New York: Praeger, 1973.

Duminy, Peter. "South African Politics: The Quiescent Years," World Today 26(6), June 1970, 228-235.

Du Toit, B. M. "Afrikaners, Nationalists and Apartheid," Journal of Modern African Studies 8(4), December 1970, 531-551.

El-Ayouty, Yassin. "Legitimization of National Liberation: The United Nations and Southern Africa," Issue 2(4), Winter 1972, 36-45; reprinted in Yassin El-Ayouty and Hugh C. Brooks (eds) Africa and International Organization. The Hague: Nijhoff, 1974, 209-229.

El-Khawas, Mohamed A. "The Third-World Stance on Apartheid: The UN Record," Journal of Modern African Studies 9(3), October 1971, 443-455.

________. "Mozambique and the United Nations," Issue 2(4), Winter 1972, 30-35.

________. "Foreign Economic Investment in Angola and Mozambique," Issue 4(2), Summer 1974, 21-28; reprinted in African Review 4(2), 1974, 299-314.

Elliott, Charles (ed). Constraints on the Economic Development of Zambia. Nairobi: Oxford University Press, 1971.

Emmanuel, Arghiri. "White-settler Colonialism and the Myth of Investment Imperialism," New Left Review 73, May-June 1972, 35-57.

Eze, Osita C. "OAU Faces Rhodesia," African Review 5(1), 1975, 43-62.

Faber, M. L. O. and J. G. Potter. Towards Economic Independence: Papers on the Nationalization of the Copper Industry in Zambia. Cambridge: Cambridge University Press, 1971. University of Cambridge Department of Applied Economics Occasional Paper Number 23.

Farah, Abdulrahim A. "Southern Africa: A Challenge to the UN," Issue 2(2), Summer 1972, 14-24.

________. "South Africa's Apartheid Policy: An Assessment," in Yassin El-Ayouty and Hugh C. Brooks (eds) Africa and International Organization. The Hague: Nijhoff, 1974, 71-102.

Feit, Edward. "Generational Conflict and African Nationalism in South Africa: The African National Congress, 1949-1959," International Journal of African Historical Studies 5(2), 1972, 181-202.

Ferreira, Eduardo De Sousa. Portuguese Colonialism from South Africa to Europe. Freiburg: Aktion Dritte Welt, 1972.

________. Portuguese Colonialism in Africa: The End of an Era. Paris: UNESCO Press, 1974.

Finger, Seymour M. "A New Approach to Colonial Problems at the UN," International Organization 26(1), Winter 1972, 143-153.

First, Ruth, Jonathan Steele, Christabel Gurney. The South African Connection: Western Investment in Apartheid. London: Temple Smith, 1972.

Freeman, Linda, Gerald Helleiner and Robert Matthews. The Commonwealth at Stake. Toronto: Committee for a Just Canadian Policy toward Africa, n.d.; reprinted in Canadian Journal of African Studies 5(1), 1971, 92-112.

Gann, Lewis H. "Southern Africa: No Hope for Violent Liberation," Africa Report 17(2), February 1972, 15-19; reprinted in South Africa International 3(3), January 1973, 147-158.

________. "Rhodesia and the Prophets," African Affairs 71(283), April 1972, 125-143.

________. "Portugal, Africa and the Future," Journal of Modern African Studies 13(1), March 1975, 1-18.

Gerber, Louis. Friends and Influence: The Diplomacy of Private Enterprise. Cape Town: Parnell, 1973.

________. "South Africa: The Peaceful Revolution," African Affairs 72(286), January 1973, 57-63.

Gervasi, Sean. "In Southern Africa - 'A Crisis of the Neo-Colonial Sustem'," Objective: Justice 4(3), July-September 1972, 21-24.

________. "The Politics of 'accelerated economic growth'," in Leonard Thompson and Jeffrey Butler (eds) Change in Contemporary South Africa. Berkeley: University of California Press, 1975, 349-368.

Geyser. O. "Detente in Southern Africa," African Affairs 75(299), April 1976, 182-207.

Gibson, Richard. African Liberation Movements: Contemporary Struggles Against White Minority Rule. London: Oxford University Press for IRR, 1972.

Girdlestone, J. A. C. "Economic Cooperation in Southern Africa," Rhodesian Journal of Economics 4, March 1970, 1-10.

Gitelson, Susan A. "The Transformation of the Southern African Subordinate State System," Journal of African Studies, 1976.

Glasgow, Roy A. "Recent Observations on the Developing Southern Strategy of Brazil, Portugal and Africa," Issue 2(3), Fall 1972, 3-8.

________. "Pragmatism and Idealism in Brazilian Foreign Policy in Southern Africa," Munger Africana Library Notes 4(23), 1973-1974.

Good, Kenneth. "South African Settler Colonialism: A Present Day Summation," East Africa Journal 9(11), November 1972, 4-13.

________. "The Intimacy of Australia and South Africa," African Review 2(3), 1972, 417-432.

________. "Settler Colonialism in Rhodesia," African Affairs 73(290), January 1974, 10-36.

Good, Robert C. UDI: The International Politics of the Rhodesian Rebellion. Princeton: Princeton University Press, 1973.

Gruhn, Isebill V. "The Commission for Technical Cooperation in Africa, 1950-65," Journal of Modern African Studies 9(3), October 1971, 459-469.

________. British Arms Sales to SA: The Limits of African Diplomacy. Denver: Center on International Race Relations, 1971-72.

Grundy, Kenneth W. "Host States and the Southern African Liberation Struggle," Africa Quarterly 10, April-June 1970, 15-24.

_______. Guerrilla Struggle in Africa: An Analysis and Preview. New York: Grossman, 1971.

_______. Confrontation and Accommodation in Southern Africa: The Limits of Independence. Berkeley: University of California Press, 1973.

Guelke, Adrian. "Africa as a Market for South African Goods," Journal of Modern African Studies 12(1), March 1974, 69-88.

Gutteridge, William. "The Coming Confrontation in Southern Africa," Conflict Studies 15, August 1971.

Hain, Peter. Don't Play With Apartheid: The Background to the Stop the Seventy Tour Campaign. London: Allen and Unwin, 1971.

Hall, Richard. The High Price of Principles: Kaunda and the White South. Harmondsworth: Penguin, 1973.

Halpern, Jack. "Polarization in Rhodesia: State, Church and Peoples," World Today 27(1), January 1971, 1-8.

Hammond-Tooke, A. "Interdependence in Commerce and Trade in Southern Africa," South Africa International 6(2), October 1975, 70-87.

Harvey, Charles, et al. The Policy Debate. London: Study Project on External Investment in South Africa and Namibia, 1975.

Hastings, Adrian. "Some Reflections Upon the War in Mozambique," African Affairs 73(292), July 1974, 263-276.

_______. Massacre in Mozambique: Wiriyamu. London: Search, 1974.

Heard, K. A. General Elections in South Africa, 1943-1970. Cape Town: Oxford University Press, 1974.

Henderson, I. "White Populism in Southern Rhodesia," Comparative Studies in Society and History 14(4), September 1972, 387-399.

Henderson, Willie. "Independent Botswana: A Reappraisal of Foreign Policy Options," African Affairs 73(290), January 1974, 37-49.

Henriksen, Thomas. "Portugal in Africa: A Non-economic Interpretation," African Studies Review 16(3), December 1973, 405-416.

Hermans, H. C. L. "Botswana's Options for Independent Existence," in Zdenek Cervenka (ed) Land-locked Countries of Africa. Uppsala: Scandinavian Institute of African Studies, 1973, 197-211.

Hill, Christopher R. "Independent Botswana: Myth or Reality?," Round Table 245, January 1972, 55-62.

Hintz, Stephen E. C. "The Political Transformation of Rhodesia, 1958-1965," African Studies Review 25(2), September 1972, 173-183.

Hirschman, David. "Southern African Voting Patterns in the UN General Assembly, 1971 and 1972," South African Institute of International Affairs, Johannesburg, August 1973.

________. "Southern Africa: Detente?," Journal of Modern African Studies 14(1), March 1976, 107-126.

Hoagland, Jim. South Africa: Civilizations in Conflict. Boston: Houghton Mifflin, 1972.

Hodder-Williams, Richard. "Afrikaners in Rhodesia: A Partial Portrait," African Social Research 18, December 1974, 611-642.

Hodges, Tony. "The Struggle for Angola: How the World Powers Entered a War in Africa," Round Table 262, April 1976, 173-184.

Homelands: The Role of the Corporations. Johannesburg: van Rensburg, n.d.

Horwood, O. P. F. "Regional Trade Cooperation in Southern Africa: With Special Reference to South Africa's Position," Rhodesian Journal of Economics 4, June 1970, 1-9.

Horrell, Muriel (ed). A Survey of Race Relations in South Africa. Johannesburg: South African Institute of Race Relations, annually.

Hough, W. "Nuclear Weapons for South Africa?," New Nation, August 1974, 11-12.

Houghton, D. Hobart and Jenifer Dagut. Source Material on the South African Economy. 3 Volumes. Cape Town: Oxford University Press, 1973.

Hughes, A. "Malawi and South Africa's Co-prosperity Sphere," in Zdenek Cervenka (ed) Land-locked Countries of Africa. Uppsala: Scandinavian Institute of African Studies, 1973, 212-232.

Hyam, Ronald. The Failure of South African Expansion, 1909-1939. New York: Africana, 1972.

Jeeves, Alan H. "The Problem of South Africa," International Journal 26(2), Spring 1971, 418-432.

________. "South Africa and the Politics of Accommodation," International Journal 30(3), Summer 1975, 504-517.

Jinadu, L. Adele. "South West Africa: A Study in the 'Sacred Trust' Thesis," African Studies Review 14(3), December 1971, 369-388.

Johns, Sheridan. "Obstacles to Guerrilla Warfare - A South African Case," Journal of Modern African Studies 11(2), June 1973, 267-303.

________. "Botswana's Strategy for Development: An Assessment of Dependence in the Southern African Context," Journal of Commonwealth Political Studies 11(3), November 1973, 214-230.

Johnstone, Frederick A. "White Prosperity and White Supremacy in South Africa Today," African Affairs 69(275), April 1970, 124-140.

Jundamian, Brendan F. "Resettlement Programs: Counterinsurgency in Mozambique," Comparative Politics 6(4), July 1974, 519-540.

Kapungu, Leonard T. The United Nations and Economic Sanctions Against Rhodesia. Lexington: Lexington, 1972.

________. "Economic Sanctions in the Rhodesian Context," in Yassin El-Ayouty and Hugh C. Brooks (eds) Africa and International Organization. The Hague: Nijhoff, 1974, 103-126.

________. "The OAU's Support for the Liberation of Southern Africa," in Yassin El-Ayouty (ed) The Organization of African Unity After Ten Years: Comparative Perspectives. New York: Praeger, 1975, 135-151.

Kay, David A. "The United Nations and Decolonization," in James Barros (ed) The United Nations: Past, Present, and Future. New York: Free Press, 1972, 143-170.

Kennan, George F. "Hazardous Courses in Southern Africa," Foreign Affairs 49(2), January 1971, 218-236.

Keppel-Jones, A. M. "South Africa in 1998: Trends and Developments During the Next Twenty-five Years," Issue 4(3), Fall 1974, 38-42.

Khaketla, B. M. Lesotho 1970: An African Coup Under the Microscope. Berkeley: University of California Press, 1972.

Khapoya, Vincent B. The Politics of Decision: A Comparative Study of African Policy Toward the Liberation Movements. Denver: University of Denver, 1975. Monograph Series in World Affairs 12(3).

Kooy, Marcelle. "The Contract Labour System and the Ovambo Crisis of 1971 in South West Africa," African Studies Review 26(1), April 1973, 83-105.

Kuper, Leo. "African Nationalism in South Africa, 1910-1964," in Monica Wilson and Leonard Thompson (eds) The Oxford History of South Africa, Volume II: South Africa 1870-1966. Oxford: Clarendon Press, 1971, 424-476.

Landell-Mills, P. M. "The 1969 Southern African Customs Union Agreement," Journal of Modern African Studies 9(2), August 1971, 263-281.

Lapchick, Richard E. The Politics of Race and International Sport: The Case of South Africa. Westport, Connecticut: Greenwood, 1975.

Larrabee, Stephen. "Moscow, Angola and the Dialectics of Detente," World Today 32(5), May 1976, 173-182.

Lawrie, Gordon G. "Britain's Obligations Under the Simonstown Agreements: A Critique of the Opinion of the Law Officers of the Crown," International Affairs 47(4), October 1971, 708-728.

Leftwich, Adrian (ed). South Africa: Economic Growth and Political Change. New York: St. Martin's, 1974.

Legassick, Martin. "South Africa: Forced Labour, Industrialization and Racial Differentiation," in Richard Harris (ed) The Political Economy of Africa. Cambridge, Massachusetts: Schenkman, 1975, 227-270.

Legge, Garth, Cranford Pratt, Richard Williams and Hugh Windsor. The Black Paper: An Alternative Policy for Canada Towards Southern Africa. Toronto: Committee for a Just Canadian Policy Towards Africa, n.d.; reprinted in Behind the Headlines 30(1-2), September 1970 and Canadian Journal of African Studies 4(3), Autumn 1970, 363-394.

Legum, Colin and Margaret. "South Africa in the Contemporary World," Issue 3(3), Fall 1973, 17-27.

Legum, Colin. Dialogue: Africa's Great Debate. London: Africa Contemporary Record Current Affairs Series, 1972.

________. South Africa: A Year of Great Decision. London: Africa Contemporary Record Current Affairs Series, 1972.

________. "The Problems of the Land-locked Countries of Southern Africa in the Confrontation Between Independent Africa and South Africa, Rhodesia and Portugal," in Zdenek Cervenka (ed) Land-locked Countries of Africa. Uppsala: Scandinavian Institute of African Studies, 1973, 165-181.

________. Southern Africa: The Secret Diplomacy of Detente. London: Rex Collings, 1975.

________. "Southern Africa: The Politics of Detente," Year Book of World Affairs. London: Institute of World Affairs, 1976, 14-29.

Leistner, G. M. E. Cooperation for Development in Southern Africa. Pretoria: Africa Institute, 1972. Occasional Paper Number 33.

________. "South Africa's Economic Interests in Africa," South African Journal of African Affairs 2, 1972, 32-46.

________. "Economic Cooperation in Southern Africa," Africa Institute Bulletin 3(8), 1975, 85-89.

Lesotho: A Development Challenge. Washington: World Bank, 1975.

Leys, Roger. "South African Gold Mining in 1974: 'The Gold of Migrant Labour'," African Affairs 74(295), April 1975, 196-208.

Lipton, Merle. "Independent Bantustans?," International Affairs 48(1), January 1972, 1-19.

________. "The South African Census and the Bantustan Policy," World Today 28(6), June 1972, 257-271.

________. "South Africa: Authoritarian Reform?," World Today 30(6), June 1974, 247-258.

Loney, Martin. Rhodesia: White Racism and Imperial Response. Harmondsworth: Penguin, 1975.

MacLear, Ian. Pattern for Profit in Southern Africa. New York: Praeger, 1973.

MacRae, Phyllis. "Race and Class in Southern Africa," African Review 4(2), 1974, 237-257.

Madavo, Callisto E. "Government Policy and Economic Dualism in South Africa," Canadian Journal of African Studies 5(1), 1971, 19-32.

Malawi - Dialogue and Development. London: Africa Publications Trust, 1973.

Malherbe, Paul. Multistan: A Way Out of the South African Dilemma. Cape Town: Philip, 1974.

Mangope, Lukas. "Will Bophutha Tswana Join Botswana?," Munger Africana Library Notes 4(20), 1973-1974.

Marco, Edmond A. "Dialogue in Africa," Optima 21(3), September 1971, 106-117.

Marcum, John A. "The Exile Condition and Revolutionary Effectiveness: Southern African Liberation Movements," in Christian P. Potholm and Richard Dale (eds) Southern Africa in Perspective: Essays in Regional Politics. New York: Free Press, 1972, 262-275.

________. "The Politics of Indifference: Portugal and Africa, a Case Study in American Foreign Policy," Issue 2(3), Fall 1972, 9-17.

________. "The Anguish of Angola: On Becoming Independent in the Last Quarter of the Twentieth Century," Issue 5(4), Winter 1975, 3-12.

________. "Lessons of Angola," Foreign Affairs 54(3), April 1976, 407-425.

Marks, Shula. "Liberalism, Social Realities, and South African History," Journal of Commonwealth Political Studies 10(3), November 1972, 243-249.

Marquard, Leo. A Federation of Southern Africa. London: Oxford University Press, 1971.

Martin, Antony. Minding Their Own Business: Zambia's Struggle Against Western Control. London: Hutchinson, 1972.

Matthews, A. S. Law, Order, and Liberty in South Africa. Berkeley: University of California Press, 1972.

Maud, Ruan. "The Future of an Illusion: The Myth of White Meliorism in South Africa," in Adrian Leftwich (ed) South Africa: Economic Growth and Political Change. New York: St. Martin's, 1974, 287-318.

Maxey, Kees. The Fight for Zimbabwe: The Armed Conflict in Southern Rhodesia Since UDI. London: Rex Collings, 1975.

Mayall, James. "Malawi's Foreign Policy," World Today 26(10), October 1970, 435-445.

________. "Black-White Relations in the Context of African Foreign Policy," International Yearbook of Foreign Policy Analysis, 1. London: Croom Helm, 1974, 181-205.

McMaster, Carolyn. Malawi: Foreign Policy and Development. London: Friedman, 1974.

Middlemas, Keith. Cabora Bassa: Engineering and Politics in Southern Africa. London: Weidenfeld & Nicolson, 1975.

Miller, J. D. B. "Notes on Australian Relations with South Africa," Australian Outlook 25(2), August 1971, 132-140.

Miller, Joseph C. "The Politics of Decolonization in Portuguese Africa," African Affairs 74(295), April 1975, 135-147.

Minter, William. Imperial Network and External Dependency: The Case of Angola. Beverly Hills: Sage, 1972. Sage Paper in International Studies Number 11.

________. Portuguese Africa and the West. Harmondsworth: Penguin, 1972.

Mnquikana, Sobizana. "Southern Africa: Realities and Illusions," Sechaba 6(6), June 1972, 2-6.

Molteno, Robert. Africa and South Africa: The Implications of South Africa's 'Outward-looking' Policy. London: Africa Bureau, February 1971.

________. "South Africa's Forward Policy in Africa," Round Table 243, April 1971, 329-345.

________. "Southern Africa: Is Federalisation a Road to Liberation? Comment on Mr. Woldring's Article," African Review 3(3), 1973, 479-489.

Moodie, Thomas D. Power, Apartheid and the Afrikaner Civil Religion. Berkeley: University of California Press, 1974.

Mtshali, B. V. "Zambia's Foreign Policy," Current History 58(343), March 1970, 148-153 and 177-179.

________. "Rough Road to Zulu Independence," Kroniek van Afrika 1, 1972, 30-34.

________. "The Mogadishu Conference and Declaration October 1971," Internationale Spectatore 24(10), May 1972, 966-977.

________. "Zambia and the White South," in Zdenek Cervenka (ed) Land-locked Countries of Africa. Uppsala: Scandinavian Institute of African Studies, 1973, 188-193.

Mubako, Simbi V. "The Rhodesian Border Blockade of 1973 and the African Liberation Struggle," Journal of Commonwealth and Comparative Politics 7(3), November 1974, 297-312.

________. "The Quest for Unity in the Zimbabwe Liberation Movement," Issue 5(1), Spring 1975, 7-17.

Mugomba, Agrippah T. "The Emergence and Collapse of South Africa's Black African Policy," Journal of Eastern African Research and Development 5(1), 1975, 19-36.

________. "The Rise and Fall of 'Pax Suid-Afrika': A Historical Analysis of South Africa's Black African Foreign Policy," Kenya Historical Review 3(1), 1975, 127-145.

________. "The South Atlantic and Indian Ocean in Western and South African Defence Strategies," Kenya Historical Review 3(2), 1975.

________. The Foreign Policy of Despair: Africa and the Sale of Arms to South Africa. Nairobi: East African Literature Bureau, 1976.

Murray, Roger, et al. The Role of Foreign Firms in Namibia. London: Study Project on External Investment in South Africa and Namibia, 1974.

Mutharika, B. W. T. Towards Multinational Economic Cooperation in Africa. New York: Praeger, 1972.

Nolutshungu, Sam C. "Issues of the Afrikaner Enlightenment," African Affairs 70(278), January 1971, 22-36.

________. South Africa in Africa: A Study of Ideology and Foreign Policy. New York: Africana, 1975.

________. "The Impact of External Opposition on South African Politics," in Leonard Thompson and Jeffrey Butler (eds) Change in Contemporary South Africa Berkeley: University of California Press, 1975, 369-399.

Nowzad, Bahram. "Economic Integration in Central and West Africa," in Paul A. Tharp Jr. (ed) Regional International Organizations/Structures and Functions. New York: St. Martin's, 1971, 201-229.

Nyquist, Thomas E. Toward a Theory of the African Upper Stratum in South Africa. Athens: Ohio University, 1972. Papers in International Studies Africa Series Number 15.

O'Brien, Jay. "Portugal and Africa: A Dying Imperialism," Monthly Review 26(1), May 1974, 19-36.

Olivier, Gerrit. "South African Foreign Policy," in Denis Worrall (ed) South Africa: Government and Politics. Pretoria: Van Schaik, 1971, 285-321.

O'Dowd, Michael. "South Africa in the Light of the Stages of Economic Growth," in Adrian Leftwich (ed) South Africa: Economic Growth and Political Change. New York: St. Martin's, 1974, 29-43.

O'Meara, Patrick. Rhodesia: Racial Conflict or Coexistence?. Ithaca: Cornell University Press, 1975.

Opello, Walter C. "Pluralism and Elite Conflict in an Independence Movement: FRELIMO in the 1960's," Journal of Southern African Studies 2(1), October 1975, 66-82.

Pachai, B. The International Aspects of the South African Indian Question, 1860-1971. Cape Town: Struik, 1971.

________. Malawi: The History of the Nation. London: Longman, 1973.

Palley, Claire. "Rhodesia: The Time-Scale for Majority Rule," Issue 2(2), Summer 1972, 52-64.

Parsons, Q. N. "The Economic History of Khama's Country in Southern Africa," African Social Research 18, December 1974, 643-675.

Pettman, Jan. Zambia: Security and Conflict. London: Friedman, 1974.

________. "Zambia's Second Republic: The Creation of a One-Party State," Journal of Modern African Studies 12(2), June 1974, 231-244.

Phatudi, Cedric and Clemens Kapuuo. "South Africa Homelands: Two African Views," Munger Africana Library Notes 4(22), 1973-1974.

Potholm, Christian P. "The Future of Africa South," Current History 60(35), March 1971, 146-150 and 178-179.

________. "After Many A Summer? The Possibilities of Political Change in South Africa," World Politics 24(4), July 1972, 613-638.

________. "The International Transfer of Insurgency Techniques: Subsaharan Pathologies," Plural Societies, Autumn 1972, 3-21.

________. Swaziland: The Dynamics of Modernization. Berkeley: University of California Press, 1972.

Potholm, Christian P. and Richard Dale (eds). Southern Africa in Perspective: Essays in Regional Politics. New York: Free Press, 1972.

Potholm, Christian P. "The Effects on South Africa of Change in Contiguous Territories," in Leonard Thompson and Jeffrey Butler (eds) Change in Contemporary South Africa. Berkeley: University of California Press, 1975, 329-348.

________. "Wanderers on the Face of Africa: Refugees in Kenya, Tanzania, Zambia and Botswana," Round Table 261, January 1976, 85-92.

Race to Power: The Struggle for Southern Africa. Garden City, New York: Anchor, 1974.

Rhoodie, Eschel M. "Southern Africa: Towards a New Commonwealth?," in Christian P. Potholm and Richard Dale (eds) Southern Africa in Perspective: Essays in Regional Politics. New York: Free Press, 1972, 276-297.

Rhoodie, N. J. (ed). South African Dialogue. Johannesburg: McGraw-Hill, 1972.

________. "The Coloured Policy of South Africa: Parallelism as a Socio-Political Device to Regulate White-Coloured Integration," African Affairs 72(286), January 1973, 46-56.

Robertson, Janet. Liberalism in South Africa, 1948-1963. London: Oxford University Press, 1971.

Roder, Wold (ed). Voices of Liberation in Southern Africa. Waltham, Mass.: African Studies Association, 1972.

Rogers, Barbara. South Africa's Stake in Britain. London: Africa Bureau, June 1971.

________. "Southern Africa and the Oil Embargo," Africa Today 21(2), Spring 1974, 3-8.

Rothchild, Donald. "Rural-Urban Inequities and Resource Allocation in Zambia," Journal of Commonwealth Political Studies 10(3), November 1972, 222-242.

Sachs, Albie. Justice in South Africa. Berkeley: University of California Press, 1973.

Sadie, J. L. "An Economic Commission for Southern Africa," South Africa International 1(4), April 1971, 167-175.

Samuels, Michael A. "Southern Africa: The Strategies of Change," Interplay 3(16), December 1970, 11-15.

Schieber, Michael T. "Apartheid Under Pressure: South Africa's Military Strength in a Changing Political Context," Africa Today 23(1), January-March 1976, 27-45.

Schlemmer, Lawrence. Political Policy and Social Change in South Africa: An Assessment of the Future of Separate Development and of Possible Alternatives to the Policy. Johannesburg: South African Institute of Race Relations, 1970.

Seiler, John. "South African Perspectives and Responses to External Pressures," Journal of Modern African Studies 13(3), September 1975, 447-468.

Selwyn, Percy. Industries in the Southern African Periphery: A Study of Industrial Development in Botswana, Lesotho and Swaziland. London: Cass, 1975.

Setai, Bethuel. "Prospects for a Southern African Common Market," Journal of African Studies 1(3), Fall 1974, 310-334.

Shamuyarira, Nathan M. (ed). Essays on the Liberation of Southern Africa. Dar es Salaam: Tanzania Publishing House, 1971. University of Dar es Salaam Studies in Political Science Number 3.

________. "A Revolutionary Situation in Southern Africa," African Review 4(2), 1974, 159-179.

Shaw, Timothy M. "South Africa's Military Capability and the Future of Race Relations," in Ali A. Mazrui and Hasu H. Patel (eds) Africa in World Affairs: The Next Thirty Years. New York: Third Press, 1973, 37-61.

________. "The International Subsystem of Southern Africa: Introduction," in Zdenek Cervenka (ed) Land-locked Countries of Africa. Uppsala: Scandinavian Institute of African Studies, 1973, 161-164.

________. "Southern Africa: Cooperation and Conflict in an International Subsystem," Journal of Modern African Studies 12(4), December 1974, 633-655.

________. "The Foreign Policy of Zambia: Ideology and Interests," Journal of Modern African Studies 14(1), March 1976, 79-105.

________. "Oil, Israel and the OAU: An Introduction to the Political Economy of Energy in Southern Africa," Africa Today 23(1), January/March 1976, 15-26.

________. "The Foreign Policy of Zambia," African Studies Review 19(1), April 1976, 31-66.

________. "Zambia: Dependence and Underdevelopment," Canadian Journal of African Studies 10(2), 1976.

________. Dependence and Underdevelopment: The Development and Foreign Policies of Zambia. Athens: Ohio University, 1976. Papers in International Studies Africa Series Number 28.

________. "International Organisations and the Politics of Southern Africa: Towards Regional Integration or Liberation? Journal of Southern African Studies, 1976.

________. "Zambia and Southern Africa: From Confrontation to Coexistence," in Olajide Aluko (ed) The Foreign Policies of African States. London: Hodder & Stoughton, 1976.

________. "Zambia and Canada: Diplomacy in Southern Africa," in Denis Stairs and Don Munton (eds) Canada in World Perspectives. Halifax, Dalhousie University Centre for Foreign Policy Studies, forthcoming.

________, with Agrippah T. Mugomba. "The Political Economy of Regional Detente: Zambia and Southern Africa," Journal of African Studies, 1976.

________, with Agrippah T. Mugomba. "Zambia: Dependence and Detente," in John Seiler (ed) Southern Africa Since the Portuguese Coup, forthcoming.

Short, Philip. Banda. London: Routledge and Kegan Paul, 1974.

Sillery, A. Botswana: A Short Political History. London: Methuen, 1974.

Simson, Howard. "Fascism in South Africa," African Review 3(3), 1973, 423-451.

________. "The Myth of the White Working Class in South Africa," African Review 4(2), 1974, 189-203.

Sklar, Richard. Corporate Power in an African State: The Political Impact of Multinational Mining Companies in Zambia. Berkeley: University of California Press, 1975.

Slonim, Solomon. South West Africa and the UN: An International Mandate in Dispute. Baltimore: Johns Hopkins Press, 1973.

Smit, P. "South Africa and the Indian Ocean: The South African Viewpoint," in Alvin J. Cottrell and R. M. Burrell (eds) The Indian Ocean: Its Political, Economic and Military Importance. New York: Praeger, 1972, 269-292.

South Africa: Black Labour - Swedish Capital. Stockholm: LO and TCO Study Delegation to South Africa, 1975.

"Southern Africa: Problems and U.S. Alternatives," Intercom 70, September 1972.

"Special Issue on South Africa's Bantustans," Third World 2(6), June 1973.

Speck, Samuel W. Jr. "Malawi and the Southern African Complex," in Christian P. Potholm and Richard Dale (eds) Southern Africa in Perspective: Essays in Regional Politics. New York: Free Press, 1972, 207-218.

Spence, J. E. The Strategic Significance of Southern Africa. London: Royal United Service Institution, October 1970.

________. "South Africa and the Defence of the West," Round Table 241, January 1971, 15-23.

________. "South Africa and the Modern World," in Monica Wilson and Leonard Thompson (eds) The Oxford History of South Africa, Volume 2: South Africa 1870-1966. Oxford: Clarendon press, 1971, 477-527.

________. "South African Foreign Policy: The 'Outward Movement'," in Christian P. Potholm and Richard Dale (eds) Southern Africa in Perspective: Essays in Regional Politics. New York: Free Press, 1972, 46-58.

________. "Plus Ca Change ... ," Government and Opposition 7(4), Autumn 1972, 529-545.

________. "Southern Africa's Uncertain Future: Adjusting to a New Balance of Power," Round Table 258, April 1975, 159-165.

________. The Political and Military Framework. London: Study Project on External Investment in South Africa and Namibia, 1975.

Stevens, Christopher. "The Soviet Union and Angola," African Affairs 75(299), April 1976, 137-151.

Stevens, Richard P. "The History of the Anglo-South African Conflict over the Proposed Incorporation of the High Commission Territories," in Christian P. Potholm and Richard Dale (eds) Southern Africa in Perspective: Essays in Regional Politics. New York: Free Press, 1972, 97-109.

Stokes, Randall G. "The Afrikaner Industrial Entrepreneur and Afrikaner Nationalism," Economic Development and Cultural Change 22(4), July 1974, 557-579.

Stokke, Olav and Carl Widstrand (eds). Southern Africa: The UN-OAU Conference Oslo, April 1973, 2 Volumes. Uppsala: Scandinavian Institute for African Studies, 1973.

Stone, John. Colonist or Uitlander? A Study of the British Immigrant in South Africa. London: Oxford University Press, 1973.

Study Project on Christianity in Apartheid Society (SPRO- CAS):

Anatomy of Apartheid. Johannesburg, 1970. Publication Number 1.

Directions of Change in South African Politics. Johannesburg, 1971, Publication Number 3.

South Africa's Political Alternatives. Johannesburg, 1973, Publication Number 10.

Study Project on Christianity in Apartheid Society Two (SPRO-CAS2). White Liberation. Johannesburg, 1972.

Stultz, Newell M. Afrikaner Politics in South Africa, 1934-1948. Berkeley: University of California Press, 1974.

Suckling, John, Ruth Weiss, Duncan Innes. The Economic Factor. London: Study Project on External Investment in South Africa and Namibia, 1975.

Sykes, John. Portugal and Africa: The People and the War. London: Hutchison, 1971.

Tandon, Yashpal. "South Africa and the OAU: The Dialogue on the Dialogue Issue," Mawazo 3(2), December 1971, 3-16; reprinted in Instant Research on Peace and Violence 2, 1972, 54-66.

________. "The OAU and the Liberation of Southern Africa," in Christian P. Potholm and Richard Dale (eds) Southern Africa in Perspective: Essays in Regional Politics. New York: Free Press, 1972, 245-261.

Thahane, T. T. "Lesotho, an Island Country: The Problems of Being Land-locked," African Review 4(2), 1974, 279-290.

Thahane, T. T., D Kowet and A. Strom. "Lesotho, an 'island' in South African Territory," in Zdenek Cervenka (ed) Land-locked Countries of Africa. Uppsala: Scandinavian Institute of African Studies, 1973, 239-260.

The Cape Route. London: Royal United Service Institution, February 1970.

Thomas, Simon. "Economic Developments in Malawi Since Independence," Journal of Southern African Studies 2(1), October 1975, 30-51.

Thomas, Wolfgang. "Separate Development and Pluralism," New Nation 5(4), November 1971, 7-9.

Thompson, Leonard. Survival in Two Worlds: Moshoeshoe of Lesotho 1786-1870. Oxford: Clarendon Press, 1975.

Thompson, Leonard and Jeffrey Butler (eds). Change in Contemporary South Africa. Berkeley: University of California Press, 1975.

Trapido, Stanley. "South Africa in a Comparative Study of Industrialization," The Journal of Development Studies 7(3), April 1971, 309-320.

________. "South Africa and the Historians," African Affairs 71(285), October 1972, 444-448.

Troup, Freda. South Africa: An Historical Introduction. Harmondsworth: Penguin, 1975.

Turner, Biff. "A Fresh Start for the Southern African Customs Union," African Affairs 70(280), July 1971, 269-276.

van den Bosch, Amry. South Africa and the World: The Foreign Policy of Apartheid. Lenington: University Press of Kentucky, 1970.

Van der Merwe, Hendrick W. and David Welsh. Student Perspectives on South Africa. London: Rex Collings, 1972.

Wall, Patrick. Prelude to Detente: An In-Depth Report on Southern Africa. London: Stacey, 1975.

Wallenstein, Peter. "Dealing with the Devil: Five African States and South Africa," Instant Research on Peace and Violence 3, 1971, 85-99.

Walshe, Peter. The Rise of African Nationalism in South Africa: The African National Congress, 1912-1952. Berkeley: University of California Press, 1971.

Weisfelder, Richard F. "Lesotho and South Africa: Diverse Linkages," Africa Today 18(2), April 1971, 48-55.

________. The Basotho Monarchy: A Spent Force or a Dynamic Political Factor?. Athens, Ohio: Ohio University, 1972. Papers in International Studies, Africa Series Number 16.

Weiss, Ruth. "South Africa: The Grand African Economic Design," in Colin Legum and Antony Hughes (eds). Africa Contemporary Record: Annual Survey and Documents, Volume 3: 1970-1971. London: Rex Collings, 1971, A11-A18.

Welsh, David. "The Cultural Dimension of Apartheid," African Affairs 71(282), January 1972, 35-53.

________. "The Political Economy of Afrikaner Nationalism," in Adrian Leftwich (ed) South Africa: Economic Growth and Political Change. New York: St. Martin's, 1974, 249-285.

Whitaker, Paul M. "The Revolutions in 'Portuguese' Africa," Journal of Modern African Studies 8(1), April 1970, 15-35.

Wilkinson, Anthony. Insurgency in Rhodesia, 1957-1973: An Account and Assessment. London: International Institute for Strategic Studies, 1973. Adelphi Papers Number 100.

Wilkinson, Anthony, Merle Lipton and J. E. Spence. Change in Southern Africa. London: Rex Collings, 1975.

Williams, Michael and Michael Parsonage. "Britain and Rhodesia: The Economic Background to Sanctions," World Today 29(9), September 1973, 379-388.

Wilmer, S. E., et al. Zimbabwe Now. London: Rex Collings, 1973.

Wilson, Francis. Labour in the South African Gold Mines, 1911-1969. Cambridge: University Press, 1972.

Windrich, Elaine. "Rhodesia: The Challenge to Detente," World Today 31(9), September 1975, 358-367.

Woldring, Klaas. "The Prospect of Federalisation in Southern Africa," African Review 3(3), 1973, 453-478.

________. "South Africa's Africa Policy Reconsidered," African Review 5(1), 1975, 77-93.

Worrall, Denis (ed). South Africa: Government and Politics. Pretoria: Van Schaik, 1971.

Worrall, Denis. "South Africa's Reactions to External Criticism," in Nic Rhoodie (ed) South African Dialogue. Johannesburg: McGraw-Hill, 1972, 562-589.

Y.M.C.A. of Canada. Investment in Oppression. Toronto, May 1973.